Sculpture in America

SCULPTURE
IN AMERICA

Wayne Craven

UNIVERSITY OF DELAWARE

Thomas Y. Crowell Company NEW YORK ESTABLISHED 1834

Acknowledgments

I WISH TO EXPRESS MY GRATITUDE TO THE ADMINISTRATION OF THE UNIVERSITY OF Delaware for the many ways they have encouraged my research in the history of American sculpture. To Dr. John Perkins, former President of the University of Delaware; to Dr. John Shirley, Provost; to Dean Arnold Lippert; to Dr. William I. Homer, Chairman of the Department of Art History; and to Dr. John Dawson, Director of Libraries, I am most grateful. And the fruition of my research is in many ways related to the stimulus provided by the Winterthur Program in Early American Culture at the University of Delaware and the H. F. du Pont Winterthur Museum.

I also wish to thank the many museum directors, curators and registrars who have contributed so much valuable information and assistance to my research.

To Lorna

Preface

NOT SINCE LORADO TAFT'S *History of American Sculpture* FIRST APPEARED IN 1903 has there been a survey study of American sculpture. In times when the arts of the United States are arousing so much interest, it is incomprehensible that one of the major fields of artistic endeavor should have gone virtually unnoticed for over sixty years. While American painting and architecture are currently beginning to receive the scholarly attention they deserve, sculpture has been generally overlooked, except for a couple of important exhibitions and biographies of sculptors. Sculpture has always been a significant component in the American arts, and has had its own very distinct ingredient to contribute to the development and evolution of the American aesthetic from period to period. One wonders how such a major artistic field could have been so long ignored. It is hoped that the present book will stimulate an interest in and enjoyment of American sculpture, and restore it to the place it deserves as an integral part of the arts of the United States. Only then can the American aesthetic specifically and the American spirit, goals, and ideals in general—as expressed in the fine arts— be fully understood.

This book represents a plateau in a research project that I have found extremely exciting, and I constantly found myself in fertile areas where scholars had scarcely tread before. Perhaps *Sculpture in America* will open the door to others who will find the problems as fascinating as I have and who will pursue what has here been begun.

Contents

Illustrations

Sculpture in America

Artisan-Craftsmen Beginnings

THE HISTORY OF SCULPTURE IN AMERICA BEGINS IN THE 17TH CENTURY WITH THE modest efforts of craftsmen who adorned gravestones, Bible boxes, and various utilitarian objects with simple low-relief decorations. These artisans were in effect the artists in a community that had no others. Thus sign painters became painters of portraits, and carpenters and stonecutters became carvers of gravestones. The art that slowly emerged in the 17th century was therefore the product of middle-class patronage and artisan talent, and was strongly affected by the colonists' religious beliefs and the social and economic conditions among them.

The meager patronage the artisans received came from groups that were not disposed to lavish riches upon the fine arts. Among those who came to settle in America in the 17th century there was no wealthy prince whose munificence built great palaces or whose patronage created an organization of artists and artisans such as Louis XIV's Gobelins. The same century that saw the construction of such magnificent edifices as the palace at Versailles and the Banqueting Hall in London also saw the austere beginnings of a new civilization manifested in the simple architectural forms of the Fairbanks House of Dedham and the Parson Capen House at Topsfield (both in Massachusetts).

The first colonists were middle-class folk—merchants, ministers, craftsmen, and laborers. Even in the Old World they had never been patrons of the arts. And in the New World, the task of securing the necessities of life from the wilderness left little time for anything else. Besides, there were no first-rate artists to accept patronage had any been offered, for the New World held little attraction for such geniuses as Bernini, Poussin, Rubens, or Inigo Jones.

The earliest settlers had hardly arrived when the need for burial markers arose. Although only a few gravestones earlier than 1660 have survived, later examples are numerous; and from the second half of the 17th century to the time of the American Revolution, sculpture in stone was the province of the gravestone carver. In about 1770 a desire for a sophisticated form of sculpture brought several monumental marble figures by renowned English sculptors to the colonies; then, in the forty years following the Revolution there was a large-scale importation of foreign sculpture and sculptors. Finally, about 1825, native-born sculptors began to create portrait busts and statues. But the first 125 years of sculpture in stone in America is found in the thin gray slates that populate churchyards from Maine to South Carolina.

The gravestones of our founding fathers were manufactured in the colonies by local artisans. At times, of course, in the 18th century, a very wealthy man might import a tomb monument: Sir William Pepperell ordered from England "a handsome marble tombstone with proper marble pillars or supporters to set it on" and engraved with the three pineapples of the family coat of arms. Several other examples of elaborate design and accomplished workmanship are housed in King's Chapel in Boston and in Christ's Church in Philadelphia. But the ordinary grave markers were cut locally, and the names of many of the men who made them are known. Their signatures are occasionally seen on the gravestones, especially on those of the 18th century. The earliest markers were made from slate, freestone, or schist; limestone, discovered in Massachusetts in 1696, was also used. Though schist weathers badly, those made of slate have survived rather well. Composed of thin laminated strata, slate was not easily workable in bold, three-dimensional forms, but it lent itself quite nicely to a shallow design or inscriptions.

The earliest stones were merely thin slabs inscribed with the name of the deceased, possibly his or her relationship to a spouse, or parent, and the date of death. In the middle of the 17th century, however, simple decorations such as rosettes or radiating sun motifs began to appear. The sides of the stones were straight, and the top was rounded, with a large semicircle in the center flanked by two smaller ones. The design was usually placed in the lunette formed by the large semicircle, and the inscription came below. This typical form is found on the marker over the grave of Ann Erinton, who was buried in Cambridge, Massachusetts, in 1653. Later in the century vertical panels often appeared at the sides under the smaller semicircles; in these there was likely to be either a geometric or a floral motif in shallow relief.

The primary motif from this time until the end of the 18th century was the winged skull. It may be seen on the gravestone of Robert Meriam (Fig. 1.1), who was buried in 1681 in a churchyard in Concord, Massachusetts. The winged skull, a stylized, two-dimensional symbol of the fleet approach of death, expresses the terror of the grave. Just below it an hourglass and the words "Fugit Hora" refer to the passage of time. The ever-present inscription "Memento

Mori" reminds the living to be always conscious of death, as do the crossed bones. Creatures of the spirit world are represented at either side by primitively rendered little faces that betray the stonecutter's inability to execute a naturalistic image or to make flesh look like flesh. Of a few years earlier is the more ambitious stone (Fig. 1.3) of Joseph Tapping (d. 1678), whose remains were interred in the King's Chapel burial grounds in Boston. The top possesses a Baroque spirit in the contour of the scrolls and in the exuberance of the leaf design. The winged skull has the hourglass resting on top of the cranium; again the viewer is confronted by the inscriptions "Memento Mori" and "Fugit Hora." In the lower part, divided into three rectangular panels by classical pilasters, the outer panels contain corbeled Gothic arches, suggesting a survival of the medieval tradition in the art of this stonecutter. At the left are the deceased's vital statistics; at the right, another message from the grave: "Vive memor Loctü/ Fugit Hora." In the central panel a skeleton carries the dart of death in its left hand, and with its right it is about to snuff out the flame of a candle, which sits upon the globe of the earth. The skeleton is assisted in this by Father Time, who carries an hourglass in his left hand while his right hand rests on the arm of the skeleton. The meaning is quite clear: Death and Time are about to extinguish the light of temporal life. This same scene was used on the gravestone of John Foster (d. 1681) of Dorchester, Massachusetts, and reappeared as late as 1745, with its components rearranged, on the stone of Rebecca Sanders, in King's Chapel burial ground. Its origin is to be found in a little engraved illustration published in Francis Quarles' *Hieroglyphiques of the Life of Man* (London, 1638).

There was no design book especially prepared for the tombstone carver that contained numerous symbols and allegories depicting death and related subjects. Images representing death were very much a part of the Protestant world, particularly the Puritan segment of it. Since late medieval times the cadaverous specter of Death and the skeleton had been familiar sights in the imagery of Western man. Woodcut illustrations of skeletons and other death motifs were often printed on broadside elegies, and gravestone carvers found them useful as models.

Stylistically the imagery remained quite flat, and no attempt was made in the 17th century to develop three-dimensional sculpturesque form. Slate itself was not conducive to anything more than surface decoration; moreover, the timidity of the craftsmen made them unwilling to complicate their work by adding the third dimension; they simply did not think in terms of sculpture but only in terms of surface design. Their lack of training made them reluctant to attempt anything very ambitious. In addition, the very nature of what might be called "Puritan aesthetics" must also be considered.

Life on earth for the Puritans was a gray existence; many of their visual images and much of their literature expressed their preoccupation with death. Uninhibited joy had no part of any art that developed within Puritan society.

When Richard Mather wrote his preface to the *Bay Psalm Book* (published in 1640), he was careful to explain that the sacred meaning of the verse had in no way been sacrificed to the art of poetry: "Neither let any think, that for the meetre sake wee have taken liberty or poeticall license to depart from the true and proper sence of David's words in the hebrew verse." Art was a means, not an end in itself. In the sister art of painting, which began in the colonies about 1665–1670, the one approved subject was the portrait, of which one may well imagine the Mathers, Jonathan Edwards, and their contemporaries commenting that "it is a fine likeness," but never that "it is a beautiful picture." There was simply no place for a pure art or art for art's sake. Puritan suspicion of almost every kind of artistic imagery was clearly spelled out by Henry Cornelius Agrippa in *The Vanity of Arts and Sciences* (London, 1694). In discussing the arts, he particularly attacked that of sculpture:

> . . . all these Arts . . . were merely invented by the Devil, for the nourishment of Pride, Lust and Superstition; the Authors were those, who first, according to the words of St. Paul, changed the Glory of the incorruptible God, into the likeness of Corruptible man . . . . For the Vanity of Men . . . invented these Arts, to tempt the Soul of Man, and to deceive the Ignorant: And the invention itself is the Corruption of Life. However we Christians above all People are so mad . . . that in all our Courts, Houses, and Chambers, we are not assham'd to keep and admire these wicked ornaments; thereby to invite Women and Virgins to wantonness, with the sight of obscene Pictures.

This same attitude was regularly expounded from colonial pulpits, as for example in the sermons of the Reverend Samuel Willard, pastor of Old South Church in Boston from 1678 to 1707. Although this was not the only view of the arts within the Puritan spectrum, it was certainly the dominant one. Therefore the art of sculpture in stone was restricted to messages from the graveyard, exhortations to be ever mindful of the passage of all things earthly and temporal, and the decay of all flesh. All this considered, the primitive, two-dimensional, stylized images of death and the flight of time become perfectly understandable both in point of style and as expressions of a civilization.

In the 18th century, the Puritanical attitude toward man's fate beyond the grave survived and even spread well beyond New England. The skull, the winged soul's head, the hourglass, and the crossed bones remained a part of the gravestone maker's repertoire. But in spite of this, another concept, that of the relationship of art to life, asserted itself. From early in the century, images on the gravestones portrayed the deceased as he or she looked in life. These were, in fact, our first portraits in stone, and their appearance coincides with a general breakdown of Calvinism, an increase of wealth in the colonies, and the rise of a philosophy that allowed men to enjoy certain honestly gained material pleasures. The Age of Reason dawned, and the colonies offered Benjamin Franklin as their representative to it—as opposed to John Cotton or Richard Mather, who were their envoys to Puritanism. Men of Franklin's time embraced a far more worldly philosophy than their predecessors had allowed. This was bound to find its way to the graveyard, just as it did to the fashionable parlors, where Chippendale furniture, imported wallpaper, and finely carved fireplaces and cornices were joined by a colonial American version of Rococo elegance in portraits by Joseph Blackburn, John Wollaston, and John Singleton Copley.

The effigy portraits appear on gravestones soon after the turn of the century, and the earliest may well be that of the Reverend Jonathan Pierpont in Wakefield, Massachusetts, signed "N. L.," in 1709. Another early portrait is that of the Reverend Grindall Rawson (d. Mendon, Massachusetts, 1715). By the 1740's, portraits appeared on gravestones from Massachusetts to South Carolina. The smiling face of Mrs. Richard Owen is seen on her gravestone (Fig. 1.6) in the Congregational churchyard in Charleston, South Carolina. Placed within a round frame, Mrs. Owen is shown in contemporary dress, in an awkward but not altogether unsuccessful attempt to represent corporeal form. The image is far from a naturalistic likeness, which was what the stonecutter was essentially searching for in his portrait.

One of the most talented of carvers of the middle 18th century was Henry Emmes, who made a bust-type portrait for the grave marker (Fig. 1.4) of Solomon Milner (d. 1757). Signed "H Emmes Boston fecit," it stands in the Congregational churchyard in Charleston, along with another signed stone by Emmes, that of Mrs. Elizabeth Simmons (d. 1740). It is a testimony to the reputation of Henry Emmes that his work was sought from so far away. The bust on the Milner marker is a portrait whose style emulates the aristocratic high art of Europe. Its three-dimensional sculptured form offers a contrast to the flattened image of Mrs. Owen. There is a greater feeling of the softness of flesh, of the texture of hair, and of the drapery about the shoulders. These same characteristics are found on another stone in the Congregational churchyard, that of the Reverend William Hutson (Fig. 1.5).

In the 1740's rather elaborate marble memorials, often with portrait busts, were imported from England to be set into the walls of American churches. These modest versions of the type being erected in Westminster Abbey represented the latest fashion in funerary monuments. Among the several to be seen in King's Chapel, Boston, is one dedicated to Frances Shirley, dating from about 1754, which contains a sculptured portrait bust. It was in imitation of such English-produced, high-style monuments that the portrait image appeared on 18th-century grave markers. Also in King's Chapel is a memorial dedicated to Carl Apthorp (d. 1758), which has a weeping infant leaning upon an urn. From imports such as this the carver of the gravestone took inspiration for the two cherubs that recline on either side of Hutson's image, resting their elbows on the old symbols of time and death. This is an early example of the nude human figure rendered as a thing of beauty rather than as an image of death and decay. The carver had observed human anatomy more often—or more accurately—than had his 17th-century counterpart. These cherubs, distantly reminiscent of classical *putti*, are truly of the flesh. But the stones of Milner and Hutson were unusual both in their development toward a true sculptural form and in their inclination toward a more naturalistic image. By far the greater number of portraits on 18th-century stones remained timid and primitive efforts of artisan stonecutters who essentially tried to follow the art of the Baroque-Rococo ateliers of Europe but without the benefit of schooling in these styles.

The 18th-century stonecutter undoubtedly relied upon a model whenever he could find one in a painting or engraving. For example, the portrait of the Reverend William Whitwell, whose tombstone is found in Marblehead, may very well have been taken from a mezzotint engraving like those made by Peter Pelham in the second quarter of the 18th century. But when no model was available and the stonecutter had to rely on his memory or imagination, the result was usually like the simple, charming, and primitive portrait of Mrs. Owen.

Besides the more stylish portrait effigy, various other images, such as coats of arms or ships, also appeared on the gravestones. One of the most popular of all was a pleasant little cherub's head with wings, which represented the flight of the soul heavenward. Abstract designs decorated many markers, like the one on the grave of Mrs. Sarah Davis (d. 1751) in Concord, Massachusetts (Fig. 1.2). The origins of this type of geometric design go back to the 17th century, and it consists mostly of pinwheels and rosettes. On Mrs. Davis' tombstone is an ovoid head, with two tangent circles for the eyes, a vertical line for the nose, and a short horizontal line for the mouth. This type of image was probably carved by a craftsman who had no experience in rendering human or floral forms; as much as he could, he relied on his cutting tools, compass, and straight edge. Such imagery is frequently found away from the main centers of colonial civilization and represents a native, unschooled tradition, as opposed to the provincial versions of European motifs discussed earlier. No trace of this abstract style is to be found in England or on the Continent.

In the years that followed the Revolutionary War the dominant symbols on grave markers became the draped urn and the weeping willow tree. The classical urn was a new motif and indicates the growing enthusiasm for neoclassial forms in America. By 1800 this design was being employed all along the seaboard. Veterans of the Revolutionary War were joining together in the Order of the Cincinnati and comparing themselves to ancient Roman soldiers, and they began to bury their dead under symbols that also were borrowed from antiquity. The skull and skeleton finally disappeared as the artisan stonecutters appropriated more sophisticated and more current styles and motifs. Eventually a classical personification of grief came to weep at the urn, and nature, too, in the form of a weeping willow, mourned the deceased.

The use of the ancient cinerary urn reveals how 18th-century neoclassical motifs became part of the artisan's stock in trade, thus narrowing the gap between the contemporary art of European studios and that produced in the shops of American seaboard towns. By the beginning of the 19th century, the gap was further reduced as Americans began to see more of the work of Italian, French, and British sculptors who migrated to this country or who sent their sculpture over to the new nation. By 1825 the day was at hand when native sons, coming mostly from stoneyards, would inaugurate the nation's first school of sculpture in stone.

At this point we must return to the 17th century to pick up the other thread of American sculpture that developed in the artisan-craftsman tradition of the colonial period—that of the wood carver.

In the 17th century, American sculpture in wood was limited to the designs that carpenters incised on the surfaces of the furniture they made. There was nothing that approached a high-style sculptural art until around 1730, when the cabinetmakers and artisan carvers began to copy the more elaborate models they found in the design books from England and the Continent. As living became more gracious and as the decorative arts became more elegant, the need arose for finely carved wooden ornament to decorate the pieces produced by colonial furniture makers. It was in the shops of these gifted craftsmen that America's first true sculptural art had its origins, and it was such men as the Skillins, Samuel McIntire, and William Rush who formed the first real "school" of American sculpture.

The first three-dimensional figural sculpture in America appeared as these craftsmen carved the furniture ornaments, the humble shop signs—standing figures of sailors or Indians—and the great vigorous figureheads that were to ride the prows of the colonial merchant fleet. These same gifted wood carvers carried figural sculpture up to the threshold (about 1830) of that first generation of native sons—Horatio Greenough, Thomas Crawford, Hiram Powers, Erastus Palmer, and Henry Kirke Brown—who turned to more sophisticated images of marble and bronze.

Seventeenth-century America possessed no genius in the art of wood carving comparable to Grinling Gibbons, the leading carver in England from about 1670 to 1720. Gibbons' repertoire included the human figure, festoons, flowers, birds, and shells. His highly decorative designs were invested with a vitality and naturalism, a beauty of form, and a Baroque exuberance that had no counterpart in the New World. Exquisite wood carving was also done in Holland in the 17th century, but little of it or its influence made its way across the Atlantic. There was simply no market for such elegant high-style art in the colonies. The churches along the eastern seaboard had no elaborately carved altars, screens, pulpits, or figural imagery. Neither were there sculptured figures or elaborate carvings in public places or in the homes of the founding fathers.

The Protestant aesthetic did not encourage art for its own sake. Aside from religious considerations, the affluence for such art had not yet been established. The determining factor was the social-religious-economic background of those who formed the civilization of the New World in the 17th century. Their suspicion of anything approaching a religious icon, plus the simplicity and austerity of their lives in general, precluded such frivolity as an elegant sculptural art in their churches, homes, gardens, or public squares. Under these circumstances, there was no inducement for a fine carver of Grinling Gibbons' ability to come to the American wilderness. And as there were no schools or shops where a native-born carver could be trained in the art of sculpture, it was the carpenter who was called upon to produce the decorative work on architecture and furniture in the 17th century, more because of his skill with the gouge, mallet, and chisel than for his talent in the fine arts.

Carved architectural decoration was virtually nonexistent on or in 17th-century buildings, with the exception of pendants beneath an overhang or turned banisters on a stairway. Finely carved moldings around doors and windows, which added so much elegance to the architecture of the following century, were not to be found, nor were there richly decorated cornices around the walls. Ostentatiousness in the home, like a display of spiritual pride in the meetinghouse, was assiduously avoided. The meager sculptural decorations in the furnishings of a 17-century home were confined to the turned leg of a table, the carved back of a chair, or the incised patterns on a chest or Bible box.

For example, an oak prayer-book box made in New England in the third quarter of the 17th century has geometric designs carved shallowly into the front and top surfaces. The box, which contained writing materials as well as the family Bible, often had the date or the initials of the owner worked into the design—as in that shown in Fig. 1.10, which bears the letters "PP" in the center of the lid. The designs were created with the simple compass and L square of the carpenter, and the carving was not intricate. The chisel, gouge, and mallet were the only tools necessary. A late 17th-century wooden chest from the Connecticut Valley reveals the same approach to carving that is found in the contemporary gravestones—the design was fashioned by cutting away to a shallow second plane from the plane of the surface (Fig. 1.8). Originally owned by Polly Warner (hence the initials PW) of Harwinton, Connecticut, the chest has a floral motif applied to the surfaces of the stiles, rails, and panels; that is, the designs were applied to the structural parts, but no extra pieces were added purely for decoration.

Such carving was done by men who were essentially carpenters and who could not aspire to anything beyond a simple low-relief surface decoration of geometric or stylized floral design applied to structural or functional parts. The designs were derived not from the high-style contemporary art of the former homelands, but rather from a folk tradition that had retained many stylistic features of the arts and crafts of the Middle Ages. The maker of the decorated chests, chairs, and boxes was not an inspired creator of sophisticated elegance and sublime beauty; he was an artisan, and the artistic tradition to which he belonged was that of the surviving medieval folk art rather than the Renaissance-

Baroque art of his homeland counterparts who worked for aristocratic, style-conscious patrons in the pursual of a lofty art based on esoteric artistic theory.

The situation of American sculpture changed very little in the early decades of the 18th century. Sculpture as an independent fine art did not exist, in spite of the progress being made in the field of painting, under the leadership of such men as John Smibert, Gustavus Hesselius, and Robert Feke. But the atmosphere grew more hospitable to fine art when the Puritan divines of New England were eventually displaced as a ruling class by the merchants. These men began to accumulate considerable wealth in goods and trade, while in the South the wealth of the land created munificent patrons on the plantations.

During the second quarter of the century a refinement in architectural decoration fostered a refinement in the craft and skill of the wood carver. In addition, there was a movement away from medieval folk-art motifs and toward the use of classical motifs. These were imported to America in design books containing engraved illustrations of architecture and furniture. The libraries of 18th-century gentlemen frequently included several of these books. The library of William Byrd of Westover, for example, contained ten books on architecture published before 1730, and by 1750 the well-known design books by Perrault, Gibbs, Langley, Swan, Kent, Campbell, and Leoni were found in the colonies. These architectural and ornamental designs, based to a greater or lesser degree on classical art and emanating from the Palladian-Burlingtonian-Rococo-Georgian fountainheads of England and the Continent, were available to the carpenter-wood carver, with the result that a great change in aesthetic taste was effected during the course of the 18th century.

The new demands placed on the carpenter-woodworker by this revolution in taste are evident in the carving in the interior of the Royall House in Medford, Massachusetts (c. 1735); the synagogue in Newport, Rhode Island (c. 1760); King's Chapel, Boston (c. 1755); and in the pediment decoration on the exterior of Brafferton Hall at William and Mary College, Williamsburg, Virginia (c. 1723). The carving in the chancel of St. Michael's in Charleston, South Carolina (Fig. 1.9; c. 1755), demonstrates how much the work of colonial wood carvers had changed in style since the preceding century. Now, with the assistance of the design books, the American carpenter-cabinetmaker was producing classical motifs (egg-and-dart, dentils, pilasters), as well as the acanthus leaves of Corinthian capitals, and flowers and vines in the festoons that decorated fireplaces. A refined and sophisticated classicism and naturalism replaced the stylized and geometric designs of the 17th century.

The shops of these carvers were frequently along or near the wharf section of the burgeoning cities of the seaboard from Boston to Charleston, South Carolina. New England was especially blessed with wood carvers such as George Robinson the younger (1680–1737) and Isaac Fowle (1648–1718). Professional carvers were active in Philadelphia as early as 1717; and Henry Burnett, an ornamental and ship carver, was at work on Elliott's Wharf in Charleston in 1750.

One of the earliest carvers to emerge as a personality was John Welch (1711–1789) who opened his shop in Town Dock, Boston, in 1733. Welch, who probably served an apprenticeship with the younger George Robinson, married the latter's granddaughter in 1734. He became a prominent citizen of Boston, holding several town offices, and served as an officer in the Ancient and Honourable Artillery Company. The first known work by Welch is his "Sacred Cod," which now hangs in the House of Representatives of the Boston State House. While the great Cod is a rather inauspicious monument, it is typical of the varied works that were produced in the wood carver's shop. The "Sacred Cod" was a symbolic image, but other wooden fish were carved and painted to hang above the doors of fish markets. The production of shop and inn signs was a regular part of the wood carver's work, along with assorted jobs of carving, repairing, and polychroming. In the spring of 1787, for example, Welch was called upon to make "sundry repairs . . . to the head of Captain Kirkwood's vessel lying at Minotts," probably a reference to the ship's figurehead. A few years earlier he had repaired and painted a "Carved rocking horse" and had also gilded the frame for a large mirror.

Other craftsmen were working in Boston in the first three quarters of the century, for example, William Codner (active c. 1711); Moses Deshon, who carved the coat of arms for Faneuil Hall in 1742; or Isaac Dupee, who set himself up in John Welch's shop when the latter went to England for a few years in 1758. They, too, were asked to carve mantels or shop signs, or to repair figureheads of ships in the harbor. Others similarly employed included Francis Dewing, who arrived from London around 1716; Richard Hubbard, who was active c. 1733; and Samuel More, who was carving ships' figureheads as early as 1736. It was among these diverse jobs executed in the shop of the carpenter or cabinetmaker that America's first figure sculpture developed.

Though no existing work can be positively assigned to Simeon Skillin, Sr. (1716–1778), he operated a very productive shop from about 1740 to the time of his death. In the deed of the house that he bought in 1741 he is listed as a carver, and in the couple of decades that followed he most likely did sundry work for the furniture shops and the shipyards of Boston. Born during that period were two of his sons—John, in 1746, and Simeon junior, in 1757—who were to become the leading carvers of their generation in the New England area; another son, Samuel, also became a carver and was active from about 1790 to 1816.

The earliest record of sculptural work by Simeon Skillin, Sr., is a bill for work on the *King George,* a ship built to patrol the coast of Massachusetts. It is possible that the "work" was a figurehead, perhaps an image of the reigning British monarch. The bill is made out to "Skillin and Comp.," suggesting that the elder Simeon had an assistant or two and possibly a couple of apprentices in his shop. Simeon Skillin, Sr., next appears on record as the carver of a bust of Lord Chatham, or William Pitt, that was placed on "a pillar of Liberty" in Dedham,

Massachusetts, on March 18, 1767. This is the earliest record of a portrait bust made in the colonies. The monument was torn down by British troops only two years later. In 1777 the shop of Simeon Skillin, Sr., produced the 6-foot 9-inch figurehead "Minerva" for the brig *Hazard*, the bill for which, along with some other work for the vessel, was receipted by Simeon Skillin, Jr.

These documents indicate that portrait and figure sculpture were within the capabilities of Simeon Skillin, Sr., and that his activity extended over nearly four decades. Moreover, he engaged in the more ordinary productions of his trade, such as carpentry and carving for the shipyards, and probably ornate decorative pieces for furniture makers as well. He may also have been called upon to carve shop signs now and again. Certainly his sons John and Simeon could have learned from their father almost any kind of work demanded of the colonial carver.

The "Little Admiral," now in the Old State House in Boston, occupies a special place historically as the earliest surviving piece of free-standing statuary to be executed in America. The wooden figure (Fig. 1.11) stands 42 inches high and at one time probably held either a beer stein or a nautical instrument in its right hand, for it was almost certainly a shop sign. The date 1770 painted on the base is probably a later additon, for the naval uniform would suggest a date a couple of decades earlier—possibly even in the 1740's. Neither the identity of the figure nor the name of the carver is known for certain. It has been attributed to Simeon Skillin, Sr., but as there is no surviving documented work by the elder Skillin with which to compare it as to style and no recorded evidence of the statue's creator, it is no more plausible to assign it to Simeon Skillin, Sr., than to any other carver of his day. Nathaniel Hawthorne, in his "Shem Drowne's Wooden Image," ascribed it to that tinsmith who had wrought the famous grasshopper atop Faneuil Hall and who later, about 1765, turned to figurehead carving; but there is no substantiation for this attribution either. Identification of the little figure is equally enigmatic. It may be a portrait of Admiral Edward Vernon (1684–1757), whose image adorned the front of the Admiral Vernon Tavern on King Street in Boston when a Mr. James Gooch became its proprietor in 1750. Drake's *History of Boston* relates that the tavern's "sign was a portrait of Admiral Vernon." Hawthorne called it simply "the Little Admiral," whereas Pinckney, in *American Figureheads*, identifies the figure as the portrait of Captain Hunnewell, which stood in front of a nautical instrument shop. Such nautical images were popular, and as early as 1712 a wooden sailor by Lemuel Beadle stood outside of the Watch House in Salem. Other similar examples existed to identify the various stores, shops, and taverns for townspeople and travelers.

The "Little Admiral" is important stylistically as well as historically. The figure is quite "wooden"; some knowledge of anatomy is displayed in the musculature of the legs, but the shoulders and arms possess virtually none at all. The style is one that might well be expected from a native wood carver of mid-18th-century New England who had never had any formal training in rendering the human figure. But for all its limitations, the statue represents a bold step toward the free-standing sculptural art, which was to grow out of a native tradition of sculpture that had artisan-craftsman roots.

John Skillin and his brother Simeon junior come into focus as assistants in their father's shop in the years 1777 and 1778. The figurehead for the brig *Hazard* was carved in that shop in 1777, and all three men were probably connected with it. But Simeon senior was sixty-one and in the last year of his life, and Simeon junior was barely twenty. John, however, was a man of thirty-one, who in the following year was commissioned to carve the figurehead for the *Confederacy*, which was built at Norwich, Connecticut. Thus it was probably John who did the actual work. Of all the ship carving done by the Skillin brothers, none has survived, or at least none has yet been identified. However, a drawing of the *Confederacy* figurehead exists in the Admiralty records in London, and John Skillin's work probably resembled this to a large degree. Another drawing (1787), signed by Simeon junior, indicates that the shop undertook the decoration of the stern of the *Massachusetts*. In 1791 the brothers submitted a bill to Elias Hasket Derby for two "Man heads," each 6½ feet high, and "other ship work"; another bill to Derby in the same year was for the figurehead (11 feet long) of the second *Grand Turk* and for "six pieces of foreside Ornament." In 1797 William Rush, the prominent Philadelphia carver, recommended John Skillin as the man to carve the figurehead of Hercules for the frigate *Constitution*, then being built in Boston. William Bentley saw this piece in the Skillins' shop and described it in his diary as a "Hercules, with the (scroll?) of the United States and the Constitution, standing upon a rock, his battoon lying beneath him." The figurehead, destroyed in the battle at Tripoli in 1804, followed the design that Rush sent to Boston, and which he described in detail in a letter to Naval Constructor Joshua Humphreys.

The Skillins also produced other types of carved work in the years following the Revolution. There were garden figures and carved capitals for architecture and ornamental carving for furniture made in the shops of local cabinetmakers. For example, in 1791 the brothers carved the three figures atop a chest of drawers (now in the Mabel Brady Garvan Collection at Yale University) that Stephen Badlam made for Elias Hasket Derby (Fig. 1.7). The figures represent "Liberty," standing in the center of the broken pediment, while "Agriculture" and "Plenty" recline on the raking cornices. The figure style is that of a ship's figurehead but sensitively integrated with the elegance of Badlam's chest. Although their posture is perhaps a little stiff, they possess a primitive naïveté, charm, and vitality. Baroque and Rococo elegance was being imitated to the best of his abilities by a provincial artisan, but the style remains that of the native American wood carver.

An example of a more sophisticated style may be seen in one of the figures atop a secretary (Fig. 1.12) in the collection of the Henry Francis du Pont Winterthur Museum. The figure of "Plenty" possesses a refined Rococo classicism, and the treatment of the anatomy and drapery suggests the work of a man of rare gifts who had been well trained in an English carver's workshop. A man of such talent and training might well have migrated to America after the Revolution, just as numerous other artists and artisans did. Certainly furniture making had developed to a sufficiently high degree of excellence to attract gifted craftsmen.

A comparison of the figure of "Plenty" on the Winterthur secretary with the Skillins' "Liberty" on the Badlam chest reveals a great difference in style. The latter emerged from the native school of figurehead and architectural carvers, whereas the former was an importation of a refined figural style from a European atelier. Still, the Skillins did aspire to the high-style sculpture that adorns the Winterthur secretary. They could have known similar pieces that served as models, or they could have taken inspiration from the numerous design books available in America at that time. For example, in Plate 114 of James Gibbs' *Book of Architecture* (Fig. 1.13) the robed female figures reclining on the raking cornices of the pediment of a tomb are similar to the figures on the Badlam chest. Further evidence of a relation between early American carving and books of furniture design is found in a design of a desk and bookcase, Plate 40 of Hepplewhite's *The Cabinet-Maker and Upholsterer's Guide* (London, 1787), where a bust of classical inspiration is placed on the pedestal in the center of a broken pediment, with another bust at each end of the pediment (Fig. 1.14). Such a bust, probably of Milton, is in the broken pediment of a secretary in the collection of the Beverly (Massachusetts) Historical Society (Fig. 1.17), and other examples exist in the Metropolitan Museum of Art and the Boston Museum of Fine Arts. On stylistic evidence the little mahogany head on the Beverly secretary has been attributed to the Skillin brothers. In 1784 the Skillins billed Elias Hasket Derby for "2 Mahogany Bustes," which, judging from the low price charged, were probably for similar use on the pediment of a chest or secretary.

Many other late 18th-century carvers in America supplied ornamental work for furniture. A chest-on-chest in the Karolik Collection (Museum of Fine Arts, Boston) contains a figure of "Liberty" in the center of the broken pediment and a magnificently carved frieze of cherubs, festoons, and a bowl of fruit; the former bears a strong resemblance to the Skillins' figure of "Liberty" on the chest of the Garvan Collection at Yale, and the relief below could be by Samuel McIntire. The Bolles secretary in the Metropolitan Museum of Art has two female personifications that have been attributed on stylistic grounds to the shop of John and Simeon Skillin, and indeed some of the peculiarities of the style—especially the treatment of the facial features—are to be seen in documented works by the two brothers (Fig. 1.18). But the drapery and anatomical form are conceived in a different manner, with greater fullness and a more complex arrangement of the folds; they have a Baroque quality about them that is not present in other works by the Skillins. The Bolles figures may have been executed in the Skillin shop, but probably by an assistant. Their inspiration also came from Europe, and they may be compared, in a general way, with the draped maidens who stand at the side of a tomb in Gibbs' *Book of Architecture*, Plate 118.

The shop of John and Simeon Skillin also produced some free-standing wooden figures of larger dimensions, ranging between 4 and 5 feet in height. The following bill, dated September 25, 1793, was presented to Elias Hasket Derby:

Elias Haskett Derby Esq. To John & Simeon Skillin

To a Figure of a Hermit for a Garden	7″ 10″ 0
To a Figure of a Shepherdess	6″ 0″ 0
To a Figure of Plenty	7″ 10″ 0
To a Figure of a Gardener	7″ 10″ 0
To Priming the Above	0″ 15″ 0
	29″ 5″ 0

And at the bottom it is receipted: "Received payment in full of/Benjn Pickman Junr/John & Simeon Skillin." The four figures occupied prominent locations in the famous Derby gardens at the farm in Danvers, Massachusetts. The "Gardener" and "Shepherdess" stood at the ends of the gabled roof of the summerhouse, which was designed by Samuel McIntire, and the image of "Plenty" was placed in front of the building. In another part of the garden was a hermitage, with its figure inside, nicely described by Eliza Southgate in a letter dated July 6, 1802:

The hermitage . . . was scarcely perceptible at a distance; a large weeping willow swept the roof with its branches and bespoke the melancholy inhabitant. We caught a view of the little hut as we advanced thro' the opening of the trees; it was covered with bark; a small low door, slightly latched immediately opened at our touch; a venerable old man was seated in the center with a prayer book in one hand while the other supported his cheek, and rested on an old table which, like the hermit, seemed moulding to decay . . . a tattered coverlet was spread over a bed of straw . . . I left him impressed with veneration and fear which the mystery of his situation seemed to create.

This follows an 18th-century English tradition of hermitages or grottoes as a part of garden design, but in New England it was quite unusual.

One of the four Derby garden figures has survived—the "Plenty" now in the Peabody Museum in Salem (Fig. 1.19). "Plenty" with her cornucopia was a popular image and frequently decorated the tops of chests and secretaries. A wooden image of her also stood on a pedestal behind George Washington when he greeted the people of Boston in 1789 from a balcony erected over the entrance of the Old State House, as may be seen in an illustration published in the January 1790 issue of the *Massachusetts Magazine*. Stylistically the Peabody "Plenty" is quite similar—in the folds of the skirt, the fullness of the arms, the rendering of the facial features, the treatment of the shoes—to the figure of "Liberty" by the Skillins on the Badlam chest in the Garvan Collection. Garden figures like the "Plenty" were, therefore, simply enlargements of the little figures that decorated the secretaries and chests.

Another pair of garden figures, the "Gardener" and the "Country Maid" in the Massachusetts Historical Society (Figs. 1.15 and 1.16), are unquestionably the work of a man who was trained in Europe. Garden figures in stone and lead had been popular in England since the 17th century and were probably of Dutch ancestry. When the idea was introduced into America, the medium was, of course, a native wood, for fine stone was not available for carving and the casting of large-scale figures in metal was not attempted for another half century.

Sculpture in the 18th century grew in the fertile soil of the utilitarian arts—such as shop signs, ship figureheads, and architecture and furniture ornamentation—rather than arising instantly and full-grown as an independent fine art. It issued slowly from the artisan-craftsman tradition in a "vernacular" artistic form. But such wooden garden figures as the Peabody's "Plenty," or the allegorical figures of "Hope" (Fig. 1.20) and "Justice" at the Henry Francis du Pont Winterthur Museum, are the American forerunners of a sculptural art independent of other forms. The figures of "Justice" and "Hope" at Winterthur may have flanked the door of a courtroom in a Massachusetts hall of justice in the last decade of the century; their back is not finished to the same degree as their front, suggesting they were placed against a wall and were to be seen only from three sides. Although it is not known that the two figures were carved by John and Simeon Skillin, they are probably connected in some way with their shop. They may be envisioned as figureheads that have been freed from the bow of a ship, for the style of carving is the same. But the figure is free-standing with an aesthetic significance of its own and is no longer an adornment of a utilitarian object. Thus during the last decade of the 18th century and the first decade of the 19th, sculpture as an independent fine art was born in America.

Mercury, like Plenty, Justice, and Hope, possessed a certain popularity in New England. His wooden image once crowned the summerhouse of Isaac Royall in Medford, Massachusetts. In the Old State House, Boston, a figure of "Mercury" (Fig. 1.21), which has been attributed to the Skillin workshop, is the earliest known representation of the nude figure in the round in American sculpture. Originally a sign that identified the Post Office in Boston, the image of Mercury, the messenger of antiquity, was quite appropriate. In form it is reminiscent of the famous "Flying Mercury" by Giovanni da Bologna (Jean Bologne). Although stocky and rather stiff in comparison with the lithe, graceful piece by the Italian master, the American "Mercury" has a primitive, naïve charm.

Another wooden figure that dates from around 1790 is "St. Paul" (Fig. 1.26), which still occupies its original position in the niche of the pediment of St. Paul's Chapel in New York City. The figure, holding the traditional sword and book, is carved from oak and painted gray to simulate stone. It is the work of a man who was trained as a figurehead carver, but the legend that attributes this work to John Skillin is, as far as is known, unfounded. There were several figurehead carvers working in New York City about this time—men such as Daniel Train, "a young gentleman of genius and ability, [who] was formerly a student of William Rush of Philadelphia." Train carved the figurehead for the frigate *Adams*, with the image of the second President in an oratorical pose, according to a notice in the *U.S. Gazette* of May 25, 1799. Though Train may have come to New York too late to have executed the "St. Paul," there were others there ahead of him who could have done it. An illustration in the *New York Magazine* of October 1795 shows the figure in its niche, thus establishing that it was carved before that time.

There remains yet another product typical of a late 18th-century wood carver's shop—ornamental carving for architecture. Simeon Skillin did the elaborate carved decoration for his own house, but little is known about it. And it was the Skillins who executed the huge Corinthian capitals for Bulfinch's new State House in Boston; William Bentley recorded in his diary that he had seen them in the Skillins' shop on May 31, 1797. In 1804 Simeon carved the capitals for the New North Church, in which he and his family had a pew. The Skillin brothers also executed architectural ornamentation for private homes—for example, that of Elias Hasket Derby for whom they carved some fancy capitals for pilasters, according to a bill dated December 10, 1799.

But in the Boston area the Skillins had a talented rival in the field of carved architectural decoration. Samuel McIntire (1757–1811) of Salem received his early training from his father, Joseph McIntire, Sr., a housewright. In partnership with his brothers, in 1779 Samuel had begun work on the house commissioned by Elizabeth Crowninshield Derby, wife of the prosperous shipowner, Elias. By 1782 the Derbys had decided to remodel the Benjamin Pitman House, and Samuel and Angier McIntire were called upon to do the interior wood carving.

Samuel McIntire now began to assert his talent in architectural decoration. Although he made occasional essays at figure and portrait-bust carving, he specialized in fine cornices and mantelpieces and exquisite relief designs for furniture. For mantelpieces, McIntire's favorite motifs were baskets of fruit or flowers, cornucopias, urns, and festoons; many of these he had seen in furniture-design books. In 1783 McIntire designed the house for Jerathmeel Pierce, which still stands in Salem. He drew heavily upon the design books of such men as James Gibbs, Batty Langley, Palladio, William Pain, and Isaac Ware; many of the details in the Pierce House, for example, were taken from Langley's *Treasury of Design* (London, 1745).

Among the finest examples of McIntire's furniture carving is the chest-on-chest (Fig. 1.24) that William Lemon made for Mrs. Elizabeth Derby in 1796. The urns, pilasters, bowl of fruit, cornucopia, and *putti* supporting the festoons endow the handsome piece with a wealth of fine carving, which in its delicacy of classical detail suggests the influence of Robert and James Adam, the eminent British architects and designers. The free-standing urns at the top and the cornu-copia on the lower sides were favorite motifs of the Salem carver. McIntire often collaborated with a furniture maker, supplying the finely carved decora-tion, just as on several occasions he produced the ornamental doorway or inte-rior work for a house designed and constructed by another man.

Like most of his woodworking contemporaries, McIntire was ready to tackle almost any wood-carving job. In 1798 he carved a striding female figure in a flowing gown for the *Mount Vernon;* in 1803 he executed a figurehead for the *Asia* and three years later one for the *Derby*—both over 8 feet in height. The sole surviving example of such work by McIntire is the small, 24-inch-high fe-male figure, now in the Peabody Museum in Salem. It may have been a model for a larger piece or perhaps a shop sign, but the familiar curvature indicates some association with figureheads.

McIntire also did other types of carving and carpentry work for ships. As early as 1788 he had done carving for two Derby ships, the *Light Horse* and the *Astrea.* And while the figurehead for the Derby ship *Grand Turk* (second of the name) was being carved in the Skillins' shop in Boston, McIntire was working on "Ye quarter galleries & sundry small jobs" and on the finishing of the ship's cabin. The versatile Salem wood carver also made a speciality of carving eagles for the tops of cupolas, over archways and gateposts.

From all this, McIntire emerges as an ornamental carver of skill and quality, but aside from the few figureheads mentioned, there is little to indicate that he was a carver of the human figure. McIntire did not think of himself as a figure carver, and ordinarily his patrons did not expect him to do figure carving; his most regular patron, Elias Hasket Derby, preferred to have the Skillins do that type of work. The one man who seems to have tried to induce McIntire to go into figural work was the Reverend William Bentley, and he soon realized that this was outside the carver's domain.

On May 12, 1798, the Reverend William Bentley noted in his diary that he had commissioned McIntire to do a portrait bust of John Winthrop (Fig. 1.25). Bentley loaned the wood carver a painted miniature portrait of Winthrop, which was returned to him with the little wooden bust (height: 15½ inches) nine days later. On May 22 the diarist wrote: "I cannot say he has expressed in the bust anything which agrees with the governor." McIntire evidently found it difficult to translate a two-dimensional image into a plastic one, for the bust presents a rather flat appearance and the quizzical, wide-eyed expression on the face of the governor is somewhat primitive. The bust belongs to the native tradition of the craftsman-carver—much closer to the figurehead style than to the high-style sculptural art then being produced in Europe.

About 1800–1805 McIntire carved a bust of Voltaire, probably also for the Reverend William Bentley. The two busts are identical in height and in the design of the pedestal, but on the base of the Voltaire there is a device composed of musical instruments. McIntire had used this same motif during this period on mantels and on an organ case. The same design is found on the base of a Chelsea Derby porcelain bust of Voltaire. In contrast to the bust of Winthrop, the better modeling of the Voltaire bust and a less stylized treatment of the clothing suggest that McIntire had before him a well-formed, three-dimensional model that may well have been the Chelsea Derby piece. There is a softer, more humanistic expression in the countenance and a greater corporeal feeling for the flesh than is found in the Winthrop bust.

Also by McIntire were the profile medallion portraits of "General George Washington," taken from Hiller's drypoint, which was in turn copied from Joseph Wright's etching. About 1805 McIntire had designed four arched gateways for Washington Square, the Common in Salem, and a medallion was carved to adorn each of these. Other sculptural efforts by McIntire include a carved pear of great naturalism, and the head and hands of a Chinese mandarin figure carved in 1801 for the East India Marine Society of Salem. In the final analysis McIntire never developed into the figure sculptor that the Skillin brothers did. A contemporary estimate of his abilities is nicely summed up by William Bentley, who wrote the following in his diary in 1802:

As a carver we place Mr. Macintire with Skillings of Boston. In some works he succeeded well. He cuts smoother than Skillings but he has not his genius. In architecture he excells any person in our country, and in his executions as a Carpenter, or Cabinet maker.

Along the coast from Maine to Connecticut there were shipbuilding centers—such as Kittery, Maine; Portsmouth, New Hampshire; Boston and New Bedford, Massachusetts; Mystic and New Haven, Connecticut—and at all of them the carver's shop was an integral part of the industry. Shipbuilding dated back at least as far as 1641, when Nehemiah Bourne built the *Trial*, the first large vessel to be constructed in Boston. By the early 18th century shipbuilding had become a flourishing industry, and it has been estimated that the colony of Massachusetts alone sent over a thousand ships into service from its shipyards. The larger ships would no doubt have had a figurehead, which at first, following the English tradition, would have been a lion. Colonial shipbuilders would have used such English publications as Sutherland's *The Shipbuilders' Assistant* (London, 1711), just as colonial carpenters drew upon English design books for inspiration in furniture making and architecture. In 1727 His Majesty's Admiralty office announced that motifs other than the lion might be used, and after mid-century the human figure began to appear on the prow. The heyday of the American figurehead was between 1785 and about 1835; after this it became a second-class art, for by then America had imported and was beginning to develop on her own a sculptural "high art."

But ships from the ports of New England carried goods around the world, and riding triumphant on their prows were the great figureheads carved by American craftsmen. The figure had a peculiar curvature which followed the line of the prow. The face usually had the rather naïve, quizzical, wide-eyed look frequently found among works done in the unschooled manner of our early wood carvers. The anatomy was not always fully understood, but this was never wholly expected of the figurehead carver. After being carved, the figure was brightly polychromed.

In the last decade of the 18th century the Skillin brothers took into their shop a young apprentice, Henry Fowle, who soon became one of the family by marrying a sister of his employers. By 1798 he was listed as owning and occupying a two-story wooden building on Salutation Alley, very near the Skillins' shop. Thus began another dynasty of woodcarvers, for the name Fowle is probably best known through the work of Henry's son Isaac, who also served an apprenticeship with Simeon Skillin, Jr.

In 1806, soon after Simeon junior's death (John died in 1800), Isaac Fowle and Edmund Raymond, also a Skillin apprentice, advertised that they were establishing themselves in the shop of their former master "to carry on House and Ship ornamental carving in its various branches." Fowle's partnership with Raymond lasted until around 1820; at about that date Isaac carved the one figure that has come down to us—a woman with billowing draperies (Fig. 1.22) now in the Old State House, Boston. One of the finest examples of the figurehead, it probably never went to sea but was used as a sign to designate the shop of the carver. Isaac Fowle also worked on a "bust head" and trail boards for an unidentified ship mentioned in the records of Benjamin Shreve, Esq., and on the brig *Arctic* in September of 1822. But the only other surviving work known to be by his hand is a hardware shop sign, showing several tools on a lunette board (Old State House, Boston). In 1833 Isaac Fowle was joined by his sons John D. and William H. Although Isaac died in 1843, the firm continued to be one of the leading carver's shops until about the time of the Civil War. But by then figurehead carving had joined circus-wagon figures and cigar-store Indians as a craft art.

In the history of woodcarving at Newburyport, Massachusetts, one encounters the amazing Mr. Timothy Dexter and his master carver, Joseph Wilson. Dexter was a businessman, sly and crafty, whose eccentric behavior was spurred on both by a nagging wife and by the belief that his son was plotting to murder him. He referred to himself as "Lord Timothy Dexter," and had his own portrait statue labeled "first in the East." Included in the bedlam that surrounded his life was his personal poet laureate, whom Dexter crowned publicly, but who—according to John P. Marquand, Lord Timothy's biographer—was "an erstwhile seller of haddock and pornography." One of the highlights of Dexter's life was his glorious funeral, attended by an estimated 3,000 people, including himself: he observed much of the event from a hiding place within his house, and later, to the consternation of the townspeople, appeared upon the streets of Newburyport, greeting the men and bowing to the ladies.

Lord Timothy entered into the history of sculpture with the same imagination and bravado that characterized the rest of his life. He had erected a toll bridge across the Merrimack River, and it was probably to persuade travelers to cross over his bridge instead of over a competitor's that he created the spectacle of Newburyport on the lawn of his house, which still stands in High Street. Here he amassed a portrait gallery of some forty eminent Americans, world leaders, and Biblical personages (Fig. 1.27), all standing figures a little less than life-size, placed on pedestals fifteen feet high. For the execution of this museum of wooden figures, Dexter called in a young figurehead carver of the town, Joseph Wilson (1779–1857), who began the work in 1801. Originally, the figures were to have been done in marble, but this soon proved to be too costly; wood, a material with which Wilson was far more familiar, was chosen instead. It was probably a painter named Babson who polychromed the figures after Wilson had carved them. The list of personages represented is indicative of the imagination of the Newburyport entrepreneur: included were the first three Presidents of the United States, the Indian Chief Cornplanter, Napoleon Bonaparte, King George, Lord Nelson, "John Hen Cock," "John Jea," Dr. Franklin, Louis XIV, the Emperor of China, the Grand Signior of Constantinople, Dr. Dwight (president of Yale), Adam and Eve (nude figures with fig leaves), Moses, kings David and Solomon, Joseph and his coat of many colors, Saints Peter, Paul, and John, and, of course, not to be excluded from such august companionship, Lord Timothy Dexter himself. Figures of lions, greyhounds, and even a unicorn lent tone to the spectacle.

It must have indeed been a spectacle, and unique in America. The brightly colored figures stood atop their pedestals and arches, until most of them were blown over in the hurricane of 1815. After that, the statute of the Indian chief became a scarecrow in a nearby garden, and the other figures were sold for as little as $3 to $5. The only known surviving pieces are two arms of a figure, now in the Newburyport Historical Society, and the figure of William Pitt (Fig. 1.23), restored and preserved in the Smithsonian Institution in Washington. The figure is rather stiff and clearly belongs to the tradition of the figurehead carver. Dexter may have gotten the idea originally from garden figures, which by 1800 were certainly not unknown in New England, but in his characteristic exuberance he carried the matter well beyond previous examples. In 1803 the peregrinating Salem diarist William Bentley observed with disgust:

There is no horrid violation of proportion in the district objects but the vast columns, the gigantic figures, the extended arches, & absurd confusion of characters, tend to convince us of the abuse of riches . . . Dexter was within doors, drunk, having just suffered from a heavy beating from his drunken son, urged on by a drunken daughter.

In the work of William Rush (1756–1833), the culmination of the native American wood carving tradition was reached. Like several of his colleagues, Rush aspired to be not merely an artisan but an artist. While representing the apex of this movement his work was also its swan song, for by the time of Rush's death the wood carver was already yielding to two other groups of sculptors—one of foreign importation and the other a native school, working in marble. No sooner had wood carving attained the elevated rank of fine art than foreign and domestic forces conspired to send it once more into the realm of a craft or folk art, where it took form in circus-wagon figures and cigar-store Indians. Except for a few pieces he modeled in clay or terra cotta, Rush remained a carver throughout his life.

William Rush's father, Joseph Rush (1720–1787), was a ship's carpenter who taught his son the skills of the mallet and chisel at a very young age. At the age of fifteen, William entered the service of Edward Cutbush, whom he served as assistant for four years. Cutbush had come to Philadelphia from London and evidently operated a sizable and busy wood-carving shop; though no extant work of his can be identified, he was one of Philadelphia's leading carvers in the period just before and after the Revolution. Such training served as an "art school" for young Rush, as it did for his fellow carvers of the colonial era. There were few art books that might have helped him, and the examples of sculpture against which he could test his own efforts were not the marble statues of Rococo gardens, but the wooden figures on the prows of ships riding at anchor in the Delaware River. Rush thus began his career in the port wood carver's tradition, which he followed for more than a quarter of a century before he began carving the portrait busts and allegorical figures for which he became famous.

Hardly had Rush left Cutbush's shop to open his own (c. 1775) when he was drawn into the American Revolution as an officer in the Philadelphia militia. With the end of hostilities, he began to produce ornamental work for ships, and his earliest known effort was the figurehead "Indian Trader," carved in 1789 for the ship *William Penn*. This piece won the accolades of local carvers when the ship called at London port; another of his figures, the "River God," brought curious and marveling Hindus out in small boats to see it when the *Ganges* visited India. Rush's reputation soon spread far beyond Philadelphia as his lively figures graced the prows of American vessels that traveled all over the world. This success in figurehead carving, which continued throughout the 1790's, evidently absorbed virtually all his efforts as a carver.

Rush did much to make Philadelphia one of the leading centers of figurehead carving in America, as is shown in the following notice, which appeared in the *Pennsylvania Journal* in 1791:

The art of carving, especially heads of ships, we may without boasting say is brought to the greatest degree of perfection in this city. A stranger walking along the wharves, must be struck with the beautiful female figures of Peace, Plenty, Love, Harmony, Ariel, Astronomy, Minerva, America, etc., etc., and also with the masculine statues of American Warriors, Alexanders, Hannibals, Caesars, etc., etc.

The inventiveness and imagination of Rush is demonstrated in a letter to Naval Constructor Joshua Humphreys, dated April 30, 1795, in which Rush outlined the iconography of several figureheads. His description of one of these will suffice to show his genius:

The Constellation should be represented by an elegant female figure characteristic of indignant Nature, at the period of the American Revolution, determined on the forming of a New Creation, from that Chaos of Ignorance, Vice and Folly, which she had long been burdened with—She should have a flaming torch in her right hand, setting fire to the bursting World under her feet, with the emblems of Tyranny, Superstition, Folly, etc. issuing from it, and thrown into Confusion and fermentation, her left arm resting on the altar of Liberty. The American Eagle in the act of flight; a Sphere resting on his pinions with the Constellation inserted; soaring to heaven with one more great offering to Nature—or to adorn the new political firmament with light and Glory, to serve as a light to the Nations that have long Wandered in Political Darkness; and to Strike with Wonder and Surprise the Wise men of the East.

[Quoted in H. Marceau, *William Rush*, p. 83]

Rush was an enthusiastic participant in the new social and political order for mankind that he saw emerging in his own time. His interest in allegorical figures is further found in his description for the figurehead "Hercules" that John Skillin carved in Boston for the brig *Constitution*. In choosing the Hercules image (because the "Union begets Strength, [and] it ought to be represented by an Herculean figure"), Rush became an early participant in the classical revival, which was then manifesting itself in the architecture of the new capitol in Washington City. In his "Hercules" he was truly combining a classical form with American concepts.

The one surviving figurehead by Rush is that of "Virtue," which was carved around 1810 but which was probably never attached to the prow of a ship. The figure of the robed lady is fully sculpturesque and possesses a vitality and animation often lacking in the work of other figurehead carvers.

During the first decade of the century William Rush's passion for personification and allegory was transferred from figureheads to free-standing statues. As early as 1808 he had carved the figures "Comedy" and "Tragedy" for the niches on the façade of the New Theatre on Chestnut Street, which had been designed by Benjamin H. Latrobe. Lively action of figure and drapery and animated expressions characterize these larger-than-life pine figures. But even more famous is "Water Nymph and Bittern" of 1809 (Fig. 1.31), now to be seen in a bronze replica in the Philadelphia Museum of Art. The original was executed in wood and was the centerpiece of a fountain in Center Square just in front of Latrobe's temple-like waterworks building; a contemporary view of the figure, the fountain, and the building is preserved in a painting by John Lewis Krimmel. A stream of water jetted from the beak of the bittern and, along with other streams from below, sprayed down upon the maiden. Nothing could have been worse, of course, for a wooden image, and by mid-century it was deteriorating so rapidly that it had to be replaced by the bronze replica.

Realizing full well that this "Nymph" was to be free-standing, the sculptor bestowed upon her a freedom of movement previously unknown among the works of our native carvers: The pelvic axis shifts properly as the weight is placed on the left leg while the right leg relaxes; there is a slight *contrapposto* as the upper torso and head bend forward and to the side; and the arms swing free as they hold the large bird, perched on the shoulder, which continues the vertical axis. The "Nymph" is not a classical figure in its proportions, nor does it possess the detached, reserved, expressionless countenance of a Greek head. On the contrary, the pupils in the eyes and the slight smile give the image a spark of life, which is characteristic of Rush's work and so often lacking in an eclectic neoclassicism.

The modeling of the body and the ease of the posture strongly suggest flesh rather than wood, and indeed an epoch-making event occurred in the creation of this figure. Strong Puritanical mores still existed with regard to the nude or seminude image. Wertmuller's painting of the unclothed Danaë had caused a scandal a decade earlier when it was shown to the public; a few years later, after receiving high acclaim in Paris, Vanderlyn's large painting of the sleeping Ariadne drew a shocked response from American gallery-goers at such indecency. Propriety was maintained by arranging special visiting hours for women to view the collections of casts of ancient statues, at which times gentlemen were not permitted in the galleries. And in Rush's time the use of the live nude model in the artist's studio had not yet won public acceptance.

In the face of all this, William Rush had a young lady come to his studio to pose in the nude for his statue of the "Nymph." (This scene was later painted by Thomas Eakins, who decades later also drew public censure for his studies of the nude.) This was a daring move indeed for Rush to make, and it would be difficult to imagine Samuel McIntire or the Skillins being so bold. Even though the result was a robed figure, the good citizens of Philadelphia blushed at the manner in which the "wet drapery" revealed the body of the woman, and the sculptor, so respected in other matters, was sharply rapped for his shameful image. While he was not able to establish a precedent for future artists who wished to express their concepts of beauty by means of the nude figure, still it was a beginning. Rush probably was a bit astonished at the uproar his statue caused; at fifty-three he surely did not think of himself as a flouter of custom and convention. But the controversy was a portent of the difficulties ahead for the figure sculptors of America, who were soon to take up the nude figure as one of the primary subjects of their art.

Rush, constantly in search of formal instruction for the further development of his art, found it in such books as *The Artists' Repository*, a copy of which he bought in 1812. In an effort to rise from his own native-craft beginnings to an art acceptable in terms of European standards, he began to incorporate into his own style the details of the face and gestures of the head and hands that were shown in the popular drawing books of the day. Further evidence of his interest in improving the artisan-craftsman status of sculpture was his collaboration some years earlier (1791) with the portrait painter Charles Willson Peale in organizing the Columbianum, an ill-fated art school. In 1811 the first of the annual exhibitions of the Pennsylvania Academy of the Fine Arts was held, and Rush was represented by three sculptures. These bore little if any imprint of the classical casts that were then owned by the Academy. Such celebrated works as "Apollo Belvedere" and "Venus di Medici" did not overpower the personal style of the Philadelphia wood carver. Details that Rush assimilated from European art books, engravings, and casts were never allowed to dominate the style that had been fostered in his youth when he was apprenticed to a wood carver. Even his recumbent maidens "Faith," "Hope," and "Charity" (1811) have only faint traces of classicism about them, and even less is found in the allegorical figures "Schuylkill Freed" and "Schuylkill Chained" (1828; now in the Philadelphia Museum of Art). In "Schuylkill Freed" (Fig. 1.28), a neoclassical coiffure and a quasi-classical urn have not essentially changed the style of Rush. Therefore, although he was more than willing to acquire certain prescribed details and employ personification to suit his needs, Rush's compromise with neoclassicism was one of idea rather than form, even though the classical revival was then at its peak in America.

Rush remained especially true to the native tradition in the field of portraiture, in which he was most actively engaged during the second decade of the 19th century. The earliest mention of a portrait dates back to 1785–1790 when Rush received some lessons in modeling from Joseph Wright, who was in Philadelphia as a die designer for the government. Few if any of the earlier or contemporary wood carvers had attempted to work the malleable media of clay or terra cotta, and Rush's venture represented a bold step beyond the confines of the wood carver. His interest in the portrait bust may have been whetted by the appearance in Philadelphia, in 1785, of the famous French sculptor Houdon, who was on his way to Mount Vernon to take the likeness of Washington. Houdon left several of his busts of eminent Americans in the Quaker City, and Rush undoubtedly knew these. A decade later the Italian Ceracchi modeled several portraits in Philadelphia, and he was followed by a host of foreign sculptors who worked in the city for varying lengths of time and with varying success. Rush's own serious occupation with the portrait bust took place during the years 1812 to 1824. Virtually all his busts from that period are in plaster or terra cotta, indicating that by then he had mastered the art of modeling. The bust of Charles Thomson, author, ardent patriot, and Secretary of the First Continental Congress (Fig. 1.29), contains the same objective rendering of a likeness that was typical of the native school of portrait painters—Ralph Earl and John Singleton Copley, for example. The same is true of the powerful image of "Philip Syng Physick" (c. 1812), the so-called Pine-knot Self-Portrait (c. 1822), the dynamic bust of Washington (1817), or the pensive Lafayette in his later years (1824). An alertness, a feeling of life, informs these portraits; despite a strong likeness they are not merely works of dry realism. A break from the woodenness or primitive style of previous attempts at portraiture by American artisans is noticeable in

Rush's work, and no doubt his ability to model in clay was a great asset in achieving this.

In style, his portraits were in the American vernacular rather than being neo-classical or Rococo imitations. By vernacular is meant a style that emerged from the new country, independent of the refinement and sophistication of the Continental styles then in vogue, and based on an unpretentious, naturalistic image. Although some of his countrymen were soon to be wooed and won by neoclassicism, an equal number withstood the courtship and created a very fine school of sculpture that stressed this indigenous naturalism. Just as Charles Thomson was known for the truthfulness of his words, so Rush was praised for the verity of his images of his fellow men. Thomson was represented in the everyday clothes of his time, as was the case in most of the busts by Rush; normal daily attire was preferred to that device of the neoclassic portraitist, the toga. Even when Rush did place the toga about the shoulders of his sitter, it was a small compromise, considering the unflinching naturalism of the head itself.

That a strength of character was attainable within this vernacular style is seen in two examples by contemporaries of Rush—a bust of Jeremiah Dodge by Charles J. Dodge (1806–1886) and one of Chancellor Robert R. Livingston (Fig. 1.30) by an unknown artist. The former dates from about 1830, the latter from about 1820; both were probably carved in New York City. Another splendid example is the figurehead-bust of Commodore Perry (c. 1830) in the Mariner's Museum, Newport News, Virginia. Thus, in the face of the imported neoclassical bust, which appeared in America after the Revolution and during the first quarter of the 19th century, the carved wooden portrait bust advanced in its own way to a state of considerable refinement.

Although Rush modeled most of his portrait busts in clay, there is one full-length portrait figure from his chisel that stands as a landmark in the history of the native school of woodcarvers—the life-size wooden image of George Washington (Fig. 1.32), carved in 1814, now in the Philadelphia Museum of Art. No other sculptured image of the first President possesses the vitality of this one, with its forceful character and animated spirit. It may well represent the zenith of the American woodcarver's art—the figurehead completely freed from its primitive style. It is an image of an American hero without the sham of a neo-classical form, and there is in this pine figure an integrity that is lacking in the multi-ton, marmorean, Zeus-like image of Washington that Horatio Greenough created two decades later.

When William Rush died in 1833—at the moment when Greenough was beginning to model his Olympian image of Washington—the high point of native American wood carving had been reached and was about to give way to the marble and bronze figures of another kind of sculpture. Nevertheless, the strength of the wood carvers' style must be recognized as one of the major ingredients that brought American sculpture to the point we find it in 1830.

Wood carvers produced many very interesting works in the period between

1825 and 1875. The best-known is that tobacco-store figure, the ubiquitous Indian; another excellent example is the "Sailor" (Fig. 1.36), now in the New-York Historical Society. Figures like these must have populated the streets of American towns in considerable number, indicating the wares to be had inside. The Indian became the symbol of the tobacco seller probably because merchants (both American and European) wanted a typically American image that would advertise their product from the New World, and what better symbol could be found than the Indian, or possibly a slave boy, as a reference to the Southern plantations that cultivated tobacco. In fact, the Indian often wore a skirt of tobacco leaves, and in place of feathers there were more tobacco leaves in his headdress.

Ship figureheads continued to be carved throughout this period, probably by the same men who created the shop-sign figures. But the great era of the figurehead had passed by 1830, for such carvers failed to follow the lead of William Rush, who had elevated wood carving to a fine art. Before long, even the craft of wood carving virtually ceased to be practical as it became a victim of the wood-carving machines of the Industrial Revolution, dying out almost altogether soon after the Civil War. Carving in wood in the 20th century is far different from the tradition that flourished throughout the 18th and early 19th century. The wooden forms that appeared in America after the Armory Show of 1913 were not of the lineage of the Skillins, Samuel McIntire, William Rush, and the others who made up the extraordinary school of the native American wood carver.

Like the other kinds of sculpture that developed in the new nation, the art of modeling in wax had its origins in Europe. Numerous examples from the Renaissance have survived, and the art of wax modeling is undoubtedly related to the revival of bronze casting, of which the wax image is the first step. It was an established skill in the Old World in the 17th and 18th centuries and was introduced to America sometime in the early 18th century. Wax was a commodity readily available in the colonies as a useful substance for dozens of various purposes around the house and in the merchants' shops. Moreover, it was easy to work and required no special knowledge for its care.

As early as 1731 Martha Gazley, living in New York, advertised that her services were available to teach gentlewomen such "curious Works [as] Artificial Fruit and Flowers, and other Wax-Work." And in 1749 an advertisement was run in the *New York Gazette* of August 28, "That the Effigies of the Royal Family of England, and the Empress Queen of Hungaria and Bohemia, and others to the Number of fourteen Figures, in Wax . . . are to be seen from 7 in the Morning to 6 in the Evening." Such diverse forms of wax sculpture are therefore known to have existed in the first half of the 18th century, and there were also attempts at small portraits in wax as well. In addition, there were small tableaux with figures representing genre, historical, or religious scenes; and of course there were the wax museums with their images of famous persons. The latter were almost always on a small scale, and they were usually rendered as profile bas-reliefs. This never became one of the major arts, and the modeler in wax might well be compared to the painter of miniature portraits or the cutter of silhouettes.

The first of the colonial wax modelers of whom much is known was Patience Lowell Wright, born in Bordentown, New Jersey, in 1725. At the age of twenty-three Patience Lowell married Joseph Wright, who died in 1769, leaving her with three children to care for. She turned to what had earlier been an amusing hobby, the modeling of wax, to support herself and her family, and she seems to have had no formal training although it is possible that she may have sought some instruction from someone like the Martha Gazley referred to above. Her little bas-relief portraits became quite popular in New York and elsewhere. In her house she had an exhibition of wax figures that could be viewed for a small admission fee, but on June 3, 1771, a fire destroyed most "of the Figures so nearly resembling Life, which have for some time past been exhibited in this City to general satisfaction." (*New York Gazette*, June 10, 1771.) Undaunted, Mrs. Wright repaired the damaged pieces and replaced others, so that her exhibition was once more ready for visitors by midsummer. She evidently concluded, however, that London offered a better market for her talents than the colonies, for on January 30, 1772, she sailed to England. In the newspaper report of her departure she was described as ". . . the ingenious Mrs. Wright, whose Skill in taking Likenesses, expressing the Passions, and many curious Devices in Wax Work, has deservedly recommended her to public Notice."

While in England she modeled countless profile relief portraits of the upper middle class, as well as those of the aristocracy including the king and queen. These were usually mounted on oval panels, which ranged from about two to ten inches on the longest axis. There is also mention of a small, full-length figure of Lord Chatham in wax. Of commissions she had plenty, and Englishmen found her frank but courteous manner to be quite engaging. Even so, she remained loyal to the colonies during the Revolution and always intended to return to her native land. Her ties with England grew stronger, however, as her son Joseph began studying painting with Benjamin West and her daughter married the portrait painter John Hoppner.

For Americans, two of her portraits made in Europe are of special interest, those of Benjamin Franklin and George Washington. Mrs. Wright was an occasional correspondent of Franklin's, and went to Paris in 1781 where she modeled his likeness in both a small wax bust in the round and a wax profile; the former was destroyed accidently years later in America. The little profile shows Franklin in his great curled wig, a rather portly man with double chin, and with cravat and waistcoat under his coat. The face is modeled in a fine Rococo style that reveals Mrs. Wright as indeed the equal of most of her English competitors. Her most celebrated profile, however, is "General George Washington," an example

of which is in the Maryland Historical Society. Washington did not become a
general and rise to prominence until several years after Patience Wright's departure for England; she had never modeled his likeness from life, but she wished
to make a profile of him—out of reverence for the man and probably with the
hope of selling several replicas. In December of 1783 she wrote the following in
a letter to Washington:

. . . you have My Most grateful thanks for your Kind attention to My Son in taking
him into your Famaly to encourage his genii and giving him the pleasing opertunity of
taking a Likeness that has I sincerely hope, gave his Country and Your Friends, Sir,
Satisfaction—I am Impatient to have a Copy of what he has done that I may have the
honour of making a Model from it in Wax work—it has been for some time the Wish
and desire of my heart to Moddel a Likeness of General Washington. Then I shall
think myself ariv'd at the end of all my Earthly honours and Return in Peace to Enjoy
My Native Country.   [Library of Congress]

Washington replied courteously that should the bust of himself that her son
had modeled reach her hands, he would be honored to have her do a likeness
from it. In time a copy of it did come into her possession, and it was from the
bust by Joseph Wright (c. 1783) that her profile bas-relief of Washington in
military uniform was made, in 1785. It has been suggested that this profile was
actually taken from the portrait by Houdon, but Patience Wright died in England in March 1786, before she could have seen the Frenchman's work.

Joseph Wright (1756–1793) returned to America in 1782 just before the end
of hostilities. Soon after his return he painted several portraits of Washington,
and in the fall of 1783 he executed a portrait bust of Washington which has
never been located. Wright began by making a life mask of the general, who
bore the discomfort with fortitude. Unfortunately, as the sculptor removed the
mask from Washington's face he dropped it, and it smashed to pieces on the
floor. There is some question whether or not Washington again submitted himself to the ordeal, and it is small wonder that he was less than enthusiastic when
Houdon had later to repeat the process.

Joseph Wright also made a bas-relief profile portrait of Washington (Fig.
1.33); an example is now owned by Winterthur Museum. A distinctive feature is
the laurel wreath about the head, putting Washington in the guise of a Roman
senator in an attempt to place him among the noblest men of that great republican epoch of the past. Designed around 1784, the profile is signed on the base of
the neck. The explanation of its numismatic character is that Joseph Wright was
at that time commissioned by the government to make designs for the coins it
was soon to mint. Wright worked in Philadelphia from 1783 to 1786 and spent
the following three years in New York City. He died in Philadelphia in 1793
during the yellow-fever epidemic.

There were others who modeled wax profiles on a more or less regular basis,
although most of them found it necessary to have additional occupations in order
to earn a living. Such a man was Daniel Bowen (c. 1760–1856), who sometime

during 1790–1795 modeled copies of Patience Wright's profile of Washington in military uniform. One of these is in the collection of the New-York Historical Society; another, in a private collection, bears the inscription "George Washington Esqre President of the United States, By Mr. Bowen, Jany 23, 1794." The modeling is weaker than in the Patience Wright profile, and the likeness is not as accurate. Bowen also fashioned a wax bas-relief profile of Benjamin Franklin. But his main source of income was derived from the museum he opened in the late 1780's in New York City.

Newspapers of that city in 1789 advertised that his museum and waxworks were located opposite Crane Wharf, with many life-size figures of famous persons. The chief attraction was the image of General Washington ". . . sitting under a canopy in his Military Dress [while] Over the head of his Excellency a Fame is suspended crowning him with a Wreath of Laurels." Prominent personalities of New York City were also represented, such as John Livingston, the Reverend Dr. John Rodgers, and the Reverend Samuel Provoost; there were also effigies of the King and Queen of England and the Prince of Wales. The heads and hands were made of wax, and it was probably Bowen himself who modeled them. From 1790 to 1795 his museum was seldom located in one city for more than a year. But by the latter date he had established his Columbian Museum in Boston, where it was to remain until fire destroyed it for the second time in 1807. This second and total destruction of his collection brought his wax museum to a conclusion, but some time later (c. 1818) he turned to the exhibition of painted panoramic views of cities. He died at the age of ninety-six in Philadelphia.

Wax portraiture continued after the turn of the century in the work of several sculptors who arrived fully trained from Europe. John Christian Rauschner was born in Frankfort, Germany, in 1760, and as a youth he learned from his father the skills of stucco work and of modeling in plaster. He had attained some success in his native land before he decided to try his fortune in America, and by 1799 he was residing in New York City, where he was described as a "wax artist." In the next decade he made frequent excursions along most of the seaboard, doing small wax profiles of sitters from Massachusetts to Virginia and possibly going even into South Carolina. He was in the Salem-Boston area during most of 1809–1810, but he appeared in Philadelphia in the fall of the latter year. Rauschner disappeared from the records sometime around 1811–1812.

More than one hundred little wax profiles by Rauschner have been identified, and there were undoubtedly many more that have not survived; but the artist, although quite gifted and prolific, did not prosper from this type of work and is reported to have taken on work of the most menial sort to supplement his income. One of his wax profiles would bring only a few dollars, and even when several replicas were ordered of a particularly popular subject—such as a governor or local bishop—the remuneration was small. Of a profile he did of Governor James Sullivan, eight replicas still survive. Several of the molds that Rauschner used are still extant. The New-York Historical Society owns both the mold and a wax profile of the likeness of John McComb, Sr. (Fig. 1.35). The New-York Historical Society has several more of his works; one of John or Joseph Reade is quite typical in the exquisitely delicate contour line of the profile, the tiny and somewhat nervously incised striations of the hair, the thick neck, and the accurate but simplified details of the clothing. These bust-length profiles frequently appear rather stiff and truncated, but the sensitivity of the face more than redeems them. Unlike Patience Wright and her son Joseph who produced a cameo effect by using only pure white wax throughout the image, Rauschner made his portraits of colored wax. A fine pigment was mixed into the wax—pink for the face, perhaps dark blue for a coat, or pale green for a dress or bonnet. Only the finest details were painted on, such as those of the eyes and mouth, or jewelry or buttons on the clothing. The profile was customarily applied to a circular or oval piece of painted glass about four or five inches in diameter.

George Miller, whose work is discussed in the following chapter, also modeled wax profiles in Philadelphia (1798–c. 1810) and in Baltimore (1810–1812). Miller's waxes are not as delicate as those by Rauschner, but share with them general characteristics of style.

About 1815, Giuseppe Valaperta arrived in America straight from his sculptural work at Malmaison in France. He, too, is discussed in the succeeding chapter, but he deserves mention here because of a group of small profile relief portraits that he modeled in red wax. Several of these were given to the New-York Historical Society by the Gallatin Family, and include images of Jefferson, Madison, Monroe, Albert Gallatin, and Andrew Jackson (Fig. 1.34); the last bears Valaperta's signature, and the others are identical to it in style. These were probably modeled in Washington, D.C., where the artist spent most of his time while in America. Valaperta so emphasized the special features of the physiognomy of his subjects that his portraits verge on being caricatures. There is a feeling for sculpturesque form in his portraits, however, that was lacking in most of the earlier wax profiles of this country.

Unquestionably one of the most gifted fashioners of cameo portraits was Robert Ball Hughes, whose major works are discussed in detail in the next chapter. By the time Hughes arrived in this country (1829) he had already received training at the Royal Academy. Several of his wax portraits reveal the English neoclassicism which had been established by John Flaxman—as may be seen in the wax-relief head of Robert C. Winthrop in the Society for the Preservation of New England Antiquities. The special qualities of Hughes' little portraits are his mastery of modeling and anatomy, and the pure whiteness of his wax. Although he is much better known today for his larger works, he was the finest modeler of wax profiles in the second quarter of the 19th century anywhere in the country. But with the arrival of the photographic image in the 1840's, the peripheral forms of portraiture—wax cameos, painted miniatures, and cut silhouettes—fell by the wayside.

[FIG. 1.1] Gravestone of Robert Meriam (d. 1681), Concord, Mass. Photo, Index of American Sculpture, University of Delaware.

[FIG. 1.2] Gravestone of Mrs. Sarah Davis (d. 1751), Concord, Mass. Photo, Index of American Sculpture, University of Delaware.

[FIG. 1.3] Gravestone of Joseph Tapping (d. 1678), King's Chapel burial ground, Boston. Photo, Index of American Sculpture, University of Delaware.

[FIG. 1.4] Gravestone of Solomon Milner (d. 1757), Congregational churchyard, Charleston, S.C. Photo, Index of American Sculpture, University of Delaware.

[FIG. 1.5] Gravestone of the Reverend William Hutson (d. 1761), Congregational churchyard, Charleston, S.C. Photo, Index of American Sculpture, University of Delaware.

[FIG. 1.6] Gravestone of Mrs. Richard Owen (d. 1749), Congregational churchyard, Charleston, S.C. Photo, Index of American Sculpture, University of Delaware.

[FIG. 1.7] "Agriculture," "Liberty," and "Plenty," by John and Simeon Skillin, Jr., on a chest-on-chest by Stephen Badlam (1791). Wood. Yale University Art Gallery, Mabel Brady Garvan Collection.

[FIG. 1.8] Chest, 17th century. Wood, 34″ high. Courtesy, Henry Francis du Pont Winterthur Museum.

[FIG. 1.9] Chancel decorations, St. Michael's Church (c. 1755), Charleston, S.C. Wood. Photo, Index of American Sculpture, University of Delaware.

[FIG. 1.10] Bible box, 17th century. Oak, 4½″ high. Courtesy, Henry Francis du Pont Winterthur Museum.

[FIG. 1.11] "Little Admiral" (c. 1750). Wood, 42″ high. Courtesy Bostonian Society, Old State House.

[FIG. 1.12] "Plenty," secretary ornament (c. 1795). Mahogany, 10¾″ high. Courtesy, Henry Francis du Pont Winterthur Museum.

[FIG. 1.13] James Gibbs, *Book of Architecture*, London (1728), plate 114. Photo, courtesy, Henry Francis du Pont Winterthur Museum.

[FIG. 1.14] George Hepplewhite, *The Cabinet-Maker and Upholsterer's Guide*, London (1787), plate 40. Photo, courtesy, Henry Francis du Pont Winterthur Museum.

[FIG. 1.15] "Gardener" (c. 1785). Wood. Courtesy, Massachusetts Historical Society.

[FIG. 1.16] "Country Maid" (c. 1785). Wood. Courtesy, Massachusetts Historical Society.

[FIG. 1.17] "Milton"(?), secretary ornament, attributed to John and Simeon Skillin, Jr. (c. 1785). Wood. Courtesy, Beverly (Mass.) Historical Society.

[FIG. 1.18] "Plenty," attributed to the shop of John and Simeon Skillin, Jr. (c. 1790). Wood. From the Bolles secretary, Metropolitan Museum of Art, gift of Mrs. Russell Sage, 1909.

[FIG. 1.19] "Plenty" (or "Pomona"), by John and Simeon Skillin, Jr. (1793). Wood. Courtesy, Peabody Museum of Salem, Mass.

[FIG. 1.20] "Hope," attributed to the shop of John and Simeon Skillin, Jr. (c. 1790). White pine, 53½" high. Courtesy, Henry Francis du Pont Winterthur Museum.

[FIG. 1.21] "Mercury," attributed to John and Simeon Skillin, Jr. (c. 1790). Wood. Courtesy, Bostonian Society, Old State House.

[FIG. 1.23] "William Pitt," by Joseph Wilson (c. 1801). White pine. Courtesy, Smithsonian Institution.

[FIG. 1.22] Figurehead by Isaac Fowle (c. 1820). Wood. Courtesy, Bostonian Society, Old State House.

[FIG. 1.24] Decorative carving by Samuel McIntire, figure of "Liberty" by John and Simeon Skillin, Jr., on a chest-on-chest by William Lemon (1796). Wood. M. and M. Karolik Collection. Courtesy, Museum of Fine Arts, Boston.

[FIG. 1.25] "Governor John Winthrop," by Samuel Mc-Intire (1798). Wood. 15¾" high. Courtesy, American Antiquarian Society, Worcester, Mass.

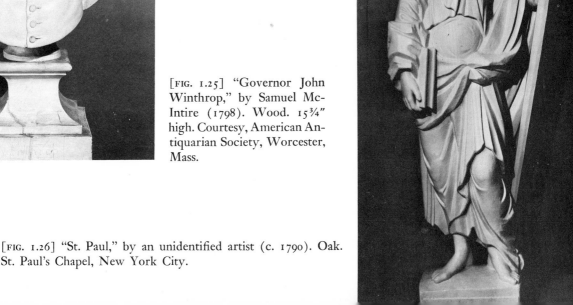

[FIG. 1.26] "St. Paul," by an unidentified artist (c. 1790). Oak. St. Paul's Chapel, New York City.

[FIG. 1.27] The Lord Timothy Dexter House, Newburyport, Mass. Lithograph published 1810 in Boston by J. E. Tilton and Company. Courtesy, Smithsonian Institution.

[FIG. 1.28] "Schuylkill Freed," by William Rush (c. 1828). Wood, 42″ high. Courtesy, Commissioners of Fairmount Park; photo, Philadelphia Museum of Art.

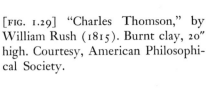

[FIG. 1.29] "Charles Thomson," by William Rush (1815). Burnt clay, 20″ high. Courtesy, American Philosophical Society.

[FIG. 1.30] "Chancellor Robert Livingston," by an unidentified artist (c. 1820). Wood, 24″ high. Courtesy, New-York Historical Society, New York City.

[FIG. 1.31] "Water Nymph and Bittern," by William Rush (c. 1828). Bronze copy of wooden original, 91″ high. Courtesy, Commissioners of Fairmount Park; photo, Philadelphia Museum of Art.

[FIG. 1.33] "George Washington," by
Joseph Wright (1784). Wax, 6″ high.
Courtesy, Henry Francis du Pont Win-
terthur Museum.

[FIG. 1.32] "George Washington," by
William Rush (1814). Pine, life-size.
Courtesy, Commissioners of Fairmount Park; photo, Philadelphia Museum of Art.

[FIG. 1.34] "Andrew Jackson," by Giuseppe Valaperta (c. 1818). Wax profile, 3″ high. Courtesy, New-York Historical Society, New York City.

[FIG. 1.35] "John McComb, Sr." by John Christian Rauschner (c. 1800). Wax profile, 3¼″ high. Courtesy, New-York Historical Society, New York City.

[FIG. 1.36] "Sailor" (c. 1868). Wood, life-size. Courtesy, New-York Historical Society, New York City.

2

The Foreign Interlude

BETWEEN THE FLOURISHING OF THE NATIVE WOOD CARVERS AND STONECUTTERS AND the appearance of the first group of American sculptors (about 1825) a sizable body of sculpture was created by foreign artists. Some of the most famous names in late 18th- and early 19th-century sculpture thus became associated with commissions destined for America. When a more sophisticated sculpture than that produced by native carvers was required in America, the commissions were of necessity sent abroad or given to foreign sculptors who had migrated to the United States. This custom had begun in the 18th century, when a man of means who wanted to leave behind a marble wall monument befitting his status in life would send to England for such a piece. The monument would be placed inside the church, along one of the outer walls, in accordance with the practice at Westminster Abbey and at countless other churches in England.

As early as the second decade of the 18th century a polychromed wooden coat of arms with a scroll and a child's head was made in England to mark the grave of Colonel John Gibbs in St. James Church, Goose Creek, near Charleston, South Carolina. It was around mid-century that the famous Sir William Pepperell of Kittery, Maine, ordered from England his marble tombstone. Three other especially fine examples are in King's Chapel, Boston. The one in memory of Frances Shirley (d. 1744) was carved in 1754 by Peter Scheemakers (1691–1781) of London, and has as its crowning feature a Rococo bust portrait of Mrs. Shirley. Against the back wall of King's Chapel is a large marble Baroque monument by William Tyler (d. 1801) that Florentius Vassall erected in 1766 as a memorial to his great-grandfather. Sir Henry Cheere (1703–1781), who is represented by no less than nine monuments in Westminster Abbey, designed the Baroque memorial for Carl Apthorp. Thus, throughout the 18th century the colonists were used to commissioning marble wall monuments from England, and when they wanted monumental statues of famous men, they naturally turned to the established English sculptors.

Before the American Revolution there were already four monumental statues in the colonies. Of these, Joseph Wilton (1722–1803) had done three: "George III" and "William Pitt" for New York, and a replica of the latter for Charleston, South Carolina. The fourth was Richard Hayward's marble memorial to Lord Botetourt for Williamsburg, Virginia.

Joseph Wilton had studied under Pigalle in Paris in the 1740's and in Rome in the early 1750's. He became an immediate success in London and by 1764 was appointed sculptor to His Majesty, George III. His large studio specialized in decorative architectural carvings, as at Somerset House, or the ornate chimney piece for the Duchess of Marlborough's dressing room at Blenheim Palace. One of his best-known monuments is that dedicated to the memory of General Wolfe, which was carved and set up in Westminster Abbey in 1772. In this work, which represents the subject nude, Wilton avoided an issue that was being hotly debated among London artists: In the representation of great men, should the ennobling garb of antiquity replace the contemporary dress? In 1771 Benjamin West had painted his famous "Death of General Wolfe" and had disregarded the advice of Sir Joshua Reynolds that the figures should wear the clothing of antiquity. West held that the men who fought at Quebec did not wear togas or cimations as they went into battle, and that the men of the ancient world did not even know of the existence of the place where the battle was fought. Only two years earlier Charles Willson Peale while studying in London had made an engraving of William Pitt clothed in a Roman toga. The artist had thus meant to ennoble Pitt, but the latter's bony knees spoiled the intended effect. Peale realized this and never again used the toga in his portraits of great men. The controversy over the use of ancient or contemporary dress was involved in nearly every major sculptural commission emanating from America, and touched upon the famous images of Washington by such men as Houdon, Canova, Chantrey, and Greenough. In his three statues destined for the colonies, executed a few years before West's epoch-making "Death of General Wolfe," Wilton chose to clothe them in the dress of antiquity.

Both the equestrian "George III" and the marble statue of Pitt had been commissioned in 1766, the latter out of gratitude for the repeal of the hated Stamp Act. The first to arrive was the lead statute of His Royal Majesty. It was probably very like Wilton's statue of the king that was erected in Berkeley Square in 1766 and copied from the image of the Roman Emperor Marcus Aurelius; evidently not well made, by 1812 it could no longer be propped up and was finally dismantled. The equestrian statue for New York was about life size and represented the king in Roman dress, with a laurel wreath upon his head. The gilded-lead statue was placed on a fifteen-foot-high marble pedestal in Bowling Green; on the pedestal was an inscription that noticeably omitted any words of praise for the monarch. The statue was dedicated in August 1770 in the presence of the most prominent citizens of the area, with thirty-two cannon being discharged at the Battery while a band played patriotic music. It must have been an impressive spectacle as the late summer sun reflected glistening rays from the gilded surfaces, for it was indeed in that day a unique sight to the eyes of the colonists. Although the subject was not popular, the statue must have done much to create a desire for monumental statuary in a part of the world where none before had existed.

Three weeks later, on September 7, Wilton's other statue for New York was unveiled and dedicated—the marble "William Pitt," which stood at the intersection of Wall and William Streets. Pitt wore the long robes of a Roman senator, with his left hand raised in an oratorical gesture while his right held the scroll of the Magna Carta, which bore the inscription: *Articuli Magna Carta Libertatum.* The inscription on the pedestal stated that "This statue of the Right Honourable William Pitt Earl of Chatham was erected as a Public Testimony of the Grateful sense the Colony of New York retains of the many eminent services he rendered America Particularly in promoting the Repeal of the Stamp Act. Anno Dom. MDCCLXX." The remains of this statue, which has lost its arms and head, may be seen in the New-York Historical Society.

The vigorous gesticulating form of Pitt was repeated in the replica (Fig. 2.1) that Wilton made for South Carolina. Although the House of Commons of South Carolina had commissioned its statue of Pitt a few months after the one for New York had been commissioned, the replica arrived in Charleston in May 1770, several months before the one for New York. It was dedicated on July 5, "in the presence of almost the whole of the inhabitants." The laudatory inscription was generally similar to that of the New York original.

All three of Wilton's statues have suffered great mistreatment, and the equestrian monument has all but disappeared. An overzealous citizenry, upon hearing the Declaration of Independence read aloud on July 9, 1776, pulled down the "George III" and dismembered it. Most of it was taken to the home of Governor Wolcott in Litchfield, Connecticut, where its lead was melted down and converted into bullets for the Revolutionary Army. The base of the statue, still showing the marks of the four hooves, was for some reason spared from the melting pot and, along with the horse's tail, may be seen at the New-York Historical Society.

In retaliation for the disrespect shown the image of the king, British soldiers in November 1776 decapitated the cherished statue of William Pitt and broke off the arms. Thus it remained in place until 1788, when it was finally dismantled. In the preceding year, in Royall Tyler's play *The Contrast,* Jonathan, wandering about in New York City, said: "Oh, I have seen a power of fine sights. I went to see two marblestone men and leaden horse that stands out in doors in all weathers; and when I came to where they was, one had got no head, and t'other weren't there." This was undoubtedly a reference to the two statues by Wilton.

The statue of the Earl of Chatham which still stands in Charleston is better preserved, although on April 16, 1780, a British cannon ball fired from James Island broke off the right arm, which held the Magna Carta. The statue was decapitated when it fell to the ground in 1794 while being moved, and it was probably at that time the left arm was destroyed. Repaired in 1808, the statue stood in the yard of the Orphan House until 1881, when it was placed in Washington Park behind City Hall.

On October 15, 1770, Norborne Berkeley, Baron de Botetourt, died in Williamsburg, Virginia. Though it was he who dissolved the House of Burgesses in 1769, when the gentlemen of Virginia had protested against the Revenue Act, he was one of the most popular of the royal governors appointed by the king. Within a year of his death, on July 20, 1771, the Virginia legislature voted "with one united voice" an appropriation for "an elegant statue in marble" of Botetourt. No one gave a thought to the possibility of a local carver executing the statue, and William Nelson, the acting governor, sent the commission to England to be supervised by the merchant John Norton. On March 10, 1772, Norton wrote to a relative that he had decided on a sculptor: ". . . his name is Hayward and he lives in Piccadilly. He's to be finished in 12 months completely, with iron rails, packed, and to be put into a ship for £1,700."

Richard Hayward (1728–1800) was a prominent sculptor of London who specialized in interior decorative carvings for such edifices as Woburn Abbey and Blenheim. His six monuments in Westminster Abbey range in date from 1765 to 1780. Hayward's statue (Fig. 2.2) shows the governor in his finest garments and a great cloak, which extends to the floor. Like Wilton's "Pitt," Hayward's "Botetourt" was heir to a Baroque legacy and is reminiscent of the grandiose and majestic portraits of Louis XIV by Hyacinthe Rigaud. In such 18th-century statues the desire for Baroque grandeur had not given way to effeminate Rococo refinement. The governor's likeness was taken from a wax medallion by Isaac Gosset, who had also made a well-known medallion of Benjamin Franklin in 1766. The statue arrived in Virginia aboard one of John Norton's ships in May 1773 and was promptly set up in a place of honor—the plaza outside the Williamsburg capitol—its high pedestal adorned with an exuberant Baroque version of classical ornament. A relief on the back of the pedestal depicts two women, one representing Great Britain and the other America, standing at the altar of peace. But peace was not to prevail, and during the Revolutionary War some overardent patriots pulled the figure from its pedestal, damaging it severely. The famous architect Benjamin Henry Latrobe, traveling through Williamsburg in 1796, wrote that "A beautiful statue of Lord Botetourt . . . is deprived of its head & mutilated in many other respects. This is not the only proof of the decay of Williamsburg." He recorded its appearance in a drawing in his sketchbook. Soon afterward the statue was purchased for the College of William and Mary, and in 1801 it was repaired and set up on the campus.

Within a decade and a half of their arrival in this country the four statues by Wilton and Hayward had been mutilated or destroyed. But once the hostilities ceased, Americans again wanted to have marble statues of their great men. Federal and state governments began voting memorials to the heroes of the Revolution, but this time the commissions were sent to French or Italian sculptors, not to Englishmen.

On December 31, 1775, Major General Richard Montgomery, leading his men of the Continental Army in an attack on Quebec, had fallen before the guns of the British, thus becoming one of the country's first heroes of the Revolution. He had given that greatest of gifts which was his to offer—his life—to the cause in which he believed, and on January 22, 1776, Congress resolved to commission a monument to his memory. A committee reported a few days later that out of a sense of gratitude to those who had "distinguished themselves in the glorious cause of liberty" and "to inspire posterity with an emulation of their illustrious actions," a proper memorial to Montgomery should be commissioned. It was resolved that a monument should be procured

. . . from Paris, or any other part of France, with an inscription sacred to his memory and expressive of his amiable character and heroic achievements; and that the Continental treasurers be directed to advance a sum, not exceeding £300 sterling, to Dr. Benjamin Franklin (who is desired to see this resolution properly executed) for defraying the expenses thereof.

In Paris, Franklin offered the commission to the *sculpteur du roi* to Louis XV, Jean Jacques Caffiéri (1725–1792), who exhibited his design of the monument at the Paris Salon of 1777. In the Salon catalogue it is described as a cenotaph ten feet high, rising from an altar supported by two wall brackets; on the altar is a broken column, with a funeral urn on top. Around the column are military trophies and several emblems of liberty, and behind it is a pyramid. Neoclassical in design, it testifies to the alignment of late 18th-century man with the spirit of ancient republican Rome. Patriotism and devotion to the cause of liberty, noble actions in the pursuit of noble humanitarian goals—these were the highest virtues of the day. In England, Benjamin West was painting them in his large historical pictures, and a decade later John Trumbull was to paint the same themes in his cycle of the struggle for independence. The Montgomery monument was finished by June 1778, but because of the war it was not until 1789 that it was erected under the east portico of St. Paul's Chapel in New York.

Also shown at the Paris Salon of 1777 was Caffiéri's portrait bust of Benjamin Franklin, which was modeled from life. The terra-cotta original—signed and dated 1777—is in the Bibliothèque Mazarine in Paris, but replicas are in the collections of the American Philosophical Society and the New-York Historical

Society. Several casts were made, a number of which Franklin ordered to give to friends. Caffiéri's bust is frequently confused with the one by Houdon, but Caffiéri's has a knotted cravat at the neck whereas Houdon's has a round neckpiece.

Another 1777 French portrait of Franklin—shown wearing his fur hat—is the little round terra-cotta relief profile by Jean Baptiste Nini, who worked at the glass and pottery factory at Chaumont sur Loire. A later image is the 8-inch terra-cotta figure made in 1793 by Françoise Marle Suzanne. Franklin, with round belly and bent knees, is in colonial dress, a three-cornered hat under his left arm, and buckles on his shoes. An example is owned by the Walters Gallery in Baltimore.

In 1778 the most famous of all French sculptors of the 18th century, Jean Antoine Houdon, also did a portrait of Benjamin Franklin. A second version was made in 1791, and replicas of both exist in several American collections. Houdon produced a number of portrait busts of eminent Americans, including Thomas Jefferson (Fig. 2.6), Robert Fulton, Joel Barlow, John Paul Jones, and several busts of Washington. In 1781 the Virginia legislature resolved that Houdon should be commissioned to make a portrait bust of the beloved French hero of the American Revolution, the Marquis de Lafayette. A replica was presented to the city of Paris, and the marble original was sent to Richmond where it may be seen in the rotunda of the State House only a few paces from Houdon's masterpiece, the life-size marble statute of George Washington (Fig. 2.3).

By the late 1770's Houdon and his work were familiar to America's leading citizens. It was only natural that he should receive the commission that was voted by the assembly of the state of Virginia on June 24, 1784, for "a statue of George Washington, to be of the finest marble and best workmanship." Although Congress had resolved in the preceding year to commission an equestrian statue of Washington, it was several decades before any action was taken; therefore, to the Virginia assembly belongs the honor of acquiring the first monumental sculptural effort of the new nation.

The governor of Virginia wrote soon afterward to Thomas Jefferson in Paris about the matter, and on January 12, 1785, the latter replied that "there could be no question raised as to the Sculptor who should be employed; the reputation of Monsr Houdon of this city being unrivalled in Europe." Jefferson wrote that to preserve Washington's true image for all ages and to uphold the reputation of the great sculptor, Houdon should come to America to study the general's features rather than make the statue from a portrait that had been painted by Charles Willson Peale. And, Jefferson continued,

Monsr Houdon . . . was so anxious to be the person who should hand down the figure of the General to future ages, that without hesitating a moment he offered to abandon his business here, to leave the statues of kings unfinished, & to go to America to take the true figure by actual inspection & measurement.

There was some disagreement for a while on the price to be paid; but with this matter settled, Dr. Franklin and Houdon, along with three of the latter's assistants, left Paris in late July 1785. Houdon took along several of his busts, but these were sent separately to Le Havre, and neither they nor his personal baggage arrived in time to make the ship. The party arrived on September 14 in Philadelphia (where Houdon bought new clothes and tools), and the sculptor was at Mount Vernon ready to begin work by October 2.

During the next two weeks Houdon completed three preliminary tasks. First, he made a life mask, which is preserved in the collection of the Pierpont Morgan Library in New York. Second, he modeled a bust in terra cotta, which was later fired and painted white; this excellent portrait with undraped chest is signed and may be seen at Mount Vernon. Third, he took Washington's measurements, so that the statue would be as exact as possible. Jefferson had remarked that there had been some discussion about making the figure larger than life to give a more imposing effect, but it was decided to make a realistic life-size statue.

The statue was modeled in Houdon's Paris studio during the next two or three years. Originally the sculptor planned to represent Washington in the classical robes of a Roman senator, and in this he had the full support of Jefferson. But the matter was brought to the attention of Washington, who wrote, "A little deviation in favour of the modern costume would be more expedient than a servile adherence to the garb of antiquity." So Houdon clothed Washington in the "boots and regimentals" of his Revolutionary army. His left arm rests upon the bundle of thirteen fasces—symbolic of the Thirteen Colonies—on which he has already hung up his sword. This last is a reference to his exchange of the duties of war for those of peace; behind the figure and leaning against the fasces is a plow, symbol of the farmer-statesman. Houdon created an 18th-century American Cincinnatus, for Washington, like the Roman hero, had left his plowshare to defend the cause of liberty, then returned to the fields when the battle was over, willingly relinquishing his military authority. The details of the clothing are simplified so that they do not demand undue attention in themselves, and the eye of the spectator is continually drawn to the head, which portrays the nobility, the pensiveness, the gentleness, and the calm dignity of the man.

Houdon finished his clay statue in 1788; the date is engraved into the base, along with the inscription *houdon citoyen français*. A fine white marble block was taken from Italy to Paris, and Houdon's model was put into stone sometime between 1788 and 1791. However, it was not until 1796 that the statue was set on its pedestal in the rotunda of the Virginia state capitol. Here it dominates its handsome quarters in lordly fashion—in contrast to the humiliation that Horatio Greenough's statue of Washington was to experience a half century later. Houdon's marble "Washington" was indeed one of the wonders of the new republic, and its success and its very presence encouraged the growth of a monumental sculptural art in America. Moreover, his busts of famous Americans were well known and highly esteemed, and they, too, played a significant role in the formation of the young nation's own school of portrait sculpture. Before the Revolution a small number of plaster and marble busts existed in the colonies, but it was only after the war that the great period of the sculptured portrait bust began; the work of Houdon, along with that of several others, was a major factor in establishing that art and determining its character.

While the Houdon statue of Washington was being carved in marble in Paris, in Philadelphia the Library Company was erecting its new building (1789–1790). On the façade at the second floor was a niche that was to contain a statue of Benjamin Franklin. In 1781 Franklin had written to Dr. Jan Ingenhousz that the arts were not sufficiently patronized in America and that "statuaries and other artists would not make a fortune in the present circumstances." Accordingly, the Library Company sent the commission, along with a bust of Franklin and a sketch showing his dimensions, to the Italian sculptor Francesco Lazzarini. Dr. Franklin had indicated that he would prefer to see himself in "a gown for his dress and a Roman head," and he was thus rendered, with a stack of books on which one arm rested; in his other hand he held a scepter turned downward, which indicated his dislike of monarchies. The statue, larger than life size, arrived in Philadelphia in 1792 and was hoisted to its niche. By the 1870's it had weathered so badly that it had to be removed. Concerning this statue, William Jones wrote the following in 1816 in a letter to Senator Nathaniel Macon of North Carolina: "It was presented by the late Mr. Bingham who employed one of the most celebrated artists in Italy to execute it, for which he was paid $6000, but unfaithful to his engagement he employed one of his pupils for that purpose and paid him $1000 for the work."

A few years later Philadelphia received another monumental statue of one of her celebrated sons: it was described in the book *Sculpture: and the Plastic Art* (Boston, 1850; p. 330):

The Statue of William Penn . . . is in front of the Pennsylvania Hospital, to which institution it was presented in the year 1804, by John Penn, Esq. of London. It is of colossal size, standing upon a marble pedestal, and represents Penn, in the plain Quaker garb and hat, holding in his left hand a scroll, containing the Charter of privileges.

About the time Lazzarini's statue of Franklin was being set in place another Italian sculptor, Giuseppe Ceracchi (1751–1802), was trying his fortune in the new nation. He had studied and worked in Rome about 1770 and a couple of years later went to England, where he made numerous portrait busts, as well as some figure decorations for the architects Robert Adam and Sir William Chambers. He returned to Rome, then journeyed to America in 1791, hoping to find sufficient patronage to produce his design for a marble monument to Liberty. It was to be more than 100 feet high, with allegorical and mythological figures among billowing clouds and the goddess of Liberty descending in a great chariot drawn by four horses. But America in the 1790's was not yet ready for such grandiose art, and the estimated cost of $30,000 dissuaded Congress from commissioning it. A feeble attempt to obtain adequate financing through private donations also failed.

Ceracchi joined with Charles Willson Peale, William Rush, and others in the early and futile attempt to organize an art academy in America. The Columbianum was the victim of internal dissension, much of which was caused by the volatile Italian sculptor. (Dr. William Thornton, designer of the U. S. Capitol, knew Ceracchi personally and reported that he had "a most violent temper," but that he was also "a man of great genius.") While in America Ceracchi made several fine portrait busts of famous Americans of the day. Most notable was his neoclassical bust of Washington, which won general acclaim for its truthfulness and dignity. The original terra cotta is now in the museum at Nantes, France, but marble examples may be seen in the Gibbes Art Gallery at Charleston, South Carolina, and in the Washington Monument in Baltimore. Ceracchi also did busts of Thomas Jefferson, Benjamin Franklin, John Paul Jones, Egbert Benson, and David Rittenhouse. Among his finest is that of Alexander Hamilton, which became the standard image of the fiery Federalist for later sculptors and painters. Several examples of the handsome Hamilton bust are in American collections, but some are actually copies by an imported Irish sculptor, John Dixey. Another of Ceracchi's fine portrait busts is the one of George Clinton (Fig. 2.4) now in the New-York Historical Society. The governor of New York is portrayed in the manner of a Roman statesman, with a toga draped about his shoulders. There is an intense liveliness and an animated expression in the portrait, and it does indeed justify the high reputation the sculptor enjoyed while in the United States. His busts, along with those by Houdon, did much to establish a new concept of sculptured portraiture here in this country—one quite unlike that produced by our native wood carvers. Ceracchi's and Houdon's busts provided a new measure of artistic excellence for native sculptors who wished to raise their craft to an art. As America's own marble sculptors came along, it was from busts such as these that they drew inspiration.

Ceracchi left America in 1795 to return to Europe. He had arrived a few years earlier with high hopes of receiving sculptural commissions from a new nation wanting to profess its dedication to liberty and the rights of man. He found instead a largely provincial civilization that did not yet regard itself as a world power or a prime mover in the destiny of the Western world. In the 1790's, America's dream was far more modest, and for the artist there remained little more than portrait commissions. Had Ceracchi chosen to stay in America a few more years, however, his talents might have been employed in decorating the new United States Capitol, which Benjamin Henry Latrobe was erecting in Washington. As it happened, Latrobe had to send to Italy for two of Ceracchi's countrymen to come over to execute the decorative work.

Christian Gullager, or Guldager (1759–1826), arrived in America not long after the end of the Revolutionary War, coming from Copenhagen where he had studied at the Royal Academy. He settled in Boston, and in 1790 he produced his best-known work, a marble bust of George Washington. Though not definitely identified, some believe this bust to be the one owned by Christ Church in Boston. That Gullager's portrait was well received is demonstrated by a notice that appeared in the April 7, 1790, issue of the *Gazette of the United States* when the bust was exhibited in New York City. By 1798 Gullager had moved to Philadelphia; by 1806 he had established himself in New York City. His total production of sculptural works during these years was small, for he was engaged more in painting than in sculpture. He died in Philadelphia in 1826.

In the decade of the 1790's, most of the foreign sculptors who decided to try their fortune in America came to Philadelphia rather than to Boston or the other seaboard cities. This is probably because Philadelphia then led the country in both cultural matters and population, and for a while was the capital of the new republic. Johann David Schoepf had observed during his travels through the States in 1783 and 1784 that

America has produced as yet no sculptors or engravers. But stone-cutters find a pretty good market. Mr. Bauer and Mr. Hafelein, at Philadelphia, make a business of preparing tombstones, chimney pieces, and other heavy decorative work, using the common marble of those parts.   [*Travels in the Confederation*, Philadelphia, 1911, p. 89]

So the foreign sculptors moved in to fill the vacuum. There were already several minor sculptors active in Philadelphia in the last years of the century, and some of them took rather active roles in the affairs of the fine arts. John Eckstein (1736–1817), who had been a sculptor at the court of Frederick the Great from about 1772, came to Philadelphia with his son, Frederick, in 1794. He, too, was one of the founders of the short-lived Columbianum, and at that institution's first exhibition in 1795 he entered the following item:

Model—the protecting Goddess of America, seated on clouds, and her Head adorned with plumage, has on her right hand two cupids; wreathing round the picture of General Washington, in Basso Relivo, a branch of laurel which they had before received from the Goddess who is in the attitude of receiving from an Eagle on her left another laurel branch for them to finish the wreath with. The Eagle rests on a shield emblazoned with 15 stars representing the United States of America.

John and Frederick Eckstein invited the citizens to inspect "an exhibition of their works of Painting and Sculpture, &c, &c, which may be seen at their house." John, active in Philadelphia until his death, was one of the founders of the Pennsylvania Academy. In 1806 he advertised that he had modeled an equestrian statue, which he exhibited several years later at the first annual showing of the Pennsylvania Academy in 1811: "An original design in clay, for a monument of General Washington." It was indicated that the model was for a statue of Washington "about to be erected in this city," but no such statue was ever executed; it is especially interesting that the general was dressed in Roman armor, probably in imitation of the equestrian statue of Frederick the Great that Eckstein remembered from earlier days in Germany. During the course of his years in Philadelphia John Eckstein exhibited regularly at the Pennsylvania Academy, usually neoclassical sculpture, but at times also drawings or water colors. No work by the elder Eckstein has at present been located, but according to Henry Tuckerman in 1867, Mr. J. C. McGuire of Baltimore owned a marble bust of Washington by Eckstein, dated 1796 and probably copied from Houdon's portrait bust. (The career of John's son, Frederick, belongs to a slightly later period and to the development of sculpture in Cincinnati, not Philadelphia; it will be discussed in due course.)

George M. Miller (d. 1819) came to Philadelphia from Scotland in the late 1790's to practice the art of wax portraiture, and over the next several years modeled numerous little likenesses "in color" of some of the city's leading citizens. That he also executed life-size busts is demonstrated by his entries at the Pennsylvania Academy. One of these, shown in 1814, was the bust "The Right Reverend Bishop White," which is now in the collection of the American Philosophical Society. The modeling is quite strong and reveals Miller to have been an accomplished sculptor, although there is a lack of richness in the textures. The same institution also owns a small plaster bas-relief profile of Jefferson by Miller, done in 1803, which is something of a caricature. A further idea of Miller's activity is gained from a letter, dated November 10, 1814, sent to the directors of the Philadelphia Athenaeum with which he deposited "the following casts, *vizt.* Washington, Franklin, Bishop White, Shakespeare, Venus de Medici, the Empresses Octavia, & Valerie, two Antique Funeral Urns, a small whole length figure of Antinous, small Busts of Susanna, & Adonis." William Jones, in a letter of January 20, 1816, to Senator Nathaniel Macon of North Carolina about that state's proposed statue of Washington, wrote:

There is a Mr. Miller in this City (Philadelphia) whose profession is that of a modeller in which art he is said to possess considerable talent, having executed some very good casts. He would undertake to make the statue, and at a rough estimate supposes the cost would be from $3000 to $4000 dollars, exclusive of a suitable block of Italian marble . . . . It is questionable whether the contemplated style [neoclassical] of execution of the work may be within the compass of his art . . . .

Miller also seems to have been ready to take on any kind of small-scale sculptural work, for in March of 1815 he advertised he would execute portraits in wax or plaster, had medallions from Italy for sale, would repair broken pieces of sculpture, and would make casts of existing pieces. But even this willingness to accept odd jobs in sculpture was not enough to support him and his family, and Dunlap wrote of him: "He would have been an artist of eminence, if he could have made bread enough to support himself and wife . . . . But he came to us before the time when merit could be appreciated, or the pretender known from the artist." Miller also worked in Baltimore around 1810 to 1812.

Giuseppe Iardella (or Jardella) was brought from Italy to Philadelphia in the late 1790's by Robert Morris to carve the architectural decorations for the mansion Morris was building. Latrobe's opinion of the sculpture that Iardella executed for Morris' house is preserved in a passage in his notebook: "There is a profusion of wretched sculpture. The capitals of the columns are of the worst taste." However, tradition has it that it was Iardella who carved the bas-relief lunettes of Comedy and Tragedy that were placed below Rush's personifications of the same figures at the theatre Latrobe had just designed in Philadelphia. Morris' financial ruin ended the work on his house, and Iardella turned to the carving of portraits, some of which were executed for James Traquair, who advertised for sale busts of Washington, Hamilton, Franklin, and William Penn. These were probably copies of works by more famous men such as Houdon or Ceracchi.

Traquair was himself a stonecutter and sculptor who specialized in ornamental carving for interiors, and Latrobe commissioned him to execute several marble mantelpieces for the United States Capitol. Men such as Traquair and Iardella probably found much more employment as carvers of decorative ornamentation for architecture than as artists who created portrait busts or free-standing statuary.

Numerous mediocre and virtually unknown foreign (mainly Italian) carvers came to America in the 1790's and early years of the new century to make ornamental mantelpieces, lintels, and the like. For example, Peter Stagi, formerly a carver of statuary to the king of Poland, arrived in Philadelphia in 1795. An idea of his work may be obtained from an advertisement that he ran in the *Federal Gazette:* ". . . several statues, busts, and portraits of the most illustrious persons of ancient, and modern times, . . . chimney pieces, fancy tables, [and] animals for garden use." Evidently his wares and his talents were not sufficiently appreciated, for Stagi returned to Europe after two years in America. John Baptist Sartori had come over in 1794 and a man named Provini in 1796. Both specialized in architectural ornament in stone, but both also advertised busts of eminent men for sale.

James Traquair had also hired an Irish sculptor, John Dixey, to copy busts. Dixey had come to America in 1789 after studying at the Royal Academy in London. It was probably around 1798–1800, for example, that he carved a replica of Ceracchi's "Alexander Hamilton"; this copy is now in the Pennsylvania Academy of the Fine Arts. Dixey's ambitions toward something more than ornamental carving are apparent in the works he exhibited at the Academy's annual shows and in New York, for there appeared such titles as "Hercules Chaining Cerberus" (1817), "Adoration of the Wise Men of the East" (1819), "Theseus destroying Phoea of Crommyon" (1818), and "Ganymede." These neoclassical subjects no doubt hark back to his student days at the Royal Academy; there he had shown such promise that he had been awarded the funds to go to Rome to study. Instead, he had chosen to come to America, where he unfortunately found little call for such work. In 1801 Dixey moved to New York City and maintained there a sculptor's studio and shop for the carving of architectural decoration for nearly two decades. It was in this shop that his son George (d. 1853) learned the carver's art and continued the work of his father until his death. John Dixey, a prominent member of the artistic circles in Philadelphia and New York, was elected vice-president of the Pennsylvania Academy and was one of the founders of the American Academy. He is probably best known for his figure of Justice (c. 1818) that was placed atop Magnin and McComb's magnificent New York City Hall. He did another figure of Justice for the State House in Albany, probably about the same time.

There were, then, several men in America, especially in Philadelphia, who had had European training in sculpture. But they were mostly men who worked in small scale, at most producing a few life-size busts. If a monumental scheme was proposed by any of them, it was soon dropped for lack of funds. So in America during the years 1790 to 1810, there was a mixture of native wood carvers, local stonecutters, and foreign sculptors who worked on a modest scale and performed odd jobs in the broadest range of sculptural work.

But for all the ornamental stonecarvers and good-to-mediocre sculptors who had come to America from Europe between 1790 and 1805, when Benjamin Latrobe needed carved decorations for the Capitol in Washington, he was convinced that no man then in America was qualified for the task.

On March 6, 1805, Latrobe wrote to Jefferson's friend in Rome, Philip Mazzei, asking him to find "a first-rate sculptor in the particular branch of architectural decorations," and an assistant for the man. He also requested Mazzei to inquire what the famous Canova would charge for carving a figure of Liberty to go in the House of Representatives chamber. Nothing came of the last, but in February of the following year Giuseppe Franzoni (d. 1815) and Giovanni Andrei (1770–1824) arrived to begin work on the sculptural decorations for the Capitol. Latrobe wrote to his superintendent of works that Mazzei had told him that "Franzoni is a most excellent sculptor and capable of cutting our figure of Liberty," and that Andrei "excels more in decoration."

Franzoni had had good training in Italy; his father was the president of the Academy of Fine Arts at Carrara. For the Hall of Representatives, Franzoni first modeled a great eagle whose wingspread reached from column to column. Then while Andrei was plodding along on the ornamental carving, Franzoni made another huge eagle for the gate of the Navy Yard; this was followed by a figure of Liberty, which was not at all to Latrobe's liking. "Liberty," cast in plaster but never put into marble, was set up in the Hall of Representatives, only to be destroyed when the British burned the building in 1814; it was later replaced with a figure by Causici. Late in 1806 Latrobe also mentioned "seventeen female figures in which his [Franzoni's] talents will be more worthily employed," but it appears that these were never executed.

Early in 1808 Franzoni and Andrei were loaned to Maximilian Godefroy in

Baltimore, where they carved the Gothic decorations for St. Mary's Chapel. While in that city they also executed a large lunette with figures of Ceres and Neptune for the pediment of the Union Bank, designed by Robert Cary Long. The lunette, carved in high relief in a brown sandstone (Fig. 2.5), is now set in the garden wall of the Peale Museum in Baltimore and provides a good example of the work of the two men. At the left is "Ceres" draped in classical robes, sitting upon a cornucopia and holding a bundle of wheat in her right hand; at the far left is her chariot. She is a 19th-century reincarnation of a Roman Tellus (or Mother Earth) image. "Neptune" is nude and resembles a Hellenistic river god or a languishing Michelangelesque figure from the Medici Chapel. He holds a trident in his right hand and reclines on a water wheel while a sea monster emerges in the corner at the far right. Between "Neptune" and "Ceres" is the emblem of the state of Maryland.

Both figures were executed in the neoclassical style of Canova and Thorwaldsen and are far removed from the type of figural work that America's native school of wood carvers was producing. It is through such men as Ceracchi, Franzoni, and Andrei, and their countrymen who followed them to America in the second and third decades of the 19th century, that neoclassical sculpture was implanted in this country. Neoclassicism was the dominant style at the opening of the 19th century, and the sculptor's greatest patrons in America—the local and national governments—found it thoroughly compatible with their political and philosophical foundations. The United States Capitol took on a Roman revival form because this nation could align itself politically with ancient republican Rome, just as Napoleon had compared his own regime to that of imperial Rome. Thus was neoclassicism successfully received in the early years of the Republic, and it was the Italian sculptors who quite naturally carried the neoclassical style to America.

Back at work in Washington by September 1808, Andrei was occupied with the carving of Corinthian capitals, and Franzoni worked on a figure of Justice for the Supreme Court room. After that, Franzoni made reliefs of figures representing Agriculture, Art, Science, and Commerce, which were placed over the entrance of the House of Representatives; these, too, were destroyed when the Capitol was burned in 1814. It was also Franzoni who carved for the Supreme Court area in 1809 the famous corn-cob capitals with which Mrs. Trollope was much impressed; she noted that they were "composed of the ears and leaves of Indian corn, beautifully arranged and forming as graceful an outline as the acanthus itself." That America should have capitals designed from one of its native plants she found especially fitting.

The two Italians continued to produce the sculptural decoration for the Capitol until the outbreak of hostilities with England. They were evidently still present in 1814 when the British entered the city and burned the Capitol, destroying much of the artists' work. Giuseppe Franzoni died in 1815, and in that same year his partner was sent back to Italy to supervise the carving of some capitals at Carrara. When Andrei returned to Washington, he brought with him two more Italian carvers: Giuseppe's brother Carlo Franzoni (1786–1819) and Francesco Iardella. Latrobe put them all to work redecorating the Capitol. Iardella is best known for his carving of the tobacco-leaf capitals of the little Senate rotunda. In the Old Supreme Court chamber is a lunette, attributed to Carlo Franzoni, with a skillfully done seated female figure holding the scales of justice in one hand and a sword in the other. For the old Hall of Representatives (now Statuary Hall) Carlo fashioned a "Car of History" in 1819, with a well-modeled neoclassical personification of History. The sculptor died soon after it was completed.

Numerous other Italian sculptors were employed at the Capitol during these years. Giuseppe Valaperta also arrived in 1815, after having attained considerable success as one of the main sculptors at Napoleon's palace, Malmaison. His early activity in America is revealed in a notice that he ran in the *Federal Gazette and Baltimore Daily Advertiser* on September 29, 1815:

Gentlemen who wish to obtain their own likeness or the likeness of any of their friends on Ivory, Wax or Plaster of Paris, [may] have that wish gratified by the excellent artist Joseph Volaperte [sic], Italian Sculptor, who arrived about three months ago at New York from Paris, where he had the honor of taking the likenesses of several Sovereigns; he has also taken the likenesses of several respectable gentlemen in New York. Mr. Volaperta now offers his services to the citizens of Baltimore . . . .

Valaperta, like many other sculptors, made a living from little profile relief portraits in colored wax or ivory. His skill in ivory carving is seen in the portraits of Archibald McVickar and his wife in the New-York Historical Society.

While Valaperta was in Baltimore the architect Maximilian Godefroy asked him to execute the female figure that was to go on the Battle Monument in that city. Agreeing to do it for $3,000, Valaperta and the architect went out to inspect the quality of the marble in the recently discovered nearby quarries. They ageed it was equal to the finest Italian marble, although no large blocks had yet been worked. The discovery of marble quarries in this country was quite important, of course, for the development of a native marmorean sculptural art. Latrobe gave the following summary of the marble supply available in America in a letter, dated January 9, 1816, to Nathaniel Macon, senator of North Carolina, concerning that state's decision to commission a statue of Washington:

We have in America marble very superior in texture to that in Italy which is the kind always used for statues . . . . The difficulty here is that our quarries are scarcely opened. An admirable Mass of Statuary Marble has lately been found very near Baltimore, and I have found as good as any in the world in Loudoun county, Virginia. From what I hear of the Baltimore Marble, as to its size it would probably be the source from which to obtain a proper block. The strata of that of Loudoun County are too thin. Vermont is inexhaustible in good statuary marble, but the transportation of so large a block as is necessary would render it inadvisable to procure it from thence.
[North Carolina State Archives, Governor William Miller's Letter-book]

Perhaps because of the long delay in obtaining the marble Valaperta did not execute the figure for the Battle Monument, but while in Baltimore he did exhibit a portrait bust of Monroe that won him high praise. It was another Italian, Antonio Capellano, who did the statue for Godefroy's Battle Monument. Valaperta instead went to Washington, where Latrobe was in great need of men to carve the decoration at the Capitol. Giuseppe Franzoni had recently died, and Andrei had temporarily returned to Italy; so Latrobe had Valaperta carve the great eagle on the frieze of the Hall of Representatives. A contemporary appreciation of the sculptor appeared in a Washington newspaper on December 16, 1816:

True connoisseurs will not fail to discover . . . the genius of the artist and the magic of his talent . . . . If Signor Valaperta were able to speak the language of the country, the amiableness of his character, and the nature of his principles, would procure him as many friends, as his talents will admirers wherever they are known.

Among others, William Thornton and Benjamin Latrobe independently recommended Valaperta as the one man then in the United States capable of producing the statue of Washington for the state of North Carolina. But with the completion of the great eagle, Valaperta's activity came abruptly to an end, and nothing more is known of him. The commission for the statue (Fig. 2.8) went instead to Antonio Canova (1757–1822) in Italy.

Because a number of the records concerning Canova's famous statue of Washington have been preserved, we can now trace how the idea for such a statue came into being, how the commission was handled by the legislators and executive officer of the state, and how the artist then created the monument. Regrettably, only a few years after its arrival (1821), the marble statue was destroyed when the State House at Raleigh burned in 1830. But in 1910 the Italian government presented North Carolina with a plaster cast, taken from the original plaster model, which still exists in Canova's studio in Possagno, his birthplace; and the cast may now be seen in the Hall of History in Raleigh.

As a result of an impassioned Fourth of July oration in Raleigh in 1815 the idea arose to commission a statue of George Washington for North Carolina. The matter was discussed in the legislative halls of North Carolina in the following months, and on December 30, 1815, Governor William Miller wrote to James Turner in the national capital that the last assembly had resolved to obtain a full-length portrait of Washington. "If a marble one can be obtained in the United States I should wish to get one . . . . I am not limited in price and should therefore wish it executed in the best manner." Miller said he had no idea of where or how such a statue could be obtained, and asked Turner to inquire of his friends in Washington. The governor's letterbooks and other sources preserve the numerous replies and suggestions that were submitted. Within a fortnight, Latrobe, Thornton, Godefroy, and a Mr. Patterson of Philadelphia, all wrote to the Honorable Nathaniel Macon to recommend Giuseppe Valaperta;

but Thornton also inquired of Valaperta how much the great sculptor Canova would charge. He further advised the North Carolinians that "Flaxman [could be] engaged to execute a fine full-length Statue of the General for seven hundred and fifty Guineas, and he is the first Artist in England, or in the world, except Canova."

Mr. Samuel L. Mitchell of New York wrote to Macon, on January 11, 1816, that Messrs. Norris and Kain, "imminent [sic] sculptors of this city," would undertake the commission and in his opinion do it properly. Norris and Kain operated a firm that specialized in grave monuments, usually encompassing little more than neatly lettered inscriptions and a small amount of decorative carving. That they were fairly well known even beyond New York City is revealed by the fact that one of their slate and marble memorials, dedicated to Theodore Dehon (d. 1817), is in St. Michael's Church, Charleston, South Carolina. In St. Paul's Chapel, New York City, is a wall memorial to George Warner (d. 1825), signed "J. and F. Kain, fecit," only a few paces from the Wells memorial by John Frazee. It would indeed have been a challenge to the abilities of Norris and Kain to produce a life-size marble image of Washington.

A Mr. Williamson of New York recommended a sculptor of that city, but he failed to give the man's name; if the statue was to be done by a sculptor in Europe, he recommended the Englishman John Bacon the younger (1777–1859). Though Williamson suggested that the full-length Landsdowne portrait of Washington by Stuart be used as the model, William Thornton had cautioned against this, saying, "though he is unequaled in a head he cannot draw a figure." From Philadelphia, however, Joseph Hopkinson wrote that there was no one in the country who could execute the commission properly, and that the gentlemen of North Carolina should try to obtain the services of Canova of Rome, who, Hopkinson believed, was anxious to have some specimen of his work in America.

This, of course, was essentially the recommendation of Thomas Jefferson, which had been made in a letter dated January 22, 1816. The Virginian wrote from Monticello that he did not know "of a single statuary in marble in the U.S. who offered himself as qualified." He praised the old Italian, saying, "No artist in Europe could place himself in a line with him; and for 30 years, within my own knowledge, he has been considered by all Europe as without a rival." He also recounted his own experiences concerning cost and length of time for execution of Houdon's statue of Washington, and added, "As to the style or costume, I am sure the artist, and every person of taste in Europe would be for the Roman . . . . Our boots and regimentals have a very puny effect." As for the model that Canova should use for the general's features, he urged that the portrait bust by Ceracchi be employed. Jefferson wrote that a Mr. Appleton, currently acting as American consul in Leghorn, was in possession of the original plaster bust by Ceracchi and that he should be contacted regarding the use of it. For the form of the body, he continued, "There are in Philadelphia, I believe, whole length paintings of General Washington, from which, I presume, old Mr.

Peale or his son would sketch on Canvas the mere outlines at no great charge."

Thomas Appleton in Leghorn agreed to act as overseer of the project and wrote at once to Canova, sending "the drawing," presumably Peale's, in the same letter. He translated Canova's reply and sent it to Governor Miller:

In truth the numerous labors to which I have obligated myself for many years to come would seem to require that I should renounce the honor proposed to me; but my admiration for the genius which has performed such sublime deeds for the safety and liberty of his country, compels me to make every effort to accomplish the statue you have proposed to me to execute; I therefore accept the commission.

Appleton advised Miller that as the ceiling of the hall that would house the statue was low, Canova believed the figure should be seated; and that the entire project would cost approximately $10,000.

Canova began work on the figure in 1819, and several small studies still survive in his studio at Possagno that show the early stages of the work. Canova used a copy of the Ceracchi bust as a model, and Washington's countenance assumed a quasi-classical Italianate appearance. The figure, dressed as a Roman general and rendered larger than life size, was shown writing on a tablet that contains the inscription *Georgio Washington Al Popolo degli Stati Uniti 1796 Amici e Concittadini.*

The *Norfolk Herald* reported that "With regard to dress . . . [Canova] could not hazard his reputation by attempting any other than that which was most familiar to him, and which is best adapted to his taste and genius." This of course did not go entirely unchallenged when the finished statue was first seen by North Carolinians in 1821, and one commentator reported that many people, "not aware of Artistic license, were . . . quite struck dumb by the fact that the Father of His Country was dressed in a Roman general's costume, with toga, bare legs, and sandaled feet." This controversy became even more heated some twenty years later when it revolved around Horatio Greenough's statue of the first President. The statue resulted in what Jefferson, referring to Ceracchi's bust, called the "ineffable majesty of expression . . . formed on the fine models of antiquity in Italy." In other words, it was an image of an American, but definitely not an American work of art. It pleased Jefferson and many people in North Carolina, but soon after the statue's arrival, the group with Jeffersonian tastes was to be outvoted in politics and art by a swelling mass of middle-class critics who had little liking for Italianate art.

Around the base of the statue were four reliefs depicting significant events in the life of Washington. These were carved by Raimondo Trentanove, "the favorite pupil of Canova." This young sculptor was known in America through his portrait of Robert Goodloe Harper (in the Maryland Historical Society; signed and dated Rome 1819), as well as by his portrait bust of Washington, carved in 1820 and presented to the Boston Athenaeum by 104 men, each of whom subscribed a dollar toward its purchase. This bust was probably modeled in Canova's studio while work was progressing on the statue for Raleigh, with Ceracchi's bust still there.

The Canova statue of Washington was carved in marble in 1819–1820 and shipped the following year on board the *Columbus* out of Leghorn. Arriving in Raleigh in November, it was erected in the newly remodeled State House. Whatever reservations there were about the attire, the people of North Carolina took great pride in the statue, and the assembly made it a crime to deface the statue in any way. But nine years later when the state capitol burned, the statue was demolished. For a while there was hope of having the statue restored by Robert Ball Hughes, who had recently arrived from England. Town and Davis were employed as architects to design a new capitol with special instructions regarding a rotunda that would house the repaired "Washington." After receiving payment, however, Hughes departed not only with the fee but also, it seems, with portions of the statue, and the project of restoration was abandoned forever. The appearance of the statue is nevertheless well known from several sources. There are the studies and models in Canova's studio in Possagno; there are several engravings and lithographs depicting it; and an Italian sculptor named Orlandi (1757–1822) made a small marble replica of it that is now in the Virginia Historical Society.

In the 1820's, Canova's statue of Washington was one of the most famous works of art in America, and it played a large role in establishing monumental marble statuary in the United States. Had it survived the fire of 1830, it would have been even more influential, for at about that time America's own young native sculptors—the generation led by Powers, Greenough, and Crawford— looked to such models as they could find in America before going to Italy, where the works of antiquity and of Canova and Thorwaldsen offered the neoclassical inspiration they sought.

In the meantime two more of Canova's gifted countrymen came to America —Luigi Persico and Enrico Causici. Persico (1791–1860) arrived in 1818 and for the next several years worked in Lancaster, Harrisburg, and Philadelphia. Rembrandt Peale, in his "Reminiscences," published in *The Crayon* in 1856, tells us that during these first years in Pennsylvania Persico could make only a "scanty subsistence . . . by miniature painting and teaching drawing" until a bust of Lafayette brought him much acclaim as a sculptor; this was probably around 1824 when the popular French marquis made a return visit to America. Persico's first exhibit at the Pennsylvania Academy, in 1825, was a bust of Dr. Nathaniel Chapman, now in the collection of the American Philosophical Society. In 1829 Dr. Chapman gave that institution a portrait bust of Lafayette by Persico, probably the one mentioned by Rembrandt Peale or a copy of it.

These busts reveal Persico as a gifted modeler who endowed his portraits with the personality of his subjects. His portraits are usually bare-chested in good neoclassical form, and possess the reserve and dignity of countenance belonging to that style. It is, of course, a Roman neoclassicism that embodies naturalism as one of its main characteristics, rather than a Greek neoclassicism, which demands an idealization of the physical features of the individual. This Roman version of neoclassicism may be observed in the exquisite bust of Nicholas Biddle (c. 1837; Fig. 2.9), also in the American Philosophical Society. It is important to realize the difference between the two, for Americans could and did accept the former for their own sculptured portraiture, whereas they could never have accepted the latter, which was reserved for "ideal" works or literary subjects.

Persico left Philadelphia in 1825 to go to Washington; John Quincy Adams was then President, and Charles Bulfinch was the architect in charge of the United States Capitol. Persico made a portrait bust of the former and worked under the direction of the latter, who was finishing the center portion—the rotunda dome and porticoes. From Bulfinch, Persico received the commission to do the pedimental sculptures (Fig. 2.7) for the east front. President Adams had cautioned against using mythological figures or personifications of Victory, and had even proposed a design of his own invention, which was described by Bulfinch:

A figure of America occupies the centre . . . , her left hand pointing to the figure of Justice, [while] on the left . . . is the eagle, and the figure of Hope resting on her anchor . . . . The figures are bold, of nine feet in height, and gracefully drawn by Mr. Persico, an Italian artist. It is intended that an appropriate inscription shall explain the meaning and moral to dull comprehensions.

The figures of the three robed women are animated and well rounded and generally of classical proportions. At the time of the remodeling of the eastern portico of the Capitol in 1959, Persico's original sandstone figures were replaced with marble copies; the originals have been placed in storage.

Between 1829 and 1835 Persico also created two heroic figures for niches under the portico—"War," the image of Mars in Roman armor, and "Peace," showing Ceres with an olive branch and some fruit. Twentieth-century copies have again replaced the originals, which have been stored. His work continued at the eastern portico of the Capitol with his ambitious group entitled "The Discovery." When it was decided to complete that portion of the building in 1836, Persico at once submitted a model for a group to go on the side of the great stairs. It consisted of Columbus striding vigorously and gazing at an orb that he held aloft in his right hand; at his side crouched a seminude Indian maiden in a very awkward position. Neither this group nor its companion, "The Rescue" by Horatio Greenough, is above criticism in point of composition and sculpturesque effect; both have been removed from the eastern front and consigned to storage crates. But Congress, after paying $24,000 for it, was not pleased with "The Discovery" when it was unveiled in 1844, and Persico's profitable employment by the government came to a close. He had hoped to do both groups that were to flank the great central stairs, but several members of Congress thought it unjust that both should be given to a foreigner when America by then had native-son sculptors, and the commission for the companion was given to Horatio Greenough. The last years of Persico's life were spent in Europe; he died in Marseilles in 1860.

Enrico Causici came to America in 1822, maintaining he had been a pupil of the great Canova. In the following year he offered a bronze bust of William Pinkney to the Baltimore Bar Assocation for $700, declaring he had cast the bust himself here in America. If true, this would have been the earliest instance of bronze-cast sculpture in America, and it is regrettable that neither the bust nor more documentation on it has survived. In 1824 he seems first to have settled in New York City and was immediately elected a member of the American Academy; but in the spring of that year William Dunlap met him in Washington, where Causici had gone in search of employment. He modeled an ornamental clock for the Senate chamber, for which he was paid $2,000. Next he turned his attention to the decoration of the rotunda of the Capitol, carving two rather cramped and awkwardly composed reliefs—"The Landing of the Pilgrims" and "Daniel Boone in Conflict with Indians." Around 1827 Causici, in treating the subject of the confrontation of the white man's civilization and the red man's wilderness, attempted to force Old World methods upon a new story, and his neoclassical, literary manner was not entirely satisfactory. One senator voiced the criticism that "A Yankee sailor with a jack-knife and a shingle, would carve images that would be better imitators of humanity." For the old House of Representatives, now Statuary Hall, Causici created a great plaster statue of Liberty (Fig. 2.10), a robust, draped, stalwart neoclassical figure with the eagle at her right and a serpent entwined around a bundle of fasces at her left.

During 1825 and 1826, Causici also had a New York City studio, where he was working on a model of an equestrian statue of Washington; unfortunately he did this without first getting the commission from the city fathers, and although the statue was cast in plaster, the city refused to make an appropriation to have it done in bronze or stone. For some time the plaster model stood outside in City Hall Park; this of course was ruinous, and the statue soon disappeared.

Causici's most famous statue is the colossal figure of George Washington that crowns Baltimore's monument to the first President. A fellow Italian, Antonio Capellano, and a Frenchman, Nicholas Gevelot, were among the nine competitors for the commission; according to Robert Gilmor, Baltimore collector and patron of the fine arts, Causici's proposal was the best of the lot and his bid of $9,000 was the lowest. The gigantic figure, wearing a military uniform under a great classical drape, is shown in the act of resigning as general; it was set in place in November 1829. The statue was carved in three sections and weighed twenty-one tons.

Causici's success in America is revealed in a letter from Horatio Greenough to his brother Henry, dated April 5, 1828: "Causici has lately left Baltimore. I miss him, for he had to a great degree the talent of interesting one in conversation . . . . This man (I know from those who have been his paymasters) has received something like thirty-thousand dollars since he has been in this country." Causici's career in America ended in the early 1830's. One of the last references to him appears in the *New York Evening Post* on November 15, 1832, concerning a statue of President Andrew Jackson he proposed to do for New York City. But nothing came of this, and William Dunlap tells us he died in Havana, Cuba.

Nicholas Gevelot is a rather enigmatic figure in the history of American sculpture. In 1822 one François Victor Gevelot (b. 1791) exhibited a bust of William Shippen at the Pennsylvania Academy, but it is not certain that Nicholas and François Victor are one and the same person. In May 1826 Nicholas Gevelot exhibited a small model of a figure of Alexander Hamilton in Philadelphia. The original final statue was to be placed in the Merchant's Exchange in New York City, but it was eventually Robert Ball Hughes who executed the New York statue of Hamilton. Moving to Washington, Gevelot executed a relief, "Penn's Treaty with the Indians," for the rotunda of the Capitol, and in the early 1830's he was working on the model for an equestrian statue of Washington, which he was unable to persuade Congress to commission. The next and last mention of Gevelot was many years later in connection with another unsuccessful attempt to obtain a commission from Congress: a memorial medallion of the late President Zachary Taylor.

Another Frenchman, J. B. Binon, had been a pupil of Chinard; his best-known work in France was the 15-foot statue "Carabinier" for the Place de Carrousel in Paris. After arriving in Boston, c. 1818, one of his first efforts was a bust of Washington, which he made from descriptions and from a portrait by Gilbert Stuart. It was heralded as an excellent portrait; historically it was important because no known bust in plaster or marble had been executed in Boston before Binon's arrival. In a letter to John Adams, dated January 21, 1819, Binon asks for a letter of introduction to Mr. Goldsborough, chairman of the committee in charge of obtaining a statue of the first President, because he wanted to make a model and submit it. Nothing came of this project, however. Probably his most famous work is his marble portrait of John Adams in contemporary attire. On February 3, 1819, Binon had written to Adams asking permission to model his portrait, and four days later the former President replied:

I am afraid that you are engaged in speculation that will never be profitable to you. The age of sculpture and painting has not yet arrived in this country and I hope it will not arrive very soon . . . . I am confident that you will not find purchasers for your bust and therefore I am sorry that you are engaged in so hopeless a speculation because I believe you to be a great artist and an amiable man.

Binon made the bust anyway, and shortly thereafter, it provided the young

Horatio Greenough with one of the few examples of contemporary sculpture that he could copy.

Binon is reported to have made busts of Generals Dearborn and Humphreys, which were "destined for Yale University." The sculptor lost his sight for a while, but it was eventually restored by a Boston physician. He was evidently the only professional sculptor of any ability then working in Boston and one of the first of the trained European sculptors to migrate to New England.

Ferdinand Pettrich (1798–1872) spent only a few years in the United States in the late 1830's and early 1840's, but during that period this especially gifted sculptor created a number of fine portrait busts and one heroic statue. Born in Dresden, Pettrich was the son of the court sculptor to the king of Saxony. His father, a follower of Canova and Thorwaldsen, taught him the fundamentals of his art, and in time the younger Pettrich journeyed to Rome where he himself studied with the great Danish sculptor, eventually gaining a considerable reputation through his own portraits and ideal pieces. In 1835 while young Thomas Crawford was crossing the Atlantic to go to Rome and Thorwaldsen's studio, Pettrich was sailing in the opposite direction. He and his wife settled in Philadelphia, where he spent several years mainly devoted to the execution of portrait busts. In 1842, for example, he modeled the bust "John Vaughn," which is now in the collection of the American Philosophical Society.

Before leaving Philadelphia, Pettrich executed (c. 1840) what has become his best-known statue, that of General George Washington in the act of resigning his commission as commander of the army. As a model for the face, Pettrich used the life mask that Houdon had made at Mount Vernon. The mask had passed from Houdon's belongings after his death into the hands of Robert Walsh of Philadelphia, who brought it with him on his return to America. The celebrated mask next became the property of John Struthers, a marble cutter, who in turn gave it to Pettrich for use on his heroic statue of Washington. Pettrich carried the mask with him a few years later to Brazil and then to Rome, where he eventually presented it to his American friend and fellow sculptor William Wetmore Story. After Story's death the mask was purchased by J. Pierpont Morgan; it is now in the Morgan Library in New York City.

From the Houdon life mask Pettrich produced several portrait busts of Washington; one in marble is in the Cooper Union collection in New York. The statue of Washington was destined for the Customs House in New York and was the first bronze statue in America. The work possesses all the heroic grandeur and dignity that the subject deserved, but there is nothing neoclassical about the figure, which is curious in view of the sculptor's having studied with Thorwaldsen in Rome. In 1842 Pettrich gave the plaster model to the National Museum in Washington.

Like most of the foreign sculptors who came to America, Pettrich eventually gravitated to the city of Washington, which was then the center for large-scale sculptural commissions. But for some reason his talents were little used in the capital city. A number of busts were commissioned, such as those of Daniel Webster, Henry Clay, and Joel R. Poinsett, and for a while it looked as if Pettrich might be awarded the commission to do the two large monuments to go on the blockings of the great stairway of the western front of the Capitol. But even though he made—and was paid for—the models, the project progressed no further.

Disgruntled with the lack of governmental patronage, Pettrich left America in 1843 for Brazil, where he became the court sculptor to Emperor Dom Pedro II. It was there that he produced his life-size marble statue "Dying Tecumseh," which was sent back to the United States and later displayed in the rotunda of the Capitol when the body of President Lincoln lay in state. Pettrich returned to Rome, where he died in 1872.

England, too, produced several sculptors who by their own presence or the presence of their works in America played a considerable role in the establishment of the art of sculpture during the first few decades of the 19th-century.

In 1816 William J. Coffee (1774–c. 1846) came to New York City to seek his fortune after several years as a modeler in terra cotta at the Chelsea Derby studios and in London. That same year he made a small bust of Hugh Williamson in plaster, which is now in the New-York Historical Society. The modeling is not strong, and the small scale suggests Coffee's earlier work at the Chelsea establishment. Coffee entered several pieces at the American Academy exhibition in 1817, but most of these were paintings of animals; there were two dogs and an "Infant Orpheus" in terra cotta, again suggesting he was not yet sufficiently advanced for monumental sculpture. About 1820 he executed in plaster the portrait of DeWitt Clinton from which Asher B. Durand made his engraving for David Hosack's *Memoirs of DeWitt Clinton*. In the 1820's he traveled a great deal; in 1821 he was in Charleston, S. C., where he did the portrait bust "General Thomas Pickney." By 1827 he had settled for good in Albany, New York. In about 1840 he was making plaster casts for Henry Kirke Brown, who was then working in the area. His work in Albany was undoubtedly among the earliest professional sculpture seen by the young Erastus Dow Palmer, later to become one of the most famous of American sculptors.

In 1826 the statue of George Washington (Fig. 2.11) by Sir Francis Chantrey (1781–1841) was unveiled in Boston. Massachusetts, following the earlier examples of Virginia and North Carolina, had voted funds for a statue of Washington to adorn the new State House, which had been designed by Bulfinch. Once again the committee in charge decided that there was no native talent available which could produce the statue competently and in the desired style. Chantrey, who was by the early 1820's the leading sculptor in England, was already known in this country through his bust of the American painter Benjamin West (New-

York Historical Society; 1811). In his statue of Washington, Chantrey attempted a compromise between naturalism and neoclassicism, for though he enveloped the figure in an enormous togalike drape, one fully perceives the contemporary dress of Washington's day underneath; the features of the head, too, are rendered naturalistically. The statue was modeled by Chantrey himself; but, as was the usual practice, the marble statue was carved by Italian artisans.

Chantrey's "Washington," the first monumental marble statue in Boston—or in all of New England, for that matter—arrived and was erected to the great joy of the people of Massachusetts. It was widely heralded as a great addition to the artistic and cultural assets of the area; but there were dissenters—for example, Davy Crockett, whom A. T. Gardner has referred to as "an *ex nato* connoisseur from the Tennessee canebrakes." Crockett, while touring through New England in 1834, articulated the feelings of countless Americans when he wrote:

I do not like the statue of Washington in the [Boston] State-House. They have a Roman gown on him, and he was an American; this ain't right. They did the better thing at Richmond, in Virginia, where they have him in the old blue and buff. He belonged to his country—heart, soul, and body and I don't want any other to have any part of him—not even his clothes.
[Quoted from *Yankee Stonecutters*, New York, 1945, p. 40]

By the time the statue was erected America's own first major sculptor, Horatio Greenough, had already been studying in Italy for over a year. But Thomas Ball, who later became one of Boston's most famous sculptors, recalls in his autobiography how he marveled at the statue when his father took him to see it, about 1830; so struck was he with the naturalism of the cloak that young Thomas, then ten or eleven, asked his father if it were a real piece of cloth that was draped around the figure. By that time many an aspiring young New England artist had at least one life-size marble statue at hand that offered a standard in the art of figure sculpture.

Very late in his life Sir Francis Chantrey produced a large mural monument dedicated to the memory of William Mason Smith, which was erected in St. Philip's Church in Charleston, South Carolina. The personification of Grief, a classical maiden, mourns at an urn covered by a cloth; she holds her forehead in her right hand. Stylistically, this ideal figure is reminiscent of the work of John Flaxman and represents a continuation of neoclassicism well into the century.

Another Englishman, Robert Ball Hughes (1806–1868), arrived in New York City in 1829, accompanied by his bride. As a young man of twenty-three, he showed promise of high accomplishment in sculpture. He had entered the school of the Royal Academy in London in 1818 and over the next several years was awarded gold and silver medals for his exceptional work, such as his copy of the "Barbarini Faun" in 1820. His precocious talent manifested itself in the bust of his father, now in the Boston Athenaeum, which was shown at the Royal Academy exhibition of 1822. The following year he modeled a neoclassic bas-relief entitled "Pandora brought by Mercury to Epimetheus," a subject taken from Hesiod's *Theogony;* this piece was awarded an Academy Gold Medal. His inclination toward neoclassicism in the 1820's is understandable, for about 1821 he went to work in the studio of Edward H. Baily, a prominent and prolific sculptor who had studied with John Flaxman. It was probably under Baily's tutelage that Hughes modeled his statue "Achilles" (c. 1824), inspired by a passage in Homer's *Iliad.* His efforts in ideal statuary were continued with his "Shepherd Boy," which was shown in the 1828 Royal Academy exhibition.

One of Hughes' earliest works in America was the portrait of John Watts; the original plaster cast was destroyed by vandalism in 1945, but there is a copy of it by Thomas Coffee in the New-York Historical Society, and a bronze cast (made by Gruet of Paris) in the Metropolitan Museum of Art. This is probably the bust that was listed in the Artists Fund Society catalogue of 1830, under Hughes' name, as "Eminent Member of the New York Bar." There is a naturalism in the details of the leathery old judge instead of an idealization of the features, a characteristic that the sculptor's American patrons found perfectly acceptable. This early bust shows Hughes to be a competent modeler of the human likeness, though it lacks the dramatic romanticism that the painted portraits of Thomas Sully or Rembrandt Peale had already begun to assume. Later busts by Hughes do have this quality.

The portrait bust was the type of sculpture most in demand, and Hughes created several in the early 1830's. One of Thomas Handasyd Perkins, eminent merchant and philanthropist of Boston, was shown in the Boston Athenaeum in 1832 and in the annual exhibition of the American Academy of Fine Arts in 1833; it was cut in marble and is now owned by the Perkins School for the Blind, Watertown, Massachusetts. There is a fine sculpturesque quality in the head, and one is reminded of the work of the Englishman Nollekens. Hughes also sent to the American Academy exhibition of 1833 a "Small model of the Bust of the Right Hon. Sir Charles Vaughn, H. B. M., Minister to the United States," and a "Model of the Bust of the Hon. D. B. Ogden, to be executed in marble."

Hughes carried portraiture in America to unparalleled heights in dramatic and heroic content in the bust he modeled (c. 1834) of Colonel John Trumbull (Fig. 2.12). The strength of character and dauntless spirit is combined with the hostile skepticism of the crochety old painter. Hanging from the toga is the badge of the Order of the Cincinnati in which, fifty years after the Revolution, the old man still took justifiable pride. Several letters from the sculptor reveal the destitute condition of Hughes and his wife at this period. A number of his busts had been impounded to be sold if Hughes did not immediately pay his back rent, and he sent Trumbull a note with a touching plea for $10. On another occasion he pathetically wrote Trumbull, "Circumstances of a very peculiar nature *forced* me *actually forced* to draw on you for Fifteen Dollars on amount of Bust. Consider that Sum as the balance for it, and forgive me for God sake the liberty I have taken. I could not my dear good Sir, *avoid it.*"

Another one of these early portraits is that of William Gaston of North Carolina. This marble bust, signed and dated 1834, is now in the state library in Raleigh. Gaston, too, wears a toga about his shoulders, and it falls over his left shoulder in folds identical to the arrangement in the bust of John Watts. Throughout the 1830's the toga was the one reference to antiquity found in American sculptured portraits. Even a squared-off bare chest was preferred to the mundane contemporary street dress; a gentleman such as Gaston could endure the truthful representation of bags under the eyes or sagging flesh at the line of the jaw, but not the nondescript and often baggy dress of the day. American sculptors never found a way of representing the attire of the first half of the 19th century in a noble manner. William Rush had attained some success with contemporary dress, and Shobal Vail Clevenger attempted it once, but it is seldom found before 1840.

It was William Gaston who seems to have been in charge of getting Canova's statue of Washington restored after it was destroyed when the Capitol burned in 1831; it may well have been at his behest that Hughes went to North Carolina. Hughes stayed long enough to model Gaston's likeness, but departed without repairing Canova's statue and thus acquired a bad name. It was William Gaston who in 1841 introduced a resolution to the state legislature proposing that "John Frazer [Frazee], of New York . . . a man of most respectable standing . . ." would undertake to restore the statue at his own expense, charge not a cent if the legislative committee was not fully satisfied, and promise not to remove any parts from the city of Raleigh. Clearly the legislature was taking care not to be deceived a second time.

Aside from doing portrait busts, Hughes was also engaged on larger works. As early as February 13, 1830, according to the *New York Mirror*, he was working on a statue of DeWitt Clinton for the Clinton Hall Association, and by November of the following year he had finished the plaster model of a bas-relief of Bishop Hobart, which was destined for Trinity Church as soon as it was put into marble. A notice in the New York *Evening Post*, November 4, 1831, stated that the model was complete and that the marble block for it had been received. Hughes represented Hobart at the moment of his death, slumping in an antique chair, with "limbs loosely wrapped in a sort of drapery so disposed around them as to give a fine classical air to his person." An allegorical female figure representing Religion stands behind the chair; with one hand she supports the bishop's drooping head while with the other she points to the sign of the cross. When completed it was placed under the great window of Trinity Church. Evidently Hughes also had hopes of gaining the commission of a sizable monument that the city of New York had under consideration; for, in addition to several portrait busts, he was represented by the following item in the 1833 American Academy exhibition:

Sketch for the proposed Monument to Washington, designed for the Park, or Bowling Green. Height to be thirty-five feet; the figures to be colossal, and cast in bronze; the pedestal to be of American marble. It represents Washington surrounded by three figures—justice, wisdom, and victory.

But nothing came of this proposal.

It was about 1833 that the sculptor began modeling the group *Uncle Toby and the Widow Wadman*, depicting an episode from Laurence Sterne's *Tristram Shandy*. In March of 1834 the artist's wife wrote to Trumbull for a loan of five dollars "to complete in *Plaster* the figure . . . which actually waits still for that." This statue was never put into marble, probably because of the great expense involved, and the model, if it still exists, is presently unlocated. In 1835 it was seen by Christopher C. Baldwin of Worcester, who recorded in his diary:

Was there ever any statuary to equal this? Uncle Toby is inimitable. Such benevolence and perfect honesty as appear in his face! How well this is contrasted with the wicked looks of the frisky and lecherous widow! There they are, snug in the sentry box, and no one can look upon them but with great pleasure.

In an effort to create something more profound than the likenesses of his contemporaries, Hughes tried modeling scenes from literature, but he found no patronage for such art.

In 1833 the directors of New York's Merchants' Exchange commissioned Hughes to do a marble statue of Alexander Hamilton—the one Nicholas Gevelot for some reason never made. In January 1834 he wrote to Trumbull, as president of the American Academy, to request permission to use that institution's statue gallery to model his "Hamilton," indicating he would require the room for about six weeks. Some time before this he had modeled several small statuettes of Hamilton, three of which still exist—one in the Museum of the City of New York, one in the Detroit Institute of Arts, and one in the Schuyler Mansion in Albany. These have assumed considerable significance since the large marble statue was destroyed by fire only eight months after it had been erected in the Merchants' Exchange. The model in Detroit (Fig. 2.13) shows Hamilton in contemporary dress about to deliver a speech; in his right hand he holds a scroll that rests upon a truncated column, with a wreath done in relief. The well-modeled figure has a fine animated and vigorous stance. As a model for the head, Hughes probably used a marble copy by John Dixey of Ceracchi's famous bust, which had become the standard likeness of Hamilton; Dixey had given his copy to the New-York Historical Society twenty-five years earlier. The figure was carved, probably by Italian artisans in New York, from a block of white Carrara marble, which soon revealed a flaw; to conceal this, Hughes added a Roman toga to his original conception. The appearance of the statue—the first marble portrait statue executed in America—is known from a wood engraving that was published in the *New York Mirror* on October 24, 1835. The statue was placed in the Exchange in April 1835 and was one of the celebrated monuments of the city—until December 17 when fire consumed the building, and the statue of Hamilton was destroyed. After noting that the Exchange resembled "the ruins of an ancient temple rather than the new and beautiful resort of the merchants," Philip Hone made the following entry in his diary on the night of December 17, 1835:

When the dome of this edifice fell in, the sight was awfully grand. In its fall it de-molished the statue of Hamilton executed by Ball Hughes, which was erected in the rotunda only eight months ago by the public spirit of the merchants.

As the holocaust raged a group of sailors from Brooklyn tried to save the statue by removing it from the building, and even got the extremely heavy mar-ble figure off its pedestal before they had to run for their lives. It was indeed a cruel blow to Hughes, whose fine marmorean masterpiece vanished before the eyes of his contemporaries and whose stature as an artist was severely diminished through the loss of what was probably his greatest completed work.

In the second half of the 1830's Hughes continued to model portrait busts and make small cameo likenesses in New York City, but his economic situation hardly improved. In 1836 Washington Irving sat for Hughes. According to the *New York Mirror*, September 10, 1836, many plaster copies were sold, but they commanded only $15 apiece—and this while Shobal Vail Clevenger and Hiram Powers were getting $150 or $200 for their work. Examples may be found in the Pennsylvania Academy and Irving's Tarrytown home, "Sunnyside." A third copy is in the Boston Athenaeum, which acquired it in 1836, along with Hughes' bust of Edward Livingston; the price for the two was $35. On one of the Irving busts Hughes inscribed: "This is the only Bust for which Mr. Washington Irving ever sat . . ." Up to that time it was, but this likeness was later eclipsed by the more famous one by Erastus Dow Palmer.

Another bust that dates from the late 1830's, and a fine sensitive one it is, is the portrait of Hughes' fellow artist in New York, Henry Inman. Somewhere be-tween 1836 and 1838 he must have made a brief trip to Boston, at which time he modeled the likeness of Nathaniel Bowditch, the eminent mathematician, astron-omer, and author of the *New American Practical Navigator*. Bowditch died in 1839, and in March of that year Hughes sold a plaster cast of his bust to the American Philosophical Society for $15. The Presbyterian Historical Society in Philadelphia owns a remarkable bust of Dr. George W. Bethune by Hughes, which dates from about 1838.

Hughes' move to Philadelphia around 1838 was probably induced by a com-petition sponsored by the Order of the Cincinnati for an equestrian statue of Washington to be erected in Philadelphia. His model, preserved in the collection of the Society for the Preservation of New England Antiquities in Boston, is the earliest surviving example of attempts at the equestrian monument in America. The sculptor had completely divorced himself from neoclassicism, and one is reminded more of 17th- or 18th-century monuments to such monarchs as Peter the Great or Louis XIV. Washington bridles the spirited prancing steed and doffs his hat as if to an admiring throng of citizens or soldiers. Unlike Canova, Chantrey, or later, Greenough, Ball Hughes did not put Washington in classical attire, but he represented him in the military uniform he wore as commander of the army. The equestrian group was to have been cast in bronze, an ambitious undertaking if Hughes did indeed plan to cast it himself here in America. Once more misfortune was to frustrate the sculptor, however, for the failure of the Bank of the United States doomed the project.

Before leaving Philadelphia in 1840, Hughes exhibited several of his works at the Pennsylvania Academy show of that year. There were several "medallion likenesses," the "Original model, Bishop White Monument," the plaster bust of Dr. Bethune, and a "Model, bust of Nicholas Biddle, now being executed in marble." But meager encouragement of his talents evidently caused the disheartened artist to look elsewhere for more munificent benefactors. The Boston Athenaeum had already purchased three of Hughes' works, and as he knew its benefactor Thomas Handasyd Perkins, he packed his belongings—among them his equestrian model—and moved to Boston.

The first few years of Hughes' activity in Boston are rather obscure. It may have been at that time that he executed the bust of General Joseph Warren for Dr. Joseph C. Warren, a marble copy of which, made by Thomas Thompson in 1855, is owned by Harvard University. By 1842 he was already well along on a model of the statue "Oliver Twist," which has disappeared but which was then immensely popular; it was sent to the Crystal Palace Exhibition in London in 1851 and may have remained in England.

In about 1845 Hughes was approached, possibly by Josiah Quincy, the chairman of the Bowditch Committee, about doing a life-size statue of the recently deceased Nathaniel Bowditch. The monument was to be cast in bronze and placed in Mount Auburn, the parkland cemetery outside Cambridge. A native-born American sculptor had had the honor of creating the first figural monument to go into Mount Auburn: Henry Dexter's marble memorial for the grave of Emily Binney had been set up in 1842. Hughes' bronze image of the old astronomer was to be the second such piece there. Bowditch was represented in the dress of his own day. Hughes was far more successful than the other sculptors of the mid-19th century in rendering contemporary attire. He included a sufficient amount of sartorial detail to render the garments acceptable, yet subordinated them to a much larger conception of the personality and dignity of the subject.

Hughes modeled the elderly scholar seated and deep in thought (Fig. 2.14), with a large globe and a sextant beside his chair. It is a fine portrayal of a man who lived the quiet contemplative life and who was one of the most erudite men of the period. The statue was cast in the sculptor's own foundry in Boston in 1847 at a total cost of $3,293.78. Although it was a brave and adventurous effort at bronze casting, it was less than successful, for by the 1880's it was in such a state of disrepair that the Bowditch family had it recast at the Gruet Foundry in Paris—as indicated by an inscription on the base. The original plaster model is in the collection of the Boston Athenaeum.

After the casting of the Bowditch statue, Robert Ball Hughes began to slip into obscurity. The Boston Athenaeum has a life-size plaster model of a work that may date from the late 1840's—"Little Nell," a young girl (from Charles Dickens' *Old Curiosity Shop*) sitting deep in thought, with a book on her lap and a gravestone under her foot. A last bit of correspondence concerns Hughes and his equestrian model once more. In 1851 Thomas H. Perkins wrote to the Athenaeum on the sculptor's behalf, asking that he be allowed to borrow the model, which the Athenaeum had acquired ten years before for $100. The city of New York was planning to erect an equestrian monument to Washington, and Hughes wished to submit his model for consideration. This was the commission in which Horatio Greenough was interested, but he died the next year without progressing beyond the model stage. The assignment eventually went to Henry Kirke Brown, whose bronze equestrian "Washington" in Union Square was the result. The defeat only hastened Hughes' withdrawal from the art of monumental sculpture. Over the years his "Hamilton" had been destroyed; his equestrian statue had twice been turned aside; and most of his other ideal works remained in plaster, for lack of a patron who would pay to have them carved in marble. The sculptor continued to do minor works—cameos, wax medallions, and so forth—and even for a while amused himself by burning images into a piece of wood with a hot poker. After the mid-1850's he seems to have given up on sculpture altogether; he died in 1868 in Dorchester, Massachusetts, where he had long been a resident.

One can only wonder why Hughes did not receive more patronage. Not only did private individuals and municipal governments fail to avail themselves fully of the genius he had to offer, but also the federal government—which between 1830 and 1860 was commissioning tons of sculptural adornments for the buildings in Washington—never once considered making use of Hughes' ability, though they employed many Italian artisan-stonecutters.

Although Hughes received his training in England, it was in America that nearly all his artistic activity occurred. But Robert Ball Hughes' special significance as a transitional figure is that he arrived at the moment when the United States was beginning to rear her own corps of gifted sculptors and no longer found it necessary to rely entirely on imported talent. As Hughes began his first works in New York City, John Frazee had already modeled his first portrait busts; Horatio Greenough had begun his career in Italy; and Hiram Powers was about to start modeling portraits in Cincinnati. Within the decade both Powers and young Thomas Crawford were to journey to Italy to begin life-long residences there. Thus, at about the time of Hughes' arrival, one epoch in American sculpture came to a close and another began.

[FIG. 2.1] "William Pitt," by Joseph Wilton (1770). Marble. Courtesy, City of Charleston, S.C.; photo, Index of American Sculpture, University of Delaware.

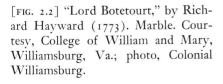

[FIG. 2.2] "Lord Botetourt," by Richard Hayward (1773). Marble. Courtesy, College of William and Mary, Williamsburg, Va.; photo, Colonial Williamsburg.

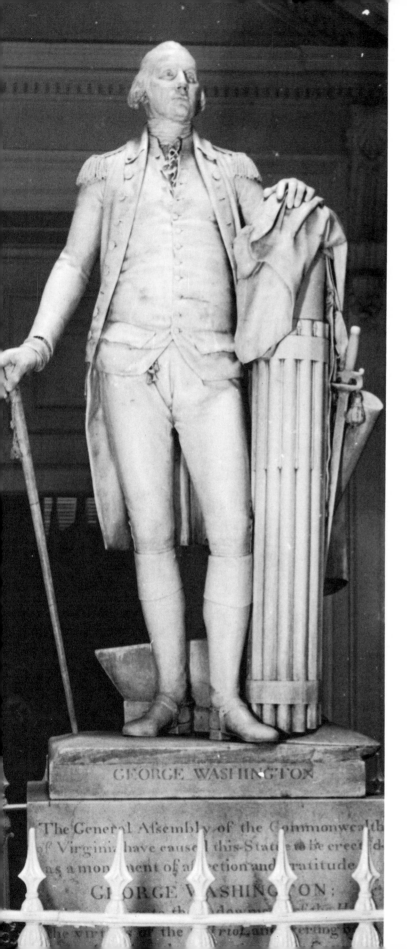

[FIG. 2.4] "George Clinton," by Giuseppe Ceracchi (c. 1792). Terra cotta, 27½" high. New-York Historical Society, New York City.

[FIG. 2.3] "George Washington," by J. A. Houdon (1788). Marble. State House, Richmond, Va.; photo, Index of American Sculpture, University of Delaware.

[FIG. 2.5] "Ceres" and "Neptune," by Giuseppe
Franzoni and Giovanni Andrei (1808). Marble,
60″ high. Courtesy, Peale Museum, Baltimore.

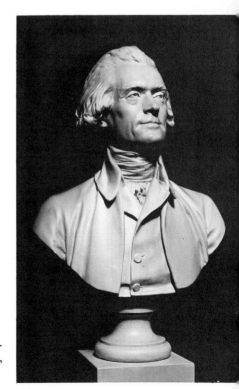

[FIG. 2.6] "Thomas Jefferson," by J. A. Houdon (1785).
Plaster, 21½″ high. Courtesy, New-York Historical Society,
New York City.

[FIG. 2.7] "Justice," "America," and "Hope," after original sculptures by Luigi Persico (1826). Marble, 108″ high. East front, central portico pediment of the U.S. Capitol, Washington, D.C. Courtesy, Architect of the Capitol.

[FIG. 2.8] "George Washington," by Antonio Canova (1818). Engraving after the original marble statue, destroyed. Courtesy, State Department of Archives and History, Raleigh, N.C.

[FIG. 2.9] "Nicholas Biddle," attributed to Luigi Persico (c. 1837). Plaster, 21½″ high. Courtesy, American Philosophical Society.

[FIG. 2.10] "Liberty," by Enrico Causici (1825). Eagle (on frieze), by Giuseppe Valaperta (1816). Marble. Statuary Hall, U.S. Capitol, Washington, D.C. Courtesy, Architect of the Capitol.

[FIG. 2.11] "George Washington," by Sir Francis Chantrey (1826). Marble. Courtesy, Massachusetts Art Commission.

[FIG. 2.12] "John Trumbull," by Robert Ball Hughes (1834). Marble, 26″ high. Courtesy, Yale University Art Gallery.

[FIG. 2.14] "Nathaniel Bowditch," by Robert Ball Hughes (1846). Plaster model for bronze statue erected in Mount Auburn Cemetery. Courtesy, Boston Athenaeum.

[FIG. 2.13] "Alexander Hamilton," by Robert Ball Hughes (1834). Plaster, about 26″ high. Courtesy, Detroit Institute of Arts.

3

"The Artistically-Inclined Stonecutter"

THE FIRST QUARTER OF THE 19TH CENTURY HAD PRESENTED BOTH ENCOURAGING AND discouraging signs for the advance of sculpture in the United States. Embittered old John Trumbull told eager and hopeful John Frazee that the art of sculpture would not arise in America for a century to come, and John Adams predicted an equally dismal future for the art. There were many who would have agreed with him. Witness, for example, the number of times the leaders of the young nation concluded there was no sculptor in America who was qualified to execute a heroic figure or a large-scale monument. Yet the number of commissions increased constantly, and sculpture did come to be a major part of the art of America. Throughout the late 18th and early 19th centuries there was a steady and deliberate progression toward a monumental three-dimensional art that was fostered by a gradual increase in private and governmental patronage.

Soon after the founding in 1802 of the American Academy of Fine Arts, New York City obtained a plaster-cast collection of famous statues that included the "Apollo Belvedere," the "Dying Gladiator," the "Laocoön" group, and busts of Cicero, Homer, Alexander the Great, and others. A notice in the New York *Commercial Advertiser*, June 15, 1803, informed the residents that the "society of Fine Arts" had received a large number of casts of excellent workmanship: "By the diligence of Mr. [Robert] Livingston . . . the society has received upwards of one hundred and fifty rare casts which will be exhibited . . . ." In June 1805 J. Delacroix and his friends presented for public viewing a number of casts of famous statues in the New York Hall. In Boston, as early as 1744, Dr. Alexander Hamilton observed in John Smibert's studio "a collection of good busts and statues, most of them antiques, done in clay and paste, among the rest Homer's head, and a model of the Venus of Medici." The Boston Athenaeum in 1823 received the Thorndike collection of casts, which contained no less than eight life-size figures and three smaller but full-length figures—among them the "Apollo," "Laocoön," "Venus de' Medici," "Capitoline Venus," Borghese "Gladiator," "Hermaphrodite," "Discus Thrower," and the "Antinous" of the Capitol— within a few years the Athenaeum had over forty busts, mostly casts of ancient works. In Philadelphia, the attempts to establish art academies resulted in plaster-cast collections as early as 1795 (The Columbianum) and 1805 (The Pennsylvania Academy of the Fine Arts). And by 1821 the South Carolina Academy of Fine Arts in Charleston also possessed an assortment of casts.

In addition to placing the finest examples of the sculptor's chisel before budding American talent, these casts made Americans in general more conscious of sculpture as one of the major arts. Certain Americans wanted to establish their country as the equal of any of the great countries of the past, and cultivation of the arts was one means of attaining this goal. Therefore, in the gentlemen's societies of the fine arts that were springing up, a collection of casts of antique statues became as necessary as copies of old masters' paintings, engraved prints, and architectural design books.

American painting executed by a native son had existed since at least 1740 when Robert Feke was first active in the Newport–Boston area. It was the better part of a century, however, before a comparable sculptor appeared. As with the painter in America, the sculptor found his prime subject to be the portrait. Around 1820–1825 several men began to model in clay and eventually put their likenesses into plaster and even marble.

Among the earliest of the native-born artists who worked in clay, plaster, and marble was John Frazee (1790–1852). Of Scotch ancestry, Frazee was born in Rahway, New Jersey, one of ten children. Shortly after his birth his mother "was deserted by an unworthy husband, and left to struggle with the ills of poverty." Young John did chores on his grandparents' farm and received virtually no formal education. He, like so many after him, entered the field of sculpture by a side door—the manual trades. In 1804 the boy of fourteen was apprenticed to William Lawrence, a country bricklayer and mason. In 1808 Lawrence completed a bridge over the Rahway River and wished to have his name chiseled in a stone, to commemorate his accomplishment. No one else being at hand, the contractor agreed to let Frazee try; the attempt was quite successful.

Frazee's cockiness is seen in a passage from his autobiography: "These were the first letters I ever made on stone and . . . they brought to me the tribute of much praise. . . . I was now about eighteen years old—active, vigorous and strong as I was skillful." The success of this venture led the ambitious young man to replace the trowel with the chisel, and, in his own words, it "begat in my mind that stonecutting was a craft much better suited to my genius and caste than bricklaying and from that period I began to ponder upon the creations of the chisel, and dream of tombstones." Frazee soon afterward moved to Newark; there he learned stonecutting, and his career was launched.

Tuckerman wrote that "the artistically-inclined stonecutter had amused himself by plastic experiments in his family before adventuring in art, having copied a head of Franklin, modeled his children eating a pie, and consoled himself for the loss of one [child] by his first ideal attempt—'Grief.'" Frazee's earliest experience with figure carving was the image of Grief leaning on an urn, done in 1815 to mark the grave of his infant son. The sculptor observed that it was a sorry thing to behold and lamented his lack of training in antique art. It was several years before he was to try the human form again.

By 1818 he had moved to New York City, where he and his brother formed a partnership in a marble shop, specializing in funerary monuments. Soon after his arrival Frazee saw his first cast of an antique statue at the Academy, and was deeply impressed by it. Though Frazee was not discouraged by Trumbull's pessimistic appraisal for the future of sculpture, he realized one could not make a living from commissioned portrait busts, so he continued doing the type of stone carving that was in demand. An early example of his work, dated 1821, is a wall memorial dedicated to Sarah Haynes in Trinity Church, New York City. It has a fine classical cornice at the top and Ionic columns at the sides, with a drape hung between the capitals. An oval tablet in the center contains the neatly cut inscription, but there was no attempt at figure work.

More ambitious, and important historically, is the mural monument to John Wells in St. Paul's Chapel, New York, which Frazee executed in 1824, and for which he received $1,000, a very high fee at that time. At the base is an inscription tablet surrounded by foliate motifs and capped with an architrave and pediment. Upon a circular pedestal rests a portrait bust of Wells, his shoulders covered with a quasi-classical drape, while at the sides are books and a lamp. This is the first portrait bust carved in marble by an American sculptor; it bears testimony to the influence of the Italian neoclassicists, many of whose works existed in New York City by that time. Since he had carved the figure of Grief, Frazee had been studying or at least observing examples of neoclassical art—probably busts by Ceracchi and Causici—and also casts of ancient portrait busts. His debt to Giuseppe Ceracchi is noticeable in a marble bust of John Jay, which he executed at the request of Congress, who appropriated $400 for it on March 2, 1831—the first such commission given by the government to an American-born sculptor. The original was placed in the Supreme Court Room of the Capitol; in 1835 a marble copy was given to the City of New York, and it now resides in City Hall. The *New York Evening Post* of November 4, 1831, reported that "a very fine marble bust of Gov. John Jay has just been completed . . ." by Frazee, and a few months later notified its readers that the portrait was on exhibition at the Merchants' Exchange. There is an element of neoclassicism in the ringlet treatment of the hair and in the rendering of the toga in the Jay portrait; but it is the modeling of the face that especially suggests the work of Ceracchi, who had produced his bust of Jay about 1795. The faces of the two busts are so similar that for a few years the Ceracchi portrait was thought to be another copy of Frazee's "Jay." Frazee had undoubtedly studied the Ceracchi portrait closely in his eagerness to improve his own art. But the likeness of the individual was not subordinated to a classical ideal, and in this Frazee adheres to native tradition in his portraiture. He would, of course, have known John H. I. Browere's "Gallery of Busts" in New York City, which opened in 1828 with its collection of life-mask portraits, and the life mask is naturally one of the most faithful renderings of the human physiognomy without intervention of an artificial ideal. Since colonial times Americans had desired a strong fidelity to the subject's features, and Frazee's portraits must therefore be seen as a compromise between neoclassicism and naturalism, with the latter usually the stronger.

In addition to the Wells memorial, Frazee also made, at the request of the American Academy, a bust of Lafayette on the occasion of the Frenchman's return visit to America in 1824. The sculptor made "a most successful mold from his [Lafayette's] face," from which he modeled the bust. In that same year Frazee had been elected to membership in the American Academy, and replied in his letter of acceptance to Alexander Robertson, dated June 10, 1824:

I am glad to learn that among my few efforts, there is something which renders me worthy to be associated with those, who, by their talents and enterprise, have gained for themselves and their country an unfading reputation. In regard to my profession, I scarcely know how to speak. I have done nothing save to grasp the chisel [sic] and approach the block; and thus I stand waiting the will of Heaven and the voice of my country to direct my stroke. If it be true that I am the first American that has lifted the tool, then it is no less true that I have before me an arduous task. Nevertheless, I am not disheartened—nor shall I shrink from the undertaking.

[Courtesy, New-York Historical Society]

Two years later, when he became one of the founders of the dissident National Academy of Design, he was the only sculptor among the charter members. In the first exhibition of that organization (1826) he showed his "Bust of Gen. La Fayette," along with a "bust of a Lady, Inscribed 'Mother.'" That he still made gravestones to earn his living is indicated by his marble tablet of 1826, "Sacred to the memory of Peter Schermerhorn," in St. Mark's Church, New York City. In 1827 he made a self-portrait; the original has disappeared, but a bronze copy exists in the Pennsylvania Academy and bears the inscription "J. Frazee/ se ipsum fecit/ Anno L. A. LII," in imitation of an antique signature.

In 1831 John Frazee entered into a partnership in the marble-working business with his former employee Robert E. Launitz (1806–1870), a Latvian-born sculptor who had studied with Thorwaldsen in Rome and who had come to New York City in 1828. During the 1830's and 1840's Launitz frequently exhibited at the National Academy, showing many classical, or ideal, pieces with such titles as "Amphitrite, Cupid and Psyche," and "Rose of the Alhambra," along with portrait busts and medallions. Meanwhile he was busy carving gravestones and marble ornamentation for architectural interiors. An example of his decorative work is the memorial urn dedicated to Andrew Jackson Downing on the Mall near the Smithsonian Institution in Washington, D.C. Launitz' style in portrait sculpture may be seen in his bust of Peter Augustus Jay (c. 1840) in the New-York Historical Society. Launitz is also an important figure because he was the teacher of several young American sculptors; for instance, Thomas Crawford, when he was first beginning to work as a sculptor, learned much from both Frazee and Launitz. The Frazee-Launitz partnership lasted until 1839, after which date Launitz continued the production of funerary markers by himself. An example of such work is the memorial he created to stand over the grave of the Indian woman Do-Hum-Me in Greenwood Cemetery in New York. On one side of the rectangular memorial with flared cornice was a relief of Do-Hum-Me's "bereaved warrior, attempting to hide, while he betrays his grief." Dating from about 1844, it is one of the earliest of the carved figures to grace a garden cemetery in this country, coming only two years after Henry Dexter's Binney memorial. A view of Launitz' monument may be seen in Cornelia Walter's *Rural Cemeteries of America*.

In the early 1830's John Frazee produced a number of portrait busts of famous men—seven commissioned by the Boston Athenaeum. When Thomas W. Ward, the treasurer of the Athenaeum, saw Frazee's bust of Nathaniel Prime in New York, he persuaded his friends in Boston to order portraits of Daniel Webster and Nathaniel Bowditch for the library. Frazee went to Boston in 1833 and began with the bust of Webster. On one occasion while posing for the artist, Webster delivered a speech for Frazee just as if he were on the floor of the United States Senate. The spirit of Webster is caught in the sparkle and fire of his eyes, though the bust still shows the strong influence of such neoclassicists as Ceracchi.

Early in 1834 Thomas Handasyd Perkins commissioned the sculptor to model the likeness of Chief Justice John Marshall and put it into marble; for this, Frazee was to receive $500, plus travel expenses to Richmond, Virginia, where Marshall would sit for the portrait. Frazee no doubt took advantage of the opportunity to study Houdon's statue of Washington and other fine pieces of sculpture while he was there. In the head of Marshall (Fig. 3.3) the sculptor captured the reserved, formal dignity of the Chief Justice, which Lorado Taft chose to characterize as "curiously rigid." But nearly everyone proclaimed it a success, even Marshall himself, who in May of 1834 supplied Frazee with a testimonial stating that ". . . so far as I can rely on my own opinion, [it] is admirably well executed. Others think it good too." A year later the old Chief Justice bought seven plaster copies of the bust at $10 each; one was given to Mr. Justice Story, another to Mrs. Ledy of New York; the other five were sent to Richmond, also as gifts. For years thereafter Frazee produced copies of his Marshall bust for various parts of the nation. On May 22, 1847, M. M. Robinson of New Orleans wrote to Conway Robinson in Virginia recommending that the Richmond Bar Association purchase a copy of "the Old Chief"; Frazee had made one for the

Louisiana bar in 1843 and it was placed in the State Supreme Court chamber. Stylistically, the Marshall is a tour de force in naturalism, comparable to Hiram Powers' portrait of Andrew Jackson, now in the Metropolitan Museum of Art, which was modeled about a year later. About this time Frazee executed his own portrait bust of Jackson in Washington, D.C. (now at Princeton in the Museum of Historic Art).

The head of the Marshall bust is obviously an American portrait, and it is a rather strange contrast to the toga-draped chest and shoulders below. Two different types exist; in the earlier (Boston Athenaeum) type the left pectoral muscle of the chest was exposed; when this drew some criticism the sculptor in a subsequent bust (in the New-York Historical Society) raised the toga to cover more of the chest. The fabric is well conceived, with a good feeling for sculpturesque form—possibly more so than in the head.

Also in the group commissioned by the Athenaeum were busts of Associate Justice Joseph Story (Fig. 3.1), Judge William Prescott, John Lowell, and Thomas H. Perkins, all of which were put into marble in 1834–1835. All these men seem to have been pleased with Frazee's work. Joseph Story, whose sculptor-to-be son was then about seventeen, wrote Frazee that he wanted to purchase copies of both the Marshall bust and his own bust. In 1840 J. A. Lowell wrote to Frazee to order a cast of his father's portrait to present to Harvard, where a collection of busts of eminent jurists was being started. Frazee gave the prices of his work: one cast, $60; six casts, $100; ten casts, $150; Lowell ordered six and received them in Boston in December of the same year.

The respect that Frazee had for his portrait busts and the care he wished them to receive are seen in a letter he wrote on August 8, 1835, to Dr. Seth Bass, the librarian of the Athenaeum:

I have just shipped to your care the Busts of Judge Marshall & Col. Perkins . . . . Now do my good Doctor have great care of these busts. They are works which I prize highly. You have none equal to them in your Athenaeum (in the modern sculptures) at least such is my opinion and if your Boston connoisseurs differ with me on this point please let me know the wherefore. Take care how you unpack them least [sic] you injure the marble and I wish you to keep the muslin cloths around them until you have them in the place where you intend to exhibit them. They never *in no case* should be handled without there being a cloth over them to keep the hand from soiling the marble . . . . N.B. In placing the Busts for exhibition great care should be taken to have the light fall quartering upon the face—so as to throw one side of the head . . . quite into the shadow.

In 1834 Frazee's interests also turned to architecture when he took charge of the building of the Customs House in New York City. In a letter dated April 18, 1837, he wrote, "The new Customs House is now reaching a critical stage of work which requires all my attention," and it was almost certainly he who designed, and probably carved, the capitals for the edifice. He was dismissed in December 1840, but continued to work on the building nevertheless.

In August 1838 J. A. Lowell wrote to John Frazee informing him that a lately deceased citizen of Boston had left money for a monument over his grave in Mount Auburn Cemetery. The executors of the will had at first considered a marble sculpture, but then decided against it because of the inclemency of New England weather. They chose instead to erect an architectural monument on the site, and Frazee was invited to submit a design. Whatever came of this is unknown, but that Frazee executed other funerary monuments for Bostonians is known—for example, those of Bishop Parker and the Rev. Dr. Jardine.

All the while the Frazee studio and stoneyard continued to turn out copies in plaster or marble of his famous busts. In the early 1840's he may have made a trip to Raleigh to look into the possibility of reconstructing Canova's "Washington," after being contacted by William Gaston of North Carolina. He also designed a monument to Washington, exhibited at the Art Union in 1848, in which he employed the Grecian style of architecture which he described as "the noblest relics of those nations where they first arose."

Frazee died in 1852, seventeen years after writing his autobiography. Although much of his time had been spent in carving marble mantels and gravestones, still he found more patronage for his work on portraits than the dour Colonel Trumbull had said he could hope for back in 1820. But he never realized his ambition, according to Dunlap, of carving a full-length figure in marble. Undoubtedly by the late 1830's and 1840's he began to hear of the successes of men who had made the journey to Italy—Horatio Greenough had been known in New York since the exhibition of his "Chanting Cherubs" in 1831, and his colossal figure of Washington arrived in the capital city in the early 1840's. Hiram Powers' "Greek Slave" caused a sensation in New York and elsewhere in the mid-forties, and his former assistant, Thomas Crawford, had made a name for himself with his "Orpheus," which was sent back to Boston in 1843. But by the time these men went to Italy, Frazee was already approaching middle age, with sizable family responsibilities and a rather good business going for him, plus the promise of considerable success in portrait modeling and carving, without traveling to Italy to study. Nevertheless, from books and whatever neoclassical works and antique casts were at hand, he became a part of the classical revival in his own way. But on looking at his total output, one realizes that he only borrowed certain neoclassical motifs and that his portrait style was actually based on naturalism and not on the neoclassicism of Canova, Thorwaldsen, or any of their standard-bearers who came to work in America in the early 19th century.

John Henri Isaac Browere (1790–1834) was also actively engaged in portraiture in New York City in the 1820's and early 1830's. He had studied with Archibald Robertson, a Scottish painter working in New York, and had gone to Europe for two years of study (1816–1817), primarily in the field of sculpture. He therefore preceded Horatio Greenough by several years as the first American to go abroad to study sculpture. He lived in Paris for a while, and it was probably at that time that he learned the technique of making life masks. Although he settled in New York City on his return to America, from 1825

Browere traveled around the country taking life masks of eminent men. He made a mask of the aged Thomas Jefferson, and poor old Jefferson is reported to have nearly suffocated in the process. In a letter dated May 22, 1826, to the New York Council Browere proposed to make a statue of Jefferson for the Fourth of July, stating that he owned the "only fac-simile reproduction" of the subject's face. Nothing came of this proposal, as far as can be determined, but it reveals that Browere was willing to attempt the full-length figure.

The Marquis de Lafayette had his likeness taken in mask form by Browere in 1824, and numerous others followed: David Hosack, the physician and professor of medicine at Columbia College; Philip Hone, mayor of New York (Browere's busts of both are in the New-York Historical Society); also, Gilbert Stuart's portrait by Browere is preserved at the Redwood Library in Newport, R.I. By 1828 he had gathered together a sufficient number of portrait busts made from life masks to open his "Gallery of Busts." He hoped to have the federal government finance the casting of these in bronze, forming a kind of national portrait gallery, but the funds were not forthcoming.

Browere's procedure was simply to apply the life mask to a toga-draped chest and shoulders, producing a portrait such as the Pierre Cortlandt Van Wyck bust (Fig. 3.2), which is now in City Hall in New York City. Again one finds the compromise between an objective and highly accurate rendering of the likeness without idealization, and the neoclassical toga-covered shoulders. The portrait is neither artless nor devoid of the feeling of character, and it was so skillfully executed that one does not suspect the technical means employed. The achievement of a rich character study through a tour de force of naturalism is one of the essential features of the American sculptured portrait in the second quarter of the 19th century—and this is as true of Hiram Powers or Thomas Crawford as it is of John Browere or John Frazee, as shall be seen in the next chapter. Browere's work, however, showed no trace of the Byronic idealization that was to appear in the portraiture of Greenough, Crawford, and Powers in the latter half of the 1830's.

Browere left his great ambition to form a national collection of bronze busts unfulfilled when he died at the age of forty-four. His collection of likenesses passed to his family and were largely forgotten until the start of the 20th century. As to the legitimacy of these portraits as works of art, it has been suggested that they are more an example of that spirit of invention and use of technical means so frequently found during Browere's day. The answer, of course, is in the work itself, for his portraits transcend a mere duplication of the features to capture the living personality—to preserve the vigor and strength of the men who were forming a nation. To deny Browere a place in the history of American sculpture would be like denying that the photograph has any validity as an artistic medium because of the technical process involved. It is curious, however, that Browere never entered a single portrait at either the American Academy or the National Academy of Design annual exhibitions, and William Dunlap took no notice of him other than mentioning his name once in passing. All this explains in part why Browere remained in obscurity for so many years after his death.

Frazee and Browere represent a transitional period between a time when there was virtually no sophisticated figure sculpture in America and 1830–1835, a time when a corps of young artists began to model portraits and ideal figures and have them put into marble. The impact of the work of Greenough, Powers, and Crawford did not hit America until the late 1830's and early 1840's, so it was native sons like Browere and Frazee, along with the many foreign sculptors, who carried forward the art of sculpture in America.

Hezekiah Augur (1791–1858) began his working career as a dry-goods merchant in New Haven, Connecticut; after going bankrupt he turned to the carving of ornamental parts and furniture legs. When his invention of a lace-making machine removed the burden of debt, he became a full-time carver. Augur also developed an early bracket saw and in 1847 introduced a machine that made piano legs.

Augur's career as a sculptor began during the period 1820 to 1825. He might easily have continued in the tradition of the native wood carvers, but about 1825 he was encouraged by Samuel F. B. Morse to try his hand with marble. Among his earliest attempts was a bust of Professor Alexander Metcalf Fisher, put in marble some time between 1825 and 1827; in the latter year it was exhibited at the National Academy of Design, of which Augur was a member. The bust was then given to Yale, and it can still be seen in the Art Gallery there. The head is well modeled and contains hardly a trace of any self-taught primitive stylization of form, which one might expect to find in an early effort of a former wood carver.

Augur is reported to have carved several ideal pieces of classical inspiration, for instance, busts of Apollo (shown at the Pennsylvania Academy in 1831 and labeled "his first essay in marble") and of Sappho, and a statue of Sappho that was in the collection of Thomas H. Perkins of Boston before 1829. Early in 1830, Ralph Waldo Emerson visited the studio of the New Haven sculptor and reported to a friend, in a letter dated March 16th, "There I saw . . . his marble people." These "marble people" were most likely the two figures, about half life-size, that are now the most famous of Augur's work—"Jephthah and His Daughter" (Fig. 3.4), taken from Judges XI, 34–35. These ambitious pieces suggest the artist's desire to create something more than portraits. Augur must have had a model of some type before him as he worked; it may have been an engraving of a dancing girl in Henry Moses' *The Works of Antonio Canova, Engraved in Outline* (London, 1824), or possibly a porcelain or terra-cotta piece such as the "Apparition of Venus to Aeneas" of the early 18th century in the Michael Friedsam Collection of the Metropolitan Museum of Art. The figures, executed about 1828–1830, are highly animated and are carved with a fine feeling for sculpturesque form. The drapery of the figure of the daughter is vigorously rendered and well designed, with cascading folds that still reveal the youthful body underneath. The influence of neoclassicism is apparent in the straight line from the girl's forehead down the bridge of the nose, in the deep-set eyes, which are placed very near the brows, and in the fullness of the mouth, neck, and chin.

There is indeed something of a triumph here for this native-born, self-taught American sculptor. Augur was something of an isolated phenomenon and evidently had no following of students or assistants, but these figures serve to show the sculptural ambitions of a new age of American artists. They have stepped across the neoclassical threshold to be executed in marble—a step that the allegorical figures of William Rush never made.

Another excellent and early example of the arrival of neoclassicism and its influence on American sculpture is the statue "Flora" (Fig. 3.5) in the Henry Francis du Pont Winterthur Museum. A wooden figure of the finest workmanship, "Flora" moves with the utmost grace, fairly dancing along with feet that hardly touch ground. Carved of white pine about 1820–1825 this "Flora" reveals a significant stylistic change from the "Plenty" by the Skillin brothers (Peabody Museum, Salem). The Winterthur figure and Augur's "Jephthah and His Daughter" clearly show the impact of neoclassicism upon the ideal works of those sculptors who had emerged from the wood-carver tradition but who did not go to Italy.

The fame that "Jephthah and His Daughter" brought to Hezekiah Augur is demonstrated in a notice in *The Literary Tablet* (New Haven) of November 1, 1832:

Mr. Augur, whose skill and taste as a sculptor are contributing so largely to the reputation, not only of our city, but of this nation, has gone to New York with his beautiful group of statuary, representing Jephtha and his Daughter. It will be a source of much satisfaction to the lovers of the fine arts at the South, to learn that Mr. Augur intends to visit Philadelphia, Baltimore and Washington—thus affording a fine opportunity for the admirers of American genius to evince their approbation of this exquisite speciman [sic] of art, by solid testimony.

In 1832 Congress gave its first large sculptural commission to an American: Horatio Greenough was asked to do a marble statue of George Washington. Greenough had lived in Italy most of the preceding seven years, and this caused some criticism; in the Boston *Transcript* in May 1832 a person who disapproved of expatriate artists wrote that the commission should have been awarded to Hezekiah Augur, the self-taught sculptor who had remained in the land of his birth. This complaint, of course, was to no avail, but two years later the Joint Committee on the Library voted to have Augur execute a marble bust of Chief Justice Oliver Ellsworth. The bust, which was not received at the Capitol until 1837, is an animated portrait with a strong angular treatment of the planes of the head and the folds of the drapery. Augur received $800 for it, with the stipulation that he supply the bracket and set the bust in place in the Supreme Court room.

This is the last record of Hezekiah Augur's activity as a sculptor. He lived for another two decades, but with the bust of Oliver Ellsworth he seems to have ended his career as a sculptor.

John S. Cogdell (1778–1847) was by profession a lawyer in South Carolina who at about the age of forty-seven took up sculpture as an avocation. During his life he was a jurist, a holder of several public offices, a musician, and the president of a bank, as well as a painter and a sculptor. After graduating from Charleston College in 1795 he entered a local law office and was admitted to the bar four years later. Poor health sent him on an ocean cruise to the Mediterranean in 1800, at which time he visited the studio of the celebrated Canova. Whatever he saw there stirred his latent talent as an artist, for thereafter he drew and painted whenever the demands of his successful law office permitted. Even during the years in the state assembly (1810–1818), he found a great pleasure in painting pictures for his friends in spare moments. In 1821 he, along with Samuel F. B. Morse, organized the South Carolina Academy of Fine Arts, which was short-lived but which "had as splendid exhibitions [as he had] seen in any other city." It was in that same year, on a trip to New York City, that he observed William Coffee modeling a portrait bust, and the encouragement to try his own hand at sculpture came from his friend the painter Washington Allston when he visited him in Boston a few years later. A bust of Dr. John Holbrook was reportedly his first attempt at modeling in clay (c. 1825), and he presented a cast of it to the Boston Athenaeum that same year, the first portrait bust to be owned by that institution. Encouraged by his initial success, the following year he modeled a portrait of General William Moultrie from a portrait; one cast was given to the Athenaeum and another, according to Dunlap, was "presented to Congress, placed in their library, and occasioned very flattering compliments on the floor of the House of Representatives." Both the Holbrook and Moultrie busts were exhibited at the National Academy of Design in 1827; the Holbrook was also shown at the Pennsylvania Academy in 1827, and the Moultrie in 1830. Thus Cogdell's work was known and admired in Boston, New York, Philadelphia, and Washington—as well as in Charleston—where he was sometimes the first, even the only, native-born American sculptor to be represented in the exhibitions of the late 1820's.

But Cogdell was more admired than patronized, and virtually no commissions came from his native South Carolina. Even the bust of the Reverend Theodore Dehon (d. 1817), executed in 1829, was undertaken on his own, although after it was finished all Charleston gave its approbation to the sculptor, and the vestry of St. Michael's sent a copy of the bust to the Protestant Episcopal Society in London. Because of the favorable reception his work continually received Cogdell planned another trip to Europe in 1830, but an investment that proved financially disastrous caused him to cancel the voyage. He became president of the Bank of South Carolina in 1832, an office he held for the rest of his life. Meanwhile his interest and participation in the fine arts continued.

Cogdell executed a number of busts throughout the 1830's and also some ideal pieces, such as "Modestia" and "Hagar and Ishmael"; the latter was a plaster group, now lost, which was given to the Boston Athenaeum in 1832 by Washington Allston. Probably his most ambitious work of all is the 1833 marble memorial (Fig. 3.6) to his mother (d. 1827), which is in St. Philip's Church in Charleston, South Carolina. Above a broad tablet bearing a long eulogistic inscription three men in classical dress mourn at an urn set on a pedestal. The figures, carved in high relief, represent the three surviving sons, including the sculptor, and are surprisingly well done, considering Cogdell's meager training. In a monument such as this the naturalism that was so necessary in portraiture was sacrificed to the neoclassicism that dominated the ideal works. It is necessary to recognize this distinction, for it existed in the work of nearly every sculptor of the period. The memorial to the sculptor's mother is reminiscent of the contemporary marble statues and reliefs in Westminster Abbey by men like Sir Francis Chantrey or John Gibson or John Flaxman. And when Cogdell executed this marble memorial in 1833, Horatio Greenough had not yet done a life-size figure in stone, and Hiram Powers had not even left Cincinnati.

Cogdell's work in sculpture continued into the early 1840's. In 1841, two years before the connoisseurs of Boston became aware of Thomas Crawford working in Rome, the Athenaeum exhibited Cogdell's busts of Sir Walter Scott, the Marquis de Lafayette, and Stephen Elliott. His last known work, a portrait of John England, was done in 1842. He died five years later, and like Browere, Frazee, and Augur, he left no students or assistants. As with the others, much of Cogdell's importance lies in the interest that his work awakened in the art of sculpture and in the realization among his countrymen that perhaps the time had come when a native-born American could model a portrait bust as good as any done by an imported European. This realization, of course, appealed immensely to Americans' growing sense of national pride.

The decade 1825 to 1835 thus saw the emergence in America of considerable sculpture in plaster and marble done by native sons, largely in imitation of the works by foreigners. The latter introduced their neoclassicism, which the Americans combined with the strong tradition of naturalism that existed in portraiture. In that decade American sculpture first became a major art form as we know it today, rising beyond the craft of the artisan which it had been earlier. While Frazee, Augur, Browere, and Cogdell remained at home, there were others who could not find the proper artistic environment in America. These men, led by Greenough, Crawford, and Powers, were contemporaries of Frazee and the others, although the careers of the last group had all ended by the 1840's, or about the time the expatriates were first gaining recognition. If, as a result of the efforts of Frazee, Augur, Browere, and Cogdell, Americans became aware of the possibility of their own country nurturing the art of sculpture through its native-born artists, the work of Greenough, Crawford, and Powers in Italy turned that possibility into a promise.

[FIG. 3.2] "Pierre Cortlandt Van Wyck," by John H. I. Browere (c. 1830). Plaster. Courtesy, Art Commission of the City of New York.

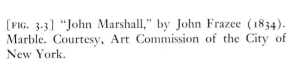

[FIG. 3.3] "John Marshall," by John Frazee (1834). Marble. Courtesy, Art Commission of the City of New York.

[FIG. 3.4] "Jephthah and his Daughter," by Hezekiah Augur (c. 1828–30). Marble.
Courtesy, Yale University Art Gallery, gift of the Citizens of New Haven.

[FIG. 3.5] Memorial to Mrs Mary Ann Elizabeth
Cogdell, by John Cogdell (1833). Marble. Courtesy,
St. Philip's Church, Charleston, S.C.; photo, Index
of American Sculpture, University of Delaware.

[FIG. 3.6] "Flora" (c. 1820–25). White pine, 57⅜"
high. Courtesy, Henry Francis du Pont Winterthur
Museum.

The First Expatriates:
Neoclassicism vs.
Naturalism

BEFORE 1825 THOSE NATIVE-BORN AMERICANS WHO EVENTUALLY BECAME SCULP-
tors—men like William Rush, Hezekiah Augur, and John Frazee—had started as
either wood carvers or stonecutters. Frequently they were first moved to try a
bust after seeing a marble portrait by one of the foreign sculptors, and they then
became sculptors while still earning a living as craftsmen. The first man born in
the United States to declare from the outset of his career that he was going to be
a sculptor and to devote his life to the creation of objects of ineffable beauty in
plastic form was Horatio Greenough (1800–1852). Often referred to as the first
American sculptor, Greenough was not the first either to take up mallet and
chisel or to model in clay, but he was the first native-born American to make
sculpture his exclusive vocation.

Horatio Greenough was the fourth of the eleven children born to David and
Betsey Greenough. The environment in which young Horatio grew up is nicely
summarized by Henry Tuckerman in his *Memorial* of 1853:

His father belonged to that respected class of merchants whose integrity, enterprise,
and intelligence . . . justly gave them a degree of consideration which is almost unknown at the present day . . . . Active in the political and social life of the town, they
almost created public opinion, and were remarkable for individuality of character not
less than a tone of mind above and beyond the mere spirit of trade. This was evinced
in the careful manner in which the children were brought up, and the intellectual
privileges afforded them . . . .

One is struck by the different surroundings of the youths of Greenough and,
say, John Frazee: When the latter was in his teens he was already a construction
laborer, whereas the former was about to enter Harvard.

In the garden of the Greenough home in Boston there stood a marble copy of an antique statue of Phocion, and this piece apparently stirred Horatio to attempt sculpture himself. While still a schoolboy he enjoyed carving toys in wood and modeling in wax, an impulse that was encouraged when his parents set aside a small room for the display of such pieces. In addition to Horatio, several of his brothers went into the arts: John, the eldest, became a painter; Richard, fourteen years younger than Horatio, became a sculptor; and Henry, perhaps the closest of all to Horatio, was an architect, writer, and painter. His novel *Ernest Carroll* deals with artist life in Italy.

The community of Boston and Cambridge provided cultural nourishment in several ways. Horatio was given entrée to the library of the Boston Athenaeum and its collection of casts after its director discovered him copying Binon's bust of John Adams in Faneuil Hall. He received instruction in modeling from J. B. Binon and from Solomon Willard, the Boston wood carver, modeler, and architect; and from Alpheus Cary he learned to carve in stone. His introduction to artistic theory came from Washington Allston, whom he came to know well while attending Harvard. On one occasion he wrote that "Allston was to me a father in what concerned my progress of every kind. He taught me first how to discriminate, how to think, how to feel." (Quoted from Dunlap, *Rise of the Arts of Design*.) At Harvard he studied the classics and anatomy, and produced a few busts, among them portraits of Napoleon (Boston, Museum of Fine Arts) and Washington. But by this time the eager youth had absorbed what art the cities on the Charles River could offer, and the conversations with Allston filled him with a great desire to go to Italy.

Arriving in Rome in 1825, Horatio took an apartment, with the painter Robert W. Wier, in a house formerly occupied by Claude Lorraine, near where Salvador Rosa and Nicholas Poussin once lived. He presented his letters of introduction to the great Danish sculptor Bertel Thorwaldsen, who gave the young American much helpful criticism and encouragement to get him started. His mornings were spent making careful drawings from the antique statues in the sculpture galleries, and visiting other art galleries and studios of Rome. Afternoons he worked in his studio, and in the evening he went to the Academy, where he drew from the nude—a common practice in Rome, but one that would have appalled Boston. Occasionally on fine moonlit evenings he and friends would roam about the ancient ruins of the city. There was a brotherhood, an international camaraderie among the artists, who gathered daily at the Caffè Greco to discuss art in all its aspects. Rome exhilarated him, and he set himself a rigorous discipline of study. In his studio he executed several portrait busts, including a self-portrait, and began modeling his first ideal work—"The Dead Abel," a subject made popular among artists and writers by Gessner's book of that title. The plaster model was brought back to America, where Allston saw it and wrote of Greenough that he "is qualified to shine in the brightest branch of his art, the inventive; an evidence of which we have in his 'Dead Abel,' . . . a

figure of beauty and truth, and such a first work as I have never before seen."
(Letter to Gulian Verplanck, Jan. 31, 1828, courtesy, New-York Historical Society.) In 1827 Greenough was struck down by a disease known as Roman fever
and was forced to return to America. The fresh air and the enforced idleness of
the sea voyage was apparently what he needed, and when he landed he was in
excellent health.

The next two years were spent in Boston, Washington, and Baltimore, where
he modeled several portrait busts of eminent men. In Boston he made a likeness
of Mayor Josiah Quincy (Massachusetts Historical Society), and in Washington,
in 1828, he modeled the bust of President John Quincy Adams (Boston Athenaeum and New-York Historical Society). On February 15 Adams noted in his
diary, "Mr. Greenough . . . a young sculptor from Boston . . . asked permission to take my bust; to which I assented. He has a room at Mr. [Charles B.]
King's, where he will give me notice when he is prepared and wishes my
attendance."

Greenough employed the bare breast of the neoclassical mode, implying that
the contemporary style of clothing added nothing of distinction to the portrait,
and he gave Adams a stern countenance, devoid of cheer or any promise of
levity. In this respect the portrait was a more accurate character study than the
President cared to admit. On February 21, 1828, the sculptor wrote to his
brother Henry, "I shall not attempt (as Sully and others have done) to make
him look cheerful . . . . Gravity is natural to him and a smile is ill at home."
(*Letters*, p. 26)

Greenough himself possessed an engaging personality and throughout his life
he was always at ease among the social elite. In Washington he conversed easily
with both President and Mrs. Adams; and he wrote of pleasant evenings spent in
the company of Charles Bulfinch, Edward Everett, William Thornton, and such
fellow artists as Chester Harding and Luigi Persico. At this time Greenough acquired the patronage of Robert Gilmor of Baltimore who gave him two commissions: one for a bust of Mrs. Gilmor, which was modeled in the spring of 1828
in the library of the family home; the other for a statue to be made when the
sculptor returned to Italy. There were other portrait commissions as well—one
of Chief Justice Marshall, for example—and these were all encouraging to a
young artist. In May 1828, with several portrait busts in plaster ready to be put
into marble, he returned to Italy.

Greenough went first to Carrara, the famous stone quarry whose mountains of
pure white marble had supplied sculptors since ancient times. During his stay of
three months, he supervised the work of putting several of his busts into marble.
Carrara marble was the least expensive anywhere—about one fourth what it
would cost in America—and there were plenty of skilled workmen who could
block out a bust and bring it to the stage where the artist need add only a few
refinements.

Late in 1828 Greenough went to Florence to begin work under the tutelage of

Bartolini, whose philosophy of beauty was that nature is the greatest of all teachers. Horatio moved into Bartolini's studio and there learned the importance of careful observation of the model. From this time it became obvious that Greenough was not going to develop along the strict neoclassical lines of Canova, Thorwaldsen, or Flaxman, and it would be a mistake to refer to him as merely a neoclassicist. He frequently found his ideal in the beauty in nature rather than in the eclectic, pre-established Greek conception of beauty. Later he was to write, "I contend for Greek principles, not for Greek things," indicating that though he was anxious to learn from classical art, he did not intend to copy it.

During the next two years commissions were few, though an occasional American traveler, like Dr. John Kirkland, would visit Greenough's studio and have a portrait bust made (Boston Athenaeum). Greenough took living quarters with the painter Thomas Cole, and in 1830 he modeled busts of Cole and of Samuel F. B. Morse, who was also painting in Florence. The one of Cole is now in the Wadsworth Atheneum; the Morse bust is in the Smithsonian. But the sculptor yearned for a commission more challenging to his talents than portraiture. This he got from the novelist James Fenimore Cooper, one of those Americans who knew the nation to be great politically and materially but was aware of its artistic and cultural inadequacies. It was in a way patriotism that caused men like Cooper and Robert Gilmor and Nicholas Longworth to subsidize young artists and thereby promote the cause of the arts in America. The matter of the commission was probably discussed while Greenough modeled Cooper's bust (Boston Public Library) in January 1829.

Cooper and his family were part of the American colony then in Florence. On a tour one day through the galleries of the Pitti Palace the novelist's daughters became quite interested in the singing *putti* in Raphael's "Madonna del Baldacchino," and it was decided that the commission should be a sculpture of the "Chanting Cherubs," the first instance of one American commissioning another to make a statue group in marble. Greenough began work on them at once. The "Chanting Cherubs" has disappeared, but it was probably similar to the "Angel and Child" of three years later (Fig. 4.1), which is now in the collection of the Museum of Fine Arts, in Boston. Both sculptor and patron were pleased with the "Cherubs" and had high hopes for the work's reception in America. It was decided to send it on tour of several cities beginning with Boston, and Cooper wrote home that the "Chanting Cherubs" was "the first effort of a young artist who bids fair to build for himself a name. . . . I hope the peculiarity of its being the first work of its kind which has come from an American chisel, as well as the rare merit of the artist, will be found to interest the public at home." (*Letters*, p. 44)

Interest them it did, at least at first; but many who went to see the group were disappointed when the infants did not actually sing! This was, of course, a time when Americans were inventing all sorts of mechanical devices: for example, within a year of Greenough's "Cherubs," Obed Hussey invented the horse-drawn reaper; Isaac Dripps invented the cowcatcher; and Peter Cooper built the locomotive *Tom Thumb*. The American public naturally expected a sculpture entitled "Chanting Cherubs" to contain some mechanism that would make cherubs sing. But a greater disappointment was that suffered by Greenough and Cooper when in New York City their countrymen were so ill-prepared for the naked infants that for a time those innocent babes were forced to wear little aprons for the sake of modesty! Such was the inclement artistic atmosphere which faced the American sculptor when he sent such a statue back to a land where an uncultivated mechanic or a glib buckskin-clad frontiersman might well represent the voice of the people on matters of art.

Cooper was appalled, and Greenough tried to be understanding, but he later wrote that he found it curious that Americans could be shocked at the nudity of his two infants, yet would gaze intently at the latest fandango dancer from Paris or Vienna. And in a related vein, on October 8, 1831, he wrote to Rembrandt Peale from Paris:

Pray Sir—convince [our countrymen] that one American work is of more value to the U. S. than 3 foreign ones even of superior merit. . . . Cooper's new book the Bravo is taking wonderfully here—If you could transfer a little of that man's love of country and national pride into the leading members of our society I think it would leaven them all and leave them quite as good men and surely much better patrons. Mr. Peale the scholars have looked so much abroad for their salvation in letters, arts and manners that they have not only overlooked home but have unfitted all under their influence for judging impartially of any thing American.

This, of course, was in answer to those who still maintained that only foreign sculptors were qualified to produce competent works of art for America.

Allston commended the "Cherubs," and young Thomas Crawford called them exquisite; others also praised them, but these few represented a cultured minority that could not carry the day. Greenough labored to give his countrymen back home a high and noble art. He and several other artists, together with a small group of intellectuals, tried to endow America with an art that would, in its own way, establish the nation as the equal of ancient Athens and Rome, of Renaissance Italy, of the France of Louis XIV. But their lofty goal met strong resistance from a powerful force that had recently come to the fore in America. That force had elected a President who was a far cry from the gentlemen-statesmen who had previously held the office. That force sought its own spokesman to champion an art "of the people" and "for the people," and it little understood the theory or purpose that was at the core of Greenough's art. He never captured the sympathies and loyalties of the great middle class of his native land, for these frontiersmen, farmers, and merchants had little rapport with the kind of art he offered. It was, in short, not *their* art.

Greenough's next "ideal," or "literary," work was "Medora," representing Conrad's dead wife in Byron's poem *The Corsair*. The sculptor's first life-size figure to be put into marble, Medora was shown laid out in her grave, with drapery covering her body from the waist down. The exposed breast caused some shock, and one lady said she would have felt more comfortable if the drapery had been pulled up a few inches more. But in sentiment it was typical of the era. Henry Tuckerman described it thus in his *Memorial:* "There is a mingled pathos and delicacy in the shape and attitude of this figure which touches the heart and awes the imagination." Greenough's "Dead Abel" and "Medora" mark the beginning of the romantic ideal in American sculpture, where a brooding pathos of considerable sentimentality replaces the unemotional detachment of neoclassicism.

The bread-and-butter work of a sculptor in the 19th century was, of course, the portrait bust, and throughout the 1830's Greenough looked to it to keep him solvent. In 1831 after arrangements had been made by Cooper, Greenough went to Paris to model the likeness of the old Marquis de Lafayette (Pennsylvania Academy of the Fine Arts), and a few other portrait commissions resulted from this visit. A fine example of Greenough's power as a portraitist is seen in his bust of Evan Philip Thomas (Fig. 4.2), modeled in Florence in 1837, along with that of his wife, Elizabeth Todhunter Thomas (both busts are in the Maryland Historical Society).

In the second quarter of the 19th century portraiture was irresistibly drawn toward a naturalism that was then still a poignant thing, full of verve and revealing a great strength of character. In the portraits by Greenough, as in those by Thomas Sully, there is an aristocratic spirit and flair combined with this naturalism. Greenough's portraits were neither Grecian nor Italianate in the manner of many of the foreign sculptors who had gone to America in the first quarter of the century. The style of the bust of Evan Philip Thomas may be described as a Byronic Romanticism that incorporates a large measure of naturalism. Byron was the arch-Romantic of the period in both his poetry and his life. Youthful, sensitive, courageous, vigorous, and touched with genius—these were all admirable qualities associated with the poet; if some features of his personality were less desirable, they were overlooked in the image his own age created of him. These qualities had been sought by American portrait painters for some years, but in sculpture they first appear around 1835 in the work of Greenough and a few years later in the portraits by Powers and Crawford.

Soon after Horatio Greenough returned to Florence in 1832 he began work on two commissions: a statue of "Cupid Bound" (Museum of Fine Arts, Boston) and his greatest undertaking of all—the colossal "George Washington" (Fig. 4.3).

James Fenimore Cooper and Washington Allston had both urged Congress to employ young Greenough to do the statue of Washington, which had long been approved but was only then being acted upon. As early as May 1, 1830, Alfred Greenough wrote to Henry that "Allston has interested himself about a statue of Washington, and has written to Webster recommending Horatio Greenough to execute it because he is peculiarly fitted for the undertaking, and the only person capable of executing it." (*Letters*, p. 64) In February 1832 Congress passed a resolution specifying Greenough to be the sculptor of the full-length marble "Pedestrian statue of Washington, to be placed in the centre of the rotunda of the Capitol." It further stated that the portrait by Houdon should be used as a model for the head, but "the accessories [were] to be left to the judgment of the artist."

Greenough received the official word from Congress the following June, but as he had other projects in progress, it was late in 1833 before anything was accomplished on the statue. At last receiving the large commission he had so long desired, he stood in awe of the task. In December 1833 he wrote to William Dunlap:

> When I went the other morning into the huge room in which I propose to execute my statue, I felt like a spoilt boy, who, after insisting upon riding on horseback, bawls aloud with fright at finding himself in the saddle, so far from the ground! I hope, however, that this will wear off.

According to a letter to his father, written at about the same time, he had completed the small clay model, and it had received favorable comment. Throughout 1834 and much of the following year, as he modeled the heroic-sized statue in his large Florentine studio, he often thought of the possibility of failure; so much was at stake here. In June 1835 he wrote to Henry that the large clay model was essentially completed and would be cast in a few months.

The usual procedure in a sculptor's studio in those days was for the sculptor himself to make the clay model of a portrait or statue; it was considered the creative part, and once this was completed the sculptor would often not see the work again for months. After the clay model had received the artist's finishing touches, it was turned over to the studio assistants—skilled Italian craftsmen—who produced a plaster mold of it from which the plaster model was made. Clay was apt to lose its form if it became too wet or too dry, and it was best to have the piece put into plaster as soon as possible. The artist's original clay model was destroyed in the process of producing the mold. If it was a portrait bust other skilled artisans in another room of the studio would put the bust into marble by a system known as "pointing":

> A pointing machine measures the depth from a given vertical, of, for example, the receding planes of the nose of a plaster cast and transfers the measurements to a hole drilled in the marble block. Scores of measured depths are thus transferred to the marble, until all that is left for the mason is to cut away surplus stone.
> [Peter and Linda Murray, *Dictionary of Art and Artists*, Baltimore, 1963]

For a larger work the plaster model would probably be shipped to Carrara, where more Italian workmen would block out and largely finish the statue, also using the pointing system. This eliminated the difficulty and expense of transporting any larger or heavier piece of marble than was absolutely necessary. The statue might be sent to the sculptor's studio in Florence or Rome for finishing touches, or with "hack" work it could be sent directly to Leghorn, where it would be loaded on board ship for the journey to America.

The artisans who did this sort of work were both expert and plentiful, and their services were relatively inexpensive. Many years later, for example, Hiram Powers wrote of his dependence on them in a letter to Edward Everett, dated March 19, 1859:

My friends who have urged me so much to come [home] . . . do not know that without workmen (marble carvers) a sculptor can do but little—and there is not a workman of this description I would trust and employ in all America. If I go home, therefore, I must leave my *hands* behind me.   [Massachusetts Historical Society]

The sculptor himself looked upon the tasks of casting the piece in plaster and then carving it in marble as laborious, physically strenuous, time-consuming, and altogether unfit work for the creative artist. Greenough had ordered that the last one-eighth-inch of marble surface be left on his "Chanting Cherubs" so that he could remove it and "finish" the statue himself; he found it so exhausting a task that he' declared he would never do it again; he admitted that the Italian craftsmen could do it better anyway.

This procedure was followed in general by Greenough's contemporaries working in Italy, and never a thought was given to their not being the ones who made the final work in plaster or marble. Indeed, they would have regarded any question about their artistic integrity as absolute nonsense.

Greenough finished the large clay model of "Washington" late in 1835, and it was then cast in plaster. In 1836 the sculptor returned to America for a joyous reunion with family and friends—and to make an inspection of the rotunda site his statue was to occupy. He returned to Florence the following year and had the plaster model transported to Carrara by November. Greenough was excited and filled with high expectation for his colossus; but it was an expectation that was tempered with doubt, for he had not convinced himself that his artistry had measured up to his ambitions. The final appraisal could not be made until the statue stood in the rotunda in Washington; Greenough was both anxious and apprehensive for the arrival of that day. Even as late as September 1839 he wrote to Henry that "the Washington is nearly done. I assure you [it] surpasses my expectations as a likeness, but what will be its reception as a work of art I know not." (*Letters*, p. 130)

Greenough's conception for his statue grew out of his vision of another great statue of the past: the gigantic ivory and gold image of the Greek god Zeus, which once reigned in the temple at Elis; it had been created in the 5th century B.C. by Phidias, who had previously supervised the sculptures of the Parthenon in Athens. One of the most famous statues of ancient times, from the early Middle Ages through the Renaissance it was counted as one of the Seven Wonders of the World, even though it had been destroyed in the 5th century A.D.

Shortly after 1800 the French archaeologist Quatremere de Quincy published a book entitled *Jupiter* (Paris, 1814) in which he made a reconstruction of Phidias' "Zeus" based on literary descriptions and ancient coins that bore its image. At the peak of the classical revival Phidias' "Zeus" was hailed as the greatest statue of the greatest god of antiquity; Zeus was the most noble being of the ancient world, and more than any other, he determined the destinies of all those who came within his sphere of influence. Greenough wished to endow Washington with these same qualities. Canova had represented Washington as an enlightened and benevolent Caesar; Greenough would portray him in the guise of the great god Zeus.

Greenough did use the portrait bust of Washington by Houdon as a model for the head, although he had some difficulty locating a copy. The countenance is serene and grand, yet resolute—an image of a man who did in fact govern the civil destinies of generations who came after him. The head, however, bears an Italianate influence as well, and one suspects that Greenough was also familiar with the Ceracchi portrait of Washington. Two small figures stand at the back of the throne; Columbus contemplates an orb while an Indian dozes in ignorance of the meaning of the new civilization born in his native land. On one side of the throne is the infant Hercules strangling the serpents—a reference to the triumph of the young republic over the political tyranny of former times; on the other side, Apollo the sun god rides in his quadriga across the sky—alluding to the bright new light that rises among the constellations. It was a well-thought-out image, embodying noble themes that had frequently been voiced in the halls of Congress or less eloquently in local Fourth of July orations. But the statue got a bewildering and unpleasant reception in America, and the conflict that developed between the artist and the public tells a good deal about the situation of the arts in the United States at that time.

In 1841 the colossal statue was shipped from Leghorn on board the merchant-man *Sea* and was set up in the rotunda of the Capitol in December of that year. While a few people like Edward Everett and Catharine M. Sedgwick had written letters or articles defending the merits of the statue, they could not convince the multitudes of its profound meaning and artistic worth. Greenough's "Washington" became the object of ridicule, and men found it easier to make jokes about it than to try to understand its significance. Soon after its unveiling one newspaper critic declared that it looked more like a Hindu god than anything else; another scornfully referred to it as "Georgy-porgy." Greenough was called to task in parlors, on street corners, and in the Senate chamber for depicting Washington as no ordinary man had ever seen him—bare-chested, risen, as it were, from the dead in his winding sheet, or preparing for his bath. Philip Hone, former mayor of New York, wrote in his diary, in April 1844:

. . . it looks like a great Herculean, warrior-like Venus of the Bath; a grand martial Magog, undressed, with a huge napkin lying across his lap and covering his lower extremities, and he preparing to perform his ablutions is in the act of consigning his sword to the care of the attendant until he shall come out of the bath.

The statue itself was profaned, and S. W. Wallis wrote in 1847 that the last time he had seen it "some irreverent heathen had taken the pains to climb up and insert a large 'plantation' cigar between the lips of the pater patriae." And Wallis came very close to the real problem when he continued: "I could not help thinking, at the time, that if Washington had looked less like the Olympic Jove, and more like himself, not even the vagabond who perpetrated the trick of the cigar would have dared or dreamed of such a desecration." (*Glimpses of Spain: or Notes of an Unfinished Tour in 1847*, New York, 1849, pp. 81–82.)

But though the people of the United States had a deep reverence for Washington the man, the general, the statesman, they could feel neither respect nor affection for this neo-Phidian, Zeus-like, bare-chested, robed and sandaled image of their idol. Greenough attempted to endow Washington with the nobility and virtues of antiquity, but the public could not see through the disguise. Thus, although the classical revival captured the creative genius of some of the artists and intellectuals of the period, it was largely at odds with the tastes of the broad mass of the American people. Greenough lost the battle when he tried to force upon a middle-class public, which had had little experience with classical fine art, a conception that was too foreign to their lives to have any meaning. American virtues in the mid-19th century could not be shrouded in classicism if the mechanics, farmers, merchants, and buckskin-clad frontiersmen were to identify with them.

Eventually the Olympic "Washington" was removed from the rotunda to a site on the Capitol grounds. This was highly inappropriate, for the statue was not meant to stand in the open, and the rain, the snow, and the soot—not to mention the pigeons—soon managed to soil it; and the great man looked extremely cold on bleak winter days. Years later it was moved into a Romanesque hall in the Smithsonian Institution; it presently occupies an unfortunate site in the low-ceiling entrance hall of the Museum of History and Technology.

While Greenough's "Washington" represented the greatest venture—and in its reception, the greatest disappointment—to its creator, it was by no means the end of his career. All the time Greenough was modeling "Washington" in Florence he was also working on portrait busts and other statues. And hardly was the statue of the first President sent off to Carrara when Greenough received another commission from the United States Government. The group "The Rescue" was begun in Florence in 1837 as a counterpart to Luigi Persico's "The Discovery." The latter was erected in 1846 on one side of the great stairs leading up to the Capitol, whereas Greenough's group was not set up as its counterpart on the other side until 1852, the year after his death. The group represented "the conflict between the Anglo-saxon and the aboriginal races," as Tuckerman put it in his *Memorial,* with the main figure being "an American settler . . . in a hunting shirt and cap, rescuing a female and her infant from a savage who has just raised his tomahawk to murder them." A curiously nonchalant dog observes the scene.

"The Rescue" was the major project for Greenough throughout many of the last years of his life. He held high hopes for it, and indeed the figure of the struggling but overpowered Indian is one of the finest 19th-century pieces of American sculpture. Characteristically, the sculptor had written to America requesting some "Indian skulls, dresses and drawstrings" so that his figure would be archaeologically accurate. The weakness of the work as a whole lies in its lack of unity: some of the major elements appear to be afterthoughts. The sculptor left no diagram showing his intended arrangement of the several separate parts, for he planned to be present to supervise their placement. After Greenough's death Clark Mills was put in charge of assembling the group, and there was some feeling that he had not composed the parts properly. At the time of the remodeling of the eastern face of the Capitol in 1959, both Greenough's and Persico's groups were placed in storage.

In addition to "The Rescue," Greenough also began work in 1837 on a life-size figure of Venus, which was completed in marble and in 1841 acquired by the Boston Athenaeum. In the Yale University Art Gallery there is a statue of the angel Abdiel which the sculptor executed in 1838, and the Boston Public Library owns a marble bust of Lucifer (1841) and one of Christ (1845), each with a coiled serpent at the base. During his last years in Florence, Greenough worked on a large oval bas-relief of Castor and Pollux (Fig. 4.4), nude except for helmets, riding spirited horses across the heavens (1847–1851; Museum of Fine Arts, Boston). It recalls the work of Flaxman and comes as close to a true neoclassicism as any of Greenough's efforts. From these several works it is obvious the sculptor maintained an active pace throughout the 1840's.

Toward the end of his life Greenough devoted many hours to writing on aesthetics and the need for the elevation of artistic taste in his homeland. He developed a "form follows function" theory during these years and published a collection of his writings in a little book entitled *The Travels, Observations and Experiences of a Yankee Stonecutter*. Greenough was strongly opposed to academies of art, for he believed they only stifled the creative talent of young artists. He compared the academy to an aristocracy that only sapped its followers for its own strength:

As the [aristocracy] came to regard the mass as a flock to be fed, and defended, and cherished, for the sake of their wool and mutton, so the [academicians] are not slow to make a band of educandi the basis of a hierarchy. . . . The pupils are required to be not only docile but submissive. They are not free.

The great teacher to Greenough was nature, as seen in the following example taken from his "Remarks on American Art":

Leonardo da Vinci coiled a rope in his studio, and drew from it, with the subtlest outline and the most elaborate study of light and shade. "Behold!" said he, "my academy!" He meant to show that the elements of art can be learned without the pompous array of the antique school or the lectures of professors.

Horatio Greenough gave America something it did not have before 1825— a sculptor of international reputation. His work attracted much interest in Italy and in England, and although his public and ideal statues were often criticized here at home, he and several others who soon joined him in his chosen profession made America conscious of sculpture as a fine art for and by Americans, whereas before, it had been the province of foreign artists.

Hiram Powers (1805–1873) was born in a rural area near Woodstock, Vermont, but while he was still a boy his family moved to a location not far from Cincinnati. His father died soon afterward, and young Hiram began working at odd jobs as his contribution to the needs of a sizable family. An aptitude for mechanical things got him a job in the Luman Watson clock and organ factory at seventeen, and it was about this time that he showed an interest in sculpture. The earliest attempt on record was a wax medallion (1823) of Aaron Corwin, but Hiram probably did not think seriously of a career in sculpture then; it was simply a pleasant avocation while he went on making a living as a mechanic. To learn more about the techniques of modeling, however, he turned to Frederick Eckstein, who had settled in Cincinnati in 1823. Eckstein taught him how to model a head in clay and how to take a plaster cast from it. In 1825 Powers is reported to have made a bust of Lafayette, which was probably copied from the Eckstein portrait of the popular old marquis. About 1828 Powers became supervisor of the mechanical section of Dorfeuille's Western Museum, an establishment in Cincinnati that exhibited an assortment of stuffed animals, rock collections, and mechanical devices for a dime. The peregrinating Mrs. Trollope was living in Cincinnati when Dorfeuille bought some battered old wax figures; it was her suggestion that these be animated with clockwork mechanisms, and to Powers went the task of making them ready for display. This involved not only inserting the mechanisms but also repairing the wax figures wherever needed. Frances Trollope suggested they be used in a tableau of Dante's *Inferno*. This was done, but the tableau's eerie realism accompanied by screams and the rattling of chains proved so successful that it had to be closed because too many ladies fainted at the sight. However, Powers' career in sculpture was thus inaugurated.

While continuing to work at the Western Museum Powers began doing portrait busts of friends, with an occasional paid commission. His innate talent had attracted the interest of Nicholas Longworth, whose land transactions and vineyards had made him one of the richest men in the nation. For several years the city's leading citizen encouraged the sculptor in numerous ways, including financial assistance in 1829 for a trip to Italy; this proved both premature and expensive and Powers only got as far as New York City before having to return to

Cincinnati. But the journey allowed the provincial mechanic to see some of the sculpture in the eastern cities.

The University of Miami in Oxford, Ohio, owns a portrait bust by Powers of the first president of the institution, Dr. Robert Hamilton Bishop; modeled around 1830, the bust is the earliest authenticated surviving work by the sculptor. It is a strong portrait in itself, which is all the more remarkable considering the sculptor's lack of formal training and the short time he had been modeling such images. Despite the classical motif of the toga, arranged in a fine series of folds around the shoulders, the likeness relies on a simple and rather plain naturalism; animation is achieved through the tilt of the head and the expressiveness of the eyes and mouth.

Longworth continued to help Powers, and in 1833 he commissioned a portrait of himself. The next year he felt Powers was ready for an artistic environment richer than Cincinnati offered and that the sculptor should go to the eastern cities where portrait commissions were more plentiful. In November 1834 Longworth provided the funds for Powers to move to Washington. But the capital city already had several Italian sculptors of established reputation, and Powers may have been a little apprehensive of such competition. He said he had not expected to find commissions at first, but wished only "to obtain a reputation as an artist."

In Washington, Powers' career got off to a fine start, for in 1835 when Andrew Jackson agreed to sit for his portrait, it was the bust of the leathery old President (Fig. 4.5) that established Powers at once as a sculptor of rare gifts. The bust was modeled in a room in the White House; Jackson gave him an hour on each of three of four days in close succession, and it is a tribute to Powers that he was able to capture so much of the man in a few brief sessions. The result was a tour de force in naturalism and epitomizes Powers' philosophy of portraiture throughout most of his career. That he sought more than just a mirror image of the sitter is evident in a letter to C. E. Lester a few years later: "It is an error to suppose that features are accidental, and nature makes them up haphazard; for the face is the true index of the soul, where everything is written had we the wisdom to read it." Therefore, to miss a single line of the physiognomy was to miss some indicator of character.

Jackson's sixty-eight years, his long battles in the military and political arenas, were permanently engraved on his face. In spite of the toga draped over the chest, Powers' image of Jackson is the antithesis of the classical Greek idealized portrait. The sculptor rendered his realistic likeness with the complete approval of the President, who instructed him "Make me as I am, Mr. Powers, and be true to nature always. . . . I have no desire to look young as long as I feel old."

Jackson was a man of the people. As such he was expressing admiration for the fidelity to physical appearance that a middle-class clientele so often demands in its portraits. But Powers knew that naturalism alone was not enough, and he endowed his portrait of Jackson with a grave heroism and a brooding sagacity.

Moreover, the idea of the individual as an individual—a man free to accomplish what he could by his wits, a man worthy of the adulation and accolade of his peers, a man of common birth who could rise to national prominence—this was one of the cardinal tenets of that era of social, political, and artistic revolution that we call Romanticism. This image of the individual called for a portraiture of naturalism, and it is found in all the busts Powers modeled in Washington from 1835 to 1837.

These qualities are apparent in his portrait of Chief Justice John Marshall (1835), now in the Supreme Court. All the imperfections of nature and the effects of time are there, but so are the artist's vision of the just and resolute character of the man. Powers captured the fiery statesman John C. Calhoun in an image that combines naturalism in his physical likeness with the fierceness and astuteness of the man's personality. This bust—marble copies of which are in the North Carolina Museum of Art and in Calhoun College, Yale University—served as the model for Powers' later statue of Calhoun and was responsible for Calhoun writing to Powers in 1850 that "if I am to go down to posterity, there lives not an artist to whom I would so willingly trust myself as you."

Powers also impressed others as he modeled portrait busts of the leading men in Washington—Daniel Webster, Martin Van Buren, John Quincy Adams, among them. In the spring of 1837 the sculptor traveled to Boston and New York City and made portraits of several of their eminent citizens. In Washington he had attracted the interest of Senator William Preston, who became with his brother a patron of Powers'. The Prestons, together with Nicholas Longworth and possibly John C. Calhoun, offered Powers the necessary financial assistance to go to Italy to study. Before leaving America—forever, as it turned out—Powers made a brief visit to Cincinnati to confer with Longworth. While there he modeled a second likeness of his patron; this was to be put into marble in Italy and the commission would help pay the expenses of the journey. (The bust is now in the Cincinnati Art Museum.)

In the fall of 1837, with his wife and two children (six more were born in Florence), Powers departed for Italy. He shipped separately thirteen plaster casts of busts he had modeled. His future as a sculptor, at least as a portraitist, was much more certain than when he had first arrived in Washington; several of his busts had been paid for in advance—$300 each—and Congress had appropriated $500 for the bust of Marshall, to be paid after it had been put in marble. These were good prices, but the commissions were few in number, and the first years in Italy were to be lean ones for the Powers family.

Hiram Powers had met Horatio Greenough in Boston the preceding year when the latter had returned to America for a brief visit, and in Florence it was Greenough who welcomed the Powers family and did what he could to get them settled. By December of 1837 Powers had found a studio, had gotten his family situated, and was ready to go to work. His first commission came when Professor and Mrs. John Farrar visited his studio; he began modeling the profes-

sor's portrait, which is now owned by Harvard University. In style the Farrar
bust is similar to the ones of Marshall and Jackson; a strong naturalism is dominant. When his plaster busts eventually arrived Powers wanted to put them into
marble right away, but recalled later to H. W. Bellows:

> I found labor cheap enough, but laborers, used to or capable of reproducing my kind
> of modelling, absolutely unattainable. After trying many, I had to go to work and cut
> four of the busts with my own hands, at a ruinous cost of time and money.
>
> ["Seven Sittings with Powers the Sculptor," *Appleton's Journal*, 1869]

The bust of Jackson and probably the one of Marshall were among the four he
carved himself. Eventually, he found an Italian who could execute his designs to
his satisfaction, and years later he employed as many as a dozen such artisans in
his studio.

Greenough continued to assist whenever he could. He commissioned a portrait
of his wife, Louise, and arranged a dinner party one night with busts by Powers
placed prominently about the house. And on April 27, 1838, Horatio wrote his
brother Henry: "Mr. Powers had suffered horribly from the long illness and
death of his eldest-born, but is at work again and cheerful. He is making an admirable bust of me. I like him very much and esteem his talent as highly as
ever." (*Letters*, p. 126) That Powers could produce a portrait of delicate sensitivity as well as of dynamic character and vital naturalism is demonstrated in his
bust of Greenough (Fig. 4.6), which is now in the Museum of Fine Arts, Boston. Powers has caught the perception and bearing of the aristocratic Bostonian.
Urbane, articulate, cultivated, sensitive—all these describe both Greenough and
his bust by Powers. Neither the derisive "bland realism" nor the derogatory
"insipid classicism" applies to this marble form of a human spirit. But a comparison with the busts Powers modeled in America reveals a decided difference, for
in the "Greenough" one finds a Byronic element, where refinement, genius,
comeliness, and the prime of life have been sought and captured. This style is seen
first in busts by Greenough himself, and if one compares Powers' "Greenough"
with Greenough's "Evan Philip Thomas" the origin of the new ingredient in
Powers' work is obvious. This style of the late 1830's and 1840's may be compared to the Romantic portraits by Thomas Sully; the antithesis of classicism,
they are examples of Romantic naturalism rather than Romantic classicism.

But this "Byronic ideal" period passed rather quickly, and Powers turned to a
dry naturalistic style. He is reported to have executed some 150 portrait busts all
told. In time he rose to pre-eminence in this field—from around 1842 to 1855
—eventually commanding $1,000 for a marble bust. The great Thorwaldsen
visited Powers' studio once and remarked that the bust of Daniel Webster was
the finest example of its type then being done. As early as 1839 the celebrated
Bartolini had "pronounced him the greatest portrait sculptor living," according
to Greenough, who was in full agreement.

For a sculptor of Powers' generation the real test and demonstration of the man's creativity and inventiveness was the "ideal" piece—sometimes a life-size marble figure, sometimes a bust—expressing a noble sentiment or an idea from history or philosophy, from literature or religion or mythology. Powers was eager to prove himself, but through the early 1840's he had not the money to put a life-size figure into marble. However, in between doing money-earning portrait busts he began to work on ideal busts.

About 1840 Powers modeled his first such bust—"Ginevra," a young woman with her hair pulled back in a classical style, knotted, and falling along her neck. Just above the hairline she wears a simple tiara, and her shoulders, upper arms, and fully-shaped breasts are draped in a cloth with sculpturesque folds. In profile, the head is a combination of the classical type and 19th century naturalism. Although the profile suggests a classical model, the woman remains flesh and blood instead of an abstraction.

The sculptor sent one of the first marble versions to the man who more than anyone else had made it possible for him to be in Italy; this bust of "Ginevra," now in the Cincinnati Art Museum, bears the inscription: "Dedicated by the author to his friend and patron N. Longworth, Esq. Hiram Powers, Sculp." There is another marble bust of Ginevra in the Corcoran Gallery in Washington, and over the years Powers had copies put into marble as they were ordered. One of the most popular of his ideal busts was his "Persephone," or "Proserpine," first produced about 1845. William Cullen Bryant saw seven marble replicas of "Proserpine" when he visited Powers' studio in Florence, and it has been estimated that more than four dozen such replicas were sold at $400 apiece.

When the "Greek Slave" became so very popular, there was a demand for busts of it, and the earliest of these dates from 1845–50. Powers' ideal piece "Psyche," was done about 1849. "Psyche," like "Proserpine," has no drapery, and the shoulders and breasts are exposed. It, too, is a combination of a classical ideal and the 19th-century Italian girl who posed for it. Another ideal bust, "Diana," was created about 1852.

The earliest of the two Eves by Powers—his first attempt at the full-length, life-size figure—was begun in 1838. Aside from a few anatomy lessons, his study of the human figure had been severely limited. He relied heavily on a cast of "Venus de' Medici" in his ideal statues of nude female figures, though in Italy models could be hired for two or three dollars a day. In January 1841 he wrote to Henry Lea that the clay model of "Eve Tempted" was almost finished and that the feet "are placed in similar position to those of the Venus de Medici's." He said that to put it into marble would require another year and a half, and he would then sell it for $5,000. But it was to be a long time before his "Eve" was perfected, and even longer before she was put into marble. In the letter to Henry Lea (now in the Cincinnati Art Museum) Powers wrote that there were "two other subjects yet to be modeled—one of a Greek Slave, and the other of a fisherboy." And about 1841 Powers did model "The Fisherboy" (Virginia Museum of Fine Arts; Fig. 4.9)—a boy holding a shell up to his ear while his right hand is placed on a fishnet thrown over a tiller.

This was the second completely nude male figure to be modeled by an American, Crawford's "Orpheus" preceding it by a couple of years. It is significant that Powers did not create an Endymion or a Ganymede from Greek mythology but chose instead a contemporary subject. The sculptor commented that it was difficult to devise a subject where the male of his own times could be represented in the nude, but that he believed sculptors should take their themes from contemporary sources and their own religion, rather than "illustrate, for the thousandth time, the incongruous absurdities and inconsistencies of idolatrous times." "The Fisherboy" was done from a living model, not from an ancient statue, and the result is truly an image of the 19th century. This is most evident in the quality of the softness of the flesh, an achievement of skill at which Powers excelled. Moreover, the proportions are not those of ancient classical art; the difference is especially noticeable in the right wrist and in the legs. There is a certain classical grace to the stance that brings to mind the "Doryphorus" by Polykleitos or Praxiteles' "Hermes." But the resemblance fades when these are actually compared. What Powers has borrowed from the ancients is a classical reserve and detachment about the boy's face, but this is a classical principle rather than a specific classical form. "The Fisherboy" is not a neoclassical figure, nor did the artist or anyone else of his generation think of it as such; to them it was a contemporary genre subject, and they took a great deal of pride in its originality.

In October 1842 Hiram Powers began work on the statue that was to establish him, according to his contemporaries, as the greatest American sculptor of the mid-19th century and rank him among the most gifted artists of all time. This was the famous "Greek Slave"—the first of his ideal statues to be put into marble (Fig. 4.10). A block of marble large enough for a life-size statue was quite an expense in itself—besides the wages of the workmen who spent long months on the carving. The usual practice was to have the statue cast in plaster where it would remain until a patron ordered a marble copy. Only then was it put into marble.

The "Venus de' Medici" influenced Powers as he was modeling the "Greek Slave:" the position of legs, the lilting curve of the torso axis, the turning of the head to present a profile. And, of course, the head is strongly Greek: the classical coiffure, the almost flush bridge of the nose, the deep-set eyes, the full chin—details that Powers frequently used in ideal heads. But the torso and limbs are 19th-century naturalism. The result is a curious blend of the seemingly incompatible styles of naturalism and classicism, but then the 19th century is known for its willingness to combine styles never before united.

Hiram Powers thought that all great ideal sculptures should have a moral as their *raison d'être*. In 1841, the heroic struggle of the Greek people to free themselves from their tyrannical masters, the Turks, some ten years earlier was still very much alive in the memories of the sculptor and his contemporaries. On January 17, 1841, Powers described the story behind his "Slave" in a letter to Henry Lea; but the clearest statement of his intention was the one he wrote to accompany the statue on its tour of the United States:

The Slave has been taken from one of the Greek Islands by the Turks, in the time of the Greek Revolution, the history of which is familiar to all. Her father and mother, and perhaps all her kindred, have been destroyed by her foes, and she alone preserved as a treasure too valuable to be thrown away. She is now among barbarian strangers, under the pressure of a full recollection of the calamitous events which have brought her to her present state; and she stands exposed to the people she abhors, and waits her fate with intense anxiety, tempered indeed by the support of her reliance upon the goodness of God. Gather all the afflictions together and add to them the fortitude and resignation of a Christian, and no room will be left for shame. Such are the circumstances under which the "Greek Slave" is supposed to stand.

In good 19th-century fashion, Powers and other American sculptors truly believed they were in a position to improve upon the art of the ancient Greeks because their contemporary art was not an art of heathen idolatry but one imbued with Christian virtues and morality. The "Greek Slave" was to them a greater work of art then the "Venus de' Medici" for that very reason; it possessed Christian "fortitude and resignation" and faith in the "goodness of God," in spite of the horrible circumstances in which the young girl found herself. It was perhaps due as much to the literary and philosophical content as to the artistic merits of the statue that it owed its brilliant success.

The initial success occurred in London, and an Englishman bought the original marble statue for $4,000. Not until 1847 did the famous statue reach America, where it was to be shown in city after city. But before the "Greek Slave" could repeat in America its London triumphs, it had to pass a purity test, and priggish America had to convince itself that it could look upon the nude female form without shame or embarrassment. For Americans, still guilt-ridden in matters of the flesh as a result of their Puritan heritage, this was not easy. Although cloistered at first, and bred in New England, Puritanism did much to establish the intellectual and moral climate of the entire country. And any art that dealt with the beauty of the flesh had to find a way to coexist with the religion and strict moral code of the New England divines of old. Previous incursions of the nude into the art of America had drawn many hostile responses. Wertmüller's "Danaë" and Vanderlyn's "Ariadne" had been early attempts to introduce paintings of the nude to the viewing public. In sculpture, there were the casts of ancient statues (complete with fig leaves), and Rembrandt Peale had a flesh-tinted wax female nude in the back room of his museum in Baltimore that could be seen for twenty-five cents; as was the custom, only gentlemen could visit the gallery on certain days, only ladies on other specified days. To be sure, America was not the only Protestant country where such a situation existed; for example, in Mannheim, Germany, in 1853, the "Venus de Milo" was tried in a court of law for her nudity, and was convicted and condemned. In this atmosphere, the "Greek Slave" made her American debut.

By what means and what rationalization were Americans, especially the clergymen who were often the spokesmen for their flocks, able to convince themselves that it was not improper to look upon the nude figure of the "Greek Slave"? First of all there was an aping acceptance of almost anything that had been approved in London; more important, Americans were subjected to a clever "brainwashing" by Minor K. Kellogg, Powers' manager, who escorted the "Slave" from city to city. Still, there was opposition to its exhibition in some communities. The statue was shipped out of Zanesville, Ohio, without having been uncrated because of the high license fee the city authorities wanted to charge before it could be shown. And it is reported that the train that carried the "Slave" had to stop outside the limits of one city while a delegation of clergymen inspected the statue; it was approved, brought into town, and exhibited. Prior to the arrival of the statue in a given area, Minor Kellogg circulated pamphlets containing the favorable critiques from London newspapers, as well as Powers' own woeful tale about the subject's pitiful circumstances. There were also proclamations from ministers, such as that by the Reverend Orville Dewey, a Unitarian, who defended the nudity of the statue with the following words:

The chasteness in this statue is strongly contrasted with the usual voluptuousness of the antique. . . . There ought to be some reason for the exposure *besides* beauty, like fidelity to history, as in the Greek girl. . . . It was clothed all over with sentiment, sheltered, protected by it, from every profane eye. Brocade, cloth of gold, could not be a more complete protection than the vesture of holiness in which she stands.

The point being made was that this was not nudity for the sake of sensuality, or even nudity for the sake of beauty, as in antique statues. So convinced were people like the Reverend Dewey that they saw chastity, piety, and holiness triumphant here, that they could allow themselves to look upon the nude marble figure without fear of entertaining prurient thoughts. The reverential and awesome mood of a viewing of the "Greek Slave" is seen in a report published in the *Union Magazine* in October 1847:

It is almost curious to observe the effect produced upon visitors. They enter gaily or with an air of curiosity; they look at the beauteous figure and the whole manner undergoes a change. Men take off their hats; ladies seat themselves silently, and almost unconsciously; and usually it is minutes before a word is uttered. All conversation is in a hushed tone, and everybody looks serious on departing.

The "Greek Slave" is not as closely linked with the classical revival as Horatio Greenough's Olympian "Washington," yet in certain respects it was related to that phenomenon. But the two statues, which arrived in America within five years of each other, could not have experienced more different receptions. The secret of the success of Hiram Powers' figure lay in creating the proper frame of mind in the crowds of people who came to see it. The sculptor and his agent spun a protective web of chastity and virtue around the lady that warded off all profane and vulgar glances. She was, after all, the innocent victim of those terrible Turks; and she was, after all, fettered by the chains at her wrists and help-less to improve her pitiful state. That her nudity was also beyond her control seemed to satisfy the throng. The "Slave" may have contained a touch of classi-cism, but more important was the host of Christian virtues it possessed. Any classical sensuousness was subdued by the personification of Christian moral righteousness, creating a kind of Neoplatonic situation where the condition and appearance of the body reflects the beauty of the soul. All of this was fraught with a Romantic sentimentality that was utterly unknown to the ancient sculp-tors, but it was the only form of the nude in art acceptable to America in the 1840's. And by being accepted, it opened the door through which other nude statues might pass.

The American tour of the "Greek Slave" was also financially successful, gross-ing the astonishing sum of $23,000. Altogether Powers sold six marble copies of the "Greek Slave" for about $4,000 apiece, and countless small replicas were profitably produced. Today, the statue may be seen in four public collections in America: the Corcoran Gallery, the Brooklyn Art Museum, the Newark Mu-seum, and the Yale University Art Gallery. The "Slave" established the fame of Hiram Powers at home and abroad, its popularity placing him in demand for both portraits and ideal works.

In the late 1840's Powers was working on a portrait statue commissioned by Mr. Wharton Green of Charleston, South Carolina—the ill-fated statue of John C. Calhoun (Fig. 4.7). Powers shipped it to America in 1850 on board the *Eliza-beth*. The ship was wrecked off Fire Island, and among those lost were Margaret Fuller Ossoli, her husband, and their baby. The marble statue was recovered, however, except for its left arm, which held a scroll inscribed "Truth/Justice/ and the/Constitution." Powers' "Calhoun" was taken to Charleston, then re-moved to Columbia during the Civil War, where it was destroyed by fire.

The marble figure was larger than life and Powers used the portrait he had made a decade earlier as the model for the head. Beside the figure was the trunk of a palmetto, the state tree of South Carolina. In this, his first full-length por-trait, Powers dressed his subject in the ankle-length robe of a Roman senator. He had a strong dislike for the contemporary dress of Americans, and avoided it in his sculpture whenever possible. The problem became quite apparent in his second portrait statue, the bronze "Daniel Webster" (Fig. 4.8), which now stands on the State House lawn in Boston. It was commissioned by a group of citizens who wished to commemorate Webster's brilliant career in public service. After it ar-rived in late 1858, there was considerable criticism of it on several points, but particularly on the bagginess of the clothing. Powers' reply to his agent, Edward Everett, was that he could not be held responsible for the inadequacies of Mr. Webster's tailor, and referred his critics to the daguerreotype of the man by Mr. Page. In a letter to Everett, dated March 2, 1859, he wrote:

Now on coats, breeches, buttons and boots no sculptor can ever expect to do a high work of Art. All he can expect is credit for fidelity to the likeness—or as much ex-pression as the human form may give, hampered up in the crude coverings of a Tailor's genius. You say that one of the criticisms of my statute of Mr. Webster is the baggy pantaloons! I copied them from his own placed upon a figure, life size of Mr. Webster, which I had prepared to dress up in his own suit which you sent out to me.

[Massachusetts Historical Society]

The Webster statue was also criticized for what was claimed to be poor workmanship in its casting. In an earlier letter to Everett, dated September 18, 1858, Powers mentioned that he had gone to Professor Papi's foundry the day the statue was cast and again after it was out of the mold, and reported that it "appeared quite perfect, even down to the nails on the fingers." Powers himself was a perfectionist when it came to the surface and the "finish" of his works. He devised tools that gave his marble figures the appearance of porous flesh, and he frequently pointed out that this was time-consuming and required special skill —and therefore cost money. But it was a point of artistic integrity with Powers, and people would just have to pay the extra price if they wanted one of his pieces.

Powers worked on several ideal figures in the late 1850's. About 1856 he produced a "Penserosa" for Mr. James Lenox of New York City, and to Edward Everett he wrote on June 22, 1859: "I am glad that you like 'La Penserosa.' You have made a just discrimination between it and the California which is 'a lower nature' although equal to the other as to form and execution; one is civilized, the other savage." (Massachusetts Historical Society)

In "Eve Disconsolate" and the "California" of these years the sculptor returned to the nude figure. Taft refers to this later "Eve" as "one of the weakest products of the time," and it certainly does lack the charm of the "Greek Slave" and the strength of the "California." Now in the Cincinnati Art Museum, it is inscribed, "H. Powers, Sculp., N.P.–N.L.," indicating it had been sent to the artist's early patron, Nicholas Longworth. The "Eve Disconsolate" glances heavenward as she places her left hand over her right breast and with her right hand points to the serpent from the tree trunk at the side.

By June of 1858 Powers' "California" was finished in marble and "detained [at Leghorn] for want of a good ship." It had been purchased by William B. Astor for $7,500 and eventually stood in his mansion in New York City; it is now in the Metropolitan Museum of Art. The statue was inspired by the gold rush of 1849, and in 1850 Powers had written to his brother that he was working on "a statue of 'La Dorado' or California." Hawthorne reported that the divining rod in her left hand was explained thus by Powers: "She says to the emigrants . . . . Here is the gold if you wish to take it." The author then remarked in his journal: "But in her face and in her eyes . . . there is a look of latent mischief, rather grave than playful, yet somewhat impish or spirit-like." Her right hand, concealed behind her back, holds a cluster of thorns, which refers to the "deceitfulness of riches." At the right side are some quartzlike formations, suggesting the precious mineral that had lured so many to California. There is something disquieting, even sinister, about the "California." Powers had hoped the city of San Francisco might buy the piece and have it put into bronze or marble in colossal scale to stand at a prominent point in the harbor. But as nothing came of this, it was later sold to Astor with the promise that no copies would be made.

Sometime in 1855 Powers modeled a figure of "America" that was put into marble about 1858. The statue itself was destroyed in a warehouse fire in Brooklyn, but several examples of the bust still survive—in the Corcoran Gallery; in the Virginia Museum of Fine Arts, Richmond; and in the Fogg Art Museum at Harvard. Despite Powers' fame and stature as a sculptor, the federal government had not given him a single commission, and Powers was naturally hurt at being ignored. Especially peeved because Thomas Crawford had been asked to execute a statue of America or the Republic to crown the great new dome of the Capitol, Powers complained to Edward Everett in October 1858 that the time was when Mr. Buchanan (President Buchanan, when the sculptor was writing) spoke out on a sculptor's behalf on the floor of the Senate: "This was all done for a foreign artist, Luigi Persico, and the result is the work called 'The Discovery of America' which now disgraces one of the blockings of the eastern stair case of the Capitol." (Massachusetts Historical Society)

In another letter to Everett that same month he revealed an unpleasant trait that is not unknown among men of the same profession—that of degrading one's fellow artist and his work. Although Powers could charm such people as Nathaniel Hawthorne and Horatio Greenough, he had his differences with Thomas Ball (who also had his studio in Florence) and especially with Thomas Crawford. Much of his animosity toward Crawford probably stemmed from the success Crawford was having in acquiring commissions from Washington, and Powers accused his colleague of turning his designs—after they had been approved—over to inferior workmen for the sake of monetary gain.

Upon the recommendation of Edward Everett in 1853, both Thomas Crawford and Hiram Powers had been invited by Captain Montgomery Meigs, chief engineer of the Capitol, to submit designs for the sculptured pediment of the extension of the Capitol. Crawford did, of course, but Powers was then at the height of his fame and evidently believed he should neither be asked to submit his designs for approval nor be expected to compete with another artist for the commission. His reply to Meigs was curt: ". . . I have not the time to prepare designs for the decoration of our Capitol Buildings even if it were a desirable object for me *to propose* for a commission from the government of my country." But by 1859 Powers was extremely pleased to receive at last a major commission from the government—to execute statues of Franklin and Jefferson for the Senate and House wings of the Capitol, for which he was to receive $10,000 a piece. These are larger than life in marble, and the two men are represented in contemporary dress. In these statues Powers succeeded more than most men of his day in regard to the representation of clothing. Though there may be nothing heroic about the attire of Franklin and Jefferson, there is nothing distracting about it either—and this, in comparison with his bronze "Webster" and with greater failures by other sculptors, was something of an achievement. For the likeness of

Franklin, Powers followed the bust by Houdon; in fact, he himself made a copy of Houdon's "Franklin," which is now preserved at Yale. Powers' "Franklin," the first to be finished, was set up in the Senate wing in 1863; "Jefferson" was installed later that year. Toward the end of his life another commission for the Franklin statue arrived from New Orleans; it was completed the year after Powers' death.

Among the finest portrait busts from Powers' last years are "James Gilmore" (1865), in the Cincinnati Art Museum; "Henry Wadsworth Longfellow" (1865) and "Robert Charles Winthrop" (1868), both at Harvard; and "George Peabody" (1868), in the Massachusetts Historical Society. All possess that spark of life and strength of character that Powers so ably infused into an accurate likeness. The "ideal" busts from the last decade of Powers' life are a second version of "Ginevra" (1865) and "Clytie" (1868). The sculptor also produced busts of the three virtues—"Faith" (1867), "Hope" (1869), and "Charity" (1871).

His last portrait statue was that of his agent and long-time friend, Edward Everett, for whom he had a genuine affection. From the 1840's, Everett had promoted Powers as America's finest sculptor, and for years he served as Powers' agent in America, often acting as a bulwark against some of the barbed harangues leveled at Powers and his work. In 1845 the sculptor had modeled the portrait bust of Everett that he used in the portrait statue. Soon after Everett's death in 1865 a committee was formed to raise funds for a monument to the statesman and educator. W. W. Story eventually received the commission, possibly because there had been so much criticism of the "Webster" Powers had done earlier. A few years later he modeled an image of Everett for Mount Vernon, to stand opposite a statue of Washington, because Everett had helped the "Ladies Mount Vernon Society" raise the money to preserve the home of the first President as a national shrine. The statue was finished in 1870, but it did not go to Mount Vernon, as was originally intended. Instead, for some reason Powers presented the statue as a gift to Everett's son William.

The last large ideal piece modeled by Powers was "The Last of the Tribe," done in 1872, the year before the sculptor's death. The statue is of an Indian girl running, looking over her right shoulder. Nude to the waist, she wears only a knee-length skirt with an Indian design worked into it. This statue brought to a close the career of one of the most famous American sculptors of all time. He had succeeded in introducing the nude figure into American sculpture, and what's more, in having it accepted—a feat without parallel in those days. After the "Greek Slave" had made her tour in the late 1840's a great flood of marble nude females all but inundated the exhibition scene, until Nathaniel Hawthorne was moved to have Miriam say in *The Marble Faun:*

Every young sculptor seems to think that he must give the world some specimen of indecorous woman-hood, and call it Eve, Venus, a Nymph or any other name that may apologize for the lack of decent clothing. I am weary, even more ashamed, of seeing such things.

Powers did a great deal to establish the ideal, or literary, work as a part of his country's sculptural art, and to carry American sculpture beyond the narrow confines of the portrait bust. Moreover, he, along with Greenough and Crawford, established sculpture as a respected profession—one that required a mixture of creative intelligence, sensitivity and great skill.

Thomas Crawford (1813?–1857), like so many American 19th-century sculptors, came to sculpture through the trades. His parents had emigrated from Ireland, and he was born in either 1811 or 1813, probably in New York City. The Crawford family harbored an atmosphere of affection for young Thomas, and his parents and older sister, Jenny, encouraged his talent for drawing and for molding designs with his fingers. He took lessons at a small drawing school in New York while in his early teens, and, quite significant for his later work, he was drawn to a study of classical literature. All the while in his room he continued to model little clay figures and study engravings, and he is reported to have had a small collection of plaster casts of his own.

About 1827 Thomas Crawford went to work as an apprentice in the shop of a wood carver in New York City. By this time the insurrection movement among artists in the city had coalesced into the National Academy of Design, and the bell commenced tolling for Colonel Trumbull's American Academy, which had refused to befriend the artistic talent of the area. As Crawford began to sketch the casts in the National Academy and express his interest in the plastic arts, he may have come to the attention of John Frazee, the sole sculptor among the thirty founding members of that institution. In any event Crawford was employed by the prominent stonecutting firm of Frazee and Launitz about 1832.

In his new position he turned from wood carving to stonecutting, working on gravestones and ornamental pieces for architecture. Both Frazee and Launitz seem to have given him instruction, but Crawford was apparently closer to Launitz. It was Launitz who persuaded the ambitious young man to come back to work for the firm after Crawford had quit because he felt he wasn't being paid enough. And it was Launitz who talked to him of Rome and the great Thorwaldsen with whom he had studied, and of Canova and the sculpture galleries of the Vatican, and of the statues everywhere in the streets, piazzas, and fountains. Conversely we can only quote Frazee's opinion from his autobiography, regarding the essentials of becoming a sculptor: "Some say it cannot be done without a visit first to Europe, to Rome and her Vatican. . . . For myself I believe not a word of this." Thomas Hicks in his *Eulogy of Thomas Crawford* (New York, 1865) said that Crawford worked on some of the busts that Frazee was doing at that period, such as "Thomas H. Perkins" and "John Marshall." Frazee undoubtedly gave the precocious aspirant many pointers in the modeling of the portrait bust and helped to instill in him the importance of naturalism in portrait modeling, but he could not have fired Crawford's imagination the way Launitz did.

Late in May 1835 Thomas Crawford began a seasick voyage to Europe, eventually arriving in Rome in September, the first American sculptor to settle there for the purpose of study and work. Launitz had given him a letter to Bertel Thorwaldsen, who greeted the American warmly and offered him space in one of his three studios. Crawford wrote his sister, Jenny, that the studios

. . . are filled with casts from his own works and from the best antiques. Clay and everything for modelling is brought to my hand, and with such opportunities before me, I was not backward in commencing. There is but one young man beside myself in the studio. He is a native of Rome. Thorwaldsen visits us once a day, corrects what he sees wrong in our work, and after some words of encouragement leaves us.

[C. E. Lester, *Artists of America*, p. 240]

Crawford continued under Thorwaldsen's tutelage for about a year. In time some began to speak of the mantle of neoclassicism, which Thorwaldsen had inherited from Canova, being passed to Crawford. In a few years the celebrated Danish sculptor would leave Rome just as the young American sculptor was beginning to attract attention there. Crawford's reception, his work with Thorwaldsen, and his decision to establish himself in this foremost center of neoclassicism had a profound impact on his subsequent development. Had he moved on to Florence his art probably would have reflected different influences. For of the three—Greenough, Powers, and Crawford—the last was by far the most thoroughly indoctrinated in the principles of neoclassicism.

Of course, Rome itself, as the greatest repository of antique statuary, also encouraged his neoclassical approach to art. In the galleries of the Vatican, Crawford studied the statues of Venus, of Apollo, of Hermes, of fauns and nymphs and the whole of Jupiter's ancient realm. Unlike Hiram Powers, who criticized the "Venus de' Medici" and found his two brief trips to Rome bewildering, Crawford was intoxicated by the cool and noble beauty of Graeco-Roman classicism, and his ideal works of these early years clearly reflect this. When not studying the statues, Crawford was apt to be at the French Academy, drawing from the nude model. And of an evening, like Horatio Greenough a decade earlier, he found a warm fellowship at the Caffè Greco. Crawford was then the lone American sculptor there, and it was not until the 1850's that there was a sizable colony of his countrymen in residence.

Commissions for marble likenesses were not often given to an unknown and largely untried sculptor, but a few came in during 1836, such as those from Commodore Hull and Mr. Ohmstead, and those of Mr. and Mrs. John David Wolfe. Crawford's appetite for study and work was apparently insatiable, and it is reported that during a ten-week period in 1837 he modeled no less than seventeen portrait busts. However, these did not bring high prices. The New-York Historical Society has his bust of Mrs. John J. Schermerhorn (Mary Hone, daughter of Mayor Philip Hone), dated 1837, and one of Judge Edmund Pendleton, which is inscribed on the back, "T. C. fect. Romae. 1839."

In the spring of 1839 Crawford met Charles Sumner, who was to be his lifelong friend and entrepreneur. That summer he modeled Sumner's portrait (Fig. 4.11). Though he leaned toward classicism in his ideal works, Crawford's portraits had a strong naturalism tempered by a Romantic sensitivity—the Byronic element already seen in the portraiture of Greenough and Powers. Charles Sumner was young and handsome, a sensitive man of rare gifts, pensive, born to greatness, and all this was captured in his bust, without resorting to the neoclassical style. The bust was not put into marble until 1842, but the plaster cast stood in the home of the American consul in Rome, George Washington Greene. It soon attracted other commissions for its creator: Sir Charles Vaughan and John Kenyon saw the bust of Sumner there and immediately ordered their own portraits. Of Crawford's portraits, Sumner himself wrote:

They are remarkable for the fidelity with which they portray the countenance, and for the classic elegance and simplicity of their composition. The bust of the late gallant Commodore Hull, made in Rome while he was in command of our Mediterranean squadron, is a beautiful production. We have also seen the bust of Mr. Kenyon, the English poet, which has great merit. That of Sir Charles Vaughan . . . we have not seen, but we have heard it mentioned in terms of high praise.
[Quoted from C. E. Lester, *Artists of America*, p. 241]

Kenyon, lamenting that Crawford was not an Englishman, compared him to Phidias, and scolded Americans for not patronizing their gifted countryman beyond a meager subsistence.

But portraiture was only the bread-winner as far as Crawford was concerned, and during the late 1830's countless ideas raced through his head about subjects for ideal works. Many of these he would sketch in a drawing pad or model in clay. The one that fascinated him more than any other was a scene of his own invention from the Orpheus myth, and that an American could conceptualize an event from an ancient legend that none of the ancients had ever represented in their art seemed amazing to his contemporaries. This in itself, aside from whatever artistic merit the statue might have, did much to establish the reputation of the sculptor. George S. Hillard, in his "Thomas Crawford: A Eulogy" (*Atlantic Monthly*, July 1869) published a letter that Crawford wrote to his sister, Jenny, in May 1839:

I have commenced modelling a statue large as life, the attitude of which throws at once in my way all the difficulties attending the representation of the human figure. When this is finished as I hope to do it, it will show that I am ambitious enough to strive with those who are moving in the highest range of sculpture. . . . You will find [the subject] in the tenth book of Ovid's Metamorphosis, where Orpheus is described as leaving the realms of light and upper air to seek his lost Eurydice in the infernal regions. . . . I have selected the moment when Orpheus, having tamed the dog Cerberus, ceases playing upon the lyre and rushes triumphantly through the gate of hell. The subject is readily adapted to the display of every manly beauty; into the face I shall endeavor to throw an expression of intense anxiety softened by the awe which would naturally be caused by such a sight as we may suppose the realms of Pluto to represent. . . . With one hand he shades his eyes . . . with the other he holds the lyre which is to charm Pluto and the Furies. At his feet is the three-headed dog Cerberus; this is important, for the attributes of lyre and wreath also belong to Apollo; but with Cerberus, anyone having the slightest knowledge of mythology must know that the figure is Orpheus in search of Eurydice.

Especially interesting is his closing statement, which demonstrates his penchant for neoclassicism.

I am trying . . . to give an antique beauty to the whole composition by keeping clear of all extravagance in the movement, and working as nearly as possible in the spirit of the ancient Greek masters.

Neither the excesses of Hellenistic works like the Laocoön nor the bombastic giants by Bernini, which abounded in Rome, could lure Crawford away from the pure classicism found in the Apollo Belvedere. From the proportions of his "Orpheus" (Fig. 4.12) he had obviously studied well the "immortal beauty" of the "divine Apollo," which was preserved in a cabinet in the Vatican. Ever since Benjamin West had seen the celebrated statue in 1759 American artists had been moved by its classic elegance, which Crawford attempted to emulate in his own first ideal work of any magnitude. This was to be the piece that would establish a place for him at the fore of a small but rising group of American sculptors, and it had to be a superlative effort.

Crawford worked on the "Orpheus" the summer and fall of 1839. And as he modeled Charles Sumner's portrait that summer, and Sumner observed the progress on the "Orpheus," the two men became good friends. The statue was cast in plaster when it was finished, but it could be carried no further because of the tremendous cost of putting a work of that size into marble. In early winter Charles Sumner left Italy; Crawford fell ill with Roman brain fever. His friend George Washington Greene answered his call for help and took him to his villa in Albano for a long period of convalescence. By spring his health was restored, but though he desperately needed money, he was slow in getting back to work. With a sense of deep gratitude Crawford repaid his benefactor as best he could—by modeling a bust of him (now in Longfellow House, Cambridge, Massachusetts).

The plaster "Orpheus" stood pale and specterlike in Crawford's studio in Rome throughout the long winter of 1840–41, haunting him like a recurring dream that has no ending. He had very few commissions, but his mind was full of ideas for sculptural projects, most of which were never carried further than the clay models. In the meantime, Charles Sumner in Boston had been promoting the purchase, through subscription, of the "Orpheus," and late that winter this was acted upon. Crawford was finally to have the funds necessary to put his "Orpheus" into marble; he signed the contract in March of 1841, to deliver the statue within twenty months for a stipend of $2,000. The marble block arrived from Carrara in October and cost $700, plus $300 for blocking it out; and in the course of 1842 the Italian stonecarvers hewed the Orphean image out of the glistening marble. It was shipped in a specially designed crate, but when it was unpacked in Boston in the early summer of 1843 it was found to be broken in several places.

The portrait sculptor Henry Dexter was employed to restore it, which he did, apparently to everyone's satisfaction. Meanwhile a separate building was constructed near the Boston Athenaeum (which had contributed $500 toward the purchase of "Orpheus") for a special exhibition, in spring 1844, of the statue and other works by Crawford. The sculptor had himself suggested the display of his work to Sumner some time earlier, pointing out that it would be the first sizable exhibition of sculpture by an American. His interest in establishing himself in his field in the eyes of his countrymen is understandable. Greenough was generally known only by his "Chanting Cherubs" and his Jovian "Washington" (both of which, for different reasons, had drawn criticism), and Powers was largely unknown to the American public, as his "Greek Slave" had not yet crossed the Atlantic. The exhibition of "Orpheus," then, was to herald a new sculptor of great talent in whom America could take pride; and the statue did establish Crawford's name, just as he had hoped.

The acclamation that greeted the "Orpheus" can best be understood when seen through contemporary eyes by way of contemporary criticism. It then becomes clear that the statue incorporated all the emotions and attitudes so popular in the 19th century—a reverence for the ancient world, a sentimentality woven about two ill-fated lovers, the hero's inconsolable grief over the loss of his beloved, and a tense adventure into a mysterious and unknown realm. It was largely because the "Orpheus" touched such sensitive romantic emotions that it was so highly regarded. Charles Sumner explained it at length:

Of all the stories of antiquity, not one is more beautiful or touching than that of Orpheus. . . . The tale is simple, and in the memory of all. Young men and maidens for ages have listened to it, and old men in the chimney corner have mused over it. To Orpheus Apollo gave a lyre. Such a gift from such a god was not in vain; and the youth charmed by his music as music never charmed before. The rapid rivers ceased to flow, the mountains moved, and the rage of the tigers was restrained, to listen to his songs. The fairest of nymphs were his companions, but he heeded only Eurydice. To her he was united in marriage. But the faithless Aristaeus saw her and loved her. She fled from his approaches, and as she pressed the grass, in her rapid flight, a serpent stung her foot, and she died. The nymphs of the woods awakened the echoes of the mountains with their sorrows; and the rocks of Rhodope, the lofty Pangaeus, the Hebrus, and the sternest parts of Thrace wept. The lover was desolate.

He resolved to regain his lost bride. With his lyre in his hand, he enters the inexorable gates of the regions below. The guardian dog Cerberus is lulled asleep by the unaccustomed strains:
"_____ tenuitque inhians tria Cerberus ora."
The gentle shades of the dead, wives and husbands, magnanimous heroes, boys and unmarried girls, came forward and wept. The grim ruler was startled. The rock of Sisphas stood still; the wheel of Ixion ceased its eternal motion; the refreshing water once again bathed the lips of Tantalus: the daughters of Danaus suspended their never-ending task; the Furies, with their necks clothed with snakes, ceased to rage. All listened rapt to the music, and forgot their pains in sympathy with the bereaved charmer. And now success has crowned his efforts. The woman's heart of Proserpine is touched, and Pluto yields to her intercession. Eurydice is restored, but with one condition. The lover shall not turn to look upon her face until they are both again

in the upper air. Joyful he leaves behind the abode of Death, and Eurydice follows unseen by him—yet still she follows. But who shall impose restraints upon the longings of love? Forgetful of the stern condition, thinking only of her, he casts one look behind. He saw his Eurydice; but with that vision she disappeared for ever, as a wreath of smoke fades into the air. He stretched forth his arms to embrace her, but she heard him not. He endeavored to retrace his steps, but the gates of Acheron closed harshly against him. What shall he do? With what words shall he seek to bend the will of the Gods? How shall he assuage his own grief? All in vain; and soon he meets with a violent death, at the hands of the Thracian women, enraged at his continued fidelity to the memory of his lost wife, and indifference to their living charms.

[Quoted from C. E. Lester, *Artists of America*, pp. 242–44]

Just as Hiram Powers was to do a few years later, Crawford even included certain Christian virtues, such as chastity and fidelity, in an otherwise pagan subject. The figure was nude except for the fig leaf, which was Crawford's own wise addition, but nevertheless the closest thing to a male nude in sculpture that America had yet seen. Crawford, in his debut, was anxious not to offend delicate sensitivities, and between the fig leaf and the description given by Sumner, there was little possibility of the statue arousing rude and improper thoughts. Thus was Boston introduced to the chastity of the white marble nude.

While the "Orpheus" was being carved in stone Crawford was also engaged on other projects. On March 22, 1842, Thorwaldsen visited Crawford's studio and saw the following works in clay or plaster: "Hebe and Ganymede," "The Bride of Abydos" (ideal bust), "Christ Blessing Little Children," "Cupid in Contemplation," "Anacreon," and several portrait busts. "Hebe and Ganymede," now in the Museum of Fine Arts, Boston, was put into marble in 1844 at the commission of Charles C. Perkins. It is probably the most purely classical of all Crawford's statues, and one is reminded of the prophecy that he was the heir to Thorwaldsen's neoclassicism. Reminiscent of Gibson and even of Flaxman, both figures are exceedingly Grecian, especially the profiles. Ganymede, the youthful messenger of Jupiter, wears only a Phrygian cap, a stole, and a fig leaf; Hebe, the cup bearer to the gods, has a drape that rests low on one hip and flows to the floor, covering her legs. The group demonstrates the strong neoclassicism of Crawford's work in his first decade in Rome, but this was to change as he acquired commissions for American subjects. This statue with its nearly nude figures was commissioned to be put into marble a full three years before the "Greek Slave" entered the United States for her triumphant tour. But "Hebe and Ganymede" went immediately into the seclusion of a Boston collection.

By November 1842 two more neoclassical pieces were to come out of Crawford's studio—the beautifully poetic "Sappho" (Longfellow House, Cambridge) and the "Vesta," both fancy, or ideal, busts. The "Vesta" was described as the sensation of Crawford's studio in the winter of 1842–43, and one commentator, when he saw it later in Boston, wrote, "It seems to me, that the mantle of the great Thorwaldsen has fallen upon Crawford." Also in 1842 Crawford modeled the "Genius of Mirth" (Metropolitan Museum of Art), a gleeful little figure, which in 1843 was carved in marble for Henry Hicks of New York City. Crawford was modeling portraits and especially ideal pieces at a rapid pace, and in that year he wrote, "I regret that I have not a hundred hands, to keep pace with the workings of my mind." He also modeled the group "Adam and Eve," which had to wait over a decade to be put into marble; it is now in the Boston Athenaeum. Clearly Crawford was gaining recognition, and all that was needed was the exhibition of "Orpheus" to put him at the very fore of his field.

Early in 1844 he met Louisa Ward, who was in Rome with her sister and brother-in-law, Julia Ward Howe and Dr. Samuel Gridley Howe. In pursuit of Louisa he returned to America that summer, and after first convincing her uncle and brothers that he was devotedly and determinedly interested in more than her money, he married the lady—his "Dearest Lou."

The couple remained in the United States for about a year. Crawford spent some time in Washington trying to persuade certain members of Congress that he should be commissioned to do an equestrian statue of General Washington for one of the remaining blockings of the eastern stairs of the Capitol; this would be placed below the groups being executed by Greenough and Persico. His mission was not successful, and when he went back to Europe he took along a number of portrait busts to be put into marble, but there was still no large commission.

The Crawfords set up residence in Rome, and the sculptor spent long days in his studio over the next four years, but about all that has come to light from this period are a portrait bust of his wife (1846; in the Museum of the City of New York) and a bust of Josiah Quincy (1846; Harvard University), commissioned by a group of Harvard students as an honor to their retiring president. In 1848 he produced a passionate image of a "Dying Mexican Princess" (Metropolitan Museum of Art), whose side has been pierced and whose life ebbs away in a final melodramatic swoon. This is the artist's attempt to translate a subject taken from the history of the Western Hemisphere (Prescott's *Conquest of Mexico*) into an art that is the equal to—and in a way based on—the art of antiquity. Feathered bonnet and skirt excepted, one is reminded of ancient prototypes like dying Cleopatras, Niobes, or Amazons; but the statue heralds a break with the pure classicism of earlier work and marks a trend toward subjects taken from the New World. An increase in naturalism and a decrease in neoclassicism become particularly evident in the major works that he created on his return to Italy in 1850 after a brief visit to America. Crawford's studio, in spite of an absence of any grandiose project, was "a shrine to travellers" in the late 1840's. In January 1846, Bayard Taylor visited it, as was the practice for touring Americans and Englishmen, and was much impressed with what he saw.

So far Crawford was the sole American sculptor in Rome, although there was quite a colony in Florence—Greenough, Powers, Ives, Mozier, and until his death in 1843, Clevenger. By 1849, however, Rome was involved in political and military strife of the same order that was to drive Horatio Greenough from Florence two years later. Louisa Crawford was anxious to see her family and have them see her two children; Crawford himself still had no large commissions that bound him to his studio. So the Crawfords left to visit the United States.

Back in America Crawford entered the competition for the monument to General George Washington that the state of Virginia planned to erect in Richmond. Since 1840 the sculptor had dreamed of doing an equestrian monument and had even made designs and models that had been shown to no avail on his previous trip to America. There was a prestige connected with an equestrian group; it was considered the supreme test of a sculptor's skill. Crawford was the last of a field of sixty to enter the Richmond competition, but he came out first, defeating a disgruntled Robert Mills.

Crawford was awarded $53,000 for the project. He received $10,000 at once, beginning a period of prosperity and of enormous activity in his Rome studios.

The history of the equestrian statue in America will be discussed below in connection with the first completed example of that type of monument—Clark Mills' "Andrew Jackson," which stands opposite the White House. Crawford's was the second to be undertaken, coming just after Mills' statue and just before Henry Kirke Brown's "Washington" in New York's Union Square, although the unveiling of the latter actually predated that for Crawford's statue of "Washington" by a couple of years.

The design that won the Richmond competition comprised three parts: an equestrian statue of Washington atop a pedestal; at a lower level, six famous sons of Virginia—Jefferson, Henry, Marshall, Mason, Nelson, and Lewis—and on the periphery of the plinth, six republican eagles. The first contract with Crawford was for the equestrian Washington and the figures of Thomas Jefferson and Patrick Henry; the other four figures would be negotiated at a later time. This was to be the sculptor's first experience with bronze, and he eventually chose Professor Ferdinand von Müller's foundry in Munich to do the casting.

The Crawford family returned to Rome that same year, 1849, and the sculptor eagerly began work on the figure of Patrick Henry. This was modeled, cast in plaster, and sent to the bronze foundry in Munich late in 1851; "Jefferson" followed in August 1852. During this period there was considerable harassment from Robert Mills, the architect in charge of the foundations and pedestals for the statues, who less than a year after Crawford had signed the contract had attempted to revise the whole design by placing all the sculptures at the base of the inevitable tower. Mills' criticism that Crawford's design lacked unity and organization was somewhat justified, but when Mills was discovered making the pedestal too small so that Crawford's equestrian group would not fit and Mills might then turn the pedestal into a tower, he was dismissed.

Crawford had in the meantime traveled about Europe, studying other equestrian groups. Bernini's "Louis XIV" would have been too wild for his tastes, whereas the "Marcus Aurelius" lacked vigor, and Rauch's "Frederick the Great" in Berlin was too confused. The result was a spirited, prancing steed of Crawford's own design, dominated by a commanding Washington in military uniform (Fig. 4.14). It, too, was cast in Munich. The equestrian group itself is not bad, but it has been severely criticized because of its precarious perch. Hawthorne saw the model in Crawford's studio in 1858, and wrote in his *Notebook*:

It is certainly in one sense a very foolish and illogical piece of work—Washington, mounted on a very uneasy steed, on a very narrow space, aloft in the air, when a single step of the horse backward, forward or on either side, must precipitate him; and several of his contemporaries standing beneath him, not looking up to wonder at his predicament, but each intent on manifesting his own personality to the world around. They have nothing to do with one another, nor with Washington, nor with any great purpose which all are to work out together.

The statues did not arrive in America until 1857, the year of Crawford's death, and the unveiling of the sculptures in place upon the monument did not occur until February 22, 1858. On December 7, 1857, Governor Wise sent a somber message to the House of Delegates:

. . . . The equestrian statue of Washington has arrived here, and is waiting to be raised to its plinth. The eminent artist who modelled it, is no more. He did his work well, and the commissioners have engaged another artist, equally eminent, to take up his chisel and complete what his brother of the arts left unfinished . . . .

At a meeting of the governor and the commissioners it had been "Resolved, That Randolph Rogers, Esq. be appointed to execute so much of the contract entered into with the late Thomas Crawford for the statues and the emblematic figures for the monument, which were not finished by him." However, Crawford had also modeled the figures of Marshall (Fig. 4.15) and Mason; Randolph Rogers had them cast in Munich. The entire monument was a little over 60 feet; the equestrian statue itself was slightly more than 20 feet high, and the standing figures were 11 feet 9 inches.

In the early 1850's, although Crawford was occupied with the Richmond monument, he had other commissions as well. The spritely "Flora," enveloped in diaphanous billowing drapery and decorated with flowers, was carved in 1853 and is now in the Newark Museum. Her dancing feet are inches above the ground in what Crawford meant to be a deceiving denial of gravity, but the weighty marble belies the trick, and one is more amused than impressed. However, "Flora" was a delight to Victorian fancies and was a great attraction at P. T. Barnum's Crystal Palace in New York City.

The year 1855 saw one of Crawford's happiest triumphs—the heroic bronze "Beethoven," which today stands in the New England Conservatory of Music in Boston. It was modeled in Rome beginning in the summer of 1853, and Crawford was undoubtedly influenced by such ancient statues as the "Sophocles" in the Lateran Museum in Rome, or the "Aeschines" in the Naples Museum. It is not, however, a neoclassical portrait, but is instead a forceful study in naturalism. The "Beethoven" was cast in Munich where the inhabitants of the Bavarian city were so taken by it that a special performance of the Munich Symphony Orchestra was arranged for its exhibition. The statue, surrounded by a "forest of flowers," was placed in the concert hall on a pedestal six feet high with a dark green velvet backdrop that was supported by gilded columns. The Bavarian court attended, from King Maximilian on down, and it was indeed a gala celebration. The success the statue had achieved in Munich delighted Bostonians, but their own reception was more reserved: The high point of the evening was when William Wetmore Story—sculptor, friend and neighbor of Crawford in Rome—read an original poem dedicated to the statue. "Beethoven" stands seven feet high, wearing contemporary dress, but with a togalike mantle over his right shoulder that envelopes him from the waist down. His eyes, looking out from under heavy brows, and his firmly set mouth give the face a thoughtful and moody expression. In his hands, crossed in front of him, he holds a quill pen and a sheaf of paper.

In August 1853 as Crawford was modeling the equestrian group for Richmond he received a letter from Captain Meigs, asking if Crawford would submit a design for sculptures to go in the Senate pediment and above the entrance within the portico. Crawford was ecstatic over this long-awaited commission from the federal government. In a few months Crawford sent Meigs a detailed outline of the pedimental sculpture, which had as its central theme the emergence of a great civilization in triumph over savage life (Fig. 4.13). In the center is the robed personification of America, holding wreaths of oak and laurel; an American eagle is placed at one side, and the sun rises at the other; with her left hand America gestures toward a pioneer who swings an ax as he cuts down the trees of the great forests. He, like the ax-toting pioneers of James Fenimore Cooper's novels, represents the advance of civilization into the new American Eden.

The figures in the remaining part of the northern angle represent the old order of the American Indian, which must give way to the new age of the white man. After the pioneer comes an Indian youth who returns from the hunt, bearing game and looking warily at the man who represents the destruction of his way of life; one is reminded of the famous "Doryphorus" by Polykleitos in this figure. Next is the seated Indian chief, whose posture reveals his aching despair as he submits to the inevitable demise of his people. A marble copy of the Indian chief is in the New-York Historical Society. Crawford, like James Fenimore Cooper and the painter Thomas Cole, extols the virtuous life that man can regain in the wilderness paradise, but at the same time, recognizing the sorrowful plight of the once proud red man, lamentingly concludes, "That's progress." In addition to the ax and the plow, the advancing white man carried with him, figuratively speaking, three banners: one for Christianity, one for civilization, and one for America herself. Thus armed he was invincible, and the fate of the noble savage is evident in Crawford's image of despair. Just behind the chief is a reclining Indian squaw who holds an infant, and near them is an open grave, a further reference to the ultimate fate of this people.

Directly to the left of the central figure of America stands a soldier in a uniform of the Revolutionary War, representing the fight the nation made for its liberty. Next, a merchant sits on some crates and studies a globe—symbolizing the worldwide expansion of the country's trade and manufacturing. Midway are four more figures: a schoolmaster instructs a boy while two more youths march off toward the center, full of dreams for the future. In the low angle a mechanic reclines, resting on a cogwheel and holding a hammer in his hand; he personifies the inventive genius the young country had already put forth so boldly. At the very end, as a counterpart to the despair of the open grave, is an anchor, an age-old symbol of hope.

Captain Meigs, who has been characterized as troublesome and insensitive as a result of his many disagreements with Benjamin H. Latrobe, showed himself in his correspondence with Crawford to be a sensitive, intelligent, efficient, and patriotic man. He, as well as his superiors (Jefferson Davis, then Secretary of War, and President Pierce), gave immediate approval to the design, and Crawford was at work on the first figures early in 1854. By the middle of the year he had completed the "civilized" half of the pediment in an almost unbelievable burst of creativity and accomplishment. At that point he became eligible for half of the $20,000 he was to receive for the pediment figures, and he turned his attention once more to the completion of the large model for his equestrian "Washington." By late summer this, too, was shipped out of the Crawford studio—by then the largest in Rome—to the bronze foundry in Munich. The models for the Senate pediment were sent to America, where they were carved in marble. Crawford tried to persuade Meigs to have the carving done at Carrara, but Captain Meigs felt that some budding American sculptor might benefit from the opportunity of working on them in Washington; also, Congress could observe the progress.

In September 1854 Crawford went to Munich to work with von Müller, the congenial master founder, on the casting of the equestrian group; by the end of the year he was back in Rome and ready to begin the right side of the Senate pediment. Summer of 1855 found most of the figures finished, but he labored a while longer on the despondent Indian chief, for it was his only opportunity to work with the nude in the entire pediment. In one part of the Crawford studio work proceeded on the marble carving of "Adam and Eve" (Boston Athenaeum); in another the sculptor was modeling his celebrated "Peri" (Corcoran Gallery), the winged creature who stood forlornly at the gates of paradise in Thomas Moore's poem. It is an example of Crawford's work that reflected the sweetness and floweriness of Victorian taste, known for its sentimentality.

Another quarter of the studio contained the remainder of the Senate pediment sculptures, and in another part the sculptor modeled his powerful, 10-foot-high statue of James Otis for Mount Auburn Cemetery (where it was to be joined by other statues by W. W. Story, Randolph Rogers, and Richard Greenough). Otis, a dramatic figure in his great mantle, is represented deep in thought after having just penned the finishing lines to his "Speech Against Writs of Assistance," which he was to deliver before the superior court of Massachusetts on February 24, 1761. On the floor behind him is a sheet of paper inscribed "The Stamp Act." Crawford may have been influenced by the statue of Goethe by Schaper which he could have seen on one of his trips into Germany. The majestic marble "Otis" is now at Harvard University.

In addition, there were the figures of History and Justice, which were eventually placed over the Senate doorway within the portico. As if all these projects were not enough, the sculptor eagerly sought more. In the autumn of 1855 he made sketches of the Senate doors, which Captain Meigs fondly thought should rival Ghiberti's "Gates of Paradise" in Florence. The theme was war and peace, and in six panels and two medallions Crawford proposed to represent famous battles of the Revolution and some of George Washington's exemplary acts of the early years of peace in the new nation. Before the doors were finished he had begun a sketch of an "Armed Freedom" in response to an invitation from Meigs; the result was the 19-foot colossus that now stands atop the Capitol dome.

The plaster model can be inspected in the Smithsonian. Its forms are boldly sculpturesque, and its expression is stark, but this figure was to stand nearly 300 feet above the eyes of passers-by, and a weak modeling and a subtle expression would have been completely lost. Moreover, when Crawford worked on the colossal form in Rome in the fall of 1856, he was suffering agonizing pain from a tumor behind his left eye, and some of the work may well have been left to studio assistants.

In July 1855 he began the sketch for the doors of the House of Representatives, continuing the same theme of war and peace that had been used for the Senate doors. Crawford's insatiable appetite for work—and probably his drive to establish himself as the sculptor of the United States Capitol—also caused him to make overtures for the 9-foot-high, 300-foot-long bas-relief frieze that was to go around the interior base of the dome—a titanic task that would, by his own estimate, require five years to complete in plaster. But Meigs soon gave up on this as too expensive.

After a brief trip to America, Crawford returned to Rome in the fall of 1856 with the contract to do the four remaining figures for the Washington monument in Richmond, with a fortified hope that he might receive the commission to execute the sculptures for the House pediment at the Capitol, with an order to do some small masks for the Post Office then being built, and with a protruding eye that was becoming more painful every day. He reported to his wife, Louisa, who had remained in the United States, that work had progressed well in his studio during his absence: "Peri" and "Adam and Eve" were completed in marble, or nearly so, and "Armed Freedom" was built up in clay and ready for his attention—if only his eye would allow him to work as he wished. The Richmond figures of Marshall and Mason were also modeled in his studio, but no details are available. The finished bronze figures bear Crawford's signature, and in the arrangements that Randolph Rogers made with the monument commission, the "Marshall" and "Mason" were specified as having been created by Crawford and needed only to be cast in bronze.

At the start of 1857 Crawford and his sister, Jenny, went to Paris in search of medical treatment. The sculptor never returned to his beloved Villa Negroni in

Rome. Louisa joined them in Paris as soon as she realized that her husband's casual remarks in his letters were meant to spare her the truth. The three proceeded to London, where an operation removed the eye as well as the tumor. But Crawford was beyond curing, and he died on October 10, 1857.

Thomas Crawford had accomplished more in his twenty years in Rome than the stamina, drive, and ambition of most men would allow in a much longer lifetime. He left countless projects as only dreams, and several unfinished pieces stood silently in his studio. "Armed Freedom" was shipped to America and cast by Clark Mills during the Civil War; the last piece of it was hoisted into place on December 2, 1863, while cannons around the capital city boomed a loud salute to this American goddess. The Senate doorway figures of History and Justice were carved in Rome after the death of the sculptor. The bronze doors for the Senate and House were finished by William Rinehart, and the plaster models were sent to the United States. Those for the Senate wing were cast in Chicopee, Massachusetts; they were set in place in 1866. But those for the House wing were not installed until 1905 because the plaster models were somehow mislaid for many years. Upon being completed in marble, "Peri" was sent to Philadelphia, and the enormous "Otis" went to Mount Auburn. Randolph Rogers eventually began the completion of the Richmond monument, for which he produced the two heroic-size figures of Lewis and Nelson, as well as the allegorical figures (which he substituted for Crawford's eagles) at the lower perimeter. Some of the plaster casts that were left at the Villa Negroni were given away to friends, but the largest portion went into a storage museum in New York's Central Park, where they were later destroyed by fire.

Thomas Crawford had begun his career in Rome as a student adhering to a flagging neoclassicism. This is especially noticeable in his "Orpheus" and "Hebe and Ganymede." But his earliest portraiture had shown the naturalism that in the late 1840's began to eclipse Thorwaldsen's neoclassical spell. As he received commissions for life-sized portrait statues his naturalism grew in expressive power —as is demonstrated in his "Beethoven" and in the "Jefferson" and "Henry" for Richmond. And by the time he was doing his various pieces for the United States Capitol, he had divested himself of Thorwaldsen's neoclassical mantle. With this naturalism he was able to blend that serene yet dramatic character that he had learned in his early days in Rome. And though he died at the early age of forty-four, he had done much to advance the art and profession to where the sculptor was respected as a man of great talent, even of genius.

All three men—Greenough, Powers, and Crawford—contributed to this end, and considering the situation of sculpture in America around 1850–1860, the debt to these three is enormous. Without them, American sculpture would not have gained the international prestige it achieved in one brief generation. They worked hard indeed to make America the artistic equal of Athens and Rome. Later critics may say that they failed hopelessly, but the 19th century did not think so.

[FIG. 4.1] "Angel and Child," by Horatio Greenough (1832). Marble. Courtesy, Museum of Fine Arts, Boston, gift of Lawrence Curtis.

[FIG. 4.2] "Evan Philip Thomas," by Horatio Greenough (1837). Marble, 28″ high. Courtesy, Maryland Historical Society.

[FIG. 4.3] "George Washington," by Horatio Greenough (1832–41). Marble, 136" high. Courtesy, Smithsonian Institution.

[FIG. 4.4] "Castor and Pollux," by Horatio Greenough (1847–51). Marble, 34½" high. Courtesy, Museum of Fine Arts, Boston, bequest of Mrs. Horatio Greenough.

[FIG. 4.5] "Andrew Jackson," by Hiram Powers (1835). Marble, 34½" high. Courtesy, Metropolitan Museum of Art, gift of Mrs. Frances V. Nash, 1894.

[FIG. 4.6] "Horatio Greenough," by Hiram Powers (1838). Marble. Courtesy, Museum of Fine Arts, Boston, bequest of Charlotte (Gore) Greenough Hervousches du Quilliou.

[FIG. 4.7] "John C. Calhoun," by Hiram Powers (c. 1845). (After destroyed marble original.)

[FIG. 4.8] "Daniel Webster," by Hiram Powers (1858). Bronze. State House, Boston. Courtesy, Massachusetts Art Commission.

[FIG. 4.9] "The Fisherboy," by Hiram Powers (1841). Marble, 57″ high. Courtesy, Metropolitan Museum of Art, bequest of the Hon. Hamilton Fish, 1894.

[FIG. 4.10] "The Greek Slave," by Hiram Powers (1843). Marble, 65½″ high. Courtesy, Yale University Art Gallery, Olive L. Dann Fund.

[FIG. 4.11] "Charles Sumner," by Thomas Crawford (1839). Marble, 27" high. Courtesy, Museum of Fine Arts, Boston, bequest of Charles Sumner.

[FIG. 4.12] "Orpheus," by Thomas Crawford (1839). Marble. Courtesy, Boston Athenaeum, on loan from Museum of Fine Arts, Boston.

[FIG. 4.13] Senate pediment, east front, U.S. Capitol, Washington, D.C., by Thomas Crawford (1855). Marble, 60″ wide. Courtesy, Architect of the Capitol.

[FIG. 4.14] Washington Monument, Richmond, Va., by Thomas Crawford (1850–57). Courtesy, State of Virginia; photo, Index of American Sculpture, University of Delaware.

[FIG. 4.15] "John Marshall," from the Washington Monument, Richmond, Va., by Thomas Crawford (1856). Bronze. Courtesy, State of Virginia; photo, Index of American Sculpture, University of Delaware.

The Quest: An Heroic American Sculpture

WHILE PART OF THE FIRST GENERATION OF AMERICAN SCULPTORS FOUND IT NECESSARY to go abroad in search of artistic fulfillment, another group drew its inspiration directly from the native soil. The latter group either felt it unnecessary to go to Italy or rejected neoclassicism and Rome and Florence to return to America in search of a truly American art. They were led by two gifted artists, Henry Kirke Brown and Erastus Dow Palmer, and an especially clever craftsman, Clark Mills. Although their art often developed along lines contrary to those of the expatriates, they frequently reached for the same expression through a different sculptural vocabulary. In brief, like Janus, these groups represent two faces of the same head—one looked to Italy, the other upon native soil. In point of time, they follow Greenough, Powers, and Crawford by some ten or fifteen years.

Henry Kirke Brown (1814–1886) was born in Leyden, Massachusetts, where his youthful artistic talents found expression first in cutting silhouettes and then in painting. By the age of eighteen he was studying portraiture in Boston with Chester Harding, and after a brief period in New York City he moved to Cincinnati, probably at the suggestion of Harding, who had painted there himself. He spent the next two years (1837–1838) doing portraits in the Ohio River city, where he was a part of the active artist colony that grew up there under the patronage of such men as Nicholas Longworth. Brown became friends with Longworth and also with Shobal Clevenger, the sculptor, who was at that time anxiously awaiting an opportunity to make his way to Italy. It may have been his contact with Clevenger that first interested Brown in modeling in clay, but in any case his initial essay in the art of sculpture did occur in Cincinnati. By March 1839, Nicholas Longworth reported to Hiram Powers in Florence that Brown had already left for Boston and was thinking of "dropping the brush and wielding the chisel," concluding that he would "succeed better with the latter than he did with the brush." (Letter, courtesy Historical and Philosophical Society of Ohio.)

That fall Brown went back east, where he married Lydia Udall of Quechee, Vermont. He painted numerous portraits of her family in the year that followed, but his inclination toward sculpture increased. From 1839–1840 date several portrait busts, among them those of William Appleton, Dr. George Hayward, Isaac Stevens, Henry Oxford, Judge Payne, and Chester Harding. Considering the competition he faced from the other sculptors then in Boston, including his friend Clevenger, Brown was doing rather well; but he, like most artists of the day, was alert to the possibility of some new locality that might offer patronage to the artist. On December 12, 1839, he wrote his sister Caroline that he was modeling the portrait of Dr. Alonzo Potter, of Union College, who wanted him to go to Albany to "take some heads." He accepted the invitation, and the warmth of his reception in the Albany-Troy-Schenectady area is revealed in the letters he wrote to his wife in Boston during the months that followed. He continued to paint portraits occasionally, since they were less expensive and more people could afford them, but he also managed to model approximately forty busts during this period. Even by March he complained in a letter to Lydia, ". . . faith I keep modeling one [bust] after another so fast that I lose interest in them. It is much like a treadmill, one thing over and over again." * But his letters home were usually filled with a jubilant enthusiasm for his work, and each succeeding bust he modeled he declared was his best. For modeling a bust his fee was from $50 to $100; plaster-cast replicas were $8 or $10 each. But he was making a living and even managing to save some money for his dreamed-of pilgrimage to Italy. In the making of casts he was once briefly assisted in Albany by William J. Coffee, who managed to spoil two of his finished busts in the process; thereafter Brown did most of his casting himself. For a while he had an arrangement with a "Mr. Carrew" (probably Joseph Carew) to put some of his busts into marble.

On November 3, 1840, the Albany *Morning Times* carried a report that the sculptor intended to take all his busts with him to Italy, where they would be carved in stone. After a year in Boston, Henry and Lydia Brown sailed for Italy in the summer of 1842. They stopped first in London, where the sculptor saw the Elgin Marbles and numerous works by Flaxman, as well as "things of more modern artists if artists they could be called." Brown was impressed by some of the statues in St. Paul's and Westminster Abbey, but appalled by others. By

* This and, unless otherwise specified, subsequent quotations from letters to, from, or about Henry Kirke Brown are published through the courtesy of the Library of Congress and with the permission of Mrs. Frances Head, daughter of Henry Kirke Bush-Brown.

early November 1842 the Browns had arrived in Florence. On November 10, the sculptor wrote to his friend E. P. Prentice that he could not see "in what respect this city possesses one charm above a dozen American cities, excepting that of antiquity. . . ." The letter continued with an interesting note of indifference toward the value of European training for an American artist: "As far as Art is concerned, . . . I am, daily, more and more convinced of the folly of studying the works of others; in no work of art is there anything beautiful but what nature fully justifies. . . ."

Thus Brown championed a home-grown American art with a simple and direct naturalism as its foundation.

It is just this attitude, which denounced the superiority of foreign styles and "expatriatism," that caused Brown's work to be thoroughly American even after his Italian experience. Unlike Horatio Greenough and Hiram Powers and their families, who in the early 1840's spoke of Florence as the most delightful place on earth, the Browns were less than enchanted, and they found the Italian people "degraded, ignorant, and indolent." As far as Brown was concerned, he would just as soon have been in Albany as in Florence.

They obtained a house near the Powerses and the Clevengers, as well as a studio, that cost only $51 a year. Eventually his tools and busts arrived from America, and Brown began putting the busts into marble himself, employing one of the newly devised pointing machines. His frugality and industry were prodigious. He complained to a friend that Italian stonecutters wanted a dollar a day and refused to work more than eight hours, and he said that he was therefore very happy that he himself had mastered the skill of stonecutting while still in America. In the evenings after dinner, Brown would go to his studio to draw from the live model where he was often joined by his friends A. G. Hoit and Clevenger.

In December 1842 Lydia wrote home that Henry had begun modeling a young Indian, hiring a thirteen-year-old Italian boy to pose; Brown had written to George Catlin, the painter of American Indians, to inquire about details of the head, so that his image would be ethnologically correct. Even in Florence he was preoccupied with a subject that came not from ancient mythology but rather from his own country's early history. Lydia wrote to a Mrs. Willard in March 1843 that the "Indian Boy" represented a subject that ". . . to an American, at least . . . possesses as much historical interest and poetry as an Apollo or Bacchus. . . ."

Brown described his Indian youth as being in an "attitude of repose, resting one hand on his bow, while in the other he holds his arrows; his drapery [is] thrown over a stump which supports the figure." On the plinth were several bas-reliefs of the Great Spirit, a chase or deer hunt, a group of Indians, and a bow and quiver. There were stag heads at the corners, with festoons of Indian corn hung between them. The sculptor stated that his statue was, as far as he knew, ". . . the first attempt that has been made to render classical objects of our own country." (He curiously ignored the Indian statue that Clevenger had modeled in his Florentine studio only a couple of years earlier, just before he died.) Brown had finished the clay model by July, and when Hiram Powers saw it in plaster he told Brown he should ask $3,000 for the marble version. The "Indian" was the major work of Brown's first year in Italy, and he hoped to have it soon carved in marble.

Before leaving Florence he shipped several busts, among them those of McConichie, Spencer, and Tibbets, back to the United States; his price for putting each of these into marble was $200. Then packing up the other models and sketches, including the "Indian," the Browns departed for Rome in early November.

They found the Eternal City as enchanting and exciting as Florence had been disappointing, and stood in awe before its grandeur and antiquity. American sculptors had not yet thronged to Rome, as they would in the next decades, but Thomas Crawford was there (his marble "Orpheus" was then on its way to Boston), and Chauncey B. Ives arrived from Florence at about the same time as the Browns. After obtaining a studio, Henry Kirke Brown got to work, and by the following February he had begun a six-foot statue of David and was modeling bas-reliefs of Spring and Autumn. Evidently the power of Rome was sufficient to lure him temporarily away from American themes, for throughout this period he took his subjects from other sources—the Old Testament, ancient mythology, Italian genre, and so on.

The "David" was completed and cast in plaster, but it was eventually destroyed by the sculptor himself, presumably because he was not satisfied with it and perhaps because no one had commissioned it to be done in marble. The "Spring" and "Autumn" bas-reliefs—later joined by "Summer" and "Winter" —were put into marble, however, and purchased by a Mr. Marquand of New York. In Brown's "Spring" the impact of Rome on his style is obvious in the classical features of the head. His conversion to neoclassicism is also found in an ideal head entitled "La Grazia" (1845). The deep-set eyes and their proximity to the brow, the straight line of the bridge of the nose, the full lips and chin, the compact treatment of the hair, all suggest the Greek ideal of the 5th century B.C. that later flourished in Rome.

Virtually all trace of America disappeared from the sculptor's work at this time. Even his "Indian Boy" which by March had been "pointed" in a beautiful block of marble, was reworked to change it into an Apollino! This act, which was tantamount to treason to Brown's earlier beliefs, seemed to have weighed heavily upon his conscience, for in June 1844 he wrote to E. P. Prentice in Albany, "I shall make amends for my treachery to this subject [the "Indian Boy"], for I do esteem it as one capable of a high poetical character." This was a promise he was to keep once he returned to the United States.

In the late summer and fall of 1844 he worked on the model of an Italianate genre piece of a little boy struggling to restrain his determined dog from getting to a bowl on the floor; it is entitled "Chi Vinci, Mangia," or "He Who Wins Gets to Eat." The infant is nude and stylistically reminiscent of the cherubs of ancient and Renaissance Rome, whereas the subject itself is playfully anecdotal. (There was at that time a demand for art depicting the ragamuffin urchins of the squalid slums of Rome and Naples.) The group was put into marble and may be seen in the New-York Historical Society. The same institution owns another of Brown's works from these years—his marble "Ruth" (Fig. 5.2). The statue was probably begun early in 1845, but Brown was incapacitated by Roman brain fever (a disease that plagued other American sculptors) during April and May, "most of the time deprived of his senses," so it was not until summer that the model was finished. The "melancholy sweetness and modesty" of the "Ruth" held great appeal for the Romantic or so-called Victorian frame of mind, and by July 1845, not only had the piece been commissioned to be put into marble by E. P. Prentice, but also two replicas at $1,000 each had been ordered. Later that year Brown designed a similar statue, "Rebecca," and another called "The Pleiades."

William Cullen Bryant saw the statue of "Ruth" and a number of other works in Henry Kirke Brown's studio when he was in Rome in the mid-1840's; during this visit the sculptor modeled the bust of the celebrated poet. The portrait, one of Brown's finest, has a Romantic flair and exuberance that are absent in most of his dry realistic likenesses. Stylistically the "Bryant" (Fig. 5.1) was a late addition to the group that included Horatio Greenough's "Evan Philip Thomas" (1837), Hiram Powers' "Horatio Greenough" (1837), and Thomas Crawford's "Charles Sumner" (1839).

As the artist modeled Bryant's portrait the two men talked about the United States—her promising future, heroic past, and unbounded natural beauty. Bryant was one of several visiting Americans who through similar conversations persuaded Brown to return to America, to bring her his maturing genius, and to do what he could to fulfill her great promise. No doubt Bryant also played some part in Brown's decision to settle in New York City, by then the hub of poetic and artistic activity. So after four years in Italy the Henry Kirke Browns sailed for home.

Brown had evidently reverted to his earlier theory that America should have an American art and that American sculptors should render their own heritage instead of that of others, for during the first several years after his return he was occupied with the Indian as a theme. He visited Indian settlements and made sketches of the people; back in his New York studio he turned the sketches into statues and statuettes, which became very popular among his countrymen. Twenty copies of a statuette titled "Aboriginal Hunter" were distributed as premiums by the Art Union; by 1850 this successful art-lottery organization had paid Brown more than $2,000 for these bronze images. Brown had cast them himself in a foundry that he devised and built in his own studio. This was not the first casting of sculpture in bronze in the United States. Robert Ball Hughes' "Bowditch" in Mount Auburn antedated it by a couple of years. But Brown's bronze casting in New York in the 1840's ranks among the earliest attempts.

Late in 1848 Brown was at work on a statue called "Quoit Player in Repose" ("a Garden Statue") and on one called "Dying Tecumseh." He had established his studio in Brooklyn by this time, and during the following year he was absorbed for a while in designing a monument to a Mr. Burd, which was to go in St. Stephen's Church in Philadelphia. His medieval-style design had a recumbent figure, reminiscent ". . . of an old knight clad in his armor." The commission ultimately went to Steinhausen, and Brown's efforts were for naught. But there were other works that year, such as the bust of President Taylor, modeled at the White House in May, and one of Julia Marquand, made in the Brooklyn studio in December. There is also mention of a bust of John H. Prentice, as well as a statue with the descriptive title "Hope Contemplating the Immortality of the Soul."

While in Washington to model President Taylor's portrait Brown saw Persico's "Discovery" group, and it made him "sick at heart to look at it." He wrote of Greenough's "Washington" that ". . . as a work of art [it] is of that disgusting mediocrity which is too good to condemn in toto and too insipid to admire." In his eyes these works had been tainted by the influence of foreign art.

The theme of the American Indian that took form in his "Aboriginal Hunter" and "Dying Tecumseh" was continued in the group "Indian and Panther." Previous historians have given 1846 as its date and declared it to be the first piece cast in bronze in this country. But it was the smaller "Aboriginal Hunter," which was done in 1846, that can rightfully claim this position. The "Indian and Panther," a statue about 7 feet high, was not created until 1849–1850. Brown wrote of it in a letter to E. P. Prentice on January 21, 1850:

Since the decision of that Phila'd affair, I have set about my "Indian Group" in good earnest;—have made the sketch for the composition, but have chosen a more general subject than that of Pocahontas. It is a fine old Indian defending his child against the attack of a panther. He has already struck one blow and is in the act of dealing another. . . . These three figures,—the strong man, the panther, his natural energy, and the child, admit of a very sculpturesque treatment; and, . . . it seems to me to present a striking idea of the Indians' mode of life, before they were disturbed by the presence of the whites.

Brown's romantic conception of the noble savage is clearly revealed in his representation of the true aboriginal hero of the North American continent. The statue was too big for Brown to cast in his own foundry, and John Quincy Adams Ward recalled that the piece was cast elsewhere by a Frenchman but finished off in the Brooklyn studio. A small model of it may be seen in Louis Lang's portrait of the sculptor.

By mid-century, Brown was a vigorous participant in the activities centered on the National Academy of Design. His bust of Asher B. Durand was shown at the 1849 annual exhibition, and the following year he was represented by portraits of William Cullen Bryant, E. P. Prentice, Thomas Cole, Dr. Parker, and a

"Bust of a Young Girl," along with the reliefs of the four seasons, "Ruth,"
"Hope," the "Quoit Player," and "The Good Angel Conducting the Soul to
Heaven." This sizable collection brought him a great deal of attention from both
the public and his fellow artists. He was elected a full member of the National
Academy in 1851, and at about this time began a period of prolific production in
his studio. Brown soon required assistance for his numerous commissions, and
among his early apprentices were John Quincy Adams Ward (beginning in
1849) and Larkin Mead (1853). Ward described his fondness for his "master" in
a letter to a friend, written in March 1852:

I find in the companionship of Mr. Brown a purer, nobler & more exalting influence
than it is possible for young persons to impart. When he speaks of art 'tis no boyish
thought, it leaves an impression, & I always try to keep at such a distance from him
as may give respect to his words. He is my Master in art & as such I will ever regard
him. Nor does that prevent him from being pleasant and agreeable.

In the early 1850's the Brown studio was busy with several pieces. Chief
among these was the statue of De Witt Clinton, destined for Greenwood Cemetery in Brooklyn. Modeled in 1851 and cast in plaster by March of the following year, "Clinton" stands in a pose that suggests animation and vitality, and looks
off into the distance, signifying his great vision. He wears the dress of his day, but
a mantle hangs from the left shoulder and covers most of the lower portion of his
body. It is once more a compromise between classical and contemporary attire,
and one of the last instances where the toga is employed. The plaster model was
sent to Chicopee, Massachusetts, to be cast in bronze at James Ames' foundry.
The Ames Manufacturing Company had specialized in making guns and swords,
and the casting of a large statue was a new experience. But the firm soon became
expert in the necessary skills, and in the last half of the century it was one of the
major foundries employed by American sculptors.

Henry Kirke Brown went to Chicopee to be present during part of the operation, and took with him Ward, Bellenout (a founder from France), and Lalou-
ette (a finisher and chaser, also from France). The legs of the model had been
broken off during the journey and had to be repaired. This accomplished, the
statue was then cast in parts, a process Brown described in a letter to his wife,
dated April 20, 1852:

. . . Mr. Lanckton told me they were nearly ready to cast the head of Clinton; of
course, I dropped all and went out to assist; we closed the mold and poured the metal;
all went fine. It was most interesting to see the quiet earnestness of the workmen,
—every man understood his business;—all orders were given by a nod of the head
or a motion of the hand. The mold filled, and I returned to my work. After dinner
we opened it and found all perfect. . . . I have got the largest pieces of the Clinton
together and shall tomorrow commence repairing them and shall mount the arms anew.
This all will take me two days at least, and may be more.

In another letter he reported that the finishing and chasing would take about a
year; all of this was done by his French assistants in his Brooklyn studio. Also in

bronze are the reliefs on the base: "The Digging of the Erie Canal" and "Commerce on the Erie Canal."

At this time Brown was also modeling the "Angel of the Resurrection" and a large bas-relief for the Church of the Annunciation in Brooklyn. More works in bronze began to issue from his own studio, such as the small (16 inches) bust of Henry Clay, one of Dr. Moffat, and a lion's head. But by the beginning of 1853 he had embarked on the equestrian "Washington" (Fig. 5.4) that stands in Union Square, a work that was to absorb nearly all his energies for the next three years.

Horatio Greenough had been approached by a group of New York City gentlemen in 1851 about an equestrian statue of Washington. Early in the negotiations, however, Henry Kirke Brown was also invited by the committee to submit a model for the statue. He agreed, but he could not understand how two master sculptors could work together on the final statue; for a while the committee evidently expected him to assist Greenough on the statue.

On May 2, 1851, Lydia Brown wrote her sister that Henry was working on "a design for a statue of Washington on horseback," and that "he is modelling it small but the statue for the monument is to be seventeen feet high. I hope he may have it to do." This model is now in the collection of the Yale University Art Gallery. The problem of the ambiguous relationship between the two sculptors resolved itself even before Greenough's death in December 1852: A few days afterward Brown wrote his friend Daniel Huntington that ". . . a disagreement between him [Greenough] and Mr. Lee and some of the subscribers was the cause of the dissolution of the whole affair when the contract was transferred to me." In September 1852 Brown drew up a contract specifying that by two years from May 1, 1853, the committee would have its statue, finished and erected, that the size of the horse and rider would be at least fourteen feet high with a suitable granite base, and that Washington would be represented in his military uniform. A schedule of payments called for a total of $25,000 to be raised through subscriptions of $500 each. Some of the pledged subscribers withdrew from time to time, and Brown finally agreed to accept $22,000, "relying on the liberality of his fellow-citizens in case the result should prove satisfactory."

A separate studio was built for the purpose of modeling the great equestrian group, and the modeling itself—in plaster rather than clay—was begun in early 1853. The next eighteen months were devoted to modeling the horse and rider; as Brown had a special interest in horses, he found the preparatory studies enjoyable. For the likeness of the general, he followed the portrait bust by Houdon, a copy of which was in the collection of Hamilton Fish. To achieve accuracy in the uniform, the sculptor studied Washington's own garments, which were preserved at the capital. The statue was well conceived; Washington has a calm dignity and nobility, and his steed has a powerful vigor. The group possesses a stability and composure that Mills' and Crawford's equestrian statues lack. One is reminded of the great equestrian masterpieces by Donatello in Padua and the ancient "Marcus Aurelius" on the Palatine Hill in Rome, which Henry Kirke Brown may have known.

The finishing touches on the model were applied in the summer of 1854, and by October it was on its way to Chicopee to be cast. Even for the skilled workmen at the Ames foundry this was an exciting challenge, and elaborate preparations were made. The head, neck, and body of the horse were to be cast in one piece, whereas the tail and legs would all be cast separately. Brown and Ward were there much of the time during the months that followed, and when they were not working on the mold, they enjoyed occasional hunting and fishing trips together. Finally on May 6, 1855, Brown wrote to a friend:

The last of the work is ready for the foundry, and as usual with me after finishing a work, I feel lost; it seems to me as though I had been pursuing a phantom and it had all of a sudden disappeared from my sight, and I am left in a miserable barren desert.

Brown then returned to Brooklyn to begin work on other projects. As the weeks passed, the pieces of the equestrian group began to arrive from Massachusetts; then followed the long, laborious, and—to Brown—monotonous task of assembling and chasing the bronze giant. It was with great relief that he finally called the statue finished and arranged for its transportation to Union Square. On June 5, 1856, he wrote his beloved Lydia that on the preceding afternoon

about 3 o'clock the men came with their ponderous truck and tackle to load the body of the horse; we . . . passed him quite into the street, then rigged a "Jim" over him and slowly laid him on his side, straddled the truck over him, and slung him underneath, and started for South Ferry; but . . . they had no boat which had a gangway sufficiently large to admit him. So we started for the Fulton Ferry and there was a boat . . . which admitted it. So we passed over Jordan. . . .

The following morning they began the task of hoisting the body of the horse up onto the base of Quincy granite, which Upjohn and Company had designed. This achieved, the legs and tail were then bolted on. The next day the rider was taken to the site and raised to "his everlasting seat." John Quincy Adams Ward wrote of the event in a lighthearted manner, telling a friend that

George with all his traps [rose to his place]; I was surprised at the coolness and unconcern he manifested while being hoisted in his awkward and stiff action in the presence of a large multitude—we accounted for it from the quality of brass in his face.

The excitement of the approaching finale to years of arduous effort by the sculptor and his assistant was quickly picked up by the crowd that gathered to watch the activity in Union Square. Brown described the scene in a letter to his wife:

A great crowd of people were gathered in the park to see it go up. I should think there were four thousand, among them I saw Mr. Green our former consul at Rome, . . . and others. Some ladies bowed to me from carriages Page said, but my back was towards them. The square was filled with people, carriages, carts and no one knows what all—and such a din and roar I never heard. . . .

In a ceremony on July 4, 1856, the statue was officially delivered from the artist to the Washington Statue Committee, and then to the City of New York. The hectic preparations for the celebration were complicated by the animosity that existed between the mayor and the chairman of the statue committee, and only Brown's personal efforts managed to salvage a respectable dedication ceremony. But bands there were, and orations; and finally the glistening image was unveiled amid loud applause and shouts of approval that warmly cheered the sculptor and his young assistant. Henry, in the quiet of his studio rooms that evening, wrote Lydia: "I have now been at work nearly four years upon this work,—this morning I bid it farewell with a sad heart; I have given so many years of my life to it,—I consign it to the future, to my country,—may it benefit them!" The equestrian "Washington" was Henry Kirke Brown's finest achievement.

In the fall of 1855, after the sculptor had returned from Chicopee, he left his Brooklyn studio to go in search of the large commissions he craved. In Washington, where he hoped to obtain an assignment from the government, he contacted Captain Meigs, who had done so much for Thomas Crawford, as well as for a host of Italian sculptors. Brown's initial impression of the engineer was most favorable, and the two seem to have gotten on quite well; but this relationship was to change drastically. Meigs told him that if he presented a design for the Senate pediment he would probably be awarded the commission. About a month later Brown returned to Washington to show Meigs his design. The captain at once placed his finger beside the figure of a slave, and the discussion that followed is preserved in Brown's notebook, dated December 1855:

After long and careful looking he said: "I do not think it would do to represent a slave in the pediment, it is a sore subject and upon which there is a good deal of feeling and I think no southerner would consent to it. . . ." He said the south talked of it as the greatest blessing both for slave and master, but that they did not like to have it alluded to. . . . [He] remarked that the figure [of the slave] would not help me any with the Secretary of War [Jefferson Davis, who had the final approval on such commissions]. I understood that.

So back to his studio Brown went, where he eagerly began the revisions. His plan reveals how an artist viewed the activities of the nation in the middle of the 19th century:

America occupies the central position in the group extending her blessing and protection alike to all, not merely to her own citizens, but to the poor and distressed foreigner who kneels at her feet on the left. On her right are the anvil, wheel and hammer representative of the mechanic arts. The first standing figure to the left of America represents a citizen depositing his vote in the ballot box, a very distinguishing feature of our country and the symbol of equal rights. Next to him is the farmer, cultivator of the soil, ingenuous and simple, resting on his plow with the products of his labor at his feet. Next comes the fisherman seated upon his upturned boat mending his nets. Lastly upon that side is the brave and athletic hunter combating the wild animals. I have placed him upon the outskirt of civilization showing him to be the hero of all border strife and hardship.

Upon the other extremity is the Indian trapper in whom I have desired to express that stillness and wariness peculiar to his race. Beside him are his dog, trap and the dead object of his pursuit. He stands for the interests of the fur trade.

Next to him I have introduced the miner, or gold seeker of California with his pick, shovel and pan. Next the American boy, frank and brave, with his little boat which he evidently intends to launch upon the first convenient sheet of water. He is the promise of commerce and navigation, the perpetual renewal of the hope of all. Next the old weather-beaten navigator and discoverer demonstrating with globe and maps the characteristics and resources of the countries he has found and exhibiting a specimen of mineral ore to the statesman, who stands attentively considering his proposition.　　[Quoted from Fairman, *Art and Artists of the Capitol*, pp. 191–192]

With nationalistic pride he pointed out that America had no need "of the symbols and conventionalities of other nations," and that the country itself had developed a "rich and beautiful history . . . , full of manliness and grandeur."

The model was submitted to Captain Meigs in February 1856, along with the above description. A month later the superintendent of works sent the design to Secretary of War Davis with the following notation: "I regret to say that I do not think it is of such pre-eminent merit that I can advise its execution in marble. . . ." The Secretary accepted Meigs' advice and instructed him to inform Brown in a gentle manner that his proposal was rejected. This did nothing to endear Meigs to the sculptor, who returned disheartened and disgruntled to New York to concentrate on the finishing of his equestrian statue for Union Square.

The depression of 1857 saw Brown established at Newburgh, New York, which was to remain his home for the rest of his life. Determined to try Washington once more, Brown conspired with the sculptor Horatio Stone to oust Captain Meigs from his position of authority over artistic matters. After Brown was elected a member of the Washington Art Association, he and Stone, operating through the Association, spearheaded the drive to have Meigs' rule over the arts brought to an end. New York artists, under the leadership of Asher B. Durand and Henry Peters Gray, were invited to join the crusade, but they failed to respond with the expected enthusiasm. Brown and Stone wanted the President to create an art commission composed of artists that would replace Meigs in all decisions relative to painted and sculptural decoration in the capital. Meanwhile, there were a few portrait busts to be done—those of Vice-President Breckenridge, of Mrs. Maynard, of Mrs. Signourey, and of General Winfield Scott; still, Brown remained optimistic about a large commission. He hoped Congress would commission a statue of John C. Calhoun, but this was dampened when he learned that Powers had been asked to do statues of Clay, Webster, and Calhoun, leaving neither appropriations nor need for his own Calhoun. (Powers ultimately chose to do statues of Franklin and Jefferson instead.) At the same time his good friend Clemson, Calhoun's son-in-law, was promoting the idea of a statue of the great statesman for his home state of South Carolina. Brown completed a statuette model, but Clark Mills owned the only life mask of Calhoun, and he was not inclined to let another sculptor use it; a copy of Powers' bust was evidently not available. These were lean times for Henry Kirke Brown, and perhaps because he did not have enough large and challenging projects to keep him occupied he participated more and more in the battle to establish a federal art commission.

There was a brief triumph in the spring of 1859 when President James Buchanan signed a bill creating the long-sought Art Commission—but it was to last less than two years. None of the men appointed to the committee—Henry Kirke Brown, James R. Lambdin, and John F. Kensett—was of the "expatriate classicist" or "Italianate" school; all three advocated a direct and honest naturalism in American art. It is not surprising, then, that the Art Commission should publish the following lines about portrait statues then being commissioned and executed:

Are portrait statues in which the Greek or Roman costume has been substituted for that worn by the individuals represented satisfactory? Do they not rather convey a feeling of shame for the paucity of invention on the part of the artists and an acknowledgment that we have sought refuge in stuffs and draperies to conceal our want of power in this special character? We want nothing thrown in between us and the facts of our history to estrange us from it. We want to be brought near it, to realize it as an existence, not as a myth. True genius presents us no nightmares, no vagaries; but is clear-seeing and by its subtleness of perception and power of expression renders truth palpable to duller senses. [Quoted from Fairman, *Art and Artists of the Capitol*]

They condemned the use of Roman togas and Greek ideals in images of American merchants, statesmen, seamen, and farmers, establishing a creed to which Brown himself adhered in the several statues that he later executed for Statuary Hall. The Art Commission presented a proposed list of expenditures for statues and paintings that came to $166,900. Congress, intending to spend only those funds needed to bring the Capitol to completion, had no wish to appropriate such a large sum for the embellishment of the building. And as the Art Commission would therefore have nothing to supervise, it was abolished in the summer of 1860.

The Washington years had been disappointing to Henry Kirke Brown, offering him no more than a few portrait busts. Toward the end of 1858 the sculptor's prospects brightened when the state of South Carolina set aside the Calhoun statue and commissioned him to do thirteen figures for the pediment of the new capitol at Columbia. The central figures were to be "Hope," "Justice," and "Liberty." But then in 1859 while working in South Carolina, Brown was run over by a team of horses. For a long period he was unable to work on the figures. Two years later the Civil War ended the project altogether. The pieces he had completed were destroyed when the city burned. Greatly depressed he returned to Newburgh in 1861, with only a few commissions in stock. But with the end of hostilities came a change in Brown's fortunes, and the years between 1865 and his death in 1886 were among the most productive of his life.

America, as always, honored her military heroes, and among the portrait busts modeled by Henry Kirke Brown at the close of the Civil War were those of Colonel Rush Hawkins, in his Zouave uniform with tasseled cap, and General Philip Kearny. But when Congress invited the several states to send statues of their most eminent men to Statuary Hall, no Civil War heroes were submitted; instead, the statues were of soldiers and statesmen from America's earlier years. The first to arrive was Henry Kirke Brown's "General Nathanael Greene" (Fig. 5.3). That this portrait statue was the first to stand in the pillared Hall was fortuitous for a country that was trying to heal its wounds. Greene, although from Rhode Island, had been commander of the Southern army in the Revolutionary War, and was so esteemed by his contemporaries in Georgia and the Carolinas that he was granted lands in those states. He was thus both Southerner and Northerner.

The statue was dedicated in January 1870. Edward Clark, the architect of the Capitol, wrote to Brown on January 2, 1870: "Your 'Greene' is admired by everyone whom I have heard speak of it, by some enthusiastically. It is, in my judgment, an honor to the Nation, and the State which presented it, to say nothing of the genius who formed it."

No one at that time criticized the excessive naturalism in the rendering of the uniform. But Brown's overattention to the details of the clothing prove so distracting that the spectator tends to lose sight of the heroic dignity of the statue itself. This was a major problem for the sculptor of this period. He could neither represent the figure in the nude (as in his ideal works) nor wrap his subject in the robes of antiquity; moreover, his attention to the naturalistic details of contemporary dress frequently brought him to grief. This dilemma was not solved until the next generation of American sculptors under the guidance of Saint-Gaudens and Daniel Chester French.

During the late 1860's Brown modeled a statue of Dr. George Bethune for the Packer Institute in Brooklyn; it, like the one of General Greene, was put into marble at Carrara. The same difficulty with regard to contemporary dress occurred in this statue as the sculptor continued to be unable to provide a solution—if indeed he ever recognized the problem. In 1868 his bronze statue of a solemn, contemplative Lincoln was placed on its granite pedestal in Union Square, not far from the equestrian "Washington."

Henry Kirke Brown rarely created a penetrating psychological study of his subject, but then neither did any of his fellow artists of the 1850's and 1860's. In the middle of the century neither the painter nor the sculptor endowed their portraits with a searching analysis of the character of the men and women they represented, for both patron and artist were largely content with a surface likeness. Not since the Romantic Byronic portraits by Greenough, Powers, and Crawford had there been much interpretation of the individual. Instead, a naturalistic likeness was all that was demanded. Brown could not go beyond this even with such a heroic figure as Lincoln—not in the one in Union Square or in a later one in Prospect Park in Brooklyn. The inability of mid-century artists to render the spirit and personality prevented the attainment of the highest level of portraiture. In the "Lincoln" in Prospect Park Brown placed his subject in a more overtly dramatic pose, but the inner character of the man was not really expressed.

The 1870's saw two more figures for Statuary Hall and two equestrian statues for the city of Washington issue from Brown's studio. Modeled in Newburgh, the equestrian group of General Winfield Scott was finished in plaster and ready for the foundry by May 1871. Brown's love of equine form is again obvious. But the horse is somewhat overpowered by a rather obese General Scott, who seems to be looking over his command, resting his right hand—which holds binoculars—on his hip. Brown chose to depict Scott at about the time of the Mexican War, "when his figure had attained its full proportions, and his intellectual faculties in their maturity had been ripened by his rich experience. The likeness is as perfect as one could desire." So wrote a critic in the New York *Evening Post*, May 30, 1871. As an equestrian group, the "Scott" is far more successful than Brown's "General Nathanael Greene," erected in Greene Square, Washington, in 1877. The horse under Greene seems far too slight to carry its rider into battle; its legs appear too short and too slender, and the neck is scrawny. The image of Greene does have a certain dynamic vitality, which is quite the opposite of the quiet, portly figure of Winfield Scott, but neither matched the calm grandeur of the "Washington" in Union Square.

For the statue of George Clinton, commissioned by the state of New York as one of their contributions to Statuary Hall, the sculptor wrote to the librarian of the New-York Historical Society in December 1872 and obtained permission to have a mask made from Ceracchi's bust of Clinton to use as a model. Brown portrayed Clinton in colonial attire, with a walking stick in his right hand and gloves in his left. The wrinkles of the clothing are less distracting in this bronze figure than in Brown's earlier marble statue of Greene, and it is easier to concentrate on the face. The style remained naturalistic, with as much forceful vitality as the sculptor could achieve, and the statue received a number of plaudits when it was unveiled in 1873.

A year later Brown modeled the statue of Richard Stockton, which had been commissioned by New Jersey for Statuary Hall. The marble figure, also in colonial dress, is similar in style to the "Greene" and "Clinton." The bronze statue of General Philip Kearny, which New Jersey also commissioned for Statuary Hall, shows virtually no trace of the new aesthetics that by the 1880's had become evident in American sculpture. By then Saint-Gaudens had completed his statue of Farragut for New York's Madison Square and was soon to start his Adams Memorial for Rock Creek Cemetery in Washington, D.C., and Daniel Chester French had already modeled his "Minute Man" for Concord.

While these young men, along with many others, were giving a new direction to American sculpture, the career of Henry Kirke Brown came to an end at his

Newburgh home in 1886. He had done much to establish naturalism as the dominant style in American sculpture in the mid-19th century; this was accomplished in the face of strong opposition from several expatriate American artists who had settled in Rome (Story, Simmons, Rinehart, and others) and who confronted their native land with images of Libyan Sibyls, of Blind Girls of Pompeii, of Circes and Penelopes and Jerusalems, of Medeas and Arcadian Shepherd Boys. There was something close to Americans themselves in the simple and direct naturalism, whereas the exotic subjects and styles that were followed in the middle of the century were usually superficial. But naturalism by itself is not synonymous with great art, and if Henry Kirke Brown and others with him are to be criticized, it is because they made naturalism their aesthetic god and did not push on beyond its limitations to seek and express the spirit and essence of their subjects.

Another early sculptor whose style developed almost wholly uninfluenced by neoclassicism is Erastus Dow Palmer (1817–1904), who was born in Onondaga County, New York. His formal education terminated when he was about twelve, and he began to acquire the skills of carpentry. After a series of odd jobs in the western part of the state he got married and settled in Utica (about 1840), where Palmer himself built the house on Genessee Street in which he and his wife were to live. In the Utica city directories of 1844 to 1847 Palmer is listed as a patternmaker; that is, he carved the wooden patterns that the local industries used to make the molds for their products. Up to this point Palmer's life had been very much like that of any other rural craftsman or mechanic of the day, with hardly any cognizance of the art of sculpture which was then growing into a major form of expression in New York City, Boston, Washington, or elsewhere in America, to say nothing of the activities of our earliest expatriates who journeyed to Florence and Rome.

Palmer's career as a sculptor began around 1845. One day he chanced to see a cameo portrait, and soon afterward attempted a similar portrait of his wife. He showed the result to a local connoisseur of the fine arts, whose high praise and encouragement reportedly brought tears to Palmer's eyes. Although he moved to Albany in the mid-1840's, his name continued to appear in the Utica directory; but in 1848 and 1849 he was listed as a *conchiglia* (Italian for "shell") artist rather than as a patternmaker. During the first two years in his new profession, he is said to have executed some two hundred little cameo portraits; collections of these are located in Utica and Albany. The New-York Historical Society owns a plaster example ($1\frac{7}{8}$" by $1\frac{3}{8}$") of an 1846 profile of Horatio Seymour, who may well have been the man who first encouraged Palmer to go into this type of work. The cameo, aside from the toga about the chest, shows no hint of neoclassicism, and although the hair is rather stylized and the folds of the drapery monotonous, the face is sensitively modeled. Even from this early period it is clear that Palmer's great teacher was to be nature rather than any borrowed or imported style.

Henry Tuckerman, in his *Book of the Artists*, described Palmer's cameos in the following manner:

The cutting is bold, distinct, unevasive; a masterly air is evident at a glance, and it seems marvelous that a hand, previously habituated to the coarser efforts of the joiner, could, in so brief a space, acquire facility in the most delicate workmanship.

But when the finely detailed work of carving small profiles in shell began to affect the sculptor's eyesight, he was forced to give it up. Converting what at first appeared to be a tragedy into a blessing, he turned to modeling in clay on a larger scale; his first effort, about the year 1848, was a bust of one of his daughters. To this portrait the sculptor gave the name "Infant Ceres," implying a quasi affiliation with ancient mythology. Palmer probably felt that a nominal association with neoclassicism was permissible so long as it went no further, for the "Infant Ceres" is classical in name only; its style has absolutely nothing to do with neoclassicism. Unlike Hiram Powers, who created a whole line of idealized mythological busts, Palmer chose to remain close to nature, at one time writing that "every face and figure is but a type of its own ideal." It was probably this portrait of his daughter as Ceres that was shown under the title "Bust of a Child" in the National Academy of Design exhibition in 1851, and from this date interest in the gifted sculptor from upstate New York began to grow.

Palmer, however, seems always to have been quite content in Albany, with no desire to move to the metropolitan center of artistic activity. The people of Albany gave him commissions, so that he could earn a decent living, and one critic wrote that

Albany has done well by Palmer, and he is crowded with orders both for portrait busts and ideal works. His ideal busts are exceedingly beautiful, yet without ever departing from individuality, or introducing any of the insipid idealities which have so much pestered and injured some modern sculptors. His ideas and feelings have been derived directly and entirely from nature, without any reference to the antique, and so have an originality and freshness which are very forcible and . . . very rare.

This favorable notice by W. J. Stillman, one of the editors of *The Crayon*, was published in that journal in 1855 in a commentary on Palmer's work. Such praise increased the sculptor's fame, and he was soon asked to exhibit his work in New York City so that those who took an interest in the art produced by their countrymen could have the opportunity of seeing it. The request was signed by twenty prominent citizens and artists, among them former Governor Hamilton Fish, the landscape painter Frederic E. Church, and poet William Cullen Bryant. Palmer cordially agreed, and in 1856 a dozen of his works were put on display in the hall of the Church of the Divine Unity on Broadway. The exhibition included the following busts: "Infant Ceres," "Infant Flora" (Fig. 5.6), "Resignation," "Spring," and "Mr. Erastus Corning." There were two medallions: "Innocence" and "A Dream of the Spirit's Flight"; an alto-relief of a head of Sappho and two bas-reliefs representing Night and Morning; and statues entitled "The Sleeping Peri" and "Indian Girl." When one recalls that Palmer had been engaged in such sculpture for only seven or eight years, it seems a rather astonishing display as to both quantity and quality. As an exhibition of collected works by one sculptor, it was second only to the one-man show given Thomas Crawford at the Boston Athenaeum in 1844.

In 1856 Powers was still working in Florence; Crawford was in the final months of his career, and Greenough had been dead four years; in New York City, Henry Kirke Brown had established his fame that very year with his equestrian "Washington"; and in the nation's capital Clark Mills' reputation rested on his statue of Jackson riding a rearing mount. The exhibition of his works at the Church of the Divine Unity placed Erastus Dow Palmer among the leading sculptors of America, where he was to remain for another two decades. Critics, artists, and ordinary visitors to the exhibition were enthusiastic in their praise of his work, as if they were pleased to find good work that was so wholesomely American, drawing its vitality directly from nature instead of from ancient art.

Several pieces were singled out for special commendation, but the one that excited the greatest interest was the statue "Indian Girl," or "The Dawn of Christianity" (Fig. 5.5). This was all the more impressive because it was the sculptor's first attempt at the full-length, seminude figure, and the numerous critics who reviewed the exhibition pronounced it a great success—both as a work of art and the story it told. Tuckerman waxed sentimental about the statue's implied story:

An aboriginal maiden is supposed to be wandering in the forest in search of stray feathers to decorate her person, when she discovers one of the little crosses placed here and there in the wilderness, by the early missionaries, as symbols of the faith to which they endeavored to convert the savage tribes. As she looks upon the hallowed emblem, the divine story of Jesus recurs to her mind, and awakens emotions of awe and tenderness; the religious sentiment thus accidently aroused, lures her into a reverie; the crucifix is held before her downcast eyes in the palm of her hand. It is a single figure, but it tells a comprehensive story—the dawn of Christianity upon savage life—the first glimmer of divine truth upon an untamed and ignorant, but thoroughly human soul.   [*Book of the Artists*]

In the eyes of many of Palmer's contemporaries, the highest form of art was one that revealed a moral in the story it told, as with Hiram Powers' "Greek Slave." In the mid-19th century, men like Tuckerman found pleasure in this literary and philosophical content, and women professed to enjoy a state of ecstasy, which may be likened to a kind of swooning, as they became thoroughly rapt in the story. As an expression of the times the "Indian Girl" was an image of the noble savage who was converted to the true faith, a triumph of Christianity and goodness in the wilderness. Palmer was putting into his first marble statue what James Fenimore Cooper had earlier put into words and Thomas Cole had painted on canvas. Here was an American artist treating an American subject in an American style, and the critics and public loved everything about it.

The critics took particular delight in both the fine sculpturesque form and excellent craftsmanship. Palmer was praised for the composition of folds in the drapery, for the treatment of the hair, for the beauty of the hands. The editor of *Harper's Monthly* (1857, p. 414) wrote on this point:

Now, as you look more curiously and closely, you will discover the characteristic of modern art—its realism—leading to exact detail, and the skill which gives superiority to the American genius. The hand, for instance, is a real hand. . . . His sculpture aims to imitate nature as far as the character of marble will allow. He is not to be satisfied with a hint or a representation. He must have the hand as Nature would have made it, had Nature fashioned Indian girls of marble.

Tuckerman published his *Book of the Artists* about a decade after Palmer's exhibition at the Church of the Divine Unity. Of especial interest is his comment that such a figure, the best executed in this country, could not have been created without the benefit of "a living model of such admirable proportions." By 1855 it was an accepted practice for the artist to work from the live nude model in his studio.

Palmer himself had known no other master than nature, and at the same time (1855) he was creating his "Indian Girl" in Albany he was also writing an essay, entitled "Philosophy of the Ideal," in which he set forth his belief in nature as the only great teacher for an artist. In fact, he actually disliked art schools because they tended to pass on to the young student the mannerisms of the instructor's style or of a particular style of art, such as that of the ancient Greeks. To him, the most beautiful thing in all nature was the human figure—endowed with a beauty not only in its "structures, forms, colors, and motions," but also in its possession of "an immortal soul." So although fidelity to nature was an important part of Palmer's art and much admired by his followers, he nevertheless maintained that it was not an end in itself. Nature was a teacher not a god, and Palmer clearly set forth this principle in his essay, which was published in *The Crayon* (1856), pp. 18–20:

The mission of the sculptor's art, is not to imitate forms alone, but through them to reveal the purest and best of our nature. And no work in sculpture, however well wrought out physically, results in excellence, unless it rests upon, and is sustained by the dignity of a moral or intellectual intention.

His own ideal thus dictates that the sculptor must seek the soul rather than mere representation of matter. But though he sought an ideal characterization, it was an ideal founded on naturalism rather than on neoclassicism or any other contrived style.

Palmer firmly held to this creed in his portraiture, as well as in his ideal works, and wrote that "the purest and best of our nature is evinced in portraiture, *not* by *copying* the forms, but by reaching after something higher—a spiritual modification of them." His ideal works were, however, so popular—because the sentiments he expressed in them were perfectly attuned to the aesthetic, literary, and philosophic mood of his day—that he did not have to rely on portraiture for a livelihood.

With the Divine Unity exhibition, Palmer's reputation was firmly established among the artists of the day, and the public was drawn to his work by a subject matter that was truly American, as well as by a naturalism and craftsmanship they could appreciate. Boston, too, wanted a look at the work of this newly discovered native-born and self-trained sculptor, and Edward Everett, Longfellow, Agassiz, and Lowell wrote to ask that the exhibition be sent to New England. From this point on, Palmer was a nationally known sculptor, even though he continued to reside and work in Albany.

Most of the early part of 1857 he spent doing a model for the pediment of the new House wing of the United States Capitol building. In all there were fifteen figures that acted out a tableau of the landing of the Pilgrims at Plymouth in 1620. Evidently the success he had experienced with "Indian Girl" encouraged him to tackle this more ambitious project. The New York City exhibition had won him a powerful lobby of admirers and apparently there was some sort of verbal commitment to Palmer, for he launched into the project with his usual enthusiasm and industry, believing that the commission was more or less his. His figures, 15 inches high, represented that first moment of prayer when the group had landed after the long journey aboard the *Mayflower*. In the center was Elder Brewster; at his side were Miles and Rose Standish, along with a young mother and her children and a stalwart young man in Puritan dress who held an ax. A few others joined this central group, which was to be executed in individual figures of colossal size. At one low angle was an Indian crouching behind a rock, motioning for his dog to be silent; at the other angle two wolves observed the scene; in bas-relief there were craggy rocks and barren trees.

The Albany *Journal* (April 10, 1857) published a description of the model, and the writer of the article proclaimed that America could take great pride in this work, depicting a subject from the nation's own history and executed by one of her own artists, and pointed out that as a work of art, it "is not disfigured by any of the so-called 'classical' adjuncts often resorted to by modern sculpture." During the summer of 1857, other friends of the sculptor wrote to President Buchanan to take action and award the commission to Palmer. But Buchanan turned the matter over to Secretary of War John B. Floyd, who rejected the model on the grounds that it represented an event of local interest and importance and was not truly a national subject.

Palmer had no further dealings with the United States government as a patron. By November he had started on what has become his most famous statue, the "White Captive" (Fig. 5.7), now in the Metropolitan Museum of Art. Several years earlier the "Greek Slave" had fought the battle of the nude figure against the ignorance and prudery in America. The success of the "Indian Girl" had encouraged Palmer to attempt a completely nude figure, but the public had not yet acquired sophistication sufficient to be able to accept the nude for its beauty alone. As the Reverend Orville Dewey had said in praise of Powers' celebrated work, there ought to be some reason for nudity, clearly implying a criticism of ancient art for its blatant sensuality.

While Palmer worked in his studio, his wife frequently read aloud the stories of James Fenimore Cooper or Sir Walter Scott. And as he began to form the statue, first in his mind and then in clay, he must have visualized one of the numerous incidents of a white girl being kidnapped from a frontier homestead by Indians. In giving marmorean form to a familiar theme, he invited a sentimental, pathos-drenched agonizing over the details. Sentimentalists like Henry Tuckerman supplied their own variations. But in fairness to Palmer it should be understood that though there was considerable emphasis on the "literary" quality of one of his ideal figures, he was still an artist and very much concerned with an artistic or formal quality. He had consciously chosen an American subject for representation, and one that might offer the opportunity of modeling the nude figure; but Palmer should not be held responsible for the gush of melodramatic prose that in the late 1850's and 1860's spewed forth about the statue, even though he may have welcomed it as a sign of the statue's success. An example of such literature is a story published in the January 1860 issue of the *Atlantic Monthly*, more than two years after Palmer had begun modeling the figure. Entitled "Palmer's 'White Captive,'" it begins, "Once upon a time. . . ." It is worth quoting a fairly lengthy passage from it to establish the flavor of the Romantic mood that certain critics created to go with the statue.

Once upon a time a maiden dwelt with her father,—they two, and no more,—in a rude log-cabin on the skirts of a grand Western forest,—majestic mountains behind them, and the broad, free prairie in front.

Cut off from all Christian companionship and the informing influences of civilized arts, all their news was of red men and of game, their entertainments the ever-varying moods of Nature, their labors of the rudest, their dangers familiar, their solacements simple and solitary. Alone the sturdy hunter beat the woods all day, on the track of panthers, bears, and deer; alone, all day, his pretty daughter kept the house against perils without and despondency within,—the gun and the broom alike familiar to her hand.

. . . Once, when the hunter was belated on his path, and sudden midnight had caught him beyond the mountain, far from the rest of his hearth and the song of his darling, came the red Pawnees, a treacherous crew,—doubly godless because ungrateful, who had broken the hunter's bread and slept on the hunter's blanket,—and laid waste his hearth, and stole away his very heart. For they dragged her many a fearful mile of darkness and distraction, through the black woods, and over the foreboding river, and into the grim recesses of the rocks; and there they stripped her naked, and bound her to a stake, as the day was breaking. But the Christian heart was within her, and the Christian soul upheld her, and the Christian's God was by her side; and so she stood, and waited, and was brave.

Horror possesses her, but indignation also; she is terrified, but brave; she shrinks, but she repels; and while all her beautiful body trembles and retreats, her countenance confronts her captors, and her steady gaze forbids them. "Touch me not!" she says, with every shuddering limb and every tensely-braced muscle, with lineaments all eloquent with imperious disgust,—"Touch me not."

Among her thronged emotions we look in vain for shame. Her nakedness is a coarse chance of her overwhelming situation, for which she is no more concerned than for her galled wrists or her dishevelled hair. What is it to such a queen as she, that the eyes of grinning brutes are blessed by her perfect beauties?

This is only part of the piece devoted to the plight of the "White Captive." Numerous other accounts were published elsewhere; for the most part they dwelt on the savage treachery and on the triumph of a chaste Christian soul. Palmer's statue was the success it was mainly because it inspired the spectators to that sort of melodramatic sentimentality in which they wallowed happily. They were pleased too that this was an American young woman rather than a classical ideal with which they could not identify. The same author who wrote the *Atlantic Monthly* story stated, ". . . it is American; our women may look upon it, and say, 'She is one of us,' with more satisfaction than the Greek women could have derived from the Venus de' Medici, with its insignificant head and its impossible spine." Although some criticized the "White Captive" because they felt the head was too large or the breasts too small or the hips too broad, and others continued the old harangue about the shameful nudity and the return of pagan idols sinfully revealing naked flesh, the statue was for the most part praised as a truly American type of ideal figure. It was bought by one of the leading citizens of New York, Hamilton Fish, who proudly placed it in his home in Stuyvesant Square.

The next decade saw a steady if unspectacular flow of sculpture from Palmer's studio in Albany. Not for many years was any of his work to attract the national attention that his "Indian Girl" and "White Captive" had received. In the Walters Gallery in Baltimore there is a marble statue by Palmer, called "First Grief," or "First Disappointment" (1861); it is of a young girl of eight or ten, holding an empty bird's nest; she wears a simple dress and is barefooted. On her face is an expression of pensive disappointment, and a puffiness about her eyes tells of her sorrow. Once again the figure is one based on naturalism rather than neoclassicism. Moreover, the sculptor has again employed considerable economy in his image, reducing the number of details to the barest essentials. As in the "Indian Girl" and the "White Captive," simplicity is characteristic of Palmer's style.

The relief "Peace in Bondage," a three-quarter-length, winged nude female bound to a tree, reflected the troubled times of the Civil War. By this time (1863) the sculptor had begun to attract attention abroad; and even Hiram Powers, upon seeing a photograph of some of Palmer's work, is reported to have said that Palmer need never travel to Italy. A review of his sculpture (from photographs), by Dr. Alfred Woltman, appeared in the Berlin *Nazional Zeitung* (November 26, 1865), and "Peace in Bondage" received special praise as the embodiment of all the "anguish and bitterness of the civil strife that has distracted [the sculptor's] native land." A number of other works date from these war years, including "Angel of the Sepulchre," which Palmer made in 1865 for the grave of General Robert Lenox at Albany Rural Cemetery. A stern-faced, heroic figure sits on the stone that had been rolled away from Christ's grave and looks directly at the observer as if about to accost him. Again thoroughly American, the statue drew some criticism for lacking the usual "angelic" quality: Contrary to contemporary fashion, Palmer made his angel male instead of female.

The large number of ideal works Palmer created during the 1850's and 1860's appears all the more impressive considering that many sculptors of the period could hardly obtain enough portrait commissions to keep them going. Palmer seems to have made no special effort to engage in portraiture, and those that he did were not among his great successes. Though his career had begun with portraiture—that is, with the small cameo likenesses—the twelve pieces he selected to exhibit at the Church of the Divine Unity in New York in 1856 included only one portrait bust, that of Erastus Corning (1855). Late in 1857 he was working on a bust of Moses Taylor, which he intended to exhibit at the Art Exposition in Washington. Occasional portraits were done between work on the large ideal statues or the numerous ideal bas-reliefs; for example, in 1860 he modeled the likeness of the daughter of George B. Warren and wrote Warren that nothing he had done surpassed it. Of the bust of Henry Burden (1862), Lorado Taft wrote that it was "a Calhoun-like head with long hair swept back in waving masses and falling below the ears," and called it "animated, kindly and responsive." The New-York Historical Society owns a marble bust of Washington Irving, which is signed and dated 1865, or six years after the death of the author. Tuckerman tells us that Palmer frequently worked from photographs in his portraits, which is known from other instances where his subject was deceased. The portrait of Irving is not extremely naturalistic or romantically Byronic, or heroic; it is quiet, gentle, unassuming. Irving is shown in casual dress, and it is altogether an intimate, informal portrait. What it lacks in impressive dignity it more than makes up for in genuine warmth.

The next major event in Palmer's life was a trip to Europe in 1873, made in connection with a commission he received from the state of New York. This was for a statue of Robert Livingston, Chancellor of New York from 1777 to 1801, that was destined for Statuary Hall in the Capitol. At the age of fifty-six Palmer's style was firmly set, and he did not go abroad with the idea of altering it. After traveling awhile, he took a studio in Paris and, in the following year, modeled his statue of the Chancellor. It is interesting that he choose to work in Paris rather than Rome or Florence, for the French capital and its schools were beginning to attract our most gifted young sculptors—such as Augustus Saint-Gaudens, who had been there from 1867 to 1870. Livingston wears a gown of state over a colonial-type waistcoat, with ruffles at the neck and wrists. In his right hand he holds a scroll; with the left he draws the great robe around him. His expression is pensive and his mood one of profound contemplation. Palmer successfully captured the greatness of the man (Fig. 5.8), far more than did most of the sculptors whose portrait statues stand near his in the Capitol. The statue of Livingston, though slightly larger than life, is nearly dwarfed by surrounding giants in marble and bronze, but few can approach it in quality. Palmer could not have realized that the other statues would be of heroic size, because his was among the first to stand there. For many of the other statues, their inadequacies become all the more obvious as they increase in size, whereas the one of Livingston wears well. Palmer preferred a quiet understatement here, just as he did in his "Washington Irving." Finished in 1874, the statue was cast in Paris, then shipped to Washington. It again drew national attention to the sculptor when it was displayed at the Philadelphia Centennial of 1876, where it received one of the first-class awards for sculpture.

Palmer was approaching his sixtieth year when he returned from France. He continued to work in his Albany studio throughout the rest of the century, but his greatest period of creativity had passed. Meanwhile, other men with other ideas about art were beginning to assert themselves, and Palmer slipped quietly into the background of the sculptural scene. His contribution to art in America, particularly sculpture, had been significant. Like Henry Kirke Brown, he had shown that the fine art of sculpture could be carried on at home. He had offered an alternative to neoclassicism by creating an American ideal based on naturalism—a style of art that Americans had no difficulty understanding and accepting. He championed the American theme and, along with Brown and others, made it thoroughly respectable. Although his insistence upon remaining in Albany kept him aloof from the day-by-day activities of the major art circles of the country, his work still had its influence on contemporary sculpture. Erastus Dow Palmer lived a long and productive life; he died in Albany in 1904 at the age of eighty-seven.

Clark Mills was born in Onondaga County, New York, on September 1, 1815. His father died when Clark was a boy, and he was sent to live with an uncle from whom he soon ran away because of excessive harshness and cruelty. There was virtually no opportunity for a formal education once he was out on his own, and young Mills began to pick up odd jobs and work as a laborer, eventually making his way south to New Orleans. By the time he was twenty he had driven a team of horses hauling lumber, cut logs in a swamp, done chores on a farm; and he had worked as a carpenter, as a millwright, and as a superintendent in a plaster and cement mill. He was a jack-of-all-trades by 1837 when he moved to Charleston, South Carolina, where he was to remain for the next decade. There he soon learned the skills of the ornamental plasterer, his first step toward a career in sculpture.

While working as an ornamental plasterer he first tried, in the early 1840's, to take a life mask in plaster. He developed a new process that caused the sitter less discomfort than previous methods and soon had all the work he could handle. His life masks were then transformed into portrait busts, always at first in plaster. What sculpture there was in Charleston from which Mills could have learned is difficult to determine. There was Joseph Wilton's marble statue of Pitt in the yard of the Orphan House, and no doubt Mills knew some of the busts by Cogdell and Coffee and such church wall monuments as the Smith memorial by Chantrey. But there was virtually no one to whom he could turn for instruction in the techniques of modeling. What he learned he acquired from the life mask itself, and this established his style as one strongly dependent upon naturalism.

In 1845 he attempted his first work in stone, a portrait bust of John C. Calhoun, the city's most distinguished citizen and at that time Secretary of State under President Tyler. The bust was modeled mainly from memory with the assistance of other portraits. Unlike Frazee, Clevenger, and other "Yankee stonecutters" who had gained a proficiency in carving stone through several years in the trade, Mills addressed the white stone block for the first time. His earlier work as a carpenter and cabinetmaker had given him considerable experience with the mallet and chisel, but still the problems of working in marble were new to him. So he launched into the project and worked out his own methods as he went along. The result, which is now owned by the city of Charleston, was a rather gaunt Calhoun with the stark expression of a man who was in his last days of fighting for the cause of the South. There is a certain primitive incisiveness about it that one might well expect from an initial effort in stone. But his fellow townsmen were extremely pleased with the portrait by their own artist-in-residence, and presented him with a gold medal with the following inscription: "To Clark Mills as a mark of respect for his genius for sculpture in his bust of the favorite son of Carolina, John C. Calhoun, and as an incentive to further exertions, this medal is presented by the City Council of Charleston." A bronze version of Mills' portrait of Calhoun is in the Corcoran Gallery of Art.

There are in Charleston several other portrait busts attributed to Mills, most of them made from life masks, that date from the 1840's: those of Benjamin Simons, Dr. Joseph Johnson, Dr. Mitchell King, George McDuffie, James L. Petigru, and Franklin Elmore. These portraits are indeed more life masks than sculptured portraits, and clearly reveal that Mills did not have an instinctive feeling for sculpturesque form. They often lack subtlety in modeling and characterization of the personality as well. But they pleased those for whom they were made, and Mills' reputation soon extended to the state capital. He was preparing for a trip to Italy to improve his art when he was invited to Columbia by John Preston, one of the Preston brothers who had assisted Hiram Powers on his way to Florence. While there he executed several busts of the Preston and Wade families. Preston urged Mills to go to Washington to see the sculpture there before going to Italy, and offered to pay his expenses plus the price of the busts of his friends Daniel Webster and John J. Crittenden.

On his way north in 1848 Mills stopped briefly at Richmond where he saw Houdon's "Washington." He was quite impressed by the Frenchman's work, which was the second life-size statue he had ever seen. The sculpture he saw at the Capitol in Washington, with the exception of Greenough's colossus, was also the work of foreign artists. Up to this time neither Congress nor Captain Meigs had felt that American sculptors were capable of creating monumental sculpture, and on the one occasion they had allowed one of their countrymen to make the attempt, the result was less than completely satisfactory. Yet they all yearned for an American art and one that was somehow a part of their way of life. At the time Mills came to Washington a new era was dawning and major sculpture commissions were beginning to be given with regularity to native-born sculptors—Crawford's Senate pediment and doorway came along in the early 1850's, followed by work by Randolph Rogers, William Rinehart, and Hiram Powers.

Though Mills admired the statue of the Olympian "Washington" by Greenough, he also heard the murmurs of discontent about its "want of historical truth." Tuckerman wrote in his *Book of the Artists* that Mills "came to the conclusion while standing there [looking at Greenough's "Washington"] that, should he ever have an order for a statue, the world should find fault for his giving too much truth, and not for the want of it."

Mills at this point had done scarcely more than a score of plaster busts, most of which were from life masks; only one of these he had put into stone. He had never done anything so ambitious as a full-length figure. These facts make all the more remarkable Mills' next project: the bronze equestrian statue of Andrew Jackson that now stands in Lafayette Park across from the White House (Fig. 5.10).

One evening quite by chance Mills met the Honorable Cave Johnson, who was then Postmaster General and also the chairman of the Jackson Memorial Committee. As the two conversed Johnson learned that Mills was a sculptor and that he was about to depart for Europe. Johnson suggested that Mills submit a design for the Jackson Memorial. Mills at first declined, realizing full well the limitations of his work. Upon reflection, however, he decided to accept the enormous and exciting challenge, and after several months he completed a model. The gentlemen of the committee, delighted with the spirited action of the group and the bold new composition, approved it, and the nation's first equestrian statue was begun.

The history of the equestrian statue in America goes back to 1770 when Joseph Wilton's leaden image of George III was erected in New York City, but this statue was destroyed during the Revolution. In 1783 Congress voted to erect an equestrian monument to George Washington, and when Jefferson and Franklin were negotiating with Houdon two years later in Paris, they dangled before him the possibility of that commission to lure him to America to make the preparatory studies for the Richmond figure; but nothing came of the equestrian statue. Thereafter, not much is heard of any such project in America until 1810, when Maximilian Godefroy proposed to include an equestrian Washington within the opening of a triumphal arch in a monument to be erected in Baltimore; the Peale Museum in that city possesses a sketch of that design. The next year (1811) John Eckstein exhibited his clay model of an equestrian Washington at the Pennsylvania Academy; but once more nothing came of his or Godefroy's proposal, and the subject was dropped for more than a decade. Then Enrico Causici, working in New York City, produced his full-scale plaster statue of Washington on horseback, which he hoped the city would commission. The sculptor's hopes were, however, not realized and his model, which stood in City Hall park, eventually disappeared, probably destroyed by the elements. In 1834 a joint Library of Congress committee voted appropriations for an equestrian statue; Nicholas Gevelot submitted a model to them the following year, but the committee turned it down. Some years later, in 1841, Robert Ball Hughes had hopes of receiving a commission from Philadelphia, only to be disappointed when hard times forced the abandonment of the project. Meanwhile Horace Kneeland, an unknown portrait sculptor of New York City, had his plaster statuette of an equestrian statue awarded as a prize in 1843 by the Art Union. By this time Thomas Crawford was working on an equestrian model—as well as on Congress to award him the commission for it—and when in 1845 Luigi Persico petitioned Congress for the assignment and asked an enormous fee, Crawford renewed his efforts by showing his model to a number of influential Congressmen. Crawford did not receive the commission from the federal government, however, and returned to Italy. But before long—although two years after Mills began work on his statue—Crawford was awarded the Richmond commission. Also, by 1851 Horatio Greenough had conceived an equestrian statue of Washington for New York City; it was ultimately wrought by Henry Kirke Brown and unveiled a few months after the dedication of Mills' statue of Jackson. Early in the 1850's, therefore, three American sculptors were working on equestrian statues—Mills on Jackson for Washington, D.C., and Brown and Crawford on images of George Washington for New York and Richmond respectively. Clark Mills had a slight edge in time; in addition, unlike Crawford and Brown, he cast his statue in his own foundry, often surmounting tremendous obstacles in the process. Finally, Thomas Ball had begun his statue of George Washington for Boston by the end of the 1850's, although it was not unveiled until 1869.

The chief tour de force of Mills' statue of Jackson is the rearing horse. In the mind of the artist, as well as his contemporaries, Jackson was a man of action, which called for an over-all presence in the statue that was far different from the one of great dignity and calm that Brown was to employ in his Union Square statue of Washington. Mills represented Jackson in military uniform to commemorate his famous victory at New Orleans. And the portrayal of Jackson as a man of action demanded a spirited rearing horse. The great problem facing Mills—how to support and balance the entire weight of horse and man on the slender hind legs of the animal—had defeated no less an artistic genius than Leonardo da Vinci in his abortive attempt at a Sforza monument for Milan in the early 16th century. Pietro Tacca had made an early effort at a Baroque equestrian statue about 1635 in his "Philip IV" in the Plaza del Oriente in Madrid. Bernini, too, had struggled with the problem of the rearing horse. His "Constantine" in St. Peter's, Rome, of 1654, circumvents the difficulty by being attached to the back wall of the niche, thus removing the weight from the hind legs; and his designs for the equestrian statue of Louis XIV at Versailles, later transformed into a conventional Marcus Aurelius type, had a stone support in full view under the belly of the horse. Falconet's solution, in his statue of Peter the Great at St. Petersburg (c. 1770), was to create a third support in the horse's tail, which was attached to a serpent, which in turn was attached to the base; this, of course, was too obviously contrived and unnatural.

Clark Mills may have known some of these early examples through engravings, but none of them offered a completely acceptable solution. Mills' statue is a credit to his ability as an engineer, and his accomplishment may be viewed as part of that general spirit of inventiveness, seeking new answers to old problems, which was then rampant in America. He designed his horse and rider so that the maximum weight stood over the hind hooves, with the rump of the horse outweighing its foreparts. That this balance was remarkable to the sculptor's contemporaries is seen in an article published in the Charleston (South Carolina) *Courier* in May 1850:

Your first question is, how, if he is not really a live horse, does he stand in that position? But Mills will go in front and throw his entire weight (156 pounds) on his fore feet, and still he stands. The center of gravity being so directly thrown over the hind feet.

From the same source we also learn that by the spring of 1850 the model had been completed.

Henry Kirke Brown visited Mills' studio one day and described the experience in a letter to his wife:

After dinner I called on Mr. Mills, native self-made sculptor: who has received twelve thousand dollars from Congress for modeling and casting in bronze the equestrian statue of Gen. Jackson. Uncle Sam provides the metal . . . .

We entered a room with one window in it and two doors, one to the main studio and one to the street. In this little room were two busts, old boots, a few books, fever and ague medicines, a hat full of eggs, his sketches for the great work, and a variety of other objects. He left a moment to arrange the light in the main studio, then he showed me in and "won an unco sight," this immense horse standing upon its hind legs balancing himself with an enormous tail which could not contain less than a barrel of plaster, but balance the thing did . . . . He then pointed out by measurement wherein the Parthenon marbles are wrong and wherein his is right. I could not but help wondering how difficult it was to measure soul by square and rule . . . . My eyes wandered around the room. I saw hanging up on the walls casts from dissections of various parts of horses like beef to dry. The tools with which he works, as you must know he models in plaster, not clay, consisted of two deck scrapers, one with and one without teeth, a hatchet and hand saw, masons hods and trowels . . . . I then, like one enchanted, followed him into the back yard, to the stable where he kept his horse from which he had modeled. Then we returned into the large studio. There I saw the boots of the old Hero Jackson. These were partly chopped out in plaster, . . . At the feet of these boots, (so to speak) lay the half formed head of the General over which the boots seemed to be enjoying a temporary triumph, and the body too stood aloof from the other members of the same family . . . . You must understand that these parts are roughed out in plaster and finished separately and are then to meet on their proper footing, and be joined, not again to be sundered.

Another triumph of Mills' statue is the successful manner in which he united horse and rider—a problem that had also plagued many of his predecessors. The stern and stoic-faced Jackson seems very much at home in the saddle, and the whole impression is that he and his spirited mount belong together; the wildness and excitement of the animal offers a foil to the cool confidence of the man. The sculptor achieved that naturalism to which he had earlier sworn allegiance as he stood before Greenough's "Washington," and yet he managed to subordinate the details to the over-all effect. The statue may appear somewhat stiff and even primitive to 20th-century eyes, but the members of the Jackson Monument Committee were delighted. Lorado Taft remarked that the committee "had expected something original and American, and they got it." From both engineering and aesthetic standpoints, the design was pronounced a success, and by the summer of 1850 Mills was ready to undertake the tremendous task of casting the group.

Mills built his own foundry in Washington and awaited the arrival of the bronze, which was to be furnished by Congress. The bronze, obtained from the old cannon that General Jackson had captured at the battle of New Orleans, was nine months in getting to the sculptor. Then followed a year and more of extremely hard work and disappointment, for not only did Mills' crane break and his furnace burst, but also the horse itself had to be recast six times before a satisfactory cast was achieved. The statue was completed late in 1852, and on January 8, 1853, it was unveiled.

There was great excitement in Washington as the dedication day approached. Plans were made for a parade from City Hall to the speakers' stand in Lafayette Park and tickets were sold for the special banquet to be held at Jackson Hall on the evening of the unveiling. The day itself marked the thirty-eighth anniversary of the battle of New Orleans. To the music of military bands and the cheering of thousands along the way the parade moved down Pennsylvania Avenue. President Fillmore was there, along with his cabinet. Then came the justices of the Supreme Court, followed by members of the Senate and House of Representatives. The entourage made its way to Lafayette Park, where Stephen Douglas of Illinois delivered an oration on Jackson the man and victorious general of New Orleans. The dramatic moment of the unveiling was described in the January 9 issue of the Washington *Daily Union:*

When the orator had concluded, amidst the shouts of the thousands who surrounded him, Clark Mills, esq., was intoduced. He had no words to express his feelings, and in lieu of words he pointed to the veiled statue; the veil was instantly withdrawn and Jackson on his steed, as if in full action, full of life and energy was revealed. That was his speech and none could have been more appropriate . . . . the scene was most picturesque . . . . At least twenty thousand people occupied the square and the neighboring house-tops. The band played a salute, and Taylor's battery answered with the guns which had done such good service against the enemies of the country.

A grateful Congress voted the sculptor $20,000, in addition to the $12,000 originally stipulated in the contract. Moreover, within three weeks of the unveiling

Congress appropriated $50,000 for "a colossal equestrian statue of Washington," and the commission was given to Mills. To execute this and other commissions, Mills needed a larger studio and foundry, which he soon began building on Bladensburg Road, three miles outside the city.

In the meantime, in 1853 Horatio Greenough's "Rescue" arrived from Italy. Greenough having died the preceding year, Clark Mills was hired to superintend the erection of the several pieces of the group, which included the pioneer struggling with the Indian, the pioneer's wife and child, and the nonchalant dog. There was no key to guide him in the arrangement, for Greenough himself had fully expected to supervise the task, and his intended plan had disappeared with his death. Mills was criticized by Greenough's friends for making a botch of the composition, but it is doubtful if the original arrangement could have very much improved matters.

Work progressed on the new studio and foundry, and by 1855 it was producing small bronze replicas of the Jackson monument; one of these is now in the collection of the New-York Historical Society. The statuette is 24 inches high and is inscribed on the base, "Patented May 15, 1855"; plaster statuettes are also in the collections of the Maryland Historical Society and in the Hall of History in Raleigh, North Carolina. It may have been about this time, or possibly a few years earlier, that Mills produced the marble portrait bust of John Walker Maury, which is now in the Corcoran Gallery in Washington. The same institution owns a bronze bust of Washington by Mills, as well as a statuette of Mills' mother. In addition to the congressional commission for a bronze equestrian Washington, the cities of New Orleans and Nashville each ordered a full-size replica of the Jackson statue. The one for New Orleans was finished and set in place in Jackson Square by early 1856.

Little is known of Mills' private life. By his first wife he had two sons, Theodore (1839–1916) and Theophilus (born c. 1842), both of whom were listed as sculptors in the 1860 census in Washington; they were assistants to their father, and Theodore gained a reputation as a modeler of Indian groups. In 1861 Mills married a second time in Baltimore.

There was indeed a promising future ahead for the runaway farmboy and laborer who had managed to turn his inventive mind and his skill with his hands to so much advantage. But there was adversity, too. A gale destroyed his new studio on Bladensburg Road, and before it was rebuilt the new foundry was consumed by fire. It was imperative that both be rebuilt at once, as several large and lucrative commissions were awaiting work. The first was the equestrian "Washington," which was set up in Washington Circle on February 22, 1860, seven years after the commission had been awarded. Washington wears his military uniform; he holds a sword in his right hand, and with his left he restrains his spirited horse. He is represented erect, determined, and unflinching while the horse prances with three feet on the ground, thus eliminating the problem Mills had encountered in the Jackson group. But all in all, the Washington statue lacks the heroic quality and the dynamics of its predecessor.

Within a few months of the unveiling of the equestrian "Washington," the sculptor's foundry was making preparations to cast Crawford's gigantic "Freedom," which was to go atop the new dome being erected over the Capitol by Thomas U. Walter. There was a controversy over Mills being awarded the commission to cast Crawford's figure, but he seems to have had strong support in high places, and the grumblings of other sculptors were of no avail. He had asked $25,000 for the task, but another arrangement was worked out whereby the government paid a rental fee for the use of his foundry, supplied the bronze and the workmen, and paid Mills a salary. The colossus was cast in five parts, and work progressed on it until May 17, 1861, when Captain Meigs ordered the job halted because of the outbreak of the Civil War. But casting was soon resumed in spite of the national calamity, and on November 11, 1862, Thomas U. Walter noted in his annual report that "the statue of Freedom . . . is completed, and removed to the grounds east of the Capitol, where it has been placed on a temporary pedestal, in order that the public may have an opportunity to examine it before it is raised to its destined position." It was not until a year later that the five pieces were completely in place high above the capital city. As the final section was lifted to its lofty perch by a steam-powered hoisting machine, shortly after noon on December 2, 1863, a thirty-five-cannon salute was fired from Capitol Hill; this was answered by rounds fired from the twelve forts that surrounded the city. When the last piece was secured in place the American flag was unfurled.

It was probably about 1865 that Mills modeled the portrait bust of Daniel J. MacGowan, for he gave a plaster replica of it in 1866 to the New-York Historical Society (Fig. 5.9). But sources of Mills' life and work are strangely silent about his career after the Civil War. There is the shadow of a scandal that hovers over his career at this time; apparently he was using bronze that was inferior to what had been specified. This may have been the reason for the abrupt withdrawal of federal patronage.

In the late 1870's Mills produced the replica of the equestrian "Jackson" for Nashville, Tennessee, for which he was paid handsomely; the statue was erected in 1880. There is also a rather mysterious and colossal monument to Lincoln (described in an 1881 issue of the *American Art Review*), that was to be several stories high and include thirty-six monumental statues, among them six equestrian groups:

On the first story will stand figures emblematic of the war and its results, with historic bas-reliefs between them; next above these the standing figures of Lincoln's cabinet and of other prominent supporters of the cause of freedom; still higher up, the statues of Liberty, Justice and Time are to find a place, and the whole is to be crowned by the seated figure of President Lincoln.

By 1881, some $100,000 had evidently been contributed toward the erection of the monument. Moreover, at least one figure—that of Chief Justice Chase—was actually cast in bronze at Mills' foundry. But no further trace of the project has come to light. It was discontinued when the sculptor died two years later, on January 12, 1883.

In truth, Mills was a greater engineer than he was a sculptor. He deserves a special place in this survey for several reasons, but none of them is based primarily on aesthetic grounds or on the value of any piece as a work of art. In the end one must conclude that his portrait busts, so often derived directly from life masks, were rather uninteresting, and his two equestrian statues have more historic than artistic importance. Moreover, a limited aesthetic sense may have been partly to blame for the faulty composition of Greenough's "Rescue." As an engineer and technician he was unsurpassed in his time in the casting of bronze; and special consideration should be given to his equestrian monument to Jackson and the brilliant solution he devised to balance the rearing horse and its rider. Nevertheless, this too was a technical problem. Although his portraits and statues possessed the naturalism he and his contemporaries cherished, they still failed to make the final step into the realm of great art. Mills made himself a good sculptor by sheer determination; but he lacked the creative imagination and sensitivity to become a really fine one.

By the 1840's and 1850's, Henry Kirke Brown, Erastus Dow Palmer, and Clark Mills demonstrated that America could produce a sculptural art on her own soil through the genius of her own native sons. Mills never went to Europe; Palmer did so only late in his career; and Brown consciously rejected what he found there and returned to spend the rest of his life in the United States. These men, moreover, did much to enthrone naturalism as the style best suited to the expression of all that America stood for; in this, they deposed the neoclassicism that had become dominant through the importation of European—primarily Italian—sculptors since the early days of the Republic. Their subject matter came from the life and history of America, from the legends about pioneers and Indians, from the great political experiment of the nation, and from the almost miraculous economic growth and expansion of the country. They proved to their contemporaries that there were men on American soil who could render images of the national heroes in a truthful manner, without recourse to some foreign historic style. This had been their quest: their search for a heroic American sculpture. If, in their zeal to provide a truly American style, they carried their devotion to naturalism too far, they nevertheless produced some remarkable monuments along the way.

[FIG. 5.1] "William Cullen Bryant," by Henry Kirke Brown (c. 1846). Marble, 26¼″ high. Courtesy, New-York Historical Society, New York City.

[FIG. 5.2] "Ruth," by Henry Kirke Brown (1845). Marble, 56″ high. Courtesy, New-York Historical Society, New York City.

[FIG. 5.3] "Nathanael Greene," by Henry Kirke Brown (1867). Marble. Statuary Hall, U.S. Capitol, Washington, D.C. Courtesy, Architect of the Capitol.

[FIG. 5.4] "George Washington," by Henry Kirke Brown (1853–56). Bronze. Courtesy, Art Commission of the City of New York.

[FIG. 5.7] "White Captive," by Erastus Dow Palmer (1857). Marble, 66″ high. Courtesy, Metropolitan Museum of Art, gift of the Hon. Hamilton Fish, 1894.

[FIG. 5.5] "Indian Girl," or "The Dawn of Christianity," by Erastus Dow Palmer (1855). Marble, 59½″ high. Courtesy, Metropolitan Museum of Art, gift of the Hon. Hamilton Fish, 1894.

[FIG. 5.6] "Infant Flora," by Erastus Dow Palmer (c. 1855). Marble. Courtesy, Walters Gallery, Baltimore.

[FIG. 5.9] "Daniel J. MacGowan," by Clark Mills (c. 1865). Plaster, 27½" high. Courtesy, New-York Historical Society, New York City.

[FIG. 5.8] "Chancellor Robert Livingston," by Erastus Dow Palmer (1874). Bronze. Statuary Hall, U.S. Capitol, Washington, D.C. Courtesy, Architect of the Capitol.

[FIG. 5.10] "Andrew Jackson," by Clark Mills (1848–53). Bronze. Lafayette Square, Washington, D.C. Courtesy, National Park Service.

6

"Dusty-White Ghosts Among Strangers of Another Generation"

BETWEEN 1830 AND THE CIVIL WAR THERE WAS A GENERATION OF SCULPTORS WHO devoted themselves almost entirely to doing marble and plaster portraits. Frequently these were of prominent statesmen or literary figures who might, with justification, be represented classically, wearing the toga. But there were also the merchants and businessmen, inventors and mechanics who commissioned busts of themselves or of their families. These pale white images so populated the land that by 1860 Nathaniel Hawthorne felt compelled to write in his *Marble Faun* the following brooding passage about the proliferation of strong likenesses of undistinguished men:

There were also several portrait busts, comprising those of two or three of the illustrious men of our own country, whom Kenyon, before he left America, had asked permission to model . . . . Other faces there were, too, of men who (if the brevity of their remembrance, after death, can be augured from their little value in life) should have been represented in snow rather than marble. Posterity will be puzzled what to do with busts like these, the concretions and petrifactions of a vain self-estimate; but will find, no doubt, that they serve to build into stone walls, or burn into quicklime, as well as if the marble had never been blocked into the guise of human heads.

And it ought to make us shiver, the idea of leaving our features to be a dusty-white ghost among strangers of another generation, who will take our nose between their thumb and fingers (as we have seen men do by Caesar's), and infallibly break it off if they can do so without detection!

But Hawthorne's low opinion of the egocentricity of the middle class' search for immortality was no hindrance to the development of portraiture in America, and throughout the century the demand for these portraits far exceeded that for large ideal works. Expressing the sentiments of most sculptors of his time, Henry Dexter wrote: "Purely ideal subjects must go begging in this country; for the present, portrait sculpture . . . is the sculptor's sole dependence." And John Albee, in his biography of Dexter, published in 1898, nicely phrased the portraitist's lament:

But portrait sculpture has this sad impediment to an artist's permanent reputation; namely, the great man of today is not the great man of tomorrow, and too often they sink into obscurity together. Marble nor bronze nor canvas can long delay the extinction of the too fond estimates of our contemporaries. And yet it is the vanity and pride of men that make possible the existence of the artist until he can free himself from their trammels and give himself wholly to ideas and beauty.

During this period an original portrait could be had for as little as $20 in plaster to as much as $1,000 in marble. Hiram Powers could command the latter figure, but the usual price was $100 to $500, depending on the sculptor and on the material. Almost all American sculptors of the time were occupied in portraiture, although most would have preferred to work on a freer, more imaginative form of art—the ideal figure or monument. There were several who seem to have been quite content working in portraiture, while others practised it almost exclusively for economic reasons. As Albee pointed out, portrait work usually had to sustain a sculptor for several years until his reputation brought him commissions for ideal pieces or sizable monuments. We have already observed that the work of Frazee, Browere, and Cogdell was confined almost entirely to sculptured busts; that Greenough and especially Powers continued to do them throughout their careers, and so did Crawford for a while, until his studio became busy with commissions for Richmond and Washington. After 1850 American sculpture entered an age when bronze became the primary medium for sculptural expression, but the first generation of portraitists followed the lead of the Italian and English neoclassicists in their preference for the pure white materials.

The style of the portraits discussed in this chapter is thoroughly naturalistic—so much so, in fact, that even the frequent use of the Roman toga draped about the shoulders can not qualify them as examples of neoclassicism. Many of the portrait sculptors began their careers in remote parts of the expanding nation as stonecutters or mechanics, and the European philosophies of art were as unavailable to them as were art schools where they could be drilled in the fundamentals of neoclassicism. So most native American sculptors relied upon the truthful representation of nature, flavored by their perception of the subject's personality and station in life. Even after some of these American sculptors went to Italy, they remained devoted to an uncomplicated naturalism in their portraiture, no matter what style they might adopt in their ideal works.

One of the active centers for the early development of a portrait school was a burgeoning town on the Ohio River, far from the major art centers of the eastern seaboard. At the start of the second quarter of the 19th century Cincinnati was not much of a town, but its mud streets and shacklike buildings were soon to give way to a thriving, bustling center of trade and industry. As the town grew some of its citizens wished to see it develop culturally as well as materially, and an active colony of painters and sculptors was soon in residence there. In August 1836 Nicholas Longworth wrote in some exaggeration to Hiram Powers, his former protégé, then in Italy, that "I scarcely meet a vagrant boy in the street who has not a piece of clay in his hands, moulding it into the human face divine . . . . There is also a mania for painting." * Frederick Eckstein had settled there in 1823, at about the same time young Hiram Powers began modeling portraits. Then came Shobal Clevenger, John C. King, T. D. Jones, Nathan Baker, Edward Brackett, T. B. Read, John Frankenstein, and Henry Kirke Brown. Many of these men spent only a few years in Cincinnati, but for most of them it was where they got their start. All of them, with the exception of Hiram Powers, remained essentially portrait sculptors throughout their careers.

The career of Shobal Vail Clevenger (1812–1843) spans little more than a decade of sculptural activity. Born in Middletown, Ohio, the son of an impecunious weaver, he received his first experience in carving when he apprenticed himself to a stonecutter working on the canal at Centerville. At fourteen he went to Cincinnati, where he was employed by the gravestone cutter David Guion, and it was in Cincinnati that he received his first impressions of sculpture as an art rather than as a utilitarian craft. The anonymous author of *Sculpture: and the Plastic Art* (Boston, 1850) tells us in his brief biography of Clevenger that on the market building of the city there was a carved wooden female figure that first inspired the youth to dream of his own pursuit of the art; we are told that, according to his own words, he "was accustomed to gaze at [the statue] for hours, wondering if the time would ever come when he should be able to imitate it." By the end of his four years with Guion (about 1830) he had already shown extraordinary adeptness with the mallet and chisel, surpassing his master to such an extent that nearly all carved ornament was given to him to execute. Clevenger learned from whatever sources were available to him in and around Cincinnati, as may be observed from the following passage in *Sculpture: and the Plastic Art* (p. 333):

Some years prior to this period [c. 1830] a monument of some pretensions, carved with allegorical reliefs, and containing a statue representing Grief, had been erected in the burial ground . . . by one John Airy, to the memory of General Ganno; and these ornaments Clevenger determined should serve him as models for study and imitation.

* The quotations in this chapter that are taken from Nicholas Longworth's correspondence to Hiram Powers are published through the courtesy of the Historical and Philosophical Society of Ohio, Cincinnati, Ohio.

Fearing that his operations might be interrupted, he would creep quietly at night into the silent grave yard, and busy himself frequently till morning in taking impressions in clay from this and other sepulchral fancies of his unknown predecessor. He turned his attention also, at this time, to reading [Nicholas Longworth referred to him as "illiterate"] and the study of books, strongly impressed with the acknowledged truism, that no one can pursue art profitably, who does not possess a refined and cultivated mind.

Clevenger had no formal education, and no opportunity to study the fine arts at an art school. Nicholas Longworth once described him in a letter (August 31, 1836) to Powers as "a plain, illiterate, unassuming man." He had an engaging personality, constantly acquiring devoted friendships, but was impatient and certainly improvident, being more like the grasshopper than the ant. In another letter to Powers, Longworth wrote on June 18, 1837: "Clevenger I have not seen for two weeks and rather believe he is displeased with me . . . . [He] has industry but no economy. His partner [Basset] had made money while Clevenger has lost. The one saved, the other spent."

It was in the early 1830's that Clevenger first began to model portraits, although he was still engaged in cutting grave monuments in 1835 when he produced the earliest surviving example of his portraits—that of Ebenezer S. Thomas in Spring Grove Cemetery in Cincinnati. Thomas, editor of a local newspaper, was much impressed with the head of a cherub he saw Clevenger carving one day in his shop. The next day he praised the sculptor's talents in an editorial in the *Evening Post,* and in return Clevenger, excited at this recognition and encouragement, asked Thomas to sit for his portrait. Without first making a model in clay, the eager young artist began carving directly on a block of stone, with the daring, adventurous, and even reckless spirit that was typical of him. The result was acclaimed a brilliant achievement. Created by the sheer force of innate genius, without benefit of formal training, the bust relied upon the eye of the artist and his ability to render with complete fidelity what he saw before him. This characteristic was found in the early work of Hiram Powers, who that same year had modeled his portrait of President Andrew Jackson with the sharp, realistic delineation of the face, but with a classical drape about the chest and shoulders. Clevenger's respect for truthfulness caused him to represent Ebenezer Thomas in the dress of the day, one of the earliest such instances among "Yankee stonecutters." He, no doubt, observed the progress being made by Powers and also studied whatever busts were available in the studio of Frederick Eckstein, but otherwise Clevenger's development had to come from within himself.

As Clevenger continued to model portraits he soon attracted the patronage of Nicholas Longworth, who wrote to Powers on August 31, 1836:

Clevenger has finished the bust of Brunet. The likeness is perfect & the execution good. I doubt his ever being able to design well, but he will admirably execute the designs of others . . . . So far as the taking of likenesses extend, he would stand high in any city of Europe.

Longworth was reportedly drawn to the sculptor's work when he saw a carving of the figure of the Clevengers' first child. In June of the following year Longworth again wrote to Powers that he intended to finance a trip to the east coast cities for Clevenger, but as hard times were then affecting the nation (over six hundred banks failed in the United States in 1837) he thought the sculptor would have difficulty finding commissions. It was the desire of both the artist and his patron that the former should go to Italy, but Longworth felt Clevenger was not yet ready for it, and instead, made it possible for Clevenger to study anatomy at the Ohio Medical College.

It may have been on commission from Longworth that in 1837 Clevenger executed the portrait of William Henry Harrison. The old Indian fighter, former governor of Indiana Territory and future President of the United States, was represented with a vigorous turn of the head, a fiery glance of the eyes, and a determined firmness of the mouth. Clevenger sought to infuse the man's personality into his likeness, searching for much more than merely flesh. The bust of Harrison, like the one of Josiah Lawrence (Fig. 6.1) done the same year, is bare-chested; thus did Clevenger avoid the problem of the toga versus contemporary attire. One can see the vitality of Lawrence here, and there is a virile strength of character in the simplified naturalism that is comparable in style to sculptured busts by such 15th-century Italian masters as Donatello and Verrocchio.

Late in 1837 Clevenger left Cincinnati for the East. Longworth, being unable to restrain the anxious young man, wrote to Powers on January 6, 1838, that he had urged him "to visit all the chief cities, & take all the Busts he can, whilst he stands without a rival." With Powers, Greenough, and Crawford in Italy at that time, Clevenger soon became the unchallenged master of the portrait bust in America, and Longworth was anxious for him to make the most of this.

In February of 1838 Clevenger was in Washington, D.C., where he made a bust of Henry Clay that was "highly praised." This became one of his most famous pieces, and there are plaster replicas of it today in numerous museums. Clevenger must have been impressed with the great dignity of the Kentucky statesman, for the bust contains a serenity and quiet self-confidence seldom exceeded in American portraiture. The heavy toga adds far more nobility than do the street clothes worn by Ebenezer Thomas in his portrait, but the real beauty of Clevenger's work lies in the head of Clay.

While in Washington the sculptor also modeled likenesses of John Quincy Adams, Martin Van Buren, and Daniel Webster. The magnificent bust of Webster, resolute and commanding, was also immensely popular, and copies are found in many public collections. The toga, fastened at the right shoulder with a circular clasp, reveals part of the bare chest and right arm of the statesman, as if Clevenger were experimenting with a solution to the toga-design problem. In an interesting letter dated February 3, 1838, written to a "Mr. Brown" (possibly Henry Kirke Brown), Clevenger outlined his recent activities:

My Dear Mr. Brown you must excuse me for not wright to you before this. I wright so badly spell so badly to and compose worse that I am a shamed to wright to any person. I have modaled a bust of John Q. Adams and Mr. Corwin's [U.S. Senator and Governor of Ohio] since I am here. My next will be your old friend Daniel Webster. he has got the finest head for a bust I ever saw. The President [Van Buren] will sit for me next.   [Courtesy, Professor Thomas Brumbaugh]

In the summer of 1838 Clevenger returned to Cincinnati, and on September 23, Longworth again wrote to Hiram Powers:

Clevenger has been here and [has] again gone East. [He] has few rivals in any Country, but I do not believe he has any bump [Longworth was a craniologist] thereby developed, but the bump of imitation. He took my Bust when here last & devoted much time to it . . . . He succeeded so well that Drake said to him, "Clevenger, you are inferior to Powers, but you have taken a more accurate likeness of Longworth than the one taken by Powers." Clevenger was delighted with the compliment, for none is more disposed than he to admit your superiority . . . . I have advised Clevenger [again!] that I thought a trip to Italy would be to him of little service, at present . . . .

By the following March (1839) Clevenger had arrived in Boston, no doubt unhappy with Longworth's advice, but accepting it—along with Longworth's recommendation to try to put still more expression in his heads. In that center of New England culture he seems to have been well received and allowed to model several of the area's prominent citizens. Boston had not yet heard of Crawford, although it was in that year that Charles Sumner saw the "Orpheus" in Crawford's studio in Rome. Clevenger stood alone commanding the field, and Boston was happy to have him in residence. He and Mrs. Clevenger dined with the portrait painter Francis Alexander and his wife, and they met the Henry Kirke Browns before the Browns departed for Europe.

For Clevenger there were brief trips to Philadelphia and New York in the spring of 1839 as he worked industriously at establishing his reputation as a sculptor of portraits. On April 29 Dr. Alban G. Smith wrote Hiram Powers that Clevenger while in Philadelphia had made a bust of Nicholas Biddle "and some others very much spoken of"; one of these was a bust of Judge Hopkinson. In 1839–1840 Clevenger was in New York City on several occasions, and about May 1839 he modeled the bust of Philip Hone, who wrote to Nicholas Longworth "lauding Clevenger highly." Several years later, on October 19, 1846, Hone made the following notation in his diary:

Twenty gentlemen of New York sent out $500. to Italy to procure my bust, which was begun by Clevenger, and finished, I believe, by Powers. It has arrived, and has been presented to the Clinton Hall Association . . . . of which I have been for so many years the presiding officer.

A plaster cast of this bust is in the New-York Historical Society, along with another of the sculptor's finest portraits—that of James Kent, Chief Justice of the New York Supreme Court (Fig. 6.2), given to the society by John Jay in 1840. In the bust of Kent the sculptor realizes fully the expressiveness that Nicholas Longworth had urged him to strive for.

Back in Boston in the summer of 1839, Clevenger modeled likenesses of Harrison Grey Otis, Joseph Tilden, John Davis, Lemuel Shaw, Jeremiah Mason, and Washington Allston. These, plus plaster busts of Webster and Clay, Clevenger sent to the first sculpture exhibition of the Boston Athenaeum that same year. Allston, by then unquestionably the elder statesman of American painting, replied to the Athenaeum, when asked to sit for Clevenger, that he was indeed pleased that "the work is to be executed by an artist of such genius as my friend, Mr. Clavinger." The trustees of the Boston Athenaeum had allowed the sculptor to work in one of their rooms; to show his appreciation, Clevenger made a gift to the Athenaeum of plaster casts of the Boston busts, and the Athenaeum reciprocated with a commission for the bust of Allston to be put into marble when the artist went to Italy. In addition, Clevenger also made likenesses of Dr. James Jackson, William Lloyd Garrison, Andrew Norton, Isaac P. Davis, Edward Everett (then finishing his term as governor of Massachusetts), Amos Lawrence, and the Reverend Dr. James Freeman. The Athenaeum owns plaster casts of the Jackson and Everett busts and the marble version of Norton. Henry Tuckerman, writing in *The Columbian* in 1884, tells us that Everett became very fond of Clevenger while his bust was being modeled and that he "took evident pleasure in unfolding his mental treasury of taste and wisdom to the young sculptor, and has ever been one of his most steady and efficient friends." The original marble bust of Everett is at Harvard University; it was put into stone at the commission of Thomas H. Perkins and is another of the portraits that were finished by Hiram Powers in Florence soon after Clevenger's death. A slightly different version in plaster, with a rearrangement of the folds of the drapery, is in the collection of the New-York Historical Society. The marble bust of Freeman was placed in a niche in the apse of Kings Chapel, Boston, on December 16, 1843. Harvard also owns a marble bust of Benjamin Bussey, and the Essex Institute has Clevenger's marble portraits of Joseph and Elizabeth Peabody, all of which were modeled in Massachusetts but carved in Italy. The sculptor portrayed the Peabodys in contemporary dress, a common practice among sculptors of a later generation, but rather unusual in 1840.

In April 1840 Longworth could write to Powers that "Clevenger has been doing well in Boston," and that instead of the $150 he had charged for a portrait in Cincinnati, he now got $500—although this included putting the bust into marble. Nevertheless, Clevenger, not a thrifty man, was always short of funds; only through the generosity of his Ohio patron was he able to go to Italy at last. Before sailing for Europe, he took the likenesses of Julia Ward Howe (Boston Public Library), Samuel Ward, and William Cullen Bryant. The portrait of Oliver Wolcott was probably done at the same time, for it was given to the New-York Historical Society in 1840 by Wolcott's grandson. Clevenger had a most impressive list of sitters, a testimony to the growth of his reputation in the few short years after he left Cincinnati.

In the fall of 1840 Clevenger and his family, along with a number of plaster

busts, some already commissioned to be put into marble, left America. Everyone wished the gifted young artist well as he embarked to join Powers and
Greenough in Florence; none could guess that he had but three years of life
remaining. After spending a few days in the sculpture galleries of the Louvre in
Paris, Clevenger hurried to Florence, where he was welcomed by Hiram Powers.
The latter assisted Clevenger in finding both living quarters for his family and a
studio for himself. Henry Kirke Brown and his wife also helped the newcomers
get settled. Clevenger took in all the art treasures that Florence boasted and
began to have some of his busts translated into marble. New commissions, however, were quite scarce.

In the spring of 1841 an eye ailment made it impossible for him to work, and
he visited Rome, where "ten days spent amid her treasure-houses, sent him back
wild with delight." And upon seeing the ideal figures—the early "Eve" and "The
Fisherboy"—taking form in Powers' atelier, he decided to attempt the "higher
art" himself. Longworth had anticipated this in his letter to Powers on April 23,
1837, when Clevenger was already pressuring to go to Italy.

I know not that a study of the arts in Italy will greatly benefit [Clevenger]. He will
always be better at execution than at design. Still, as he is illiterate and entirely self-
taught, he may catch a glimpse of the higher branches of the art, when he has seen
the works of first masters.

In 1841 and 1842 Clevenger worked on an ideal bust, the "Lady of the Lake,"
and an ideal figure entitled "Indian Chief," inviting speculation as to what else
might have come from his studio had he but had the time. Regarding the "Lady
of the Lake," almost nothing is known except what appears in the letter to his
friend and patron George Peabody in Paris, in April 1843:

I have finished more than half of my busts in the marble, and have modelled an ideal
bust, the lady of the Lake, from Scott's little Poem. I have taken her at the moment
she hears the hunters horn. I also have a Statue of an Indian Warrior nearly done in
the clay, and I hope to be able to make one or two other statues before leaving Florence.
[Courtesy, Professor Thomas Brumbaugh]

Numerous reports did make their way back to America about his "Indian
Chief." Longworth was skeptical, however, and wrote to Hiram Powers on
November 23, 1842, concerning their friend's work:

I recently had a letter from Clevenger . . . . He speaks of his Lady of the Lake & his
Indian Group. To succeed he should have had material subjects to copy from; but
it may answer for Italy where they never saw an Indian Chief or his squaw.

Evidently the sculptor planned to have an Indian woman as a companion to the
"Chief," but this was probably never modeled. A line engraving of "Clevenger's
Indian Chief" was published in the February 1844 issue of the *U.S. Magazine &*

Democratic Review (Fig. 6.3). The Indian is nude, except for feathers atop his head and a fig leaf; his head turns to his left and his left hand rests on a tree trunk (structural support for the heavy marble); his right hand holds a bow, which is as high as the Indian is tall. The "Indian Chief" is reminiscent of the "Achilles Borghese" in the Louvre, but whatever the prototype, the sculptor very likely had the vision of some ancient work in mind as he posed his own model in his studio.

Clevenger received considerable encouragement for choosing the subject he did, and in March 1843 Lydia Brown expressed an idea that was very much on her husband's mind when she wrote to relatives back home regarding Clevenger's "Indian Chief":

It is a fine subject, and I am glad if our artists can find enough of poetry and of interest in the early history of their own country for the employment of their imaginations without recurring to the oft-repeated stories of Grecian and Roman mythology.

[Courtesy, Library of Congress]

Henry Tuckerman also praised Clevenger's choice of subject, in his memorial published in *The Columbian* in 1844, calling the statue "one of the most characteristic products of the American chisel"; he added that it excited much attention in a land where heathen mythology has furnished nearly all the subjects for sculpture.

Lydia Brown tells of Clevenger's situation in Florence in early 1843:

Clevenger . . . has overlooked [supervised] the cutting of his busts in marble which he brought with him, for [he does not] do anything or but very little to them [himself] . . . . His busts are considered, I believe, as equal to Powers' . . . . Clevenger has many friends here and has received assistance from his friends at home besides that received for his work. He is also in debt as well as Powers . . . .

[Courtesy, Library of Congress]

Then suddenly the first symptoms of tuberculosis appeared, and Clevenger found it increasingly difficult to work in his studio. There stood the "Chief" and possibly the first crude form of an Indian squaw and the model of the "Lady of the Lake," along with a row of plaster busts, waiting to be placed in marble. As summer drew to a close it was obvious that the Clevengers should return home.

The last days in Florence for Shobal Vail Clevenger, his devoted wife, and their several children are related in a letter from Lydia Brown to her sister Adoline, dated September 10, 1843:

[Clevenger] has not been well since last spring [and] for the last six weeks he has been confined to bed most of the time. We now fear it is too sure he has the consumption and they have concluded to go home immediately as the Doctor says a sea voyage is his most probable if not his only chance of cure . . . . Mr. Clevenger and his wife have full confidence in his recovery. They are both forming plans for the execution of his work when he gets home. I pray they may not be disappointed.

[Courtesy, Library of Congress]

When the time came for the Clevengers to leave, numerous friends, mainly from among the artist colony there, provided the funds for the return journey. But time had run out, and the young artist died of "consumption" on board ship, not far off Gibraltar, on September 28 at the age of thirty-one.

To assist the destitute family, Hiram Powers had some of the commissioned busts put into marble by his own Italian stonecarvers. He also had them carve the "Indian Chief" from a marble block that had been paid for by Clevenger's good friend Edward Everett, so that Mrs. Clevenger might receive the full amount paid for the statue. But who bought it or what has happened to it is not known; should it ever be located it will be especially valuable, for it was Clevenger's only ideal figure put into marble. With the death of Clevenger, America lost a sculptor of unusual ability in the truthful and precise rendering of a likeness. Yet Clevenger had not included every detail of the physiognomy to achieve a realistic portrait. He selected and rejected, as an artist must, and the result was a portrait in which every essential feature was included and the unessentials eliminated. American sculpture—especially portraiture—came a little more of age with the help of Shobal Vail Clevenger.

Edward Augustus Brackett (1818–1908) was seventeen when he moved to Cincinnati from Vermont with his parents in 1835. In the next few years he began working with clay, no doubt encouraged by the fame Powers had acquired locally and the praises he heard of Clevenger's portraits. Among his earliest efforts were a bust of his sister and a medallion of Washington. Impatient to attain fame, Brackett exhibited a statue, "Nydia," at the Cincinnati Academy of Fine Arts before he had become proficient in his art; at least Longworth thought so. In a letter to Hiram Powers on September 22, 1839, Longworth wrote: "A young man by the name of Bracket [sic] has completed a statue of Nydice [sic], the blind girl in The Last Days of Pompeii. It is creditable to him, but he had not the sense enough to destroy it when finished." Brackett is reported to have finished the statue within six weeks; and though this feat astonished some people in Cincinnati, most agreed with Longworth. Brackett also modeled portrait busts in the area, and his likeness of William Henry Harrison, which he exhibited at the Apollo Association in New York in September 1840, was probably done while he was still in the Midwest.

In the fall of 1839 Brackett left Cincinnati to try his luck in the East, settling first in New York City. In 1840 and 1841 he was represented by several busts in the National Academy and Apollo Association exhibitions. He did the likeness of Rufus Dawes, the editor and poet, early in 1840, and later did one of Dr. Alban G. Smith, a correspondent of Hiram Powers, who described Brackett as "promising." The bust of Dawes may have been one of the two Longworth referred to when he wrote to Powers on April 30, 1840, that "the stupid Gothamites let him starve while they give Clevenger $500. for Busts. I understand he has got but 2 Busts at $40." Portrait busts of the Reverend Mr. Orville Dewey and of Charles

F. Grim also date from this period, and probably one of William Cullen Bryant as well. But the future did not seem promising in New York, so in the summer of 1841 Brackett moved to Boston, where he made his permanent home.

At first Boston offered no better patronage to Edward Brackett than it did to Robert Ball Hughes, who had taken up residence there a little earlier. Commissions were few, and the price remained low. In 1843 Brackett sent a bust of John Sheridan to the Athenaeum exhibition and began what is probably his most famous portrait—that of his friend Washington Allston. When the famous painter died, Brackett made a death mask, and from this came the portrait bust in 1844. His "Allston" (Fig. 6.4) is a fine piece of sculpture that does credit to its creator, but one is reminded of Clevenger's bust (1840); Brackett must have been influenced by Clevenger's plaster cast of Allston in the Boston Athenaeum. The handsome features are framed by Allston's long wavy hair in a likeness that achieves, through a selective naturalism, a certain stateliness and decorum. There is in addition a timeless quality about it, due in part to the absence of both ancient toga and contemporary dress. Probably dating from the late 1840's are the busts of Henry Wadsworth Longfellow, George H. Baker, and S. V. Merrick. All three were exhibited at the Pennsylvania Academy in 1850 when Brackett was in Philadelphia for several months.

During the years 1850–1851 Brackett worked on what seems to be his only story piece that has survived—"Shipwrecked Mother and Child." The subject was selected partly because it offered an opportunity to model the nude figure and partly because it allowed the artist to indulge in the sentimental pathos so popular in his time. In 1855 Thomas Ball modeled "Boy on a Raft," and some years later James MacDonald produced his "Shipwrecked Boy"; similarly, in Rome in 1857 Paul Akers modeled his "Dead Pearl Diver," hoping to move the spectator with the assistance of a pitiful tale that accompanied the statue. Brackett's group, modeled in Boston and carved in Woburn, is perhaps more ghastly than pathetic; it depicts an unfortunate woman who, with her babe still clutched to her side, has been washed ashore after a wreck at sea. Such disasters were not uncommon in the mid-19th century. So realistic was the image that medical men recommended its study because of the accuracy of the bloated lifeless forms. Although it was a little too brutally realistic and morbid for many people who saw it in the Athenaeum in August 1852, the astute critic Horatio Greenough praised the work. He wrote a letter to Richard Dana—who frequently visited Brackett's studio in Tremont Row—stating that he would contribute to a fund to purchase the group for some local institution. This letter was published in the Boston *Daily Advertiser*, as well as in New York papers, and was printed in the Athenaeum catalogue of 1852 when the group was shown:

I have several times sat for an hour in the same room where Mr. Brackett's group, the "Wrecked Mother and Child," is exhibited, and always with a new sense of power which has made that block of stone the vehicle of so many sad and tender thoughts, expressed in the language of beauty. I have admired the art by which he has so placed the head, that a glance tells us her sufferings are passed, and so swept every limb and tress, that we see the surge has lodged her there, and there left her.

But there was not sufficient interest and support to carry out Greenough's proposal. "Shipwrecked Mother and Child" remained in the Boston Athenaeum until around 1900 when it was placed in Mount Auburn Cemetery. It eventually found a home in the Worcester Art Museum in 1904.

Throughout the 1850's and 1860's Brackett continued to model portraits. At Harvard there is a marble bust of Charles Sumner (c. 1855). Following the common practice, the shoulders were draped in a toga. At about this same time he made the "Model for Bust of J. Sartain," which was displayed at the Pennsylvania Academy in 1856. The following year he executed a marble statue of Hosea Ballou, which still stands in Mount Auburn Cemetery. The bust of General Benjamin F. Butler probably dates from about 1865, since Butler rose to prominence during the Civil War. Sometime in the early 1860's Brackett made an imaginary portrait—based on other images—of John Brown; James Jackson Jarvis, a critic who was usually quite contemptuous of contemporary American art, praised the piece for capturing the ". . . intense moral heroism of the reformer," and called it "one of those rare surprises in Art . . . which shows in what high degree the artist was impressed by the soul of his sitter."

But commissions were not plentiful, and the Brackett family had financial difficulties so long as Brackett relied on sculpture for a livelihood. By this time he had become quite absorbed in work connected with conservation and wildlife and had hothouses and game-bird preserves at his own home. His wife, in a letter addressed to the Metropolitan Museum of Art in 1903, said that he finally gave up his sculpture studio in 1873. Thereafter he devoted himself to writing poetry, a collection of which was published in 1904, and to serving as head of the Massachusetts Fish and Game Commission, a more secure vocation.

Out of Cincinnati came two other sculptors, Nathan F. Baker and John C. King. Little is known about Baker, who was born around 1822, the son of a wealthy landholder. His earliest attempt in the plastic art dates from about 1841 when he made a copy of Clevenger's portrait of Henry Clay and busts of his grandfather, Hezekiah Flint, and his father, John Baker; the last was carved in freestone and was his first experience with the chisel. Baker went to Italy in the summer of 1842, and Nicholas Longworth wrote Powers in Florence to expect him. How long he remained in Italy is uncertain, but he was back in Cincinnati in 1851. A bust he made of John James Audubon was shown at the National Academy of Design in 1847, and one of James P. Wilson is in the collection of the Cincinnati Art Museum. He made a statue entitled "Egeria" (from Byron's *Childe Harold*), which was exhibited in the "Orpheus Room" at the Boston Athenaeum in 1847, and for which he asked $1,500. The following year he requested that it be removed from the Athenaeum, and by 1851 it was at the Art Union in Cincinnati. His "Cincinnatus" arrived in that city in 1847 and eventually made its way to the local college. Nothing else has been recorded about his brief career.

John Crookshanks King (1806–1882) emigrated from Scotland in 1829, and after working as a machinist in New Orleans and Louisville, he settled in Cincinnati from about 1832 to 1836. While there he became friends with Powers and Clevenger, who soon rekindled in him a childhood interest in the arts. The story goes that in 1834 a young friend of Powers died of cholera, and Powers was asked to model a bust of him from memory. King, invited to watch the procedure, was given some clay to make a bust of himself or his wife. This he did, receiving criticism and encouragement from Powers. He later wrote, "I finished the bust [of my wife], and from 1836 to 1837 several busts and medallions." He continued working as a machinist, but whenever leisure time permitted he would model in clay; around 1834 he made a bas-relief portrait of Hiram Powers, and Nicholas Longworth gave a plaster copy of it to the Boston Athenaeum in 1838. Before Powers left for Italy he gave King a large assortment of "odds and ends," among which was the first bust he had ever modeled.

It was difficult for King to leave a reliable trade to take up sculpture, and for a while he was occupied with both. On August 31, 1836, Longworth sent the following information to Powers: "I am not certain that King might not be induced to desert his profitable business and follow you to Italy. He is now engaged on a Bust of himself and it promises to be equally good with the one taken of his wife."

With the depression and bank failures of 1837, King had little work as a machinist and so devoted more time to making portraits—such as that of a Mr. Neville, which "does him much credit." Longworth observed that he was a slow worker, the opposite of Clevenger in this respect, but that practice should improve the situation.

Late in 1837, having made the break from machinist to sculptor, King decided to try his fortune in New Orleans, where he had lived briefly when he first came to America. But never during the two years he was there did he manage to earn more than a bare subsistence. In the winter of 1838–1839 he produced only two busts and was forced to turn to cameos to eke out his income. This was considered rather degrading to a sculptor, comparable to a portrait painter having to paint miniatures to earn his daily bread.

At last he gave up on the delta city and in 1840 moved to Boston, joining Brackett and Hughes who had just established themselves there. Full of hope and ambition, King was represented in the 1841 exhibition of the Boston Athenaeum by plaster busts of James Savage, John Lowell, Judge Samuel Putnam (now at Harvard), the Reverend Francis W. P. Greenwood, and a "bust of a Child," possibly one of his own children. The portrait of Greenwood is one of his best; it presents the minister of King's Chapel in his clerical robes, which look almost like a toga draped about the shoulders. Several plaster copies were made, and a marble version (Fig. 6.5) was placed in a niche in King's Chapel in March 1845.

Years later, in 1856, a marble version of the Lowell bust was also set in a niche in the same chapel. There were also busts of James Gallier, Joseph Ames the artist, and Benjamin Russell, but for the most part King fared only slightly better than Brackett and Hughes in portrait commissions. To find a patron who would pay for a bust was difficult enough, and King was not in a position to command high prices for his work.

It is small wonder, then, that King did not attempt large ideal pieces or fancy busts. He worked away as best he could at portraiture, probably never even daring to dream of Italy and large governmental commissions, equestrian monuments, or even life-size statues. He was undoubtedly hesitant to attempt the full-length figure, as he had not studied anatomy. Moreover, not moving in the upper social circles of Boston, he had no way to meet wealthy citizens who might want portraits of themselves. Greenough had been born into this group; Crawford had educated himself and had married well; Clevenger had overcome similar difficulties with his engaging personality. But King was destined to remain one of countless men who made a bare subsistence, from one meanly paid portrait commission to another.

On February 23, 1848, John Quincy Adams died as he addressed the House of Representatives; that same year King exhibited his bust of Adams at the National Academy of Design. The government chose King's bust to be put into marble and placed in the Vice-President's room in the Capitol. The bust, modeled a few years earlier, was done with utter realism. There was no attempt to put youth into the sagging flesh or fullness at the wasting neck and shoulders. John Quincy Adams seemed to transmit to the artists who made his likeness an insistence upon exactitude, for the old Yankee preferred to see things as they really were.

Two other unrelated items occurred in 1848. Along with the bust of Adams, King exhibited a bust of Robert Burns, a fond recollection of the poet-idol of his native Scotland. More important, King gave love-sick Thomas Ball a lump of modeling clay with which to soothe himself when he was unable to work at his easel, and thus instigated Ball's great career as a sculptor.

In March 1852 King's studio burned, destroying his plaster models of portraits. It was a severe blow to one already used to hard times.

It is to be expected that we who are *pioneering* sculpture in this new country should experience some ups and downs of life. The most distressing calamities that have befallen me were the death of my oldest son, on his way to China, and the destruction of my studio, by fire, with all its contents, in March last, 1852. The gatherings of fifteen years were swept away in an hour, and but for the kindness of friends, I should not have been in a position to proceed with the orders I have on hand.
[Letter to Hannah Lee, dated January 22, 1853]

In the New Hampshire Historical Society is a 17-inch plaster bust of Daniel Webster by King. Stamped into the base is the inscription, "Published June 1853," the year of the death of the great orator. The portrait, by no means the most distinguished one of Webster, is interesting because it is one of the earliest instances of "copywriting" or "patenting" pieces of sculpture that were intended to be produced and sold in large numbers. Thomas Ball also patented his statuette of Webster in the same year, allowing Webster's devoted admirers to obtain inexpensive likenesses of him. King produced a larger marble version of his Webster, and wrote to Hannah Lee, "I have executed two marble busts of Mr. Webster and have orders for two more."

Several other busts by King should be mentioned here. Harvard University has one of the Reverend James Walker, and the Concord [Massachusetts] Free Public Library owns a marble bust of one of its benefactors, Sherman Hoar, signed and dated 1857. Other likenesses done in Boston include those of Ralph Waldo Emerson, Louis Agassiz, and Dr. Samuel Woodward; the Corcoran Gallery in Washington owns a marble bust of Commodore Charles Morris. Probably the one element lacking in King's portraits was that which Nicholas Longworth had urged Clevenger to try for—an expressive countenance. The gentlemen of Boston and elsewhere may have sensed this lack and given their patronage to more gifted men. Although John Crookshanks King lived until 1882, not much came out of his studio after 1860.

Perhaps one reason that neither Hughes, Brackett, nor King found the patronage they had hoped for in portrait commissions in Boston after Clevenger departed for Italy was the success there of Henry Dexter (1806–1876). Like all of the above-mentioned except Hughes, Dexter began his working career as an apprentice to a tradesman. Not content with his lot as a blacksmith, he sought advice about pursuing a natural but limited talent in painting. His wife's uncle, the painter Francis Alexander, at first discouraged him, but after several years of continued determination finally assisted young Dexter in establishing himself in Boston. His first painted portraits in late 1836 were not especially praiseworthy. Then, legend has it, one day he picked up some clay that had been left behind by Horatio Greenough and began modeling a head; this was his start as a sculptor.

Early the following year the "blacksmith sculptor," as he was then called, received his first commission. In a letter to Hannah Lee, Dexter wrote: "Alexander . . . introduced a sitter, Colonel Samuel Swett. This time I made an effort to do my best. They pronounced it good, all around." The bust of Colonel Swett was only the third attempt at modeling a portrait. Sometime later it was put into marble by Dexter himself, and on the flat shoulder plane of the undraped bust he inscribed these words with obvious pride: "This is the first bust ever made by Henry Dexter, Feb. 1837." But of greater importance for the establishment of his professional reputation was the bust he executed in the spring of 1838 of the mayor of Boston, Samuel A. Eliot. In his diary Dexter made the following notation: "I have this day completed a marble bust of Honorable Samuel A. Eliot, June 9, 1838,—it being the first bust I ever made,—the first time I ever struck marble with mallet and chisel." It would seem that Dexter meant the Swett portrait was the first commissioned one he had modeled, whereas the Eliot was his first venture at carving marble. There is a plaster cast of the Eliot portrait in the Boston Athenaeum.

The busts of Eliot and of Colonel Swett were the first of more than 180 portrait busts that were to be done in the next thirty years—a remarkable production. After Clevenger left for Italy, Dexter took his place as the favorite portrait sculptor resident in Boston. He almost always had commissions awaiting his pleasure, and he made quite a decent living from his art while other sculptors in the area barely got along or gave up to enter other professions.

In 1839, at the request of Thomas H. Perkins, Dexter modeled the likeness of the celebrated actress Ellen Tree, of whom he had already done a painted portrait. He exhibited it the same year in the first sculpture exhibition of the Boston Athenaeum and also at the Apollo Association exhibition. In 1841 Charles Dickens visited America, and while in Boston he had his portrait done by Henry Dexter. Years later Dickens' secretary, G. P. Putnam, recorded the event and described Dexter's *modus operandi:*

While Mr. Dickens ate his breakfast, read his letters and dictated answers, Dexter was watching with the utmost earnestness the play of every feature, and comparing his model with the original. Often during the meal he would come to Dickens with a solemn, business-like air, stoop down and look at him sidewise, pass around and take a look at the other side of his face, and then go back to his model and work away for a few minutes; then come back and take another look, and go back to his model; soon he would come again with his calipers and measure Dickens' nose, and go and try it on the nose of the model; then come again with the calipers and try the width of the temples, or the distance from the nose to the chin, and back again to his work, eagerly shaping and correcting his model. The whole soul of the artist was engaged in his task, and the result was a splendid bust of the great author. Mr. Dickens was highly pleased with it, and repeatedly alluded to it during his stay as a very successful work of art. [*Atlantic Monthly*, Oct. 1870]

Dickens and his wife not only gave the portrait their wholehearted endorsement, but ordered several copies to take back to England. Numerous replicas were also produced and sold by Dexter's representative wherever Dickens spoke on his lecture tour in America.

Dexter's initial experience with the full-length figure was the image of young Emily Binney, shown in repose, as if she were asleep, which was placed at her grave in Mount Auburn Cemetery. Although a statue had earlier been contemplated for this cemetery, the project was abandoned because of the bad effect New England weather would have on exposed marble; John Frazee was invited to design an architectural monument instead. Mount Auburn had been dedicated in 1831; ten years later Henry Dexter began work on what was not only the first piece of sculpture to go into America's first garden cemetery, but was also the first statue carved in marble in all of New England. It is a testimony to Dexter's reputation that he, inexperienced as he was with the full-length human figure, was selected over Robert Ball Hughes, who had previously produced several life-size statues in marble. Bostonians took great pride in their beautiful new parkland burial ground, as well as in the gleaming white marble image, which was erected in June 1842. It became one of the special attractions to be seen in the area. Even Nathaniel Hawthorne paid tribute to it in *Mosses from an Old Manse*.

Unfortunately the statue soon began to suffer from the elements, and by 1860 it had to be enclosed in a glass case. In 1934 it was in such a state of deterioration that the authorities, with permission of the family, had it removed. Nothing was left of Dexter's fine workmanship. We know something of its appearance, however, through several engravings. Emily Binney slept on a full pallet, hands crossed, as were her bare feet; at the four corners were Doric columns supporting a canopy that was crowned by an urn in the center. The Binney monument certainly established the reputation of the man who had made it, and more and more of the local citizens presented themselves at his studio to have their portraits made.

After Thomas Crawford's "Orpheus" was found to be broken in several pieces as it was uncrated in Boston, it was Dexter who repaired it in the winter of 1843–44. He may have been a little envious the following spring when he saw the mended "Orpheus," along with several other works from Crawford's Rome studio, in the impressive exhibition at the Athenaeum, and he surely pondered the possibility of taking a trip to Italy. But in the end it seemed unnecessary, and he was never lured abroad; indeed, he firmly believed in the primacy of American subjects and that a sculptor could learn all he needed to on his own side of the Atlantic.

On August 4, 1845, George C. Shattuck wrote the following letter to Henry Dexter:

While sculpture among the ancients has given life to an imaginary being,—Hercules—why may not modern sculpture give body and form to that real being, the pioneer of civilization,—The Backwoodsman?

A West and Clevenger have celebrated the figure of the Indian, why may not a Dexter chisel life into that benefactor of man, the tamer of the wilderness, who, with axe in hand, constructs a habitation for his dependent family? The moral sublime is exhibited in the life of the Backwoodsman.

This Romantic concept of the American pioneer was nothing new to the arts and literature of this country. James Fenimore Cooper had praised the homespun hero of intuitive moral righteousness in his novels, and Thomas Cole, chief among a whole generation of painters, had portrayed him as a virtuous new Adam in a wilderness that he compared to the Garden of Eden. The idea that Shattuck had proposed struck Dexter as a noble one, for the very reason that it dealt with an American subject and contained a moral lesson as well. Between work on commissioned portrait busts he began modeling his sylvan giant, and by 1847 he had completed it. The following was published in *Dexter's Latest Marble Statues* (Boston, 1848):

This statue is intended to represent the impersonation of American genius, in the figure of a hardy pioneer of civilization, as he goes forth into the wilderness to endure the difficulties of his new life, embodying both the physical and the moral suggestions of the lot of an Anglo-Saxon adventurer. The attitude is erect with an inclination forward. The arms are uplifted and thrown back over the right shoulder, while the hands grasp the helve of the axe which is about to descend into the trunk of the tree that springs at the feet. The dress is in keeping, being only a shirt, which with its rolled up sleeves, leaves the muscularly developed arms nearly bare—coarse trousers are girded about the loins, while the feet are covered with a primitive kind of shoe, being rough undressed leather, folded up to the ankles, threaded and tied about with leather thongs. The expression of the head and face is designed to be that of inflexibility of purpose, intellectual power, and high moral aim, mingled with manly beauty, and the gentler sympathies of humanity.

Several gentlemen of Boston contributed to the cost of having the statue translated into marble, and it was afterward placed on view in the Boston Athenaeum for several years. It was later given by the artist to Wellesley College, but has since disappeared.

In the late 1840's, Dexter worked on busts of several members of the Cushing family of Boston, and did portrait statues of the children of John P. Cushing. Young Thomas Cushing, about two years of age, intently studies his pet squirrel; his sister, Mary Louise, reads from a book. The two figures were called "Observation" and "The First Lesson" respectively, typifying "the progress of science by the simplicity of childhood." Thus again we see the poetic, philosophical, storytelling urge coming out in Dexter's work. If he had found regular patronage for ideal works he, like many others, would have been happy to do them; but the "vain self-estimate" ruled the day, and Dexter had little choice. Occasionally he worked on the models of statues—"Yankee Boy" (1853), "Dog" (1854; Forest Hills Cemetery), even a marble statue of General Warren for Bunker Hill (1857); and there was also a pedimental design for a public building in Washington, representing the Settlement of America (1858). But a catalogue of his works shows his time was devoted largely to portraits. As the decade drew to a close Henry Dexter conceived a bold plan that carried him both far and long from his Boston studio, a plan that offered a measure of spice to an otherwise monotonous vocation.

In 1859 Henry Dexter undertook at his own expense to travel to Washington, D.C., and to nearly every state then in the Union to model the portraits of the governors and the President. In the national capital he took the likeness of James Buchanan (Fig. 6.6). He traveled by stage, by train, by riverboat, and by any other means of transportation available. In Maine, Governor Morrill was his host in his modest home, where the sculptor listened to good music while the governor's daughters performed pirouettes. He modeled the bust of Governor Wickliffe in New Orleans, where his Yankee sense of propriety was shaken at the wild abandon of the Mardi Gras carnival; he crossed the Gulf of Mexico to Galveston (where there was no sweet milk, where people ate only pork, and where his favorite Northern apples cost $10 a barrel) to take the likeness of Sam Houston, governor of Texas. In Kentucky he saw black slaves for the first time, was hospitably entertained by his sitter, Governor Magoffin, and visited Mammoth Cave; in Tennessee he observed that the slaves were the "happiest of human beings," and if "there is slavery, it is the master who is in bondage"; and while in Tennessee to model Governor Harris' portrait he heard a brimstone-and-hell-fire preacher who spouted tobacco juice as he harangued the local sinners. This was an exciting journey through the South, where he was on occasion suspected of being a Northern spy sent to eavesdrop as he modeled the portraits of Southern governors. Up the great wide Mississippi he went, and through the Midwest, always carrying a few personal belongings and a cask of clay with him. It was always his hope, of course, that there would be commissions from the governors themselves, as well as from their friends and supporters, for copies of his portraits, or even that a few might be ordered in marble, as with the one of Governor Ellis of North Carolina. But his ultimate plan was to assemble a kind of national portrait gallery of his own making that would exhibit the likenesses of the men who governed the nation in 1860. It was doomed to failure, however, with the approach of the Civil War. Back in Boston, in January 1861 he exhibited his thirty-two portraits in the Doric Hall of the State House, and received many fine words of praise for his efforts. The busts were in time given to the National Museum in Washington, where they soon collected the dust of forgotten art. For Dexter in the 1860's it was back to the quiet production of portrait busts of distinguished and undistinguished Bostonians, frequently duplicating portraits made in earlier years. It provided a good income for the sculptor and his family, but he must have longed for something more challenging.

In 1870 Dexter made his last attempt at an ideal work—"Nymph of the Ocean."

The Nymph is of the water, a young Thetis, represented as reclining on the seashore. She leans upon a shell, and there are other emblems of the sea. The face and head are modeled on Greek lines. The half human and half divine are blended in the expressive mythological manner of the classic artists.

[Quoted from J. Albee, *Henry Dexter*, 1898, p. 100]

The sculptor had invited Dr. Oliver Wendell Holmes to see the "Nymph" in his studio, and Holmes looked at it in long silence, finally commenting that it was "a Yankee girl," not Grecian. This evidently piqued Dexter, for the next day he gave the face a classic profile, and when his friend Longfellow came around to see it, the poet at once called it "Thetis" and praised its grace and chasteness. Dexter's first attempt to affiliate his art with that of the ancient Greeks came at the end of his career, an isolated instance in the continual stream of naturalistic portraiture that carried his work into the early 1870's. Henry Dexter died in the year of the Centennial, 1876.

Joel Tanner Hart (1810–1877) was born of impecunious parents on the American frontier—Winchester, Kentucky—and was sent into apprenticeship with a stonecutter when in his teens. His formal education had been virtually nonexistent, although he had eagerly studied books on architecture and sculpture that belonged to a neighbor. It was in Pruden's stone yard in Lexington that he had his first glimpse of the sculptor's art when young Shobal Vail Clevenger visited the city for the purpose of taking the likeness of Henry Clay. While working in the stone yard in the 1830's he began modeling his first busts, among them Henry Clay and General Cassius Clay—and former President Andrew Jackson, whose likeness was taken at the Hermitage. Jackson commissioned his portrait to be put into marble—a task that Hart could perform himself. The New-York Historical Society owns a plaster bust of Clay that bears the inscription: "M. Pruden from J. Hart," and this may well be his early portrait of the statesman (Fig. 6.9), which he presented as a gift to his employer. Dependent upon an acute observation of nature, the strength of its style comes from a forthright presentation of the sitter's features plus the artist's respect for the man himself.

By 1845 Hart was anxious to visit the cities of the eastern seaboard, to see the art he had heard was there, and to try his fortune among cultured patronage of the East. The best he could have found in local culture would have been in Cincinnati, and Hart had by then attracted the attention of Nicholas Longworth. But he longed to see Philadelphia and Baltimore, and the rest, so off he went with his busts of Henry and Cassius Clay, which he exhibited at the annual show of the Artists Fund Society in Philadelphia in 1845. "Henry Clay" especially drew much praise to the unknown sculptor, and when shown in Richmond, Virginia, it attracted the attention of the Ladies' Clay Association, which promptly bestowed upon the sculptor a commission for a full-size marble statue of its hero. As he traveled back to Lexington, he must have felt a warm confidence in his future career, and the dream of going to Italy probably began to assume a reality.

That Joel Tanner Hart was never to be hurried in his work is an understatement. Although he received the commission for the statue of Henry Clay in 1846, it was not until three years later that he sailed for Italy to put it into marble. (Fig. 6.7). He was to receive $5,000 for the statue—$500 when he signed the contract, $1,000 when he embarked for Florence, and the balance when the work was completed. As methodical as he was slow, Hart not only took Clay's measurements, but also took casts of parts of his body and had numerous daguerreotypes made from different angles. From all these he modeled the figure in Lexington in 1847 and wisely made two plaster casts of it. The head of the statue is nearly identical to the early one now in the New-York Historical Society. He dressed Clay in the clothes he wore as United States Senator and as Secretary of State, and posed him in the act of delivering an oration. The figure suffers somewhat from being almost exactly life size, thereby failing to achieve the heroic stature of a figure larger than life. Moreover, it inclines forward slightly, creating a disturbing lack of equilibrium. The baggy, ill-fitting coat and trousers are distracting, and the blame cannot be laid on the tailors of the time, as the sculptors were prone to do. It is an artist's task to eliminate any element that diverts the eye and thought of the spectator from the total conception of the work. That American sculptors, in their fidelity to the creed of naturalism and truthfulness, frequently failed in this respect and thereby injured their art must be acknowledged, albeit with regret. In Hart's statue of Clay, as in Powers' of Webster, the problem arose at least in part from a dependence on the daguerreotype, with its infinitesimal details.

For over two years Hart remained in Lexington working on his statue. Finally in September 1849, he sailed for Italy, his precious plaster model being sent on another ship.

In Florence he met Powers, and at first they seem to have gotten along well enough. He found living quarters and a studio, and began exploring the museums and galleries of the art-rich city. He was especially impressed with the sculptures by Michelangelo, but there seems to have been no impact on his work from that source. His time was relatively free, as his model of Henry Clay had not yet arrived. To improve his knowledge of anatomy he went to London, where he spent several months studying at the medical college; then he returned to Italy by way of Paris, wandering about the galleries of the Louvre and the sculpture-laden boulevards, gardens, and parks. On his return to Florence he learned that the ship carrying the model of the Clay statue had gone down at sea, and another period of waiting had to be endured while a second plaster model was shipped from Lexington. But even had Hart found his model waiting for him when he returned, he could not have worked on it, for he became ill with cholera and fever, and his recovery was slow.

Very little work other than the final carving of the statue of Henry Clay was done in Hart's first half-dozen years abroad. In the Corcoran Gallery in Washington there is a marble bust of Agnes Maxwell Kearny dated 1854 (Fig. 6.8), but little else is known to have come from these early years. Even the Clay statue was not completed until 1859, ten years after Hart had left America.

Much of his time during the mid- to late 1850's was devoted to the invention of a pointing machine, which by means of about two-hundred needlelike rods could transfer the forms and proportions of a head directly into clay. This allowed the sculptor to make a portrait bust in about one-third the time normally needed; his fellow artists—for example, Powers and Ball—criticized the machine for making art too mechanical with a resultant lack of imagination and feeling in the portrait. Nevertheless, they both devised their own pointing machines in time, although they were less dependent on them than was Hart. The novelty of such a mechanically produced bust intrigued many people, and several commissioned their likenesses to be taken by Hart and his contraption. It was after all an era when the potential of the machine was becoming recognized, and machines had made many former mechanics and laborers enormously wealthy. But the novelty eventually wore off, and Hart never became prolific in the production of portrait busts, even though at one time he maintained he could make a bust in from three to six days.

In 1859 and 1860, Joel Hart returned to America to be present at the unveiling of his marble statue of Henry Clay in Richmond. The ladies for whom he had executed the image were generally pleased, although their judgment of the artistic merits of the statue may have been clouded by hero worship. The Ladies' Clay Association petitioned the Virginia Assembly in February of 1860 to allow the statue to be placed under the portico or in the rotunda of the State House, evidently as a counterpart to Houdon's "Washington." But the Democrats would not hear of it, and a compromise was finally reached in the construction of a little circular, columnar "Pagoda" on one corner of the capitol grounds. After a couple of decades of exposure to the elements, the statue had to have money appropriated for its renovation, but it was not until the 1930's that "Clay" was brought inside the State House and placed in an unobtrusive corner of one of the chambers.

The acclaim Hart received for his statue of Henry Clay afforded him a triumphant return to his native Kentucky. Before he returned to Florence he had two commissions, at $10,000 each, for replicas of his famous statue for Louisville and for New Orleans, enough money to make him financially comfortable for the rest of his life in Italy. The one for Louisville was completed in 1867, the one for New Orleans a few years later. A more ambitious man could certainly have produced the two replicas in considerably less than ten years, especially with the assistance of talented Italian stonecutters.

Although Hart is usually thought of as a portraitist because of his pointing machine and his famous busts and statues of Henry Clay, the freedom from financial worries allowed him to indulge his fancy in ideal sculptures and in writing poetry from the time of his return to Florence, in 1860, until his death in 1877. He made a copy of the "Venus de' Medici" and an ideal bust of his own design, "Il Penseroso." Also from these years dates a statue, called "Morning Glory," of a little girl holding a morning glory in her hand. But the one ideal piece he worked on during the years 1865 to 1877, never bringing it to completion, was the statue "Woman Triumphant." This statue actually went under several names ("Venus and Cupid," "Beauty's Triumph," "The Triumph of Chastity"), and Hart described it in a letter to Henry Clay:

I gratified my passion in modelling a life-size virgin and child in a group—not a Christian virgin, however. The figures are nude—Beauty's Triumph. She being assailed by Cupid, rests her left foot on his exhausted quiver, and holds his last arrow in triumph, for which he pleads, tiptoeing, reaching after it. It gives the most graceful and finest attitude possible, both in the woman and the boy. The idea is modern and my own.   [Quoted from W. W. Price, *Old Masters of the Blue Grass*, 1902, p. 170]

For years he labored at his group, while in between times he would write and rewrite his poetry, which he soon began to dream of publishing in a book.

Friends urged him to call the statue finished and put it into marble; his reply was, if God Almighty needed eighteen or twenty years to create a perfect woman, why should he be expected to do it in less time? When the end came for Joel Tanner Hart the group was only half carved from the marble block. On April 26, 1877, Thomas Ball wrote the following about Hart's last days in a letter to young Daniel Chester French:

Poor old Hart has passed away without seeing his labour of so many years accomplished. After having half finished his figure in marble, he was obliged to give up and his friends succeeded in getting him out of that horrid den he had lived in upwards of a quarter of a century. He lived about six weeks after as comfortable as we could make it for him. The poor old man was surprised to find he had so many friends outside of his studio. His figure is being finished with the hope of selling it and with the proceeds to carry out the twin idea of his life, of publishing to the world his book of poetry with his biography. This was his last request.

[Courtesy, Houghton Library, Harvard University]

The sculptor was buried in Florence, but ten years later the Kentucky legislature appropriated funds to have his remains removed to his native soil.

Soon after the sculptor's death his admirers back home expressed the hope that the "Woman Triumphant" could be finished, to become what the Lexington *Observer* called a "distinctive landmark in Lexington's culture sustaining reputation." One critic even paid the statue the high honor of saying it would "do more to attract the admiring gaze of the world than all our fine horses and cattle have done for fifty years." The statue was finished in marble by the British sculptor Saul and shipped back to America. It was sold for $5,000 and sent to Lexington, where it was given an impressive reception. "Woman Triumphant" was placed in the Court House there, where it remained until the fire of May 14, 1897, destroyed it.

Joel Hart is known to us today mainly for his portrait busts and statues of Henry Clay. There was an honest strength in his work when he limited himself to portrait heads, but faulty anatomy and composition and too many details in the clothing left something to be desired in his full-length figures. Throughout his portraiture he remained loyal to the American credo of naturalism, in spite of his foreign surroundings. So little of his ideal work of the later period has survived or can be located that it is difficult to make an estimate of it.

Powers, Clevenger, King, Brackett, and others left Cincinnati in the 1830's, but the art of sculpture was maintained there by a second generation that came to replace them in the 1840's. Chief among these was the portraitist Thomas Dow Jones (1811–1891), who also first served an apprenticeship in stonecutting before attempting any sculptural work of his own. He was working in a stone yard in Cincinnati in 1841 when he made his first essays at reproducing the human likeness. Of course, by that time there was something of a sculptural tradition in the Ohio River city, at least so far as the modeling, casting, and carving of portrait busts were concerned; and there were far more examples for Jones to learn from than there had been for his predecessors a decade earlier.

His first effort was a bust of John H. Coleman in 1841, followed the next year by a "Colossal Bust in Stone" of General William Henry Harrison. Evidently ambitious to try his hand at something more than portraiture, in 1843 he made a monumental piece, "The Resurrection," a high-relief group comprising eight figures. By 1844 he had joined the ranks of those who had modeled the likeness of Henry Clay. Cincinnati newspapers praised his bust of Clay, but Nicholas Longworth confided to Hiram Powers that he thought it a failure. Jones, who was also carving in wood during these years, produced a colossal wooden "Fireman" (1844) in full regalia and a wooden figure of General Marion (1845), which was larger than life. He also worked in bronze, for in 1846 he made a "Basso Relievo, Three Figures in Bronze, Arabesque Style, for Catholic Cathedral, Cincinnati, O." This would be one of the earliest examples of sculpture being cast in bronze, if we may believe this information, which was taken from a published list of Jones' works.

In the late 1840's several portraits—among them those of Lewis Cass and General Winfield Scott—were commissioned from the Detroit area, and Jones may have been working in Michigan at that time. In any case, he had left Cincinnati for the East by 1850, doing portraits all along the seaboard from Boston to Washington. Settling in New York City in 1851, he opened a studio at 300 Broadway and entered into a partnership with S. H. Drennon, who was his "business associate" rather than a fellow artist. The firm manufactured and sold replicas of busts, medallions, and reliefs created by Thomas Dow Jones. Among the many medallion portraits is one of Henry Clay which Jones said he modeled from life in Washington, D.C. From this medallion, so he advertised, was made the gold medal presented to Clay by the Whigs of New York. Two copies of the medallion exist in the collection of the Maryland Historical Society; it is a plaster oval, 12 inches high, and is signed and dated. Especially interesting is the inscription "Copy-Right secured," placing it among the earliest of instances where American sculptors endeavored to prevent the "pirating" of their sculptured works. Italian cast-makers, notably guilty of this offense, would sell them at low cost, glutting the market, not caring how the artist's reputation might suffer from their careless methods of reproduction. On an advertisement, which was sometimes pasted on the back of his medallions, Jones included the following notice: "Letters Patent have been secured on all the works above mentioned, and those having possession of any of them . . . are earnestly enjoined not to permit them to be copied . . . . All persons are warned against copying any of the said BUSTS and MEDALLIONS, as the same are Patented."

Many of these medallions are rather uninspired and appear to have been produced with a minimum of care; perhaps this was done because the sculptor and his partner were trying to produce an item at a price that the general public could afford, but they no doubt also recognized the lack of discernment in their clientele. For example, in the medallion profile of Daniel Webster, a replica of which is in the New Hampshire Historical Society, the portrait has little more than a resemblance to recommend it. There is nothing of the vital, forceful personality that was Webster's. As a work of art it is totally lacking in sensitivity of outline and form. There is another medallion portrait, thought to be of Arthur Garfield, in the New-York Historical Society, which contains a greater sensitivity in the line of the profile and in the subtle modeling of the head; but the observer still searches in vain for any expressiveness.

From the year 1852 date several works connected by their subjects with England (a bas-relief portrait of Queen Victoria, for example), and Jones may have made a journey to London to see the Crystal Palace, with its wondrous exhibitions of industry and art. But no substantiating evidence of this has yet come to light. Between 1853 and 1855 he exhibited several of his medallions at the National Academy of Design, of which he became an Associate Member in 1854.

Jones executed portrait busts as well as medallions, and as a rule the former were somewhat more successful than the latter. But even in his bust of Abraham Lincoln (Fig. 6.10), which was very popular, he again failed to achieve any feeling for the character of the man. Lincoln was given the appearance of being smaller than life instead of the giant that he was, and the countenance possesses nothing that reflected his inner qualities. It must have been one of those busts produced more for commercial expediency than as a serious study of form and character.

About 1865 Jones returned to Ohio to settle once more in Cincinnati. There he produced, around 1865 to 1870, one of his finest busts, that of Griffin Taylor (Fig. 6.11). Although it is a tour de force in naturalism and possesses a simple dignity and quiet self-confidence, it is nevertheless generally unexciting, and in this it is typical of post-Civil War portraiture.

In the 1860's American portraiture reached its nadir as painters and sculptors alike turned to an increasingly uncomplicated, unromanticized naturalism, and one could easily compare a painted portrait by Charles Loring Elliot with a sculptured bust by Thomas Dow Jones. Gone is the romantic, sensitive, refined, and elegant image of Powers' "Greenough" or Crawford's "Sumner." In the bitter years that surrounded the Civil War it would seem Americans lost their faith in the romantic dream, and in the next years would only permit a coarse, factual description of the world they faced. Romantic pretension and eulogy were stripped away, leaving a naked, prosaic naturalism. Since the 1840's the photographic image had supplied a factual realism that could not be questioned in accuracy of detail; it provided an indisputable truthfulness, but it took a couple of decades or more before it was generally realized that this was not synonymous with the highest form of art. Thomas Dow Jones was not the only one of our sculptors whose portraits relied upon this dry naturalism, as a look at the later busts by Hiram Powers will demonstrate. This is especially to be found in the portraits of ordinary middle-class merchants, lawyers, or business men. That such men wanted to purchase ghostly-white three-dimensional likenesses to immortalize themselves is perhaps not unnatural, but the sculptors and painters of the third quarter of the century refused to see these men as being anything more than they outwardly appeared or to endow them with any virtue they did not manifestly possess.

The career of Thomas Dow Jones extended through the decade of the 1870's. In about 1874, for example, he did the marble bust of Chief Justice Salmon P. Chase in the old Supreme Court in the United States Capitol. But after forty years of making portraits, Jones put aside his clay and tools; by then Saint-Gaudens was beginning to inject a new dynamic vitality into the exhausted naturalism of American portraiture.

John Adams Jackson (1825–1879), born in Bath, Maine, received his first instruction in art from the famous book illustrator of Boston, David Claypoole Johnston. Between 1845 and 1850 he made his way to Paris, being among the first American sculptors to go to the French capital instead of Florence or Rome. There he studied drawing and anatomy under the guidance of Charles Suisse. By 1851 he had returned to Boston, determined to go into sculpture rather than painting or illustration; from that year dates "Daniel Webster," one of his earliest portrait busts. Jackson returned to Europe in 1853, this time going to Florence to put into marble the portrait busts he had modeled in the past couple of years. Among the finest of the group is that of the Honorable James Edward Macfarland (1853), which is now in the Confederate Museum in Richmond (Fig. 6.12). It is a well-modeled portrait, its air of refinement and sensitivity a survival of that type of Romantic bust created by Greenough, Powers and Crawford in the late 1830's. The drapery of the toga that covers the chest falls in simple but exquisite folds. Avoiding a coarse realism, the sculptor has emphasized the sophisticated elegance of the man. The same characteristics are found in his bust of the traveling author George S. Hillard, done the same year (Boston Athenaeum). The following year Jackson moved to Paris; while there, he modeled the portraits of Lyman Beecher and Wendell Phillips. By 1858 he had returned to America to establish himself for a couple of years in New York. It was then that he modeled the bust of William Lloyd Garrison. A letter from Garrison to Oliver Johnson, dated May 1, 1858, describes the difficulty Jackson encountered with his portrait:

One thing is certain—for some reason or other, I have one of the most difficult faces in the world to take (owing, probably, to its changeableness of expression); all artists, at home or abroad, having failed to get a likeness generally satisfactory to my personal friends . . . . Jackson acknowledges that he has never had one sit to him whose living expression it has been so difficult to catch as in my own case; nor has he ever had one sit to him so many times, or for whom he has exerted himself so laboriously to achieve success. Besides, there is an inherent difficulty with which he has had to contend, and which it is not possible for even genius to surmount, in making a bust of me. My spectacles are a part of my face,—few ever see me for a moment without them,—and

they greatly modify the appearance of my eyes, and my general expression of countenance. In fact, when I lay them aside, I am almost another man.

[Quoted from *Life of Garrison*, 1885, IV, p. 288]

Jackson returned to Florence to join the American colony, which included
Powers, Ball, and Hart; there, except for a brief trip to America in 1867, he
spent the rest of his life. He evidently went to Italy to execute a monument to
Dr. Elisha Kent Kane, who in 1853–1855 headed the Second Grinnell Expedi-
tion into the Arctic; but Jackson never completed the monument, and Lorado
Taft hinted that that was the reason for Jackson's self-imposed exile in Florence.
He executed a bust of Louis Agassiz in the coat, vest, and bow tie of the day,
and managed to subordinate the inconsequential details of contemporary dress to
the characterization of the man himself. The bust is skillfully modeled and cap-
tures the pleasant manner of the Harvard zoology professor. There is a bust of
General Chamberlain by Jackson in the State House at Augusta, Maine; and the
State Library at Augusta has a plaster statuette of General Henry Knox, the first
Secretary of War. For the city of Lynn, Massachusetts, Jackson made a Soldiers'
Monument.

Although he was primarily a portraitist, Jackson produced several ideal works,
including a bust called "Dawn" and a medallion titled "Morning Glory." In the
Boston Athenaeum there is a low-relief portrait of Dante. Probably his most
famous work was "Eve Mourning over the Dead Body of Abel," executed soon
after his return to Florence; shown at the Pennsylvania Academy in 1869 and
1870, and elsewhere in America, it attracted much attention. Like Brackett's
"Shipwrecked Mother and Child," it is part of the necromania of the period.
Europeans and Americans alike seemed to relish the masochistic contemplation
of death. While women swooned in the presence of such works as Jackson's
"Eve and the Dead Abel," men were supposedly moved to reflect upon the real
values of life and the purpose of existence.

Jackson died in Pracchia, Italy, on August 30, 1879.

As a young man Thomas Ridgeway Gould (1818–1881) became a successful
dry-goods merchant. When time permitted, however, he engaged in drawing and
modeling as a hobby, for a while in the early 1850's working alongside William
Wetmore Story in the studio of Seth Cheney. When his business collapsed during the Civil War, Gould turned to modeling portraits for a living. Among his
earliest surviving work is a bust of Ralph Waldo Emerson; a marble version is
owned by Harvard University, and a plaster cast, signed and dated 1861, is in the
Concord (Massachusetts) Public Library. Other well-known citizens of Boston
sat for their portraits—for example, Governor John Andrew and actor-manager
Junius Brutus Booth. Gould was quite taken by the latter and some years later
published a book on Booth's life and career. Thomas Gould exhibited his work at
the Boston Athenaeum only once—in 1864, a pair of heads of Christ and Satan in
plaster; these were later put into marble in Florence (1878), and for them Gould

received $1,000, which had been raised by subscription. They were presented to the Athenaeum where "Satan" still resides; in 1906 the head of Christ was sent to St. John's Ecclesiastical Seminary in Brighton, Massachusetts. In 1867–1868 Gould worked on the model of a statuette of William Ellery Channing, which he patented. By that time he had decided to go to Italy, and in 1868 he left America, returning on brief visits in 1878 and in 1881, the year of his death.

In his Florence studio Thomas Gould devoted considerable time to ideal works; his best known piece was of a light-footed girl, nude to the waist, who looks over her left shoulder as she scampers along: the once-celebrated "West Wind." There is something quite uncomfortable about the tight, confining drapery of her skirt, and the star-studded belt is extremely banal. The statue was very popular when it was exhibited at the Philadelphia Centennial, but most people today would agree with Lorado Taft, who criticized it scathingly. Nevertheless, it brought commissions for seven lucrative replicas, and the income from these kept the sculptor comfortably in Florence for several years. At one time it was insinuated that "West Wind" had been plagiarized from Canova's "Hebe," but this was denied.

The 1870's saw a large production of ideal works in Gould's studio. Taft lists several of these fancy works, which have long since been removed to dim corners of storage rooms. Gould also modeled quite a few busts in those years, including one of William Munroe (1874) in the Concord (Massachusetts) Public Library. In 1875 he made a full-length statue of John Hancock for Lexington, Massachusetts, and one of John Andrew, for the cemetery at Hingham. His most unusual commission was for a statue of King Kamehameha, which was erected in the Sandwich Islands.

In his last years Gould was busy modeling a statue of John Bridge in his Puritan dress, but the sculptor died before it was completed. The statue, which now stands little noticed on the Common in Cambridge, Massachusetts, was finished by his son, M. S. Gould, who had it cast in bronze; it is inscribed: "Florence 1882."

As a youth in Norfolk, Virginia, Alexander Galt (1827–1863) made cameo likenesses and pencil and crayon portraits, and seems to have had no formal artistic training. By the time he reached twenty his thoughts were filled with visions of Italy, and in 1848 he sailed for Florence to join the small colony of American sculptors there. In Florence he received his first disciplined instruction as he drew from models during the day and modeled in clay in his studio at night. Because commissions were scarce, he had plenty of time to attempt some small ideal pieces. One of the earliest was a bust titled "Virginia," wrought in homage to his beloved birthplace; it was put in marble and sold at the American Art Union sale in 1852 for the rather low price of $110. Another, "Bacchante," is in the Corcoran Gallery (Fig. 6.13), and an ideal bust of the ancient poetess Sappho is unlocated. After nearly six years in Italy he returned to Virginia in

1854. The South had not had a great many sculptors, and young Galt's talent soon attracted much attention. He modeled numerous portrait busts of Southern gentlemen and their ladies, and in 1856 the federal government commissioned him to execute a portrait bust of the second Chief Justice of the United States, John Rutledge, who had died over half a century earlier. The portrait was modeled from painted likenesses, and the result, which may be seen in the U.S. Capitol, is a bust that possesses a serene dignity, strength, and integrity (Fig. 6.14).

In 1856 the sculptor packed up the plaster portraits that were to be translated into marble and returned to Florence for two very productive years. On February 21, 1854, the Virginia state legislature had voted to commission a statue of Thomas Jefferson and awarded it to Galt. The statue, modeled and carved in Florence, was finished by the time the sculptor returned to America in 1860. The statue is now at the University of Virginia.

Back home, Galt established his studio in Richmond, and when war came he stood ready to serve the cause of the South. While on the staff of Governor John Letcher, Galt modeled the portrait of the governor, dressing him in a Roman toga. He also produced a portrait of the president of the Confederacy, Jefferson Davis, while he was in office in Richmond. Another of Galt's works at this time was an ideal bust, "The Spirit of the South." Late in 1862, while making studies for a portrait of Stonewall Jackson, Galt contracted smallpox in the general's camp, and died. Much of the work of his brief fifteen-year career was destroyed when the warehouse in which it was stored was burned in 1863.

In Boston there were three sculptors by the name of Carew active in the middle part of the century. John Carew, born in England, may have been a son of the British sculptor John Edward Carew (active 1810–1855); in any case, in the 1840's he came to America and settled in Boston. Next to nothing is known of his work except that he listed himself as a sculptor in the city directories. Groce and Wallace, in their *Dictionary of Artists in America*, give the year of his birth as c. 1820, but it could easily have been earlier; he died in Boston in 1850, leaving a widow. It is not known at present what relationship, if any, John Edward or John Carew bore to the brothers Joseph and Thomas A. Carew, active as sculptors in Boston from about 1843. Joseph exhibited a "Marble Bust of a Child" at the Boston Athenaeum in 1843, and in the following year he was joined by his brother Thomas in a partnership that lasted eight years. They did decorative plaster work and plaster casting in their studio on Harrison Avenue in Boston. In 1847 Joseph sent a "Marble bust, modeled after death," to the Athenaeum exhibition, but his brother was not represented at the annual shows until 1853 when he displayed his marble portrait of the Reverend John Pierce and another portrait, of "a gentleman." The latter may be the same marble "unidentified gentleman" now owned by the Concord (Massachusetts) Public Library, which bears the signature "Thomas Carew, Boston, 1852." The Carew brothers probably did their own stone carving, since in later years they were often occupied with the creation and construction of stone memorials in the cemeteries around Boston. An example of this latter is an obelisk in Mount Auburn, dedicated to the memory of the Reverend Charles T. Torrey, who died in 1846. Sometime between that date and 1851 the brothers not only designed and carved the obelisk, but also modeled and had cast in bronze a small weeping female figure in relief, as well as a *tondo* relief portrait of Reverend Torrey; these were applied to the monument. The woman is a somewhat primitive approximation of a classical personification of grief; although a large drape envelopes part of the figure, most of the torso is nude. The positions of the arms and hands are rather awkward, suggesting a lack of formal training in anatomy.

Thomas Carew exhibited a bas-relief at the Boston Athenaeum in 1859, which, though unidentified, was probably the portrait of Theodore Parker that he patented in 1860. In 1865 and 1866 he worked on a very large monument that was erected over the grave of William Frederick Harnden, the founder of the first express company in the United States. The monument has several panels that contain scenes of the life and work of Harnden; on the base is a St. Bernard dog keeping a vigil at his master's grave. This is the last we hear of Thomas A. Carew, although it is possible that some of the other sculptured monuments in Mount Auburn Cemetery may be by his hand. One of the brothers, however, was still active in 1870 when Thomas Ball wrote to Otis Norcross on August 29 that one of the Carews had agreed to set up his marble statue of Governor Andrew for $100, but had died before he could do it. The careers of both brothers had come to an end by 1870.

David M. French (1827–1910), born in Newmarket, New Hampshire, received some training from Peter Stephenson in Boston, and finally settled in Newburyport. Not much has come to light about his life and career, but several pieces by him still exist. "Portrait of a Child" (1862) is in the New Hampshire Historical Society, and the Phillips Brooks House at Harvard has a marble bust of Andrew Preston Peabody. The Newburyport Historical Society owns two marble busts by French. One, tentatively identified as William Swaysey, is signed "1867 Newburyport." In the same collection is a marble bust of John Greenleaf Whittier, dated 1876, which the sculptor exhibited at the Philadelphia Centennial. Stylistically the portraits are competently rendered with greatest emphasis placed on an objective treatment of the facial features. Their fidelity to nature no doubt made them highly satisfactory to those who posed for them, and in this respect David M. French was like countless other practitioners of the trade in marmorean likenesses in the 1860's and 1870's. His only departure from the portrait bust seems to have been a standing figure of William Lloyd Garrison.

Horatio Stone (1808–1875) was born on a farm in New York State, and as he grew up, his father saw no future in what he considered the boy's foolish whit-tling and insisted he attend instead to his farm chores. To this, young Horatio reacted by running away from home. After several odd jobs he managed to study medicine and eventually set up a practice, which he pursued for a number of years. Then, quite abruptly, he put aside medicine to take up sculpture in the national capital. There his career became closely tied to the decorations for the federal buildings, and at the Capitol may be seen his marble statues of Alexander Hamilton (c. 1868, Fig. 6.15), John Hancock (1858), and Edward Dickinson Baker (c. 1873). For many years during the 1850's and 1860's he made a career of executing portrait busts which were good likenesses, but which lacked any spark of life. In 1857 his bust of Chief Justice Taney (Supreme Court Building) was awarded a medal by the Maryland Institute of Mechanic Arts. He applied for at least one big commission in the pedimental decorations of the Capitol, but in this he was unsuccessful. Stone is probably best remembered for the part he played in the formation of a Federal Art Commission for the purpose of obtain-ing better quality in the decorations for the buildings in Washington. Henry Kirke Brown, one of the three artists named to the Commission, was quite taken with Stone, and in February of 1858 wrote to his wife, Lydia: "This Stone has been for the last eight years a kind of martyr to the cause of Art in Washington; through poverty, neglect and scorn he has urged increasingly the claims of American artists to the consideration and patronage of the government."

Stone, with the help of Brown and some others, was finally successful in get-ting Captain Montgomery Meigs removed from his position of authority over works of art for the Capitol. But his dream of a Federal Art Commission was short-lived, being abolished in 1860 by an act of President Buchanan.

Doctor Stone, as he was usually called, remained one of the leading figures in Washington art circles until his death in 1875, which occurred at Carrara on his second trip to Italy.

Very little is known about the career of Anthony W. Jones, who was active in New York City from 1818 to 1861. He was not listed as a sculptor in the city directory until 1850, but as early as 1844 he exhibited a plaster portrait bust of General James Tallmadge at the American Institute Fair. In the last decade of his life he specialized in medallion portraits of eminent men. Three of these are in the collection of the New-York Historical Society: The one of John Pintard in plaster was the model for a medal that was struck in 1857 to commemorate the opening of the new building of the Historical Society of which Pintard was a founder; in 1858 Jones patented a cast-iron bas-relief oval medallion, 30 by 39 inches, of George Washington; the third was a bronze oval relief portrait of Charles Ira Bushnell, 9 inches in diameter. Plaster medallion portraits such as these were sold at modest prices in large numbers during the middle of the 19th century. There were numerous sculptors who turned out popular works for a large middle-class clientele, and like the Currier and Ives prints, examples of sculpture could be found in almost any home with pretensions to an appreciation of art.

Charles Calverley (1833–1914) perpetuated the white marmorean portrait down through the bronze age of American sculpture and right up to the threshold of the new century. He was born in Albany, where at the age of thirteen he was contracted to a seven-year apprenticeship in the shop of a marble cutter. By his twentieth birthday he had become an assistant in the studio of Erastus Dow Palmer, who was then producing many of the marble statues and busts that were to receive such acclaim at his New York City exhibition in 1856. Young Calverley, experienced at marble carving, no doubt assisted Palmer in the execution of several of those pieces. He remained as Palmer's assistant for fifteen years, and not until 1868 did he set out on his own. In 1868 he executed a low-relief profile of the portrait painter Charles Loring Elliott (Metropolitan Museum of Art), who died that same year. The influence of Palmer is quite unmistakable.

Calverley took the Elliott portrait with him when he moved to New York City, and entered it in the 1868 exhibition of the National Academy of Design. He set himself up as a portrait sculptor and during his entire career only twice undertook anything more ambitious than a bust or a profile relief. In 1875 he was made a full member of the National Academy, and the following year he exhibited two portraits at the Philadelphia Centennial—a bas-relief of Peter Cooper and a bronze bust of John Brown. Also in 1876 he modeled the likeness of Horace Greeley. These were competent enough and satisfactory to his sitters for their physical likeness, but in their bland naturalism they rarely became exciting works of art. In the face of competition from men such as Quincy Ward and Augustus Saint-Gaudens, who were then working in New York, plus his reluctance to attempt ideal or symbolic figures, Calverley became a part of the "rear guard" of American sculpture in the last quarter of the century. There were, however, numerous medallions and busts each year, such as those of Elias Howe (1884) and Edward C. Moore (1890), both cast in bronze. In a biographical letter (dated 1903) sent to the Metropolitan Museum of Art, Calverley reported that he had executed approximately 250 busts and medallions "since coming to New York City." In the same letter he stated, "I finished all my own marble work, and pointed much of it." An example of his work may be seen in the marble bust of Nathanial Boynton (1891), which is in the collection of the New Hampshire Historical Society (Fig. 6.17).

The Metropolitan Museum of Art owns a bronze bust of Robert Burns by Calverley, executed in 1890 when he was working on one of the two full-length figures of his career. The statue of Burns was erected in Washington Park in Albany; a figure representing "Meditation" marks the location of the Boulware lot in the Albany Rural Cemetery. Yale University owns a bronze bust of Sir

Walter Scott, dated 1896. Both of the imagined portraits and the symbolic figure lack characterization, and as Lorado Taft puts it, "Calverley's permanent reputation will rest largely upon his medallions."

By the turn of the century Calverley's sculpture career had come to an end, outdistanced by younger men and outdated by a more vitalized naturalism. He died at the home of his daughter in Essex Falls, New Jersey.

When Preston Powers (1843–1904) decided to pursue the art of sculpture in the Florence studio of his famous father in 1868, he had already tried several different professions. He inherited from Hiram Powers a talent for making mechanical things work, and he had been employed in the railroad barns in Florence and by the Grant Locomotive Works of Paris and New Jersey; serving in the United States Navy, he had acted as chief's clerk and interpreter aboard the U.S.S. *Canandaigua*. But at the age of twenty-five he decided to settle down in Florence and continue the work of his aging father. He quickly became adept at modeling physical likenesses, probably with the assistance of a pointing machine applied directly to the face and head of the subject. Then, as his father had done before him, he turned the clay model over to Italian craftsmen who made the plaster cast and perhaps translated it into marble.

Though Powers made several trips to America, Italy remained his home thereafter, and in Florence he perpetuated what was essentially the late portrait style of his father. American, British, and Continental tourists continued to come through the city, and a sufficient number came to the studio to have their likenesses modeled that the sculptor made a respectable living. Typical of his work are the marble busts of Professor Louis Agassiz (1874; Corcoran Gallery and Harvard University) and of Justin Smith Morrill (1875; National Collection of Fine Arts). Each piece reveals the competent manner in which marble was converted to flesh or fabric or strands of hair. The "Agassiz" (Fig. 6.16) is undoubtedly one of his best, and possesses that elusive quality of human existence so frequently missing from other examples of his work. The bust of Morrill, for example, seems to be more likeness than life, although admittedly one could find little fault with that likeness.

Like many other sculptors of his day, Preston Powers made a bust of Charles Sumner. It was shown at the Philadelphia Centennial in 1876, and Americans were reminded of the Powers' tradition, which was being continued by a second generation. That tradition is also found in the portrait busts that mark the graves of the two Lowndes women, dated 1878 and 1882; the busts stand quietly amid the wild natural growth of Magnolia Cemetery in Charleston, South Carolina. But in following the established style of his father's portraiture, Preston Powers failed to keep stride with the changes that were occurring in American sculpture—changes that emanated from the *Beaux-Arts* style of Paris. Moreover, there was no "Greek Slave" or "Eve" to create any special aura about the work of the younger Powers. There were practically no attempts at ideal pieces. Around 1880 he was working on one of the few life-size, full-length figures of his career—the marble statue of Jacob Collamer, which the state of Vermont presented to Statuary Hall in the Capitol. Competent but unexciting, it is again a continuation of mid-century aesthetics, which in portraiture willingly settled for a fidelity to realistic physiognomy and tailoring. By this criterion, Preston Powers succeeded well.

American portrait sculpture in the years immediately following the Civil War developed a character all its own. The bitter experience of the Civil War created a people who had lost their ability to idealize, and could only recognize a reality they could see. Naturalism became a jealous god that purged completely the elements of Romanticism—be they classical, Gothic, Byronic, or whatever—with which it had found a certain compatibility in the first half of the century. We can see naturalism as an end in itself in the late portraits of Hiram Powers, where the earlier Byronic ideal was swept aside. It can also be seen in the work of Henry Kirke Brown, whose marble statue of General Nathanael Greene is no match for his equestrian "Washington." And it can be recognized in countless other sculptors of the period. It has gained for the sixties and seventies the reputation of an art that is crass and banal in its naturalism, devoid of any poetry. With some justification, the question has been asked whether a sculpture that was so captivated by objectivism and the pursuit of reality could attain the level of the highest form of art. The painted portrait in America experienced the same disastrous result. An excessive naturalism had been encouraged by the appearance of the camera, which produced an image of total objectivity and accuracy, and unfortunately both patron and artist accepted this as the true form of art. The photographic naturalism of the painted portrait was not to be outdone by the modeled portrait, and American portraiture had to await the arrival of such men as John Singer Sargent, Thomas Eakins, and Augustus Saint-Gaudens to restore Art with a capital *A* upon the throne usurped by Naturalism with a capital *N*. To rise above the dull mediocrity it had achieved, naturalism had to be revitalized with elegance and heroism.

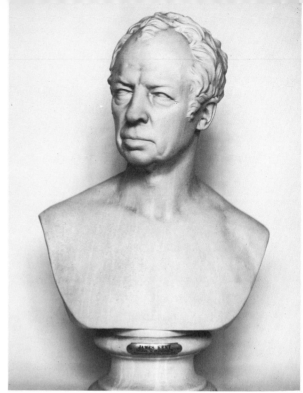

[FIG. 6.1] "Josiah Lawrence," by Shobal Clevenger (1837). Plaster. Courtesy, Cincinnati Art Museum.

[FIG. 6.2] "James Kent," by Shobal Clevenger (1840). Plaster, 26″ high. Courtesy, New-York Historical Society, New York City.

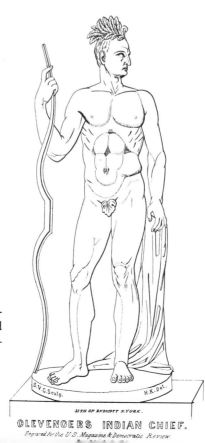

[FIG. 6.3] "Indian Chief," by Shobal Clevenger (1842). Published in *The U.S. Magazine & Democratic Review*, February, 1844.

[FIG. 6.4] "Washington Allston," by Edward Brackett (1844). Marble, 26″ high. Courtesy, Metropolitan Museum of Art, gift of Children of Jonathan Sturges, 1895.

[FIG. 6.6] "James Buchanan," by Henry Dexter (1859). Marble, 25½″ high. Courtesy, National Collection of Fine Arts, Smithsonian Institution.

[FIG. 6.5] "The Reverend Francis William Pitt Greenwood," by John C. King (1841). Marble. Courtesy, King's Chapel, Boston.

[FIG. 6.8] "Agnes Maxwell Kearny," by Joel T. Hart (1854). Marble, 22½" high. Collection, Corcoran Gallery of Art, gift of Miss Virginia Livingston Hunt.

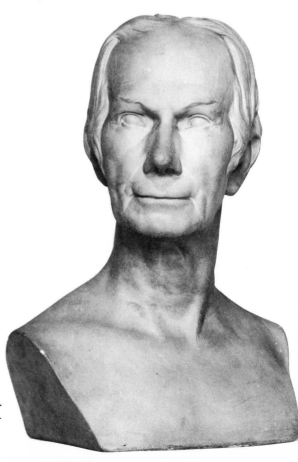

[FIG. 6.7] "Henry Clay," by Joel T. Hart (1847). Marble. State House, Richmond, Va. Courtesy, State of Virginia; photo, Index of American Sculpture, University of Delaware.

[FIG. 6.9] "Henry Clay," by Joel T. Hart (c. 1834). Plaster, 19" high. Courtesy, New-York Historical Society, New York City.

[FIG. 6.10] "Abraham Lincoln," by Thomas Dow Jones (1861). Plaster, 32½" high. Courtesy, New-York Historical Society, New York City.

[FIG. 6.11] "Griffin Taylor," by Thomas Dow Jones (c. 1865–70). Marble, 32½" high. Courtesy, Cincinnati Art Museum.

[FIG. 6.12] "James Edward Macfarland," by John Adams Jackson (1853). Marble, 29½" high. Courtesy, Confederate Museum, Richmond, Va.

[FIG. 6.13] "Bacchante," by Alexander Galt (c. 1852). Marble, 21″ high. Collection, Corcoran Gallery of Art, gift of William Wilson Corcoran.

[FIG. 6.14] "John Rutledge," by Alexander Galt (1856). Marble. U.S. Capitol, Washington, D.C. Courtesy, Architect of the Capitol.

[FIG. 6.15] "Alexander Hamilton," by Horatio Stone (c. 1868). Marble. Statuary Hall, U.S. Capitol, Washington, D.C. Courtesy, Architect of the Capitol.

[FIG. 6.16] "Louis Agassiz," by Preston Powers (1874). Marble. Collection, Corcoran Gallery of Art.

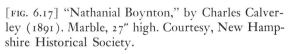

[FIG. 6.17] "Nathanial Boynton," by Charles Calverley (1891). Marble, 27″ high. Courtesy, New Hampshire Historical Society.

7

The Bronze Age and the Galvanized Heroes

IN THE SECOND QUARTER OF THE 19TH CENTURY AMERICAN SCULPTORS HAD CHOSEN to execute their finest efforts in glistening white marble or dull chalk-white plaster. No doubt this was a legacy from the neoclassicism that dominated European art in the second half of the 18th and the beginning of the 19th century. In the 1840's there had been only a few adventurous experiments with bronze casting in the sculptors' own studios, but after the middle of the century a high degree of competence in the techniques of casting was rapidly achieved, and American sculpture entered its "bronze age." Although European foundries, such as von Müller's in Munich, were used frequently, year by year sculptors, such as Clark Mills, Henry Kirke Brown, and John Quincy Adams Ward, came to rely increasingly on their own abilities and those of American foundries.

The nation wanted statues of its heroes in public squares and parks. Marble sculpture does not long survive exposure to the American climate, and bronze weathers very well; its only reaction to the elements is an enriching patina that forms over the years. Moreover, bronze offered a greater freedom and versatility than marble; the latter because of its sheer weight could not be employed for an equestrian monument, as the bulk of the horse's body and the rider could not be supported by the animal's four spindly legs. Even with standing figures in marble, it was usually necessary to contrive some support in addition to the statue's legs, and tree trunks or bundles of fasces or some other device had to be worked into the design. A bronze figure, however, could stand alone, for the hollow mass of the torso posed no threat to the slenderness of the legs; in a bronze equestrian monument the horse could even be represented rearing on its hind legs.

The sculptors discussed in this chapter were mainly makers of public monuments, their work being largely devoted to portrait statues, commissioned by the local or federal government. And though several of them began their careers in the closing years of the marmorean age, the group as a whole is chiefly known by their works cast in bronze. The character of the portrait style that emerged may in general be described as a naturalism that lacks drama and that frequently fails to convey anything very significant in the way of intellectual or emotional experience; nor do these works, as a rule, possess in themselves a dynamics of sculptural form sufficient to lift the spectator to aesthetic heights. An accurate rendition of the appearance of the statesman, merchant, clergyman, educator, soldier, and so on, was the main objective, and it formed the basis of the aesthetics of this bronze age. At times all these factors combined to produce some very fine, straightforward, unpretentious portraiture. This phase of American sculpture developed in a place and among a people where there was no tradition in or conception of powerful, glorious sculptural form. Still, the art of this period expressed the aesthetic taste of the nation, and it was accordingly praised. The sculptors and their patrons took an honest look at the Americans being portrayed and decided that their great men were great just as they were; and so they were represented without embellishment, sham, or pretension. If there was a certain measure of brass in American society, it was the result of a society of self-made men, of whom mid-19th-century America was not prone to be critical; therefore, a measure of brass was also permitted in their portraits. No better example of this brand of portraiture exists than that of Thomas Ball.

One of the very few artists to write an autobiography, Thomas Ball (1819–1911) in his *My Three Score Years and Ten* allows us to know the warmth of his family ties and friendships, and provides us with an intimate commentary on the struggles of an artist to attain perfection in his work. Ball's father was a sign painter who was sensitive to the first manifestations of his son's native talents in both art and music. When Ball was a lad of about ten or eleven, his father took him to see Chantrey's "Washington" in the Boston State House. After his father's death the boy held a series of odd jobs that included bricklaying and clerking in a museum. At the latter post he began to cut silhouette profiles and to paint miniature portraits, exhibiting his efforts in the early 1840's at the Boston Athenaeum and the Apollo Association in New York. In this manner he was led into a painting career that showed little promise of success. By 1848 and 1849 he was exhibiting such ambitious paintings as "Christ in the Temple" and "Scene From King Lear" at the American Art Union.

Meanwhile, Ball's interest in music was still strong, and he supplemented his income by singing in church choirs and the like. He sang the role of Adam in Haydn's *Creation* and the title role of Elijah in the first American performance of Mendelssohn's oratorio. By 1850 the production from his easel showed every sign of remaining inauspicious; moreover, the sensitive, sentimental young artist had experienced a disappointment in love that left him unable to concentrate on his painting. His friend John C. King, the portrait sculptor, one day gave him a lump of clay "about the size of two fists . . . to play with" when he was unable to paint. As Ball began to work with the clay in his own studio, the prescribed therapy worked its magic as one small head after another took form, each being destroyed to become another. His career as a sculptor was launched.

His first serious attempt at portraiture was inspired by the Swedish Nightingale, Jenny Lind, who was brought to this country by the great showman P. T. Barnum in 1850. So moved was Ball upon hearing her sing that he collected all the photographs of her he could obtain and from these modeled her likeness. The result was such an immediate success that Ball could not produce replicas of the bust fast enough, until an "Italian pirate in New York" got hold of one, manufactured copies himself, and sold them at starvation prices. By the middle of the century this piracy of sculptors' designs had become so common that sculptors began to obtain patents or copyrights, but even this was frequently ineffective. Ball, in fact, had paid $30 to patent his "Jenny Lind." On one occasion Ball discovered copies of two of his own busts of close friends being peddled on the streets of Providence; and upon asking the peddler about them, he was told they were "the man that was hung the other day in Boston, and the man he killed." It was not unusual to find peddlers in the larger cities, with trays of plaster busts and statuettes, hawking their wares on street corners or from door to door; Nicolino Calyo recorded just such a scene in a little water color illustration in his book *When the Old Streets Talked*, now in the Museum of the City of New York. All this may be interpreted as a means of meeting a demand for a mass-produced sculptural art at a low price for America's increasingly art-conscious middle class. Two other manifestations of it occurred in the same decade: John Rogers' genre groups and Currier and Ives' lithographs.

Ball continued working on a smaller-than-life scale for another year, probably because he was a little timid in attempting anything monumental and also because his small busts, or "cabinet" busts, as they were commonly called, were quite popular. It was the custom of the day to have several such portrait busts of eminent persons about the house; a "Jenny Lind" might be placed on the piano, for instance. During this period (1851 and 1852) Ball modeled several cabinet portraits of his friends, many of whom were musicians; among them are busts of George J. Webb, George F. Hayter, and Charles C. Perkins. He also modeled a cabinet-size portrait of Daniel Webster, a man he greatly admired. Thoroughly dissatisfied with the small portrait, he at once destroyed it, but the desire to portray Webster lingered. And in the course of his career he was to produce two portrait busts, a statuette, and two heroic-size bronze statues of the Massachusetts orator.

Ball undoubtedly felt that the greatness of Webster could not successfully be reduced to a cabinet-size image, and so was led to undertake his first portrait bust of dimensions slightly larger than life (Fig. 7.2). This time he achieved the fiery spirit and the resolution with which his subject was imbued, and instead of putting him in contemporary street clothes, as he was to do in later images of Webster, he draped the shoulders in a wrap that bears resemblance more to those used in Baroque and Rococo busts than to the classical toga. Webster, of course, did not pose for this portrait, which was modeled on a stake placed upright over an ash barrel. In fact, Ball had only one fleeting glimpse of the man when he passed through Boston at that time on his way to Marshfield, where he died shortly after. The sculptor recalled the incident in his autobiography:

As [Webster's] procession was to pass through Tremont Street, you may be sure I was at [my studio] door to have a good look at him . . . . It seemed but a few days before the bulletins began to record his rapid decline, and then came the final announcement of his death. My bust was finished but a day or two before, and as you may suppose, at such a time attracted a good deal of attention. It was pronounced a wonderful success, and numerous demands were made for casts of it. I put a subscription paper in front of it, and in a very few days had nearly a hundred names upon it . . . . This bust, my first of life-size, is the only one I have ever used, without alteration, for my several statues of the great man.*

Soon after Webster's death there was talk in Boston of a statue of the great man to be placed in one of the public parks. Though Ball did not believe he would get the commission for a full-length heroic figure, he was led to model a statuette. In his first encounter with the entire figure he tells of being in such a rush to model it that he used as a makeshift armature an umbrella stick, and while observing his work one day, "had the satisfaction of seeing it slowly tip forward and go crashing to the floor." Only the head could be salvaged; the figure had to be made again. In the statuette Webster is represented as he might have been seen addressing Congress, in contemporary dress, his right hand placed inside his coat in the familiar "Napoleonic" manner. As Ball's first attempt at the human figure it was quite successful, but unfortunately it missed its heroic objective by too close a fidelity to Webster's ill-fitting trousers and coat and to his protruding belly. Nevertheless, on the first day that the model was exhibited, C. W. Nichols offered the sculptor $500 for it, which he accepted, granting the purchaser permission to reproduce it. Nichols may have begun with plaster copies only, but over the next several years both plaster and bronze replicas were produced in great number. An inscription on the base of the bronzes shows that the patent was actually assigned to C. W. Nichols, not to Thomas Ball. Replicas in bronze or plaster exist in numerous public collections throughout the country. Historically it is important as one of the earliest sculptures to be mass-produced and patented.

The success Thomas Ball experienced during his first three years as a sculptor encouraged him to try for wider opportunities. In pursuit of these, he and his

---

* Unless otherwise noted, quotations are taken from Thomas Ball's autobiography, *My Three Score Years and Ten*, Boston, 1892.

wife sailed for Italy on October 11, 1854, on the steamer *America*. In Florence, Joel T. Hart helped them find an apartment—one formerly occupied by the painter William Page and the sculptor Shobal Clevenger. On the first evening the painter and poet Thomas B. Read came to call and took Ball to one of the regularly held social evenings at the home of the Hiram Powerses. A friend from Boston, the painter Francis Alexander, was there, along with the Brownings.

We found assembled quite a roomful of Americans and Englishmen. Hiram Powers . . . welcomed me very cordially. Those receptions we afterward found very pleasant, —conversation interspersed with music or an occasional recitation, and refreshed by tea and cakes.

Ball took a studio in the Piazza Indipendenza, "with an adjoining room for a marble workman to cut three or four busts I had brought with me to put in marble." One of those, signed and dated 1855, is the bust of little Herbert Skinner now in the Boston Athenaeum. Of the several portraits dating from this first Italian sojourn (1854–1857), one of the finest is that of the Reverend Ephraim Peabody (Fig. 7.1), minister of King's Chapel in Boston from 1845 to 1856. The bust has a quality that had come to dominate American portraiture: an unpretentious rendering of the physiognomy, faithful in its likeness, but plain and lacking drama. In painting, one thinks of the portraits of George P. A. Healy or Thomas Hicks. Ball did not participate in the classical revival, which was not to have its final dissipation until the third quarter of the century. Instead his style was based on a simple and direct naturalism. But he sought something more, too, and in his autobiography is the following exhortation: ". . . to make the most satisfactory portrait . . . the character and expression should first be attended to; the exact form of each individual feature is of minor importance." The Reverend Mr. Peabody was represented with a quiet, self-confident bearing yet an intent expression in the eyes and mouth. Also, the surface treatment and general rendering of the clerical robes are as fine as any to be found in American portraiture.

From these first Italian years date other works which reveal the prolificacy of Thomas Ball. There is a fine bust of Napoleon and statuettes of Washington Allston and George Washington, as well as several essays at ideal works. "Boy on a Raft, Shipwrecked" proved to be too ambitious for him, and "Pandora" (1855) was never carried beyond the clay model. The latter was his first experience in working from the nude model, and he naïvely wrote that he was surprised to discover that all Italian women were not like the Venus de' Medici.

In 1857 Ball returned to Boston, where he remained for eight years. There are several busts from this period—"President Lord" of Dartmouth, "Henry Ward Beecher," a cabinet-size "Rufus Choate," and "William H. Prescott," the historian and author of *The History of the Conquest of Mexico*. Almost immediately after his return Ball was asked to execute two relief panels, depicting events from the life of Benjamin Franklin, which were to be applied to the pedestal of Richard Greenough's statue of Franklin at the City Hall, Boston. But his two greatest triumphs of these years were his little statuette of Henry Clay and his heroic equestrian statue of Washington for the Public Garden.

In the late spring and early summer of 1858 Ball modeled his statuette (31 inches high) of Henry Clay (Fig. 7.3), and on July 8 he invited Edward Everett, who knew Clay well, to come to his studio to see it before it was sent off to the foundry. Everett was impressed with the statuette and wrote a testimonial praising it. Ball's statuette is perhaps the most excellent full-length figure of Henry Clay ever made, as a work of art surpassing even Joel Tanner Hart's "Clay," which Ball must have seen in Hart's studio in Florence. In this piece the sculptor was far more successful in mastering the difficult problem of contemporary dress than were most of his contemporaries. There is a verve, a pugnacious defiance, in the stance and the wiry frame of Clay. The paper in his hands and the fragment of a column at his side suggest that he is in the act of delivering one of his orations in the pillared hall of Congress. In his statuettes of Clay and Webster, Ball has created portraits of two of the ablest statesmen of their day, achieving an artistry that was never reached in the heroic-size statues of great men that he made in later years.

The statuette of Henry Clay was placed in the hands of C. W. Nichols, who contracted with the Ames foundry of Chicopee, Massachusetts, to produce bronze replicas of it. This foundry was one of the first to cast sculpture by American artists in bronze. Only a few years earlier (1855) it had cast Richard Greenough's statue of Franklin and Thomas Ball's relief panels that went with it, and three years before that it had successfully cast Brown's equestrian "Washington," no small accomplishment. Ball's "Henry Clay" and perhaps his "Daniel Webster" were, then, among the first to be cast by Ames.

Also in 1858 Ball began work on his most famous statue, the equestrian "Washington" in Boston's Public Garden (Fig. 7.4). Discussion of such a statue had periodically come up in Boston, and it was this general interest that induced the sculptor to make a model completely on his own. When it was finished, the model (now in the Boston Athenaeum) was shown to several friends who soon spread word of its success throughout the city. A committee was formed to raise the necessary funds, and before long the sculptor had the commission. While still in Florence Ball had heard that Boston was about to commission an equestrian statue of Washington, and he had begun to study the anatomy of the horse. But this was temporarily abandoned when in 1857 he learned that Thomas Crawford had been chosen for the job. It was, of course, never carried out by Crawford, who died later that year.

The artistic and technical problems of creating a heroic-size horse and rider were indeed challenging to a man who had not yet modeled a life-size full-length figure. But with his characteristic enthusiasm, Ball launched into the project at once. In his great barnlike studio (60 feet by 40 feet and 30 feet high) with its dirt floor, he erected an ingenious armature on a large round turntable at one end.

Screwed firmly to my platform was an iron post about ten feet high, and four or five inches square. A horizontal timber about the length of the body of the horse rested on top of the iron post . . . the timber intended to lie along just under the lowest part of the back and together with the iron post support the entire weight. I then formed of plaster a series of rough slabs, ten inches wide, three inches thick, and in the form of a half circle of the diameter of the body of the horse. As soon as they were hard I simply hung them up to the timber, a dozen on each side, their lower ends coming together under the belly, supporting each other until I could join them with plaster. Thus I had a hollow cylinder . . . forming a foundation upon which to build the "barrel" of my horse. I drew next on the floor the outlines of the legs in their right proportions and positions, bending a strong iron to lay in the middle of each leg . . . . Of course, my small model told me where to place the hoofs. After this, the building up of the neck and head of the horse was a simple matter.

To model his statue the sculptor used plaster instead of clay, for the great weight of the work (four to six tons) could have caused clay to give and sag; moreover, with the inadequate heat in his studio, clay would have frozen and cracked. The use of plaster, which hardens right away, eliminated these problems. Ball purposely placed his plaster at the far end of the studio and mixed it in two-quart batches, so that while he stirred up a fresh supply he could study his work from a distance and decide where the next portion should be applied. For the figure of Washington he made a straw man, that was then coated with plaster. The figure was modeled as a separate piece, and by means of a derrick it could be raised and then lowered into the saddle or brought back to the ground.

During this period (1858–1861) Ball did little but work on his great statue, and only a half-dozen portrait busts diverted his attention. The statue was 16 feet high and 16 feet long; the figure of Washington sat a heroic twelve feet tall in the saddle. The horse is a sturdy yet spirited animal, and reveals the sculptor's sound knowledge of equine anatomy. Washington sits very erect, controlling his mount with a light touch on the reins, and gazes into the distance. Even from below—at a distance of about twenty-five feet—the strong and forceful naturalism of the portrait may be seen. Details of the Revolutionary War uniform are minimized and do not detract from the statue's over-all simplicity and boldness.

When the group was finished the people of Boston were invited into the studio to see it, and they marveled at what one of their own had done. Even school children, we are told, were brought around in groups to see the wonderful image. But the Civil War had already begun when Thomas Ball put the finishing touches on his equestrian "Washington," and all available bronze was being cast into cannons, not statues. The completion of his great work would therefore have to wait for several years yet.

It was time for Thomas Ball to return to Florence. But late in 1864, before he left, he modeled a bust of Edward Everett. He also took a life mask of Everett's face and made measurements of the head or perhaps of the entire figure, no doubt with the hope of one day doing a full-length statue. The need for such a statue arose sooner than expected, for not long after Ball had finished the bust,

Edward Everett died. An Everett Statue Committee was formed immediately, and several sculptors submitted designs for a commemorative statue. Ball wrote the committee in January 1865 that he and Powers were the only living artists who had modeled Everett from life, that he was sailing for Europe in a few weeks, and that he would make the statue in Florence for $10,000 if he should receive the commission—which he didn't. The committee chose William Wetmore Story instead, who seems to have behaved in a rather ungentlemanly and quarrelsome fashion toward Ball, who generously offered both bust and measurements of Everett to whomever was selected by the committee. Neither of the sculptors ever forgot the incident. More or less as a consolation prize, the committee, which raised more money than it needed, commissioned Ball to put his bust of Everett into marble, offering him the inordinately high figure of $2,500. This bust is now in the Boston Public Library; other copies are at Harvard (marble, 1865) and the Massachusetts Historical Society (plaster, 1865).

Thomas Ball's Florence studio was a busy place in the years following his return. He had brought along several portraits besides the one of Everett, and he was then employing two Italian stonecutters full-time. In 1866 he was at work on the statue of Edwin Forrest in the role of Coriolanus for the Actor's Home in Philadelphia; it was put into marble the following year. Another bust of Daniel Webster was designed in 1868, which was later given to the Metropolitan Museum of Art by the artist's daughter. He also began work on the marble statue of Governor John Andrew, commissioned in 1868, for the State House in Boston; the statue, signed and dated 1870, was unveiled on February 14, 1871. Meanwhile his great equestrian statue had been cast at the Ames foundry in Chicopee, had been set upon its 15-foot-high granite pedestal, and dedicated on January 29, 1869. In 1869 also Ball executed his fine statue "St. John the Evangelist," which was ordered by Aaron Williams of Boston for his home, but which was later placed in Forest Hills Cemetery; Hiram Powers thought this statue was Ball's masterpiece. During this period he modeled several ideal works as well—"Love's Memories," a cupid seated on an Ionic capital; "La Petite Pensée"; and "Eve Stepping into Life," a standing figure.

In 1868 Thomas Ball had bought the property adjoining the land where Hiram Powers was building his new house. There, atop a hill overlooking Florence, Ball built for his family the "Villa Ball" on the site of a vineyard near an old monastery.

In the early 1870's the sculptor was at work on a monument for the plot of his wife's family, the Chickerings, in Mount Auburn Cemetery. The two figures atop the marble memorial represent, in the sculptor's own words, "The Realization of Faith." The Angel of Death, holding a torch pointed downward in his left hand, raises the veil that covers the eyes of a kneeling young woman, "Faith," who holds a cross to her breast. In a *tondo* on the pedestal is a bas-relief of a sleeping muse of music; she holds the laurel wreath and the lyre of Apollo, an appropriate image for the Chickering family of piano makers.

Soon after Thomas Ball's return to Italy he had modeled the small composition showing Abraham Lincoln with an unshackled figure of Liberty, which is now in the Houghton Library at Harvard. The composition was repeated in 1873–1874 when he executed a larger work of Lincoln bidding a Negro, with broken chains at his wrists, to rise (Fig. 7.5). This is the "Emancipation Group," or "Freedman's Memorial," which was cast at von Müller's Royal Foundry in Munich and set up in Washington, D.C., in 1875. The group was extremely popular among Northerners, and two years later the Honorable Moses Kimball ordered a duplicate of it for the city of Boston. In the earlier model the sculptor had made an "ideal" slave, but in the statues for Washington and Boston he was more specific. The head of the slave is that of Archer Alexander, the last man to be recaptured under the Fugitive Slave Law. Ball had modeled the likeness from Alexander's photograph, which had been sent to him from America. This gave the group an authenticity that Americans greatly admired. One critic wrote that the "ideal group is thus converted into the literal truth of history without losing anything of its artistic conception or effect." Objective truthfulness and literal naturalism is again seen to dominate the art of Thomas Ball. For something that had so touched the American people's lives, no fanciful ideal would do. The significance of the statue was increased by the fact that the figures were accurate portraits of the men themselves. There is a bold resolution in the face of Lincoln, and the half-clad figure of the slave is quite well executed. But in the figure of Lincoln the broad planes of the coat and trousers are simplified to the point of monotony, a characteristic weakness found in several of Ball's full-length portrait statues of the 1870's and 1880's. For the occasion of the unveiling of the group, John Greenleaf Whittier wrote a poem that was read aloud to the assembled spectators.

During the period 1873–1878, Ball was so busy with heroic-size statues that he seems not to have had time for portrait busts. In 1876 he produced an enlargement of his Webster statuette for New York's Central Park, a statue that already by 1900 was mentioned as among those "bad statues" in the Park that ought to be destroyed. Boston commissioned two more monuments of her worthy sons, and in 1877 and 1878 Ball modeled the statues of Charles Sumner (Public Garden; Fig. 7.6) and Josiah Quincy (in front of City Hall, Boston). The sculptor had at first refused to enter into a competition for the Sumner statue, then changed his mind. His first model wore slippers, and when questioned about this by a committee member Ball answered that "it was simply a fancy of mine to represent the great man in his study, from whence emanated his great thoughts." This original conception was replaced by one of the statesman delivering a public oration. Altogether twenty-six sculptors submitted plaster models in the competition. The committee found none of the models satisfactory as they were, however, and deliberated further. Finally three prizes of $500 each were awarded to Martin Milmore, Anne Whitney, and Thomas Ball; and to Ball went the commission and its $12,000 stipend. While Ball was at work on the "Sumner" in his studio in Florence he was visited by Ulysses S. Grant, who is reported to have said, "Charles Sumner! That's the fourth Sumner I've seen this morning!" The statue, which was cast in the Barbedienne Foundry in Paris, was unveiled in Boston on December 23, 1878. The head is an excellent portrait study, but the rest of the figure is uninteresting. The same may be said of the statue of Josiah Quincy. Although there is a certain dramatic intenseness and vigor in the head, the figure itself is an anticlimax. Ball never solved the problem of the complete portrait statue in which every part of the figure participates in expressing the whole man. The "Quincy" was cast in Munich and erected in Boston in 1879.

One of Thomas Ball's finest compositions in point of sculptural form was the heroic-size "Christ with a little Child" of 1880, which drew high praise from Dupré, one of the leading European sculptors of the day. The head is one of serene and manly beauty, and in the folds of Christ's robes the sculptor achieved a variety and excellence of composition that was absent from most of his portrait statues. "David," a defiant, scantily clad youth who leans backward in the act of flinging the stone at Goliath, was modeled in 1885 and put into marble about 1890. Also about 1885 Ball was busy on another large bronze of Daniel Webster, this one for the State House lawn at Concord, New Hampshire. The result was an improvement on the one he had done for New York City a decade earlier, both statues in general following the statuette of 1853. In 1883 Ball had modeled a bust of P. T. Barnum, and shortly thereafter he was given a commission for a full-length portrait of the man. This was done in 1886–1888, cast in bronze, and erected in Bridgeport, Connecticut. All these works are evidence of the reputation Thomas Ball enjoyed; he received numerous extremely lucrative commissions from various parts of the country, even during economic crises when money was not plentiful. America liked his brand of naturalism and did not find it dull and banal as later critics did.

In the late 1890's Ball worked on his one last great project—the Washington monument, now destroyed, that was erected in the city of Methuen, Massachusetts. At the base sat four historical and allegorical figures; one of the finest was that of Cincinnatus, a middle-aged man in the dress of a Roman general. Between the seated figures American eagles clutched flags in their talons. Higher up were busts of four of Washington's generals in the Revolutionary War. Crowning the entire monument was the colossal figure of General George Washington, right arm extended, as if addressing a gathering below. The monument, in its blending of naturalism and allegory, carried Ball through the period that saw the arrival of a new generation of American sculptors led by Augustus Saint-Gaudens and his own former student, Daniel Chester French. While in one sense this new generation of sculptors turned their backs on the plain naturalism of Ball and some of his contemporaries, they also drew much of their strength from the "truth in nature" their predecessors so highly prized.

Thomas Ball returned to America soon after he completed the several parts for his Washington monument, and went to live with his daughter and her husband, the sculptor William Couper, in Montclair, New Jersey. Not much dates from this period except a small self-portrait of an old, bearded sculptor, a copy of which is in the Addison Gallery in Andover, Massachusetts. Ball died in 1911 at the age of ninety-two.

Active during the same years as Thomas Ball was Anne Whitney (1821–1915), youngest of the seven children of Nathaniel R. Whitney II, a gentleman farmer and clerk in Middlesex Courts, and Sarah Stone Whitney. As she was growing up in Massachusetts, her interest in the arts was encouraged both at home and at school. At first her attention centered on poetry; then one day she chanced to come upon a lump of moist clay in a neighbor's greenhouse. The material took form readily under her touch, and it is said that this is how her career as a sculptor began. Her earliest portraits were of members of her family—busts of her father and mother (1855) and of her brother James (about 1858). She modeled busts of friends and relatives in her studio in Watertown, and sought instruction in New York and Philadelphia. In 1861 she made the likeness of her life long friend Adeline Manning; the portrait possesses a delicate animation in the tilt and turn of the head; the style is a plain but refined naturalism. The subject wears contemporary dress, with a shawl about the shoulders; there is a simplicity in the folds of the drapery and in the hair that prevents them from detracting from the face itself. The essential characteristic of Anne Whitney's style is an uncomplicated naturalism, which was to govern her work even during several years spent in Europe.

One of her earliest ideal works is "Lady Godiva" (1861), a sculpture perfectly suited to the typical Victorian parlor or vestibule. It is essentially a costume piece, with careful attention lavished on ruffles, patterns, and pleats. In this it appealed to mid-century tastes, which reveled in a profusion of surface detail, even though some of the more basic sculpturesque qualities were sacrificed. The marble "Lady Godiva" was shown in both Boston and New York City, where it drew considerable attention to the heretofore unknown sculptor. That this was the sculptor's first effort at a full-length, life-size figure was impressive; that it had been created by a woman made it an object of extraordinary curiosity, for Anne Whitney, Harriet Hosmer, Emma Stebbins, Margaret Foley, and Edmonia Lewis had just begun to establish woman's place in the field of sculpture. It had previously been acceptable for women to dabble in watercolor sketches or to paint little still lifes in oil, but before the middle of the 19th century, sculpture had been considered a masculine art, requiring more exertion and involving more of a mess than was thought proper for womankind.

During the years of the Civil War, Anne Whitney was in America while many American sculptors went to or remained in Italy. That she was much concerned with the issues is shown by her statue "Africa," a colossal reclining figure, which was cast in plaster in 1864 and shown in Boston and New York, but which was destroyed by the sculptor herself many years later. Inscribed on the base was the

Biblical text: "And Ethiopia shall soon stretch out her hands to God." Her anti-slavery sentiments were even more strongly expressed a few years later in her statue of Toussaint L'Ouverture in prison. In the mid-1860's she also modeled a number of busts and medallions of children, which sold well throughout the next several years. Her work progressed mainly under her own direction all the while, although she did study anatomy in Boston in 1862 with William Rimmer.

When the Civil War ended, she began to dream more and more of study abroad, and in 1867 she joined the American colony in Rome. Here her inclination toward ideal subjects was stimulated. She had modeled a "Lotus Eater" in Boston, and in 1864 it was put into marble. But she was evidently not satisfied with the result and took the sketch to Rome, where she remodeled it in 1867; a plaster statuette of this second version is in the Newark (New Jersey) Museum. Similar to the "Lotus Eater" is her statue "Chaldean Shepherd," or "The Astronomer" (1868), which may have been inspired by William Rimmer's statue of the same subject. Both the "Lotus Eater" and the "Shepherd" are idealized nude youths, although in a final version of the latter a sheepskin covers the loins. In these figures there is the influence of classical Roman art, of which Anne Whitney was quite aware. In 1869, again influenced by her environment, she modeled what she held to be one of her most successful works—the "Roma." It was one of her most popular pieces and several copies of it in different media were made during the following decades. The "Roma" is a bent, seated beggarwoman in long robes, with a scarf over her head and an expression of hopelessness, suggesting the destitute situation of Italy before its unification. It may very well have a prototype in images of Hellenistic and Roman beggarwomen, and of course there was a well-established tradition of figures of women personifying cities of the ancient world.

Anne Whitney's stay in Europe lasted four years and included study in Paris and Munich, as well as in Rome. In 1871 she returned to America and opened a studio in Boston. She was by then one of the leading sculptors living in New England, and within a year of her return she received the commission from the Commonwealth of Massachusetts to create the marble statue of Samuel Adams for Statuary Hall in Washington. Adams is represented in a defiant pose in the dress of his day, his arms folded across his chest and a scroll grasped tightly in his right hand. The commission stipulated that the carving be done in Italy, so after the small sketch was approved and the actual model (a little larger than life size) executed and cast in plaster, the sculptor returned to Florence. She supervised the selection of the block of marble, but once carving was underway she left Italy to spend the summer and winter in Ecouen and Paris. The marble carving was completed in 1875 in the studio of Thomas Ball, with Anne Whitney herself applying the finishing touches. The following year the statue was exhibited in the vestibule of the Athenaeum in Boston before being presented to Congress in July. The forceful image of Adams was well received by Bostonians, who showed their approval by commissioning a bronze replica; this was cast at the Ames foundry in Chicopee and erected in Adams Square in front of Faneuil Hall in 1880 (Fig. 7.8).

Before Anne Whitney went to Florence to have the statue of Adams carved, she made a small model of a statue of Charles Sumner, which she submitted anonymously in the competition held by the Sumner Memorial Committee. When her design—representing the senator seated, in contemporary dress—was chosen as one of the best three (of twenty-six entries) there was much consternation over its having been made by a woman. She was awarded $500 as a prize, but the commission was given to Thomas Ball. Her disappointment was bitter indeed, and she—like Augustus Saint-Gaudens, who had also entered a design —vowed never again to enter a competition. Many years later she produced her statue of Sumner on her own and, with the help of several Harvard professors, arranged to have it erected in Harvard Square. This bronze version dates from 1900. It is a well-done portrait, representing the senator deep in thought; there is a fine incisiveness in the character study of the head.

By this time traces of the influence of French sculpture had begun to show in Anne Whitney's work, indicating the shift of interest from Rome to Paris that occurred in the 1870's. It was in 1874, for example, that Saint-Gaudens returned to America after several years of study in France and Italy, but with virtually no trace of the influence of Italian classicism. The more impressionistic French style, with its lively surface and flickering lights and shadows, can be perceived in Anne Whitney's "Le Modèle," a bronze bust in the Boston Museum of Fine Arts. Modeled in 1875 and cast in Paris by the Gruet Foundry, it represents an elderly peasant woman dozing, her turbaned head bent low and away from the spectator. Also dating from this French period are "Faun of Fontainebleau" (a head of a child with the ears of a faun) and "Head of a Young Girl."

Anne Whitney's association with the main currents of New England intellectual activity, especially the abolitionist movement, was demonstrated when she modeled the portrait bust of William Lloyd Garrison. Several plaster and marble examples survive. In the life of Garrison written by his children, there is an account of the modeling of this bust:

A new friendship, which [Garrison] greatly enjoyed, was formed in the spring of 1878, when he became acquainted . . . with the gifted sculptress, Miss Anne Whitney of Boston, and was invited by her to sit for his portrait bust. During the months of March, April, and May he made frequent visits to her studio, and gave her full opportunity to study his features and character.
[*William Lloyd Garrison, 1805–1879: The Story of his Life Told by his Children*, 1885–89, vol. 4, p. 288]

The bust was carved in Italy in late 1878 and returned to Boston in March the following year. That Garrison himself was highly satisfied with the likeness—preferring it to those made earlier by Clevenger and Jackson—is shown in a letter to his daughter, written only a few days after seeing the bust in marble: "It is admirably executed and the marble is of the purest white . . . . I do not think a more accurate 'counterfeit presentment' of your father's features could possibly be made; and I am particularly pleased that it has been achieved by a woman."

Olin Warner, after winning a competition conducted by the Garrison Memorial Committee, produced his bronze image of Garrison, which now resides on Commonwealth Avenue in Boston. Garrison's family disliked the statue intensely, and in 1880 they commissioned Anne Whitney to do a statuette of the celebrated abolitionist. The result (Fig. 7.7) was one of the finest specimens of her work. Five bronze replicas were made, one for each home of the Garrison family. In it, Anne Whitney managed to overcome the problem of contemporary dress that had plagued sculptors for decades. The necessary details are present, but emphasis is successfully centered on the man himself, especially on his thoughtful expression. This is as close to the vital naturalism of Saint-Gaudens and Daniel Chester French as Anne Whitney comes, and a comparison between her "Garrison" and French's marble "Emerson" (1914) in the Concord Public Library is instructive. It is, however, the smoothness and finish of the surfaces —in which Hiram Powers and Thomas Ball took great pride—that ties the "Garrison" to the older style.

In the fall of 1880 Anne Whitney executed an equestrian statuette of Robert Gould Shaw as a model for a memorial to the man who gave his life while leading a regiment of Negro soldiers in battle during the Civil War. But though there was an initial show of interest in erecting a suitable memorial, the necessary funds were not obtained for many years, and the commission was ultimately given to Augustus Saint-Gaudens. Earlier in 1880, however, she had modeled a statuette of Leif Ericson, in response to the Norumbega theory that the Vikings had landed in America around A.D. 1000. The city of Boston commissioned a heroic-size statue to be cast in bronze, and the full-scale model was begun in her studio on Mt. Vernon Street. Cast in plaster in 1885, the statue was sent to the foundry at Chicopee, where it was cast in bronze at a cost of $11,000. On October 29, 1887, it was unveiled on its pedestal on Commonwealth Avenue; about two weeks later a bronze replica had its presentation ceremonies in Milwaukee, Wisconsin. In the library of the Boston Athenaeum, Anne Whitney had consulted every available source on Viking costume so that her statue would be historically correct. But in the details of the chain-mail armor and other paraphernalia, it became a costume-history piece, and the total effect of the statue suffered as a result.

In 1878 Anne Whitney was commissioned to make a life-size statue of Harriet Martineau, an English author and economist who had joined the antislavery movement in 1835 and had led the international movement for women's rights and other reforms. Working from photographs, Anne Whitney modeled the statue in clay in her Boston studio, creating an idealized portrait of the subject, trying for the spirit of the woman rather than for her physical appearance. The original plaster cast was shipped to Florence, where it was carved in marble in

1883. On December 26 the 8-foot-high seated statue was unveiled in Old South Church after an oration delivered by the eminent author and avid abolitionist Wendell Phillips. Two years later it was presented to Wellesley College, to be "an incentive and an inspiration to young women"; placed in College Hall, it was destroyed by fire in 1914. The original plaster bust of the Martineau statue still exists, however, in a private collection.

In the last part of the nineteenth century Anne Whitney modeled many portrait busts, an activity she had avoided earlier in her career. In the Wellesley College Library there are three of her portraits: a plaster bust of Ann Mary Hale (1877), a marble bust of Eben Norton Horsford (1890), and a plaster bust of Alice Freeman Palmer (1891). In the early 1880's she modeled a portrait of the famous lawyer for women's rights Samuel Edmund Sewell, and in 1888 she did one of Edward Charles Pickering, the Harvard astronomer. She also made medallion profiles of Jennie McGraw Fiske (1891; bronze replica at Cornell University), Mary Tileston Hemenway (c. 1892), and George H. Palmer (1894; Wellesley College Library); marble busts of two famous American women of the day, Harriet Beecher Stowe and Frances Elizabeth Willard, date from 1892.

The likeness of Lucy Stone was taken in 1893. The details of this commission are given in a letter from the subject's daughter to a friend. Apparently Lucy Stone had refused the request of Frances Willard and others to have a portrait done for exhibition at the Chicago World's Fair of 1893 because she thought the money should not be diverted from the suffrage cause. At a meeting of the New England Women's Club, which Lucy Stone did not attend, a committee was formed, and Anne Whitney was asked if she would model a bust for the $150 that had been subscribed. The sculptor was willing (although her usual fee was $300), and Lucy Stone, upon learning that the money had been subscribed for this purpose only, agreed to pose. The result was a fine likeness, and the marble bust was proudly exhibited in the Woman's Building at the World's Fair and later presented to the Boston Public Library.

There were other portraits from the last decade of the century, such as the bust of Mary Ashton Rice Livermore (1895; Melrose, Mass., Public Library) and medallions of Polly Brown Austin and Almena Baker-Flint. In the winters of 1899 and 1900 Anne Whitney, nearing eighty, was busy working on the statue she had wished to do many years before—the one of Charles Sumner. This was her last major undertaking. She had begun her career in the pre-Civil War era of unrestrained naturalism in American sculpture, but she perceived the vitality and strength that was reborn in the art of some of the younger sculptors of the 1870's and incorporated them into her own work. Anne Whitney lived until 1915, spending pleasant summers at her farm in Shelburne, New Hampshire, and winters in Boston, where she loved to entertain her fellow Bostonians, especially poets. She died at the age of ninety-three.

Martin Milmore was born in Ireland in 1844 and brought to America by his mother in 1851 after the death of his father. Joseph, an elder brother, and Martin were educated through Latin School. Immediately afterward, Joseph began an apprenticeship to a cabinetmaker and then became a stonecutter, whereas Martin started taking art lessons at the Lowell Institute, where he drew from casts, did some watercolors, and possibly studied anatomy. It was, however, from his brother that Martin caught the first spark that led him into sculpture. Joseph taught him how to use the mallet and chisel and some of the fundamentals of carving, but he could furnish no assistance when young Martin modeled his first work in clay—a self-portrait. The boy had heard there was a sculptor in Boston who might take a student, and so he applied to Thomas Ball, who was about to begin work on his equestrian "Washington." Ball, reluctant at first, said he did not take students, but when the persistent Martin, then fourteen years old, re-appeared the next day the sculptor gave in.

I told him if he would like to come to me for a year, I would do all I could to help him on, and charge him nothing; but if he would keep my studio tidy (which I never could) and attend to the fires, I would furnish his fuel, clay and all his necessary studio-utensils in a room by himself . . . . [He] remained with me the next four years on these terms.   [T. Ball, *My Three Score Years and Ten*]

During those years Milmore watched the great equestrian group take form and undergo its final refinement. He also observed the sculptor modeling the likenesses of several eminent men and creating the magnificent statuette of Henry Clay. By the end of his four years with Thomas Ball, Martin Milmore had learned well how to model in plaster and clay.

Toward the end of his apprenticeship he began modeling works that attracted considerable attention. In 1863 he produced in high relief his first ideal work, "Phosphor," which was also his first piece of sculpture to find buyers, for he sold not only the original but also two replicas. In that same year he produced another ideal subject, a figure entitled "Devotion," for Boston's Sanitary Fair, and a foot-high plaster portrait bust of Henry Wadsworth Longfellow that reminds one of the cabinet-size busts Thomas Ball made in the late 1850's. These were small and inexpensive, and they were made with the hope that the subject's popularity would bring about the sale of many replicas. One such copy of Milmore's "Longfellow" is in the New Hampshire Historical Society. It possesses the same plain and undramatic naturalism that dominated Ball's sculpture. On the base is found the inscription "Copy-write of Devries, Ibarra & Co., Publishers, Boston." Milmore evidently turned the bust over to a publishing firm to have numerous copies produced, just as Ball had done with his statuettes of Webster and Clay.

At this time a committee approached Ball with a commission to execute three colossal figures for Horticultural Hall in Boston. But Ball was planning his return to Italy and turned down the proposal, and Martin Milmore, then not yet twenty years old, asked the older sculptor if he might apply to the committee for the commission. Ball agreed, recommended his protégé highly, and before he departed for Italy saw the career of Martin Milmore launched with a very

important and sizable commission. The three figures were classical personifications of the plenitude of nature—"Ceres" was 12 feet high and "Flora" and
"Pomona" were 8 feet tall. Classical studies dominated most learning in the
United States, and the science of horticulture was no exception; therefore, as was
typical of the times, classical symbols were chosen instead of purely American
images to express the bounty of Mother Earth. In point of artistic style, however, the classicism remained rather vague.

The three figures for Horticultural Hall did indeed launch the sculptural career of Martin Milmore; with the contract secured, the young sculptor opened
his own studio, bright visions of more great commissions ahead of him. After
Ball's departure there was no sculptor in Boston who ranked ahead of Milmore
for any monumental commission that might come from the city fathers or from
private individuals. Henry Dexter was confining his efforts almost wholly to portrait busts, and William Rimmer had managed to destroy his reputation for public statues with the hastily modeled statue of Hamilton. Richard Greenough was
in Paris; W. W. Story and John Adams Jackson had forsaken Massachusetts for
Italy—as had Anne Whitney, temporarily. Boston, and most of New England
with it, suddenly loomed as Milmore's territory. By then, Joseph Milmore had
become Martin's assistant, and during the two years devoted to the statues of
"Ceres," "Pomona," and "Flora" the brothers worked side by side. Martin conceived the designs and modeled them in plaster, and Joseph translated them into
stone.

The mainstay of any sculptor's studio was, of course, the portrait bust. Among
Milmore's earliest was one of Charles Sumner executed in 1865 as a gift from the
Massachusetts legislature to George William Curtis. Although rendered in the
somewhat dry naturalism of the day, there is animation in the tilt of the head
and determination in the set of the mouth. Within the limited aesthetics of objective naturalism the sculptor still managed to capture something of the personality of Sumner. Milmore dressed his subject in the toga drape of the ancient
statesman-philosopher rather than in contemporary attire; this was seldom done
at this date. Milmore's contemporaries saw a perfect likeness and an aura of the
greatness of Sumner himself in the bust, thus establishing Milmore as an
accomplished—even inspired—portraitist. Other portrait commissions of Boston's
more outstanding citizens followed, such as the "George Ticknor" (1868; Boston
Public Library) and the "Wendell Phillips" (Bostonian Society, Old State
House). The latter (Fig. 7.11), modeled by Martin but carved and signed by
Joseph Milmore, was presented to Phillips as a Christmas gift. Wendell Phillips
wrote to Milmore thanking him for it, wishing him a happy new year, and expressing his admiration for the portrait. Phillips frequently championed Milmore's cause. For example, in June 1870 he asked Ralph Waldo Emerson to go
by the sculptor's studio to see his work and if possible pose for a portrait bust,
which Emerson eventually did.

Among Milmore's other busts of notable men were those of George S. Boutwell, Cardinal McCloskey, Daniel Webster, Abraham Lincoln, and Ulysses S. Grant. Actually, however, his fame among his contemporaries grew out of his Civil War monuments in and around Boston. In fact, credit has been given to Milmore for establishing the prototype of the countless monuments to those who fought and died to preserve the Union, which seem to mark every crossroads and village square in the Northeast. In truth, there were a few earlier ones, but Milmore unquestionably did much to create the Civil War type of monument. Hardly had Appomattox become history when the city of Boston declared it only fitting to honor her brave dead with a monument in Forest Hills Cemetery. The commission went to Milmore, the first of many such memorials he was to create in the next two decades. The first one consisting of the figure of a Union soldier, standing, leaning on his rifle, contemplating the graves of his fallen comrades, possesses a certain humble dignity in its very simplicity; the modeling is competent, if not exciting. On its completion another one like it (Fig. 7.9) was commissioned by the town of Claremont, New Hampshire, where the monument was unveiled in the public square in 1869. The statue was cast at the Ames foundry, which could then boast of more than a decade of successful casting of bronze statues for American sculptors.

The success of this monument marked the beginning of a period of intense activity in Milmore's studio, with numerous large commissions being assigned to him. In the early 1870's Martin modeled and Joseph carved the colossal American Sphinx (Fig. 7.12) that now keeps guard outside the Gothic Bigelow Chapel at Mount Auburn Cemetery. Its form, of course, was derived from the great Sphinx of the Nile, but its iconography became American when the Egyptian asp of the headpiece was replaced by the American eagle, and a star was placed over the chest. On the left side of the base is a Latin inscription; on the right side is its English translation: "American Union Preserved/African Slavery Destroyed/By the Uprising of a Great People/By the Blood of Fallen Heroes." The significance of the image to post-Civil War America is explained in the following passage from the dedication speech delivered by Dr. Jacob Bigelow, former president of the Mount Auburn Association and donor of the great Sphinx:

It stands as a landmark of a state of things which the world has not before seen,—a great, warlike and successful nation in the plenitude and full consciousness of its power, suddenly reversing its energies, and calling back its military veterans from bloodshed and victory to resume its still familiar arts of peace and good-will to men. What symbol can better express the attributes of a just, calm and dignified self-reliance than one which combines power with attractiveness, the strength of the lion with the beauty and benignity of woman?   [*An Account of the Sphinx*, Boston, 1872, pp. 13–14]

Even before the dedication of the Sphinx of Mount Auburn had taken place the city of Boston had determined to erect a memorial to those who had served in the great war, and in 1870 Mayor Gaston officiated at the ceremony of the laying of the foundation stone in Boston Common. The commission for the monument was awarded to Martin Milmore, whose design (Fig. 7.10) again became a model for other large and complex memorials. At the base, on separate blockings are four figures representing the Army (a soldier), the Navy (a sailor), Peace, and the Muse of History, the last two being personified by seated, robed women with laurel wreaths upon their heads. Between these blockings are two reliefs depicting the departure for and return from the war. The monument then rises out of a rectangular base to a circular shaft, at whose base stand four robed female figures; the column itself is thrice encircled with decorative bands, culminating in a Doric capital adorned with American stars. Atop the capital is a platform with four American eagles and a colossal bronze statue of a woman holding a flag and personifying the Union preserved. Upon its dedication, ex-Mayor Frederick O. Prince made the comment, "Their deeds are a Union restored—a Constitution saved—a Nationality preserved."

The War of 1812 had brought forth many fine painted portraits of military officers in their handsome uniforms of bright colors—altogether Romantic visions of a generation of heroes. The soldier and the sailor on Milmore's monument, however, are ordinary men, without the flair of the earlier images, but valiant and stoic defenders of the cause. A few years after the Civil War the North became increasingly aware of just how much valor and sacrifice the bitter struggle had demanded of the rank-and-file soldiers and sailors. In this and in countless other memorials that followed, the foot soldier and the yeoman were eulogized in bronze and granite, and it is they who are placed alongside the allegorical maidens of Peace, Victory, and so on; no longer were war memorials to be limited to images of generals and admirals. In Milmore's monument, the high-ranking officers and civilian leaders are hidden among the numerous figures in the bas-reliefs on the base, and the ordinary soldier and sailor are given the honored positions.

Like so many before him, Martin Milmore felt he could not produce this, his greatest work, here in America, and therefore, departed for Italy, where he modeled the several figures and bas-reliefs for Boston's Civil War Memorial. He worked mainly in Rome, and it was there that he created the angel with the horn that stands atop the Coppenhagen tomb in Mount Auburn Cemetery; it is a life-size figure executed in marble, signed and dated: Rome, 1874. While in the papal city he also modeled a portrait bust of Pope Pius IX. In 1875 Milmore returned to America, his reputation at its peak. The city of Boston at once presented him with another commission: a statue of John Glover of Marblehead. The bronze heroic figure is represented in the military uniform of the Revolutionary War, with a great mantle thrown across the shoulders and trailing nearly to the ground behind; the left foot rests on a cannon barrel, and the right hand holds a sword whose tip is on the ground. Again Milmore approached the verge of dramatic power in expressiveness, but did not quite succeed. Lorado Taft has written of him:

Mr. Milmore stands for good workmanship rather than for poetic expression. Few, if any, of his productions seem inspired; they never thrill. There is nothing epic in his grasp of war subjects, nothing lyric in his treatment of gentler themes; no trace of sweetness at any time. But we find throughout good honest construction, adequate modeling, and, rarest of all, a sense of the monumental in line and mass.

[*History of American Sculpture*, 1903, p. 255]

It was, incidentally, about this same time that young Daniel Chester French's "Minute Man" was unveiled in Concord, and a comparison of it and Milmore's "Glover" points up the stylistic confrontation of the two generations. Other commissions came into the Milmore studio in the late 1870's and early 1880's, such as the one of Colonel Sylvanus Thayer, cast in bronze and erected at West Point. Thayer, "Father of the Military Academy," is represented in military uniform with a large, nearly full-length Inverness cloak about his shoulders. He stands at ease, but with a military erectness. Although the sculptor seems to have tried to represent Thayer as a man of vision, he failed to capture any sense of heroics in this statue; the style is best described as a competent naturalism that is somewhat limited in expressive power. Civil War monuments by Milmore may also be found at Charlestown and Fitchburg, Massachusetts; at Erie, Pennsylvania; and at Keene, New Hampshire.

Martin Milmore's death came in 1881—when the sculptor was only thirty-seven—ending prematurely one of the nation's fine talents. He was buried in Forest Hills Cemetery in Roxbury, not far from his first monument of a Civil War soldier. Milmore's own grave is marked by the famous memorial by Daniel Chester French, "Death and the Young Sculptor," which shows the Angel of Death beckoning to a young man who models in relief a huge Sphinx. French once described Milmore, in a letter to Adeline Adams, in the following manner:

Milmore was a picturesque figure, somewhat of the Edwin Booth type, with long dark hair and large dark eyes. He affected the artistic (as all of us artists used to, more or less), wearing a broad-brimmed soft black hat, and a cloak. His appearance was striking, and he knew it.   [Quoted from *Dictionary of American Biography*]

Launt Thompson (1833–1894) is one of the most fascinating and, toward the end of his life, enigmatic and tragic personalities in the history of American sculpture. His career soared on professional accomplishment and easy movement within the highest social circles of his day, then collapsed to a sordid life as a derelict and finally confinement in a state institution for the insane.

He was born in Queens County, Ireland, where his father died when he was still a small boy. When Launt was fourteen, his mother brought him to America, and they settled in Albany, New York. Launt, a bright and winsome boy, was soon studying the fundamentals of anatomy in the office of Dr. James H. Armsby. He made drawings of the bone structure of the human figure and read the doctor's medical books, learning the muscles, tendons, and organs. It may have been the bust of Dr. Armsby modeled by Erastus Dow Palmer that first inspired Launt to become a sculptor; in any case, within a year Palmer was attracted by the precociousness of Thompson's drawings and invited him to become his studio helper. Albany, while not rich in sculptural monuments, was not insensitive to the new art forming in its midst. William J. Coffee and Henry Kirke Brown had both worked there previously, leaving behind numerous examples of their art.

At the time Thompson came to him, Palmer had only a few years before turned from carpentry to cutting cameo shell profile portraits, and his greatest period was just beginning. Palmer's development was meteoric, with an incredible production in plaster and marble by the time of his exhibition in New York City in 1856, and his young apprentice observed it all. In a manner of speaking, the master and the assistant developed together.

In 1857 Thompson decided that Albany was no longer the place for him. Anxious to test his own abilities, he left to establish his own studio in New York City. He found a place on Tenth Street, in a building with several painters, and set up shop. Almost at once he fell in with the group of artists that clustered around the National Academy of Design, then at its apogee as the main art institution of the country. Thompson began work modestly, cutting cameo portraits to provide some income, and in free hours he would model ideal reliefs, much in the manner of Erastus Dow Palmer. To the National Academy exhibition of 1859 he sent a "Case of Cameos" and a marble medallion, "Girlhood." An example of his profile portrait work is an oval medallion (22 inches on the long axis) of Miss Candace Wheeler (Fig. 7.13), carved in marble in 1863 for the actor Edwin Booth. Stylistically it is very similar to the profile reliefs by Palmer. His work was sufficiently admired by his colleagues so that in 1859 he was elected an associate member of the Academy and became a full member three years later. In 1860 Thompson sent two more marble busts ("L'Allegra"; "La Penserosa") and a portrait bust to the annual exhibition, indicating a departure from the peripheral art of cameo cutting.

The decade of the 1860's saw a continual development of Thompson's career accompanied by a rise to social prominence through his friendship with William Waldorf Astor (who was also his pupil) and his marriage to the sister of Henry Codman Potter, rector of Grace Church and later bishop of New York. Thomas Bailey Aldrich wrote an article about a visit to Thompson's studio in 1865 and mentions seeing several medallions on the walls depicting such subjects as Elaine from Tennyson's *Idylls of the King*, and a profile of a small child with a bunch of flowers; lined up along one wall were three portrait busts—"Rocky Mountain Trapper," "Edwin Booth as Hamlet," and "William Cullen Bryant." The "Bryant" was exhibited in 1865 at the National Academy and listed as a "study for a colossal bust for Central Park." A bronze replica of it, cast in 1867 and intended for Bryant Park, is in the Metropolitan Museum of Art (Fig. 7.14). The bust has some extremely fine modeling in it and possesses a boldness of sculptural form, frequently lacking in the work of others of the period. Thompson was developing in the same direction as John Quincy Adams Ward, and he might, like

Ward, have given a poignant vitality to the literal naturalism of his contemporaries had his life been different.

Aldrich also commented that he saw in Thompson's studio a large plaster cast of a statue of Napoleon I, which was nearing readiness for the foundry. This was Thompson's first major work, and it attracted a good deal of attention. The sculptor portrayed Napoleon in a quiet, pensive mood, wearing his military uniform, his hands clasped behind his back. There is a special sensitivity in the face. Thomspon took great pride in his work and sent the plaster cast, along with his bust of the "Rocky Mountain Trapper"—an unusual combination, to say the least—to the Paris Exposition of 1867. The statue, which was not cast in bronze until 1889, was acclaimed at the Exposition, and this no doubt encouraged its creator to make a journey to Europe—which he did in 1867. For two years he lived and worked in Rome, always hoping for a monumental commission of the type he saw being executed in the studios of Story, Rinehart, Hosmer, Ives, and others. But such a commission was not forthcoming, and in 1869 he returned to America to marry Marie L. Potter of Schenectady.

A number of very fine portrait busts date from the early years of the next decade. In 1870 he modeled the likeness of his friend and fellow Academician Charles Loring Elliott, the leading portrait painter of the day. It was translated into marble and is now in the Metropolitan Museum of Art. In the same collection is the bronze of Sanford R. Gifford (1871). Its modeling is bold but careful, and there is a great sensitivity about the eyes, in a manner which prefigures the work of Saint-Gaudens. The sculptor, carrying his portraiture well beyond a mere likeness, combines vigor and delicacy to produce a bust that is both handsome and dignified. Thompson also took the likeness of the aged Samuel F. B. Morse, and in 1872 produced the marble bust, now at Yale, of Joseph Perish Thompson.

In the year he returned to the United States (1869) Thompson received the commission to model the portrait statue of General John Sedgwick for the Academy at West Point. This marked the beginning of a period of great productivity in his studio. In 1871 he was awarded the commission to execute a memorial portrait statue of Charles Morgan, which was erected in Clinton, Connecticut. For the Old Soldiers' Home in Washington, D.C., he produced a full-length portrait of its founder, General Winfield Scott, and for the same city he made a statue of Admiral Samuel du Pont, which stood in Du Pont Circle until 1921 when it was moved to Rockford Park in Wilmington, Delaware. Admiral du Pont stands with feet apart, as if firmly planted to maintain balance on a rolling deck; his shoulders are squared and his eyes scan the horizon; he has binoculars in his hands. There is a decided vigor and animation in the figure, and the sculptor has succeeded in avoiding a concentration on the inconsequential details of the uniform. One is aware of the character of the man himself without being distracted by the handiwork of tailors. The head, with its full side whiskers that join with a heavy mustache, is well modeled and expresses the wary determination of a man on guard. At the core of the style, of course, is naturalism, but it is a naturalism with the art restored. Comparison is naturally invited between Thompson's statue of Admiral du Pont and Saint-Gaudens' statue of Farragut, modeled in the late 1870's. Though the statue of Admiral du Pont lacks the dynamic quality found in the "Farragut" and is basically a figure of the usual Civil War monument type, Thompson was, nevertheless, moving in the direction of that vitalized naturalism that was to dominate American sculpture in the last quarter of the century.

In 1874 Thompson was elected vice-president of the National Academy of Design and that year received the commission for a portrait statue of the first rector of Yale Collegiate School, Abraham Pierson. It is a striking figure, reminiscent of Erastus Dow Palmer's "Livingston." The sculptor sent it to the Robert Wood foundry in Philadelphia for casting in bronze.

With several major commissions behind him, Thompson returned to Europe in 1875, settling in Florence for six years. It was while he was in Florence that a change began to occur in his personality. Few finished works issued from his studio during these years, and when he returned to America in 1881 it was apparent that trouble lay ahead. The one major piece that he produced during the 1880's was the bronze equestrian statue of General Ambrose E. Burnside, erected in a park in Providence, Rhode Island. As in all Thompson's work, a calm dignity dominates the statue, and there is a fine feeling for sculptural form.

The completion of the "Burnside" concluded a career that barely missed brilliance, but one that was eventually dissipated in periods of drunken wanderings through New York City. Friends and relatives were unable to help him and finally had him placed in a hospital. By 1890 his condition had deteriorated so badly that he had to be confined to a mental institution, where he died of cancer of the throat and general paralysis.

The reputation of Leonard Volk (1828–1895) rests almost entirely upon his portrait of Abraham Lincoln, which was used by nearly every other sculptor who later modeled Lincoln's likeness. Volk was born in Wellstown, New York, the son of a stonecutter. Learning his father's trade, he left home to apply his skill in several parts of the country before he was out of his teens. In St. Louis he decided to attempt a career in sculpture and began to take art lessons there in the early 1850's; among his first efforts was a copy of Joel T. Hart's bust of Henry Clay. By that time word of Harriet Hosmer's activities in Rome had begun to reach St. Louis, for she had formed an affiliation with the city that was soon to result in her first commissioned statue. Volk decided that he, too, should go to Italy in pursuit of further training; this he did—with money borrowed from Stephen A. Douglas, a relative of his wife. The years 1855 to 1857 were spent in Rome, where he not only studied the ancient sculptures and architectural ruins, but also photographed them. When he returned to America he established himself in Chicago, taking a studio on the fifth floor of the same building in which he and his wife and son had an apartment. Not much is known of these early years before he took the life mask of Lincoln, although he did write of being in Washington, D.C., in the winter of 1859–60, "publishing a statuette of Senator Douglas." There is also mention of "a statue of Judge Douglas for Governor Matteson's new house."

It was in April 1860 that Volk took the life mask and modeled the first portrait bust of Abraham Lincoln (Fig. 7.15). The sculptor and the lawyer had met two years earlier during the Lincoln-Douglas debates, and it was then agreed that one day Lincoln would pose for Volk. Upon learning that Lincoln was in Chicago on legal business in the spring of 1860, the sculptor reminded him of his promise and Lincoln warmly consented. Volk recorded his memories of the occasion in an article published in the *Century* magazine. Every morning after breakfast Lincoln went to the sculptor's studio to pose until about ten o'clock when court opened. First, the general form of the bust took shape in clay, but then Volk made the life mask in order to save several sittings.

He sat naturally in the chair when I made the cast, and saw every move I made in a mirror opposite, as I put the plaster on without interference with his eyesight or his free breathing through the nostrils. It was about an hour before the mold was ready to be removed, and being all in one piece, with both ears perfectly taken, it clung pretty hard, as the cheekbones were higher than the jaws at the lobe of the ear. He bent his head low and took hold of the mold, and gradually worked it off without breaking or injury; it hurt a little, as a few hairs of the tender temples pulled out with the plaster and made his eyes water . . . .

It was from this mold that the original life mask, now in the Smithsonian Institution in Washington, was taken and from which numerous replicas were made in the decades that followed; a copy is in the Philadelphia Museum of Art. At the last sitting Volk asked Lincoln to remove his coat, vest, shirt, and collar so the sculptor could model the shoulders and chest. Lincoln obliged and even slid his undershirt down around his waist, tying the long sleeves loosely behind his back. At the end of the session, Mr. Lincoln dressed, bade goodby to the sculptor, and left. Volk continued the account:

A few moments after, I recognized his steps rapidly returning. The door opened, and in he came, exclaiming: "Hello, Mr. Volk! I got down on the sidewalk and found I had forgotten to put on my undershirt, and thought it wouldn't do to go through the streets this way." Sure enough, there were the sleeves of that garment dangling below the skirts of his broadcloth frock-coat! I went at once to his assistance, and helped to undress and re-dress him all right, and out he went, with a hearty laugh at the absurdity of the thing.

The result of all this was the bust, plus a good many replicas, most of which have a drape about the shoulders and chest. The Metropolitan Museum of Art has one that was cast in bronze in 1914, reportedly from the original made by Volk in 1860; the portrait stops at the base of the neck with no indication of the shoulders and chest. In this sensitive portrait, which caught the subject in a thoughtful mood, Volk produced an image far superior to a mere reworked life mask. It possesses the raw, manly vigor of Lincoln's countenance in the years preceding the trying period, which soon enough engraved deep lines and hollowed caverns in his face. Far from an idealized portrait, the likeness finds its greatest strength in a simple naturalism that one associates with Abraham Lincoln. But Volk avoided the traps of excessive naturalism into which others of his generation had fallen.

A few months after the life mask had been made Volk called on the Lincoln family in Springfield, Illinois. On that occasion he made a cast of Lincoln's hands. As it happened, Volk arrived in the Illinois capital on the same day that it was announced that Abraham Lincoln was to be the Republican candidate for President. Volk declared that he wanted to make a statue of the man who would be the next President, and it was for the statue that the casts of the hands were made. This statue, along with Volk's "Stephen A. Douglas," is in the State House in Springfield.

Volk became very active in the artistic affairs of Chicago and rose to considerable fame on the basis of his portrait of Lincoln, which was in great demand. He was not only one of the founders of the Chicago Academy of Design, but was also its president for eight years. Other portraits of famous and unknown men followed in the succeeding decades, such as those of Douglas, William Henry Seward, and Generals Ulysses S. Grant and John Adams Dix. At the Columbian Exposition, held in Chicago in 1893, Volk was represented by marble busts of Colonel William Hale Thompson, a "Colonel Hascall," and a "Bust of a Lady." Taft also mentions busts of "Elihu B. Washburne, David Davis, Zachariah Chandler [and] J. H. McVickar." The sculptor also produced the Douglas Monument in Chicago and a Soldiers' Monument for Erie County, New York; another Soldiers' Monument was for Rock Island, Illinois. Late in life he modeled the statue of General James Shields, which was cast in bronze and unveiled in Statuary Hall in 1893, a presentation from the state of Illinois. Two years later the sculptor died at the age of sixty-seven, survived by his son, Douglas, who was a painter of some accomplishment.

Another of those men who made a specialty of the bronze hero image was James Wilson Alexander MacDonald (1824–1908). He was born in Ohio, but ran away from home at an early age to avoid apprenticeship to a blacksmith; he eventually made his way to St. Louis, where he grew up. It is reported that the sight of a bust of George Washington—probably the first piece of sculpture he had seen—inspired him with the desire to model forms in clay; but such an impractical urge was temporarily subdued while his time and energy were devoted to business affairs. Being a bright young man, he soon rose to the position of ranking partner in a publishing firm, with a handsome income. In time, this allowed him to give up the business world for a career in sculpture. He had begun taking lessons in the evenings in St. Louis, and these continually whetted his appetite; he studied sculpture with Alfred Waugh and received instruction in anatomy from a Professor McDowell.

In 1849 he left the Midwest and his business interests to go East and devote his full time to sculpture; but he was evidently not captivated by New York City, for within a year he had returned to St. Louis. Soon afterward he made a bust of Thomas Hart Benton, which was the first marble portrait to be carved west of the Mississippi. Sometime in the interval between 1850 and his final return to New York City—just after the Civil War—he made his first attempts at ideal sculpture—a bust of Joan of Arc and a full-length figure, "Italia."

The latter piece would suggest an interest in and perhaps a desire to journey to Rome and Florence with their rich collections and galleries and their numerous ateliers and exciting artist's life. But MacDonald never left this country, probably because he became so busy in the creation of Civil War monuments that it seemed unnecessary, as well as unwise, to quit a nation which was so eager to commission statues.

In the decade and a half after MacDonald re-established himself in New York City, his studio was perpetually busy filling orders for everything from portrait busts to equestrian statues—all in bronze and almost all commemorating men of the 1860's and 1870's.

There were busts of John Van Buren, General Winfield Scott Hancock, Charles O'Connor, Peter Cooper, William Cullen Bryant, and James T. Brady; there was also a colossal head of Washington Irving for Brooklyn's Prospect Park. MacDonald was reported to have had Houdon's original model for the bust of George Washington, with which he turned a handsome profit through the sale of numerous replicas; many orders came as a result of its exhibition at the Philadelphia Centennial. His other works on a larger scale included a bronze statue of Fitz-Greene Halleck (1877) for Central Park in New York, another of Edward Bates for Forest Park, St. Louis (1876), one of General Custer for West Point (1878), and an equestrian group of General Nathaniel Lyon (1878). The sculptor was so occupied with portrait commissions that there was little time left for ideal works, but he did manage to produce a "Shipwrecked Boy."

MacDonald, as much as any other sculptor of his day, had his hand on the aesthetic pulse of his patrons and provided them with both the objective naturalism they demanded in their portraiture and the Romantic pathos they sought in their ideal works. Very little is known of MacDonald's life and career after about 1880, although some works were executed after that date. He died in Yonkers, New York, at the age of eighty-seven.

The sculptural career of George Edwin Bissell (1839–1920) did not begin until the 1870's, and he might have been placed with the men who were active between the Philadelphia Centennial and the First World War; but stylistically he definitely belongs to the preceding generation. In his work one finds a continuation of the prosaic naturalism that characterized many of the sculptured portraits of the late 1860's and 1870's.

Bissell's ambition to become a sculptor was excited by his father, who was a quarryman and marble worker in New Preston and Waterbury, Connecticut. But as a youth, Bissell was put to work as a clerk in a store, a position he retained until he enlisted in the army at the beginning of the Civil War. After the war, he married and settled in Poughkeepsie, New York, where he joined his father and brother in the marble business. During the next several years, between the routine work in the stone yard, he began to execute ambitious designs for architectural ornament and elaborate gravestones. His special talent being recognized locally, he was commissioned in 1871 to carve a marble figure of a fireman that was to stand outside the fire station in Poughkeepsie. It was probably the success of this statue that encouraged Bissell to leave his job as craftsman in the stone yard and take up sculpture, and by 1875 he had determined to go abroad to study.

In Paris he worked in the studios of Aimé Millet, Tabar, and Dubois; in Rome he studied at the English Academy. Returning to Poughkeepsie in 1876, he set himself up as the sculptor in residence and executed a number of portrait busts over the next several years. Larger commissions were exceedingly rare, although he did produce a granite figure for the John C. Booth family monument. In 1883, however, he began work on a Soldiers' Monument for Waterbury, Connecticut, thereby contributing to the vast army of galvanized heroes that date from this period. Another monument for Waterbury, his portrait statue of Colonel John L. Chatfield (1887), clearly reveals the sculptor's dedication to a naturalism that was more academic than living. His work was not influenced by the invigorating new naturalism that was reviving American portrait sculpture. Occasionally his work showed a superficial influence of the Beaux-Arts style, as in his marble bust of Mary Justina de Peyster (1886; Metropolitan Museum of Art); but although he was then maintaining a studio in Paris, as well as in Poughkeepsie, his art was essentially unaffected by the rich modeling and impressionistic surfaces of the French school. His devotion to mid-century naturalism may be seen in the busts of Frederic de Peyster and John Watts de Peyster in the New-York Historical Society.

Just as Quincy Ward carried naturalism to supreme heights in some of his portrait statues, so Bissell at times attained greatness through it, as in his bronze image of John Watts for Trinity churchyard in New York City. This portrait, containing "an air of great dignity and composure" and "a statuesque effect," as Taft described it, represented the sculptor at the Chicago Exposition of 1893 and drew general acclaim from the critics. His studio was busy in the 1890's with commissions for statues of Lincoln (1893) for Edinburgh, Scotland, and of General Gates for the Saratoga Battle Monument at Schuylerville, New York. The creation of Civil War effigies continued with a "Standard Bearer" for Winsted, and a "Union" for Salisbury, Connecticut. His bland naturalism is evident in the bronze statue of President Chester Alan Arthur (Fig. 7.16), which was unveiled in New York City on June 13, 1899. Bissell avoided overemphasizing details of the clothing, and the head is rather sensitively done, but the figure lacks verve.

A statue that offered an opportunity for greater "color" through its 17th-century costume and wig was that of Abraham de Peyster, which was produced at Bissell's new studio in Mount Vernon, New York. Depending more on his imagination and less on the appearance of the everyday world, the sculptor produced a statue of greater sculptural richness in form and stronger contrasts of light and shadow than existed in his earlier work. A marked similarity exists between Bissell's "Abraham de Peyster" and Michelangelo's "Moses" which the American had undoubtedly studied in Rome. Another historical piece, the "Lycurgus," was created in 1900 for the Appellate Court Building in New York City. In this, one is reminded of the Roman senator-philosopher statue of antiquity, such as the "Sophocles" in the Lateran Museum in Rome; there is also a reminiscence of such Italian Renaissance sculpture as the bronze saints that Ghiberti and Donatello created to adorn *quattrocento* Florence. This borrowing from the Renaissance masters, strangely overlooked by the earlier generations of Americans who studied and worked in Italy, is not unique with Bissell, for Saint-Gaudens had incorporated their special vitality into his own work as early as the 1870's.

In the years around the turn of the century Bissell participated in several of the country's large-scale sculptural projects. Perhaps his finest statue is the figure of Chancellor James Kent for the upper area of the rotunda of the new Library of Congress (Fig. 7.17). Bissell achieved a forceful expression in the face and a richness of modeling in the great fur-trimmed robe that was never again matched in his sculpture. In that statue he came as near as he ever did to a mastery of the new brand of naturalism of the last quarter of the century. His part in the famous Dewey Arch, which was hastily erected to honor the visit of the celebrated admiral to New York City in 1899, was the creation of the groups representing the Army and Navy, on the piers some distance in front of the Arch. For the Pan-American Exposition at Buffalo he made the statue of Hospitality; his "Science and Music" adorned the Louisiana Purchase Centennial in St. Louis. His colossal bust of Admiral Dahlgren was a part of that complex of bronze images that made up the Smith Memorial in Fairmount Park, Philadelphia. Thereafter the largest part of his work was concerned with portrait statues or busts for memorials, such as the "Lincoln" for Clermont, Iowa; the "Samuel Sloan," which was erected in Hoboken; and "John Starin" in Fultonville, New York.

One of his biographers, writing in the *Dictionary of American Biography*, described Bissell as "A genial, kindly person, in temperament and appearance [and] was affectionately termed 'Père Bissell' by the younger sculptors who knew him . . . ." The end of his career came just as the revolution of modern art burst upon the scene. By the time of the Armory Show in 1913 he was seventy-four years old, and his active years as a sculptor had come to an end. He died on August 30, 1920.

The most celebrated exponent of the galvanized hero was John Quincy Adams Ward (1830–1910), who for several decades represented the highest aesthetic standard of undramatic objective naturalism. Unlike many of his contemporaries, midway through his career Ward recognized the merits of the new, lively naturalism, which was introduced into American sculpture in the last quarter of the 19th century, and he incorporated some of it into his own style. In so doing, his portraiture was strengthened immeasurably. Ward, in a sense, belongs to two movements: the Civil War era of naturalism, and the French-influenced, impressionistic, invigorated naturalism. Although he participated in the latter to a certain extent, his place in the history of American sculpture is properly with the former.

Ward was born on a farm west of Columbus, Ohio, near the little community of Urbana. His father, a man of some feeling for education and culture, provided accordingly the best the area offered for the upbringing of his children. Quincy, as he was called, attended school irregularly; he found a much greater attraction in the nearby workshop of a potter named Chatfield, and he spent as many hours as he could modeling toylike animals and men in clay. One biographer tells of a statuette of Venus, made from wax stolen from his sister's flower-making paraphernalia, that young Quincy modeled away from the house and hid in the tall grass in a shady field. His father, failing to make a farmer of him, tried to persuade him to become a physician, and for a while he was absorbed with human anatomy in his study of medicine. But this did not satisfy young Quincy, who continued to dream of becoming a sculptor.

When an older sister returned from New York for a visit in 1849 and learned of Quincy's secret desire, she promised to speak to Henry Kirke Brown, a sculptor who had a studio in Brooklyn not far from her home. Quincy's hopes fell a little when she wrote back that Brown had not been encouraging. But when Quincy traveled east to visit her, she agreed to take him to the sculptor's studio. He was then nineteen years old and was fascinated by the activity and works he saw all around him. At Brown's suggestion he modeled a nude female figure as a demonstration of his ability. Anxiously he awaited the sculptor's reaction, knowing his longed-for career was at stake. Brown at once declared the figure's merits and invited the youth to become a paying student in his studio. Ward was overjoyed. So rapid was his progress that before long he was a full-fledged assistant to Henry Kirke Brown, actually earning his living in the work he loved.

Brown was a kind and generous man, and under his guidance Ward learned how to prepare the clay, erect an armature, make casts, carve marble, and even how to prepare for the casting of a work in bronze. In the evening the two of them, sometimes joined by a couple of other artists, would frequently draw from the live model. All that Brown knew he was ready to impart to his eager and talented young assistant. They became the best of friends, sharing many interests other than art; on numerous occasions they went hunting or fishing together, both enjoying the robust outdoor life. Ward stayed with Brown for seven years during which time the major project was Brown's equestrian "Washington" for Union Square. Brown even inscribed on the statue, along with his own signature, "J. Q. A. Ward, Asst." Ward once commented that Jonah had spent less time in the belly of the whale than Ward had spent inside the belly of the horse. Although Brown did most of the final modeling, the two men worked side by side on the statue throughout its creation.

During this time Quincy Ward received the finest training in sculpture available in America. In addition, he was exposed to the dominating doctrine of Brown's art, an honest naturalism—the only art that could truly claim to come from the soul of this nation itself, according to Henry Kirke Brown. When Ward left Brown's studio in 1856, he was thoroughly competent in sculptural techniques and devoted to a bold naturalism, which he would learn to control in a very short time.

Quincy Ward spent the next two years in Washington. Those who posed for the young sculptor were men who were very much involved in the enormous controversy of the times. For example, he modeled a bust of Hannibal Hamlin of Maine, soon to become Abraham Lincoln's Vice-President, and a bust of Senator John Parker Hale of New Hampshire. He also did busts of Alexander H. Stephens, who would become vice president of the Confederacy under Jefferson Davis, and of Congressman Joshua Reed Giddings of Ohio, the first of the abolitionists who as early as 1842 had attempted to introduce an antislavery bill into Congress. These men he represented in the direct naturalism that was to remain the basis of his style. No hint of neoclassicism would ever appear in his art.

In 1860 the sculptor visited his home state of Ohio before establishing himself in New York City. From this trip dates the bust of Governor Dennison, modeled in Columbus. But Ward was anxious to return to the vigorous activity of New York City, where he felt increasingly a part of the circle of painters, sculptors, and architects; within about a year of his return he was elected an associate member of the National Academy of Design. Taking a studio in the Dodworth Building, he devoted himself mainly to the execution of the busts he had already modeled, plus several new ones—such as those of the Reverend Orville H. Dewey and Dr. Valentine Mott. He supplemented his income by modeling elaborate handles for presentation swords, which were being manufactured by the Ames Manufacturing Company in Chicopee; he had gotten to know the people at the foundry when he had accompanied Brown there during the casting of the equestrian "Washington." One of his biographers recalled "a delightful little table-bell of silver, with figures in high relief, a marvel of delicate beauty. His hand seemed as happy in shaping a cane-top for a clergyman as in designing pistol-handles for a Sultan."

Quincy Ward was then thirty years old, and he was anxious to make his first serious attempt at an ideal piece. He chose to enlarge a subject he had modeled on a small scale years before while still in Brown's studio—a statuette of an "Indian Hunter," which had been considerably admired. But to do it properly he decided a journey among the Indians of the West and Northwest was essential; so off he went for several months to make studies of the Indians as they lived, dressed, and hunted. Back in his New York studio he began to work from the sketches made on his western trip. The clay model took form in 1864 as he worked long and carefully on it. Finally it was finished, cast in plaster, and put on exhibition in the gallery owned by John Snedicor on Broadway (Fig. 7.18). It was received most enthusiastically, and critical notices in newspapers praised it for its American theme and the manner in which it captured the spirit of both the hunter and his dog. Several prominent citizens initiated a movement to raise the necessary funds to have the work cast in bronze and placed in Central Park. After its exhibition at Snedicor's it was packed off to the foundry, and the sculptor was jubilant with the acclaim and widespread interest that his first subject piece had aroused.

The sum of $10,000 was raised and presented to Ward for the bronze "Indian Hunter," which was eventually placed in Central Park; another in bronze was given to the City of Buffalo and placed in Delaware Park. Permission was given the sculptor to first send the original bronze abroad to the great exposition in Paris in 1867. There, too, it attracted favorable attention, just as it did once more in New York City when it was exhibited at the National Academy of Design before being set up in Central Park.

The anatomy of the figure is quite good. Here, as in his portraiture, Ward relied on direct observation of nature instead of on a classical system of proportions—as Crawford had done in his first ideal work, the "Orpheus." As an ethnic type, the young Indian was accurately portrayed in the structure of the head and body. Details, such as the long, flowing, coarse strands of hair, the animal skin draped about the loins, and the bow and arrow tensely clutched in the hand, were held to a minimum; for although Ward aimed at a certain objectivity and realism, he was highly selective in the details he included. In addition, his "Indian Hunter" possessed an animated quality. Through the intense concentration of the glance of the Indian and his dog, whose snarling is quieted by the gentle pressure of his master's hand at the throat, one can imagine the presence of their prey, even though it is not shown. Man and dog seem to move quickly and lightly through the forest as they approach their quarry.

Americans found it easy to appreciate such imagery, and from that time on Ward's studio never lacked commissions. But these were seldom for ideal or literary works like his "Indian Hunter"; instead, with but a few exceptions, his career over the next thirty-five years was devoted to portrait statues. This was a mixed blessing, for though it was quite lucrative, it prevented the sculptor from doing what he felt was a higher form of art. It may have been just this situation that forced him to strive to make the portrait statue a higher form of art than it had been.

However, a couple of other ideal works date from the early years of his career. The "Freedman," which was modeled and cast in 1865, is a statuette of a seminude Negro seated on a tree stump; on his left wrist is a remnant of the chain that once bound him; in his right hand he holds the rest of it. The pose is casual, as if he is contemplating his newly acquired freedom with some uncertainty, and he turns his head as if looking for some sort of guidance from either God or man. Once again, there is no hint of classicism in the style, as it would have been sorely out of character in a subject which sprang from one of the most burning issues of American civilization of that day. With regard to subject matter the "Freedman" represents the sculptor's involvement in the abolitionist movement; he, like John Rogers, Thomas Ball, Anne Whitney, and others, could not resist the impulse to put into sculptured form the plight of the Negro. Numerous bronze replicas were cast and the "Freedman" proved to be a popular piece in the North.

Ward had no desire to live in Rome or Florence, to join the American colonies of sculptors there, or to study at the marmorean schools of antiquity. His views on the matter were published in an article in *Harper's Magazine*, in June 1878:

There is a cursed atmosphere about that place [Rome] which somehow kills every artist who goes there. The magnetism of the antique statues is so strong that it draws a sculptor's manhood out of him . . . . A modern man has modern themes to deal with; and if art is a living thing, a serious, earnest thing fresh from a man's soul, he must live in that of which he treats. Besides, we shall never have good art at home until our best artists reside here. God knows how much we sculptors suffer from not living in an art atmosphere . . . . But an American sculptor will serve himself and his age best by working at home. I do not blame artists who live abroad; they have a right to do so. But those of us who remain behind must needs suffer and struggle the more.

Ward shunned all foreign styles and subject matter in favor of American themes and a relatively straightforward and honest naturalism, which he considered befittingly American because the people could understand it. However, in the same article in *Harper's* he declared that naturalism must be the tool and not the god of the artist:

Art means the selection and the perpetuation of the noble and beautiful and free—else we might as well have photography. In portraiture especially the best movements, forms, and expressions should be taken. The true significance of art lies in its improving upon nature.

Another ideal piece, the group for the "Good Samaritan" memorial in the Boston Public Garden, was less successful. It commemorates the discovery of the use of anaesthetics in surgery, and consists of a patriarchal figure administering to a limp, nude youth, who slumps in his arms. Ward dressed the Samaritan in a turban and robe and gave him a long flowing beard. In making it an exotic costume piece, Ward lost the strength of his innate naturalism. He received $5,000 for his plaster model of the group, which was then cut in granite and placed high atop a quasi-Gothic pier of four polished red granite colonnettes.

The dedication of the "Good Samaritan" was held on September 26, 1868, to the accompaniment of band music and eulogistic orations. Less than one week later, on the afternoon of October 2, Ward's statue of Commodore Matthew C.

Perry was unveiled in Newport, Rhode Island. The monument had been commissioned by August Belmont, Sr., of whom the sculptor was to make a full-length, seated bronze statue nearly half a century later. With the "Perry," the sculptor's long career in portrait statuary was successfully launched.

Barely was the plaster model of "Commodore Perry" packed off to the foundry before a heroic statue of a Civil War soldier began to take form; this was commissioned by the state of New York to commemorate the bravery of its Seventh Regiment of the National Guard. For this statue he received $23,000, and before it was finished, the city of New York had approved the small model of a statue of William Shakespeare, for which he was to be paid $20,000. Ward's work by this time commanded prices comparable to those of almost any living sculptor; with such omens of the success ahead of him, he bought some property at the corner of Forty-ninth Street and Fifth Avenue, where he built a fine house and a large studio. It was there that the "Shakespeare" for Central Park was modeled.

Ward described his method of building up and modeling a statue in the afore-mentioned article in *Harper's Magazine:*

Take an iron rod long enough to reach to the neck of the figure and fasten it securely in a perpendicular position. The upper end must be directly under the pit of the throat, else the body will not stand well. Put some cross-pieces near the pelvis to support the clay, and see that the clay is thick enough. If not thick enough it will have a tendency to roll down. For the bent leg and arm use pieces of lead pipe, which will bend easily, and can be adjusted at the proper angle after being covered with the clay . . . . All over the skeleton thus made put little iron crosses, still further to support the clay. The nearer the clay to the skeleton and crosses, the stiffer it must be. This will make the figure more compact, and enable you to use softer clay in modeling the exterior.

He then instructed that the masses of the body should be developed simultaneously and the finishing work proceed generally throughout the figure, and concluded with "No matter how the figure is to be draped, always model it in the nude first, so as to feel the masses and the movement of the figure."

The "Shakespeare" was the third of Ward's statues to be erected in Central Park within five years. Unfortunately, it turned out to be not much more than a costume piece. At first it delighted the Victorian taste for such things, but a quarter of a century later there was much sharp criticism of it and a movement to have it removed from the Park. The sculptor signed his name to the finished model in 1870, but the bronze version was not unveiled until May 1872. Neither the "Shakespeare" nor the "Seventh Regiment Soldier" were portrait statues in the usual sense, and therein lies the explanation for their failure. Ward often lacked the vision to create a successful imaginary portrait, and his images of men who could actually stand before him were, as a rule, much stronger as works of art. This same weakness is found in the heroic-size bronze statues of General Israel Putnam (signed 1872) for Hartford and of General George Washington for

Newburyport, Massachusetts (1878), both in the military uniform of the Revolutionary War; they are well executed, but they lack the vital force that informs the sculptors' greatest works. This vitality was most often captured in portrait statues of his contemporaries such as Greeley, Beecher, Belmont, Conkling, and Garfield.

In the 1870's and 1880's the fervor to perpetuate in bronze the likenesses of the military and political heroes of the great rebellion reached it peak, and until Saint-Gaudens' "Admiral Farragut" was unveiled in New York City, no American sculptor enjoyed a higher reputation in—or received more commissions for—such work than Quincy Ward. In the early 1870's, he created a large statue of General John F. Reynolds, which was erected at the Gettysburg battlefield where the general had fallen in combat. A few years later the first of his equestrian statues was commissioned—"General George H. Thomas," for Washington (Fig. 7.19). The man who had led his Union troops to victory in the battles of Mill Springs, Missionary Ridge, and Nashville in the Kentucky-Tennessee campaigns had died in 1870. The small model was made in the Newburgh, New York, studio of the sculptor's friend and former teacher, Henry Kirke Brown, in February and March of 1877. Work on the large model, however, was carried out in Ward's own studio during the next year, and the casting in bronze took place in 1879. Unveiled in Thomas Circle on November 19, 1879, it stood high (some have said too high) on a pedestal silhouetted against the sky. The horse reveals a nervous energy that contrasts sharply with the calm confidence of its rider. The animal's mouth is open, its head tossed back slightly; its mane flutters from the action and its ears are erect—all suggesting a spirited beast that is imperceivably restrained by the rider. There was some criticism because Ward represented the reins falling loose, "giving the horse its head," which a superb equestrian would never do. The pose of the general is relaxed, and his hat is in his right hand at his side, to allow a better view of his head. His countenance is serene, thoughtful and well modeled, and is unchallenged by the details of the uniform or the trappings of the saddle, bridle, and so forth. One's eye is drawn at once to the head of General Thomas where a sharp naturalism was combined with certain expressive qualities. In this monument John Quincy Adams Ward reached the highest level of his capabilities for the first time.

Curiously enough, Ward was not represented at the great Centennial Exposition of 1876 in Philadelphia. During those years he was occupied with several rather sizable commissions, such as the "General Washington" for Newburyport, the equestrian "General Thomas," and also six figures personifying Agriculture, Law, Commerce, Science, Music, and Equity for the State House in Hartford, Connecticut. In addition, there were always the requests for portrait busts, like the one in bronze that crowns the monument to the poet, novelist, and historian William Gilmore Simms, which was unveiled on June 11, 1879, in Charleston, South Carolina. This was soon followed by another commission from South Carolina—the statue of General Daniel Morgan (1881), one of the heroes of the

Revolutionary War in the southern colonies, which stands in Spartanburg.

Then came a request from New York City for a bronze statue of George Washington to go in front of the Sub-Treasury Building at the corner of Broad and Wall streets. Since it was at that very location that Washington took the first presidential oath of office, Congress voted to permit the statue to be placed in front of the building. The funds, $35,000 in all, were raised under the auspices of the New York Chamber of Commerce. In his statue Ward sought an expression of dignity and dedication by modeling a benign and confident countenance. The well-modeled colossal figure is tall, anatomically well formed, and poised. The clothes, representing the style of dress worn by men in 1789, are subdued in all details to the total demeanor of the figure and the serene, almost majestic expression of the head. The statue was cast in New York City at the foundry of the Henry Bonnard Bronze Manufacturing Company; though founded only a few months earlier (February 1883), the company was already a spectacular success and was preparing to enlarge its facilities to handle sculpture from several foreign countries as well as from the United States. The unveiling ceremonies were held on November 26 in a drizzling rain. Flags fluttered from the windows of the surrounding buildings; the national colors were draped around the Grecian columns of the Sub-Treasury Building and also covered the statue. Ward was on the platform along with his friend, architect Richard Morris Hunt. The most distinguished guest was President Chester Arthur, but it was Governor Grover Cleveland who pulled the cord that unveiled the bronze statue while the band played and the cannon roared a salute.

In the middle years of the 1880's Ward worked on two statues. One, "Lafayette," was for Burlington, Vermont, and was dedicated on June 26, 1883; the other, the "Pilgrim," was for Central Park, and its presentation ceremonies were on June 6, 1885. The "Lafayette" is reminiscent of Houdon's "Washington" in Richmond, and there seems to have been a conscious avoidance of the strong naturalism that dominates Ward's statues of men of his own time. In the stance, which suggests the aristocratic bearing of the Frenchman, one is even reminded of the pose of Louis XIV as painted by Rigaud. Certainly this is not the casual pose of Ward's statues of contemporary men. In the "Pilgrim," Ward placed too much emphasis on the costume, thereby detracting from the personality of the figure as a whole. Some years later, the critic Russell Sturgis summarized his remarks on the statue by saying,

. . . in short, one would enjoy getting rid of the excessive call upon his attention made by the costume part of it, and getting at the man, with the hope of finding there the kind of human nature out of which the real Mayflower Pilgrim was made . . . . It is sculpture we are talking about, and not costume, nor archaeology . . . . and sculpture has as little to do as the conditions may allow with creased leather and crumpled cloth.

The "Pilgrim," ordered by the New England Society of New York City, predates Saint-Gaudens' famous and more successful "Puritan" in Springfield,

Massachusetts, by a couple of years. Ward's statue of William Earl Dodge was erected in New York City in 1885 under the auspices of the Chamber of Commerce, of which Dodge had served as president for many years. In comparison with the aristocratic "Lafayette" and the costume-piece "Pilgrim," the sculptor was clearly at his strongest when portraying the political and commercial leaders of his own day in his direct, straightforward and selective naturalism.

By the time the foundries had cast the "Lafayette," the "Pilgrim," and the "Dodge" statues, Ward had begun work on the multifigured Garfield Monument, which occupies a site near the western face of the Capitol in Washington (Fig. 7.20). On a granite pedestal, designed by Richard Morris Hunt, stands the bronze figure of James A. Garfield, who had been assassinated in 1881. At the base of the statue are three seated bronze figures that refer to the three parts of Garfield's life: the first, a seminude youth, quietly contemplative and reading from a parchment, represents Garfield the student; the second is a vigorous and forceful Germanic warrior, wary and watchful, and clothed in the furry hides of wild animals; the third personifies statesmanship. In the well-modeled, animated portrait statue of Garfield the attention of the viewer is drawn to the head, where the sculptor, as always, achieved a fine likeness. But the three exquisite figures at the base make the statue above appear rather commonplace. In these figures Ward's imagination carried his gifts to unexcelled heights, and he was never again as successful in ideal images. The over-all design of the monument is derived from contemporary French sources; Ward's awareness of current Continental art is thus illustrated, as well as his willingness to accept any part of it that was compatible with his own work and the aesthetic inclinations of his patrons. The monument was dedicated in 1887.

A couple of fine portrait busts from the late 1880's deserve mention. In Central Park on a marble pedestal with Grecian decorative motifs is the bronze likeness of Alexander L. Holly, with the following inscription on the base: "In honor of Alexander Lyman Holly foremost among those whose genius and energy established in America and improved throughout the world the manufacture of Bessemer steel, this memorial is erected by engineers of two hemispheres." In a monument dedicated to the memory of a 19th-century American industrialist, Ward's contemporaries found it perfectly acceptable to combine the vital living, naturalism of the portrait bust with architect Thomas Hastings' eclectic academic design for the base, which was derived from the classicism of the École des Beaux-Arts.

The bust of Silas Packard (1890) reveals the solid structure that is typical of Ward's work. It is as if the sculptor began with the bony structure and then applied the flesh to it; in this respect he surpassed most of the other sculptors discussed in this chapter. In addition to likeness and structure, there is an alertness about the eyes, an animation around the mouth, and a liveliness in the tilt of the head that endow the portrait with spirit and verve—a composite of the humor, temperament, energy, and intrepidity of the man himself. Another of Ward's finest heads is that of Roscoe Conkling (about 1892), in which the naturalism rivals Italian Renaissance portraiture of the 15th century in its incisive portrayal, its feeling for sculptural form, and its exquisite sense of design (Fig. 7.22). The last is especially evident in the wiry hair and beard, which are splendidly contrasted to the solid structure of the head and the flesh. But Ward was not imitating the style of Verrocchio or of Donatello, as some of his fellow sculptors had already begun to do; he had not made the pilgrimage to Italy as Augustus Saint-Gaudens had done, and if there is any trace of a foreign style in his work, it is in the enlivened surfaces that come from contemporary French sculpture. No longer were the planes smooth, flat, and dull as Ward's surfaces became vibrant with a myriad of tiny lights and shadows that gave it a luster unknown to America's earliest bronze images. This feeling for the life-quality of the flesh is especially noticeable around Conkling's eyes and cheeks, and is also present on the broader planes of the forehead, neck, and chest. In this portrait, which actually went beyond naturalism to what one may call realism, in the best sense of the term, Ward created a sensitive yet objective image of the gentlemanly, astute, and controversial senator from New York. This sort of character portrayal parallels perfectly the Silas Lapham image created by William Dean Howells in his book *The Rise of Silas Lapham*, first published in 1885. The "Conkling" presents the kind of truthful, objective view of a man that such a person as Lapham could appreciate. The Conklings and Hollys, the Laphams and Greeleys, the Fricks and the Carnegies, the Dodges and Coopers, were all self-made men—statesmen and industrialists who could be as generous as they were brash, as confident in business as they were unsure of themselves in art galleries or polite salons, as gruff and good-natured as they were ill at ease in the midst of genteel company; they were realists in their arenas of commerce and politics, and it was realism that they could most respect in works of art. But the term "realism" has taken on a bad connotation of late, and it is not of that prosaic and lifeless realism that we now speak. The realism in Ward's "Conkling" is one that sought impartially the good and the bad without "idealizing away" the weaknesses of the man. There are to be sure strength and determination in that face, but there are also lines of age and strain, of long years of hard work, and of hard-fought failures as well as victories. It is an art that matches the man pefectly, and in this is found the key to Ward's success.

The same exacting naturalism, or tempered realism, may be found in the portrait statue of Roscoe Conkling in New York City, for which the bust of the senator was modeled. The figure stands in a casual pose, the left side of his knee-length coat held back by the left hand, whose thumb rests in the pocket of the trousers; the right hand is at his side but the palm is turned toward the observer, as if the subject were giving a quiet oration. The clothes have the textured surface of the French manner, but there is an excess of wrinkles—a heritage Ward received from his mid-century predecessors. The memorial statue of Roscoe Conkling was dedicated in 1893.

A couple of years earlier Ward completed two other monuments, "Greeley" and "Beecher." The bronze statue of Horace Greeley was erected in front of the Tribune Building in 1890, and it remained in that unglamorous setting—with a huge lettered window just behind it—for twenty-six years, until it was given to the City of New York and placed in City Hall Park. The founder of the *Tribune* is seated in a large upholstered chair with tassels at the arms and a long fringe around the base. He sits at ease, his left arm on an arm of the chair; in his right hand he holds a newspaper resting on his right knee; one may read the title *New York Tribune* across the top of the paper. His shoulders and head lean forward, breaking the ease of complete repose and adding a liveliness to the figure. Greeley's glance is directed beyond the newspaper, as if contemplating the news he has just read.

In 1891, in front of the Borough Hall in Brooklyn, one of Ward's best known works, the "Beecher Monument," was unveiled (Fig. 7.21). The mountainous image of Henry Ward Beecher stands solidly, almost defiantly, atop a stone base; three additional figures of a smaller scale are at the sides. At the left is a Negro woman who places a palm branch at his feet as she looks up toward Beecher with an expression of devoted admiration and gratitude for the role he played in the abolitionist movement. On the other side a little boy assists a little girl to climb up the base to lay flowers upon the pedestal. These youthful figures are also of bronze and form a fine group in themselves. Once again, as in the Garfield Monument, some of the best of Ward's work is to be found in these adjunct figures. He avoided the problem of a rivalry for the eye's attention in the Beecher Monument, however, by the enormous bulk and larger scale of the nine-foot-high image of Beecher. Ward made good use of the Inverness type of cloak, which the preacher was accustomed to wearing, to enclose the large form within simplified contours and planes.

The monument was enormously popular, and on the day of its unveiling, June 24, 1891, an estimated 15,000 people gathered in Brooklyn's City Hall Park for the ceremony. A military band played as members of Beecher's family mounted the platform along with numerous dignitaries. Spectators watched from the windows of buildings and stood several deep along the platform of the elevated railway to see the statue of the borough's most famous citizen unveiled. After the band had played several appropriate numbers and a prayer was said to open the ceremony, five-hundred school children began singing what had been Henry Ward Beecher's favorite hymn, "Love Divine, All Love Excelling"; during the second stanza the granddaughter of the celebrated minister, accompanied by the sculptor himself, approached the monument and pulled the silk cord, allowing the fabric shrouding the statue to fall. At that moment applause and cheers rang throughout the square, while Beecher's widow sobbed at her daughter's side, so moved was she by the striking likeness of the bronze image before her. President Seth Low of Columbia University delivered an oration on the life and work of Henry Ward Beecher, after which the band played and the entire multitude sang

"America." The services were concluded by a prayer offered by Rabbi Gott-heil.

The Beecher Monument is frequently considered the culmination of Ward's career, although at the age of sixty-one he still had two full decades of consider-able productivity ahead of him. By that time he already wore the mantle of elder statesman among American sculptors. He was perhaps not quite as progressive in his art as Saint-Gaudens and Daniel Chester French, who were the unquestioned leaders of the younger generation, but he was nevertheless respected as one of the most eminent and capable sculptors of the day: At the founding of the Na-tional Sculpture Society in 1893 Ward was elected the first president.

Dating from the mid-1890's are a bronze relief portrait of young James Hazen Hyde in the New-York Historical Society and a colossal bronze bust of Abra-ham Coles in Newark, New Jersey; a marble version (1897) of the latter is in the Newark Museum. Also in 1897 Ward produced the personification of Poetry as one of the many decorative figures for the Library of Congress in Washing-ton. Two years later when New York City hastily erected a wood and plaster triumphal arch to celebrate the visit of Admiral Dewey, it was Quincy Ward who received the commission to create the victory group that crowned the attic: six spirited horses splashing in the sea pulled the prow of a barge in which rode the winged goddess of Victory, unmistakably like the Victory of Samothrace. Ward, like the other sculptors who worked on the decorations for the arch, do-nated his time and efforts, making a small clay model about eight feet across, which was then enlarged and put into staff (a mixture of plaster and a fibrous material) by his studio assistants.

At the turn of the century Ward was seventy years old, but several large projects still lay ahead of him. The most challenging of these was the sculptural decoration for the pediment of the New York Stock Exchange. In this he was assisted by one of the most promising of the young American sculptors, Paul Wayland Bartlett. The theme, "Integrity Protecting the Works of Man," was expressed allegorically. The building itself, of a severe classical design, dictated a well-balanced, harmonic, reserved composition. The whole area, about 100 feet long on the base, is divided into five units: In the center, with arms outstretched and accompanied by two infants, stands the key figure, Integrity; flanking her are groups of a mechanic and his helper on one side, and a farmer with his wife on the other; in the low angle areas are groups representing designers and pros-pectors. The iconography is thoroughly American, but the vital naturalism of Ward's portrait style has been replaced. Ward recognized full well that the classi-cal style of the building necessitated some sort of compromise. That he was able to reconcile his American manner with the demands of classicism is to his credit as an artist. The figures were executed in marble. Ward and Bartlett seem to have had a difference of opinion regarding the style of the work in general, but Ward's reserved "naturalistic classicism" prevailed; when Bartlett had his own way, however, in the House pediment of the U.S. Capitol, the decorative features, busy composition, and flickering surfaces of the French school became the salient features.

In 1907 Ward created a Soldiers' and Sailors' Monument for Syracuse, New York, followed the next year by his second equestrian statue—"General Philip Sheridan," for Albany. And there is no indication of a disintegration of his creative powers in the seated figure of his old friend and patron August Belmont, modeled in 1910. The subject, wearing his fur-lined overcoat, relaxes comfortably in a chair, the fingers of his left hand toying with his chin, a thoughtful expression on his face. Volume and mass are well rendered and there is a fine variety of texture in the garments and in the unusual chair in which Belmont sits. There is throughout a contemplative animation that typically culminates in the head. Although it may lack the dynamic power of the Beecher, still it is a fine portrait statue.

The last major undertaking of the Ward studio was a third equestrian statue, that of General Winfield Scott Hancock (1910) for the large Smith Memorial gateway in Fairmount Park, Philadelphia. Ward himself made the quarter-size model and modeled the full-scale figure of the general. But his health was failing, and after eighty years he did not have the strength to make the larger-than-life horse; this was done by studio assistants. As the work on the "Hancock" came to a conclusion it is reported that Ward sighed to his wife, "Now I can go in peace." Very soon after that he did.

John Quincy Adams Ward had begun his career at a time when American idealism took its sculptural shape in nude or seminude Indian maidens or in the Sibyls and Cleopatras wrought by the second generation of expatriate sculptors in Italy. But in portraiture, naturalism prevailed, forming the foundation of his art from the very first; it was he who during the third quarter of the century gave the greatest vitality to that naturalism, which in the hands of lesser men had occasionally degenerated to something rather commonplace, unimaginative, and lacking in any kind of dynamics. Ward removed the banalities from naturalism in American sculpture and ended up with a sharp, character-defining naturalism. And he, like the painter Thomas Eakins, gave a new vigor and verve to the truthfulness and objectivity that this nation found so desirable in art, especially in portraiture. Ward had practiced his art for twenty-five years when Augustus Saint-Gaudens began his career as a sculptor; these two men, along with Winslow Homer and Thomas Eakins, gave a renewed vitality to American naturalism in the last quarter of the century—before Sargent's English elegance and the French Impressionists sent the art of this country off in other directions.

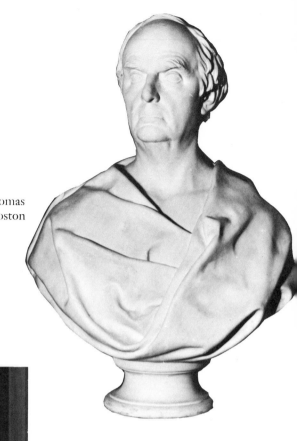

[FIG. 7.2] "Daniel Webster," by Thomas Ball (1853). Plaster. Courtesy, Boston Athenaeum.

[FIG. 7.1] "The Reverend Ephraim Peabody," by Thomas Ball (c. 1855). Marble. Courtesy, King's Chapel, Boston.

[FIG. 7.4] "George Washington," by Thomas Ball (1858–61). Bronze. Public Garden, Boston. Photo, Index of American Sculpture, University of Delaware.

[FIG. 7.3] "Henry Clay," by Thomas Ball (1858). Bronze, 31½" high. Courtesy, North Carolina Museum of Art, Raleigh.

[FIG. 7.5] "Emancipation Group," by Thomas Ball (1874). Bronze. Washington, D.C. Courtesy, National Park Service.

[FIG. 7.6] "Charles Sumner," by Thomas Ball (1877). Bronze. Public Garden, Boston. Photo, Index of American Sculpture, University of Delaware.

[FIG. 7.7] "William Lloyd Garrison," by Anne Whitney (1880). Plaster, 27½″ high. Courtesy, Smith College, Northampton, Mass.

[FIG. 7.8] "Samuel Adams," by Anne Whitney (1878). Bronze, 90" high. Adams Square, Boston. Photo, Index of American Sculpture, University of Delaware.

[FIG. 7.9] "Civil War Memorial," by Martin Milmore (1869). Bronze. Courtesy, City of Claremont, N.H.; photo, Index of American Sculpture, University of Delaware.

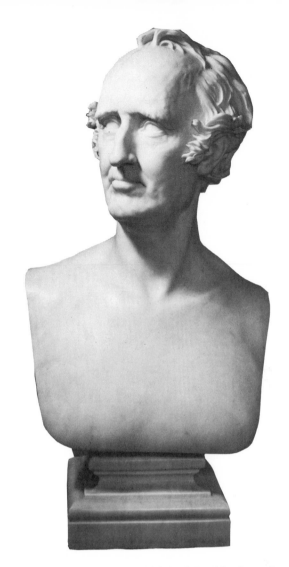

[FIG. 7.11] "Wendell Phillips," by Martin and Joseph Milmore (c. 1870). Marble. Courtesy, Bostonian Society, Old State House.

[FIG. 7.10] Civil War Memorial, by Martin Milmore (1874). Boston Common. Photo, Index of American Sculpture, University of Delaware.

[FIG. 7.12] "The American Sphinx," by Martin Milmore (1872). Granite. Mount Auburn Cemetery, Cambridge, Mass. Photo, Index of American Sculpture, University of Delaware.

[FIG. 7.13] "Candace Wheeler," by Launt Thompson (1863). Marble, 22½" high. Courtesy, New-York Historical Society, New York City.

[FIG. 7.15] "Abraham Lincoln," by Leonard Volk (cast in 1914, after the original of 1860). Bronze, 20¾" high. Courtesy, Metropolitan Museum of Art; gift of Theodore B. Starr, Inc., 1914.

[FIG. 7.14] "William Cullen Bryant," by Launt Thompson (1865; cast in 1867). Bronze, 46½" high. Courtesy, Metropolitan Museum of Art; property of the New York City Department of Parks.

FIG. 7.16] "Chester Alan Arthur," by George Bissell
(1899). Bronze. Courtesy, City of Philadelphia.

FIG. 7.17] "Chancellor James Kent," by George Bissell
(c. 1899). Bronze. Courtesy, Library of Congress.

[FIG. 7.19] "General George H. Thomas," by John Quincy Adams Ward (1878). Bronze. Washington, D.C. Courtesy, National Park Service.

[FIG. 7.18] "Indian Hunter," by John Quincy Adams Ward (1864). Bronze, 16″ high. Courtesy, New-York Historical Society, New York City.

[FIG. 7.20] "President James A. Garfield," by John Quincy Adams Ward (1887). Bronze. Washington, D.C. Courtesy, Architect of the Capitol.

[FIG. 7.21] Henry Ward Beecher Monument, by John Quincy Adams Ward (1891). Bronze. Brooklyn. Courtesy, Arts Commission of New York City.

[FIG. 7.22] "Roscoe Conkling," by John Quincy Adams Ward (c. 1892). Bronze, 23½" high. Courtesy, New-York Historical Society, New York City.

The Second Generation of Americans in Italy: Part I

THE FIRST WAVE OF AMERICAN SCULPTORS MIGRATED TO FLORENCE AND ROME BE-tween 1825 and 1837. Horatio Greenough, Hiram Powers, and Thomas Craw-ford constitute a special group, for they were pioneers who first sought to create a high-style art in sculpture and establish America as the equal of Europe in that art. The second group is much larger, and for convenience it has been divided into two chapters—Part I and Part II of "The Second Generation of Americans in Italy." The period of greatest activity for this second wave spans three dec-ades—about 1840–1870—and among its primary representatives are Richard Greenough, William Wetmore Story, Chauncey B. Ives, Paul Akers, Harriet Hosmer and the "White Marmorean Flock," William Rinehart, Randolph Rogers, Franklin Simmons, Edward Bartholomew, Larkin Mead, P. F. Connelly, and Moses Ezekiel. There were many others who went to Italy, of course, some of whom have been discussed in preceding chapters.

The men and women who make up this second generation are set apart by the spell that the grandeur of antiquity worked upon their sculpture; for instead of turning to American themes, they found their greatest challenges in "Medeas," "Clyties," "Cleopatras," and "Sibyls." While they certainly produced their share of portraits and memorial statues, they almost always turned to antiquity instead of to America for inspiration and subject matter in their ideal works. This group was far more neoclassical than were Horatio Greenough, Hiram Powers, and Thomas Crawford. But to call them neoclassicists would be an oversimplification, since naturalism remained the basis of all portrait busts and statues, and the inci-dental details of a lady's dress or a gentleman's coat and vest were rendered with an exactitude nearly equal to that of the features of the head. And in their concentration on literary accuracy or picturesque quaintness in ideal works they tended to ignore the concept of real sculptural form.

In their detachment from their native soil, this group's native roots often withered. Their imaginary subjects failed to reflect the major social and philosophical movements of America; theirs was in many ways an attempt to create a culture apart from these movements, and to keep it unspoiled by them. As a style of art, their work was ill suited to express the burning issues which then plagued the nation. Neoclassicism, in truth, held even less validity in mid-century than it had in Horatio Greenough's earlier career, for the broad base of American society was not oriented towards the time-honored classical solutions to the economic, political, moral, and artistic problems that confronted it. While many interesting pieces of sculpture came out of the studios of this group, it must be said that as a movement it had more than its share of aesthetic pitfalls. Its chief glory was in the wild, eclectic, sentimental, nostalgic, escapist manner in which it reflected the Romantic-Victorian era.

Richard Saltonstall Greenough (1819–1904), was the youngest son of David and Betsey Greenough, and he therefore experienced in general the same cultural environment that his older brother Horatio had known. He had a Boston Latin School education, but chose not to go on to Harvard, taking instead a job in the accounting department of two of his brothers' business. By the time Richard was seventeen, Horatio had already begun to make a name for himself in America—especially in the Boston-Cambridge area, where the support for his intellectual sort of art was always strongest. The young boy greatly admired his older brother and aspired to follow in his path, and Horatio and the other members of the family encouraged Richard's early efforts at drawing and modeling. In 1837 Richard sailed for Italy to join Horatio, who had just finished the colossal "Washington."

In Florence he followed the usual course of study for a young student. The collections of sculpture he found there fascinated him and much of his time was spent drawing from antique statues or casts. He visited the studios of other artists, especially the Italians'. He worked from the live model in drawing classes, then soon began modeling from the nude figure as well. It was a splendid beginning, and he was exhilarated by the "new world" he had found in Italy. But, as had happened with his older brother, he soon became ill, and after only six months abroad he was forced to return home.

Back in Boston Richard's health improved and he returned to accounting work in his brothers' office. In 1839 he opened a studio in Boston, but in the years that followed he could hardly meet the competition of Clevenger, Dexter, Hughes, and others who were working in or near the city. It was not until 1844 when he sent his plaster bust of William H. Prescott to the Boston Athenaeum exhibition that his work began to attract attention. In March of that year Prescott wrote to

Horatio Greenough in Florence that all who had seen the bust approved of it, and that "it augurs well for his success in a profession where mediocrity is not tolerated by gods or men" (*Correspondence of William Hickling Prescott*, 1925, p. 455). The younger Greenough had demonstrated he could accurately render the physiognomy, and his career as a sculptor gained momentum. Commissions began to come to him, and one biographer, Shurtleff, relates that he was always busy modeling "portraits or fancy heads, and occasionally a statuette." Another example from this period is "Bust of a Child" (Museum of Fine Arts, Boston), which clearly shows the influence of Horatio Greenough in its quiet, pensive reserve. He continued to work in Boston, and in 1846, on the strength of his promising future as a sculptor, he got married. At the Athenaeum that year he exhibited his medallion head of Thomas H. Perkins, which he himself had cut in marble. Several other portrait busts date from this period, among them that of Samuel May (Boston Athenaeum); but with each success his desire to return to Italy increased. In 1848 the Richard Greenoughs settled their affairs in Boston and sailed for Rome, where they established themselves for a stay of several years.

Thomas Crawford and William Wetmore Story were already there, and Richard Greenough would soon be followed by a host of others who preferred Rome to Florence. One of Greenough's first works in Rome was a portrait of Cornelia Van Rensselaer (Fig. 8.1). The head is a fine compromise between a stately idealization and naturalism. A faint smile of pleasure is on the lips, yet there is also a feeling of cool aloofness in the position of the head and in the eyes. But whatever measure of classicism is contained in the head, naturalism dominates, as it always does in mid-century portraiture. Careful attention is given to details of the contemporary dress. There is a prosaic quality in the lace of the collar, a characteristic that becomes more and more predominant in the years that follow. It is attention paid to such frilly incidentals that in part distinguishes the work of this second generation from that of the earlier men, though even Powers and Crawford succumbed to it at times. This preoccupation with intricacy of pattern and surface design has come to be associated with the style referred to as Victorian. Richard Greenough carried it to its apogee in his own work a few years later in the statue of Governor Winthrop.

Also dating from the late 1840's and early 1850's are Richard Greenough's little "Cupid Warming an Icicle with his Torch" and "Psyche," which represent his continued interest in neoclassicism. The nature of his amalgamated style is further seen in his "Shepherd Boy and Eagle," which, although modeled in Rome, is an example of the sculptor's concern with American subject matter. Like the architecture and decorative arts of the period, sculpture might be done in one of a number of styles or in a combination of several styles. The "Shepherd Boy" is pleasant and anecdotal, with numerous details that arrest the eye. The sculptor brought it to America with him in 1853 and had it cast in bronze by the Ames foundry; it was therefore one of the first pieces of sculpture to be cast by that firm and one of the earliest examples of the bronze age in American sculpture. When Richard Greenough exhibited it at the Boston Athenaeum in 1857, $1,500 was subscribed to buy it and present it to that institution, where it may be seen today.

By 1853 Richard Greenough had established himself as one of the leading American sculptors who had migrated to Rome. And because he was a local artist he was chosen to execute the statue of Benjamin Franklin, which was to be erected in the city of Boston (Fig. 8.3). No statue since Chantrey's "Washington" had been commissioned for the city; more important, the monument was to be wrought by one of their own—a member of a gifted and cultured Boston family. Heretofore Boston had been one of the centers that most encouraged the growth of sculpture in the United States, and it no doubt wanted to perpetuate its reputation as patron of the arts. The statue of Franklin, seldom mentioned in histories of American art, was therefore a major commission.

Bostonians wanted an image of their very own Franklin, not some toga-draped abstraction of the man. Greenough's busts had convinced them he could achieve a facial likeness, and to insure accuracy in the rest of the figure a suit of Franklin's clothes was provided by the Massachusetts Historical Society. The statue was modeled in Boston, where the committee could observe the progress on their $20,000 project. Aware of the aesthetic bias of his patrons, the sculptor produced an image that was indeed their very own Franklin. In May 1854 he wrote the Committee:

I would have [the Franklin] thoughtful, dignified, of kindly expression, and unconscious [sic; unselfconscious]. In pursuing this course I am gratified to feel that the same principle was observed in the most eminent portrait statues of antiquity. The statues of Menander, Demosthenes, Sophocles and Agrippina are signal examples in support of simplicity . . . .
[Shurtleff, *Memorial of the Inauguration of the Statue of Franklin*, p. 359]

Greenough clearly sought sanction for his work in the art of antiquity, even though he did not follow it stylistically. His "simplicity" was, of course, relative, for he gave considerable attention to details. But it was largely because he held in check his impulse toward overelaboration of details that the statue turned out to be one of his most successful works. He made every effort to capture the bent frame, the wobbly legs, the kindly countenance and witty expression of the man, without excessively emphasizing the details of the costume. When the model was completed the sculptor signed it, "R. Greenough fecit. Boston 1855." Because the city was anxious to have the monument finished and erected, Greenough suggested that another sculptor be engaged to do some of the bas-reliefs that were to go on the base. Accordingly, Thomas Ball provided "The Declaration of Independence," taken from Trumbull's painting in the Capitol, and "The Peace Treaty of 1783." Greenough himself was able to do the other two panels, "Franklin's Experiments with Lightning" and "Franklin in his Print Shop." All of these were cast at the Ames foundry in Chicopee, along with the statue itself, and were installed in front of City Hall, on a pedestal designed by Henry Greenough. On a beautiful day in September 1856 the statue had its unveiling, followed by a celebration that involved most of the town. Nearly all were pleased with their bronze "Franklin," and Richard Greenough's reputation soared.

Even before he had completed work on the "Franklin," he received a commission for a life-size figure of Governor Winthrop in marble. Mount Auburn Cemetery, already possessing several marble and bronze statues in its parklike burial grounds, "looked forward," as Brumbaugh has observed, "toward creating a Westminster Abbey in the midst of a necropolis on the outskirts of Boston." When the directors of the cemetery commissioned him to do the "Winthrop" statue, Richard Greenough went to Paris to make the model and was thus the first American sculptor of any consequence to choose the French capital over Italy. The seated figure (Fig. 8.2) was modeled in an incredibly short time: It is signed and dated 1856, indicating little over a year for its completion in clay. The sculptor altered his style significantly from that of the "Franklin," for the "Winthrop" is no more than a clever costume piece with a display of virtuosity in the numerous and elaborate details. The face has a vacant stare and the figure seems ill at ease. Nothing of the personality of Winthrop is conveyed, and the eye of the spectator is overpowered by the veneer of minutiae in the clothing and chair. That tendency toward a reliance upon surface patterns and "prettiness," which first manifested itself in the lace collar of the "Cornelia Van Rensselaer," was carried to excess in this statue, and the sculptor lost sight of the primacy of sculptural form. Nevertheless, the statue appealed to the taste for quaintness and elaborate decoration held by many of Greenough's contemporaries back in Boston.

Other works from the Paris period included a bronze equestrian statuette of Washington (1858), at the United States Military Academy Museum at West Point, cast by the Williams Foundry of New York; the plaster model is in the collection of the Louvre. John Rogers, who came to know Greenough quite well in Paris, saw the model in his studio and praised it in a letter to his mother. Unlike his older brother's earlier image, Richard depicted Washington in his regimentals and seems to have been influenced by Houdon's statue. The marble bust of George Hayward at Harvard was executed in 1860, and that of John Winthrop Motley in the Boston Public Library is signed and dated, "Paris 1862." Contemporary hair styles and dress, as well as a factual, rather dry likeness, distinguish these busts from American sculptured portraits of the late 1830's. Certainly the "Byronic ideal" has been replaced by a more pedestrian image. There is also the bust of Mrs. R. C. Winthrop, now in the collection of the Society for the Preservation of New England Antiquities.

Greenough's factual portraiture was often in strong contrast to his fancy or ideal works. For example, in 1863 he perpetuated the neoclassical theme with his stylistically quasi-classical "Carthaginian Girl" (Fig. 8.4), which has been in the Boston Athenaeum since 1869. Modeled in Paris, about three-fourths life-size, it shows a Carthaginian girl about to cut her hair to make strings for the bows of the defenders of her city at the time of the Second Punic War. The dichotomy of styles within the work of one artist was no reason to doubt his artistic integrity, for in the third quarter of the century the sculptor was free to employ any style from the past or present that the occasion demanded. Just as there is a dim reminiscence of the "Venus de' Medici" behind Powers' "Greek Slave," so may the form of the "Venus de Milo" be perceived in the torso and draped lower portion of the "Carthaginian Girl." One must wonder at the survival of such academic neoclassicism this late into the century, but survive it did. And as a work of art the statue does seem to surpass some of the sculptor's works that were more directly connected with his own cultural origins.

The classical is combined with the quaint in Richard Greenough's little statue of "Cupid riding the Tortoise" (1865), now in a private collection. It reminds one of the enormously popular statuettes of "Puck" by Harriet Hosmer. A change of subject matter is found in his "Mary Magdalene" (The Cooper Union Museum), and his "Alma Mater crowning her Heroes" reveals the many directions the artist's fancy could take. The latter was, in a way, prophetic of the sort of heroic abstractions that were to become so popular in the last quarter of the century in the work of Saint-Gaudens and Daniel Chester French.

By the middle 1870's the Richard Greenoughs had moved from Paris to Rome, where they made their home more or less permanently for the rest of their lives. It was there that the sculptor modeled his standing figure of John Winthrop, which was put into marble for Statuary Hall in Washington (1876) and into bronze for Scollay Square, Boston (1880; now on the grounds of First Church in Boston). It is more animated than the earlier seated version of Winthrop, but it is still little more than a costume piece. Try as he might, Richard simply did not have Horatio's profound intellectual wherewithal to give to his sculpture. In his last major undertaking, Richard Greenough attempted to combine the overindulgence in picturesque details of his seated "Winthrop" with a classical subject, and the hybrid style that resulted was quite remarkable: "Circe" (1882; Metropolitan Museum of Art) represents a coquettish, quasi-classical female figure who tempts the spectator to drink from her cup. Although the subject is obviously classical, the style is a corrupt version of pure classicism, but quite typical of bastardized Victorian classicism. As if to make up for what was lacking in stimulation for the mind, the sculptor included a wealth of distracting details on the footstool, the chair, and the miserable creature that slinks beneath the chair. Furthermore, the face of Circe lacks that reserved elegance one expects in a work purporting to be a descendant of the classical tradition.

In the end, Greenough failed to achieve any kind of aesthetic theory that would give validity to his ideal works, and no amount of decorative detail can conceal that fact. After "Circe" he continued to produce portraits that possessed a literal accuracy that could not be challenged, but they often lacked verve. Among these was one of William W. Greenough (1889; Boston Public Library) and another of George Bancroft (1889; Harvard University). With all the experiments that Richard Greenough tried in search of substance and greatness in his sculpture, his portraiture achieved only a bland verisimilitude that had been deprived of that elusive quality called Art somewhere along the way.

His wife died in 1885, and over her grave in a cemetery in Rome Richard

Greenough placed his figure of Psyche. His own death came in 1904 in Rome, but his remains were interred at Mount Auburn.

The sculpture of Richard Greenough had very little intellectual basis, whereas that of William Wetmore Story had too much, which is equally unfortunate if intellectualism becomes the substitute for form in art. Story (1819–1895) was the second son of Joseph Story, Associate Justice of the United States Supreme Court, and his early home life in Salem and Cambridge provided numerous cultural advantages that were to have a great impact on his life. His father, who had been appointed professor of law at Harvard University in 1829, was frequently host to the most brilliant personalities of the area. William graduated in 1838 from Harvard, where he formed a close friendship with his fellow student James Russell Lowell. Two years later, he received his law degree from the same institution and followed his distinguished father into jurisprudence. Young Story set vigorously to work, and the several publications that came from his pen during those first years forecast a successful law career. His three-volume *Reports on Cases Argued and Determined in the United States Circuit Courts* appeared in 1842, followed in 1844 by his important *Treatise on Law of Contracts;* in 1846 he added three more works. He took a position in the law offices of George Hillard and Charles Sumner, and later worked with George Ticknor Curtis, practicing law until after his father's death in 1845. This event may have released him from something of a filial obligation, for soon afterward his life as a sculptor began. Even while he practiced law, he had an avid interest in literature and the arts. In 1841, for instance, he was a member of that little group of literati and dilettantes of the Boston-Cambridge community that included Margaret Fuller, the Reverend George Ripley, Sophia Dana, Ralph Waldo Emerson, and Mrs. Nathaniel Hawthorne. Once when a question was raised as to why Greek art was more inspiring than Greek poetry, William Story replied that it was "because the poets wrote for popular applause [while] sculptors labored more purely for art."

Justice Joseph Story was one of the community's best loved leaders, and on his death prominent citizens of Boston and Cambridge formed a committee to arrange for a monument to him. Surprisingly, they asked his son William to execute the portrait statue for it. Up to this time Story had merely amused himself with painting, sketching, and a little modeling. There is a drawing he did in 1843 of a young man, for example, which is in the Essex Institute in Salem. But before 1846 he had not considered art as anything more than a pleasant pastime, and he had certainly never thought of attempting anything so ambitious as a statue. Henry James quoted a letter from W. W. Story that explained his reaction to the invitation:

I had hitherto amused myself, in hours of leisure, with modeling, but more with painting, and I used to get up early in the morning to work at these before going to my office . . . . On receiving the commission . . . I declined it, from a sense of incapacity —I didn't think I could carry it out. But I was so strongly urged to try that I finally consented on condition that I should come abroad first and see what had been done in these ways. [Quoted from *W. W. Story and His Friends*]

On the basis of his culture, his intellect, and what little evidence of his ability in drawing and modeling they had seen, the committee insisted that Story be the one to model the full-size figure of his father. He went to Europe in 1847 to explore the various solutions to the portrait statue, visiting England, traveling on the Continent, and falling in love with Rome. Returning to America, he presented the committee with a small sketch of the statue of his father, which was at once accepted. For eight months he remained in the United States, devoting himself to his law practice and to a biography of his father. "I was haunted, however, by dreams of art and Italy, and every night fancied I was again in Rome and at work in my studio. At last I found my heart had gone over from Law to Art, and I determined to go back to Rome." (Quoted from *W. W. Story and His Friends*)

Story was delighted to be in Rome again, and even while work progressed on the statue of his father, he was modeling from the live female figure and generally improving his art. At one point, in March 1849, he wrote that his thoughts abounded with hundreds of statues that he might make in the future. By May of that year he had completed another clay model for his father's statue and hired an Italian artisan to cast it in plaster. His mission to Rome completed for the time being, he and his wife left Italy to begin a tour of the Continent and England before returning to Boston. This model, too, was approved at once, but other matters detained the Storys in New England for over a year. Although Story made a pretense of returning to his law practice, Rome continued to beckon, and its artist life seemed more attractive all the time. At last he decided to give up the law altogether, and late in the summer of 1851 he and his wife, Emelyn, departed for the expatriate but cosmopolitan life they had come to cherish. In 1848, James Russell Lowell had written to Story in Rome: "It is hardly possible that pure pleasure should exist [so] far from Cambridge," to which the sculptor had replied: ". . . as the time draws near I hate to leave Rome . . . . How shall I ever again endure the restraint and bondage of Boston?" Thus did the Storys give up Boston for Rome, and law for art.

On his return to Italy, Story began to work on the full-size plaster model of the statue of his father. By February 1853 this was nearly finished, and soon afterward work was begun on the marble version. Before leaving America, Story had written to Powers in Florence asking him to procure a suitable block for the statue; when Powers after several years was unable to do so, the relations between the two sculptors became quite strained. Story eventually obtained the marble, and while the Italian artisans proceeded with the laborious task of carving the statue, the Storys enjoyed a social whirl with such friends as the Robert Brownings, the Thomas Crawfords, Margaret Fuller, the Jaspar Cropseys, the Nathaniel Hawthornes, and William Makepeace Thackeray, who joined with the Storys for strolls among the Roman gardens, walks through the ruins by moonlight, tea in the afternoon, or evenings of poetry readings or of discussions on art.

The carving of the statue of Justice Joseph Story was finally completed and shipped to Boston, where it was well received. Hawthorne called it "very noble," and the proprietors of Mount Auburn Cemetery, where it was to be placed in the newly constructed Bigelow Chapel, voted a glowing appreciation for the "exact and living likeness of its distinguished original; . . . and a truthful and lifelike embodiment of what marble can give successfully to commemorate the dead." Although praised by many of William Story's contemporaries, its fame was not enduring; even Tuckerman, who was seldom critical, hinted at certain weaknesses, and Lorado Taft wrote that "the expression is weak, the gesture obtrusive, and the modeling lamentably absent."

In his second full-length marble figure, Story, like Nathaniel Hawthorne and his *Marble Faun*, was drawn to a marmorean image of a pastoral being out of antiquity—the "Arcadian Shepherd Boy" of 1852, now in the Boston Public Library. This was the first work devised completely on his own: a seminude, flute-playing youth seated upon a rustic, leaf-wreathed tree trunk. Though the figure is not in itself classical, in subject matter it belongs to the timeless Roman Campagna. The impact of his beloved Rome and all its hoary antiquity caused Story to foresake forever the artistic traditions of the land of his birth; during the next two decades he attempted to align himself with this antiquity. The result was a classical Romanticism of a rather superficial sort. Another work of the early 1850's was the statue "Marguerite" (Essex Institute, Salem), inspired by Goethe's *Faust*. In it Story provided a wealth of incidental detail, such as the daisy on the ground, the little cross on a chain about the neck, the costume's surface pattern at the waist, and the purse on a chain at the side. But all these refinements could not compensate for the poor proportions and the lack of spirit in the figure.

News of his mother's illness brought Story and his wife back to Boston, where they remained for a year. During that period Story worked on a book of verse. Poetry was another facet of his diversified creative urge, and when Crawford's "Beethoven" was unveiled at the Hall of Music in 1856, William Story added luster to the occasion by reading some of his own verse. By July 1856 the Storys were again aboard ship headed for Rome, where they established residence in one of the spacious apartments on the second floor of the Palazzo Barberini, built by Urban VIII "out of the quarry of the Colosseum."

Story's studio was an active place as a few of the "hundreds of statues" that swirled in his head began to take form. Often in the afternoon he would be joined by Robert Browning, who amused himself by modeling small pieces in the sculptor's studio. In the late 1850's Story was working on a bust of Theodore Parker (Boston Public Library) and a statue of Josiah Quincy (Harvard University), both of which were put into marble around 1860. The statue of Quincy is probably the sculptor's finest effort; only the later bronze portraits of John Marshall and Joseph Henry equal it in dignity, poise, and character. Story was usually at his best in this "official" or "state" kind of portrait, which seems to possess a far greater artistic integrity than his ideal works.

In comparison with Hiram Powers, Chauncey B. Ives, or others of his contemporaries, Story did not do very many portrait busts; unlike most of his fellow Americans in Italy, he was not dependent upon them for his livelihood. In 1853 he had executed a bust of his close friend James Russell Lowell; and a marble bust of his father probably dates from about that period, since it was shown at the Boston Athenaeum in 1857. But he much preferred the "inventive" subjects, and he modeled likenesses only if he was particularly interested in the subject. The sculptor had made a bust of Robert Browning as a gift for Elizabeth Barrett Browning, and after her death he modeled her likeness for the bereaved husband. The original was executed in the summer of 1861, while the copy in the Boston Athenaeum (Fig. 8.5) is inscribed, "In Memoriam Roma 1866." Although the face is sensitively rendered, the artist's Victorian preoccupation with prettiness and surface pattern are somewhat distracting. This piece is a counterpart to Richard Greenough's "Cornelia Van Rensselaer," with its clever display of sculptural virtuosity in the treatment of the crocheted cap and collar, the masses of curls, and the brocade work on the edge of the jacket.

The statue that brought Story the greatest international fame in his own time was "Cleopatra." The original (1858) is in the Goldsmiths' Company Hall in London; the replica in the Metropolitan Museum of Art was carved in 1869. This statue and his next major piece, "Libyan Sibyl" (Fig. 8.6), done in the early 1860's, represent the Romantic search for heroic and exotic subjects out of the ancient past. But Story felt that the cool, detached reserve of the ideal Greek style of the 5th century B.C. was altogether too lacking in expression and emotional content, and he consciously avoided the pure classicism of Phidias and his contemporaries. He sought his inspiration in the mysterious, tragic women of Egypt or the Near East as readily as in the heroines of Greek mythology. This element in Story's work was quite compatible with the spirit of an age that sent the early archaeologists into the valleys of the Nile, the Tigris and Euphrates, and into the deserts of the Holy Land to unearth the remains of the once-grand civilizations that preceded the Greeks. There was unquestionably a kind of escapism involved as the sculptor turned his back on subjects of his own time and his own people. But this is, after all, quite typical of the 19th-century with its impassioned Romantic attraction to heroic, weird, and exciting legends from distant lands.

In his "Cleopatra" Story attempted to create a statue that would recall all the events surrounding the fall of the great Egyptian queen nearly two thousand years earlier. To accomplish this he relied on a wealth of props and costume accessories. His contemporaries marveled at all the detail that recreated the scene so vividly before their eyes; they could "read" it in all its color and incidental richness, very much as if they were reading some archaeological or literary account of the treasures found in some long-hidden Egyptian tomb. Archaeological correctness was of the greatest importance, outweighing even a desire for beauty in sculptural form. Henry James wrote of the "critical" standards by which the "Cleopatra" and the "Libyan Sibyl" were judged when they were shown at the London Exposition of 1862:

. . . we can only feel, as we pass, a certain envy of a critical attitude easier, simpler and less "involved" than our own. "Critical" attitude is doubtless even too much to say; the sense to which . . . the work of art or of imagination, the picture, the statue, the novel, the play, appealed was not, in any strictness, the aesthetic sense in general or the plastic in particular, but the sense of the romantic, the anecdotic, the supposedly historic, the explicitly pathetic. It was still the age in which an image had, before anything else, to tell a story, and that had much to do with the immense welcome offered to the Sibyl and the Cleopatra of the new American sculptor . . . . Story . . . was frankly and forcibly romantic, and with a highly cultivated quality of his romance, so that he penetrated the imagination of his public as nobody else just then could have done . . . . He in any case offered the observer a spectacle and, as nearly as possible, a scene. His imagination, of necessity, went in preference to the figure for which accessories were of the essence; which is doubtless a proof, one must hasten to recognize, that he was not with the last intensity a sculptor.

[Quoted from *W. W. Story and His Friends*]

The exoticism of Story the Romantic is further revealed in a long poem by him, most of which is quoted in Gardner's *Yankee Stonecutters;* a few stanzas will suffice to show the mood of the sculptor and the aura he spun about his statue. Cleopatra speaks, in a kind of reverie about her earlier love in the desert when her spirit inhabited the form of a tigress:

> I will lie and dream of the past time,
> Aeons of thought away,
> And through the jungle of memory
> Loosen my fancy to play;
> When, a smooth and velvety tiger,
> Ribbed with yellow and black,
> Supple and cushion-footed,
> I wandered, where never the track
> Of a human creature had rustled
> The silence of mighty woods,
> And, fierce in a tyrannous freedom,
> I knew but the law of my moods.
>
> . . . .
>
> His yellow eyes flashed fiercely
> As he crouched and gazed at me,
> And his quivering tail, like a serpent,
> Twitched, curving nervously.
> Then like a storm he seized me,
> With a wild triumphant cry,
> And we met, as two clouds in heaven
> When thunders before them fly.
>
> . . . .
>
> Come to my arms, my hero,
> The shadows of twilight grow

And the tiger's ancient fierceness
In my veins begins to flow

. . . .

Come, as you came in the desert,
Ere we were women and men,
When the tiger passions were in us,
And love as you loved me then!

Nathaniel Hawthorne wrote in his *Italian Note-Book* that Story had designed the statue "with depth and power"; but W. J. Clark, in his *Great American Sculptures*, was quite right in observing that Hawthorne was in large measure responsible for the fame of the "Cleopatra," for the novelist immortalized the statue in his *Marble Faun*, published in 1860.

Much the same may be said of the "Libyan Sibyl" with regard to its historical and literary content. The sculptor was recreating a visual image of an era long-past, and his contemporaries found it as fascinating as *Ben Hur* or *The Last Days of Pompeii*. In August 1861, he wrote to Charles Eliot Norton:

It is a very massive figure, big-shouldered, large-bosomed, with nothing of the Venus in it, but, as far as I could make it, luxuriant and heroic. She is looking out of her black eyes into futurity and sees the terrible fate of her race. This is the theme of the figure—Slavery on the horizon, . . . it is thoroughly African.
[Quoted from *W. W. Story and His Friends*]

To an intellectual and dilettante living and working in Rome it may have made perfect sense to disguise his sentiments on a Civil War issue in such a historic form, but to the people as a whole back in America it was far too remote. It was, in truth, more a Romantic fascination with the subject than a commentary on a burning contemporary issue.

It was in England that Story established his reputation, writing to friends on several occasions that America did not understand his work and felt no affinity with it. In November 1862 Story wrote again to Charles Eliot Norton:

I get the best appreciation in England . . . . It is of no use in America for me to hope for anything. I do not expect to find a public there until I have obtained it elsewhere. They will resist to the last considering me anything but a poetaster, dilettante and amateur.   [Quoted from *W. W. Story and His Friends*]

The sculptor's friend Charles Sumner urged him to take up once more with his native land and become its sculptor: "Give us, give mankind, a work which will typify or commemorate a redeemed nation. You are the artist for this immortal achievement." This was a challenge Story did not accept.

Dating from the middle 1860's are such pieces as the statue of "Saul" (one at the Essex Institute, another in the M. H. de Young Museum, San Francisco) and the standing "Venus" in the Museum of Fine Arts, Boston. There is a strong reminiscence of Michelangelo's "Moses" in the face of Saul and in the hand toying carelessly with the beard. One of Story's more classical ventures in stone is the "Medea" (1864), of which there are examples to be found in the Essex Institute and the Metropolitan Museum of Art (Fig. 8.7). At that time the play *Medea* was being performed in Rome and the celebrated actress Ristoni, who played the title role, was a close friend of the Storys. The sculptor's "Medea" stands thoughtful and sinister, pondering the revenge she is intent upon, unconsciously playing with the beads at her neck with one hand while in the other she holds the menacing knife. In general, it is one of the sculptor's better heroic marble women, but this type of academic eclecticism by 1865 was in its final decade of popularity. Throughout the rest of the 1860's and on into the 1870's, there issued from Story's studio in Rome statues entitled "Delilah" (1866–1867; de Young Art Museum), "Polyxena" (1869–1870; Brooklyn Art Museum), "Salome" (1870; Metropolitan Museum of Art), and "Jerusalem in her Desolation" (1870; Pennsylvania Academy of the Fine Arts).

During this period the only connection Story's sculpture had with his native land came from his commissions for portrait statues, such as that of Edward Everett. After Everett's death a committee discussed the subject of a suitable memorial with several sculptors, among them Henry Dexter, Thomas Ball, and William Story. Although Ball wanted the commission desperately, the committee finally chose Story. The result stands today in the Boston Public Garden. Modeled in 1866, it marks the beginning of a twenty-year period when the sculptor was mainly occupied with portrait statues. Although he had never modeled the likeness of Everett himself, and therefore did not have his own bust from which to work, Story, as noted in the previous chapter, for some unknown reason took offense when Thomas Ball offered him his portrait of Everett along with his life mask and the measurements of his figure. Story's portrait was therefore done from photographs and possibly from the bust of Everett that Hiram Powers had made thirty years earlier. The pose is that of the orator, with one arm raised. By the spring of 1866 the clay model was finished, and Story left it to be cast in plaster by his Italian workmen while he joined his family in England. The von Müller foundry in Munich finished casting it by March 1867; it was then shipped to Boston and set up on its pedestal. But many Americans did not care for Story's statue of Everett any more than they cared for his ideal pieces. Soon after it was unveiled, a critic wrote the following perceptive remarks:

It is humiliating to compare such statues as this of Everett with that of Demosthenes in the Vatican; and, in view of the fact that our sculptor is a man of culture and acknowledged ability in his art, it seems evident that the study of classicism in Italy does not give the modern artist the power of the ancients, or else that it does not make that power available for present needs. Instead of taking root in the new soil, and growing healthily and vigorously from it, the artist who gives himself up to the classic influence flourished bravely as a parasite on the firm old trunk, but yields us no fruit.

[*Atlantic Monthly*, November 1868, p. 560]

The contract had left the matter of dress entirely up to the sculptor, who placed the former president of Harvard in contemporary clothing. Still Story expressed the wish that the "unsightly pantaloons" might somehow have been covered, demonstrating that the problem of how to render mid-19th-century attire continued to plague American sculptors.

Other, more successful, full-length portrait statues followed, such as the "George Peabody" (London and Baltimore), in which the subject is seated comfortably, his countenance endowed with a stern vigor; the colossal statue of Colonel Prescott (1880) at Bunker Hill Park; and in front of the Smithsonian in Washington stands the robed image of Professor Joseph Henry (Fig. 8.8), which was done in 1881. There is a fine rhythmic design in the folds of the academic gown and a quiet self-confidence in the professor's face. Though it lacks drama it is a dignified likeness and avoids the slavish adherence to literal realism to which much American portraiture degenerated after the Civil War. Also in Washington is the bronze statue of Chief Justice John Marshall on the Capitol grounds. The chapel at Cornell University has a portrait statue of Ezra Cornell, modeled in the mid-1880's; and from the same period is the Francis Scott Key Monument in Golden Gate Park, San Francisco. These portrait commissions brought to a conclusion the sculptural career of William Wetmore Story. Among his last works was a monument to his dear departed Emelyn, to mark her grave in the Protestant Cemetery in Rome.

Lawyer, poet, critic, musician, and altogether a cultivated gentleman, W. W. Story took all these facets of his personality quite seriously, and perhaps for that reason never really threw himself whole-heartedly into the art of sculpture. As an incurable Romantic with a definite leaning toward literary subjects from exotic places and ancient times, he reflected a segment of the 19th-century spirit in general. In search of other things, he forgot the real pleasure in sculptural form. But in his own day, he was one of the most famous American sculptors who lived and worked abroad.

Just as William Wetmore Story in his "Cleopatra" and "Libyan Sibyl" epitomized one facet of mid-19th-century escapism—a mystical, reverend absorption in the civilizations of remote antiquity—so the Romantic, hypersentimental preoccupation with death was epitomized in the "Dead Pearl Diver" by Paul Akers. Each in his own away might be said to materialize an important aspect of the ethos of the period. Largely on the basis of this monument, which permitted his contemporaries that strange pleasure of indulging in a languishing contemplation of death, Akers became one of the most famous of the expatriate artists. In a very responsive but thoroughly uncritical way—as regards formal matters of art—these Romantics mistook their emotional experiences for aesthetic ones, and in this confusion it was widely held that the "Dead Pearl Diver" moved them more than any other sculpture.

Benjamin Paul Akers (1825–1861), born in a small village in Maine in the year Horatio Greenough first sailed for Italy, was the eldest son of eleven children of the wood carver Deacon Akers and his wife. His formal education was modest, but his parents seem to have enjoyed bringing whatever culture they could into their home. At about the age of sixteen Paul went to work in his father's wood-turning shop, where "in graceful and original design in ornamental woodwork [he] first discovered his artistic ability." Though the area offered little to encourage an aspiring artist, he always remembered the beautiful Maine countryside with deep affection and once wrote, in a poetic passage,

. . . while my body has been wandering by the Tiber, and my eyes have looked along the line of the Sabine mountains, and I have listened to the lowing of herds, the laughter of children and the bells remotely ringing, my soul has been where purer streams do flow and the sounds are far dearer.

[Quoted from *The New England Magazine*, 1895, p. 461]

Eventually moving to Portland to try a career as a printer, Paul chanced to pass a shop window that displayed a portrait bust by Edward Brackett; it evidently reawakened in him the desire to make beautiful things in sculptural form. He acquired some clay from the Dodges, who at that time operated a pottery shop near Deering Oaks in Portland, and began modeling faces and small figures.

In 1849, no doubt having heard of the sculptures in the Athenaeum, Paul Akers went to Boston where he learned the rudiments of modeling and plaster casting from Joseph Carew. Returning to Maine, he established himself in a studio shared with landscape painter John R. Tilton. He barely scratched out a living at first, but over the next three years a fair number of commissions for portrait busts came his way. Among these were likenesses of the Boston publisher Samuel Appleton, John Neal, the Reverend Doctor Nichols of Portland, and Professor Parker Cleveland of Bowdoin. On June 12, 1851, Henry Wadsworth Longfellow noted in his Journal, "Mr. Paul Akers of Portland has arrived [in Cambridge]. He is to pass a week or so with me and make my bust. A young man of superior talent and high ideals." There are also reports of a medallion head of Christ and a portrait of his artist friend Tilton, as well as a bust of Charlotte Corday. In time, Portland and the Boston-Cambridge area provided sufficient income to finance a trip abroad.

Akers sailed for Italy in 1852, and for one year settled in Florence, joining the colony of American sculptors there. His first project was to put into marble some of the plaster busts he had brought with him. He also modeled two bas-reliefs, "Night" and "Morning," commissioned by Samuel Appleton of Boston. But thoughts of home were always with him, and in 1853 he returned to America.

In his studio in Portland he modeled his first large ideal work, "Benjamin in Egypt," representing the moment when the cup was discovered in Benjamin's sack. Unfortunately, it was destroyed by fire, but from accounts of the statue it must have been a "literary piece," with much attention given to picturesque details. In the winter of 1854 Akers went to Washington, D.C. Clark Mills was already there, basking in the success of his equestrian "Jackson"; but as Mills was too busy with larger commissions to become the "portrait sculptor" of the nation's capital, Akers found plenty of work available. Unlike some American sculptors of that day who liked to do as many ideal works and as few portraits as possible, Akers found a challenge in the portrait bust, as may be seen in a quotation from an article he wrote for the *Atlantic Monthly*:

Than a really great portrait, no work of art can be more truly historical . . . . No artist was ever great enough to invent the combination of lines, curves and planes which compose the face of a man. There is the accumulated significance of a lifetime, subtle traces of failures or of victories wrought years ago . . . . The modifications are infinite, and each is completely removed from the region of the accidental.

This is, in essence, a theory of aesthetics in support of a strong naturalism: As every line, curve, and plane in the face has been developed by the man's experiences throughout his life, to remove or alter these would be tantamount to depriving him of character, and the portrait would then fail in its historical accuracy. One of the portraits that Akers modeled while in Washington in 1854 was of Edward Everett (Fig. 8.9), which was put into marble two years later in Rome. It is an example of the sculptor's theory that he could represent the soul through a naturalistic rendering of the physical features. That this theory met with general and enthusiastic approval is obvious from the many portraits he modeled in the nation's capital—Sam Houston, President Franklin Pierce, the Honorable Gerrit Smith, and Judge John McLean among others. He also executed the "Head of a Drowned Girl," a forecast of the sculptor's fascination with morbid themes.

Although Akers enjoyed portraiture and dearly loved his native land, the attraction of Rome constantly pulled at him. "I have a work to do," he wrote, "it is always before me, demanding fulfillment, reproaching me when I am swayed by other than its own power, and I must obey or I am lost . . . . So very soon I shall go to Rome, where I belong." In 1855 he set out once more for Italy. There, in the few years left to him, he produced an enormous quantity of work. He took a studio in the Via del Crecie, within earshot of the sound of nuns singing in a nearby convent. Altogether there were seven rooms which were, to use his words, "peopled by a race which maintains perpetual peace." Rome excited him beyond anything he had ever experienced, and he wrote:

All that my intellect craves is within my reach. All the demands of my taste may be here satisfied . . . . Here are the great silent strivings for immortality and the noble struggles for true language and worthy utterance. Here are gathered the finite creators, and here is the world they have made with their undying people.

He frequented the long sculpture galleries of the Vatican, where he made copies of the famous busts "Ariadne," "Demosthenes," and "Cicero," as well as a replica of the "Dying Gaul," or "Gladiator" as it was then known; these were made at the request of Edward King of Newport, Rhode Island, who gave them to the Redwood Library. Akers' acquaintances in Rome included Robert and

Elizabeth Browning, Charlotte Cushman, and Nathaniel Hawthorne, along with the international community of painters and sculptors. He often had lunch with Harriet Hosmer and Emma Stebbins, and the latter was his pupil for a while. In 1856 he toured Switzerland, Germany, and France, ending up in England, where he did extensive research on portraits of Milton before doing his own bust of the Puritan poet. Robert Browning saw it in Akers' studio and praised it.

He began one ideal piece after another and frequently had several in progress at the same time. "Within my studio the daily music is the sound of ringing marble," he once wrote. There was his "Undine," being put into "stone as fair as pearl," and studies of works yet to be given to the world." There were models for statues such as "Una and the Lion" from Spenser's *Fairie Queen*, and an "Isaiah," as well as a "Diana" and an "Endymion." There is also reference to a "Girl Pressing Grapes," a statue of "Peace," and a "Reindeer." His most famous works, however, were the statues of "St. Elizabeth of Hungary" and the "Dead Pearl Diver." The former—of which two copies were made, one for New York and one for Boston—is essentially a costume piece; it drew much attention in his studio when visitors from Europe and America came to call. But the stellar attraction was unquestionably the "Dead Pearl Diver" (1857), now in the Sweat Art Museum in Portland, Maine (Fig. 8.10). The mid-century Victorian mind swooned at the woeful tale of the beautiful youth who sought the largest and most precious jewels of the pearl beds and who drowned when they were just within his grasp. A pathos hovers over the limp white body, and Akers' contemporaries were greatly moved by this image of the mysterious eternal sleep. They stood in the presence of death, or at least its very image, when they looked upon this statue. They were amazed at the virtuosity displayed in the execution of the details, such as the texture of the sand and the occasional shell; but especially did they marvel at the rendering of the net over the pelvic area. If the composition of the figure seems awkward and ungainly, if the work as a whole appears too mawkish or artificially emotional to 20th-century eyes, it was not so to Akers' contemporaries, who reveled in such melodrama.

The "Dead Pearl Diver" was Paul Akers' last major work. In 1858 he became ill and returned to America. His health improved for a while, and he married Mrs. Elizabeth Taylor, who accompanied him to Europe within the year. Before he reached Rome, he experienced a severe hemorrhage, and once in the city his condition deteriorated. He nevertheless did a portrait of the Reverend John Frothingham, which had to be completed later by his brother Charles. Paul also worked on the model of a statue of Commodore Perry, which was to be placed in New York's Central Park, but it never got beyond the clay stage. Eventually his illness forced him to return to America, and he died in Philadelphia on May 21, 1861. Although he lived only thirty-six years, Paul Akers had experienced the sweet taste of popular success, thanks to his "Dead Pearl Diver."

Among the permanent members of the American colony in Rome was Chauncey Bradley Ives, one of the most prolific portrait sculptors in the city and a creator of marble ideal statues of tremendous popularity. One of seven children, Ives (1810–1894) was born on a farm in Hamden, Connecticut, and his childhood was typical of that of any boy growing up in rural 19th-century America. About 1825 he was apprenticed to a New Haven craftsman, R. F. Northrop, from whom he acquired the skills of a wood carver. In time he began to model in clay and even to try the direct carving of likenesses in stone. Ambitious to become something more than a craftsman, he may have sought some instruction from Hezekiah Augur, then at the pinnacle of his fame. Among Ives' earliest works is the bust of David Daggett (1839); a plaster copy is now in the collection of Yale University. Ives also modeled likenesses of Professor Benjamin Silliman and the architect Ithiel Town, the bust of the latter resting upon a copy of Stuart and Revett's *Antiquities of Athens*. Ives, who was about thirty years old when he did these busts, took them with him when he went to Boston in search of commissions and further training. Exhibited at the Boston Athenaeum in 1841, they drew favorable comment, and Ives' career as a portrait sculptor was launched. Two other busts at Yale (c. 1840) are those of Jeremiah Day and Thomas Day, and another of this period is that of young William Hoppin in the New-York Historical Society.

But Ives, like many others around 1841, may have found competition in Boston to be too keen, for though Clevenger had just left, Robert Ball Hughes had just arrived; and Henry Dexter was there, as was John C. King and others. Moving to New York City, Ives established a studio and in the next three years produced a number of portraits. In the catalogue of the 1841 exhibition of the National Academy of Design, he was represented by five portrait busts; there were those of Town and Silliman, plus likenesses of Noah Webster (Yale University), Park Benjamin, and the Reverend Dr. Wainwright. It was probably at this time that he also did the bust of William Henry Harrison, now in the New-York Historical Society. Then sudden ill health, possibly tuberculosis, made him seek a warmer climate, and as soon as he could, he sailed for Italy.

When Ives arrived in Florence in 1844, he found only three other American sculptors there—Horatio Greenough, Hiram Powers, and Henry Kirke Brown. Richard Greenough had already returned to America, and Clevenger, while returning home, had died at sea. Portrait commissions were few at first, so Ives had time to study the treasures of Florence and familiarize himself with Bartolini's doctrine of naturalism. Hiram Powers' "Greek Slave" was just beginning to draw international attention, and while Ives was in Brown's studio, he no doubt saw the statue of "Ruth" and the classical bust "La Grazia." These inspired him to try his own ideal works, and when Bayard Taylor visited Florence in 1845, he noted that "Mr. Ives . . . has just completed the clay models of two works—a boy with a dead bird, charmingly simple and natural, and a head of Jephthah's Daughter" (*Views A-Foot*, 1855, vol. I, p. 384). The idea for the latter very likely came from Augur's group "Jephthah and His Daughter," which Ives would have seen in New Haven. It is not known if these two pieces were ever carried beyond the clay model, but they mark the beginning of his work with ideal subjects. In 1847 he sent a piece entitled "Flora" to the National Academy of Design exhibition in New York, but the great period of his ideal works came after his removal to Rome. Meanwhile, a good many portrait busts date from his seven years in Florence. One of the most striking busts he ever produced is that of Mrs. William Gage Lambert (1848). Ives endowed it with a human warmth, so often lacking in the prosaic literalism of many of its contemporaries, and in the softness of the face one feels that stone has been turned into flesh (Fig. 8.11). At the bodice is a trace of that fancy surface patterning that was to delight Americans from the late 1840's through the 1860's and become an important feature of Ives' later works.

In 1851 Ives moved to Rome, where he worked in the courtyard of a house occupied by William Page and other artists. In 1854 he produced his first "Pandora," which is in the Virginia Museum of Fine Arts; another, dated 1864, is in the New Hampshire Historical Society in Concord. The naturalism of the Florentine portraits gave way noticeably to the neoclassicism of Rome, for in style as well as subject the sculptor was inspired by the art of antiquity. The classical influence is most obvious in the face and hair, whereas the rest of the figure has a greater degree of 19th-century naturalism than is at first suspected. Pandora is shown at the moment she can no longer resist the temptation to open the jar. Spectators would lapse into a kind of reverie as they recalled the tale, which was sometimes printed in a catalogue that accompanied its exhibition:

Pandora was sent by Jove to Prometheus, with a jar containing all the evils of life in punishment for his stealing fire from heaven. She was equipped by the gods with every charm. Venus gave her beauty; Mercury persuasion; and Apollo, music. Prometheus refused to accept her or her jar, and sent her to his brother Epimetheus, who gladly received her. Pandora was charged by Jove not to open the jar, but being seized with curiosity, she cautiously raised the lid, and at once there issued forth all the ills that beset mankind in body and in soul. Hastening to close the jar, she saved only hope which lay at the bottom, and thus, though a victim of every evil, man ever retains hope.

The literary flavor appealed strongly to the people of the 19th century. Analytical art criticism was virtually nonexistent, and a statue was judged primarily on the basis of its literary success, the religious or philosophical moral it contained, or its quaintness or cuteness—none of which has anything to do with the quality of its artistic form.

That same year Ives modeled his "Rebecca at the Well"; he sold twenty-five replicas of it over the next forty years. "Pandora" and "Rebecca" were two of the main attractions of his New York City exhibition in 1855, for which the sculptor returned to America. His work had such popular appeal that within two months everything was sold, and Ives returned to Rome with many orders for replicas. To fill the orders, Ives' enlarged his studio and hired several Italian artisans.

About this time (1855) he modeled "Undine" (Fig. 8.13), the water nymph. This, too, proved popular, and over ten replicas were commissioned and sent to America over the following decades. Its literary source was Friedrich Heinrich Karl de la Motte-Fouqué's *Undine*, published in England in 1818 and in New York in 1823 as *Undine, or the Spirit of the Waters, a Melodramatic Romance*. Around 1860 several editions appeared in America, indicating the book's popularity about the time that copies of Ives' statue were being produced. The subject was one of mystery and enchantment, and Ives chose to represent a scene from Chapter XVIII: "But an appearance, from the opening of the fountain, filled them with awe, as it rose like a white column of water; at first they imagined it to be a spouting fountain . . . until they perceived the form to be a pale female, veiled in white." The body of Undine stretches upward, covered by the thin wet veil, which in itself was a display of sculptural virtuosity that dazzled Ives' contemporaries. Such clever, unusual, and decorative surface treatment was something his patrons could admire, even though most of them had not had an education in the arts which would allow them to discriminate between relative values of sculpturesque form.

On a trip to America in 1859 Ives married Maria Louisa Davis, and they returned to Rome the following year. Though he produced a number of ideal pieces for the profitable American market, he continued to model portraits of the Americans and Englishmen who visited his studio. The New-York Historical Society has the bust of the Reverend Thomas Church Brownell in clerical robes (Fig. 8.12), signed and dated 1860; the Newark Museum owns "Bust of a Ward Child," and at Yale there is a marble likeness of Nathaniel William Taylor, both from this period. The Maryland Historical Society has in its collection an extraordinary "Alexander the Great" type of bust of Thomas de Kay Winans, executed in marble in 1861. Although the style of the face is naturalistic, as expected, one is unprepared for the soft flesh of the bare chest and shoulders. In the portrait bust, everyday street clothes had generally replaced the toga and bare chest some fifteen years earlier, but in Rome the classical tradition persisted with some sculptors through the 1860's. In his portraiture Ives managed to avoid a dry literalism, and somehow smoothed off much of the coarseness of the American physiognomy; he ignored the unessential details and emphasized his patrons' handsomer features, which of course pleased them immensely. That there was little of their personality in these portraits caused them no concern.

Among the ideal pieces Ives made throughout the 1860's and 1870's are "Jephthah's Daughter" (Buffalo and Erie County Historical Society); "Egeria" (1876, Virginia Museum of the Fine Arts); "Fisher Boy"; the popular "Sans Souci," which sold over twenty replicas; and "The Scholar" (Corcoran Gallery). The nude "Egeria" is taken from the ancient legend of the nymph who befriended Numa, the second king of Rome, and helped him rule wisely; when Numa died, Egeria "pined away and was changed into a fountain, which is still shown in Rome." One can see the waters of the fountain issuing from her right foot as the metamorphosis commences. There is a faint hint of neoclassicism in the face, but the figure is that of the 19th-century Italian girl who posed for the statue. Ives sold ten marble copies of the "Egeria"; another very popular piece, "The Truant" (New-York Historical Society), is a barefoot little girl on her way to school, stopping to listen to the roar of the sea in a shell held to her ear; one of those countless images of sweet or impish children at play, it appealed to the public's taste for quaintness. In the full-length "Jephthah's Daughter," Ives displayed his ability to incorporate surface patterns and intricate modeling into his statues. He had no difficulty modeling such things as brocade and fringe in clay; and of course it was the Italian artisans who reproduced them in marble.

Always busy with portrait busts and ideal pieces, Ives never bothered to seek large commissions from the government of the United States. It was not until late in his career that two of his works, his only life-size, full-length portrait statues, went into a government building in Washington, and even these were commissioned by the state of Connecticut. For Statuary Hall, Ives produced marble statues of two of Connecticut's favorite sons—Jonathan Trumbull and Roger Sherman. Only H. K. Brown's "Nathanael Greene" and Franklin Simmons' "Roger Williams" preceded the Connecticut statues' arrival in the Hall in 1872. Both figures were represented in colonial attire, and were accordingly turned into costume pieces by the sculptor, who was better at rendering ruffles and buttons than at modeling the male figure. The very poor understanding of the proportions of the male anatomy—especially noticeable in the legs of the "Trumbull"—is rather surprising in a sculptor who had produced so many full-length female figures. Moreover, in both statues the head is considerably too large for the body; and though some individual parts are well done, Ives failed to integrate them into a harmonious whole. Another "Trumbull" was made for the state of Connecticut capitol at Hartford, and it fared no better.

Ives was by then past sixty, and his most productive years were behind him. His finest period had been from 1851 to about 1865; during these years he created those smooth-skinned female figures and sweet children that were to invade so many Victorian parlors and libraries in America. His style was that curious amalgamation of neoclassicism and 19th-century naturalism; his subjects were usually drawn from ancient literature or American genre, melodramatic and picturesque themes that either amused his patrons or caused them to swoon. Although Ives' studio continued to turn out replicas of his earlier statues, and the sculptor himself still modeled some portrait busts, his career was essentially over by 1875. The rest of his life was spent in Rome, where he died on August 2, 1894.

William Henry Rinehart (1825–1874) more than any other sculptor perpetuated the neoclassical tradition throughout the third quarter of the 19th century while still retaining something of its original verve. Rinehart is the first American sculptor to be the subject of a modern monograph (written by William S. Rusk and published in 1939). And in 1948 many of his works were gathered together for a sizable exhibition held jointly at the Walters Gallery and the Peabody Institute in Baltimore, the American city with which the sculptor maintained his strongest ties. There is no question that he was one of the most gifted of the 19th-century sculptors, a fact that is apparent despite his involvement with eclecticism.

Rinehart was born on a Maryland farm, which his father owned and tilled. The boy's mind continually wandered from his chores, and Israel Rinehart, a stern but compassionate father, came to the realization that his son's future was not to be that of a farmer when one day he found young William modeling an earthen bust of his mother while the team of horses and plow stood idle nearby. The boy's formal education extended through high school, but he was not really scholastically inclined. In a happy arrangement, he began by an apprenticeship at a quarry that had just then started operations on the Rinehart farm. His introduction to working with stone consisted of polishing surfaces and carving inscriptions on gravestones, but in time he advanced to the more complicated carving of moldings and decorations for architecture. His proficiency with stone increased rapidly, and he was barely twenty when in 1844 he left the Carroll County farm to live and work in Baltimore.

Young Rinehart arrived in Baltimore just as American sculpture was witnessing the end of the "foreign interlude" and the emergence of native talent. Whereas two decades earlier, sculpture in America hardly existed except for foreign importations, by the middle 1840's it showed signs of really maturing. Such was the situation when William Rinehart took a job in the stone yard of Baughman and Bevan, where he became foreman in two years. By day he worked as a stonecutter, and at night he took art courses at the Maryland Institute. In 1851 he sent a small marble bas-relief entitled "The Smokers" (Peabody Institute), copied from a genre scene painted by the 17th-century Dutch master Teniers, to the fair held at the Institute. The catalogue of this exhibition carried the committee's recommendation of the artist "as entitled to the most favorable notice and highest regard," and the aspiring young sculptor must have been thrilled when his relief was awarded a gold medal. Thus encouraged, in the 1853 exhibition of the Maryland Historical Society Rinehart was represented by three pieces: a reclining ideal figure, "Faith"; a portrait bust of Samuel Christian Friedrich Hahnemann, the founder of homeopathy; and a portrait bust of the Reverend John Gottlieb Morris, one of Baltimore's distinguished citizens and scholars. These works further demonstrated Rinehart's genius, and he soon acquired the support of William T. Walters, for whom he had earlier done some skillful repairs on a carved mantelpiece. This patronage gave him the opportunity to study in Italy.

In 1855 William Rinehart arrived in Florence where he met Hiram Powers, Thomas Ball, Joel T. Hart, and the other Americans living there. During his two years in the city, he helped pay his expenses by doing stonecutting. There were virtually no portrait commissions to be had as a result of competition from such established men as Powers and Ball. So Rinehart worked on ideal conceptions, many of which were of subjects drawn from America, such as "Backwoodsman," "Indian Girl" (which he later destroyed), and "Pioneer and Family."

These were subjects that had been undertaken by Horatio Greenough in his "Rescue" group and by Crawford in his Senate pediment sculptures, but they had been special commissions for the Capitol of the United States; when American expatriates in Italy chose their own ideal subjects, they usually turned to ancient mythology or history. Rinehart, too, soon fell under this spell. For example, in these early years he also executed two small pairs of bas-reliefs: one set was of Winter and Spring; the other was of Morning and Evening. In every case the images were neoclassical female figures representing the abstractions of time and the seasons by means of personification. The first manifestations of the sculptor's attraction to neoclassicism, they recall the ancient reliefs of the Hours and the Seasons and also the reliefs of Antonio Canova and John Flaxman.

Rinehart returned to Baltimore in 1857 to establish a studio where he could execute the commissions he hoped would be forthcoming. A small group of wealthy and influential men presented him with several requests for works, and there was a carved chimney piece and an Indian fountain for the United States Capitol. But Italy had won his heart, and by September of 1858 he had established himself in Rome.

There were a few portrait commissions, such as the busts of Robert Garrett and H. A. Stone; but due largely to the continuing patronage of William T. Walters, Rinehart was able to devote much of his creative energy to ideal works. Late in 1859 and through the first half of 1860 he worked on "The Woman of Samaria," commissioned by Walters. The Christian subject is rendered in a thoroughly neoclassical form, with the head reminiscent of the style of Phidias or Polykleitos. Thomas Crawford had inherited the neoclassical mantle of Canova and Thorwaldsen, but his death in 1857 left it unclaimed until Rinehart with such works as "The Woman of Samaria," donned it. Referring to this statue in a letter to Frank Mayer (November 1860), he expressed his devotion to classical Greek principles and attacked the frivolous Victorian fascination with decorative details:

> I have treated [the subject] with as much simplicity as I could & perhaps with more severity than is common in modern works. I hold that these are essential to every good work in sculpture . . . . I have made no effort to get Prettiness [for] I believe it to be unworthy of Sculpture intirely [sic].
>
> [M. C. Ross and A. W. Rutledge, *William Henry Rinehart*, p. 39]

The life-size statue was put into marble and shipped to Walters in 1861; it is now in the collection of the Walters Gallery in Baltimore. A life-size marble copy and several small replicas were subsequently made.

Also dating from the year 1859 is the statue of Leander, the youth who nightly swam the Hellespont to be with his beloved Hero, a priestess of Venus. The style reminds one of the work of Praxiteles, for the artist sought to attain the nobility and heroic quality with which the Greeks invested their idealized figures. However, in an effort not to offend the priggish sensibilities of his patrons, the sculptor in a rather self-conscious manner covered the area of the statue's genitals with drapery, and a touch of the prettiness for which he professed contempt crept into the rendering of the little waves at Leander's feet.

By 1860 Rinehart had committed himself to neoclassicism in his ideal works, but this did not hold for his memorial statues and portraits. Moreover, in typical mid-19th-century fashion, his genre subjects were done in a style that might be called sentimental naturalism. In late 1859 and early 1860 he produced the first of his "Sleeping Children," a group that was to become extremely popular during the next fifteen years when twenty replicas were sold. The original group of two sleeping babes cuddled together, a pillow under their heads and a light blanket drawn about their lower bodies, with the arm of one tenderly laid across the stomach of the other, was made for the Sisson family of Baltimore, and it eventually found a place in the Sisson lot in Green Mount Cemetery. The Victorian love for the innocence of the sleeping child was mingled with the association of sleep with death—also a very popular subject of the time. Only a few years earlier Thomas Crawford had made a similar group (Metropolitan Museum of Art), except his children were older and clothed, and slept out of doors.

Rinehart also made portrait busts in the next few years, such as "James M. Mason" (Peabody Institute, Baltimore) and "Mrs. John Shoenberger" (St. Margaret's Hospital, Pittsburgh). The likeness of William W. Corcoran (1864) is characterized by a prosaic naturalism typical of many of Rinehart's portrait busts, along with a lack of vitality or any sense of drama or heroics. There is, of course, a simple honesty in the unadorned plainness of Rinehart's portraits, for most of his patrons belonged to the middle class. Having only lately acquired their wealth, they were neither aristocratic nor effete and would therefore be only falsely represented as such. Rinehart's likenesses stand in marked contrast to the earlier portraits painted by Thomas Sully or those sculptured by Horatio Greenough, Powers, and Crawford in the late 1830's, whereas they may be compared to the styles of Charles Loring Elliott and George P. A. Healy, the leading portrait painters of Rinehart's day. This rather unexciting naturalism, which dominated his portraiture throughout the remaining fifteen years of his life, may again be seen in the bust of Mrs. William T. Walters (Walters Art Gallery), executed in 1862, the year of her death.

At the time of Thomas Crawford's death in 1857, his studio contained a number of major pieces in various stages of completion, chief among them being the doors for the United States Capitol. One panel of the Senate doors (Fig. 8.14) had been cast in plaster (the "Death of Warren at Bunker Hill"; top panel, right valve), and there were four others more or less as clay sketches. Louisa Crawford eventually received permission from Captain Meigs, chief engineer of the Capitol, to see that the doors were completed according to her husband's designs. The legend starts at the upper right rectangular relief, moves down the right valve, then across to the lower left rectangle and up the left valve: the Death of Warren at Bunker Hill; Washington at Monmouth; Hamilton at Yorktown;

then, Washington at Trenton on his way to the Inauguration at New York; Washington taking the Presidential Oath; and finally, at the upper left, Washington laying the Cornerstone of the Capitol in 1793. The right valve represents War, symbolized in the oculus at the lower right by a New Jersey farmer defending his family against a Hessian soldier; the left valve represents Peace, embodied in the oculus below of a farmer with a plow and with his family gathered around him.

Gustave Kaupert, a German who had often worked in the Crawford studio, was asked to complete the panel of Washington taking the Presidential Oath. But in June 1861 Crawford's widow wrote to inform Captain W. B. Franklin, Meigs' successor, that she had "given the whole work into the hands of Mr. Wm. Rinehart, the most promising of the American Artists now in Rome—confident that he will in every way do it fullest justice." In the same letter she explained that Rinehart was not only equal to Kaupert in "artistic merit," but was also more reliable, and she further reported that "a feeling existed among the Americans, strongly opposed to the employment of foreign talent, where a countryman could with equal success carry out the designs." Nationalistic feeling ran high among American artists at home and abroad, and although Crawford had intended to have the doors cast at von Müller's Royal Foundry in Munich, the desire to make the Capitol as much as possible the work of native talent resulted in their being sent to the Ames foundry in Chicopee. Thomas U. Walter, architect of the Capitol, wrote to the Secretary of the Interior on June 22, 1863, about the matter:

I deem it proper to suggest that these models be brought directly to this country, to be put in bronze by American artists instead of sending them to Munich to have the doors cast from them by Mr. von Miller [sic], as was originally intended . . . . I consider it by no means a settled question that a work in bronze, equal in every respect to that of the Munich foundry, cannot be produced in the United States. But even admitting that our workmen are inferior to those of the Bavarian workshops, it is but just and appropriate, that our National Capitol, at the date of its construction, should be an exposition of the state of the arts in our own country, and not a museum of foreign art.   [Quoted from Fairman, *Art and Artists of the Capitol*]

Walter recommended that the door for the House entrance not be started, but by that time Rinehart had already begun work on it. Once again Crawford was responsible for the iconographic program, which from top to bottom on the left valve, deals with War: the Massacre of Wyoming Valley; the Pursuit of the British at Lexington; the Surrender of the British Flag at Charleston, South Carolina; the Death of General Montgomery. On the right valve, from top to bottom, are scenes of Peace: the Public Reading of the Declaration of Independence; the Signing of the Peace Treaty with Great Britain; Washington's Farewell to His Officers; Benjamin Franklin pursuing His Studies of Electricity. This plan had been outlined in a letter from Crawford to Meigs, and Rinehart followed it. Crawford also had roughed out clay sketches of the panels and had sent Meigs a photograph of them. Crawford, however, had been dead over five years by then, and Thomas U. Walter was not so devoted to the man and his memory as Meigs had been. In addition, Louisa Crawford had married Luther Terry in 1861 and was no longer occupied solely with carrying out her first husband's unfinished business. Rinehart therefore had a fairly free hand in executing the panels in his own style. In 1866 both sets of doors were shipped to the Ames foundry, and within two years the Senate doors were cast—the first great bronze doors to be produced in this country. Somehow the models for the House doors were misplaced, and not until 1905 were they found and cast in bronze.

Traveling Americans began to visit the Rinehart studio in increasing numbers, and in 1865 the Honorable and Mrs. J. Thompson sat for their likenesses there. In 1869 Bishop William Ingraham Kip had his portrait done by Rinehart; the plaster copy in the Peabody Institute, Baltimore, shows Rinehart's work at its finest. The bishop is manly and handsome, and exudes an air of confidence and dignity. The drapery over the shoulders and chest is in both style and conception reminiscent of Baroque busts, with a liveliness in its folds and a rich play of light and shadow. Here the sculptor rises well above the usual modeled likenesses of the period, having captured a Byronic element in the portrait. This is also true of the bust of Dr. Robert V. McKim (Peabody Institute) whose portrait suggests a youthful vigor and a sensitive spirit beneath the handsome features.

Rinehart's interest in ideal works continued unabated in the mid-1860's. "Juno" and "Penseroso" are ideal busts of neoclassical inspiration, and full-length classical figures were modeled for the tombs of the Walters and Fitzgerald families in cemeteries near Baltimore. At the Walters' site in Green Mount Cemetery stands the bronze statue of a classical, robed woman, holding a bunch of flowers in her left hand while strewing blossoms with her right. This was Rinehart's first major work to be cast in bronze, and in 1866 he sent the plaster model to the Royal Foundry in Munich while he returned to America with the models for the Capitol doors. The figures of Christ and the angel of the Resurrection and two funerary urns for the Fitzgerald tomb in Loudon Park Cemetery were modeled in 1865, then carved in marble by his studio assistants. Rinehart also did a statue of Hero, sitting upon a rock by the shore, gazing across the water in expectation of her lover, Leander. As in his earlier statue of Leander, a few small scalloped waves ruffle at the base of the statue. Rinehart wrapped mid-19th-century sentimentality in a neoclassical guise: There is a romantic pathos in the young girl who waits for her true lover who will come to her no more, and there is a melancholy preoccupation with death, for upon realizing that Leander has drowned, Hero throws herself into the waves. As testimony to the popularity of this piece, no less than eight marble copies were sold.

The last seven years of the sculptor's life saw a constant increase in the number of commissions for portrait busts, most of which are listed in the catalogue compiled by Ross and Rutledge. One example will suffice—the marble image of William P. Wilstach (Fig. 8.16), modeled in Rome in 1870. Rinehart's likeness of the Philadelphia merchant and art collector has an alertness of countenance that suggests an animated spirit; unlike many of the "dusty white ghosts" of this period, there is something more of the man in this portrait than a petrified likeness.

In the late 1860's and early 1870's, Rinehart worked on the finest of his several statues for cemeteries and public squares in the vicinity of Baltimore. There was the seated bronze of Chief Justice Roger B. Taney in his judicial robes, listing slightly to his right, deep in thought. "An admirably monumental work," Lorado Taft called it, and further conceded that it was "a fine, dignified characterization of the man." But Taft also lamented that it lacked the "charm of modern technic," meaning that Rinehart did not participate in the new French Beaux-Arts movement, which was to captivate American sculptors of the last quarter of the century. In comparison, Rinehart's surfaces are dryly naturalistic instead of decorative and flickering. The glory of the Taney statue lies in its boldness, simplicity, and monumentality. It is a sturdy representation of Taney the jurist, the contemplative American and quiet citizen who guarded the laws of the nation. The sculptor achieved the same selective naturalism in this statue that he did in the best of his portrait busts. The Taney commission was awarded by the state of Maryland in 1869, and the statue was unveiled December 12, 1872, on the grounds of the State House at Annapolis. A replica was dedicated in Mount Vernon Place in Baltimore in 1887, several years after Rinehart's death.

While his design of the Taney statue was being considered in Maryland, Rinehart began work on what was to be his most famous nude female figure—"Clytie" (Fig. 8.15). The nymph who fell in love with the sun-god, Apollo, and thereafter turned into a sunflower was represented in graceful form and stance, with the symbol of unwavering love held gently in her right hand. Executed in a purer neoclassicism than other sculpture of the time, it did not have the same emotional appeal as Powers' "Greek Slave." Still, such men as W. T. Walters and W. W. Corcoran succumbed to its charm, and after the sculptor's death even the British Academy in Rome asked if it might have a plaster cast of it. Marble versions are in the collections of the Peabody Institute and the Metropolitan Museum of Art, and a plaster copy is in the Corcoran Gallery. "Clytie," along with "Latona and her Children" (Fig. 8.17) done in 1874, represents the epitome and the swan song of American neoclassicism in the third quarter of the 19th century. Rinehart's success was in large measure due to his ability to provide his patrons with both a fine naturalism in their portraits and a lofty ideal art of Olympian heritage for their parlors. But when death cut short his career at the age of forty-nine, his purer strain of neoclassicism died with him. In the following decades sculptural imagery was to center on personifications and allegorical figures in which a majority of Americans could recognize their own highly esteemed virtues and aspirations—economic growth, material achievement, technological progress, military and political victory. These, of course, were the symbols of the crass, muscle-flexing, gilded age of Mark Twain and William Dean Howells.

Rinehart left his accumulated wealth in trust for the purpose of elevating the taste of his countrymen and "of assisting young men in the study of the Art of Sculpture, who may desire to make it a profession." The executors, W. T. Walters and B. F. Newcomer, supervised the sale of many of the pieces in the studio in Rome, and added the money to the trust fund, which by 1891 had grown to $100,000. At that time the fund was turned over to the trustees of the Peabody Institute, which established in Baltimore the Rinehart School of Sculpture and created scholarships to send promising young sculptors abroad for study. (A. Phimister Proctor was the first recipient of a Rinehart scholarship, and in 1895 he quite naturally elected to go to Paris rather than to the Rome of his benefactor.)

Franklin Simmons (1839–1913) joined William Rinehart in the attempt to perpetuate a pure classical ideal in the second half of the 19th century. He was born in Webster, Maine, but from 1867 until his death he lived in Rome, a permanent member of its expatriate colony. Simmons spent his boyhood in Bath, Maine, and as a youth of fifteen got a job in the counting room of a cotton mill in Lewiston. It was then, around 1854, that he first took drawing lessons and began modeling in clay as a pastime, reportedly inspired by a description he read of Hiram Powers' "Greek Slave." Among his earliest efforts, modeled in the evening hours, was a bust of Dr. Nathaniel Bowditch, which attracted much favorable local comment. But Lewiston offered no fine and noble examples of sculpture, and there was no one there who could provide the disciplined instruction he then needed and desired. Accordingly, in 1856 he went to Boston in search of professional training, which he found in the studio of another native son of Maine, John Adams Jackson. The duration of Jackson's instruction was brief, but Simmons learned the rudiments of modeling in clay and of making plaster molds and casts. In Boston he looked at the many portrait busts in plaster and marble, also at Chantrey's marble "Washington," Richard Greenough's "Franklin," and Hughes' bronze "Bowditch," as well as at the casts of ancient sculptures in the Athenaeum. Thus trained and inspired, the eighteen-year-old Simmons returned to Lewiston and opened his first studio—a seven-by-nine-foot cubicle.

His first commission was for a bust of the Reverend George Knox, a local minister. This was successfully completed and was followed by several others: At Colby College there is a bust of President Champlain, dated 1859; President Woods and Professor Alpheus Packard of Bowdoin also sat for their portraits, as did the Reverend Nathaniel Butler (1861) and the Honorable Lot M. Morrill. Each portrait was deemed more successful than its predecessor, and young Simmons decided to test his ability in Portland, the largest city in the state. There was no sculptor in Portland then, although the residents followed intently the career of Paul Akers in Italy. But they immediately took to the new artist in their midst, and the prominent men of the city—such as John Neal, William Pitt Fessenden, the Reverend Horatio Stebbins, and F. O. J. Smith—sat for their portraits. Simmons' facility in rendering a good naturalistic likeness was soon established.

During the first half-dozen years of his professional career, Simmons' talent had not been tested beyond the portrait bust. A greater opportunity—his first commission for a full-length figure—came in 1863 when he was asked to do a memorial statue of General Hiram G. Berry, who had been killed at the battle of Chancellorsville. In October John Neal wrote to Mrs. Berry that he was confident that Simmons' work would be ". . . not only a comfort and consolation to the family, but an honor to the state and country." The statue was unveiled in Acorn Cemetery, Rockland, on October 31, 1865, the first of many Civil War memorials Simmons was to do. The favorable reaction to this statue encouraged Simmons once more to think of the greater opportunities that awaited him elsewhere. So he left Portland and set up his studio in Washington, D.C. Congressmen, senators, and members of the Cabinet posed for him, as well as military heroes of the day. From the years 1865 and 1866 date portrait busts of William Henry Seward, of Generals Sherman, Grant, Sheridan, Meade, Thomas, Hooker, Wright, and Warren, and of Admirals Farragut and Porter. Grant was evidently pleased with his likeness, for he is reported to have recommended Simmons as the sculptor to do a life-size marble statue of him some years later. The bust of General Sherman has a calm countenance and an icy stare, and the squared shoulders and erect carriage of the head reveal the iron man that he was. Done with a naturalism full of verve, it is one of the sculptor's most accomplished portrait busts.

It was not until the fall of 1866, however, that he obtained the type of commission he had hoped for—a public Civil War monument—and from his former home town, Lewiston, Maine. It consists of a bronze soldier standing atop a large granite base, on which are bronze plaques with the more than one hundred names of the boys and men of Lewiston who had fallen in battle. Modeled and cast during 1867, it was one of the first public commemorative monuments of the Civil War.

But the work that was to bring Simmons a national reputation was the earliest of his two statues of Roger Williams (Fig. 8.18), a commission for Statuary Hall. Like Henry Kirke Brown's figure of General Nathanael Greene, which was the first statue placed in Statuary Hall, it was the gift of the state of Rhode Island and the second statue to arrive. Ulysses S. Grant had recommended Simmons for the commission. No portrait of Roger Williams existed, but the countenance was to express those qualities for which the "apostle of religious freedom" stood. Simmons did research on Williams' personality, his times, his conflicts, and his dress, so that his image would contain everything Rhode Islanders held to be a part of the man. Simmons also felt that it was again time to widen his artistic horizons, so late in 1867 he and his young wife sailed for Italy.

The Simmonses went first to Florence, where the sculptor renewed his acquaintance with John Adams Jackson and met the aging but redoubtable Hiram Powers, as well as Thomas Ball. The following spring the couple moved on to Rome. It was all they had imagined and far more, and there they were to make their home for the rest of their lives. Before long the sculptor began work on the model for his statue of Roger Williams, which was cast in plaster, then cut into marble by Italian craftsmen. The statue was sent to the United States late in 1871, set up in the Capitol, and formally dedicated on January 9, 1872.

Simmons succeeded in giving an expression of careworn benevolence to the face, but like most sculptors of the time, he was unable to solve successfully the problem of the attire. Like other artists, also, Simmons had to appeal to the taste of his patrons, who took an abundance and accuracy of detail as their standard for artistic quality, rather than good sculptural form. To later generations, the gestures of this statue seem hollow and the details of the clothing prosaic. But Simmons' contemporaries were immensely impressed with both the authenticity and execution of the statue in these respects.

Thus the style of the Williams statue was typical mid-19th-century naturalism. But, as with many other sculptors of his time, the spell of Rome soon overwhelmed Simmons, also. He had hardly arrived in Rome before he began to follow and perhaps envy a little the spectacular success of William Wetmore Story's heroic images of the "Libyan Sibyl," "Cleopatra," and "Medea" and Rinehart's "Clytie" and "Woman of Samaria." Once Simmons finished modeling the figure of Williams, he began work on his first ideal statue, "Mother of Moses" (Portland [Maine] Museum of Art). Rejecting a subject from his native land, he turned instead to the ancient past. "Promised Land" (1870; in the Metropolitan Museum of Art and the Portland [Maine] Museum of Art) is a young Hebrew woman in sandals and long gown, a veil about her head, sitting beside the trunk of a palm tree. Her expression is dreamy and peaceful, and she represents a symbol of the end of the search for the good life and the land of her forefathers. There was also a "Medusa," a bronze life-size "Galatea," a standing figure of Miriam, and a marble "Penelope," all of which are in the Portland museum. In "Penelope" (Fig. 8.19), Simmons carried his neoclassical ideal to its finest point. A lovely figure, graceful and animated, is perceived beneath the drapery of Penelope's gown, and the head—which has a pronounced Greek profile—is as delicate and sensitive an example of neoclassicism as any ever produced by a member of the American colony in Italy. Moreover, the sculptor captured a mood, an expression of the resignation that had overtaken Penelope after long years of waiting for Ulysses. The exquisite modeling of the torso and head is sufficient to overpower the many details the sculptor included, such as the sphinxes on the chair and the embroidery on the hem of the gown. The "Penelope," like Rinehart's "Clytie" and "Latona," was of sufficient quality to give life once more to the moribund neoclassical movement, though only temporarily.

Franklin Simmons' greatest artistic achievements were not realized in his ideal works, however, but in several portrait statues and war memorials done in the naturalistic style that had roots deep in American tradition. And his work of the 1880's and 1890's acquired a new vitality and strength.

On a visit to America in 1873 Simmons was commissioned to do a bronze statue of Edward Little, which was four years later erected in front of the Edward Little High School in Auburn, Maine. There were other portrait busts, of course, and another monument to Williams, which was set up in Roger Williams Park in Providence, Rhode Island. The bronze figure atop the large granite pedestal is a replica of the marble figure in Statuary Hall; a bronze female figure, representing History, stands beside the base. This auxiliary figure embodying an abstract idea was a bold innovation, one of the earliest appearances of the personifying figure that became so popular in the last quarter of the century.

While these figures were being cast in Munich, Simmons began work on the statue of William King, which was commissioned by the state of Maine for Statuary Hall. The result was, by and large, another costume portrait. Although Simmons tried to present King in the guise of a Roman senator by wrapping him in a great togalike cape, the large tasseled boots attract the eye every bit as much as the head, and the ruffles at the cuffs and neck are equally distracting. Congress was satisfied with Simmons' work, however, and awarded him $20,000 for a Naval Monument dedicated to the seamen who lost their lives in the Civil War. Erected in Washington, the 40-foot-high pedestal was crowned with a group composed of a figure of a grief-stricken America mourning on the shoulder of History. On one side of the base is the figure of Victory, who holds high a laurel wreath, and on the opposite side is Peace, who stands amid farm implements, two infants playing at the feet of these lower figures.

Thus far in his career Franklin Simmons had remained faithful to the aesthetics of most mid-19th-century American portraiture—a dry, smooth naturalism, with greater emphasis on accuracy of detail than on powerful sculptural form. But by 1880 American art had reached a turning point, and a decided change in Simmons' own style may be seen in certain works that date from the mid-1880's on. The first monument in which this is evident is the imposing seated figure of Henry Wadsworth Longfellow, which dominates a small square in Portland, Maine. The city of the poet's birth commissioned the statue in October 1885, and Simmons modeled it in Rome during the next year and a half. It was unveiled in Portland on September 29, 1888, while a chorus of school children sang Longfellow's "Psalm of Life." In the bold massiveness of the figure Simmons attained a measure of greatness never before realized in his work. The eye is not distracted by details, and the real climax of the work is reached in the head, where the spectator is captivated by the pensive and sensitive expression. Longfellow sits with his cape nearly off his shoulders but wrapped snugly about his legs; his left hand, holding a manuscript, rests in his lap; his right arm is on the arm of the chair. There is the quality of real life in it, a quality noticeably lacking in Simmons' earlier pieces for Statuary Hall. The style remains that of naturalism, and the only trace of any revival eclecticism is in the quasi-classical decoration of the chair. It is indeed a finely conceived, well-wrought image of a 19th-century American sage.

Even before the "Longfellow" was cast in bronze, the sculptor had begun work on another commission for the city of Portland—the large monument to the Union and to the sons of Portland who died to preserve it. High on a massive granite base (designed by Richard M. Hunt) stands a colossal bronze figure of a robed woman representing the Union (sometimes referred to as the Great Republic, or Our Lady of Victories); on her head is a liberty cap with a wreath, and in her hands she holds a sheathed sword, a shield, and the olive branch of peace. The size of this figure tends to overpower the two bronze groups on the sides of the base; these are by far the best parts of the monument and would stand up well against any other work done in the last quarter of the century. They represent the Army and the Navy (Fig. 8.21), and in each group an officer stands in the middle, flanked by two of his men. Behind and above them are flags and laurel wreaths; at their feet are assorted paraphernalia of war. In the flags and elsewhere, the sculptor nearly achieves a sensation of color by clever design and modeling. But the richness of the detail does not detract from the whole; the real strength and beauty of each group is in the figures themselves. Their faces show determination, pride, alertness; and one gets a feeling that the noble and heroic has returned to American sculpture. This was sparked in large measure by the work of Saint-Gaudens, whose influence is clearly seen in the strong resemblance between Simmons' naval officer and Saint-Gaudens' "Admiral Farragut" in New York's Madison Square. Naturalism remains at the core of this style, but in the last quarter of the century several American sculptors perceived that naturalism by itself was not the same as Art—a fact that was not understood in the preceding quarter of the century. In these boldly sculptured groups of the Army and Navy, with their good composition, their animated figures, and their expressive faces, Franklin Simmons raised his art well above the banality of most American sculpture in the previous thirty years. Portland took justifiable pride in its monument, which was unveiled on the main thoroughfare on October 28, 1891; and Simmons, who was present for the occasion, must have been immensely pleased.

In the course of his career, Simmons is reported to have modeled more than one hundred portrait busts. But these were generally unspectacular, possessing not much more than a good likeness of the subject. There are marble portraits of Vice-Presidents Hamlin, Fairbanks, and Stevenson in the Capitol at Washington; and in the Baxter Public Library in Portland is a bust of James Phinney Baxter (1886). Simmons' studio in the Via San Nicolo Tolentino was one of the places that Americans in Rome visited, and many of them posed for their portraits in clay. The constant demand for his work had made Simmons a relatively wealthy man, and his Villa Settembre reflected his prosperity.

About 1895 Simmons received a commission from the Grand Army of the Republic for a life-size marble statue of General Grant. After the statue was put into marble it was rejected by the G. A. R. for not being a true representation of Grant. Simmons then began work on a second one, which was accepted and unveiled in 1900; it is now in the Capitol. The first statue, now in the Portland Museum of Art, seems far superior to this second one, however. The former is the more thoughtful man, who has laid aside his sword, with the branch of peace, or victory, at his feet; this is Grant the President, and Simmons attempted to endow him with all the dignity that the office deserves. The second version shows Grant in full military dress, more the man of action, and evidently that was the way the Grand Army wished to remember its general.

Simmons' other major project in the 1890's was an equestrian statue of General John A. Logan (Fig. 8.20), which drew exclamations of delight and approval from visitors as they saw the model reaching its final form in his studio. Simmons worked on it for several years, for not only were the horse and rider to be of bronze, but the entire base as well. The latter provided space for two exquisite reliefs, which dealt with Logan's careers as a general and as a statesman, and for a rich quasi-classical decoration in the enframing parts. The group was cast in Rome. On its completion a ceremony was held at the foundry and attended by the King and Queen of Italy, who honored the sculptor by knighthood. The monument was then shipped to Washington, where President McKinley delivered the oration in Iowa Circle at the unveiling ceremony on April 9, 1901. General Logan sits very erect in his saddle, sword drawn, awaiting the moment to command the charge. Both horse and rider are animated and skillfully done. On the base, the same heroic quality seen in the Portland groups of the Army and Navy is present in the seven solemn-faced officers who listen to General Logan as he plans his offensive. Again, a naturalism filled with verve is achieved in the figures, and the only equestrian statue of this period that rivals it is the "Sherman" by Saint-Gaudens in Central Park, unveiled a few years later.

The equestrian Logan was the last of Simmons' major commissions, although he was active in his Roman studio during much of the remaining 15 years of his life. Several projects for ideal works and portrait statues occupied him during these years, and strangely enough the spell of neoclassicism lingered. This is seen in the heroic-sized group "Hercules and Alcestis," which was carried only as far as the plaster model. The sculptor, who died in 1913, willed it and many other pieces in his studio to the Portland Museum of Art. Simmons had begun his career in the rather dark days of a tyrannical, bland, and banal naturalism, but he participated in the renaissance that American sculpture experienced in the last quarter of the century. He was one of the few men of the older generation who, like Quincy Ward, caught up the spirit of the new movement, especially in his portrait statues. He died in Rome at the age of seventy-four.

[FIG. 8.1] "Cornelia Van Rensselaer," by Richard Greenough (1849). Marble, 25″ high. Courtesy, New-York Historical Society, New York City.

[FIG. 8.2] "Governor John Winthrop," by Richard Greenough (1856). Marble. Courtesy, Harvard University; photo, Index of American Sculpture, University of Delaware.

[FIG. 8.3] "Benjamin Franklin," by Richard Greenough (1855). Bronze. City Hall, Boston. Photo, Index of American Sculpture, University of Delaware.

[FIG. 8.5] "Elizabeth Barrett Browning," by William Wetmore Story (1866, after the original of 1861). Marble. Courtesy, Boston Athenaeum.

[FIG. 8.4] "Carthaginian Girl," by Richard Greenough (1863). Marble. Courtesy, Boston Athenaeum.

[FIG. 8.8] "Professor Joseph Henry," by William Wetmore Story (1881). Bronze. Washington, D.C. Courtesy, National Park Service

[FIG. 8.7] "Medea," by William Wetmore Story (1868 after the original of 1864). Marble, 76½″ high. Courtesy, Metropolitan Museum of Art, gift of Henry Chauncey, 1894.

[FIG. 8.6] "Libyan Sibyl," by William Wetmore Story (1868; after the original of c. 1861). Marble, 54″ high. Courtesy, National Collection of Fine Arts, Smithsonian Institution.

[FIG. 8.9] "Edward Everett," by Paul Akers (1854–56). Marble. Courtesy, Maine Historical Society, Portland; photo, Index of American Sculpture, University of Delaware.

[FIG. 8.10] "Dead Pearl Diver," by Paul Akers (1857). Marble. Courtesy, Portland (Maine) Museum of Art.

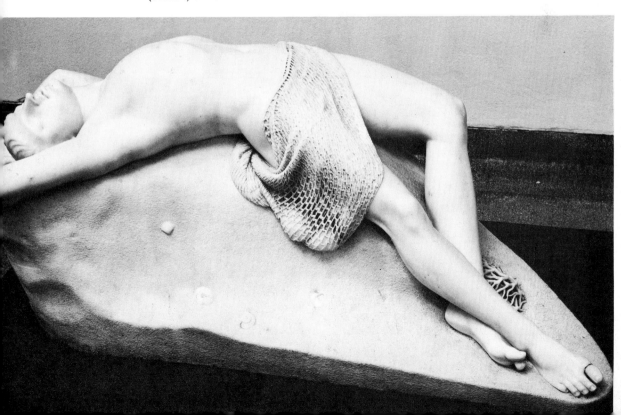

[FIG. 8.11] "Mrs. William Gage Lambert," by Chauncey B. Ives (1848). Marble. Courtesy, New-York Historical Society, New York City.

[FIG. 8.12] "The Reverend Thomas Church Brownell," by Chauncey B. Ives (1860). Plaster, 32½″ high. Courtesy, New-York Historical Society, New York City.

[FIG. 8.13] "Undine," by Chauncey B. Ives (c. 1855). Marble, 61″ high. Front and back views. Courtesy, Yale University Art Gallery, gift of Mrs. Alice A. Allen.

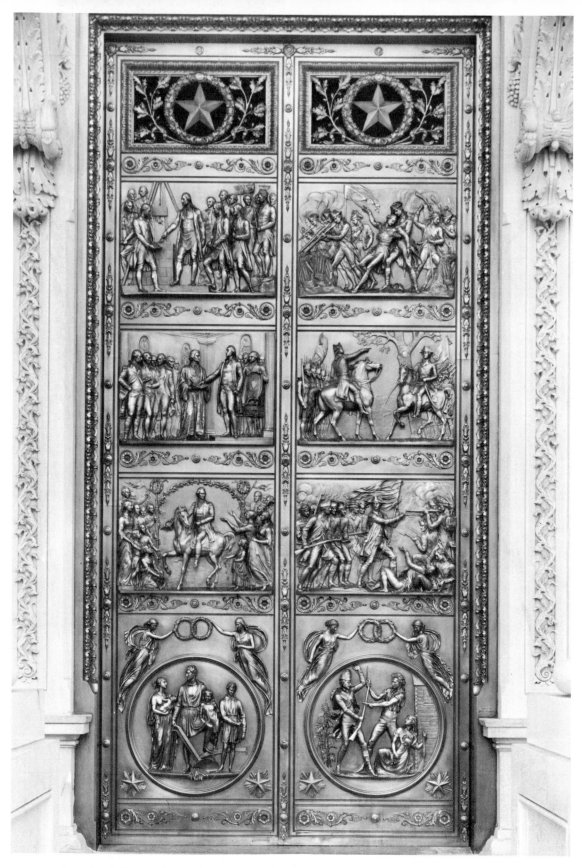

[FIG. 8.14] Senate doors, designed by Thomas Crawford (1855), executed by William Rinehart (1863–65). Bronze, 14′ 5″ high. Eastern entrance, Senate Wing, U.S. Capitol, Washington, D.C. Courtesy, Architect of the Capitol.

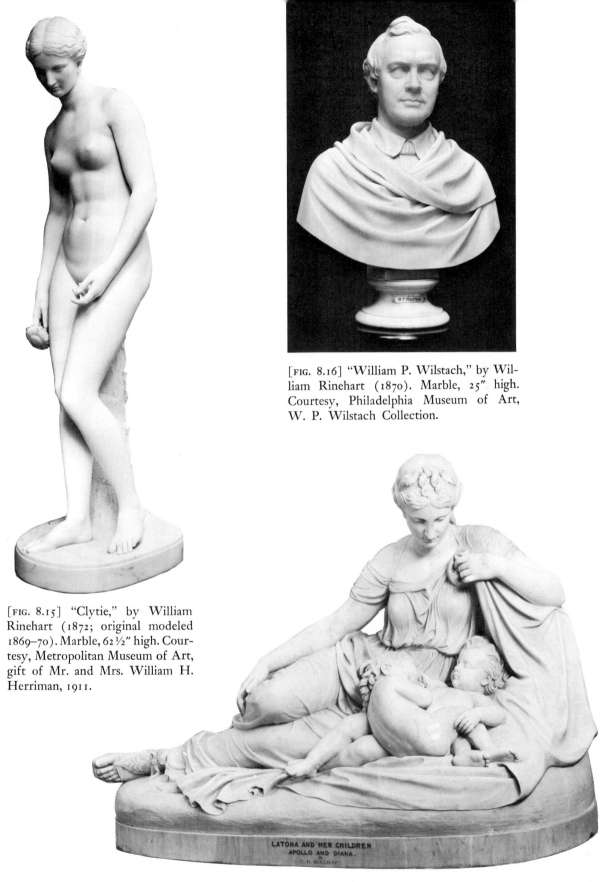

[FIG. 8.16] "William P. Wilstach," by William Rinehart (1870). Marble, 25″ high. Courtesy, Philadelphia Museum of Art, W. P. Wilstach Collection.

[FIG. 8.15] "Clytie," by William Rinehart (1872; original modeled 1869–70). Marble, 62½″ high. Courtesy, Metropolitan Museum of Art, gift of Mr. and Mrs. William H. Herriman, 1911.

[FIG. 8.17] "Latona and her Children," by William Rinehart (1871–1874). Marble, 46″ high. Courtesy, Metropolitan Museum of Art, Rogers Fund, 1905.

[FIG. 8.18] "Roger Williams," by Franklin Simmons (1868). Marble. Statuary Hall, U.S. Capitol, Washington, D.C. Courtesy, Architect of the Capitol.

[FIG. 8.20] "General John A. Logan," by Franklin Simmons (1897–1901). Bronze. Washington, D.C. Courtesy, National Park Service.

[FIG. 8.19] "Penelope," by Franklin Simmons (c. 1880). Marble. Courtesy, Portland (Me.) Museum of Art; photo, Index of American Sculpture, University of Delaware.

[FIG. 8.21] "Navy Group," Civil War Memorial, Portland, Me., by Franklin Simmons (1891). Bronze. Photo, Index of American Sculpture, University of Delaware.

9

The Second Generation of Americans in Italy: Part II

THE SECOND GENERATION OF AMERICAN SCULPTORS TO EXPATRIATE THEMSELVES IN Italy continued during the third quarter of the nineteenth century with such artists as Randolph Rogers, Edward Bartholomew, Larkin Mead, Harriet Hosmer and the "White Marmorean Flock," P. F. Connelly, and Moses Ezekiel. Each of them contributed to the lively social and artistic life of Rome while the American colony in Florence dwindled steadily. By the end of the third quarter of the century, however, Rome itself would be forsaken in favor of Paris and the new Beaux-Arts style being taught in the academies there. But between roughly 1850 and 1875 Rome was the Mecca to which nearly every aspiring young sculptor made his pilgrimage. Furthermore, those who came to Rome found it an exceedingly difficult place to leave. They fell under the city's spell and were invariably affected by its neoclassical traditions, so that this generation of American sculptors continued to produce its great marble "Zenobias," "Blind Girls of Pompeii," "Sapphos" and "Oenones." The other half of this split artistic personality continued, of course, to create portrait busts and statues in a highly naturalistic style that was frequently too smooth of surface, too detailed, and too lacking in verve and sculptural form to attain the rank of great art. Yet these artists with their colorful lives are fascinating personalities in their own right, and a careful study of their art reveals an interesting insight into that strange epoch known as the Victorian Age with all of its wild array of eclectic, Romantic ornamentation.

One of the most gifted of these expatriate American sculptors was Randolph Rogers (1825–1892) whose "Nydia, the Blind Girl of Pompeii" became through its literary associations a symbol of the age, just as Story's "Cleopatra" and Akers' "Dead Pearl Diver" had in their own way. Randolph Rogers was born in Waterloo, New York, but grew up in Ann Arbor, Michigan, showing little inclination toward art in his youth. At about the age of twenty he moved to New York City, where he became a dry-goods clerk. Although previously his artistic efforts had been confined to some drawings and cartoons, in 1848 he held what Lorado Taft called "an impromptu exhibition of . . . several figures and a bust of Byron"; also included was a portrait of little Lycurgus Edgerton, son of one of his employers. So well received was this exhibition that he was given the opportunity to study in Italy, the trip being financed by his two employers.

He left that year, going first to Florence, where he studied with the celebrated Bartolini at the Academy of St. Mark. By 1851 he had settled in Rome, where he studied ancient statuary, drew at the academies, and modeled in his own studio. Hiram Powers, Horatio Greenough, and Joel T. Hart were in Florence; Thomas Crawford, Richard Greenough, W. W. Story, Paul Akers, and C. B. Ives were in Rome; and young Rogers entered happily into this growing fraternity of American sculptors. In their studios he saw rows of plaster portrait busts and observed the ideal works then in progress. He also joined them and other artists for lively discussions and strolled with them among the ruins of the ancient cities. All of this supplied a kind of nourishment not to be found back home.

In 1852 he sent an ideal bust entitled "Night" across the Atlantic to the National Academy of Design exhibition, and word about this promising young sculptor began to spread. Several busts were modeled during these years, as was what seems to have been his first ideal figure, "Ruth." The statue was not put into marble until 1855, but some fifteen to twenty replicas were afterward produced. Ruth is shown kneeling, while gleaning in the wheat fields, looking up with a startled air, no doubt at the arrival of Boaz. There is a faint classicism in the profile of the head and in the proportions of the figure. But the emphasis on the grass, leaves, and on the strands of hair reveal the anecdotal style, full of naturalistic details so much in favor in the middle of the 19th century. The statue was highly praised, and when the sculptor applied to Captain Meigs in Washington for a commission from the government, he sent Meigs a photograph of "Ruth." Meigs later (May 1855) wrote to Secretary of War Jefferson Davis about the sculptor's proposal for a set of bronze doors: "If he can succeed as well with these as with his Ruth, of which you have a photograph, it will be well enough." Certainly the statue was consonant with the canon then prevailing in aesthetic taste: The figure of Ruth was taken directly from the sacred pages of scripture; it offered the artist a noble subject, appropriate to the pursuit of a lofty art. It was both a challenge to the sculptor and an acceptable subject in the religious and moral atmosphere hovering over mid-19th-century America.

One of the most celebrated of Rogers' statues was "Nydia, the Blind Girl of Pompeii" (Fig. 9.1), done in 1853; something like one hundred replicas were sold over the following decades. A visitor to Rogers' studio once saw seven Nydias "all in a row, all listening, all groping, and seven marble-cutters at work, cutting them out." It was still a stellar attraction when shown at the Philadelphia Centennial of 1876. The subject is taken from Bulwer-Lytton's novel *The Last Days of Pompeii,* first published in 1834, and once more an American sculptor proved to be under the spell of Graeco-Roman antiquity. In "Nydia" the sculptor attempted to wring every bit of pathos and sentimental empathy from the beholder, just as the author had done when he wrote of the blind flower girl who groped her way amid the mobs and rubble on that fateful day in A.D. 79 when Vesuvius erupted:

> Poor girl! her courage was beautiful to behold! and Fate seemed to favor one so helpless. The boiling torrents touched her not . . . but spared that frail form . . . Weak, exposed, yet fearless, supported by but one wish, she was the very emblem of Psyche in her wanderings . . . of Hope, walking through the Valley of the Shadow; a very emblem of the Soul itself—alone but comforted, amid the dangers and the snares of life.   [Quoted from Bulwer-Lytton, *The Last Days of Pompeii*]

Here was yet another literary sculpture, following the Romantic tradition of the "Greek Slave" in its moralistic content, and faintly hinting at authenticity by being conceived in a form similar to a specific ancient statue—in this case the "Old Market Woman" in the Vatican. There are copies of the "Nydia" at the Metropolitan Museum of Art and the Newark Museum, at Harvard and Princeton, at the Pennsylvania Academy, at the University of Michigan, and at the Buffalo and Erie County Historical Society.

   Although he was not yet thirty when he completed the "Ruth" and the "Nydia," Randolph Rogers yearned for a large commission that would test his ability and establish his reputation. Having heard of Crawford's commission to do the bronze doors for the new Senate wing, Rogers suggested that he, too, might produce a set of doors—for the Rotunda entrance. Meigs wrote Rogers that he hoped the government would soon be able to give him a commission; the sculptor thereupon took the initiative and asked for tracings of the Rotunda doorway, which were promptly supplied. For this portal the artist proposed executing ten panels and a lunette devoted to the history of Columbus. Fairman has published the proposal in his *Art and Artists of the Capitol,* and it reads in part:

> . . . the subject to be the life of Columbus, which will be illustrated by eleven alto-reliefs, which will contain in all about one hundred and fifty figures, besides twelve portrait statuettes and twelve heads of the distinguished contemporaries of Columbus, together with suitable ornamental work for the rails and stiles of said door, such as animals, fruit, foliage, etc., etc.

Rogers asked $8,000 for the doors completed in plaster, and he estimated the cost of having them cast in bronze would be an additional $2,000. His proposal, accompanied by a sketch, was submitted on May 24, 1855, and was approved on the following day by the Secretary of War, with a promptness that seems unbelievable today.

Rogers had been active as a sculptor only about seven years when this, his first important commission, came along. He had gone to America to discuss his proposal; upon receiving the commission, he again returned to Rome, firm in the opinion that only there could he accomplish such a work, in spite of Captain Meigs' hope that while executing their commissions for the Capitol, more of the nation's sculptors would find it possible to remain in their native land.

That same year the sculptor opened what was to become one of the most prolific studios in Rome. Work progressed slowly on the models for the Columbus doors for the Capitol (Fig. 9.2). In May 1857 the sculptor wrote to Captain Meigs not to pressure him, but to allow him time to do the work properly. As they took form, the doors constituted one of the earliest examples of a "Renaissance revival" in American art, for the sculptor had before him the vision of Ghiberti's "Gates of Paradise" on the Baptistry at Florence. In the same letter, Rogers wrote:

I am willing you put this photograph by the side of any of the panels of the Ghiberti Gate and have no fear of comparison. This may seem to you like vanity, but to me it is only common sense, for I am not willing to acknowledge that an American of the nineteenth century cannot produce a work equal to that of any Florentine of any period.

Finally wrought as eight panels (four on each valve), instead of the ten originally planned, the illustrations of Columbus' life and adventures are enframed by statuettes of the discoverer's contemporaries in conch-shell niches and with small portrait heads in occuli; the resemblance to Ghiberti's doors is further marked by low-relief floral and military decorations on the frames and the door jambs. Above is a lunette that contains the main scene of the landing of Columbus with his men and the planting of the Spanish flag in the soil of the New World while Indians watch from behind a tree. In all the panels the main figures are placed up stage in fairly high relief, whereas the architectural and landscape backgrounds are either incised or in low relief. Stylistically this, too, is derived from Ghiberti's prototype. Seen from a short distance these reliefs are effective and handsome enough as narrative compositions, but upon closer scrutiny one observes a peculiar awkwardness in many of the anatomical details. Several years were devoted to these doors, while other projects in the sculptor's studio were initiated and concluded, and it was not until 1861 that the doors, jambs, and lunette were sent to Munich to be cast in bronze. They were shipped to America the following year to be installed at the entrance to the hall leading from the Rotunda to the House chamber, although they were ultimately placed at the entrance to the Rotunda itself. This was quite a prestigious accomplishment for Rogers and attracted a great deal of attention to his work. Moreover, although Crawford's doors in the Senate had been commissioned earlier, they were left at his death in an incomplete state, and it was a long time before they were finally finished and set up in the Capitol. Rogers' doors were therefore the first bronze doors in the building to be installed.

While his Italian stonecutters were turning out copies of "Ruth" and "Nydia,"
Rogers was modeling the life-size statue of John Adams (1859), which was to be
placed in the Gothic pantheon of New England dignitaries in the cemetery at
Mount Auburn. The marble statue, now in Memorial Hall at Harvard, represents
Adams in the pose of an orator, dressed in 18th-century attire; his right hand is
outstretched, and his left rests on the scroll on the post beside him. As a costume
piece, it is quite a display of virtuosity, with a great amount of decorative, naturalistic detail, especially in the lace ruffs at the wrists and neck and in the em-
broidered flower pattern on the waistcoat. Once again this preoccupation with
minute details deprived the statue of the heroic quality the subject deserved.
Rogers, like many of his fellow sculptors and their patrons, had lost sight of
what constituted truly great portraiture. Perhaps realizing the errors made in his
statue of Adams, Rogers achieved more than merely technical cleverness in his
next major commission.

In November 1857, while work was continuing on the models for the Capitol
doors, Rogers was asked by Governor Wise of Virginia if he would make the
remaining figures and decorations for Richmond's Washington Monument, left
unfinished by Crawford at his death. Rogers had been a frequent visitor to
Crawford's studio during Crawford's last years. When he returned there several
years later, he found in the gray silent rooms the models for the statues of Marshall and Mason, which needed only to be sent to Munich, where von Müller was
already preparing to cast Crawford's figures of Patrick Henry and Thomas
Jefferson. Of the six standing figures, Rogers was to model only the ones of Nelson and Lewis. Crawford had endowed the "Patrick Henry" with a dynamic
vigor; he had made the "Jefferson" and "Marshall" pensive and calm, and the
"Mason" resolute. Following his example, Rogers sought more than blandness of
character and accuracy of detail in his figures. Rogers' statue of Meriwether
Lewis, dressed in buckskin and leaning on his rifle, is a heroic figure of a man of
courage and confidence (Fig. 9.3). The artistic strength of this figure lies in its
simple yet noble naturalism. The statues of both Lewis and Nelson represent the
highest achievement in portraiture of Rogers' career.

In addition to doing the two statues, Rogers replaced the attendant eagles of
Crawford's original design with seated allegorical figures accompanied by trophies of war. The figures personified such things as the Bill of Rights, Justice, Independence, and on the shields beside them were inscribed the names of the
famous battles of the Revolution. The figure representing the Bill of Rights was
signed and dated by the sculptor 1860, but von Müller's date of casting is inscribed 1868. These well-modeled seated maidens belong more to the robust style
of the Second Empire than to the purity of neoclassicism, and Rogers seldom
again achieved their fine sculptural form.

Rogers' progress on the various pieces for the Richmond monument is outlined in the following letter he sent Governor Francis H. Pierpoint in November
1866:

My last letter to the commissioners, before the war, was dated March 7th, 1861. I then stated that I had just received a letter from [von Müller], the bronze founder at Munich, stating that the statue of Marshall had been completed in bronze, and would be forwarded to Rotterdam without delay, and that Nelson was nearly finished, and that Lewis would be ready for shipping before the first of July; also, that two of the allegorical statues, with military trophies, had been for several months in the hands of bronze founders, and I believe they were well advanced.

At the time of the statue arriving in Rotterdam, the aspect of political matters looked so threatening that I was advised not to send it forward, for fear of seizure and confiscation. The statues of Nelson and Lewis have been finished and packed ready for shipping ever since the summer of 1861, the balance due upon which, and one of the allegorical figures and trophies finished and another advanced, I am expected to pay interest since that time.

My contract with the state of Virginia is, in substance, as follows:

For casting in bronze the statue of Mason after the plaster model by Crawford	$ 4,500 00
For casting in bronze the statue of Marshall after the plaster model by Crawford	4,500 00
For moulding and casting in bronze statue of Nelson	9,000 00
For moulding and casting in bronze statue of Lewis	9,000 00
For six allegorical figures, with military trophies (5,000 each)	30,000 00
Boxing, baling, insurance and transportation to Richmond	3,500 00
Making	$60,500 00

In the late 1850's and early 1860's Rogers had three major commissions going at once: the Columbus doors, the statue of John Adams, and the sculptures for the Washington Monument in Richmond. Not all of the pieces for the latter were produced at once, of course, but still his studio must have been one of the busiest of the period. That his work commanded high prices is seen in the fact that the government paid him one third again as much for his bronze doors as it had agreed to give Crawford. And there was other work as well. In 1861, for example, he modeled a figure of Isaac, which was eventually put into marble, and the following year he produced an "Angel of the Resurrection" for the Colt funerary monument in Hartford, Connecticut. In 1863 he received a commission from the city of Cincinnati for the first of his large military memorials, "Soldier of the Line." Two others followed later in the decade, for Providence and Detroit. Although the sculptor sincerely sought something of a grand conception in these designs, they frequently lack a formal unity. In addition to all these large commissions, there were endless requests for portrait busts; in the winter of 1866 he is reported to have produced nearly a score. For the most part they were competent likenesses, but tended toward the prosaic portraiture typical of the Civil War period. In 1870 he produced the colossal bronze statue of Lincoln for Fairmount Park in Philadelphia; its total cost was $33,000. Lincoln is shown seated, in a relaxed pose, with his legs crossed, deep in thought. The head is the strongest part of the statue; but the details of the clothing detract from the overall force of the characterization. It was almost this exact figure that Rogers used a few years later for his bronze portrait of William Seward, signed and dated "Rome, 1875." Seward is seated, a quill pen in his right hand and some papers in his left; books and various documents are under the chair. Although widely praised at its unveiling in Madison Square in September 1876, it was later severely criticized; one newspaper reported that Rogers had admitted he merely substituted a head of Seward for that of Lincoln and used the earlier seated figure for the rest of the statue. These two statues were Randolph Rogers' contribution to that phenomenon known as the "galvanized hero."

Work on the huge monuments for Providence and Detroit, which entailed the execution of numerous large figures, occupied Rogers well into the 1870's. The Providence memorial was dedicated in 1871 and the one in Detroit in 1873. At the top of the Providence memorial stands a colossal figure of a robed woman, wearing a liberty cap (Fig. 9.4), who symbolizes both the union of the states under a republican form of government and the freedom of all men within that republic. Bronze figures, on pedestals halfway up the monument, represent the armed forces; on the lower level, four angels (done in relief) hold swords that point down and palm branches that point up. Flights of steps lead up to the main pedestal, and small cannon rest on blocks between them. Late in the decade Rogers worked on another Civil War monument for the city of Worcester, Massachusetts; and for the state capitol at Hartford he produced the statue known as the "Genius of Connecticut" (1877), which now stands atop the dome of the building.

Aside from the several state and municipal commissions that occupied Rogers during the last years of his career, he wrought a few ideal pieces on his own. Returning to classical mythology, he found the subject for one of his most popular works, "The Lost Pleiad," which over the years brought the sculptor some one hundred requests for replicas; as these came in, of course, he needed only to inform his Italian workmen that yet another copy of the "Pleiad" was desired, and it would be produced with little more attention required from Rogers himself. The "Pleiad" is perhaps too theatrical for 20th-century tastes, but it suited perfectly the taste of the wealthy Americans of Rogers' day. Typically it recalls a moving episode from the literature of the past, and is one of those figures that mark the culmination of the mid-century tradition of literary and historical ideal works, faintly veiled in Romantic neoclassicism.

In 1880 Rogers modeled an equestrian group whose subject was taken from American history. Called "The Last Arrow," it shows one Indian turning around on his rearing horse to fire his last arrow at the onrushing enemy—no doubt the white man. Beneath the horse another Indian—recalling the "Dying Gaul"—has fallen mortally wounded and raises his left hand to ward off the final stroke of death. The bronze group, about 45 inches high, is now owned by the Metropolitan Museum of Art. With this statue Randolph Rogers' career essentially ended. Less than two years later he was stricken with a disabling paralysis that prevented further pursuit of his art. Although his studio continued to function awhile longer, in about 1885 he shipped all his plaster casts—an enormous body of work—back to America, where they found a home in Ann Arbor, Michigan. Rogers remained in Rome, where he died in 1892.

The sculpture career of Edward Sheffield Bartholomew (1822–1858) lasted only a little more than a decade and was devoted to a continuation of neoclassicism in its mid-19th-century Romantic form. Born in a small town in Connecticut, Bartholomew moved with his parents to Hartford while still a child. His father, a cordwainer, was opposed to the boy's artistic inclinations, and Edward was forced to serve an apprenticeship, first with a bookbinder and then with a dentist. In the early 1840's he left Hartford and went to New York City, where he began studying drawing at the National Academy of Design, supporting himself by a practice of elementary dentistry. Meanwhile in Hartford a group of enlightened citizens, led by Daniel Wadsworth, had organized to create an art museum; the architects Town and Davis designed a sizable Gothic structure, which was opened to the public on July 31, 1844. This was the home of the Wadsworth Atheneum, and in the following year the position of janitor-curator was offered to, and accepted by, Edward Bartholomew; he remained there for the next five years. Bartholomew had returned to Hartford as a hopeful young painter, but not long afterward he discovered he was color-blind, unable to distinguish red from green. At first terribly depressed at having to give up painting, he suddenly found he had a talent for modeling.

For assistance, Bartholomew turned to a local marble cutter named Batterson, from whom he learned to carve stone. One of his earliest pieces was a marble bas-relief of Mrs. Lydia H. Sigourney (Wadsworth Atheneum; Maryland Historical Society), a popular writer of the time, which was shown in 1847 at the National Academy of Design. Another early work was an ideal bust, "Flora." The success of these and other works encouraged Bartholomew to return in 1848 to the National Academy for further study. In New York City he also studied anatomy with a Dr. Watts, to prepare himself for modeling the whole figure, and all proceeded well for a time. But then he fell ill with smallpox, which settled in his hip and left him lame for the rest of his life; he was never to enjoy good health again. Determined to pursue his art, however, he soon began to make plans to go to Italy.

Establishing himself in Rome in 1850, he began his studies under the then well-known Italian master Giorgio Ferrero. His work almost immediately betrayed the impact of Roman antiquity—for example, the marble relief entitled "Blind Homer led by the Genius of Poetry," now in the Maryland Historical Society. The classical theme and the pure white marble captivated his imagination, and it did not discourage him in the least that he made the head of Homer too large, the legs of the poet's guide too short, and her right arm grotesquely long. Though he could draw confidence from his successful treatment of the details of the drapery, the hair, and the lyre, the total effect left something to be desired.

One finds similar errors of proportion in his relief of "Belisarius," although the figure of the youth is certainly an improvement.

The first couple of years in Rome saw very few commissions for portrait busts, although American and British travelers frequently visited Bartholomew's studio. There is a bust of Washington from this period, as well as one of Sappho. Baltimoreans soon learned of the sculptor through the enthusiastic reports of George Read and James McHenry, whose portraits Bartholomew executed in 1852—a bust and a bas-relief respectively. Now in the Maryland Historical Society, they mark the beginning of a considerable patronage from Baltimore. The next year the sculptor produced a bas-relief portrait of Read, this time cast in the character of the great 6th-century general of the Eastern Roman Empire, Belisarius. Read became a generous patron, ordering copies of many of Bartholomew's works.

Enoch Pratt, a benefactor of both Baltimore and Bartholomew, was in Rome in 1855 and took an immediate interest in the sculptor. Pratt escorted Mr. and Mrs. John Knight and their daughter Fanny to Bartholomew's studio, where all three posed individually to have their likeness modeled by the frail young man. (A few years later it was the Knights who took Bartholomew to Naples and cared for him until another friend came to look after him.) Before Enoch Pratt left to return to Baltimore, he commissioned the sculptor to make busts of William Ellery Channing and Henry Payson; later he gave these to the First Unitarian Church in Baltimore, where they may still be seen. Pratt also ordered a portrait of himself and an ideal piece, "Shepherd Boy," which are now in the Pratt Library and Peabody Institute, Baltimore, respectively. In 1855 Bartholomew returned briefly to Baltimore to supervise the erection of the wall monument to Charles Carroll (Chapel, Doughoregan Manor, near Baltimore); its chief motif is two mourning nude angels holding down-turned torches.

Back in Rome by 1856 Bartholomew did marble busts of Mr. and Mrs. Frederick Marquand (Yale University); he also did portraits of Mr. and Mrs. Samuel Colt and their children, as well as of Millard Fillmore, all now in the Wadsworth Atheneum; a plaster copy of the Fillmore (Fig. 9.5) is owned by the Maryland Historical Society. The modeling of the Fillmore head is competent if unexciting, typically dry in its naturalistic style; under the spell of Rome and its traditional neoclassicism, Bartholomew draped a toga about his subject's shoulders. Things were going rather well for the sculptor in 1856, and in March of that year he wrote to his friend the painter Frederick Church:

I am full of orders and works of all kinds. I am making any number of portrait busts, I counted them a week ago and there were *ten*, since then I have given up counting them. Expresident Fillmore is among them and is so much liked that I have got to make seven copies of it for different persons and places.
[Quoted from W. G. Wendell, "Edward Sheffield Bartholomew, Sculptor"]

In the half-dozen years before his death Bartholomew worked on several ideal statues. His subjects, as was the fashion, were taken from mythology, history, or the great literature of the past, and as such were illustrative images conceived by a basically literary-oriented mind. Bartholomew drew inspiration from the Bible, for example, and made such pieces as "Hagar and Ishmael"; "Ruth, Naomi and Orpah"; and "Eve Repentant." The last mentioned, one of his most famous works, is a figure well designed to convey the idea of Eve's despair after the Fall. She sits with her head bowed, her hands resting limply in her lap. Details, such as the head of the serpent and the apple on the ground, are somewhat distracting. This was a tendency exhibited by the sculptor in many of his ideal pieces, and again it is a characteristic shared with such American contemporaries in Rome as W. W. Story and Richard Greenough. Hawthorne saw the statue in Bartholomew's studio and noted in his *Journal* that he did not much care for it. But then, Hawthorne did not really understand the spirit that lay behind such grandiose literary themes, for he was too much oriented toward the history and traditions of his own land. The first marble replica of the "Eve" was purchased by Joseph Harrison of Philadelphia for $5,000, but the sculptor was not alive to enjoy the money, and it went to his creditors. Another replica in marble was purchased for the Wadsworth Atheneum, also after the artist's death.

Bartholomew often turned to classical mythology for what he considered to be worthy subjects, finding Calypso, Diana, and Ganymede much more fascinating than pioneers, New England merchants, or Southern statesmen. His life-size marble statue of Sappho (Fig. 9.6) is as obvious an attempt as anything of its time to continue the neoclassical tradition by direct imitation of Graeco-Roman proportions, profile, garment, and hair style. It is eclecticism of a kind generally held in disfavor today, but to Bartholomew and others—William Rinehart, for example, or Franklin Simmons—working in the waning days of neoclassicism, it represented a continuation of a fine and noble tradition.

Bartholomew also did two statuettes entitled "Morning Star" and "Evening Star," and one of his most successful works was the statue of George Washington in military uniform with a great cape about his shoulders. In his right hand he holds a scroll, and his left rests on a book on a pedestal at his side. There is a manly vigor, even a heroic quality about the image conspicuously lacking in Bartholomew's work derived from ancient themes. The statue was commissioned by a Baltimore dry-goods merchant, Noah Walker, who reportedly paid $6,000 for it and proudly placed it in a niche on the façade of his store, where it remained until the structure was demolished in the early 1890's. A new niche was then erected for the statue at an entrance to Druid Park, where it may still be seen.

In the early spring of 1858 Bartholomew became ill, and at the suggestion of a doctor he moved to Naples, where he died within a few months at the age of thirty-six. Most of the works in his studio were crated up and sent back to Hartford, where they became possessions of the Wadsworth Atheneum.

Larkin Goldsmith Mead (1835–1910) was one of the last of the expatriate American sculptors in Italy. He grew up in Brattleboro, Vermont, where he was born, one of several talented children of a prominent lawyer. His first employment was in a hardware store, where he served as a clerk for several years until he could no longer resist the desire to become a sculptor. At the age of eighteen he went to New York City and became one of the studio assistants to Henry Kirke Brown, joining young Quincy Ward. After two years he returned to Brattleboro to begin working on his own. Not much is known of his early work there, except that on New Year's Eve 1856, Larkin Mead and two of his friends perpetrated a sculptural joke that was reported in the local newspaper:

The denizens of "Toad Hill" in our village were agreeably surprised, when coming down from breakfast Tuesday morning to find a beautiful statue at the fork of the roads opposite the schoolhouse. It was about eight feet in height and represented the Recording Angel that may be supposed to wait upon time, making up her record at the close of the year. In her right hand was a stylus, while in her left she held the tablet on which the events were noted. It was modeled in snow the previous evening by Larkin G. Mead, and in a manner which was of itself sufficient evidence of his superior claims as an artist. [*The Vermont Phoenix*, January 3, 1857]

A notice similar to the above is reported to have been seen by Nicholas Longworth of Cincinnati, the man who had assisted Hiram Powers, Clevenger, and others in their efforts to get to Italy. Longworth is said to have written to the postmaster at Brattleboro for information about the young man who had created the colossal snow angel, and upon learning his identity, offered his patronage and encouragement. James Russell Lowell later memorialized Mead's "Snow Angel" in his poem "A Good Word For Winter." Meanwhile, in 1857, Mead executed his first monumental work, a colossal figure 19 feet high representing Vermont (or Ceres) for the State House in Montpelier. Early the following year he journeyed to the national capital, one of several artists who endorsed a plan calling for a "Convention of the Artists of the United States at the City of Washington," a project headed by Horatio Stone and Henry Kirke Brown. In a letter dated February 22, 1858, Brown wrote his wife that

Larkin Mead has just come in. Says he is going home tomorrow or next day. He has been leading a very gay life here among the young ladies. He has made more acquaintances in Washington than I have since coming here. He has been a good deal of company to me. I am sorry to have him go.

Once more Mead returned to the state of Vermont, which had commissioned him to make a statue of Ethan Allen. When he finished, it was carved in marble (1861) and placed in the State House. With the outbreak of the Civil War, Mead began doing illustrations of the activities of the Army of the Potomac for *Harper's Weekly*. But by 1862 he had decided to go to Italy. On his journey to Europe he was accompanied by his sister Elinor, who was on her way to marry William Dean Howells. Howells was then scarcely known, although a collection of his poems and a biography of Lincoln had been published, the latter having won for him the post of United States consul at Venice. Larkin Mead gave the bride away in the Christmas Eve wedding ceremony in Paris, and immediately after the service the entire party departed for the Louvre to view the art treasures. Howells and his bride then traveled to Venice, and the sculptor went to Florence, where he was greeted by Hiram Powers, Joel Tanner Hart, and Thomas Ball. Hart occupied an apartment in the Casa Grazzini, and there Mead settled, also. The Kentuckian offered his newly arrived countryman the use of part of his studio in the Piazza Indipendenza, and it was there that Mead's first works in Italy were made. John Sartain describes those early days in *Reminiscences of a Very Old Man* (1899, p. 238): "Here, as a study, Mead modeled in clay a copy of an antique, a female torso. On Mr. Hart's suggestion that it be good practice, he added a head and arms and legs according to his judgment of what should be the movement, with successful result." With some modification Mead turned the statue into an image of Echo. W. W. Corcoran visited the sculptor in his studio, saw the nude female figure, and commissioned a marble copy of it; the statue is now in the collection of the Corcoran Gallery in Washington. Tuckerman tells us in his *Book of the Artists* that "Echo" was one of the pieces the sculptor brought with him when he returned to America in 1865, along with several other pieces—"Thought of Freedom," "La Contadinella," and "Returned Soldier, or The Battle Story." The collection was well received and demonstrated a variety of subject matter that ranged from an ancient mythological motif to the American Civil War.

Among the other sculptures Mead had brought with him was an ambitious model for a memorial to Abraham Lincoln, which was to be erected in Springfield, Illinois. It consisted of a portrait statue of the President in front of a high obelisk, which had at the four corners of its base representations of the infantry, navy, artillery, and cavalry. One of the earliest of the Civil War monuments to be commissioned, but one of the slowest to be completed, it was judged a magnificent design; the sculptor, then thirty years of age, returned to Italy to begin work on it.

Larkin Mead's studio remained in Florence, but Venice frequently attracted him. So enchanted with the city was he that he modeled an ideal head called "Venezia," a marble copy of which is now in the New Hampshire Historical Society (Fig. 9.7). It is an image of an attractive young Italian girl; on her head is a diadem that contains the image of a gondola set against a shell; the lower part of the bust is covered with a plant motif that resembles seaweed. Mead had good cause to be charmed by Venice, for on several occasions when his sister and brother-in-law went vacationing, he would go there to act as vice-consul. And it was from a window of their apartment that he first saw the lovely Marietta di Benvenuti strolling in the piazza with her parents. She and her family lived in the rooms above the Howells apartment, and Mead began to see her with increasing frequency. The courtship progressed, although she knew no English at first and his Italian was not too fluent. On February 26, 1866, the two were married—against the wishes of the Pope and without a dispensation. It may have been Marietta who posed for the ideal portrait of Venezia.

In his Florentine studio, with his new bride, with many good friends and travelers dropping in, and with the large commission for the Lincoln monument before him, Mead worked away in absolute contentment. But work progressed slowly on the base of the Lincoln Memorial in Springfield; construction was not begun until 1869. In the early years of the following decade Mead modeled the plaster statue of Lincoln, which was eventually shipped to Chicopee, Massachusetts, to be cast in bronze. But Mead's portrait is hardly known except to visitors to Oak Ridge Cemetery. The statue failed to achieve the quiet force of the man, and Lorado Taft, who stated that ". . . Mr. Meade's 'Lincoln' is by no means a bad statue," also succinctly summarized: "The essence of greatness is not in it." What was lacking in the spirit and vitality of the Lincoln, the sculptor sought to make up for in the frantic animation of the four accompanying groups.

In July 1871 the citizens of Chicago had raised the $13,700 to commission the first of the peripheral groups, and 137 men in New York City each contributed $100 so that work might begin on the second group as well. The Naval group was the first to arrive, soon followed by the Infantry, and both were dedicated in September 1877. There are three figures in the Naval group, gathered around a thick, squat mortar that rests on the deck of a gunboat. The Infantry has three figures rushing into battle; an officer holds a flag, with a young drummer boy at one side and a soldier, charging with bayonet, at the other. The Artillery and the Cavalry were set in place in 1882 and 1883 respectively. In the sculptor's attempt to capture the fury of battle, the compositions themselves became chaotic and disorganized. Although adequately done with regard to naturalistic details, the groups lack cohesion, and in the total design, the monument was something less than a success. In the fury of these fighting men one is apt to forget that Lincoln would have chosen to be remembered not as a perpetrator of violence, but as a bringer of freedom.

Mead is represented in Statuary Hall by his marble image of one of Vermont's most celebrated sons, Ethan Allen (Fig. 9.8). Given to Congress and dedicated in 1876, it is largely a reproduction of the statue the sculptor had made for the Vermont State House in 1861. The statue represents the Revolutionary War colonel in a bellicose pose as he demands the surrender of Fort Ticonderoga; all the details of his military uniform are carefully rendered, and one is reminded of Henry Kirke Brown's "Nathanael Greene." But in the stance, in the position of the arms, in the slight turning of the torso, and even in the profile it is obvious that the model for this statue was Michelangelo's "David," which stood not far from Mead's Florentine studio. In a typical example of 19th-century eclecticism, Mead appropriated the nude form of the Renaissance giant and dressed him in a Revolutionary War uniform. But Larkin Mead in his work never really absorbed those qualities of 15th-century sculpture that were to influence Augustus Saint-Gaudens so much.

By the early 1880's Mead had become one of America's most famous sculptors working abroad. Wealthy Americans and Englishmen touring Italy were sure to visit his studio, as did art critic James Jackson Jarves in 1883 when the sculptor modeled his portrait in bas-relief; the bronze plaque is now owned by Yale University. In the mid-1880's, Mead returned to the playful subject of his youthful years—the "Recording Angel." The white marmorean image stands almost enveloped in its great wings, hands crossed in front, holding a quill pen and the record book, its head tilted upward, apparently listening to the dove that sits chirping on the tip of the left wing. The figure (now in All Souls' Church, Brattleboro, Vermont) was a part of the American exhibition held in 1887 at Earl's Court, near London, where it was praised for the beauty of both concept and form. But such marble images were already on their way out. Marble was replaced by bronze and the smooth finish gave way to the textured, more decorative surface of the French school.

Larkin Mead in the early 1890's began work on the pedimental decorations for the Agriculture Building at the Chicago Exposition, of which McKim, Mead (the sculptor's younger brother), and White were the architects. It was wrought in plaster, as were nearly all the temporary decorations for the exhibition buildings of the fairs held in Chicago, Buffalo, and elsewhere, and has long since disappeared. The central theme was "The Return of Proserpine from the Realms of Pluto," a subject that offered a splendid opportunity for a very colorful group: "Ceres, in the center with Cybelle drawn by lion's cubs on the left, and King Triptolemus drawn by winged dragons on the right, going forth to teach agriculture to the earth." At this exposition Larkin Mead served as a member of the jury of acceptance for sculpture. But by this time his career was approaching its conclusion. He worked on a reclining figure of the Mississippi, which was put into marble at the commission of a gentleman from New Orleans, who, in the end, could not pay for it; the statue is now in Minneapolis. The kindly, warmhearted old sculptor still retained a goodly amount of respect and affection among his colleagues, and occasionally a young sculptor would come to his Florentine studio to study, as did Bessie Potter in 1897. Little more came from his hand, and Mead died in Florence on October 15, 1910.

Among the American sculptors in Rome one of the most picturesque personalities was Harriet Hosmer (1830–1908). Born into a family where tuberculosis claimed the lives of her mother, two brothers and a sister while Harriet was still very young, her physician father took every precaution to see that his surviving daughter led a healthy existence in the outdoors, with plenty of vigorous exercise. The two of them would hike through the Massachusetts countryside, and Harriet became especially fond of swimming and horseback riding; she was taught to row and skate and to shoot pistols and bow and arrow. During her explorations of wooded hills and rocky creek beds Harriet collected objects of natural history, and she enjoyed modeling little animals in local raw clay. The robust activity in the fresh air and her father's love and care created an active way of life, an independent spirit, and a self-confidence that was to be hers for the rest of her life.

Having lost the rest of his family, Dr. Hosmer was more concerned with his daughter's health than with her formal education. But in an effort to add a touch of polish to his fifteen-year-old tomboy he sent her to Mrs. Sedgwick's school in Lenox, Massachusetts, in the Berkshire Mountains. There she found several other emancipated females with whom she was to form lasting friendships; among those were the actress Fanny Kemble and the novelist Catharine M. Sedgwick, sister of the headmistress. Surrounded by women of accomplishment she was encouraged to seek an active career for herself, and by the time she left the school she had decided to became a sculptor.

At her father's home in Watertown, a studio was constructed on the property, and Harriet began to pursue her art in earnest. This, of course, caused considerable talk in the neighborhood. There were no other women sculptors at the time, and it seemed much too unladylike an occupation. Aside from the physical labor involved, there was also the business of learning human anatomy, which meant dissecting corpses and drawing and modeling from the nude. But Harriet Hosmer was immune to all talk of her scandalous behavior and followed her own gay course. In the late 1840's she went into Boston regularly to take lessons with the sculptor Paul Stevenson, but she was unsuccessful in her attempts to enter a medical school. Not until 1850, when she renewed her school friendship with Cornelia Crow in St. Louis, was she finally able to study anatomy. Dr. J. N. McDowell, an acquaintance of Cornelia's father, Wayman Crow, was soon convinced of the extraordinary young woman's sincerity; although he could not allow her to enter the all-male classes at the medical school in Columbia, Missouri, he met with her each day in his office for private study. When the course was completed Harriet took and passed the regular examination.

Before returning to Massachusetts the 20-year-old girl struck off on her own to see more of the West. She traveled down the Mississippi on a riverboat to New Orleans and back up again to St. Paul; she smoked a peace pipe with some Dakota Indians, and she beat several young men in a race that involved climbing the highest bluff along the Mississippi. Back in Watertown she resumed her sculpting, her first piece being an ideal bust titled "Hesper," or "Evening Star." After modeling the work, she obtained a fine block of white marble and had a workman knock off the corners, but the rest of the carving she did herself, wielding a 4½-pound mallet for nearly ten hours every day. A critic writing in the New York *Herald Tribune* in 1852 said of the "Hesper":

This beautiful production of Miss Hosmer's hand and soul has the face of a lively maiden gently falling asleep . . . Her hair is gracefully arranged, and intertwined with capsules of the poppy. A polished star gleams in her forehead and under her breast lies the crescent moon. The hush of evening breathes from the serene countenance and the heavy drooping eyelids. The swell of cheek and breast is like pure young healthy flesh and the muscles of the beautiful mouth are so delicately cut that it seems like a thing that breathes.

The "Hesper" was well received by the critics and by friends, such as the actress Charlotte Cushman, who encouraged her to go to Italy. Harriet Hosmer would have gone alone, of course, but she was accompanied by her father and Miss Cushman. They arrived in Rome in 1852 and at once met the other American artists who were living and working there. Even before leaving America, Harriet had harbored the desire to study with John Gibson, the most prominent English sculptor working in Rome and heir to the neoclassical tradition of Flaxman; Gibson, who had studied under Canova and Thorwaldsen, was almost as renowned as his celebrated masters, but unlike them he was extremely reluctant to accept students into his studio. A friend laid daguerreotypes of the "Hesper" on the table before Gibson one morning while he was having coffee at the Caffè Greco. Indifferent at first, he agreed to meet the young American woman and was taken at once by her spirit and determination. The Englishman was by then an old man and the ebullient, effervescent Harriet Hosmer brought a great pleasure into his life.

She was given a little studio in the garden, a studio that to her seemed enchanted because it had once been occupied by the great Canova. Under the influence of Rome and Gibson her work of these years was generally neoclassical in style and subject matter. After drawing antique statues and making copies of famous classical works for a while, she was allowed to attempt an ideal bust or two. The first was a Daphne, followed by a Medusa. Copies of these were sent to America and England, where they brought considerable recognition to their creator. John Gibson was quite pleased with her progress.

A kind of legend continued to grow around this free-spirited young lady, and interest in her as a personality equaled interest in her as an artist. Her unusual character soon made her one of the attractions of the city, and she was frequently pointed out as she rode her fine saddle horse through the streets or across the countryside, boldly unchaperoned and with as much skill in horsemanship as any man. Even more colorful was her attire—long pantaloons, smock, and a beret cocked on one side of her head, with long curls tumbling from under it. Most of those who knew her well became very fond of her; even Elizabeth Barrett Browning wrote in admiration:

She lives here all alone (at twenty-two); dines and breakfasts at the cafes precisely as a young man would; works from six o'clock in the morning till night, as a great artist must, and this with an absence of pretension and simplicity of manners which accord rather with the childish dimples in her rosy cheeks than with her broad forehead and high aims.
   [Percy Lubbock, *Elizabeth Barrett Browning in Her Letters*, 1906, p. 321]

A testimonial of the friendship between "Hattie," as she was called, and the Brownings is seen in the clasped hands of Elizabeth and Robert that the sculptor modeled; several bronze replicas were produced, one of which is in the Art Institute in Chicago.

Harriet Hosmer had sent a copy of the bust of Daphne to her friend Wayman Crow, who responded by commissioning a life-size figure in marble of a subject of her own choosing. This was her first full-length figure, and for it she predictably selected a theme from ancient mythology; her subject was Oenone (Fig. 9.12), the shepherdess who was deserted by Paris for the beautiful Helen of Troy. The young girl is seated, head lowered, a melancholy expression on her face. This statue, done about 1855, reveals that the sculptor, like nearly all her contemporaries, was more concerned with the storytelling content of the work than with sculptural form. As long as such pieces were judged mainly according to a literary criterion, they were praised most highly. But it was not a sound basis for sculpture, and in time these works drew sharp criticism from even such a kindly critic as Lorado Taft.

Harriet Hosmer's ability to model the human form is nowhere better revealed than in her reclining figure of Beatrice Cenci, done in the middle 1850's. Beatrice Cenci is asleep on the floor of her prison cell on the eve of her execution, her head and upper torso resting on a pillow, a rosary in her right hand. The features of the head are generally classical, and the sculptor came closest to understanding the true principles of ancient art in her design of the folds of the garment and in its relationship to the body underneath, although there is excessive emphasis on details and on surface decoration. England and America praised the "Cenci" wherever it was exhibited, and it was the pride of the first public art collection in St. Louis, that of the Mercantile Library.

Another popular piece at this period was her naked, impish figure of Puck seated on a toadstool (Fig. 9.10) which can only be described as cute. Altogether about fifty of these were executed in marble at about $1,000 each; even the Prince of Wales and the Duke of Hamilton bought copies of it. Depicting the uninhibited joys and devilment of childhood, it "provokes a smile and is suggestive of mischievous intent." "Puck" was followed some years later by an equally charming piece, "Will-o'-the-Wisp," which contributed significantly to the sculptor's financial independence. Her father's support had ceased in 1854 when he'd had some financial difficulties, and from then on Harriet Hosmer supported herself through the sale of her work.

She was still sharing the studio of John Gibson when Nathaniel Hawthorne visited her in 1858. The author was favorably impressed with her sincerity and talent and ready to overlook her eccentricities. He noted in his Italian journal that among the pieces he saw was "a 'Puck,' doubtless full of fun." When Harriet Hosmer greeted the Hawthornes she was busy modeling her colossal queen of Palmyra, "Zenobia." In March 1858 she wrote to her friend Cornelia Crow Carr, "I am busy now upon Zenobia, of a size with which I might be compared as a mouse to a camel."

Again borrowing from the great legends and history of antiquity, in typically 19th-century Romantic manner she sought the exotic subject of a remote land and a queen whose name and destiny were hardly known to most Americans. Harriet Hosmer's "Zenobia"—a great queen in the disgrace of captivity, an unbroken regal spirit that refused to be intimidated, a monumental woman who triumphed in her darkest hour—appealed strongly to the emotions. The spectator could also marvel at the craftsmanship in the execution of the chains and the ornaments on the crown and the sandals. Judging the statue by the standards of its day, "Zenobia" was a successful piece, and Nathaniel Hawthorne referred to it as "a high, heroic ode." Wherever it was shown it received the highest praise— even in London at the 1862 exhibition, where it was assumed to be the work of John Gibson rather than of Harriet Hosmer. In America, the statue went on tour and earned a handsome sum for its creator, as well as orders for replicas from Mrs. Potter Palmer of Chicago and Robert Emmons of Boston; the original was purchased by Almon Griswold of New York City. "Zenobia" brooded over the exhibition halls of her day in no less awesome magnificence than William Wetmore Story's "Libyan Sibyl" or "Cleopatra." They were all sisters of the same titanic family.

Up to this time, about 1860, Harriet Hosmer had withstood the pressures to do portraiture. She received a good income from copies of both "Puck" and "Will-o'-the-Wisp," and besides, there was more prestige in ideal works because of the greater challenge to the artist's imagination than portraiture offered. Then in 1860 she made her first return visit to the United States to see her father who was ill. At this time she received a commission from the state of Missouri for a full-length statue of Thomas H. Benton, the distinguished senator and author. Back in Rome, she started on the clay model at once, but hardly had it begun to take form before Fort Sumter was fired upon. Although she completed the statue not long afterward and had it cast in bronze at the Royal Foundry in Munich, it was not unveiled in Lafayette Park, St. Louis, until 1868—before an estimated crowd of forty thousand. The statue looks toward the west and the inscription on the base reads: "There is the East. There lies the road to India." Remaining true to her adopted classical style, the sculptor draped the Missouri statesman in a voluminous Roman toga and put sandals on his feet. This was one of the last instances where an image of an American was clad in the garments of antiquity, and it was already a rare occurrence by that time. Harriet Hosmer recognized that American sculptors had not solved the problem of contemporary dress, and took pride in having been "bold enough to represent a modern without trousers, substituting drapery," as she put it.

That neoclassicism remained at the heart of her work throughout the 1860's may be seen in her "Sleeping Faun" of 1865, of which Sir Charles Eastlake wrote, "If the 'Sleeping Faun' had been discovered among the ruins of Rome or Pompeii, it would have been pronounced one of the best Grecian statues." She also did a "Waking Faun," as well as such subjects as "African Sibyl," "Pompeian Sentinel," and "Hylos with Nymphs." These neoclassical images were especially praised in the English art journals of the day.

After the Benton statue, Harriet Hosmer received several portrait commissions; she did busts of her good friends Charlotte Cushman and Wayman Crow, and a medallion relief of John Gibson. For an Englishwoman living in Rome, she produced a memorial to her daughter, "Mademoiselle Falconnet," which was erected in San Andrea della Fratte. And for some time she worked on the model of a memorial to Abraham Lincoln, which was never completed. On the base were four reliefs representing various periods in Lincoln's life; above, in a classical temple resting on an octagonal plinth, was a sarcophagus bearing the inscription "A. L., Martyr Pres. U.S., Emancipator of four millions of men and preserver of the American Union."

One of the outstanding personalities in Rome, Harriet Hosmer was a favorite with the royalty that frequented the Eternal City, such as the Czar of Russia, the Empress of Austria, and the Queen of Naples; with the last two she shared a love of fine horses. She was usually in the lead of the chase in Roman fox hunts, and both her studio and her home were visited by the distinguished figures of the day. We have seen expressions of the Brownings' fondness for her freshness and independence, as well as Nathaniel Hawthorne's respect for her as a woman and an artist. From time to time such eminent persons as Thomas Carlyle, William Dean Howells, W. W. Story, Alfred Tennyson, and Dr. Samuel Osgood called on her; and William Page, Charlotte Cushman, and Fanny Kemble were her friends and companions. Even Pope Pius IX found her company amusing, and she was quite close to Lady Marion Alford, Lady Ashburton (with whom she later lived in England), and J. Pierpont Morgan. She chose not to marry because she said she could not be both wife and artist, and she wished to devote herself to her art; also, her independence might have been jeopardized, and that she could not have endured.

Her sculpture followed along lines similar to those of William Wetmore Story and Richard Greenough, for she found her greatest inspiration in subjects far removed in time and space from her native land, and she attempted to create an art out of a literary bias and a borrowed pseudo-classical style plus what seems today to have been an excessive amount of inconsequential surface decoration. A diluted academic classicism resulted, as it did in the work of many another artist in the third quarter of the 19th century.

From the 1870's on, much of Harriet Hosmer's attention was given to mechanical devices, especially to a perpetual motion machine. There were a few sculptures, such as the statue of Queen Isabella of 1892 for the city of San Francisco, but generally speaking Harriet Hosmer's career was over by 1875. She lived for a while in England, but returned to America in 1900, where she died eight years later.

In addition to Harriet Hosmer and Anne Whitney, several other women took up sculpture around the middle of the century. Henry James called them "the White Marmorean Flock" when he wrote of them in his biography of W. W. Story, and the epithet has stuck. The group included Margaret Foley, Louisa Lander, Emma Stebbins, and Edmonia Lewis, all of whom settled in Rome.

Margaret Foley (c. 1820–1877) was born in Dorset, Vermont. Her natural gift for sculpture began to reveal itself in whittling and wood carving; then in 1848 she went to Boston to carve cameos. There she saw the sculptures in the Boston Athenaeum and the larger works about the city—Dexter's "Binney Monument," Hughes' bronze "Bowditch," Chantrey's "Washington," and even Richard Greenough's "Franklin." All these filled her with a desire to do more than cameo-cutting, at which she had become quite proficient. She, like many another, dreamed of going to Rome, and in 1855 she did.

At first she supported herself by carving little cameo likenesses of British and American visitors to Rome. The next logical step was an enlargement of these into medallion portraits, which became quite popular, an example of this sort of work being the marble bas-relief of Charles Sumner, signed and dated, Rome, 1866, in the collection of Harvard University. Then followed busts of S. C. Hall and of Charles Sumner, as well as medallion portraits of Longfellow and Bryant. The general spirit of reverence that Boston felt for Major Robert Gould Shaw eventually reached the expatriate colony in Rome, and about 1864 Margaret Foley created a bust of him—probably from photographs—which drew a great deal of favorable comment both there and at home. A portrait bust of Henry Farnam was put into marble in 1868; it is now at Yale University, which also owns a second version carved in 1875. The location of a bust of Theodore Parker is currently unknown. Thus Margaret Foley began her career in Rome like most of her fellow sculptors, that is, as a portrait artist.

But she was anxious to obtain larger, more challenging commissions. The first of these came from Richmond, Virginia, for a statue of General Thomas J. (Stonewall) Jackson. Modeled in the early 1870's, it was cast in London in 1873 and set up in Richmond within the year. This was one of the first statues of their Civil War leaders to be commissioned by the South, which was so engrossed in recovering economically and politically that very little was expended on the arts during the years 1865 to 1875. Naturalism, of course, dominated the artist's treatment of the celebrated general, who was shown in his military uniform.

In the 1870's Margaret Foley worked on a fountain, whose basin was supported by three little children—two boys and a girl—playing underneath. This was eventually put into marble and sent to the Philadelphia Centennial of 1876, but being placed in the Horticultural Building, it escaped the notice of art critics. She also sent to the Centennial several other pieces that received quite favorable comment. There were the medallion portraits of her close friends William and Mary Howitt, and a bas-relief of Mrs. J. B. Read, as well as ideal busts of Jeremiah and Cleopatra. But the exhibition was financially a disaster for Margaret Foley, and after it was over, she found herself not only in wretched health but short of funds. When the fountain was not sold at the Centennial, it was a severe blow to the sculptor's purse and pride. In time, it was purchased and placed in a park in Philadelphia; by then, however, it was too late to help its creator.

When the Centennial closed, Margaret Foley was already suffering from an illness from which she was not to recover. She went to the mountains of Austria for her health, but after returning to Rome, her condition worsened. In an effort to restore her health, some kind friends took her to Medina, but to no avail; she died there in the summer of 1877.

As a child, Louisa Lander (1826–1923) had amused herself by modeling little heads in wax for her dolls, and in these early manifestations of her special gift, she was encouraged by her family. She first emerges from obscurity in Washington, D.C., where by 1853 she was modeling portraits. Two years later she, too, went to Rome and worked as a student-assistant in the studio of Thomas Crawford. There may have been a trip back to America about 1858, however, for on November 1 of that year John Rogers wrote to his mother from Paris that Miss Lander had arrived in that city and was anxious to get to Rome, and that Richard Greenough had seen her and reported that she had "some orders besides the bust of Governor Gore which she is taking [to Rome] to finish."

The portrait of Gore, now owned by Harvard University, has a softness of form that suggests a weakness of structure; she draped the chest and shoulders in a toga, rejecting contemporary attire for the mantle of the ancient philosopher-statesman. In Rome she modeled the bust of Nathaniel Hawthorne, which was put into marble in 1858; it is slightly larger than life and the author was represented with bare chest. Years later, Hawthorne's children presented it to the Public Library in Concord, Massachusetts.

About this time Louisa Lander seems to have committed some indiscretion in Rome that not only alienated her from many of her fellow artists and from British and American visitors, but also was the subject of a kind of court of inquiry—made up of several sculptors and led by W. W. Story—that investigated the scandal. The committee suggested she go before the American minister and swear there was no truth to the rumors and accusations, but her pride would not permit this. The wagging tongues of Rome would give her no peace, and there is no doubt that a judgment was generally passed against her, although the committee seems to have taken no formal action. Though all this was quite damaging to her career and certainly contributed to her continual exclusion from Roman society, it did not break her spirit. But she received few commissions, and today very little is known about her, although she lived over half a century after the incident was reported to have occurred.

John Rogers did see her occasionally in Rome, but evidently he felt it imprudent to encourage a close relationship. On February 13, 1859, he wrote home that "she snaps her fingers at all Rome," but he also told of a considerable activity in her studio:

Miss Lander's work must be all money out of pocket—I don't think she has sold anything yet but her little Virginia Dare—She has made a [reclining] figure of Evangeline and put it in marble which is not sold—a bust of Hawthorne which is very good but he does not notice her now and I don't know whether he will take it or not. She is modeling a large Virginia Dare which she is having put into marble, but it is not ordered and she has another little figure two or three feet high in marble and she is going to model an Undine on an uncertain order from Mary Warren.

[Courtesy, New-York Historical Society]

In addition, there were also ideal figures of a "Sylph" and "Ceres Mourning for Persephone." But there was never a rush to Louisa Lander's studio, and as Rogers reported, many of her pieces were put into marble at her own expense. After 1860 her life and work slip into historical oblivion, and she is not heard of again until 1913 when her name appeared in the Washington, D.C., *Who's Who*.

Emma Stebbins (1815–1882) began her career as a painter in the 1830's in New York City, but it was not until about 1857 that she became interested in sculpture. Making the decision to take up her new-found interest seriously, she went to Rome where she immediately fell in with Harriet Hosmer and began to study in the studio of Paul Akers. The three of them frequently had lunch together and saw each other regularly. It was probably Akers who introduced Emma to Charlotte Cushman, of whom she modeled a bust in 1859 at the request of R. D. Shepherd. Shepherd's daughter presented the marble portrait to the Handel and Haydn Society of Boston, but at least three other marble copies were made. So infatuated was Emma Stebbins with her subject that she wrote a biography of her many years later, and was her constant companion, even returning to America with her in 1870.

There were several other portrait busts, of course, such as the one of John Stebbins, which was presented to the Mercantile Library in New York; but as with most of her fellow sculptors, the full-length figure or the ideal piece represented the greatest challenge. There were statuettes of the Biblical figures Joseph and Samuel; the latter, about 40 inches high, was produced in 1868 and is in the collection of James Ricau. There was also a statue of Columbus for New York City, as well as "Angel of the Waters," a fountain figure (c. 1862), for Central Park. Probably her best-known work is the bronze statue of Horace Mann in front of the State House in Boston (Fig. 9.11). Commissioned by the city, the statue was modeled in Rome and cast in Munich in 1864, and today stands as the counterpart to Hiram Powers' bronze "Webster." Emma Stebbins modeled her subject holding a book, but she covered his contemporary clothes almost completely with a full-length Roman drapery. His right hand is extended, as if to invite all who come his way to a greater life through study and knowledge. The head is especially sensitively rendered.

After Emma Stebbins' return to America in 1870 much of her energy was devoted to her biography of Charlotte Cushman, which was published in 1877. Very little is known of her work thereafter.

Edmonia Lewis (1845–?) was born in upstate New York, the daughter of an Indian mother and a Negro father, both of whom died when she was three years old. Raised by her mother's tribe, the Chippewas, she was educated at Oberlin and then sent to Boston with a letter to William Lloyd Garrison, who, it was hoped, would be able to help the bright young girl get a start. As she sat alone on the steps of City Hall, she became fascinated with Richard Greenough's bronze statue of Benjamin Franklin. Garrison provided her with an introduction to Edward Brackett, who gave her a portion of clay and a cast of a foot, telling her to take it home and model it; the sculptor had her repeat the exercise several times, and perceived in her a seriousness and an eagerness, along with an obvious talent. Among her first efforts were a medallion head of John Brown and a bust of Colonel Robert Gould Shaw, who had recently been killed while leading his Negro regiment in the Civil War. Many of her subjects, both portraits and ideal figures, were to be drawn from the struggles of the Negro cause or from the life and legends of the Indians. About 1866, for example, she modeled a statue entitled "The Freedwoman." It was her bust of Shaw, however, that brought her widespread attention in Boston, for after it was exhibited at a Soldiers' Relief Fair she sold in the neighborhood of one hundred plaster copies of it. The money from these paid for her trip to Italy in 1867, and she was welcomed to Rome by Paul Akers, Harriet Hosmer, John Gibson, and Charlotte Cushman.

There was a bust of Lincoln, one of Longfellow, and one of Charles Sumner, among others, and her several ideal pieces attracted a great deal of attention in the next decade. The first of these was the image of Hagar, destitute in the wilderness, and the sculptor remarked that she had a common bond with "all women who have struggled and suffered." There were two statuettes taken from Longfellow's popular *Hiawatha;* these drew considerable comment, such as that published in *Revolution* in April of 1871:

Hiawatha's Wooing "represents Minnehaha seated, making a pair of moccasins, and Hiawatha by her side with a world of love and longing in his eyes." In the Marriage [statuette] they stand side by side, with clasped hands. In both, the Indian type of feature is carefully preserved, and every detail of dress, etc., is true to nature; the sentiment is equal to the execution. They are charming bits, poetic, simple and natural, and no happier illustrations of Longfellow's most original poem were ever made than these by the Indian sculptor.

About this same time she modeled another Indian subject, the "Old Arrow-Maker and his Daughter." In 1871 she created a pair of ideal statues, "Asleep" and "Awake," which were put into marble; they, like the "Old Arrow-Maker," have been loaned to the Tuskegee Institute by Cooper Union in New York. She also created "Madonna with the Infant Christ" (an altarpiece) and "Rebecca at the Well"; the locations of these are presently unknown.

The climax to her career came with the "Death of Cleopatra," which she sent to the Philadelphia Centennial of 1876. Intended to illustrate that at the time of death even the rarest beauty may become a ghastly sight, the statue both amazed and repelled those who saw it; for Edmonia Lewis had chosen to represent Cleopatra after the venomous asp had done its work. One critic wrote of it:

This is not a beautiful work, but it was a very original and very striking one, and it deserves particular comment, as its ideal was so radically different from those adopted by Story and Gould in their statues of the Egyptian Queen . . . . The effects of death are represented with such skill as to be absolutely repellent. Apart from all questions of taste, however, the striking qualities of the work are undeniable, and it could only have been produced by a sculptor of very genuine endowments.

[Quoted from W. J. Clark, *Great American Sculptures*]

For some reason, after this spectacular statue was completed, the life and work of Edmonia Lewis fade into obscurity. It is known that she was still active in Rome in 1885, but after that, nothing.

One of the very last to join the American expatriate coterie in Italy was Pierce Francis Connelly (1841–after 1902), who rose to prominence just as the neoclassical movement he espoused had completely exhausted itself. A young man of no mean talent, had he turned to Paris instead of to Rome around 1870, as Saint-Gaudens had done, his story might have been quite different. Connelly was born in Louisiana; his father was an Episcopal minister, who had been converted to Catholicism, and his mother later founded the Order of the Holy Child. His grandfather Henry Connelly was an accomplished cabinetmaker in Philadelphia. As a child Pierce was taken to Florence, where his family resided for several years, before moving to England after his father returned to the Episcopal fold. Thus the boy grew up and was educated in Italy and England, and as soon as he was able to, he made his way to Paris to study briefly at the Ecole des Beaux-Arts. Next came Rome during these early student years; then in 1865 he returned to Florence, where the work of Hiram Powers offered just that inspiration he was seeking. He remained in Florence for several years, doing portrait busts for a living and occasionally modeling an ideal piece. Only one ideal work seems to have been put into an enduring material, "Honor Arresting the triumph of Death" (1869), now at Rosemont College—an institution operated by the organization his mother had founded. This bronze statue represents one of the very few times Connelly chose an ideal subject reflecting contemporary American life; it was inspired by those who died for their cause in the Civil War. Death rides an active steed in the midst of the vanquished figures of Courage, Perseverance, and Strength; and only Honor is able to thwart what would otherwise be a total triumph over warring mankind.

By 1871 Connelly had left Italy for England where he settled briefly, exhibiting at the Royal Academy in London that year busts of Algernon George, Henry George, and Earl Percy. Several other busts of Englishmen also date from this period. But Florence remained his favorite, and it was there that he made his home for most of his life. Back in his studio amid the narrow streets and magnificent *palazzi* of Florence, not far from the ateliers of Thomas Ball, Hiram Powers, and other American sculptors, he worked at a feverish pace, producing numerous ideal pieces that were soon to be shown at the Philadelphia Centennial.

As Connelly stood in Memorial Hall at the Centennial, reviewing his several works, he was well aware that his was the largest group exhibited by any one sculptor, and that the nature of his subjects gave his work a prestige beyond its acknowledged high quality. His list of exhibited works reads as follows:

141. Honor Arresting the Triumph of Death.
142. Ophelia.
1187. Horse's Head.
1189. Queen Philippa.
1190. Thetis Thinking How She May Regain the Birthright of Her Son Achilles.
1191. Lady Clare.
1193. Helen of Troy.
1194. Diana Transforming Actaeon.
1195. The Thread of Life.
1196. Viola.
1227. St. Martin Dividing His Cloak.

All but "Thetis" and "St. Martin" were owned by the artist and were for sale. "Thetis" (Fig. 9.9) had already made its way into the Metropolitan Museum of Art; Hiram Powers' "California" had been the first piece of American sculpture acquired by that young museum in 1872, but the "Thetis," not actually listed in the registrar's records until 1877, must have been among the very first monumental pieces by an American to join the collection. The statue was carved in the same year, 1874, as Rinehart's "Latona." Connelly's group of sculptures represented a kind of swan song for the expatriate neoclassicists of Italy—the Storys, Rineharts, Hosmers, and so on—for also at the Centennial were the "Minute Man" by Daniel Chester French and the bust of William M. Evarts by Augustus Saint-Gaudens, the two men who would very soon lead the way out of an exhausted neoclassicism and into a new revitalized American sculpture.

In spite of his impressive array of bronze and marble works shown at the Centennial, Connelly began to slip into near oblivion soon afterward. It seems rather curious that after a successful exhibition of his work at the Centennial, Connelly should thereupon sail to New Zealand to paint the wild landscapes of volcanoes, craters, lakes, and forest-covered mountains. Although he rejoined his father and sister in Florence in 1879, when he executed the portrait bust of Napoleon III that is in the collection of the University of Pennsylvania, virtually nothing is known of his life and work over the next two decades. He was at his father's bedside when he died in 1883, and with his sister when she died in 1900. The last word of him that has so far come to light is the autobiographical note that he sent the Metropolitan Museum of Art in 1902: "Born 1841 in Louisiana U.S.A. (Father and Mother both born in America)."

One of the more prolific American sculptors whose years of activity fall between the Civil War and World War I was Sir Moses Jacob Ezekiel (1844–1917) who maintained a studio in the ancient Baths of Diocletian in Rome during most of that period. Today hardly remembered, he was in his prime one of the most acclaimed artists on either side of the Atlantic and was even knighted by three monarchs of Europe. Born and reared in Richmond, Virginia, he attended the Virginia Military Institute, and after serving in the Confederate army, was graduated in 1866. Afterward he studied anatomy at the Virginia Medical College, and at about that time made the decision to become a professional sculptor. From this early period are a bust of his father and an ideal work titled "Cain," both at present unlocated. In 1868 he moved to Cincinnati, where he studied at the art school of J. Insco Williams and worked in the studio of Thomas D. Jones. Under Jones' instruction he modeled a statuette called "Industry," which attracted a good deal of attention. After little over a year he departed for Europe to study at the Royal Art Academy in Berlin, where he worked mainly under the direction of Albert Wolff. Toward the end of his five years in Germany he carved a number of reliefs for the interiors of several of the finest homes in Berlin; among these were the "Welcome" and "Farewell" for the Leo Villa in 1873. Other reliefs were "Confession" and "Consolation," but it was a group called "Israel," with figures representing Jesus, Jesse, Jerusalem, and Ahasuerus, that won for him a scholarship in 1874, enabling him to go to Rome for two years of study. As it turned out, he was to spend nearly all the rest of his life in Rome, with only several short visits to America.

In good Romantic style he established himself in the spacious decaying grandeur of that part of the Baths of Diocletian that still were habitable, and there he modeled his first large commission from America, the "Religious Liberty." The group, shown at the Philadelphia Centennial and now in Fairmount Park, consists of a robed female figure of America wearing a liberty cap, extending a protecting hand over a child who represents Religion; the latter holds the burning lamp of Faith in his hand. On the other side of the woman is a great American eagle, which conquers the monstrous serpent of Intolerance. The statue drew a good deal of interest to the previously little-known sculptor, and thereafter his studio was a busy place, with many commissions progressing at once and several assistants employed. His heroic-size bronze portrait of Benjamin B. Hotchkiss of 1879 (University of Cincinnati) was followed by a bust of Abraham Lincoln (1880) and one of his friend Franz Liszt (1881), a frequent visitor to his salon. He also received a commission for twelve large marble statues of the world's greatest artists, destined to inhabit the exterior niches of James Renwick's new Corcoran Gallery of Art in Washington, and he worked on these in the late 1870's and early 1880's. The image of Thomas Crawford was among them, and it is preserved at the Virginia Museum of Fine Arts; the others are now owned by the Botanical Gardens of Norfolk, Virginia. Crawford was in good company, for the other artists represented included Phidias, Michelangelo, Durer, Canova, Titian, Rubens, Leonardo, Rembrandt, Murillo, and Raphael.

At the Columbian World's Fair in Chicago, 1893, Moses Ezekiel was represented by a bronze figure of Christopher Columbus for the Columbus Memorial Building. His career as a portrait sculptor was firmly established by then, and numerous busts and full-length figures followed. For Charleston, West Virginia, he produced a bronze statue of Stonewall Jackson, with a replica later being erected on the grounds of the Virginia Military Institute. His "Anthony Drexel," a bronze seated figure, is in Fairmount Park, Philadelphia, as is his bust of Governor Curtin, which is a part of the Smith Memorial. In 1900 he modeled a figure of Thomas Jefferson that stands upon an enormous Liberty Bell, with four female figures around it representing Liberty, Justice, Equality, and Brotherhood; a replica of this curious piece was placed on the campus of the University of Virginia. Perhaps his finest portrait statue came very late in his career—that of Edgar Allan Poe, in bronze, for Wyant Park in Baltimore. The author is shown seated in the "chair of fame," leaning forward.

There were numerous ideal works, too, such as the bronze "Homer and Guide" at the University of Virginia and the "Virginia Mourning her Dead" on the campus of VMI. He also produced several pieces of religious subjects, such as the "Ecce Homo" in the Cincinnati Museum of Art and the relief of "Christ Entombed" in a little chapel in Paris. At the San Francisco Exposition in 1915 he was represented by a bronze statue of "Eve." There were too many other monumental sculptures to enumerate here.

Successful though he was in his own day, Ezekiel's works lacked an enduring quality, for he and his sculpture were soon forgotten after his death in 1917; and as a perpetuator of an outdated style, he was never hailed by the younger men. About the time Ezekiel established himself in Rome, the European center for the study of art shifted from Rome to Paris. With the exception of an occasional American sculptor who passed through for a brief period, Rome ceased to be the great magnet that it had been for the preceding generation. In the last quarter of the century, the aesthetic tide was with the French art of the Ecole des Beaux-Arts.

The Philadelphia Centennial of 1870 was the last great showplace for the mid-century expatriates of Florence and Rome. It marked the end of a movement in which subjects drawn from the antiquity of Rome or the ancient Near East predominated over American themes, and in which a highly Romantic version of neoclassicism was the style of the day. In portraiture, the bronze and marble effigies of Americans reached their most prosaic depths, as naturalism was, with few exceptions, drained of both verve and art. By 1870 American portraiture and American ideal imagery stood in dire need of revitalization. Both naturalism and neoclassicism, as practiced by these expatriates—and by many who remained in America, too—had become totally exhausted as a means of expression.

[FIG. 9.1] "Nydia, the Blind Girl of Pompeii," by Randolph Rogers (1853). Marble, 55″ high. Courtesy, Metropolitan Museum of Art, gift of James Douglas, 1899.

[FIG. 9.2] "Columbus Doors," by Randolph Rogers (1855–58). Bronze, 16′ 8″ high. Eastern entrance to the Rotunda, U.S. Capitol, Washington, D.C. Courtesy, Architect of the Capitol.

[FIG. 9.3] "Meriwether Lewis," by Randolph Rogers (1861). Bronze. Washington Monument, Richmond, Va. Courtesy, State of Virginia; photo, Index of American Sculpture, University of Delaware.

[FIG. 9.4] Soldiers' and Sailors' Monument, by Randolph Rogers (c. 1870). Providence, R.I. Photo, Index of American Sculpture, University of Delaware.

[FIG. 9.5] "Millard Fillmore," by Edward Bartholomew (1856). Plaster, 32″ high. Courtesy, Maryland Historical Society, Baltimore.

[FIG. 9.6] "Sappho," by Edward Bartholomew (c. 1856). Marble, 68″ high. Courtesy, Wadsworth Atheneum, Hartford, Conn.

[FIG. 9.8] "Ethan Allen," by Larkin Mead (1875). Marble. Statuary Hall, U.S. Capitol, Washington, D.C. Courtesy, Architect of the Capitol.

[FIG. 9.7] "Venezia," by Larkin Mead (c. 1865). Marble, 26″ high. Courtesy, New Hampshire Historical Society.

[FIG. 9.10] "Puck," by Harriet Hosmer, (1856). Marble, 28″ high. Courtesy, National Collection of Fine Arts, Smithsonian Institution.

[FIG. 9.9] "Thetis and Achilles," by P. F. Connelly (1874). Marble, 56″ high. Courtesy, Metropolitan Museum of Art, gift of Mrs. A. E. Schermerhorn, 1877.

[FIG. 9.11] "Horace Mann," by Emma Stebbins (1864). Bronze. Courtesy, Massachusetts Art Commission; photo, Index of American Sculpture, University of Delaware.

[FIG. 9.12] "Oenone," by Harriet Hosmer (c. 1855). Marble, 27″ high. Courtesy, Gallery of Art, Washington University, St. Louis.

The Brooding Enigma
and a Sculptor
of American Genre

BEFORE TURNING TO THAT NEW STYLE IN AMERICAN SCULPTURE THAT SPRANG FROM
the Ecole des Beaux-Arts in the last quarter of the 19th century there are two
more sculptors to be considered—William Rimmer and John Rogers. These men
had nothing in common so far as their work was concerned, and for that matter
their art was quite unlike that of other sculptors in the third quarter of the century. It is because their work had a unique character and because their periods of
greatest activity were generally contemporary that they have been brought together in this chapter.

There are some men whose originality of expression and extraordinary visual
imagery place them well outside the main artistic currents of their times; such
were Albert Pinkham Ryder and Elihu Vedder in American painting, and such
was William Rimmer in American sculpture. Rimmer (1816–1879) found portraiture as it was practiced by his contemporaries too prosaic for his turbulent
mind, and their quasi-classical ideal pieces lacked the vitality and boldness he always sought in his own work. To him, an art based on eclecticism was insipid
and uninspiring, so he struck off on a new path entirely of his own charting.

The origins for Rimmer's extraordinary personality must be sought in the social upheaval of the French Revolution and the deposing of the Bourbon line of
kings. His father had been taken out of France hurriedly and placed with an English family by the name of Rimer, to be raised in the genteel manner; the expenses of all this were reportedly paid out of the treasuries of the British and
Russian monarchies. Thomas Rimer, encouraged in the belief that he was the escaped Dauphin, grew up with the secret conviction that one day he should have
his triumphal return to France. His education included mathematics, music,

fencing, and riding, and also curiously enough, he was taught the craft of shoemaking—a skill that would be valuable to him later. Thomas Rimer became an officer in the British army, but upon learning that another king had ascended the throne of France, he resigned his commission and, before long, married and moved to Nova Scotia. His departure for Canada was made in the hope that he might thereby escape from the dangers of detection by those in France who must now view Rimer's mere existence as a threat to the established monarchy of Louis XVIII. Once in Canada he guarded his identity for what he believed to be the very safety of himself and his family. He changed his name to Rimmer, and for a period the family moved frequently, first to the isolation of northern Maine, then southward, until they finally settled in Boston, Thomas working as a cobbler all the while. His own education in the arts, sciences, and languages was passed on to his children, and young William grew up in a very culture-conscious home. He was, in fact, unlike many American artists, always encouraged to pursue art and make it his profession.

By the age of fourteen William Rimmer had become fascinated by the activities in the stoneyard near his home, and it was probably from the workmen there that he learned the rudiments of handling the mallet and chisel. About 1830, when Horatio Greenough had barely started his career, Rimmer, a mere boy, wrought the emotionally charged, tension-filled little image of his father, entitled "Despair" (Fig. 10.1). The nude figure sits on a rock, the left hand clamped over the mouth; the right knee is drawn up to the chest and the leg is held at the ankle. This is one of the first—perhaps the very first—sculptured nude figures to be executed in the United States, and it was done fifteen years before Powers' "Greek Slave" was to storm the barricades of American prudery. In choosing the nude in this first work the artist manifested his fascination with human anatomy—both for its physical beauty and for its expressiveness. His training in anatomy and sculpture had been limited to what he heard at home and learned at the stoneyard; there was then no sculptor of any consequence in residence in Boston, and his only conception of a statue was probably derived from Chantrey's marble, cloaked "Washington" in the State House or the casts in the Athenaeum. Essentially, Rimmer's very personal style evolved from the man himself, and its dominating characteristics are present in this his earliest work. The skin ripples as tensed muscles push against it; highlights and shadows flicker across the surfaces, creating a lively animation such as was never achieved in the smooth-skinned marble images by his contemporaries.

Aside from the sculptural style, which prefigured the art of Auguste Rodin (1840–1917) by nearly four decades, there is also the strong emotional statement. The figure expresses the fright, the anxiety, the potential explosiveness, the total despair, that circumstances had made of his father's life; the hand over the mouth seems to repress an anguished cry. It is not a happy image, and the macabre mood was to be part of almost every piece of sculpture William Rimmer created. The cool, detached, unemotional neoclassicism of Thorwaldsen or

Canova would hold no attraction for Rimmer, and the later Victorian frivolities would appear to him altogether artificial in expressing basic emotional experiences.

Such a forceful rendering of human feeling in good sculptural form by a boy of fourteen would seem to presage an early and brilliant career. But it was not to be; not until the 1860's would William Rimmer's major works in sculpture appear. For a while he worked at a variety of odd jobs—from soapmaker to sign painter. He drew designs on stone for Moore's lithographic firm in Boston, and eventually painted scenery. There was even a period when he took a studio and painted religious pictures for nearby Catholic churches; one of these early works, in the heroic tradition of Washington Allston, was entitled "After the Death of Abel." A friend tells of entering Rimmer's studio one day in 1836 as the painter was beginning his "Death of Abel"; the friend was astonished to find eight unclad women lined up while young Rimmer looked them over to select a model for his figure of Eve. Then, after working from the model for a while, Rimmer decided that Boston was not yet ready for the nude in painting, so he covered her with what looked like a kind of "door-mat."

These were lean years for Rimmer. In 1840 he married Mary Peabody, and during the next years the couple lived in several cities in the vicinity of Boston while William tried to earn a living from his art. His personality did not facilitate matters, for he was at times reticent and withdrawn, at other times brash and outspoken. Erratic and opinionated, he was capable of making scathing verbal attacks, even against those who befriended him. He was not attracted to the social leaders of the day, nor they to him, and his clientele usually paid from $5 to $20 to have their portraits painted.

From the painting of likenesses he was drawn to the study of anatomy, and thereafter to medicine. By 1845 he and his family had settled in Randolph, Massachusetts, where he worked as a cobbler, painting a few portraits on the side. In Randolph he formed one of the few lasting friendships of his life—with Dr. A. W. Kingman, who first interested him in the study of medicine. Dr. Kingman and his library provided all the teaching necessary for a brilliant mind to acquire what was then a sufficient knowledge of medicine to hang out a shingle and start treating patients. As time passed, he seems to have even gained the respect of his colleagues who had had more formal training in the physician's skills. He was admitted to the dissecting room at the Mason Street medical center in Boston, which furthered his knowledge of anatomy.

During his residence in Randolph, the only piece of sculpture mentioned dates from 1849—a head of his three-year-old daughter, carved directly in marble. T. H. Bartlett, Rimmer's biographer, had described the manner in which this little bust, which has disappeared, was made:

He worked sitting on the floor, and holding the block between his knees, illustrating in the process a cardinal principle of his nature and teachings . . . . In executing this bust, he relied upon the glimpses he caught as his daughter passed him in the room, as reminders of his memory . . . [And he] sought to go directly to the result without any preliminary steps, such as first making a model in clay, casting it in plaster, and then learning the use of tools.   [*Art Life of William Rimmer*, p. 20]

So far as Rimmer was concerned, his sculpture had thus far been merely an avocation, an amusing pastime; so it was to continue throughout the decade of the 1850's. In 1855 he moved to East Milton and began to practice medicine in earnest. By that time he had been invited to join the Suffolk County Medical Society and been awarded a medical degree. The community into which he settled was a rather poor and dreary one; most of the local men worked in the quarries in the vicinity. Rimmer was a good doctor to the people thereabouts, but outside the sickroom he had nothing in common with the community, for intellectual, artistic, and cultural attractions were altogether absent. To add to the gloom of this period, the last of Rimmer's three sons died. Yet not until his financial situation became so strained that he was about to be arrested for nonpayment of his butcher's bill was he drawn out of his seclusion. When a friend paid the debt for him, Rimmer repaid him by carving a head out of granite to adorn a building in Boston. Through this same friend, Rimmer was introduced to Stephen H. Perkins, a wealthy Boston patron of the arts, who was to encourage and assist him from their very first meeting. It was Perkins who at this point in Rimmer's career, after numerous discussions on anatomy, painting, and sculpture, advised him to "be an artist; there are plenty of doctors, but few artists." The doctor, then nearly forty-five years old, took his advice, and his serious pursuit of sculpture began.

Rimmer's first work was a head of St. Stephen, a subject chosen no doubt out of gratitude to his new friend. The artist attacked the block of granite directly, without preparatory sketches or models. He had worked stone with mallet and chisel many times before, so the technique was familiar to him, and through his medical studies he had a great understanding of human anatomy. The final ingredient—a dynamic expressiveness—came, as it must in all art, from Rimmer the man and the artist. The result was no quiet, comforting image of the saint, but one that connoted anguish and pain. The head, set upon a thick, muscular and heavily veined neck, looks upward over the right shoulder; the forehead is furrowed, the brow pinched, and the lips parted, as if to emit a cry. The bust is full of animation, with every part contributing to the agonized whole. Though in its emotionalism and to some extent in its naturalism, it is reminiscent of Hellenistic sculpture, it is by no means an eclectic piece. The head of St. Stephen was finished late in December of 1860, at a time when the photographic image, with its uncompromising realism, was having a strong influence on American portraiture. It was in the face of this mania for objective realism that Rimmer's career as a sculptor began anew; his art was to have nothing to do with photographic likeness or surface exactitude.

The bust was exhibited at Williams and Everett, the leading art gallery in Boston, and received several favorable notices in the Boston newspapers. Perkins became the champion of Rimmer's cause, frequently explaining that the artist, who had had no formal training, was "another Michael Angelo"; he hoped that his fellow citizens would encourage the sculptor by purchasing the "St. Stephen" for $500. Many admired it, especially because it had been cut directly in granite without preparatory sketches or model. But no one offered to buy it at any price, and both patron and artist were disappointed.

On January 27, 1861, Rimmer noted in his diary, "Received from Mr. Perkins a hundred dollars, with which to begin the statue of the Falling Gladiator." Within a week the sculptor's first life-size full-length figure was begun, and he worked on it when he could steal a few hours from the demanding profession of physician. He did not employ a model, which would have cost money, and besides he preferred to work from his own knowledge of anatomy, studying his own body when necessary. He lacked proper training in the fundamentals of working in clay; he did not even know about the use of an armature, a necessary item to support the weight of the clay, especially in a life-size figure. Various parts kept falling off and were damaged, the sculptor resorting to a rather makeshift arrangement of props, braces, and supports. Moreover, he seems not to have known how to prepare his clay; he was unable to keep it in workable condition; when it was not unworkable from drying out, it was freezing and cracking. Much of the statue was modeled in the winter months of 1861, and there was no heat in the spare room of his home in East Milton that served as a studio. He built up large forms of clay, then cut them down to the shapes desired, choosing to carve rather than to model. As he worked, he made drawings on the walls of his studio; these, it seems, were his only preliminary sketches.

A certain amount of curiosity was aroused in Boston over the dramatic anatomical wonder that was being wrought in the shabby studio of a physician down in East Milton, and interested persons even traveled the few miles by carriage to get a peek at both the creator and his statue. Colonel E. C. Cabot, Professor W. R. Ware, and of course Stephen Perkins were among those who spread the word of the unusual talent that existed unattended on the periphery of the Boston art world. But Boston's connoisseurs and dilettantes were concerned with more conventional talents—with Thomas Ball, then working on his equestrian "Washington"; or Richard Greenough in Paris; or Henry Dexter, at that time exhibiting his thirty-two busts of the governors; and, of course, the activities of their own W. W. Story and Harriet Hosmer in Rome were eagerly followed through newspaper and magazine articles. Little attention was paid to Rimmer, who had neither been to Italy nor exhibited at the Athenaeum.

By June 1861 the "Falling Gladiator" was finished (Fig. 10.2), but Rimmer did not know how to cast it in plaster. The expenses of having it done were paid for by the sale of photographs of the head of "St. Stephen"; and after it was cast, photographs of the "Gladiator" itself were circulated by the sculptor's friends, but to little avail. Boston seems not to have taken the whole affair very seriously.

Stephen Perkins was a determined man, however; and if the work of his protégé was not to be appreciated in America, he would show it elsewhere. When
he departed for Europe in 1862, he took casts of the "St. Stephen" and the "Falling Gladiator" with him. They were shown in London, where they received
some favorable reviews, but in Paris the "Gladiator" fell victim to the same
accusation that many years later would be leveled at Rodin's work: it had been
taken from a mold of a man's body and could not therefore be considered as a
work of art. Perkins regretted all this derogatory nonsense, but he was helpless.
So he took the casts to Florence, where they at least attracted the admiration of
the eminent sculptor Dupré, who sent Rimmer a note encouraging him to
persevere.

The original plaster of the "Gladiator" was exhibited in Boston several times
in the next few years and eventually helped establish Rimmer as a sculptor—but
not in the one glorious burst of public recognition that he, Perkins, and a few
others had hoped. The "St. Stephen" was purchased by Perkins for $150, but the
"Falling Gladiator" ended up in a storage room at Cooper Union in New York
City. Not until 1906—after a committee for the purpose had been organized by
Daniel Chester French—was the statue cast in bronze. Bronze replicas are now in
the Boston Museum of Fine Arts and the Metropolitan Museum of Art, plaster
versions in the Smithsonian Institution and at Avery Library, Columbia University.

In the late fall of 1861 Rimmer began giving anatomy lessons in Boston. For
two years his lectures and demonstrations, his drawings, and his breadth of
knowledge of the human figure fascinated Bostonians as his sculptures had never
done. In October 1863 he began a series of ten lectures at the Lowell Institute,
for which he received $1,000—enough to permit him to move from East Milton
to a suburb of the city. He also gave instruction in anatomy at the Boston Athenaeum to a group of artists, and in time a separate art school was organized with
Rimmer as its director and teacher. From 1864 until he went to New York in
1866, William Rimmer conducted art courses in what was essentially his own
school. All of this, of course, was rewarding enough, and Rimmer enjoyed his
new role immensely, but it so absorbed his time and energy that it interfered
with his own creativity.

In 1864 Rimmer published the first of his instructional art books, *Elements of
Design*, with forty-nine steel-plate engravings and forty-two pages of text. The
purpose of the book was to teach the drawing of the human figure, from the
elementary stick-figure representations of the body in movement to the completed anatomical forms in action and repose. This publication spread his reputation as an art teacher far beyond the Boston area, and years later there was still
sufficient demand for the book to warrant a second edition (1879).

In 1864, Rimmer also got his first commission for a public monument—the
"Alexander Hamilton" that now stands in Commonwealth Avenue. For it, he
was to receive $5,000, not a large sum for such an undertaking, and he noted this

fact in his diary: "Five thousand dollars is but half the amount that other sculptors receive for similar work; but it is best to do it for that price, for reputation." It appeared as if Rimmer was about to create the work of art that might bring him countless commissions in the years ahead (Boston was certainly monument-conscious then) and establish him as one of the leading sculptors of the day. To make the clay model of the "Hamilton," he rented an abandoned church near his home. Hurling himself into the project in his characteristic manner and driven by nervous energy, he benefited little from his experiences with the "Falling Gladiator." Once again he did not use an armature, and although the pose itself provided greater stability for the statue, parts toppled off and had to be remodeled and replaced. Once again his studio was not adequately heated for work in the middle of winter, the clay freezing and becoming too stiff to work properly. But in spite of all these adverse conditions, the sculptor built up the form to nearly ten feet in height and finished the details in the incredibly short time of eleven days—truly an accomplishment in itself, although he was later to regret that he had not given the statue more time and careful attention. He also modeled three overlapping profile relief portraits of Washington, Hamilton, and Jay to go on the base.

The members of the committee must have felt some uneasiness when, only a fortnight after the sculptor had started on the "Hamilton," they received an invitation to come to his studio in Chelsea to inspect the clay model. With some misgivings, they bestowed their approval—after several suggestions about the refinement of certain details—and the statue was sent to Quincy to be put into stone. It was probably Rimmer himself who selected the silver-gray mottled Concord granite instead of pure white marble, probably because of granite's greater durability outdoors. But even for pieces that were to remain indoors —such as the "Head of a Woman" (Fig. 10.3)—he seems to have been attracted to the color and over-all pattern of granite. In his own time, as today, he was criticized for using a kind of stone whose innate qualities compete with sculptural form. But it should be observed here that a willingness to experiment with an unusual combination of color, pattern, and form was in general characteristic of the mid-19th century.

Because he had seldom, if ever, been out of the Boston area since childhood, Rimmer very likely knew only a few statues that had been done as public commissions: Chantrey's marble "Washington" had recently been joined by Powers' bronze "Webster"; and Richard Greenough's "Benjamin Franklin" now stood in front of City Hall. Obviously Rimmer was drawn to Chantrey's image as the model for "Hamilton" because of its dignity and calm. Hamilton was represented in the attire proper to his time, and as with the "Washington," a great cloak was draped over much of the figure. It is very possible that Rimmer had the picture of Robert Ball Hughes' "Hamilton" in mind, too, for there is quite a similarity in the over-all form; Hughes' statue had been destroyed in a fire in New York City thirty years earlier, but Rimmer could have seen an illustration of it in the October 24, 1835, issue of the *New York Mirror*. Hughes was still alive in 1864, living in Dorchester, between Milton and Boston, and it is very possible that Rimmer communicated with the older sculptor sometime before beginning his own work on Hamilton. There were, of course, small models of Hughes' "Hamilton" around, and Rimmer may have seen one of these, although on the models there is no toga. For the head of his subject, Rimmer may have used one of the several copies of Ceracchi's bust of Hamilton.

There was indeed a controversy over the successfulness of Rimmer's "Hamilton." In spite of the efforts of his friends—including William Morris Hunt, who by then was one of his devoted admirers—the balance of opinion was decidedly not in Rimmer's favor. In this greatest of opportunities the consensus was that the sculptor had blundered, ". . . thereby debarring himself further opportunity in Boston," as Lorado Taft succinctly phrased it. Bartlett summarized the reaction to Rimmer's abilities as a sculptor when he wrote that it was generally held that

he had no loyalty to his art, so that art . . . was simply a convenient method of earning money, or a pleasant pastime for a passing moment. It followed, according to this view, that he could not respond to a great occasion, from the meagerness of his nature; that he could not continue the long struggle necessary for the consideration of a statue, but must do whatever he did at all quickly and without the long and concentrated [effort] from which alone has resulted whatever is great and noble in art.
[*Art Life of William Rimmer*, p. 46]

Bostonians turned instead to the studied naturalism of Thomas Ball, Anne Whitney, W. W. Story, and others for their public monuments.

Hardly had the clay model of the "Hamiliton" been delivered to the stonecutters at Quincy before Rimmer, buoyant and hopeful over the prospects of the fame and distinction he thought would result from his first public commission, began another monumental statue, "Osiris," in an outburst of enthusiasm. Once again the clay model was completed in an incredibly brief time—barely more than a week. The artist employed a live model this time, but for a few hours only. The subject was drawn from the exotic repertoire of ancient mythology, a colorful and exciting god from the far-off land of the Nile. In style, "Osiris" is reminiscent of such classical Greek works as Polykleitos' "Doryphorus" or Praxiteles' "Hermes with the Infant Dionysus." The curious but imaginative mind of William Rimmer is revealed by his having made two interchangeable heads for his "Osiris": One was a human head, a youthful bacchanalian type, with curling ringlets of hair; the other, and the one he preferred, was the head of a hawk, symbol of Osiris' son, Horus. After being cast in plaster the statue was exhibited in the gallery of Childs and Jenks, only to be removed almost at once when objections were raised to its nudity. This is curious, for the battle of the nude in American art had been largely fought and won decades earlier. But Boston had not been one of the battlegrounds for this controversy and was therefore not as quick to accept the undraped figure as, say, New York City. The "Osiris" was exhibited at Cooper Union in New York after Rimmer moved there, but it was eventually broken and finally destroyed. Bartlett published a photograph of it in his monograph on the artist.

In 1866 William Rimmer was asked to give a lecture at the home of one of his students, a prominent Boston woman. Present that day as a guest was Peter Cooper, the founder of Cooper Union, who was fascinated with what he heard and especially with the doctor's ideas on the methods for teaching art. As a result, Rimmer was invited to New York City to become director of the School of Design for Women. For some time the trustees had thought that the school lacked proper direction, and all were convinced that Rimmer was the man for the job.

During the next four years while he was the chief administrator and teacher, it became a very respected institution. He introduced a new curriculum, and his own inspired instruction contributed immeasurably. The students drew from plaster casts and from the draped model. At the core of Rimmer's instruction were his lectures on "art anatomy," that is, an analysis of human and animal anatomy especially devised for the artist. Instruction was also given in design and composition, oil painting and water color, drawing, modeling in clay, and wood engraving. Administrative duties and teaching absorbed virtually all Rimmer's energies at the School of Design, just as they had earlier in Boston, with the result that there was little attention given to his own sculpture. He reworked earlier models of the statues of "Endymion" and the "Chaldean Shepherd," both of which were still in clay. In time, both of these were destroyed. No new major piece was attempted during his New York years; it is quite possible that after the "Hamilton" and "Osiris" not only failed to bring him the fame he hoped for but actually damaged his reputation as a sculptor, Rimmer was content to devote himself to teaching, at which he was unquestionably successful.

But after two years at Cooper Union some of the trustees began to challenge the direction Rimmer's course of instruction was taking: it was so decidedly oriented toward the fine arts instead of toward the industrial arts; and after all, it was for the latter that the school had been founded. The controversy swelled over the next two years, and when Rimmer returned to the school in the fall of 1870, he discovered that in his absence the program of instruction had been completely revised, another person had been put in charge as administrator, and his role was reduced to that of teacher, with an accompanying reduction in salary. His purse could have recovered from the blow but not his pride; he could not tolerate interference with his instruction. In spite of pleas from the trustees to remain as teacher, with his former salary of $3,000 a year restored, William Rimmer went back to Boston.

In Boston he immediately gave notice that he was going to conduct classes in art, again with special emphasis on art anatomy; over the next several years his school usually had about two dozen students. He was constantly called upon to give lectures before various groups of Bostonians, who found him both stimulating and controversial. Even in New York City, he was in demand, giving a series of twenty-five lectures at the National Academy of Design; these were enormously popular, but were ended prematurely by Rimmer's desire to return to Boston. He also lectured at the Technical School in Worcester and at the School of Fine Arts at Yale, and in the late fall and early winter of 1871 he gave a series of twelve lectures in Providence, Rhode Island. The subject of these lectures was almost always art anatomy, with the artist illustrating his talk with chalk drawings on a blackboard.

In the year after his return to Boston, Rimmer modeled two of his finest sculptures—the "Dying Centaur" (Fig. 10.4) and the "Fighting Lions." These were both executed whenever he could find time between his art classes and the demands of his domestic life. The plaster originals are in the Boston Museum of Fine Arts; replicas in bronze—cast about 1906–1910, long after the artist's death—are in the Metropolitan Museum of Art. Each is highly animated, with rippling surfaces that are as exciting as anything produced in American sculpture in the 19th century. Rimmer's knowledge of animal anatomy is clearly as profound as that of the human figure, and he frequently taught comparative anatomy. The subjects themselves are also quite revealing; looked at in this light, Rimmer's work often reflected violence and anguish. His imaginative works are "Despair," the agonized image of his father; "St. Stephen," experiencing fear and mental torment; the "Falling Gladiator," the last violent reflex and jerking movements of a man mortally wounded; "Osiris," the king of the dead; a "Centaur" in the last anguished moments before a painful death; and finally the uncontrolled fury of two lions attacking each other. In these subjects, and in others of similar motifs found in his numerous drawings, there is a preoccupation with violence and tension, anguish and pain. It is the repertoire of a man beset with many anxieties himself.

The "Lions" and the "Centaur" have been called Rimmer's finest works in sculpture, and A. T. Gardner in his *Yankee Stonecutters* quite rightly observed that the "Lions" make the much-touted animals by the Frenchman Barye look like "tame desk ornaments, paperweights." As to the "Dying Centaur," Gardner says it is a perfect symbol for the life and work of Rimmer himself:

A wild pagan creature, half man, half myth, sinking to the earth, with amputated arm stretching its handless stump to a pitiless Puritan sky. This was what society could do to an artist who loved art more than literature, who dared to express ideas by form rather than by the trumpery props prescribed by convention. They could let him squander his great talents and exhaust his mind lecturing on anatomy before a blackboard on whose surface he cast a thousand masterly sketches . . . .

It is the expressive power combined with an innate drive toward true sculptural form that sets the work of William Rimmer apart from the work of his contemporaries. Nowhere is this more clearly seen than in the Michelangelesque sketch "Torso" (Fig. 10.5).

One can only regret that the artist's reputation was so thoroughly injured by the statue of Hamilton, for no one paid much attention to his renewed efforts to return to sculpture with "Dying Centaur" and "Fighting Lions," and throughout the 1870's he had to content himself with the role of teacher. In 1875 he was commissioned to make a 9-foot model of a figure of Faith (which was to be cut in stone, 36 feet high) to go on the National Monument to the Forefathers at Plymouth, Massachusetts. Rimmer made the model, based on the Venus de Milo—as specified by Hammatt Billings, the architect of the monument; and for his efforts he received $2,000. Bartlett reproduces a photograph of the model, but the man who carved the final version altered it considerably, replacing Rimmer's delicate, diaphanous drapery with volumes of material and cascades of folds.

In that same year, Rimmer embarked upon an unsuccessful venture that he hoped would bring him considerable financial reward. He joined several other men in a business to mass-produce portrait busts of eminent men—a kind of portrait counterpart to the enormously successful genre groups by John Rogers, then being issued by the hundreds and even thousands. But the project never picked up momentum and soon expired altogether.

Rimmer's second book, *Art Anatomy*, which he worked on after the portrait-making fiasco, appeared in 1877 containing "nearly nine-hundred drawings, illustrating in the fullest manner, the ethnological, bony, anatomical, and artistic construction, movement . . . and purposes of the human form, of both sexes and all ages, as well as the expression of the passions, with full explanatory text on the same page with the drawings." (Bartlett, *Art Life of William Rimmer*, p. 85.) An admirer of his work had placed $2,000 with the treasurer of Harvard University to cover the expenses of the publication, and an edition of fifty copies, each with eighty heliotype plates printed in red ink, was produced. Selling at $50 a copy, the book did not move rapidly, although the artist did receive some remuneration. In 1879 the plates and all copies that had not been sold were destroyed by fire, but a new edition was issued in 1884, followed by two others in later years.

The year his *Art Anatomy* was published, Rimmer gave a series of lectures on the same subject at the Museum of Fine Arts in Boston. By then over sixty, Rimmer found the task of lecturing increasingly arduous, and he could not manage to complete the course. His mind remained charged with new projects to undertake, but his energy and physical stamina ebbed with every passing day. Finally the end came while he was resting at the home of a daughter, on August 20, 1879.

Many friends and institutions paid tribute to him at his death, and within the year a memorial exhibition of his paintings, sculptures, and drawings was held at the Museum of Fine Arts in Boston. Altogether nearly 150 examples of his art were shown; the exhibition was a counterpart to that given the work of Rimmer's friend William Morris Hunt, who had also died in 1879. The show made

New England shamefully aware of the rare gift that had been neglected in its midst; but after a period rife with eulogy, Rimmer's name again became obscure until another exhibition was organized—in 1946 by the Whitney Museum in New York City. Although he was essentially a sculptor out of his time, his extraordinary talent now begins to assume its rightful place in the history of 19th-century American sculpture.

Like William Rimmer, John Rogers represents a unique phase of American sculpture in the 19th century. With his little plaster genre and theatrical groups he was, in effect, a movement unto himself, for none of the other sculptors of the era chose to depict the everyday scenes of contemporary American life. Unlike Rimmer, Rogers created an art that was typically 19th-century America, reflecting American life with a poignancy that the ideal creations of the expatriates never approached.

John Rogers (1829–1904) was born into one of the leading families of the Boston area; his mother, Sarah Ellen, was the granddaughter of Elias Hasket Derby, the famous Salem merchant and shipowner. Although he did not grow up surrounded by wealth—due to his father's poor management of his inheritance—young John was provided with a fine cultural environment and a good education; at the Roxbury Latin School he did admirably. When he was nineteen, he was dissuaded from the pursuit of drawing and painting, and instead, he studied to be a mechanic; this seemed a wise decision, as the family fortunes continued to dwindle. But his interest in art was not to be thwarted, and one day, upon seeing a little figure modeled by a friend, his enthusiasm became so fired up that he procured some clay of his own, made a few primitive modeling tools, and "set-up [his] first figure." Shortly afterward the young artist took a job as a mechanic in Manchester, New Hampshire, where he produced a number of little figures, which he modeled by candlelight after long hours in the machine shop. In Manchester in the early 1850's, he thus became increasingly engrossed in small figures of ordinary folk or characters from literature.

Rogers was a prolific letter writer, and in his many letters to his mother, father, and sister we can perceive the character of the man and establish the general outline of his career. They disclose, for example, the subjects of some of his earliest works—such as "The Black Knight with Friar Tuck" (1855) or "The Old Oaken Bucket" of a year or two previous, and an early version of "Checker Players." There was also "Little Nell in the Curiosity Shop," taken from Dickens and for which Kitty Dodge posed; he may have been influenced in this by Robert Ball Hughes who had modeled a similar subject only a short time earlier. These were the hesitant efforts of a beginner who was quite self-conscious about his work. The state to which Rogers' career had advanced by the late summer of 1855 is shown in a letter to his mother, dated August 26:

I told her [Ellen, his sister] that I would rather make a figure than think of a subject. She wanted me to try something in the beautiful order but I should certainly get out of my depth there. That would require an accurate knowledge of the human figure which I have never had the least opportunity of studying—so I must content myself with everyday scenes.*

He continually urged his sister to give him a subject to model, but he wanted something not too ambitious for his limited talents. He would not venture into the realm of ideal beauty, and as he had not studied anatomy, that eliminated the nude figure. Besides, Rogers wanted people to like his little creations, and his personality and his background would hardly have allowed him to invite friends and relatives into his room to see a nude figure. From the very beginning he was drawn to the commonplace in American life and quaint and colorful scenes from literature.

By spring of 1856 he was traveling westward, to try his luck in a machine shop in Hannibal, Missouri. He found the frontier town to be like something out of the recent books by a man named Mark Twain, and very like the scenes we know today from the paintings by George Caleb Bingham. Whatever he expected Hannibal to be, it was a disappointment: There were no interesting people in the whole town, he reported, and the area was sorely troubled by the "curse" of slavery; it was a rowdy place, and at the hotel he had to share his room and sometimes even his bed with strangers of the most despicable sort; the streets were muddy, and so was the drinking water, which he described as "opaque." In something less than the good old pioneer spirit he once wrote his father that "Unless they import some Yankees I am afraid they will never make much of a place of Hannibal." But there was a dancing school and an occasional dance; and once he was invited to join a debating society when the crucial issue was: "Resolved, that reading of the works of fiction has a tendency to injure both mind and morals." Parties there were, with young ladies who were quite impressed with the clever young man from the East. And he took a steamboat ride down the Mississippi River to St. Louis to hear Edward Everett deliver his celebrated oration on George Washington.

During these years modeling small groups in clay was his favorite pastime, and in April 1857 he wrote his mother that he was modeling "a nightmare scene to ornament my room which is expected to be surpassingly horrible." This little scene amused his acquaintances, who continually stopped in to see it—a ghoulish spectacle, according to Rogers' description.

The victim is in bed and is being hugged by a skeleton from which he is squirming to get away. The old devil himself is leaning over the headboard, quietly grinning & admiring the scene. Two little imps are sawing the man's leg off and a few small imps are scattered around engaged in various kinds of mischief—I have it understood that the poor fellow has been boarding lately at the same house where I board and the hard fare don't agree with him.

The "Nightmare" (in the Gladys A. Hawkins Memorial Museum) reminds one of some of the bizarre scenes painted by John Quidor. There were probably other

---

* The letters from John Rogers quoted in this chapter are in the collection of The New-York Historical Society, through whose courtesy they are published.

groups as well from this Hannibal period, but Rogers seems not to have tried selling any of his pieces. In the fall of 1857 a depression hit Hannibal, and John Rogers was ordered to dismiss nearly all the men in the machine shop who worked under him; in time he himself left Missouri for Massachusetts.

It was at this point—sometime in early 1858—that Rogers finally decided to have a go at it as a sculptor, encouraged by the popularity of his diminutive groups wherever they were seen. He also decided that to become an artist he must go to Europe, and when the *Ariel* sailed in September 1858, John Rogers was aboard.

Toward the end of September he arrived in Paris, where Richard Greenough helped him get established. He visited the Louvre and was "overwhelmed" by the city of Paris itself. Although it was too late to enter the Academy, with Greenough's assistance Rogers was admitted to the studio of Dantin, then reputed to be one of the best sculptors in Paris. Rogers went to Greenough's house frequently in the evenings, and the two sculptors went about the city together —to the tailor's one day, to visit the Emperor's stables another, and so on. Rogers got along famously with his French instructor, but he did not care for Dantin's other two students. Nor did he think highly of the French mode in sculpture; he could not believe it when he saw some of his fellow students' work that had won medals, and he wrote home that he could already do as well with only two hours of work on a piece. That his Yankee attachments were never seduced by France is evident in a letter written to his mother on October 6, 1858:

I have seen nothing remarkable yet that the artists have done here and flatter myself that I stand a pretty good chance with them *now* . . . I look forward to the time when I shall feel prepared to go back and settle down in the good old city of Boston, for you need have no expectations that I am going to live abroad after I have acquired what I have come for.

In the same letter he articulated sentiments quite unlike those of his friend Greenough and others, who then believed the sculptor could live and work only in Europe:

I am convinced that after the rudiments are acquired and after having had the advantages of models & seen the works of the old masters, all after that lies in the artist himself, and he can bring it out as well in one place as another. The advantage that an artist has in going to Rome or any other great center of art like that is in copying from old statues. Now I think the very reason why sculptors are so poor is on that very account. They are kept copying all the time till at last they are scarcely more able to work from their impressions of anything that is beautiful than they were in the first place . . . . I have always worked from impressions alone for it gives me an immense advantage now.

In December 1858 John Rogers left Paris to go to Rome, carrying letters from Richard Greenough to Randolph Rogers, Christopher Pearse Cranch, and Luther

Terry. He met William Wetmore Story and his wife who entertained him in their apartment in the Palazzo Barberini, and there he also made the acquaintance of Charlotte Cushman, John Gibson, Harriet Hosmer, and Emma Stebbins. But he remained convinced that Boston was as good a place as any on earth, and wrote home that in spite of being surrounded by glorious antiquity he would never take up the classical style; it was too high an art for him, he said, and confided to his father in a letter dated December 14, 1858, that he would be "out of his depth" if he should try it. He also wrote that before leaving Rome one thing he wanted to master was the method of working in plaster—a skill that was to be of great importance to him later when plaster copies of his groups would be produced by the thousands.

He had approached Randolph Rogers about working in his studio, but was told that the place was so busy doing the Capitol doors that it could not then be arranged. A British sculptor named Spence, however, took him into his atelier at once. Rogers liked the sculptor, but the confrontation of two opposing styles—Spence's neoclassicism and John Rogers' homey naturalism—occurred immediately, and was duly reported in a letter by Rogers:

. . . according to the classical ideas prevailing here, and no doubt they are the true principles, statuary should be as simple as possible, with very little drapery and no *accessories,* as they call all the little odds and ends that I used to put around my groups to help tell the story. You see when you leave all those out it is difficult to make any particular action or position tell the story. It may be true in theory to leave all the accessories out but I don't believe in it altogether. Look at Powers' Greek Slave—there is nothing in the world that made that so popular but that chain. The chain told that she was a slave and the whole story was told at once.

From the start, these "accessories" were a fundamental part of Rogers' style, basic to the storytelling quality in his groups. These cleverly worked incidental details were soon to amuse and enchant his public and make him one of the nation's favorite sculptors.

By spring of 1859 Rogers had had his fill of Rome and returned to America. After a visit with his family in Massachusetts he tried Hannibal again, hoping to find work as a machinist. He evidently felt he could not make a living from his sculpture and so gave it up, and for a long time his letters home made no mention of it. Hannibal had changed, however, and there was no work to be had, so he went to Chicago, where he got a job in the office of the city surveyor.

Then in August 1859 he wrote his mother about a little group he had modeled—"Checker Players,"—that he intended to send to a bazaar in early September. He had set it up in his office, and even before it went to the bazaar it began to attract considerable attention: An article about it appeared in one of the Chicago newspapers. The group fetched, so it seemed to Rogers, an enormous sum at the bazaar. Robert Collyer, writing to Henry Kirke Brown on October 27, reflects the sculpture's popular reception:

Now, among my friends over whom I have oversight, is John Rogers; a young man with what I believe to be a wonderful talent for sculpture. He has done a small group in clay for our Bazaar, that sold for seventy-five dollars. He is just now absorbed in a new work—A Slave Auction. I do not possess more than the taste to *feel* a good thing, but when I went the other day to see *that*, I "felt all through my bones," as Candace would say, that this was a success and ought to be known . . . . You can, and will advise him . . . . John Rogers is struggling just as somebody else did once.

[Courtesy, Library of Congress, Manuscript Division]

The career of John Rogers was thus truly launched with the "Checker Players," which scored a spectacular success at a Chicago fair. Within the month the sculptor wrote home requesting his father to ask Thomas Ball about the procedure for obtaining a copyright for a statue; Ball had had experience copyrighting his statuettes of Daniel Webster and Henry Clay. Hardly had the clay of the "Checker Players" dried before Rogers started his second group, "The Slave Auction" (Fig. 10.8); and it was from this little piece, 13 inches tall, that the first casts of Rogers' groups were made.

The success of his group at the fund-raising fair started Rogers thinking of the demand that might exist for other subjects; his experience with machines made him aware of the possibility of mass-producing plaster copies at reasonable rates. But Chicago was not the place to do it. Packing "The Slave Auction" in his trunk, and with a letter from the Reverend Robert Collyer to an Italian craftsman in New York who knew how to work with flexible molds, he set off for the East. From the Italian, Rogers learned the process of making plaster copies, and he was soon duplicating "The Slave Auction" on his own, in his attic studio high above Broadway.

The group is well calculated to touch the emotions of the beholder: The impending tragedy of the family's separation and the whole concept of human bondage are expressed in the forceful and poignant image. The sign tacked up on the auctioneer's platform reads: "Great Sale of Horses, Cattle, Negroes & Other Farm Stock—This Day at Public Auction."

"The Slave Auction" had an immediate appeal for the leading abolitionists of the day; Henry Ward Beecher endorsed it heartily, and word soon spread of how effectively the young sculptor had put their thoughts into visual form. But though it won favor with antislavery advocates, it incurred the censure of Southern sympathizers; and there were enough of those for the New York shopkeepers to refuse to put the group on sale in their establishments. Rogers solved the problem by opening his own outlet: He hired a man—as it happens, a Negro—to sell them on the street. And sell they did.

Within the year Rogers had modeled two more groups and produced copies of them. There was a second version of "Checker Players," a little over 8 inches high, with two men seated on a bench; the other was an illustration of a line from Goldsmith's poem *The Deserted Village*. In these first three pieces one finds the major themes of Rogers' work throughout his career: a piercing social comment; a genre piece that may be either sly and amusing or gentle and warm; and finally an illustration of a scene from literature. With excitement, pride, and expectation he entered the three groups in the 1860 National Academy of Design exhibition, where they attracted a great deal of attention. The wisdom of his move to New York was apparent, and for the next thirty years his little plaster groups would become more and more popular. They were the sculpture counterpart of the Currier and Ives prints—an answer to the demand of an art-conscious middle class for works of art at modest prices. Both prints and plaster copies are the mass-produced result of the union of art and the Industrial Revolution.

With the outbreak of war, Rogers' next groups extolled the gallantry of the Union soldier and showed his more casual moments, somewhat like Winslow Homer's illustrations of army life behind the lines for *Harper's Weekly*. There were the crafty "Sharp Shooters" and the alert "Picket Guard," as well as the "Town Pump," "Camp Fire, or Making Friends with the Cook," and the "Card Players." These ranged in height from 8 to 13 inches. The "Picket Guard" sold for $6, and as with the very first group, "The Slave Auction," Rogers obtained patents on his designs so no one could copy his pieces.

Rogers began to hire artisans to produce the copies, and before the decade was over he had a staff of some twenty men working in his studio. At first the molds were made directly from his clay model, but when a breakdown of detail was observed the sculptor had his clay model cast in bronze (by the Frenchman, Guerin, who had a foundry in the city) and had the molds taken from the bronze. A square wooden form was set up around the bronze model, and a gelatinous glue was poured in around it; when the glue had set, it was pliable yet held its shape, so that the wooden form could be taken away, the mold cut up and removed from the model, and the careful details preserved. The mold was thus ready to be reassembled, held together by cords and pegs, and the plaster was poured in. Later, a wire armature was used to give strength to the fragile or vulnerable parts of the piece. When the plaster had hardened and the molds were removed, the group was painted either slate gray or putty brown. It was then ready for sale at Williams and Stevens or at Goupils—the main New York art dealers of the day—or at any number of stores throughout the city. Soon many of the cities along the seaboard were handling Rogers' groups, and eventually they were available in the major centers of the Midwest. Rogers seems to have supervised most of the business end himself.

Rogers began modeling groups on a larger scale in 1862, with the 23-inch-high "Wounded Scout, or Friend in the Swamp." A Union soldier, weak and exhausted, has escaped from Libby Prison and is helped through the swamp by a sturdy Negro. The peril is compounded by a copperhead coiled near by. The appeal of such groups lay in the ability of the sculptor to express a sentiment held by Northerners of that day, to achieve a vitality in the figures, and to include a sufficient amount of detail to give the realism that his patrons wanted. There is in the group "The Wounded Scout" a real sense of drama, of impending danger, of a common cause for which men gave their lives. And it was presented in a way that was immediately understandable to Americans of the 1860's. Abraham Lincoln, who received a copy as a gift from the sculptor, was immensely pleased with it.

Other groups followed: "Union Refugees" (1863) and "Wounded to the Rear" (1864), and one of a Union soldier explaining to a blacksmith and a little girl "How the Fort was Taken" (1863). One of the finest to come from the Civil War, and one that the sculptor himself considered to be among his best was "Taking the Oath and Drawing Rations," which sold for $15 in 1865. A study in mood, a contrast in feelings, and a representation of the chivalry so much admired by the Victorian generations made this one of the sculptor's more popular groups.

From 1865 on there were such genre pieces as "The Charity Patient" and "Uncle Ned's School" (1866) and "The School Examination" (1867). But Rogers did not forget the gravity of the conflict that had split the nation. In 1868 he produced his splendid group titled "The Council of War" (Fig. 10.7), fine portraits of General Grant and of Secretary of War Stanton standing behind a seated Abraham Lincoln. There is a simplicity about such groups that lets the viewer concentrate on the import of the situation. The carefully selected details Rogers supplied always enriched the story he wished to tell; they were never distracting. Lincoln's lankiness, for example, is subtly captured by the way in which his right foot rests a little awkwardly on its side behind the left one. The portrait head of Lincoln has the gaunt pensiveness that caused his son to describe it as among the finest portraits ever produced of his father. And Secretary of War Stanton wrote Rogers that ". . . you were especially fortunate in your execution of the figure of President Lincoln. In form and feature it surpasses any effort to embody the expression of that great man which I have seen." It was Rogers' first attempt to portray nationally known personalities, and all reports agreed he succeeded admirably.

Another of Rogers' finest groups was "The Fugitive's Story" (1869), which reveals the sculptor's passionate belief in the cause of the abolitionists even several years after the Civil War had ended (Fig. 10.10). A young Negro mother holds her child in her arms while she speaks to three of the leaders of the abolitionist movement—John Greenleaf Whittier, Henry Ward Beecher, and William Lloyd Garrison. Rogers caught fine likenesses of the three men, who are easily recognizable. But it is the compassion and concern in the countenance of each man that places Rogers' work in the realm of excellent portraiture. All three are intent upon the story the woman tells, and determined that the injustice of it all must be corrected. As a contrast to the three men with their august bearing and their fine attire and grooming, the woman wears tattered clothes and seems slumped under her burdens, in virtual resignation to her situation. There is a lackluster look in her eyes that again contrasts sharply with the determination in the eyes of her audience. Henry Ward Beecher had earlier expressed his admiration for Rogers' work when he wrote to him on January 18, 1865:

I am especially gratified in the moral element that so plainly appears in all that you do. I deem him to be an artist who employs . . . form and color to express some worthy thought or emotion, and so allies Art directly with the Soul and makes it the tongue

of the heart, and not merely the nurse of the senses. You have the true and highest
Artistic impulses.   [Quoted from C. and M. Smith, *Rogers Groups*, 1934]

And upon seeing the group, William Lloyd Garrison wrote to the sculptor com-
plimenting him on the lifelike quality of the portraits and on the expressive quality of the slave mother. Rogers gave a copy of the group to William Cullen
Bryant, who wrote to tell him that he had "succeeded in a higher degree than
almost any artist of any age in making sculpture a narrative art, and giving to
motionless and speechless figures the power to relate their own adventures."

Rogers typically gave just the right amount of detail to tell his narrative, but
held it in check so that it became neither tedious nor too literary. One tear on
the Negro woman's right sleeve was enough to suggest tattered attire; the bundle
at her feet was sufficient to indicate what her destitute situation was, for it was
readily understood that all her earthly belongings were gathered there. On her
head she wears the scarf typical of her people, and in her ears are the rings one
might also expect to find. It is not by chance that the three men are gathered
around a writing desk, for it was by means of the pen as well as the spoken word
that they waged their abolitionist campaign. The desk is an accurate representation of the furniture style of the day, as is the chair in which Garrison sits.

Rogers could blend his human warmth and wit with the more pleasant, even
humorous side of 19th-century American life. Many of his pieces achieved this,
but one of the most popular was "Coming to the Parson" (Fig. 10.11); about
8,000 copies followed its first appearance in 1870. Many a Victorian parlor contained this little tan-colored group on a marble-top table, alongside velvet sofas
and potted plants. It was also a favorite wedding gift because of its subject; 22
inches high and 40 pounds, it originally cost $15. By 1870, it and others could
be ordered from a catalogue that contained illustrations of Rogers' various
groups, gave their prices, and also showed pictures of tables and marble pillar-
type stands that one could buy along with the sculpture. Rogers' groups were
sold directly through his firm by mail order, as well as in art galleries and general
stores from the East Coast to Chicago and even farther west.

Once more Rogers sought a psychological study in the contrasts between his
characters. The wizened elderly parson looks up from his copy of *The Union*
with an expression on his face that reveals both a quiet pleasure in the young
couple and a knowing concern for the vicissitudes ahead. The fact that he is in
his dressing robe, indicates that he has not been expecting his visitors and that
their decision has perhaps been a rather spur-of-the-moment one—all the more
cause for the way he looks at them. The delight on the face of the shy young
girl while she nervously nibbles at one corner of her scarf and hides behind her
young man is a study of the excitement and hesitancy that comes to many a
bride. She is petite, wholesome, and pretty, in contrast to the groom, an awkward youth who seems to have outgrown his clothes. He is, however, equally
self-conscious as he points to the girl whose hand he tenderly holds, and the
look on his face is one of mingled earnestness, joy, and embarrassment. In his
preoccupation with the matter at hand, he is not aware that he is knocking the

minister's book off the table. His only embellishment for the wedding ceremony is a freshly picked flower adorning his lapel, whereas the bride has put on her best and most stylish dress. The mongrel dog has doubtless made the young man's approach more faltering, darting between his feet in order to snarl at the hissing, hunch-backed cat placed beside the parson's chair. All of these details add up to a richness in the narration of the event. One may well be touched by the simple, genuine, and uninhibited reactions of these figures to the circumstances depicted.

Other genre groups followed, such as the "Parting Promise" (1870), "The Foundling" (1870), and "The Favored Scholar" (1872), as well as three scenes depicting events from the story of Rip Van Winkle (1871). The Rogers firm usually brought out from one to three new groups each year; but no new piece was produced in 1876, perhaps because the sculptor's studio was occupied with filling the many orders that resulted from Rogers' display at the Philadelphia Centennial.

The year 1877 saw the creation and production of another great favorite, "Checkers up at the Farm." The sculptor had done this theme before, but this last one has more people and a greater richness of detail. Like so many others before it, the group centered on a homey subject with which 19th-century America could easily identify. There were also the keen delineations of mood and personality of the several characters. Somewhere around 5,000 copies of this group were sold at $15 each over the next fifteen years.

In 1879 Rogers modeled his first sports group, "Polo," and the next year the first of five pieces inspired by Shakespeare's plays—"Is it so Nominated in the Bond?" from *The Merchant of Venice* (Fig. 10.9). Included are the four characters Antonio, Bassanio, Portia, and Shylock; the great actor Edwin Booth posed for Shylock. These theatrical groups were often overburdened with details of costume and setting and with excessive action, and therefore seem not as successful as his genre pieces. His interest in the theater is also manifested in a portrait statuette of Fighting Bob (1889), a character from Sheridan's play *The Rivals*. The noted actor Joseph Jefferson posed for this image, and it bears his likeness in the 18th-century costume he wore in his role of the cowardly Bob Acres. For some reason, however, only seven copies were made of it. "Fighting Bob" is as much a costume-theatrical piece as anything else, and in the late 1880's and early 1890's many such groups were created, as well as several history pieces such as "The Watch on the Santa Maria" and "Why Don't You Speak for Yourself, John?" The "Santa Maria" was the last of such groups to be designed for mass production (1892); a year later John Rogers sold his business to his foreman, under whose guidance the firm soon collapsed—largely because Americans had no further craving for that kind of sculpture. It has been estimated that between 1860 and 1892 more than 80,000 copies were produced by a shop that employed from twenty to sixty workmen.

The relative position of John Rogers' genre pieces was nicely summed up by an anonymous critic in the *Atlantic Monthly* (November, 1868): "The little groups by John Rogers, simplest realism as they are, and next to the lowest orders of true art, carry more significance than all the classic sculpture in the country, and will possess historic value which we cannot overestimate."

There were many works by John Rogers that were not mass-produced. In size and ambitiousness they range from a drowsy little puppy, barely 8 inches high, to an equestrian statue of General John Reynolds (outside City Hall, Philadelphia; 1884) and a memorial to Abraham Lincoln (1892) for Manchester, New Hampshire. There were models for memorials to John Elliot and General Stark, and there were groups called "Ichabod Crane with the Headless Horseman" (1887) and the "Landing of the Vikings" (1893), both cast in bronze, about one-third life size, and both in the New-York Historical Society.

There are also portraits of his family and acquaintances, such as the charming bust of his daughter, Katherine Rebecca Rogers (1874), and a fine likeness of the aged poet William Cullen Bryant (1890; Fig. 10:6). In these, naturalism remained at the heart of his style; unlike many of his contemporaries, especially those who had settled in Italy, the same naturalism dominated Rogers' work whether he made a portrait or an ideal piece. The bust of his daughter captured all the sweetness and impishness of a six-year-old girl. In contrast, the portrait of Bryant is a study of reflective old age—a bearded American naturalist-philosopher and poet-sage, with character in the wrinkled face and the bushy brows. Aside from the statuette of Henry Ward Beecher (1887), John Rogers did not publish portraits of famous men and women of his day, though this was done by such sculptors as Bernard Dreyfuss and Thomas Dow Jones.

John Rogers died at his home in New Canaan, Connecticut, on July 26, 1904, at the age of seventy-five. From 1860 to 1890 he was something of a one-man phenomenon in American sculpture. It is strange that as popular as his groups were, there were not more attempts to imitate his work, and thereby get in on what was a very lucrative business. But no one achieved the success in this line that he did, and of those who tried none was the combination of creative artist and businessman that John Rogers was. Occasionally a little genre piece turns up that was made by one of Rogers' less talented contemporaries, and these have sometimes been assigned to Rogers himself. But the test of quality sooner or later separates the true Rogers from another's work. In the New Hampshire Historical Society there is an unsigned little plaster statuette, 17 inches high, entitled "By Jingo"; a Tom Sawyer type with bare feet, the figure lacks the refinement of details and the good proportions of a figure by John Rogers. The New-York Historical Society has in its collection a plaster statuette of "Frank Mayo as Davy Crockett," which is signed and dated, "D. B. Sheahan, Sculptor, N.Y. 1883." The same institution owns a plaster group of two men in what appear to be clerical robes seated at a table and having a hearty laugh; this piece, entitled "A Capital Joke," also lacks the finesse and delicacy of a Rogers group. Caspar Hennecke, who was active in Milwaukee during the 1870's and 1880's, produced a group of Faust and Marguerite (about 1886). Though similar little genre, theatrical, and historical groups done by other sculptors may come to light with further research, it is certain that none will equal the work of John Rogers.

[FIG. 10.2] "Falling Gladiator," by William Rimmer (1861). Bronze, 63″ high. Courtesy, Museum of Fine Arts, Boston; gift of Miss Caroline Hunt Rimmer, Miss Adelaide R. Durham.

[FIG. 10.1] "Despair," by William Rimmer (c. 1830). Gypsum, 11″ high. Courtesy, Museum of Fine Arts, Boston; gift of Mrs. Henry Simonds.

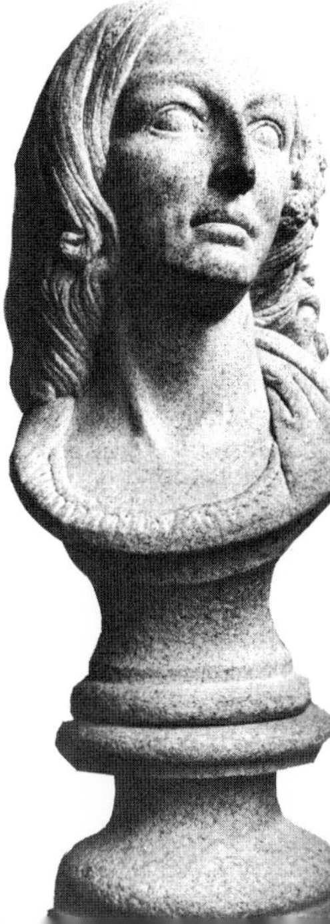

[FIG. 10.3] "Head of a Woman," by William Rimmer. Granite. Collection, Corcoran Gallery of Art, gift of Mrs. Henry Simonds.

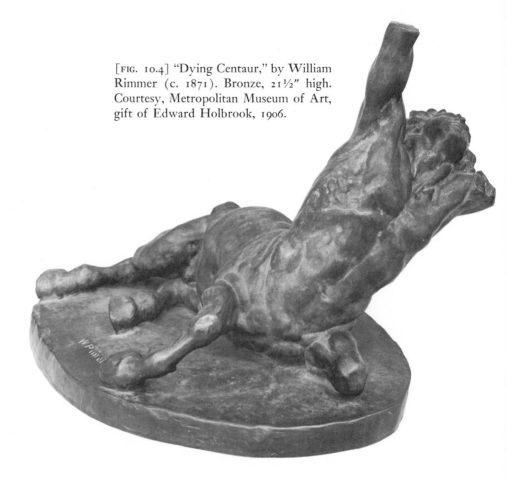

[FIG. 10.4] "Dying Centaur," by William Rimmer (c. 1871). Bronze, 21½" high. Courtesy, Metropolitan Museum of Art, gift of Edward Holbrook, 1906.

[FIG. 10.5] "Torso," by William Rimmer (c. 1877). Plaster. Courtesy, Museum of Fine Arts, Boston.

[FIG. 10.6] "William Cullen Bryant," by John Rogers (1890). Plaster (bronzed) 24¼" high. Courtesy, New-York Historical Society, New York City.

[FIG. 10.7] "The Council of War," by John Rogers (1868). Bronze, 24" high. Courtesy, New-York Historical Society, New York City.

[FIG. 10.8] "The Slave Auction," by John Rogers (1859). Plaster, 13⅓" high. Courtesy, New-York Historical Society, New York City.

[FIG. 10.9] "Is it so Nominated in the Bond?", by John Rogers (1880). Bronze, 23" high. Courtesy, New-York Historical Society, New York City.

[FIG. 10.10] "The Fugitive's Story," by John Rogers (1869). Plaster, 22″ high. Courtesy, New-York Historical Society, New York City.

COMING TO THE PARSON

[FIG. 10.11] "Coming to the Parson," by John Rogers (1870). Plaster, 22" high. Courtesy, New-York Historical Society, New York City.

11

Direct from Paris: Saint-Gaudens, French, and Warner

THE DYNAMIC PORTRAIT AND THE NEW IDEAL

WHEN PRESIDENT ULYSSES S. GRANT OPENED THE PHILADELPHIA CENTENNIAL ON May 10, 1876, the event marked the end of one phase of American history and the beginning of another. For art, the Centennial was the last great showcase of the academic realists and the expatriate idealists, and the place where the sculpture of Augustus Saint-Gaudens, Daniel Chester French, and Olin Warner was shown together for the first time. America faced a new period of unity and growth under its Presidents, from Hayes through Theodore Roosevelt. They presided over the nation during its meteoric rise in commerce, industry, and finance, led by such giants as Andrew Carnegie, Jay Gould, J. P. Morgan, William H. Vanderbilt, John D. Rockefeller, Henry Clay Frick, Henry Ford, and Edward H. Harriman. Along with the unparalleled economic growth, there were disastrous bank failures and recessions.

It was a dark era of dirty mining towns and company stores, of strikes and strike busters, of labor unions—like the American Federation of Labor and the United Mine Workers—and labor leaders such as Samuel Gompers, who organized the working man to protect his interests against the ruthless owners. And it was the period of trusts and antitrusts. All of this turmoil and struggle to discover and establish an equitable arrangement between men and the vast materialistic society in which they suddenly found themselves was reported in the newspapers of William Randolph Hearst, Joseph Pulitzer, and James Gordon Bennett, Jr. Americans had begun to communicate with each other by telephone and typewriter, both machines being displayed and demonstrated at the Philadelphia Centennial. In 1877, Thomas Edison invented the phonograph; in 1879 came his first incandescent light. All this materialistic growth and power was proudly displayed at the spectacular world's expositions, not only at Philadelphia in 1876, but also at Chicago (1893), Buffalo (1901), St. Louis (1904), and San Francisco (1915).

Between 1876 and 1915, America created a unique gilt-edged society that was both crassly materialistic and loftily idealistic. And it demanded of its art a bold naturalism that would be compatible with its materialism and an idealized imagery that would reflect its destiny, its aspirations, and its enormous pride and confidence. The first to create such an art were Augustus Saint-Gaudens, Daniel Chester French, and Olin Warner, who brought renewed vitality to American sculpture just as a dynamic new vigor propelled American civilization in general to amazing new heights of achievement. These sculptors and those who followed them found their inspiration in the art schools of Paris—especially the Ecole des Beaux-Arts—rather than in the studios of the expatriate neoclassicists of Rome and Florence.

Augustus Saint-Gaudens (1848–1907) was born in Dublin, the son of a French father and an Irish mother. Brought to America when still an infant, he grew up in New York City, where his days were devoted as much to mischief as to learning his lessons. He often joined in street brawls with rival clubs, but most of his after-school hours were spent in his father's shoe-making shop. The elder Saint-Gaudens, who was something of a character but devoted to his family, told Augustus at thirteen that it was time for him to learn a trade and asked what he would like to do. "I should like it if I could do something which would help me be an artist," Augustus replied. Bernard Saint-Gaudens had seen sketches his son made on the walls of the shop, on fences, or on almost any other suitable drawing surface, and he arranged for Augustus to begin an apprenticeship with a Savoyard named Avet, a cutter of stone cameos. For three and a half years Augustus worked for the man, recalling the period as one of "miserable slavery." But it was a beginning. His task was to prepare the stone cameos for Avet to finish, and occasionally he would get to finish one himself. Avet was a volatile man who frequently lost his temper; one day in a rage he told Augustus to get out, which he did, and no amount of pleading could induce the headstrong lad to return.

He was next employed by a shell-cameo carver, Jules LeBrethon, with whom he worked for three years. LeBrethon was a gentle man who never scolded him; he allowed him an hour each day to work with clay, and he gave young Saint-Gaudens helpful criticism. After work Augustus began to take drawing lessons at Cooper Union. Before long he was also studying at the National Academy of Design, where he drew from antique casts and from the nude figure, and where he saw the works of the leading painters and sculptors of the day. But there is no mention in his *Reminiscences* of visits to the studios of Ward or Henry Kirke Brown or any of the other sculptors then active in New York City.

Bernard Saint-Gaudens watched his son's interest and ability develop during these years and recognized the rare gift of artistic genius. When Augustus was nineteen, his father offered to send him to Paris, realizing that a few years in the art schools of Europe would do much to bring out his son's talent. Before he left for France, Augustus modeled the likeness of his father in a bust that showed the feeling for form and structure of a true sculptor, though its style was the typical naturalism of the period. This bust, now at the Boston Athenaeum (signed and dated 1867), is the earliest surviving example of his sculpture.

On a cold winter day in February *The City of Boston* pulled out of New York harbor with Augustus Saint-Gaudens aboard. His seasick trip in steerage was forgotten on his arrival in Paris as he walked up the Champs Elysées toward the home of his uncle. He was most warmly received by his relatives, but he soon found quarters of his own in Montmartre. At the Paris Exposition of 1867, Saint-Gaudens saw the work of the eminent French sculptors of the day, such as Jouffroy and Dubois. Their works excited him, just as earlier Americans had been excited by the ancient statuary in Rome and Florence. Paris was unquestionably the place for him to study; Rome could wait awhile.

It was many months before he was admitted to the Ecole des Beaux-Arts, and in the meantime he led the life of the Parisian art student. To support himself, he began cutting cameos (an early example is the 1869 profile of William Root Bliss in the Boston Athenaeum). At night he drew from the live model in one of Paris' many smaller art schools. Finally word came of his admission to the Ecole des Beaux-Arts—which had to be arranged through the U.S. minister—and he chose to enter the classes of the celebrated Jouffroy:

> . . . at that time Jouffroy's atelier was the triumphant one of the Beaux-Arts, his class capturing . . . most of the prizes. From here Barrias had received his Prize of Rome three years before I arrived, Falguière two years before, and Mercié the year after . . . .
>
> I was the only American in the class, though Olin Warner followed me some six months later. [*Reminiscences*, vol. I, pp. 74 and 77.]

In the Jouffroy atelier Saint-Gaudens modeled from the nude figure and essentially laid the foundation of his later art. His master was a patient man who encouraged him with helpful criticism. Saint-Gaudens devoted himself to his studies yet enjoyed the camaraderie of the school; his favorite activities outside the classroom were swimming and long hiking trips. But with the outbreak of the Franco-Prussian War, Augustus Saint-Gaudens went to Italy. Though no major work had resulted from his two years in France, he was more a professional, ready to start work, than an art student when he reached Rome in 1870.

Saint-Gaudens was fascinated by Rome, by the superb works of art, and by the Italian people and their "extraordinary gift for celebrations," which he witnessed with the formal arrival of King Victor Emmanuel into the city. He took a trip with friends to see the exciting spectacle of Vesuvius erupting, and he spent pleasant evenings of talk and levity with fellow artists over cups of strong black coffee at the Caffè Greco. He found living quarters and shared a little studio with a Portuguese friend and fellow student named Soares; a large sheet was suspended in the middle of the studio to give each a measure of privacy, but it failed to protect Soares from Saint-Gaudens' incessant, jubilant singing. Rents, models, food—all were cheap in Rome, and he was able to make a little money regularly by cutting cameos.

Anxious to attempt a monumental work of sculpture, he chose a subject—Hiawatha—from the literature of his native America. The Indian was represented seated, "pondering, musing in the forest, on the welfare of his people," to use the sculptor's own quotation from Longfellow's poem. No doubt, Saint-Gaudens recalled Quincy Ward's "Indian Hunter," which he had admired in New York, and he probably hoped to create his own epic figure in a similar vein. But whereas Ward had spent several months among the Indians, there is no evidence that Saint-Gaudens had ever seen a real live Indian. Moreover, he did what Ward had earlier warned against: He modeled his Indian in Rome under the shadow of the art of antiquity. Ward's misgivings seem well-founded when the "Hiawatha" is studied, for it appears to be another Victorian ideal or literary figure. Saint-Gaudens included many inconsequential details in the manner characteristic of countless ideal pieces of the mid-19th century; in this respect he was reacting to Rome just as many had before him.

He worked hard, but frequent seizures of Roman fever interrupted his progress. And he was concerned over the cost of having "Hiawatha" cast in plaster. Then one day a wealthy American, Montgomery Gibbs, came to the studio; the event is recorded in a letter written by one of Gibbs' daughters:

Upon going [to Saint-Gaudens' studio], Mr. Gibbs found only a little boy, who told him that his master was very ill, but that he had taken care of "the model" and had kept it wet. He then undid the wrapping from the clay figure of Hiawatha, which so impressed Mr. Gibbs that he hastened to discover the sculptor. He found him dangerously ill in a low attic, and immediately had him removed to better quarters and nursed. On his recovery, Mr. Gibbs undertook to support him while he finished the Hiawatha . . .

[Quoted from *Reminiscences*, vol. I, p. 121; letter from Belle Gibbs to Mrs. John Merrylees]

By March 1871 Saint-Gaudens was ready to cast the "Hiawatha" in plaster. Gibbs had offered to cover all the expenses if the sculptor would model portrait busts of his daughters, Belle and Florence. Saint-Gaudens agreed, and in May 1872 he informed Gibbs that the bust of Belle was finished but that the one of Florence had to be cut again because a flaw had appeared in the marble. Meanwhile his "Hiawatha" was cast in plaster and became the pride of his studio.

Gibbs introduced the sculptor to the family of Senator William M. Evarts. Hettie Evarts at once commissioned marble copies of the ancient busts of Demosthenes and Cicero; the senator himself agreed to pose for Saint-Gaudens, although this was not to take place for some time. Gibbs, realizing a visit home would be well-advised for Saint-Gaudens, provided the funds for the journey.

When the sculptor's first European period came to an end after five years, he had his "Hiawatha" in plaster, two marble portrait busts of young ladies, and a couple of marble copies of ancient Roman portraits, as well as a lot of experience in both sculpture and life, to show for it. In 1872 Saint-Gaudens walked unannounced into his father's shop for a joyous reunion with his family.

He remained in New York for two years. Probably his most important work during this time is his portrait of William M. Evarts, a bronze copy of which is at "Aspet," Saint-Gaudens' home and studio in Cornish, New Hampshire. There is no trace of either Roman classicism or Victorian frills in the bust, which contains the first touches of the invigorated naturalism that would in time replace the prosaic realism to which American portraiture had fallen victim. Although structural form and the lively surfaces of rich modeling are not as apparent in this bust as in works of a few years later, there is at least the hint of them. Other works of this period include busts of Edward Stoughton and Edwards Pierrepont and copies of the heads of Demosthenes and Cicero for Elihu Root.

When in 1874 Saint-Gaudens returned to Europe, he carried with him a couple of commissions from L. H. Willard—one for a sarcophagus and the other for a figure, "Silence." In Rome he rented the studio that he had earlier shared with Soares and began modeling the "Silence." Meanwhile his plaster "Hiawatha" came to the attention of E. D. Morgan, who commissioned the piece to be put into marble. Saint-Gaudens was delighted; it meant he could give up cameo cutting for more ambitious projects. His studio became a busy place as he began modeling sketches for other imaginative pieces—such as a peculiar image of "Mozart, nude, playing the violin," and "a Roman Slave holding young Augustus on the top of a Pompeian column and crowning him with laurel." The latter he took seriously for a while; the former he did not. There was also "a little Greek girl . . . lying on a low Pompeian bed and kissing an infant." But the work that occupied him most was the figure "Silence." Even though he continued to model such subjects from antiquity as "Ave Caesar Imperator," his image of "Silence" did not succumb to the faltering neoclassical tradition. It shows a girl standing, wearing a full-length robe and a veil; a finger at her lips conveys the message "silence," and her left hand is forward in a further quieting gesture.

In her nondescript gown and veil, "Silence" belongs to no specific era of the past, and thus a new kind of personification was born. Mr. Willard had evidently proposed that the figure be Egyptian, but Saint-Gaudens thought otherwise and wrote his patron:

. . . the subject being abstract, I think it better after all not to follow any exact style, for the reason that Silence is no more Egyptian that it is Greek or Roman or anything else. I think in that case "Le Style Libre" is the best.

[Quoted from *Reminiscences*, vol. I, p. 141]

Thus the sculptor proposed an imagery that was freed of the hackneyed motifs of revival styles. His use of the term "abstract" is significant. In the last quarter of the century the personification of ideas and values in American sculpture took on a new form, expelling the images of the revival styles; a new breed of robed maidens who possessed a kind of timelessness was devised to represent such ideas as Justice, Peace, Victory, Industrial Power, and so on. Saint-Gaudens' "Silence" was the prototype for the many allegorical and personifying maidens that were to follow in the next decades. They became abstract symbols of things Americans thought and felt and did, and they replaced the Nydias, the Medeas, and the Clyties. Augustus Saint-Gaudens played a leading role in the invention of this new kind of American sculptural imagery.

While in Rome Saint-Gaudens knew that older group of expatriates; there was William Wetmore Story and William Rinehart, Harriet Hosmer and Franklin Simmons. But Saint-Gaudens seldom mentioned these people in his *Reminiscences*, and it would appear that he had early determined not to follow their example. Though he dearly loved the city of Rome, his stimulation came from sources other than classical antiquity. His three years of modeling at the Ecole des Beaux-Arts had had its effect on his way of working. No longer was the surface completely smooth and highly finished in the classical academic manner; instead, it had the texture of a spontaneous sketch, with a lively and decorative quality in its modeling. Also, Saint-Gaudens began to study the sculpture of the 15th-century Italian masters—Ghiberti, Verrocchio, della Robbia, and especially Donatello. It is known that when he returned to America to set up his studio in New York, he had several casts of reliefs by such men hanging on the walls, and that he despaired of ever matching their beauty. To be sure, native American naturalism remained at the heart of his work, but the new elements that he introduced into American sculpture were those from the Ecole des Beaux-Arts and from the 15th-century Florentine Renaissance.

"Silence" was cut in marble and shipped to New York, where it was placed at the head of the main staircase in the Masonic Temple on Sixth Avenue. In 1875 Saint-Gaudens returned to the United States and the next year sent three pieces to the Centennial Exhibition in Philadelphia. Among the works of W. W. Story, Randolph Rogers, Anne Whitney, Moses Ezekiel, and many others, neither his busts of Evarts nor his statue of "Hiawatha" made much of an impression—nor did a handsome portrait head of Admiral David Farragut, which in a few years would appear in the monument that was to establish Saint-Gaudens' name and style in the vanguard of American sculpture.

In the next couple of years Saint-Gaudens met Stanford White and Charles McKim, later of the architectural firm of McKim, Mead, and White. He also met John La Farge, one of the leading painters of the day, whom he assisted in the decorations for St. Thomas Church, New York City. These acquaintances were to prove important to the sculptor.

About that time a clash occurred between Saint-Gaudens and the National Academy of Design. Just as that institution had been founded by a group of artists in rebellion against the outdated principles and policies of the American Academy, so a new organization was needed to provide a rallying force and a place of exhibition for the generation of the 1870's. It was time for a change from the insipid naturalism that dominated American art through the National Academy, the insurrectionists cried, and as their revolution could not take place within the existing institution—honored, prestigious, and powerful though it was—a new organization had to be formed. Heated controversy had been raging for years, but in the spring of 1877 it reached its greatest fury. The Art Students League had already been formed to offer the instruction that the Academy failed to provide. The National Academy was reluctant to take younger men into its organization, and those who were rejected felt they had been deprived of the professional standing and recognition that was rightfully theirs. It was a decade of conflict in the fine arts when the old guard fought desperately to retain its privileged status.

When the National Academy in 1877 rejected a piece Saint-Gaudens had submitted for exhibition, it was symptomatic of the attitude that the Academicians held toward most of the younger men, nearly all of whom had been trained in Paris. Saint-Gaudens was enraged by the rejection, and immediately joined forces with several other discontented artists to form a new group. Fortunately they had the assistance of one of the leading critics of the day, Clarence Cook, who on June 5, 1877, published in the New York *Tribune* the whole story of the dissension between the two factions, treating quite sympathetically the plight of the younger men. Cook attended the meeting at which the Society of Artists was formed; also present were Saint-Gaudens, Wyatt Eaton, Walter Shirlaw, and Helena De Kay Gilder. This small but highly motivated nucleus quickly increased their numbers, and by autumn the group had established itself as the American Art Association. Its purposes were quite simply specified at a meeting held on October 29, 1877, where it was

Resolved, That an Association be formed by those present, with the object of advancing the interests of art in America, the same to be entitled "The American Art Association."

Resolved, That the Association hold annual and special exhibitions of paintings, sculpture, and other works of art, and that the first exhibition be held in the city of New York during the coming winter.

Another critic, Sheldon, writing for *Harper's Monthly* in April 1878 (pp. 764–768), began his article in the following manner:

Were you to talk with almost any member of the American Art Association, now holding its first annual exhibition in the Kurtz Gallery in New York City . . . , he would tell you that the principal reason why the Association was formed is that the National Academy of Design seemed unwilling to aid the progress of art in this country. He would say that the Academy is concerned too much with the comfort and the prejudices of Academicians; that it does not serve art energetically or disinterestedly; that it appears to be jealous of young artists who are or have been studying in Europe; that it does not represent the truest and freshest impulses in art; that, in a word, it is a mutual admiration and sustentation society, sluggish, easily satisfied, and wholly out of sympathy and patience with the rising children of light.

Sheldon further listed the members of the new organization, fifteen in all:

Walter Shirlaw, president; Augustus St. Gaudens, vice-president; Wyatt Eaton, secretary; Helena De Kay Gilder; Olin L. Warner; R. Swain Gifford; Frederick Dielman; Louis C. Tiffany, treasurer; Francis Lathrop; Homer Martin; Samuel Colman; Julian A. Weir; John La Farge; Thomas Moran; and William Sartain.

During the two years he was in New York, 1875–1877, Saint-Gaudens worked on several sculptural projects, many of which came to naught. He did a sketch of some angels for the E. D. Morgan tomb for Hartford, Connecticut; these were put aside until later. He entered Boston's competition for the monument to Charles Sumner, but he lost out—first to Anne Whitney, then to Thomas Ball. Nor did anything come of his proposals to execute statues of Sergeant Jasper for Charleston, South Carolina, and Chancellor Kent for New York City. But when he was ready to return to France he had commissions for a large relief for St. Thomas Church and portrait statues of Captain Richard Randall and Admiral David Farragut. With these secured, so seemed his future. He married Augusta F. Homer in Roxbury, Massachusetts, on June 4, 1877, and a few days later sailed with his bride for France.

By summer the Saint-Gaudenses were settled in Paris. The first task in the studio was the modeling of the relief the "Adoration of the Cross," for St. Thomas Church in New York, done in collaboration with John La Farge who was in charge of the interior decor of the building. In eight bas-relief panels, fourteen *quattrocento*-type angels kneel and adore the large cross. The influence of 15th-century Italian art, obvious in the angels themselves, is substantiated numerous times in letters the sculptor wrote to La Farge. For example, on August 29 he wrote that he had been to the Louvre to see the paintings of the early Renaissance, stating that ". . . the next relief will be more in that character." Later his friend Wyatt Eaton wrote to him that he felt the angels had ". . . the purity and sincerity of the early Italians and the force and effect of the later and modern art." The reliefs were cast in plaster and then painted, using the color scheme of the *quattrocento* masters; in the painting Saint-Gaudens was assisted by Will Low. The relief, completed in the incredibly short period of a little over a month, was shipped from Paris on September 20. New Yorkers went to see the "Adoration of the Cross" after it had been installed and gave it high praise. When S. G. W. Benjamin wrote his short history of American sculpture for *Harper's Monthly* in 1879, he concluded the article with a brief reference to Saint-Gaudens and reproduced an engraving of the Adoration relief, describing it as "one of the most important and beautiful works in the country." Benjamin praised Saint-Gaudens, saying he was "superior in technical skill, [and] moved by a genius thoroughly trained in the best modern school of plastic art, that of Paris. . . ." It is unfortunate that this early work by the sculptor was destroyed when the church burned in 1905; luckily its appearance is preserved in an engraving by Timothy Cole.

The completion of the relief brought Saint-Gaudens large commissions and saw the development of a modeling style that was new to American sculpture—the low relief, of subtle and exquisite delicacy. Among the finest medallion reliefs are two that were done in 1880: one of the artist Bastien-Lepage; the other of Saint-Gaudens' friend Dr. Henry Shiff. An additional innovation was an inscription worked into the design of the relief; this introduced a decorative linear element that was a fine counterpoint to the modeling of the figure. The subject, almost always shown in profile, was rendered in a manner that clearly reveals the sculptor's delight in the act of modeling. The fresh, exciting surface was in sharp contrast to the smooth, untextured surface of the art of Saint-Gaudens' predecessors.

Three larger works date from this period. The angels wrought for the Morgan tomb in Hartford, Connecticut, were destroyed by fire in 1882 before their unveiling; they were of the *quattrocento* type, and bore a strong similarity to the style of the 19th-century Pre-Raphaelites. The model for the statue of Captain Richard Randall was for Sailor's Snug Harbor, on Staten Island; but his real triumph was the "Farragut" (Fig. 11.1). On all three the sculptor collaborated with Stanford White, who designed the architectural settings for them; thus began an intimate friendship that was to endure until White's tragic death.

Soon after the death of Farragut in 1870, a committee was formed to erect a monument to him. By the time the Farragut Monument Association was ready to vote on a sculptor, the choice lay between the untried Saint-Gaudens and the proven John Quincy Adams Ward. Saint-Gaudens was anxious for this great opportunity and courted the favor of several members of the committee, but the deciding action seems to have come from Ward himself, who was then very busy with other commissions, and who spoke to the committee on Saint-Gaudens' behalf. The decision was finally made in December 1876, but it was not until early in 1878 that the sculptor began to model his sketches of the statue—at first in Rome, and then in Paris.

From his studio in the Piazza Barberini, Saint-Gaudens wrote to Stanford White in March 1878:

I've been pegging away at my "Farragut," but its a hard "tug," with our infernal modern dress. I have only the cap, sword, belt, and buttons, and the resource of trying to strike away from the stuff [portrait statuary] we have in America. When you come over I want to talk with you about the pedestal. Perhaps something might be done with that . . . .   [Quoted from *Reminiscences*, vol. I, p. 256]

Something was done about the pedestal, and something very special at that. When White joined Saint-Gaudens in Paris they designed a pedestal that was indeed a departure from the type previously used. Instead of the prismatic block with a carved molding or two, the base became an integral part of the monument, decorated with reliefs and inscriptions that sang the praises of the heroic Farragut above them. Something so new was bound to face opposition, not only on aesthetic grounds but also because the extra costs had not been included in the original agreement. Stanford White, back in America, fought countless battles to get the approval of the committee, although in the end the architect and the sculptor took it upon themselves to cover the additional cost of several hundred dollars. While White was pleading with one member and then another, Saint-Gaudens worked at his model in Paris, assisted all the while by his brother Louis, who lived with Augustus and his wife.

Slowly the 8-foot statue of Farragut took form. It has been suggested that Saint-Gaudens' figure was copied after Donatello's "Saint George" at Or San Michele in Florence, mainly because of the stance and the turn of the head. But although "Farragut" shares this with Donatello's statue, Saint-Gaudens' figure is an original piece and not an eclectic reinterpretation of a historic style.

Naturalism remained at the core of Saint-Gaudens' art, but it was no longer treated as an end in itself. Though retaining the essentials of the physiognomy and the proportions of the admiral, all extraneous detail was eliminated; what detail was retained was applied with great sensitivity. This was a naturalism born of American aesthetics and tempered by what Saint-Gaudens had discovered in the highly selective naturalism of the 15th-century masters of the Italian Renaissance. But for all this naturalism, the spirit of a hero was returned to American imagery; it became a naturalism that was vigorous and selective, truthful and bold, never banal or monotonous. With this monument naturalism in portraiture became a means to an end, and the end was that noble concept, that aura of greatness, that invincible confidence and determined drive toward victory which the artist envisaged as surrounding the subject of his statue. The whole idea of the image revolved around the character of the naval commander who stood watch on the bridge of his ship, and the emphasis was truly on the character of the man rather than on his appearance. The coattail is blown by a brisk sea breeze, and the feet are placed apart, as if to maintain balance on a rolling deck. With a pensive glance and a stoic expression the admiral gazes out to sea, his binoculars in hand. This is a portrait statue that far surpasses the typical costume piece of the third quarter of the century; even more important, an American sculptor finally mastered the problem of how to render contemporary attire.

Saint-Gaudens finished his figure in time to have the plaster cast of it exhibited at the Paris Salon of 1880, along with several of his medallions. The French critics were captivated by his work, and one, in the *Revue des Deux Mondes,* wrote:

The city of New York may congratulate itself on the choice that it has made of one of its sons, Mr. Augustus Saint-Gaudens, for the statue to be erected to Admiral Farragut . . . . In this sailor and admiral may be found the peculiar character of a race: the tenacious and clear-sighted will, and along with large experience of life, a boldness of conception, and an initiative force, which are peculiar to Americans, and of which Farragut was a living example . . . . In the exercise of an art new to his nation he has been able, while profiting by the instruction of our school, to preserve native qualities of strength and spontaneity—qualities which could not have had a better employment than here.

Other critics also praised the statue, all perceiving in it a departure from the previous style of American statuary and recognizing the spark of genius in its creator.

The "Farragut" was cast in Paris at the Gruet Foundry while Stanford White went about supervising the construction of the pedestal in New York City. Gruet's first casting was not successful, and Saint-Gaudens' return to America was delayed while another casting was made. The statue was shipped to America, and in May 1881 the unveiling ceremonies took place. As a band played military music and cannon were discharged nearby, the covering fell away to reveal what marked a new era in American sculpture.

The bronze image stood mighty and bold upon an exquisite pedestal that represented a triumph of the artistic creativity and integrity of both Augustus Saint-Gaudens and Stanford White, who had held to their design in the face of long months of opposition from the committee and much personal annoyance and financial loss. The base was not merely a support for the statue, but an integral part of the memorial itself. The reliefs were in Saint-Gaudens' low-relief style and fused with the decorative inscriptions. On the central block of the pedestal, under the statue, is the sword of the warrior set against the ocean currents. The currents continue into the wings, which have personifications representing two of the admiral's finest qualities—Courage and Loyalty. The exedra-plan seat of the pedestal ends in fish, which form the curves for the arms of the bench. The elegant bas-relief offers a subtle and perfect contrast for the bold sculptural quality of the statue above it. The lines of the pedestal are clean and neat, and the strong horizontal axis along the top accentuates the stalwart image above. The entire monument is a triumph of both subtlety and boldness.

The sculptor established himself in New York City, where he was to maintain his studio for seventeen years. Louis, his brother and trusted assistant, was again with him. In 1885 Saint-Gaudens was persuaded to buy a farm in the serenity and remoteness of the beautiful hills of Cornish, New Hampshire. In the summer months he worked at his country place, but during the rest of the year he was in New York City. One of the first projects after the "Farragut" was the completion of the statue of Captain Richard Randall. The model, which he had made in Paris, was reworked and enlarged, cast in bronze, and finally erected, but the sculptor was never really satisfied with it. There were also a good many low-relief profile portraits—for which Saint-Gaudens became quickly famous—done in the years after 1881; most of these appear in the chronological checklist at the back of Volume II of the *Reminiscences*.

The first new major undertaking after the "Farragut" was the Shaw Monument for Boston, a project that was to occupy Saint-Gaudens off and on from the early 1880's until 1897. During this period the Shaw model often stood in the shadows of the studio while other more lucrative works absorbed his energies. First there was the Bellows mural-portrait, followed by the standing "Lincoln" and the "Puritan"; then came the McCosh portrait and the Adams Memorial, followed by the enormous "Diana." And there were countless portrait medallions and busts.

From 1881 to 1885, Saint-Gaudens executed about twenty bronze medallions and also several sculptural decorations for the Vanderbilt and Villard houses. A period of great activity was inaugurated in 1885, with his purchase of the country place in New England. He wrote in his *Reminiscences* (vol. I. pp. 311–12):

Now let me turn to other pleasures, and chief among them my coming in 1885 to Cornish, New Hampshire . . . .
To persuade me to come, Mr. [Charles C.] Beaman had said there were "plenty of Lincoln-shaped men up there." He was right. So during the summer of my arrival, and in the one-hundred-year-old barn of the house, I made my sketch for the standing Lincoln, and for a seated Lincoln which was my original idea, as well as another sketch, the study for the mural monument to Dr. Bellows in All Souls' Church, New York, and completed my relief of the children of Mr. Jacob H. Schiff. I had several assistants with me, Mr. Frederick MacMonnies and Mr. Philip Martiny, besides my brother Louis Saint-Gaudens . . . .

The mural-portrait of Henry Whitney Bellows (Fig. 11.2) made for All Souls' Church in New York City, is signed and dated: "Cornish, N.H. 1885." The plaster model for it and numerous other models of the sculptor's work are preserved at "Aspet" (his place in Cornish was named after the little French town his father had come from). The "Bellows" is a full-length heroic-size portrait of the minister in his clerical robes, rendered in relief—the first of Saint-Gaudens' major works to be attempted in this style. Though the relief of the figure itself is quite bold, that of the semiclassical arch, pilasters, and moldings of the back plane is much lower. An inscription of neat, crisp letters was again worked into the design; there is a beautiful design in the wrinkles around the sleeves of the robe and a large simplicity in the folds of the front. Once more the sculptor has taken an imaginative approach to the art of portraiture, for this form had never before been used in America. This original, experimental, and creative bent is one of the outstanding features of Saint-Gaudens' genius. This same form, which again clearly owes a certain debt to *quattrocento* sculpture, was used a few years later in the McCosh Memorial for Princeton University.

The Lincoln statue committee in Chicago first wrote to Saint-Gaudens to inquire if he would participate in a competition for their statue. When he refused—because he, like many other American sculptors, would not enter competitions—they asked him to do the statue, and he accepted. When Saint-Gaudens was in his teens, he had seen Abraham Lincoln campaigning in the streets of New York City. A quarter of a century later he was to create what is perhaps the most famous, successful, and expressive memorial portrait statue of the Great Emancipator (Fig. 11.3). His standing "Lincoln," in Chicago's Lincoln Park, is 11 feet 6 inches high, and as a portrait image it was indeed a worthy successor to the "Farragut." The initial sketch was modeled that first delightful summer at the Cornish farm, but the full-size clay model was executed in the shadow of the Shaw monument in the studio on West 36th Street; the sculptor would work awhile on one statue, then switch to the other for a few days or weeks. In addition to his youthful remembrance of the great man, he had at his disposal the life mask and casts of Lincoln's hands, which had been made in 1860 in Chicago by Leonard Volk.

Saint-Gaudens' image seems to be the very incarnation of Abraham Lincoln. Tall, gaunt, and meditative, he has just risen from a chair, and his whole demeanor suggests the momentous words he is about to utter. One senses the orator who delivered the moving address at Gettysburg. M. G. Van Rensselaer expressed very well the characterization the sculptor captured:

The dignity of the man and his simplicity; his strength, his inflexibility and his tenderness; his goodness and his courage; his intellectual confidence and his humility of soul; the poetic cast of his thought, the homely vigor of his manner, and the underlying sadness of his spirit,—all these may be read in the wonderfully real yet ideal portrait which the sculptor has created.   [*Century Magazine*, vol. 35, Nov. 1887, p. 39]

The image is naturalistic in style, but Saint-Gaudens exerted a remarkable control over that naturalism, whereas his predecessors had all too frequently become enslaved by it. The viewer, absorbed with the character of the subject, is not distracted by the details of "the tailor's art."

Replicas of the standing "Lincoln" were made many years after the sculptor's death. One was given to the Carnegie Institute in Pittsburgh; another was sent to England and presented to the British people. A smaller replica, 38 inches high, was also made, and an example may be found in the Newark (New Jersey) Museum. In the last years of his life Saint-Gaudens created another Lincoln, this one seated, for the city of Chicago.

The standing "Lincoln" was unveiled on a rainy day in 1887; that same year saw the presentation ceremonies of Saint-Gaudens' striding image of the "Puritan," in Springfield, Massachusetts. In his autobiography the sculptor wrote that the statue "was to represent Deacon Samuel Chapin, but I developed it into an embodiment . . . of the 'Puritan.'" Quincy Ward's "Pilgrim" had been unveiled in Central Park two years earlier. Its quiet, meditative mood finds a sharp contrast in the spirited "Deacon Chapin." Nor did Saint-Gaudens' figure degenerate into a costume piece, for in the determination, the vigor, the confidence, and the sternness, the sculptor captured the sober and austere Puritan personality; with the large Bible clutched in the left hand, he included a note of righteous piety as well. This was a very popular piece: The New England Society of Pennsylvania at once ordered a replica for Philadelphia, and around the turn of the century Saint-Gaudens had a number of smaller replicas about 30 inches high, produced in bronze. This was probably the result of the statue's being shown in the United States exhibit of the 1900 Paris Exposition, where it won a Grand Prix.

While the enormous relief of the Shaw Memorial stood in one section of the studio, slowly progressing and changing form, and while the standing "Lincoln" and the "Puritan" were being completed, along with several other smaller works, Augustus Saint-Gaudens began work on one of his finest pieces—the figure for the Adams Memorial (Fig. 11.7) in Rock Creek Cemetery, Washington, D.C. The "Farragut" and the "Lincoln" had been public memorials of national heroes. The Adams Memorial, however, was not a public statue, and that point can hardly be overstressed. From the very beginning it was a highly personal and private conception, in which four of the most fertile minds of the day worked together to produce the most abstract image of 19th-century American sculpture.

When Henry Adams returned to America from Japan in 1886, he wanted a fitting memorial to mark the grave of his wife, Marian, whose life had tragically ended in suicide. In matters of artistic taste, Adams relied heavily upon his close friend John La Farge, then at the height of his career as a painter and a consultant on large-scale decorative projects. It was probably La Farge who recommended Saint-Gaudens for this particular commission. The fourth man involved was Stanford White, who designed the architectural portions of the monument. Although Saint-Gaudens began work on the figure in 1886, it was only after five years of work and thought, procrastination and uncertainty, that the figure was set in place in its cemetery grove.

The reasons for the unusually long time were twofold. First, Saint-Gaudens would never let a piece out of his studio until he was fully satisfied with it. Second, the delay was due in large measure to the unique conception and abstract nature of the memorial itself. Previously cemetery monuments had been either a portrait statue of the deceased, an angel of the Resurrection, or a quasi-classical or quasi-Gothic personification of Grief. But Adams did not want any of these and left it up to Saint-Gaudens, with La Farge passing on the design, to create an image that would express what Adams had in mind. Certainly the result was not a portrait likeness of Marian Adams, nor was it meant to represent the spirit or personality of one particular person. What, then, does this shrouded sibylline figure represent?

Henry Adams on his return from Japan discussed with La Farge the philosophy of the Kwannon, whose basic principles were to become the heart of the Adams Memorial figure. Years later La Farge recounted the first meeting of Saint-Gaudens and Adams to discuss the commission; Adams gave no instructions about his visualization of the image, but explained that "he wished the figure to symbolize 'the acceptance, intellectually, of the inevitable.'" (Quoted by E. Scheyer in *Art Quarterly*, 1956, p. 195.) The sculptor, not entirely sure of the form he was searching for, tried first a *penseroso* pose, then several studies of a more or less classical solution in a stele type of monument; in the latter he represented Socrates as the personification of reflection, introspection, and the search for truth. Finally he hit upon the pose that struck the response Adams sought. He instructed Saint-Gaudens to "go to La Farge about any original ideas of Kwannon," declaring that he did not want to see the statue until it was finished.

Adams, long interested in the enlightened philosophies of the East and finding Christianity increasingly hollow, shared a point of view with the Boston "Brahmins," who had created a kind of cult around Nirvana; according to Webster, Nirvana is an "extinction of the flame of life; final emancipation; the dying out, in the heart, of passion, hatred and delusion. This emancipation involves a beatific spiritual condition, and freedom from the necessity of future transmigration." In one of Saint-Gaudens' notebooks there is a faint ink sketch of the figure, with an inscription in his own hand that reads: "Adams / Buddha / Mental repose / Calm reflection in contrast with the violence or force in nature." This was indeed a blow struck for artistic freedom, representing a break with middle-class tastes. It contained the seed of a new art that was the product of intellectual and artistic genius; this art would have little rapport with the nonintellectual public. Though they flocked to the site of the monument in Rock Creek Cemetery, they went to see the figure as a curiosity, and not as an expression of something which they could themselves understand and experience in its deepest significance.

A few knew the Adams Memorial for what it was, and thrilled to it. John Hay wrote to the traveling Henry Adams on March 25, 1891, that

The work is indescribably noble and imposing. It is to my mind Saint-Gaudens' masterpiece. It is full of poetry and suggestion, infinite wisdom, a past without beginning and a future without end, a repose after limitless experience, a peace to which nothing matters—all are embodied in this austere and beautiful face and form.

Adams himself, in *The Education of Henry Adams*, wrote of his own reaction to the statue, and of his observations about those who came to see it:

[Adams] first step, on returning to Washington, took him out to the cemetery known as Rock Creek, to see the bronze figure which St.-Gaudens had made for him in his absence. Naturally every detail interested him; every line; every touch of the artist; every change of light and shade, every point of relation; every possible doubt of St.-Gaudens' correctness of taste or feeling; so that, as the spring approached, he was apt to stop there often to see what the figure had to tell him that was new; but, in all that it had to say, he never once thought of questioning what it meant. He supposed its meaning to be the one commonplace about it—the oldest idea known to human thought. He knew that if he asked an Asiatic its meaning, not a man, woman or child from Cairo to Kamchatka would have needed more than a glance to reply. From the Egyptian Sphinx to the Kamakura Daibuts; from Prometheus to Christ, from Michael Angelo to Shelley, art had wrought on this eternal figure almost as though it had nothing else to say. The interest of the figure was not in its meaning, but in the response of the observer. As Adams sat there, numbers of people came, for the figure seemed to have become a tourist fashion, and all wanted to know its meaning. Most took it for a portrait statue, and the remnant were vacant-minded in the absence of a personal guide. None felt what would have been a nursery instinct to a Hindu baby or a Japanese jinricksha-runner. The only exceptions were the clergy, who taught a lesson even deeper. One after another brought companions there, and, apparently fascinated by their own reflection, broke out passionately against the expression they felt in the figure of despair, of atheism, of denial. Like the others, the priest saw only what he brought. Like all great artists, St.-Gaudens held up the mirror and no more. The American layman had lost sight of ideals; the American priest had lost sight of faith.

This statue represents not an art of the great middle class, which patronized John Rogers and Currier and Ives, but an art of the union of the intellectual and artistic genius of the highest order that American civilization could nurture to maturity. Somehow, one cannot imagine Henry Adams being at all aesthetically moved by the little genre groups by John Rogers (still being produced in the 1880's and '90's) such as the "Checkers up at the Farm," or the "Coming to the Parson." A new type of art appeared on the horizon, and after considering the story behind the figure of the Adams Memorial, it becomes apparent that the way was being prepared in the late 19th century for the abstract, even nonobjective, art of the early 20th century, where an abstract concept is the prime consideration.

The Adams Memorial figure, however, is in most respects atypical of Saint-Gaudens' sculpture, which was largely concerned with portraiture in which less abstract means of expression were employed. In 1887 and 1888, while both the Shaw and the Adams commissions underwent their languid metamorphoses in separate parts of the studio, Saint-Gaudens modeled a number of fine bas-relief portraits. There were profile likenesses of his artist friend William Merritt Chase and of the children of Jacob Schiff, and the first of the reliefs of Robert Louis Stevenson. In the "Stevenson" the refinement and exquisite sense of design of the low-relief portraits reaches a peak (Fig. 11.4). Saint-Gaudens was fond of Stevenson's writings, and he told the author of his desire to do his portrait when Stevenson visited America in 1887. The sculptor tells of the circumstances surrounding the modeling of the medallion in his *Reminiscences* (vol. I, p. 373):

I began the medallion at his rooms in the Hotel Albert . . . not far from where I lived in Washington Place. All I had time to do from him then was the head, which I modeled in five sittings of two or three hours each. These were given me in the morning, while he, as was his custom, lay in bed propped up with pillows, and either read or was read to by Mrs. Stevenson.

At first the portrait was to be of the head only, but by the following spring the sculptor had decided to include the hands as well. Another sitting was arranged, and the figure of the author was modeled at his house in Manasquan, New Jersey. Stevenson himself was very fond of the result and once wrote to Saint-Gaudens that everyone who saw it hanging above a fireplace in his house in Samoa thought it "a first-rate but flattering portrait," and in his own opinion it was a "speaking likeness." Several versions resulted.

While working on the Stevenson portrait, Saint-Gaudens also modeled the bold, vigorous, and square-shouldered bust of his ideal of the American soldier—General William Tecumseh Sherman. There were eighteen sittings, each of about two hours' duration, and every moment in the presence of the general was a memorable one to the sculptor. Saint-Gaudens always had a special desire to create a truly grand statuary art for the commemoration of Civil War heroes, and in his "Farragut," "Shaw," and "Sherman" figures he fully achieved his ambitions. Of the three, the "Sherman" offered the keenest challenge. Years later his bust of 1888 served as the model for Saint-Gaudens' famous equestrian statue in New York's Central Park.

On July 18, 1863, Colonel Robert Shaw fell mortally wounded as he led his Negro troops in an attack on Fort Wagner in Charleston Harbor. In the fall of 1865 a group that included Senator Charles Sumner, Dr. Samuel G. Howe, Governor John Andrew, Henry Lee, and Henry Wadsworth Longfellow formed a committee to erect a memorial to Shaw. Within a few months a little over $3,000 was raised; by 1883 it had grown to more than $16,000. The eminent architect Henry Hobson Richardson recommended Augustus Saint-Gaudens for the commission, and on February 23, 1884, the sculptor met with members of the committee to sign the contract.

The idea of an equestrian monument was rejected by the Shaw family as pretentious, but when it was suggested that the whole monument be treated as a relief, they agreed. The relief, 14 feet wide and 11 feet high (Fig. 11.5), was set up in Saint-Gaudens' 36th Street studio and occupied a large portion of it for the next twelve years. Several times as it neared completion the model was destroyed, and the sculptor began anew. The group eventually evolved into higher and higher relief until it was almost free-standing.

In one part of the studio Saint-Gaudens kept a gray horse of which he made clay studies; he finally modeled the animal in large scale on a specially erected platform. Next he did the rider, in his officer's uniform, carrying his unsheathed sword in his right hand and sitting very erect in his saddle—an image of confidence and of determination and of a quiet pride in his command. The relief of the marching soldiers reveals the ingenious inventive powers of Augustus Saint-Gaudens. There was no prototype to which he could turn for solutions to the many problems that arose in connection with the numerous figures. The legs of the marchers, for example, posed an especially severe test for the sculptor's ability, but Saint-Gaudens ultimately devised a remarkably ordered arrangement that, with the torsos, suggests the impellent surge of a military troop. There is indeed a rhythmic movement, a vigorous shuffling cadence, which is echoed in the spirited prance of the colonel's horse. For the heads of the soldiers, Saint-Gaudens sought out models from Boston to New York, on the streets and in bars and anywhere else he might find them, to achieve just the right expression of the ethnological type and the sober stoicism with which they marched to war. Countless times the sculptor persuaded individual Negro men to pose for him only to destroy the portrait when the countenance or expression was at odds with the effect he sought for the group as a whole. In the end, these heads warrant close scrutiny, for they are among the highest achievements of Saint-

Gaudens' portraiture. The sculptor masterfully subordinated the details of the uniforms to these portraits, just as he had done earlier in the "Farragut." The linear forms of the rifles and flags are reminiscent of the "Surrender at Breda" by the 17th-century Spanish painter Velasquez, but there is no trite eclecticism here.

The robed personification flying above the soldiers holds a laurel branch, symbol of victory, and poppies, symbol of the sleep of death. In the swirling folds about her upper torso and the fine rhythmic folds that trail from her waist, the sculptor revealed his exquisite sense of design. No dichotomy exists between the real and the imaginary worlds represented by the soldiers and the personification; each is rendered in the same naturalistic style. Saint-Gaudens' imaginary being is appropriate as the guide to these American soldiers, whereas a borrowed goddess of neoclassical form would have been out of place.

Many years after he had begun work on the monument, Saint-Gaudens applied the last touch—his signature and the date: October 10, 1896. The piece was sent to the foundry, and in the meantime Charles F. McKim designed an architectural frame of classical inspiration for the bronze relief; the site was just opposite the Boston State House. On the frame were inscriptions by James Russell Lowell and Charles W. Eliot, president of Harvard. By 1897 the relief had been cast and set in place. At the dedication, about sixty-five Negro troops—and several officers—who had served under Colonel Shaw marched in as a military band played "John Brown's Body." Augustus Saint-Gaudens occupied a seat in the front row of the unveiling stand, feeling very self-conscious and quite uneasy for fear that someone should ask him to make a speech. As the veil slipped away from the monument, the cheers and applause made the sculptor's heart swell with pride and satisfaction.

In that same year the residents of New York saw Saint-Gaudens' bronze statue of Peter Cooper unveiled in its Ionic nichelike temple, which Stanford White had designed. In the "Cooper," the sculptor captured the sagacity and dignity of the bearded old man. Also in 1897 was the dedication of Saint-Gaudens' equestrian statue of General John A. Logan in Chicago. The success of large commissions such as these certainly established the fame of Augustus Saint-Gaudens and placed him along with Quincy Ward in the leadership of American sculpture.

But we must retrace his career momentarily to consider the figure of Diana (1892), which he created to go atop the tower of Stanford White's Madison Square Garden building. This was the only nude figure Saint-Gaudens ever produced, and he was quite pleased when the opportunity presented itself, since so much of his time and energy had been devoted to portraits. He could have worked more in the ideal realm had he chosen to accept Daniel Burnham's invitation to execute several of the sculptures for the spectacular Columbian Exposition of 1893, but with so much other work pressing him, he declined and recommended Daniel Chester French and Frederick MacMonnies for the major commissions. The "Diana," a svelte, graceful image of the goddess, possesses all the noble detachment of expression of ancient Greek sculpture without itself being Greek. Made of hammered copper sheeting, the original was 18 feet high. But when she was hoisted to her perch on the tower both sculptor and architect realized there had been a miscalculation in scale, and down she came to be replaced by a second version, 13 feet high—all of this at considerable expense to Saint-Gaudens and White. Once permanently established, the graceful huntress with her bow and arrow reigned over the Manhattan skyline—to the shock and indignation of some and the profound pleasure of most Americans, who could by then accept a nude goddess in full sight of all who passed her way. The "Diana" stood atop the tower until the demolition of Madison Square Garden in 1925; then she languished in a Brooklyn warehouse for several years while her owners sought a suitable recipient for her. None was found in New York, and in 1932 the statue was given to Philadelphia to be placed in the new museum of art near the banks of the Schuylkill. A lady minister, the Reverend Mary Hubbert Ellis—a leader of the "youth protection committee" and a "crusader against pornography"—attempted to block Diana's entry into the Quaker City, but her campaign fell flat in the face of an art-conscious public that had finally acquired some sophistication in matters of aesthetics.

In 1892 the Sherman Monument Committee asked Augustus Saint-Gaudens to model an equestrian statue of General William Tecumseh Sherman. The proposal delighted him, for the subject had long been his ideal of the American military hero. There were, however, many projects then in the works in his busy studio, and it was not until 1897 that the statue could receive his full attention. Moreover, the sculptor was never one to rush an important piece through his studio, to have it come forth ill-conceived and poorly rendered. In those early days of the Sherman commission he did devise the design that was ultimately to take form on a heroic scale many years later. The Victory leading the group was part of the initial conception, and was a highly original addition to the design of the equestrian monument. It may have been inspired by some of the sculptures at the Columbian Exposition in 1893. In the general design he copied no other equestrian statue, although he admired Dubois' "Joan of Arc" and kept a photograph of it in his Paris studio.

Soon after his arrival in Paris in 1897 Saint-Gaudens established himself in a studio off the rue de Bagneux and began to work on the large model of the horse and rider. For the head of the general he followed the portrait bust he had made in 1888; for the body he posed an Italian model astride a large barrel. The figure of Victory caused the sculptor a great deal of difficulty; at one point he had four nude models in his studio, arranging drapery on them in an attempt to find a satisfactory design for the flowing folds of the material. The model for the horse and rider was finished in time to be cast in plaster and sent to the Salon of the Champ de Mars in 1899, where it was one of the more sensational exhibits. Meanwhile Saint-Gaudens continued to rework the Victory until he produced the surging, vigorous figure that now leads the way for the general. There were many lesser works in the years 1897–1900, such as his exquisite medallion relief of "William Dean Howells and his Daughter" (1898) and the studies for the never-completed groups for the Boston Public Library. But after the several parts of the "Sherman" were completed and cast in plaster, the sculptor turned the model over to a foundry in Paris and went back to America.

He returned a sick man. The long years of overwork had taken their toll on his general physical condition, and he went straight to his home in Cornish. He had never been completely satisfied with the "Sherman," and although it had already been sent to the foundry, he began reworking the horse's mane, the right hand of the general, and some of the folds of the Victory. After revising them he sent them off to Paris to be worked into the already cast monument. Such was Saint-Gaudens' desire for perfection, a desire that knew no limits in terms of hard work and extra effort.

When the bronze group finally arrived from the Paris foundry, the sculptor applied a double layer of gold leaf to the surface. Then there was the matter of a proper pedestal, and he set up the entire group in the isolation of a nearby field—much to the delight of his farmer-neighbors—to study the scale and elevation of the work. The fame of the Sherman Monument had spread well before it was unveiled in New York City. The whole group had been shown together for the first time in 1900 at the Paris Exposition, where it and several other works won for the sculptor a Grand Prix. A year later it was exhibited in Buffalo at the Pan-American Exposition; there the jury awarded it a special diploma and had a medal of honor struck for it. Both Europe and America sang the praises of this true successor to Donatello's "Gattamelata" and Verrocchio's "Colleoni," and when the work at "Aspet" was completed, New York City excitedly prepared for the famous monument's reception.

Although the sculptor would have preferred a site on Riverside Drive in front of Grant's Tomb, the monument was placed at Fifth Avenue and 59th Street, at the southeast corner of Central Park (Fig. 11.6). In the spring of 1903 the gilded bronze equestrian group was erected atop the polished pink granite pedestal and unveiled on Memorial Day. The military band filled the air with the strains of "Marching through Georgia," and all recognized the fallen pine branch by the left rear hoof of the horse as a symbol of Sherman's march to the sea through the state of Georgia. Saint-Gaudens experienced a feeling of ecstasy as the crowd cheered its approval of his statue. Newspaper accounts agreed that the sculptor had produced a fitting memorial to Sherman. As in the "Farragut," the spirit of the hero was presented in a naturalism that was vigorous and selective, truthful and bold, and never banal or monotonous.

The "Sherman" capped a brilliant career that placed the sculptor at the fore of his art. Critics repeatedly praised his work and proclaimed his eminent position; younger artists paid him the highest of tributes by copying, or at least taking inspiration from, the style he had devised. Though Saint-Gaudens kept to the hills of New Hampshire, there was no cessation of work. Aging and sometimes ailing, shocked by the murder of his close friend Stanford White, grieved by the fire that destroyed his studio and many of his works, as well as countless personal mementoes, still Saint-Gaudens was a sculptor to the end. Numerous medallions, portrait busts, and bronze statues were produced, along with several reductions of such earlier works as the "Puritan" and "Amor Caritas." During these last years he modeled a heroic figure of Lincoln, seated, for the city of Chicago. There was a magnificent memorial to the Reverend Phillips Brooks, with the image of a solemn Christ towering behind the subject as he preached from his pulpit; it stands in a niche outside Trinity Church in Boston's Copley Square.

These were the last works of a man who had brought to American sculpture a new vitality in its naturalism, a new spirit of heroics in the images of its leaders, and an elevated standard of professional workmanship. There was also a new enthusiasm for innovation that expelled the diluted artistic forms of 19th-century eclecticism. Though Saint-Gaudens was not the one to make the break with the naturalistic tradition in American art, he was instrumental in providing it with one last flowering moment. In this he was joined by an extremely talented contemporary, Daniel Chester French.

Augustus Saint-Gaudens was essentially a sculptor of portraits, whereas Daniel Chester French was more a sculptor of the new ideal imagery of the late 19th and early 20th centuries. French's sculpture became the epitome, the final glorious outburst, of the representation of abstract concepts by personification. The latter was the heritage of a classical, Graeco-Roman-inspired outlook on the life and experience of mankind—of man's relationship to his fellow beings, to his own potential, to the forces of nature, and to the universe and the divine being that controlled his destiny. In brief, all of these elements could be and were personified in the form of the human figure, and the supreme master of such imagery was Daniel Chester French. The generation that came to maturity in the years just before and after World War I, however, would challenge the basic principles of such art, and seek an abstract, even nonobjective form in art to express the intangible concepts of the mind. But at the height of his long and prolific career, French had no equal in American sculpture.

Exeter, New Hampshire, with its tree-lined streets, white churches, and handsome academy, was a quiet, lovely New England town in the mid-19th century. Prominent among the residents was the lawyer Henry Flagg French—cultured, urbane, and witty. Into these surroundings his son Daniel Chester French (1850–1931) was born. When the family moved to Cambridge, Massachusetts, about ten years later, the boy began to display a talent for carving the little animals that he knew from the countryside. Then in 1867 the Frenches moved to Concord, Massachusetts, and young Daniel, then seventeen, found himself in the midst of such giants as Emerson, Thoreau, and the Alcotts, any of whom might be encountered daily on the streets or walking in the woods.

Abigail May Alcott, a painter and sculptor, gave Daniel his first instruction in modeling in clay, which his father purchased in Boston. Few of these early pieces have survived, even though the family and neighbors treasured them highly; they were simple subjects, depicting such things as the boy knew from the woods and fields or from the books in his father's library. There was a popular pair of owls, whose ornithological accuracy was a result of Daniel's love of birds and his hobby of taxidermy. The New-York Historical Society owns a piece entitled "Joe's Farewell," a picturesque, homey scene of Dolly Varden and Joe Willet from Charles Dickens' *Barnaby Rudge*. Not quite 10 inches tall, it was inspired by the Rogers groups, and like them, "Joe's Farewell" was mass-produced; the young sculptor made arrangements with a man in Bennington, Vermont, for its reproduction in Parian ware and plaster. Essentially a costume-literary piece, it was skillfully done, and the figures possess a verve that in 1871 forecast a brilliant future for Daniel Chester French.

In the early 1870's he did a low-relief portrait of Mrs. Edward Waldo Emerson in plaster that was proudly signed "D. C. French, Sculptor; Concord Mass." He had clearly begun to consider himself a professional sculptor and soon afterward sought training from accomplished sculptors. This he found at Boston in brief courses in anatomy with Dr. William Rimmer and in drawing with William Morris Hunt. Though he was not drawn to Rimmer's sculptural style, he had a high regard for the man's genius in anatomical draftsmanship. One month's study with John Quincy Adams Ward in New York City turned French's interests from the genre art of John Rogers toward a sculpture of greater monumentality. And not long afterward the first real test of his ability presented itself.

The little community of Concord, Massachusetts, took pride in its resident geniuses, and when the town elders decided to erect a monument to those who fell at Concord Bridge a century before, they naturally turned to Daniel Chester French. That French was untried in any sculptural effort as ambitious as a full-length life-size figure did not disturb them; they were well aware of his special talent and asked him to produce an image of Captain Isaac Davis, the first commissioned officer killed at the battle of the North Bridge. The result was the famous bronze statue "Minute Man" (Fig. 11.9). French contributed his services, although the town voted $500 for any expenses he might incur. Judge Hoar pledged ten cannon, which could be melted down to supply the bronze for the statue, and Concordians began going through their attics to find any attire worn by the revered militiamen of 1775 that would help the artist achieve accuracy in the details of the clothing.

The sculptor took a studio in Boston in the winter of 1873–1874. Several young men from Concord posed for head studies, and a cast of the "Apollo Belvedere," borrowed from the Boston Athenaeum, served as the model for the figure. French's statue was a poised, alert, and confident man of Concord—handsome, rugged, and square-shouldered, with one hand on a plow and the other hand holding his rifle. The image represented a man of local farmer stock, a man of homespun philosophy, common sense, and determination. It was an imaginary portrait that characterized those early New Englanders who first defended their liberties, and the colonial attire stretched across the raw-boned frame bore little

resemblance to the pasty-white "Apollo." French probably employed the celebrated antique statue only because he had no nude model from which to work; it
was never his intention to make his "Minute Man" another member of the preceding generation's neoclassical brotherhood. Upon its completion the plaster
model was sent to the Ames Manufacturing Company in Chicopee to be cast.
Thus a monument was created that was truly a product of New England genius
and resourcefulness. The "Minute Man" was unveiled in a lovely wooded site
near the bridge, and an august gathering admired a work created by one of their
own. President Grant was present, as were Henry Wadsworth Longfellow,
James Russell Lowell, Ralph Waldo Emerson, and other local dignitaries. But
Daniel Chester French, on that April day in 1875 was already on his way to join
Thomas Ball and pursue his studies in Italy. The fame of the "Minute Man"
began to spread when a bronze replica, owned by the Boston firm of Doll and
Richards, was exhibited at the Philadelphia Centennial of 1876. French heard of
all this while working in Florence.

Daniel Chester French was among the last of the new generation to choose
Florence or Rome over Paris, and in later years he would often admit that he regretted not having gone to the exciting center where the new art was developing. But word of the Ecole des Beaux-Arts had not reached him as he was finishing the "Minute Man." Only that year, 1874, had Augustus Saint-Gaudens returned to America bearing the standard of the Parisian style, and it took several
more years to establish its primacy. The names French had heard most frequently in Concord, Cambridge, and Boston were those associated with
Italy.

The young sculptor lived with the family of Preston Powers, the son of
Hiram, but worked in the studio of genial Thomas Ball, who took great pleasure
in the promise of his fellow New Englander. French got to know the Ball family
well and even accompanied them in the summer of 1875 on an extended trip to
Munich, where he saw Thomas Ball's large bronze group of President Lincoln
and the freed slave in the process of being cast at the Royal Foundry. In Florence, French was not especially impressed by the virile naturalism of the works
of Donatello and Ghiberti, but he was inspired by the art of antiquity, and he
benefited immensely from the almost daily presence of a nude model in Thomas
Ball's studio.

French showed the impact of his surroundings when, forsaking the themes of
his homeland, he modeled an "Awakening Endymion"—a nude reclining youth
with Cupid whispering into his right ear. When Bronson Alcott saw the "Endymion" in the sculptor's studio in America a few years later, he wrote in his
diary (July 25, 1879) that it was "a work of rare merit," and added, "We now
have an Artist." French's attitude toward antiquity was clearly not the same in
the "Endymion" as it had been when he transformed the "Apollo Belvedere"
into his "Minute Man," and made of it a truly American piece. The classical
profile of the "Endymion" reveals a capitulation to the style of Canova and
Thorwaldsen that, to quote Lorado Taft, sent many an American sculptor "to a

vast burying ground of all their ambitions." But in the end French was not captivated by the fading cry of the neoclassical sirens, and after two years abroad he returned to America, anxious to establish himself among the nation's professional artists.

Judge Henry French met his son's boat at the Boston docks, and the two of them journeyed to Concord to a splendid reception that family friends and relatives had arranged for the creator of their beloved "Minute Man." It was a joyous moment when French saw for the first time his statue in gleaming bronze mounted on its pedestal. The visit to Concord was brief, and he accompanied his father to Washington, where the elder French was assistant Secretary of the Treasury. Establishing his studio in the home of a relative, Daniel Chester French entered the second phase of his career at a moment when Augustus Saint-Gaudens was challenging the entrenched academic naturalism that had long held the official sanction of the National Academy of Design. In brief, French arrived on the scene just as a significant change was occurring in American art; and he would become one of the foremost masters of the new movement, eventually succeeding even Saint-Gaudens himself as its leader.

During the years between his return to America and his departure for Paris in 1886, French made numerous portrait busts, two portrait statues, and received several sizable commissions for heroic personifications of national ideals. Among the portrait busts were those of his father (1878), of Amos Tuck (1881; New Hampshire Historical Society), of James Elliot Cabot (1880; Concord [Massachusetts] Antiquarian Society), and of A. Bronson Alcott (1882; "Chesterwood," Stockbridge, Massachusetts). Probably his finest bust, the one that brought him the most acclaim, was of Ralph Waldo Emerson (1879); examples of it in plaster, marble, or bronze may be found in numerous collections from New York City to Boston (Fig. 11.8). The style is an animated naturalism that far transcends a dull realism. When one of Emerson's friends saw the bust, he observed that it "represents the man as he now is, touched with age yet youthful in his manly features and expression. It is the form in which we wish to perpetuate our friend." And upon seeing it, the subject himself was moved to make the now much-quoted remark: "That is the face I shave." It reveals the extraordinary ability of Daniel Chester French to infuse that elusive spark of life into his portraits and to endow them with a spirit peculiarly theirs.

The seated portrait statue of John Harvard (1884; Harvard University), holding a great Bible in his lap and deeply absorbed in the Puritan world of philosophy and theology, is an image of the spirit as well as of the flesh. The sculptor concentrated on the quiet, profound, contemplative power of the subject instead of on the details of the Puritan dress; in this respect it was more successful than Ward's "Pilgrim" (1885) in Central Park and in its own way equaled the physically dynamic "Puritan" (1887) of Saint-Gaudens.

The decade following the Philadelphia Centennial saw the rise of allegorical groups on governmental and commercial buildings—great imposing figures personifying such virtues and ideas as Justice, Truth, Progress, Time. Daniel Chester French was among the earliest to put these abstractions. into monumental form, developing in the process a new artistic mode of expression that would reflect the emergence of the titanic industrial and commercial ventures and a government that seemed blessed to endure after its first turbulent century. The earliest of these groups was for the St. Louis Customs House, obtained perhaps with the help of his father's influence. He modeled two mighty stone maidens and a youth, classically draped and seminude, for the U.S. Court House at Philadelphia, in 1879; the figures represent "Law," standing in the center, with "Power" and "Prosperity" seated on either side. Other personifications by French decorated the Boston Post Office (about 1882) and represented two groups: "Science Controlling the Forces of Steam and Electricity," and "Labor, Art, and the Family." The reputation of the sculptor soon spread across the country as he embodied the lofty ideals of a nation filled with a sense of its own power, prosperity, and eagerness for culture.

In 1886 a commission from the state of Michigan for the portrait statue of Lewis Cass, destined for Statuary Hall in Washington, took Daniel Chester French back to Europe. This time he chose Paris, which by then had become the recognized artistic capital of the western world. There was a brief stop in London, where the sculptor met Henry James, Sir Edward Burne-Jones, and Robert Browning. But Paris beckoned; in about a week he had crossed the Channel and soon found a suitable studio in the rue Champagne. Edward Potter had a studio nearby, as did the son of Robert and Elizabeth Barrett Browning. Several evenings a week French attended Mercié's sculpture class, where he found the training in modeling he sought. During the winter he completed the model for the "General Cass," working from a portrait bust and a daguerreotype of the subject. He also had the benefit of criticism from G. P. A. Healy, then living in Paris, who had painted a portrait of Cass many years earlier. The Cass statue, like many others standing in Statuary Hall, was a successful likeness but a rather unexciting work of art. While it was being translated from plaster into marble, there was time for a trip to Rome. The sculptor was anxious to return to America, however, to put into practice the results of his Parisian experience.

In 1888 French set up his studio in New York City. Ward was there, and so was Saint-Gaudens, as well as many other sculptors. His first major commission was for "Gallaudet and his First Deaf-Mute Pupil," for the Columbia Institute for the Deaf in Washington, and it was one of his greatest successes. Gallaudet, who is seated in a chair, has his arm around a little girl alongside; she looks intently to him for help as both make identical signs with their right hands. The Parisian style of modeling, with its lively textured surfaces, has replaced the smooth polished surfaces of French's earlier style, and there is a fine feeling for sculptural form. Just before the date set for French's wedding, Saint-Gaudens saw the model and remarked that the legs were too short. French thereupon wrote to his fiancée, his cousin Mary Adams French, that the wedding might have to be "put off . . . for a month" while he made the necessary corrections.

A wedding planned for June thus took place in July, 1888, much to the consternation of everyone but the sculptor.

In New York City the Frenches fell in with a glittering array of artists, writers, and social celebrities. There were the Kenyon Coxes, the Saint-Gaudenses, Will Low and his wife, and Mr. and Mrs. Richard Watson Gilder. There was William Dean Howells, "whose 'Silas Lapham' was just then the rage." At social gatherings they mingled with the Morgans and the Tiffanys, the Vanderbilts and the Astors, the Appletons and others who made the 1890's the Gay Nineties. The Frenches spent the winters in New York City and the summers in Concord, Massachusetts, or in the little colony that had gathered around Saint-Gaudens near Cornish, New Hampshire.

From French's busy studio issued a procession of works that ranged from portrait busts to the large figures of "History" and "Herodotus" for the new Library of Congress; in 1891 he produced the statue of Starr King for the city of San Francisco. In the summer of 1891, at the request of the family of his deceased friend Martin Milmore, French worked on a memorial to mark the sculptor's grave in Forest Hills Cemetery near Boston. The result was the large relief known as "The Angel of Death and the Sculptor" (Fig. 11.13). There had been earlier angels that stood on pedestals over graves, sounding trumpets, or recording the name of the deceased in a book, or taking the deceased by the hand; but the Milmore Memorial represents the finest example, the culmination, of this tradition. For some time French had had an image of an Angel of Death in mind, and this was his opportunity to develop it to its fullest. He sought to create a sublime being, one that moved in majesty yet was veiled in mystery; a gentle creature who carried a small cluster of poppies, the flower of sleep. From the shoulders grew great wings, with enormous feathers that curved down the entire length of the body. The Angel reaches out gently to stay the hand of the young artist. The sculptor himself, in the customary attire of his studio, is shown busy at work on one of his own pieces—the great Sphinx that stands outside the Bigelow Chapel at Mount Auburn Cemetery near Cambridge. His chisel is poised, and his arm is drawn back; but his action is halted as he looks over his shoulder at the Angel, whose touch he has just felt. The implication is that the Angel came too soon, that Milmore still had years of work ahead of him, and that he was surprised to be called away from it prematurely. In his hooded Angel, French sought an image of a sublime and somewhat mysterious woman that would be comparable to Saint-Gaudens' enigmatic figure for the Adams Memorial.

The excellent sculptural form of the figures is especially noticeable in the dramatic sweep of the folds over and around the head of the Angel and in the heavy drapery of her gown. The head is placed in the deep cavern of the hood, creating a rich play of lights and darks, with the darkness of the cavern offering a splendid foil for the sensitive profile of the head. The firm and youthful figure of the sculptor is full of verve and life. The main difference between this and earlier versions of similar themes is that this is a truly sculptural work of art, whereas in previous versions sentimental or literary elements dominated over good form.

French took the model for the Milmore Memorial with him when he returned to Paris in 1892 and had it cast in bronze. The plaster model was exhibited at the Salon and won for its creator a medal, as well as high praise from critics of many countries. Augustus Saint-Gaudens, then in Paris, saw it and declared that Daniel Chester French must be included in the army of artists he was organizing to create the decorations for the Chicago World's Fair of 1893.

Chicago in the winter of 1892–1893 was host to a gathering of artists, the likes of which, Saint-Gaudens excitedly declared, had not been assembled since the great days of the Renaissance. Frederick MacMonnies was there, as were Henry Augustus Lukeman, Edward Potter, Saint-Gaudens himself, and Karl Bitter; also Isidore Konti, Philip Martiny, Alexander Phimister Proctor, and Carl Rohl-Smith. Daniel Chester French was assigned the colossal figure representing the Republic, which was to tower 65 feet above the Lagoon; at the opposite end was MacMonnies' triumphant Barge of State in the company of splashing dolphins and Tritons. The colossal scale of the great "White City," as the fair was called, required that the figure of the Republic be enormous if it were truly to be a focal point of the Lagoon and work well with the twelve palaces and the triumphal arch that were to surround the grand basin (Fig. 13.7).

In French's studio, which was set up at one end of the large Forestry Building, the clay model was enlarged to five times its own size. The colossus was assembled section by section, each part constructed on a wooden frame over which the staff mixture of plaster and straw was built up in rough form. The final details were then "pointed," much as if they were being carved in marble. The figure, except for the head and arms, was then covered with gold leaf. Clothed in a full-length robe with ample folds, "The Republic" had a kind of classic majesty that worked well with the neo-Renaissance architecture that surrounded the Lagoon; around her head was a wreath containing electric lights. It was a grandiose spectacle, but like all the decorations made of staff, it did not last long after the closing of the fair. A smaller, gilded bronze replica was produced in 1916 and may still be seen in Chicago.

For the triumphal arch behind "The Republic," French collaborated with Edward Potter to produce the quadriga group "The Triumph of Columbus"; then the sculptors moved their studio to the Agricultural Building, where they created four groups of animals led by pages. French's wife described the scene:

. . . here the models came to pose for them, some in Greek draperies and sometimes, I imagine, without draperies, and Mr. French discovered that the workmen outside were making holes in the plaster walls of the studio—pinholes on the inside, but large enough on the outside to accommodate a human eye, and allow the curious to gaze upon the mysteries of studio life!   [*Memories of a Sculptor's Wife*, p. 177]

Potter did the animals while French modeled the figures walking beside them. Daniel Chester French was thus well represented at the Columbian Exposition.

Not only were his three pieces—along with MacMonnies' Barge of State—considered to be the most brilliant and monumental displays of sculptural genius at the fair, but by the time the fair opened, French's Milmore Memorial had been cast in bronze and shipped over from Paris. It was displayed in the Palace of the Fine Arts, where it received international acclaim.

During the next ten years commissions poured in at such a rate that it was necessary to make a waiting list, and several large works began to take form at once in French's 11th Street studio in New York. About that time the Frenches discovered the old Marshall Warner farm near Stockbridge, Massachusetts, in the Berkshires. French asked his friend Henry Bacon, with whom he had worked on some memorials, to draw up plans for remodeling the several buildings. The result was "Chesterwood," now a museum of plaster models of the sculptor's work. A new studio was built, with a 30-foot-square main room that had skylights, a revolving platform, and a "railroad track" on which a large piece could be moved outdoors so the artist could see how his work would appear in full daylight.

In the closing years of the century French produced several large sculptures. Three figures for the John Boyle O'Reilly Monument (c. 1895), in Boston, represented a robust lady of Erin seated between two youths personifying her favorite sons, Poetry and Patriotism. For the city of Philadelphia he collaborated with Edward Potter on a striking equestrian statue of Ulysses S. Grant, which was unveiled in Fairmount Park on April 27, 1899. Potter made the horse, and French made the general. The two sculptors again joined forces to produce an equestrian "Washington" for France, the gift of an organization called Women of America. The statue was modeled at "Chesterwood" one summer, with the assistance of Augustus Lukeman, who enlarged the figure of the rider from French's small sketch. One of the local farm boys was sent to New York City to be outfitted in a Revolutionary War uniform, and during the hot days he proudly posed while Lukeman and French wrought their image. The statue was unveiled at the Paris Exposition on July 3, 1900, in time to commemorate both America's Independence Day and France's Bastille Day. A replica, which was shown at the great fairs held in Buffalo (1901) and in St. Louis (1904), was made for the entrance to Washington Park in Chicago.

There was also a statue of Rufus Choate (1898) for the Court House in Boston and the figure of General Meade, which stands atop a column in the Smith Memorial in Fairmount Park. But more than portraiture, the personification of abstract ideas and concepts absorbed French's talents, and he became increasingly noted for his success with these. For the Dewey Arch in New York City he produced a personification of Peace, and for the Appellate Court Building in New York he modeled the figure of Justice. The nearly superhuman pace continued with personifications of Bounty, Wisdom, Prudence, Courage, Truth, and Integrity for the Minnesota state capitol in St. Paul and culminated in the two exquisite figures and portrait bust for the Richard Morris Hunt Memorial in Central Park. In the Hunt Memorial, maidens in full-length gowns stand at the sides of an Ionic colonnade: On the left, the personification of Painting and Sculpture holds a painter's palette, a small replica of the reclining "Dionysus" from the pediment of the Parthenon, and a sculptor's mallet; her counterpart, Architecture, holds a small model of a building (Fig. 11.12). In their attire and coiffure, in their stately posture, the figures fit well with the neo-Renaissance style of the exedra. Centered in front of a shallow niche that is hung with classical ornamental sculpture, stands the bronze bust of Richard Morris Hunt. The inscription on the pedestal reads: "IN RECOGNITION OF HIS SERVICES TO THE CAUSE OF ART IN AMERICA, THIS MEMORIAL WAS ERECTED 1898 BY THE ART SOCIETIES OF NEW YORK. French's style was perfectly attuned to the noble dignity of the Renaissance revival, which was then at its peak; the last of the great revival styles of the 19th century, it had been resurrected to satisfy the industrial barons, who sought a grandeur in their mansions and memorials, their commercial palaces and office buildings.

After the unrelenting pace of the 1890's French, his wife, and their daughter, Margaret, traveled to Greece, to Rome, and finally to Paris, where they attended the unveiling ceremony for the equestrian "Washington." French returned home to a long list of commissions: There was the full-length uniformed portrait of Commodore George Hamilton Perkins (1901) for Concord, New Hampshire, and the Francis Parkman Memorial (1906) in Jamaica Plain, just outside Boston. Collaborating again with Edward C. Potter, French produced two more equestrian statues—one of General Joseph Hooker for the lawn of the Boston State House (1903); the other of General Charles Devens (1905), destined for Worcester, Massachusetts. The citizens of Boston, having banished MacMonnies' impish nude "Bacchante" from the courtyard of their Public Library on stately Copley Square, were far more pleased with the propriety of French's maidens who adorn the doorways in bas-relief panels, representing the sober themes of Knowledge and Wisdom, Music and Poetry, Truth and Romance. Several of his works were exhibited at the World's Fair in St. Louis in 1904, for which he made a statue of Napoleon I—the emperor who negotiated with Thomas Jefferson for the Louisiana Purchase, whose centennial the fair celebrated.

All this work, of course, carried large financial rewards, and the French family lived very well, with a town house and a country home, three house servants, two handymen, a coachman, and splendid driving horses. French enjoyed his family and his in-laws, and also a certain amount of social life among the wealthy and well-placed in New York and New England society. He was both respected and liked by his colleagues in the arts. Polite, gentle, thoughtful of others, he was resolute in his own opinions and in the direction he gave to his life. In recognition of his contributions, a number of honors were bestowed upon him in the years before World War I. He was elected to the National Academy of Design in 1901; in 1910 he was made a Chevalier of the Legion of Honor in Paris. He was awarded the First Medal of Honor by the New York Architectural League in 1912, and in 1913 Yale and Columbia conferred honorary academic degrees upon him.

All the while, work continued. A large commission came in for four groups —representing the continents of Europe, Asia, Africa, and America—for the U.S. Customs House in New York City. The theme was chosen because the great port was constantly receiving peoples and products from all parts of the world. Each of the groups, solidly pyramidal and carved from Tennessee marble, contains a seated female figure, personifying one of the continents, along with various symbolic trappings. "America" and "Europe" sit erect and alert, whereas "Africa" and "Asia" are shown brooding and only half-awakened. French did not miss an opportunity to indulge in an exotic kind of imagery, which was united with the allegory of the four stages of development of the continents.

Slumbering "Africa" rests one arm on a lion at her left; at her right is the Great Sphinx. "Asia" is represented as a mother of religion, sitting in a contemplative trance, with eyes closed, aloof from the changing world of the European and the American. She holds a little Buddhist figure on her lap, and in one hand is a lotus flower with a serpent coiled around the stem. The prostrate youth before her represents unquestioned obedience to the gods of her various ancient cults and religions; near him, and serving as her footstool, is a collection of skulls.

"Europe" in a Grecian gown rests her right arm on the prow of an ancient galley; decorations from the Parthenon frieze adorn her throne. The book under her left arm symbolizes her contributions to the arts and letters. Behind her sits a gloomy hooded figure who studies a scroll and a skull; this is "History," who has at her feet the "crowns of dynasties long leveled to the dust." "America," alive, her vision intent upon the future, holds in her right hand the illuminating torch of liberty; on her lap are stalks of corn. A North American Indian in feathered war bonnet represents her recent, savage past; her foot rests upon a remnant of ancient Central and South American civilization—the serpent-headed symbol of Quetzalcoatl.

In the massive groups that adorned the approach to the Customs House such concerns of men as religion and the arts, commerce and agriculture, social and political achievement, were all included in the rich imagery. In them is found that element in American sculpture that Adeline Adams described as "moral earnestness," where lofty ideals and concepts are put into three-dimensional form, employing personifications and symbols to express abstract ideas. America found in the work of Daniel Chester French the answer to her yearnings for a grandiose sculptural art encompassing enormous iconographic programs that reached to the core of her national pride, her material achievements, and her philosophy.

The "Four Continents" were finished in 1907, the same year that saw French's statue of Governor Roger Wolcott take its place in the Boston State House and his Alice Freeman Palmer Memorial unveiled in the Wellesley College Chapel. In 1908, statues of Edward I and John Hampden, destined for the Cleveland Court House, were completed, along with the splendid portrait statue of Senator George F. Hoar, which was erected in Worcester, Massachusetts. The most significant piece in 1909 was the Melvin Memorial—"Mourning Victory"—which stands in Sleepy Hollow Cemetery in Concord, Massachusetts (Fig. 11.10). A gift of James Melvin, who dedicated it to his three brothers—Asa, John, and Samuel—who lost their lives in the Civil War, it is quite unlike earlier Civil War monuments. In the 1870's and 1880's, Martin Milmore and countless others who produced bronze tributes to fallen heroes usually chose to make portrait images to stand over the graves or anonymous portrait statues of soldiers or sailors for the public squares. French, however, carried the image of a mourning nation, grieving over the loss of her fine men, to its highest pinnacle of expressiveness within the scope of the personifying figure and academic idealism. A monumental maiden, whose torso and arms are undraped, emerges from a prismatic block. There is an Art Nouveau element in the swirling curvilinear design of her hair, the shroudlike American flag about her head, and the draperies at her side. Her expression is one of deep sorrow, not openly displayed. In her right hand she holds up a laurel branch, for she represents Victory, but a Victory saddened by the loss of three young men. As a boy, Daniel Chester French had known the four Melvin brothers, and he invested the monument with considerable personal feeling.

Also in 1909 French did several figures for the Brooklyn Institute; they personify "Greek Epic Poetry," "Greek Lyric Poetry," and "Greek Religion," plus "Art and Science." In the following years he produced several memorials, such as the Slocum Memorial in Forest Hills Cemetery, the Governor Oglethorpe Monument in Savannah, the statue of Samuel Spencer in Atlanta, and the figure "Memory" for the Marshall Field Memorial in Graceland Cemetery, Chicago. Two winged beings, a youth and an aged woman, representing both Modern and Ancient History, were carved for the New Hampshire Historical Society and may still be seen above the main entrance of the building in Concord.

One of French's great challenges was the standing "Lincoln" he created for Lincoln, Nebraska, in 1912. Several fine images of the Great Emancipator had been produced in the preceding thirty years. There were those by Thomas Ball for Boston and Washington, and one by Larkin Mead in Springfield, Illinois; the most celebrated was the standing "Lincoln" by Augustus Saint-Gaudens in Chicago. French's statue was undoubtedly influenced by this last, as he sought to achieve its solemn pensiveness. He also aimed at a natural dignity in the rugged, unpolished personality and appearance of the man, instead of concentrating on his gangling, self-conscious awkwardness as George Grey Barnard and Andrew O'Connor were to do a few years later. Lincoln was the man who had to make the decisions necessary to preserve the Union; he is, therefore, more than any other President, represented in portrait statues as a man of profound solemnity and gravity. French showed him with his head bowed, his jaw firmly set, and his hands held before him in his easy characteristic manner. A natural dignity is thus combined with a natural, unpretentious pose. Lincoln seems best remembered this way. French's friend Henry Bacon, the architect, designed the architectural setting for the memorial. Behind the figure he placed a stone wall on which the

Gettysburg Address was engraved. When the statue was finished, the sculptor held open house in its honor, inviting people from miles around to come see it and have tea. Later, accompanied by his daughter, he took the long train ride from New York to Nebraska to attend the unveiling.

As always, during the years 1912–1914 there were several commissions in progress at the same time in French's studios, such as the equestrian "General Draper" (horse by F. H. Packer) for Milford, Massachusetts, and the bust for the Longfellow Memorial in Cambridge. One the sculptor found especially interesting was the portrait statue of Ralph Waldo Emerson, which was ultimately carved in marble and placed in the Concord (Massachusetts) Public Library. The famous author is shown in contemporary dress and enveloped in a great lounging robe, which gives him the appearance of an ancient philosopher. The sculptor borrowed from the Emerson family the favorite robe, affectionately referred to as "Gaberlunzey," which the subject wore on cold winter days as he worked in his study. He is shown seated, erect and alert, his right hand grasping the arm of the chair as his head juts forward slightly. It is a quiet image, as the subject was better known for his contemplative rather than his active life, but it still possesses a certain vigor and energy. Although French employed the portrait bust he had made some forty years earlier, the naturalism is not as sharp in the countenance of the seated figure. There was a happy reunion of Concordians when they congregated at the library for the unveiling of the statue of Emerson.

Daniel Chester French's career was at its crest when the Armory Show of 1913 flashed before the eyes of the American people with the strange new experiments in form, color, and the interpretation of nature that had been forming in Europe over the preceding decade. By no means was there an instantaneous revolution in artistic taste in the United States, and French maintained his lofty position in the eyes of critics and the general public in the years which followed. After the Armory Show—with its simplified abstraction of the human head by Constantin Brancusi and its expressive elongation of the human figure by Wilhelm Lehmbruck, to mention only two of the many modern experiments— French continued in his usual style, apparently untouched and unmoved by the work of "the wild men of art." In 1915 several of his most notable works were erected on their pedestals, and not one bears a trace of the abstraction of natural forms that the new art of the Armory Show had advocated. There was his monumental "Alma Mater," with outstretched welcoming arms, who sits in her throne on the steps leading up to Columbia University's Low Library; the figure is very like "The Republic" of the Columbian Exposition of 1893, only seated and on a less heroic scale. For the entranceway to Manhattan Bridge he executed two groups personifying Brooklyn and Manhattan, and for Boston's Public Garden he produced the exquisite bronze portrait statue of the ardent abolitionist Wendell Phillips. The major piece to be unveiled in 1917 was the elegant memorial to Lafayette, in Brooklyn's Prospect Park. In the next few years there were numerous commissions for memorials to gallant leaders and fallen heroes of the

Great War. By that time, however, the sculptor was approaching his seventieth birthday, and his yearly output began to wane a bit—but only a bit. The list of ambitious works that date from these years is amazing, and it includes the gigantic marble "Lincoln" that sits in the Doric temple in Washington, D.C.

The project of a suitable memorial to Lincoln for the national capital had been revived in 1911, and much debate and controversy ensued as to the most appropriate kind. Finally a site in Potomac Park was chosen, overlooking the river and on a direct line with the towering obelisk that honors Washington; Henry Bacon was selected as the architect. Because a building of great dignity was desired, Bacon designed a Doric temple. Thus rose up in glistening white marble one of the last great monuments of the classical revival. At Bacon's recommendation, French was chosen as the sculptor. The Doric temple took form first, and the architect and the sculptor frequently stood before it discussing the sort of statue it should house. By 1918, after nearly three years of thought and work, French had produced a seated figure, more grave and pensive than his standing "Lincoln" for the Nebraska capital. It was reminiscent of the seated "Lincoln" Saint-Gaudens had created ten years earlier for the city of Chicago. French designed a statue that would suit the classical dignity of the building, a statue that would show Lincoln in his most difficult hours of decision. The sculptor's daughter aptly described the portrait when she wrote in her monograph on French that the sculptor had "always felt great character and power in the bony structure of Lincoln's face, and . . . he tried to show the true spiritual grandeur shining through the rugged likeness of a homely man."

In February 1918 the sculptor and the architect stood and gazed at a plaster model that had been set in the temple in the position the marble version would later occupy. This first model, only 8 feet high, was dwarfed by the surrounding architecture. To obtain some idea of the proper scale, gigantic photographs—from 14 to 18 feet high—were made of the statue and put together on a wooden framework; one by one, each was erected on the site, and only the largest proved adequate. The statue would ultimately be set upon a pedestal 11 feet high, placing the head of Lincoln nearly 30 feet above the floor.

The task of carving such a monumental figure was certainly too great for French to undertake himself, and he turned to the six Piccirilli brothers, noted marble carvers of New York City. Their enormous studio was described by W. M. Berger soon after they had begun work on French's "Lincoln":

[It was] a vast workshop, where amid the apparent confusion of great masses of rough and uncut marble, fantastic shapes of plaster and clay (surrounded by scaffolding and ladders, forges and benches, and the indescribable litter of chips and broken stone), [one] may discern dimly through fine clouds of marble dust and smoke, crowds of workmen in blouses, unconventional overalls and paper caps, busily engaged with their humming pneumatic chisels, hammers, and measuring instruments in liberating from these crude blocks of stone the form of some graceful nymph, or, perhaps, the robust figure of one of our distinguished statesmen. It is in such a studio that the great statue of Lincoln by Daniel Chester French has been in the process of development during the past year.   [*Scribner's Magazine*, Oct. 1919, p. 424]

Twenty-eight blocks were required, and they were carved separately in the several studios of the Piccirilli complex, which extended over an entire city block. Gradually the forms emerged, following French's 8-foot model in every detail by means of pointing machines. When all the extraneous parts had been removed 170 tons of Georgia marble remained. Not until they had all arrived at the memorial site in Washington were the finished pieces assembled, but they fit together perfectly (Fig. 11.11).

French had been traveling abroad when the statue was set up in its appointed place, and with great anxiety he made his way to Washington after his return. He knew that his first view of the statue in its final size and in marble would mark the climax of his long career. But when he finally saw it he was horrified! The entire effect was wrong, all wrong: The benign dignity had somehow been transformed into a blank stare—almost imbecilic in its lack of expression. Both sculptor and architect realized suddenly what had happened: It was the lighting. Bacon had originally planned a glass skylight that would allow the greatest amount of light to come from above; when he employed translucent marble instead of glass, this diffused and reduced the overhead light and changed all the shadows that had been so carefully worked out by the sculptor. Light flooded in through the broad doorway opposite the statue, reflecting from both the great pool outside and the polished floor inside. The light thus striking from below flattened many of the forms and made the face quizzically expressionless.

Several experiments were made to rectify the situation but to no avail. The day of the dedication arrived—Memorial Day 1922—and still the lighting was creating an entirely unsatisfactory effect, at least so far as the sculptor and the architect were concerned. But neither Chief Justice Taft—chairman of the Lincoln Memorial Committee—who presented the statue, nor President Harding, who received the statue on behalf of the nation, was aware that anything was wrong. Nor were the assembled guests disturbed. Everyone was thoroughly pleased with the statue of the great President, with the temple, and evidently, with the lighting.

In subsequent years French and Bacon continued their efforts to correct the lighting. With the help of engineers from General Electric they finally solved the problem with floodlights, placed above the ceiling, that shone down on the statue through louvered panels. Thus the lights could not be seen as one approached the statue, and the beauty of Bacon's architecture was in no way impaired. French was even a little surprised at how effective the new lighting was, and how well it could be controlled both day and night—even outshining the sun's reflection on the brightest days. Daniel Chester French was at last at peace with his enormous marble "Lincoln."

The indefatigable sculptor was seventy-two years old when his "Lincoln" was unveiled. Lorado Taft, in the revised edition of his *History of American Sculpture* (1925), continued to refer to French as "the dean of American sculptors." He created several busts for the Hall of Fame at New York University: the exquisite "Edgar Allan Poe" of 1922, and one of Phillips Brooks the following year; "Emerson" in 1924 and "Nathaniel Hawthorne" in 1925. For the Engineers Club in New York he produced a striking likeness of George Westinghouse (1925), and for the Irving Memorial at Irvington-on-Hudson he modeled a sensitive portrait of Washington Irving (1928). There were also several large groups and statues, such as the "Lafayette" in Easton, Pennsylvania, a "Victory" for the First Division Monument in the national capital, and the ideal marble group in the Corcoran Gallery, entitled "The Sons of God Saw the Daughters of Men That They Were Fair."

In 1930 French, at the age of eighty, was still at work in his studio. He was by then active as a trustee of both the Saint-Gaudens Memorial in Cornish, New Hampshire, and the Metropolitan Museum of Art in New York City. Then, in 1931, in the lovely afterglow of an extremely successful life and career, in the balmy fragrance of his cherished garden in the wooded Berkshires, the end came to a productive, creative, well-ordered, and generous life.

The third man who was responsible for the introduction of a new style and a new type of imagery into American sculpture in the 1870's and 1880's was Olin Warner. Although he was highly regarded among his fellow artists, his extraordinary genius was not generally recognized until long after Saint-Gaudens first became prominent; and then his career was cut short by his untimely death. Warner did not create the scores of magnificent monuments the other two men produced, and his name is therefore not as well known. Nevertheless, he holds a special place in the history of American sculpture as one of the first to transplant the style of the Ecole des Beaux-Arts to the United States.

Olin Levi Warner (1844–1896), the son of a Methodist minister, grew up in rural New England, where he attended local schools in Amsterdam, New York, and Brandon, Vermont. His innate artistic talent for sculpture first manifested itself when he molded a block of plaster, let it set, and then carved a bust of his father from it. The result was a remarkably expressive character study for the work of a beginner. The praise accorded this first serious effort gave young Warner the desire to become a professional sculptor. However, neither he nor his family possessed the financial wherewithal to allow him to go to Europe to study, so for the next six years he worked and saved the money he earned as a telegrapher. Having accumulated the necessary funds by 1869, he sailed for Paris.

Saint-Gaudens, who had arrived in Paris a few months earlier, helped Warner get settled, and in time he entered the Ecole des Beaux-Arts. The tuition was free, but all would-be students had to pass various examinations, as well as do an acceptable life drawing to gain admittance. At the school were some of the most celebrated French sculptors, the greatest of whom was old Jouffroy, who nearly forty years before had won the Ecole's highest award, the Prix de Rome; it was in his atelier that Warner first began his studies. He got to know the two younger men who were, in the 1870's, to become leaders among the French sculptors—Jean Alexandre Joseph Falguière and Marius Jean Antonin Mercié.

When Warner first arrived in France, Jean Baptiste Carpeaux had just finished his decorations for the Pavilion of Flora at the Louvre and his group of "Dancers" for the brilliant new Opéra; he was then beginning his last monumental effort—an ambitious fountain for the Luxembourg Palace, with personifications of the four great continents supporting the orb of the earth. Carpeaux took the talented Warner into his large, busy studio, and in time Warner was invited to become his assistant rather than his student. He accepted the position, but the troubles of France, and of Paris in particular, soon brought an end to the relationship. The plush, gilt-edged Second Empire crumbled, and the Republic succeeded it only to be overthrown by the Commune. Out of sympathy for France, Warner enlisted in the French Foreign Legion for the duration of the conflict. Eventually he chose to return to America rather than take up work again in Carpeaux's studio. Warner came back to the United States with much valuable experience behind him; between the Ecole des Beaux-Arts and his work in Carpeaux's studio, he had been exposed to a new kind of sculpture with its new methods of modeling and its exciting, lively new surfaces.

The years between 1872 and the Centennial of 1876 were extremely difficult for the sculptor, about whom America knew virtually nothing. The reputation he had had in Paris had not made its way across the Atlantic, and America took little notice of his talent. He found a few odd jobs designing such household objects as gas fixtures, but he was soon forced to abandon his art and the art world of New York City for the security of his father's farm in Massachusetts. At the Centennial in Philadelphia, however, Warner drew some attention with his medallion portrait of the famed actor Edwin Forrest.

In the late 1870's and early 1880's, Warner joined Augustus Saint-Gaudens in the development of the low relief as a vital form of expression in American sculpture. The refinement of his style may be seen in his small medallions of Thomas Fenton (1878) and of his mother and father (1879), as well as in the portrait of his friend, the painter A. Wyatt Eaton, modeled in 1883 and cast by Tiffany and Company. It is a handsome head done with freedom and gusto, which is especially noticeable in the rendering of the hair, moustache, and beard; there is a sensitive expression in the eyes and in the set of the jaw, as well as liveliness in the surfaces.

Two other factors that contributed to Warner's rise to prominence after the Centennial were his participation in the formation of the Association of American Artists, and his friendship with Daniel Cottier, the art dealer. Cottier invited the artist to exhibit his work in his gallery, and soon afterward the sculptor modeled a bust of him that was much admired. It is a pleasant, bearded, Hellenistic-like head, with eyes that smile and a warm gentle demeanor. Warner's exquisite poetic touch in the portrait bust is readily seen in the likeness he produced in 1880 of his fellow artist Julian Alden Weir (Fig. 11.14) and in that of the noted harpist Maud Morgan. In 1880 Olin Warner took a studio in the Benedict Building, where Weir and Wyatt Eaton also had rooms; in the ensuing years they developed a camaraderie, which later included the painter Albert Pinkham

Ryder. In the bust of Weir there is a feeling for sculptural form, especially in the tufts of hair and in the sharp, well-modeled features; the portrait has a spark of life and a dashing, heroic, sensitive quality that was so often lacking in the portraiture of the preceding generation. It represents one of the earliest appearances in America of the new Parisian style of modeling. There is also intense expression in the bust of Maud Morgan, as well as a lovely refinement in the rendering of the feminine features. Naturalism remained at the heart of the style, but the heroic sensitivity produced a new ideal—one that was also being developed by Daniel Chester French and Augustus Saint-Gaudens. Years later, in 1903, Alden Weir had several replicas of Warner's bust cast in bronze to present as gifts, one of which was sent to John Singer Sargent in England.

Other portraits from this period include those of the literary critic William C. Brownell and of the railroad tycoon John Insley Blair (1883), and one of the daughter of Daniel Cottier, also in 1883. Warner's ideal pieces were beginning to attract attention, too. His little marble figure "Twilight," a draped female form slightly under 3 feet high, appeared in 1879. Four years later he created his "Diana," a late-19th-century interpretation of a goddess from ancient mythology (Fig. 11.15). Warner combined the classical beauty of the refined nude form with the lively surface and naturalistic rendering of the figure, achieving a merger of seemingly incompatible artistic elements. Contemporary critics often spoke of his work as classical, but by 1880 the term had a connotation that was quite different from the connotation in the earlier part of the century. Of the "Diana" one critic wrote that its "perfect simplicity, reserve, purity of line and almost severe beauty have nothing in common with the affected pseudo classicism which was begotten by Canova" (*Art Review*, March, 1887, p. 5).

Though Warner was never inundated with commissions the way Quincy Ward, Saint-Gaudens, and Daniel Chester French were, he was getting more encouragement than before. He received a commission for a full-length portrait statue of Governor Buckingham for Hartford, Connecticut, and from Boston came requests for bronze statues of General Devens and of William Lloyd Garrison. The "Devens" is a splendid embodiment of the staunch yet debonair military man. The figure of Garrison the abolitionist sits in contemplation, leaning forward slightly as he grasps a newspaper in his right hand. In the Garrison statue Warner reached the summit of his art; he obtained not only an expressive likeness but also a portrait that stands as a work of art on its own intrinsic formal values. Lorado Taft compared this statue to Saint-Gaudens' "Farragut," which had been unveiled a few years earlier.

Like Saint-Gaudens and French, Olin Warner had learned to be highly selective in modeling only the essential details of physiognomy, anatomical form, and attire. The eye of the viewer is not overburdened or wearied by an excessive accumulation of details, for the sculptor sought a spirit and a character study in his work, instead of a mere physical representation.

In 1889 Warner embarked on a trip through the Northwestern Territories that was to last more than two years. He modeled medallion profile likenesses of a number of the Indian chiefs he encountered on his wanderings; many of these pieces are now in the Metropolitan Museum of Art. He also made a profile medallion of Charles Erskine Wood (1891), who wrote an article about Warner's Indian portraits that was published in *Century Magazine* in 1893. Wood, a lawyer in Portland, Oregon, was instrumental in obtaining the commission for the fountain Warner later designed for Portland.

After his return from the West, Olin Warner was occupied with sculptures connected with the Columbian Exposition of 1893—not only with his own contributions, but also as a member of the jury who selected the works submitted by fellow sculptors. For the exposition, Warner designed the commemorative silver half dollar, which thousands took with them as souvenirs; he also did a statue of Hendrik Hudson and busts of Governors DeWitt Clinton and Roswell P. Flower for the New York State Building. Warner exhibited a plaster version of his "Diana" there, and several medallions of Columbia River Indians, a model for a caryatid, a portrait of an infant, and his bust of Alden Weir. The sculptor was at last achieving the recognition and respect among the public that he had long enjoyed among American sculptors.

This recognition, however, came too late. Warner, who was finally awarded a monumental commission by the Federal Government, did not live long enough to complete it. After the Columbian Exposition Warner began work on a set of great bronze doors for the Library of Congress. The two valves were to illustrate the way man has transmitted his knowledge from one generation to another by means of oral tradition. Other doors were projected, illustrating the advent of the age of writing and the revolution brought about by the printed word. In the center of the lunette-shaped tympanum, Warner placed the personification of "Oral Tradition"—a robed female figure, who instructs the child at her knee. At the corners, four representatives of primitive man sit listening intently, for such was their only way of perpetuating the knowledge of their forebears. In low relief on the valves below, "Memory" carries objects of the past while "Imagination" holds a lyre. Unfortunately, Olin Warner died before he could enjoy the general acclaim accorded the portal. The doors were cast in New York at the John Williams Foundry, and the remaining two doorways were assigned to Herbert Adams and Frederick MacMonnies.

In 1896 Warner was fatally injured when a carriage struck him while he was riding a bicycle in Central Park. He was fifty-two years old, and his career had only recently reached its peak. By the time of Warner's death the new Beaux-Arts style was firmly implanted in American sculpture, and he had been one of the earliest to introduce it. A host of younger men would reap what he along with Saint-Gaudens and French had sown as an exciting new period of decorative architectural sculpture, colorful imagery, and dynamic portraiture appeared on the sculptural scene.

[FIG. 11.1] "Admiral David Farragut," by Augustus Saint-Gaudens (1881). Bronze. Courtesy, Art Commission of the City of New York.

[FIG. 11.2] Model for the Dr. Henry Bellows Memorial, by Augustus Saint-Gaudens (1885). Plaster. Courtesy, Saint-Gaudens National Historic Site, Cornish, N.H.; photo, Index of American Sculpture, University of Delaware.

[FIG. 11.3] "Abraham Lincoln," by Augustus Saint-Gaudens (1887). Bronze. 11′ 6″ high. Courtesy, Chicago Park District.

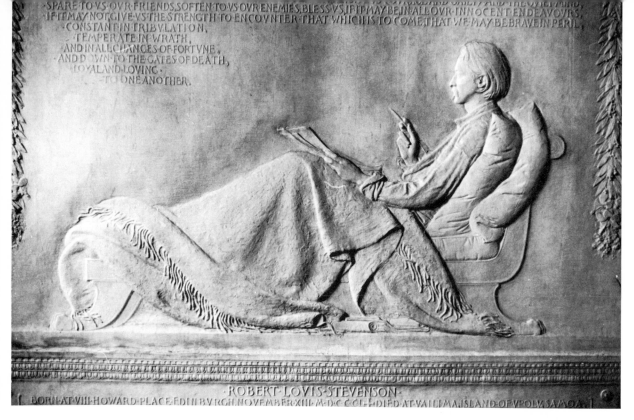

Within the relief, the inscription reads:

SPARE TO VS OVR FRIENDS, SOFTEN TO VS OVR ENEMIES, BLESS VS, IF IT MAY BE IN ALL OVR INNOCENT ENDEAVOVRS, IF IT MAY NOT GIVE VS THE STRENGTH TO ENCOVNTER THAT WHICH IS TO COME, THAT WE MAY BE BRAVE IN PERIL, CONSTANT IN TRIBVLATION, TEMPERATE IN WRATH, AND IN ALL CHANGES OF FORTVNE, AND DOWN TO THE GATES OF DEATH, LOYAL AND LOVING TO ONE ANOTHER.

ROBERT LOVIS STEVENSON
BORN AT VIII HOWARD PLACE EDINBVRGH NOVEMBER XIII M·D·C·C·L· DIED AT VAILIMA ISLAND OF VPOLV SAMOA

[FIG. 11.4] "Robert Louis Stevenson," by Augustus Saint-Gaudens (1887). Plaster. Courtesy, Saint-Gaudens National Historic Site, Cornish, N.H.; photo, Index of American Sculpture, University of Delaware.

[FIG. 11.5] Model for the "Robert Gould Shaw Memorial," by Augustus Saint-Gaudens (1884–96). Plaster. Courtesy, Saint-Gaudens National Historic Site, Cornish, N.H.; photo, Index of American Sculpture, University of Delaware.

[FIG. 11.6] "General William Tecumseh Sherman," by Augustus Saint-Gaudens (1903). Bronze. Courtesy, Art Commission of the City of New York.

[FIG. 11.7] Adams Memorial, by Augustus Saint-Gaudens (1886–91). Bronze. Courtesy, Rock Creek Cemetery, Washington, D.C.

[FIG. 11.9] "Minute Man," by Daniel Chester French (1874). Bronze. Courtesy, Town of Concord, Mass.

[FIG. 11.8] "Ralph Waldo Emerson," by Daniel Chester French (1879). Bronze. Courtesy, Daniel Chester French Museum, "Chesterwood," Mass.

IN TH
AS IN THE HEA
FOR WHOM HE
THE MEMORY OF
IS ENSHR

[FIG. 11.10] "Mourning Victory," by Daniel Chester French (1909). Marble copy (1915) of the Melvin Memorial, Sleepy Hollow Cemetery, Concord, Mass. Courtesy, Metropolitan Museum of Art, gift of James C. Melvin, 1922.

[FIG. 11.11]"Abraham Lincoln," by Daniel Chester French (1922). Marble. Lincoln Memorial, Washington, D.C. Courtesy, National Park Service.

[FIG. 11.12] Richard Morris Hunt Memorial, by Daniel Chester French (1898). Courtesy, Art Commission of the City of New York.

[FIG. 11.13] "The Angel of Death and the Sculptor" (Milmore Memorial), by Daniel Chester French. Marble copy (1926) of original bronze (1891–92). 92" high. Courtesy, Metropolitan Museum of Art, gift of a Group of Trustees, 1926.

[FIG. 11.14] "Julian Alden Weir," by Olin Warner (1880). Bronze, 22½" high. Collection, Corcoran Gallery of Art, gift of Ferargil Gallery.

[FIG. 11.15] "Diana," by Olin Warner (1883). Bronze, 23½" high. Courtesy, Metropolitan Museum of Art, gift of National Sculpture Society, 1898.

Mansions, Monuments, and the Beaux-Arts Style: Part I

ALTHOUGH IN AMERICAN SCULPTURE MID-CENTURY NEOCLASSICISM AND A SOME-
what prosaic naturalism lingered on well after the Civil War, they were replaced
in the last quarter of the 19th century by a style that emanated from the numerous art schools and ateliers of Paris, as was seen in the preceding chapter in the
work of Saint-Gaudens, Daniel Chester French, and Olin Warner. The many
sculptors discussed in the present chapter and the one following it represent a
direct extension of this prevailing French sculptural style.

In the memorials commemorating famous men, in the decorations of the magnificent private dwellings and civic buildings, in an architectural era dominated
by Richard Morris Hunt and by McKim, Mead, and White, and in the grandiose
sculptural projects of the great international expositions held in the United States
from 1876 to 1915, the direct influence of the Ecole des Beaux-Arts is apparent.
In sculpture naturalism in portraiture was infused with a new vigor and animation, and both subject and form showed a marked increase in decorative qualities. It was the period of the last of the great architectural revivals—the neo-
Renaissance, of either the French châteaux or the Italian *palazzo* type, which in
revival form came to incorporate considerable amounts of sculptural decoration.
In scope this architectural revival ranged from the more restrained classicism of
the New York and Boston public libraries, the Metropolitan and Brooklyn
museums of art, Columbia University, and the Henry Clay Frick mansion to
the lavish decor of some of the most important artistic projects of the time, such as
the four great world's fairs: the 1893 Columbian Exposition in Chicago which followed the pattern of that held in Paris in 1889; the Pan-American Exposition in
Buffalo (1901) which reflected the influence of both the Chicago fair and the

one held in Paris in 1900; the Louisiana Purchase Exposition held in St. Louis in 1904, and the Panama-Pacific Exposition held in San Francisco in 1915. These architectural and sculptural extravaganzas were actually neo-Baroque in their exuberance. The same was true of other, more permanent monuments—the new Library of Congress building of the late 1890's, and the Appellate Court, the Hall of Records, and the Customs House in New York City. There was also the Dewey Arch, hastily erected in New York City to celebrate the return of Admiral Dewey in 1899. These projects frequently involved a collaboration between architects and many different kinds of artists.

In the midst of all this activity the National Sculpture Society was organized, which—although presided over at first by the venerable John Quincy Adams Ward—soon became the American center for the promulgation of the Beaux-Arts style of sculpture. The Sculpture Society was founded in late May 1893 to provide American sculptors with an organization of their own and in the words of the original announcement of the Society's goals:

To spread the knowledge of good sculpture, foster the taste for, and encourage the production of, ideal sculpture for the household, promote the decoration of public buildings, squares, and parks with sculpture of a high class, improve the quality of the sculptor's art as applied to industries, and provide from time to time for exhibitions of sculpture and objects of industrial art.

After its first seventy years as one of the fine arts, sculpture finally achieved equality with painting and near-equality with architecture. To a large degree it was the union of architecture and sculpture that brought the latter to the status of a truly monumental art, and that union can again be traced back to the Beaux-Arts style in architecture that developed in Paris.

Although portraiture remained basically naturalistic, it had impressionistic overtones as flickering surfaces and spontaneous modeling replaced the smooth, often labored, dry literalism of the preceding period. The origins of this new technique are found in the works of Rodin, Falguière, Mercié, Chapu, Frémiet, Dampt, and Dalou, all of whom maintained large ateliers. In the 1880's Paris was the undisputed sculpture center. The famous annual Salons were there, and foremost among the many art schools were the Ecole des Beaux-Arts, the Académie Julian, the Académie Colarossi, and the school in the Jardin des Plantes. As if it were a magnet, Paris drew the younger American sculptors, some spending a year or two, some much longer, and many returning again and again. Young Paul Wayland Bartlett was there at the start of the 1880's, and so was John Talbott Donoghue; Frank Edwin Elwell arrived in 1882, George Grey Barnard in 1883, Frederick MacMonnies and George Edwin Bissell in 1884; Herbert Adams was there between 1885 and 1890. In 1886 Daniel Chester French went to Paris for the first time; Gutzon Borglum appeared the next year; Charles Grafly and Hermon MacNeil joined them in 1888. Meanwhile only a few went to Rome for protracted study. Karl Bitter and Isidore Konti came to America from

Vienna, and John Massey Rhind came from Edinburgh, but all bore the imprint of the Ecole des Beaux-Arts and its satellites.

Although the sculpture of this period was dominated by the triumvirate of Saint-Gaudens, French, and Warner, a host of other men contributed variety to the general stylistic trend. Chief among them were Frederick MacMonnies, Paul W. Bartlett, Herbert Adams, Charles Grafly, George Grey Barnard, and Charles Niehaus. But there were many others whose work must be considered in the aggregate in order to gain a clear picture of the art of this period. The sculpture by these men was buoyant, decorative, and often highly expressive. In addition to the spirit of inventiveness and experimentation that prevailed, there was a prolificacy that in sheer quantity carried this large group of sculptors far beyond anything in the arts that America had yet seen.

This was the generation of men who met head on a revolutionary "modern art" that they could not understand and therefore could not absorb. The result was a two-pronged divergence in the course of American sculpture that can still be recognized today. What might be called the abstract-nonobjectivists emerged triumphant and represented the leading spirit in contemporary American sculpture; but the old guard continued to perpetuate itself through a number of organizations, which generally failed to carry meaningful creativity into the present day. The main confrontation of these two forces became clear in the years between the two World Wars, and by 1945 it was obvious that the United States, along with most of the Western World, had recognized the necessity for a new art to express her joys, sorrows, and beliefs. But though many lived to see the art they stood for besieged by the abstractionists and nonobjectivists, they did enjoy their own great flowering for thirty or forty years.

In his sculpture, Frederick William MacMonnies (1863–1937) was daring, decorative, inventive, exciting, and prolific, and therefore is typical of his artistic generation. Rejecting the old lifeless neoclassicism, he followed the lead of his master, Augustus Saint-Gaudens, and the contemporary French sculptors with whom he studied in Paris. MacMonnies was born in Brooklyn, the son of a Scottish emigrant. As a boy, he modeled small figures and animals in white wax, and was barely in his teens when he carved from stone an image of a pet frog, using an ice pick for a chisel. Though his efforts were admired by his parents, for pecuniary reasons it was necessary for the boy to go to work as a clerk in a jewelry store. By the time he was eighteen, however, he was working in the Augustus Saint-Gaudens studio, where he did odd jobs and menial labor for months before the sculptor became aware of his talent. "His duties [were] . . . mixing clay and serving it up as requested, keeping the models wet and covering them with cloths at night, attending to fires in winter, answering the door and running errands" (R. de Quelin, *Arts and Decoration*, 1922, p. 424).

One day Saint-Gaudens entered his studio in a volatile, fractious mood; his assistants avoided him at first, but when the sculptor began throwing wads of clay at some of the works in progress, they persuaded him to go home for a while and rest. When young MacMonnies asked how he should occupy himself in Saint-Gaudens' absence, he was told to do anything he pleased. He got two crates, one to sit on and one to serve as his modeling stand. The four or five little statuettes he produced in the next few days attracted the attention of the assistants, Louis Saint-Gaudens (the sculptor's brother) and René de Quelin. When Saint-Gaudens himself returned after three weeks' absence, he was amazed at the competence of the young man's work and promoted him to the rank of an assistant. MacMonnies' facility in modeling rapidly increased. At first he built up rudimentary forms for statues, then enlarged others from his mentor's small sketches; he modeled drapery on projects where the two worked side by side, and worked on the lettering of the long inscriptions that were part of Saint-Gaudens' style. In addition, he began attending drawing classes at both the National Academy of Design and the Art Students League.

By 1884 the time had come for MacMonnies to go to Europe. Choosing Paris, he carried with him letters to John Singer Sargent, Paul Baudry, and Jean Alexandre Falguière, evidently with the intention of studying painting. But Sargent, after the scandal of his "Madame X," had left Paris, and Baudry (famous for his paintings in the Paris Opera House) had died. That left Falguière, the sculptor, a circumstance that led MacMonnies right back to sculpture. He arrived with the sound technical skills and sense of art that had developed during his four years in Saint-Gaudens' studio, and when he entered Falguière's class at the Ecole des Beaux-Arts, his progress continued to be rapid. But the outbreak of a cholera epidemic soon sent him to Munich, where he spent more time studying painting than sculpture. Back in Paris he resumed his work in sculpture, but his studies were again interrupted when Saint-Gaudens asked him to return to New York to assist him with numerous projects then in progress. It was a year before MacMonnies was back in Paris again. The Ecole could teach him nothing more, however, and Falguière invited him to become his assistant in his private studio.

MacMonnies had gained recognition in France earlier when, in two successive years, he won the highest prize available to foreigners at the Ecole—the Prix d'Atelier, second only to the Prix de Rome. But it was his "Diana" that really brought him international acclaim when it was awarded an honorable mention at the Salon of 1889. Although it is a classical subject, there is nothing of neoclassicism in the style. Falguière had himself found great pleasure in the suppleness and grace of the female figure that the subject of Diana offered; under his influence, MacMonnies wrought his own image of the goddess, which emerged in a style nearly identical to the Frenchman's. This is noticeable in the slender proportions, in the fluid transformations of forms, and in the soft modeling of the flesh and hair. The massive proportions of antiquity's women are replaced by a svelte and delicate figure. Even in the head there is no trace of neoclassicism, and the face is that of the French woman who posed for the statue. Only in the crescent in her hair and in the bow in her left hand is this maiden associated with the antique tradition.

MacMonnies' increasing recognition soon brought him commissions. The first of these was a request for three life-size angels for St. Paul's Church in New York City; of greater consequence were the commissions for the statues of Nathan Hale and James S. T. Stranahan, which were destined for City Hall Park, New York City, and Prospect Park, Brooklyn, respectively. The sculptor was actively engaged on all these works in his own Paris studio in 1890, and by the following year the two portrait statues had been cast in plaster and were exhibited at the Salon. Stranahan, who became one of the artist's most ardent patrons, was represented in the attire of his day; the statue was praised for the vividness of the portrayal of the subject's likeness and personality, and the critics maintained that MacMonnies had solved the sculptor's problem with contemporary dress. Moreover, MacMonnies sought to endow the naturalism of his portraiture with the same dynamic life spirit that Augustus Saint-Gaudens, Daniel Chester French, and John Quincy Adams Ward had discovered only a few years earlier.

The "Stranahan" received far more favorable criticism than the "Nathan Hale," which some held to be "too picturesque" (Fig. 12.1). The unsmooth surfaces gave the latter a spontaneity that was sometimes confused with a lack of finish, and it encouraged suspicions that the sculptor had been too anxious to call his work complete in order to get on to the next piece. Theodore Dreiser, however, described it as "one of the few notable public ornaments of New York." Hale, wearing 18th-century dress, is represented in an imaginary portrait, since no likeness taken from life was available. The moment MacMonnies chose is when the young hero, waiting to be hanged, spoke his immortal words: "I only regret that I have but one life to lose for my country." The figure portrays a man of great calm but fierce pride who has utter scorn for his fate and his captors alike. The smooth surface of mid-century statuary has been replaced by the lively, textured ones typical of the Parisian school, and the entire image is endowed with a spirited animation that was seldom obtained before the last quarter of the century. With the face alive with emotion and the hands betraying the helplessness of the bound man, the artist sought to carry his work beyond mere portraiture.

While the statue was being cast at the Gruet foundry—along with the small replica now in the Metropolitan Museum of Art—MacMonnies' studio was in a flurry of activity. From the early 1890's came the impish "Pan of Rohallion," the first of his fountain statues, destined for the garden of Edward Adams of Seabright, New Jersey. In it, the exuberance of MacMonnies' style was criticized as excessive, and one critic described it as "nothing more than a fanciful conceit." The same impressionistic characteristics are to be found in the "Young Faun with Heron," a bronze statuette about 28 inches high, examples of which are in the Metropolitan Museum of Art and the Cleveland Museum of Art. Here, too, was that gay *joie de vivre* that animated several of MacMonnies' creatures from pagan mythology. There was less of the godly reserve and decorum of the earlier "Diana," and more of the uninhibited frivolity of the celebrated "Bacchante with an Infant Faun" (Fig. 12.3).

The gleeful and spritely "Bacchante" (1893) again focused the attention of the American art world upon Frederick MacMonnies. While modeling the figures for the Barge of State for the Columbian Exposition, the sculptor had become infatuated with the sparkling, laughing face of a model named Eugenia, and after his work at Chicago was finished, he hurried back to Paris to model her dancing form and spirit. The famous illustrator Charles Dana Gibson, creator of the Gibson girls, once represented MacMonnies and Eugenia sitting at a sidewalk café in Paris, and la belle jolie and her impish, gleeful face are easily recognizable. In December 1894, P. L. Binon wrote in The Critic that

Without tricks of prettiness, without concessions, sternly correct in reproduction, the statue is a true portrait from head to foot, of a nude young woman. The uninitiated will probably fail to understand clearly the merits of this work, which may, or may not create a school.

The "Bacchante" was a full-length portrait of a real woman—not an abstraction or an idealization—and this was to bring it much adverse criticism in America. Aside from its merits as a work of art, it was too much of the flesh, too immediate, and therefore too vulgar for public display.

The original was given to the architect Charles F. McKim, who in turn—with the sculptor's consent—placed it in the courtyard of the neo-Renaissance library that he and his partners had designed for Boston's Copley Square. The trustees of the library were somewhat hesitant, but accepted the gift anyway, and one Saturday night the statue was set up in the fountain basin of the courtyard. The great bells of the nearby churches had not yet ceased their ringing after Sunday morning services before the good citizens crowded through the portals of the Public Library, eager to see what they already knew was an image of wanton, blatant nudity and drunkenness. Most appalled of all was Harvard's Charles Eliot Norton, who headed the list of petitioners demanding the removal of the scandalous lady. The Women's Christian Temperance Union railed against what they considered the inebriated condition of the maenad and saw in it only an image depicting a wild, drunken spree. Pressure to have the statue removed continued to mount, and finally the trustees asked McKim to consult with Augustus Saint-Gaudens and Daniel Chester French about the matter, probably in the hope that a favorable statement from such respected artists would put an end to the controversy. But the architect and the two sculptors decided that it would be best if they said nothing, and McKim offered to remove MacMonnies' statue if the trustees so desired. They did, and expressed their sincere regrets.

McKim then offered the "Bacchante" to the Metropolitan Museum of Art, where it was enthusiastically accepted. But as the bronze lady made her way to New York the American Purity League and the Social Reform League circulated petitions against her. This time, however, the trustees stood firm, and the "Bacchante" took an honored place in the entrance hall of the great museum. Numerous artists and critics had come to MacMonnies' assistance, although the sculptor himself had remained largely aloof from the controversy, as he was in Paris. Several years later, H. H. Greer called the statue the embodiment of grace and beauty and saw in it "aught but purity"; chiding those who had condemned it, he continued,

Had MacMonnies planted both feet firmly on the pedestal, stroked off some of the rotundity of form so as to give a suggestion of consumption or piety, substituted a rattle for the grapes, taken the laugh out of the eyes and given them an upward pensive cast, and compressed the joyous mouth into sedate seriousness, the merits of the work might have been better appreciated.   [*Brush and Pencil*, vol. X, April 1902, p. 10]

As if to mock America's priggish morality, which continued to interfere with the development of a sophisticated aesthetic sense, the French government ordered a full-size replica of the "Bacchante with an Infant Faun" for the Luxembourg Museum in Paris. The Luxembourg collection consisted of the works of contemporary artists, mostly French, with a small area devoted to the work of foreign artists. MacMonnies' "Bacchante" was the first American piece to be included. In the same year, 1896, the sculptor received the Order of the Chevalier of the Legion of Honor from the French government.

Controversial though the "Bacchante" may have been, it once more brought attention to MacMonnies, and the nation began to think of him as one of the leaders in American sculpture. Olin Warner died in 1896, and MacMonnies stepped forward to take his place in the company of Augustus Saint-Gaudens and Daniel Chester French. By that date another of his celebrated works had already helped establish his fame—the great barge representing the "Triumph of Columbia," which dominated one end of the lake at the Columbian Exposition in Chicago in 1893 (Fig. 12.2). In a ship vaguely reminiscent of the one that carried Christopher Columbus across the Atlantic four centuries earlier (the event the Exposition celebrated), were numerous allegorical figures, led by a winged Fame at the prow. The "Barge of State," as it was also called, was propelled by eight mighty maidens who represented the Arts (Music, Architecture, Sculpture, Painting) and the Industries (Agriculture, Science, Industry, Commerce), and it was guided by an aged and bearded Father Time at the helm. Perched high on a throne, which rests on a pedestal decorated with *putti* and festoons, sits triumphant Columbia, holding a torch in her right hand. What probably was intended to be an imitation of the Renaissance style actually became Baroque in its exuberance and in the lavishness of its classical decorative motifs. In the spirit with which he appropriated, or misappropriated, the stylistic forms of bygone periods, MacMonnies was a true product of his age. He, along with Saint-Gaudens, French, and McKim, Mead, and White, perpetuated the eclecticism of the 19th century by helping to make the Columbian Exposition a gigantic showplace for the Renaissance revival in both sculpture and architecture.

The "Barge of State" was made of staff (plaster and straw) and, of course, did not long endure exposure to the elements, but it played its bravura role well during the Exposition's run. Although MacMonnies received $50,000 for the work, he reportedly spent considerably more than that on it. The "Barge of State" repaid whatever financial loss he incurred, however, through an enormous gain in reputation and the numerous commissions that followed as a result. The great success of this work and the controversy over the "Bacchante" brought him to the very fore of American sculpture in the mid-1890's.

The pace of activity in MacMonnies' studio from 1888 to 1896 was amazing, causing his friend, the painter Will Low, to observe that it was

> . . . a pace . . . which no one could hope to keep up, and something of this haste has left its impress on certain of his conceptions, though rarely or never on his execution . . . . There are already signs of moderation of this gait in his last completed work, the figure of Shakespeare . . . where it is evident that perhaps for the first time a larger measure of reflection has wisely restrained the effervescent quality of execution heretofore predominant. [*Scribner's Magazine*, 1895, p. 617]

The enthusiasm that caused MacMonnies to leap from one work to another, hardly pausing to let his original conceptions mature, did not go unnoticed by his contemporaries. His method of working during these years was very different from that of his former teacher Augustus Saint-Gaudens, who frequently kept unfinished models of major pieces in his studio for years before releasing them to be cast in bronze. Their difference in approach is quite evident in the results, for the one offers what is mainly a shallow spontaneity and excitement whereas the other presents a profound long-pondered study.

But Will Low was wrong, for MacMonnies' torrid pace continued throughout the remaining years of the decade. From the mid-1890's date two costume pieces—the "Shakespeare" (Library of Congress) and the "Sir Harry Vane" (Boston Public Library). The "Vane" is a stylish piece, animated and dashing in its over-all effect, which greatly overshadows any true sculptural qualities. Vane is represented in rich 17th-century attire, with a large-brimmed, plumed hat, a walking stick tucked under his arm, tall leather boots with spurs, and a short cape hanging freely from his shoulders. There is a foppishness about this figure that is somehow contrary to the religious convictions that the subject held so dear. In the "Shakespeare," the surface pattern of the costume is extremely elaborate, but this is not distracting, because the statue is at a distance—high up in the Library rotunda. It is a good conception of the sensitive, courtly author, who stands lost in thought as he writes in the book he holds before him.

These works and those that were done in the next few years were modeled in MacMonnies' studio on the Rue de Sèvres in Paris. In one part of the studio stood the models for the pedimental sculptures for the Bowery Savings Bank, while in another was the study for the winged, trumpet-blowing maiden, in quasi-classical attire, that personified Victory and was destined for a monument at West Point. Soon the models for the spandrels of the Washington Arch in New York began to take form, along with two groups representing the Army and Navy for the Soldiers and Sailors Monument in Indianapolis. The Library of Congress also had commissioned MacMonnies to execute a set of bronze doors; its central figures represented the Humanities and the Intellect in low relief; Minerva occupied the tympanum, flanked by her owl of wisdom and a printing press, and winged creatures offered the world's great books to a people eager to receive them.

Meanwhile MacMonnies and his assistants had begun work on the three ambitious groups for the Brooklyn Memorial Arch, which was dedicated "To the Defenders of the Union, 1861–1865." On top of the arch stands a bronze quadriga driven by the Republic, or Union, and led by winged, robed Victories, who herald her approach with long trumpets. Bold reliefs of enormous scale on either side of the arch represent the Army and Navy. The Army relief bears an unmistakable resemblance to Rude's "Le Depart" on the Arc de Triomphe, which was not far from MacMonnies' studio in Paris. It contains a chaotic excitement: Troops advance as a wounded drummer continues to urge them on; horses stumble and fall as a young officer leads his men over a barricade that reminds one of Delacroix's famous painting "Liberty Leading the People"; above the scene a helmeted and armored goddess sounds a trumpet while riding a winged horse and grasping a dying soldier to her bosom. The Navy counterpart is less chaotic; it is reminiscent of Franklin Simmon's reliefs on the monument to the Republic in Portland, Maine, and the officer in charge bears a marked similarity to Saint-Gaudens' "Admiral Farragut."

At the turn of the century MacMonnies created the colossal Baroque "Horse Tamers," which would become part of the sculptural adornments of the Pan-American Exposition at Buffalo (1901) and ultimately end up flanking an entrance to Brooklyn's Prospect Park. The nude athletes, who strain every muscle to control the mighty beasts they ride, represent the triumph of the mind over brute force, again an attempt to depict an abstract concept through a symbolic, but naturalistic, image. MacMonnies and his contemporaries realized full well that they had great and noble ideas and concepts to represent, but they could not free themselves from the standardized, centuries-old ways of showing them.

Although he lived in the Paris of Picasso, Matisse, and Kandinsky during the exciting years of 1905 to 1913, MacMonnies resisted any alliance with the new art. Even after World War I he continued to follow the style of academic personification he had helped create. MacMonnies would have been unable to take seriously the wild atrocities of Picasso's "Les Demoiselles d'Avignon" anymore than he would have Diaghilev's production of Stravinsky's ballet *Le Sacre du printemps*. All the while MacMonnies was more confident than ever that the art he taught his students and assistants in his studio-school—which he opened in 1905 at Giverny, outside of Paris—was as vital and expressive an art as could be desired. Students and commissions flocked to him, and the established artists' societies on both sides of the Atlantic continued to praise his work.

At Giverny, MacMonnies was surrounded by a whole colony of admiring young American sculptors. There was also his bride, Mary Louise Fairchild of St. Louis, whom he married in 1905 and whose paintings of landscapes and people pleased him immensely. In his studio MacMonnies modeled the equestrian statue of General Slocum for New York City, and followed it with one of General McClellan for Washington, D.C. The latter was unveiled on May 2, 1907, with President Theodore Roosevelt as the guest of honor. These were among the last in the long parade of equestrian military heroes that extended back to Clark Mills' "Jackson" in Washington's Lafayette Park. Whereas once they had represented the noblest form of portraiture, Western man no longer traveled on horseback; an era was passing. But Frederick MacMonnies and most of his fellow artists went blithely on their way, secure in the numerous large commissions that awaited them each morning in their studios.

During the years preceding World War I, MacMonnies produced a number of large works. There was the frontier scout on his spirited pony for the "Pioneer Monument" in Denver, and for Princeton, New Jersey, he made the monument "Washington Refusing Defeat at the Battle of Princeton." The latter has a painterly rather than a sculptural approach, indicating the artist's resurging interest in painting. Again one comes to the conclusion that MacMonnies was more concerned with surface effect or a colorful conception rather than true sculptural form.

In 1915 the plaster models of his "Truth" and "Intelligence" were set in place on either side of the main entrance of the New York Public Library to see how they worked with the rest of the building; they were approved and ordered in marble. That year MacMonnies returned from war-ravaged Europe to establish himself in America for the rest of his life. And in a few months he announced he was giving up sculpture for painting, and declared that he wanted no more large public commissions—which had, incidentally, made him both wealthy and famous.

First of all I shall paint [and] develop some ideas which I have long had in mind. I shall do some sculptural work, but only along such lines as appeal to me, and none of it is to be in the form of commissions. I shall be working for myself. That is, I shall not consider anything from any other point of view than that of expressing my own ideas. [Quoted from *The New York Times*, December 7, 1915]

MacMonnies' desire to express himself through his art, to produce "art for art's sake," was becoming a credo among those who wanted to work without any artistic restrictions imposed by a public whose aesthetic taste was severely limited. For the next several years he painted much more than he modeled in clay; his work could at best be called competent, but never exciting or original. And when he returned to sculpture he picked it up once more as if there had been no flight of freedom, no unrestricted soaring of the artist's will.

In the 1920's MacMonnies created two allegorical pieces—one of Civic Virtue for New York City, and the other, commemorating the Battle of the Marne, for Meaux, France. The "Civic Virtue" was a failure in almost every way. Derided by most of the general public, it soon became known as "the fat boy." An overly muscular nude youth, with a club on his right shoulder, stands on a writhing nude female, who represents the siren of temptation and political corruption: it is a sculptural group reminiscent of 16th-century Italian Mannerism. The general public began to find such personifications boring and inadequate; many found the "Civic Virtue" ludicrous, whereas some even took offense at it. In March 1922 it was necessary for Mayor Hylan to hold a public hearing in New York City Hall on whether or not the statue should be allowed to remain standing in City Hall Park. The Women's Christian Temperance Union and other women's organizations spearheaded the verbal attack as they mobbed the hearing room, and one after another stood up to denounce the statue as degrading to womanhood because the vanquished "Civic Corruption" had been represented as a woman. One declared, "We do not believe that the human race regards man as a symbol of virtue and woman as a symbol of vice. Neither has a monopoly on virtue." For more than a dozen years the statue engendered heated controversy; it was then moved to Foley Square, but even there it was obviously unwanted by the residents of Manhattan. Finally it was taken off the island of Manhattan and placed in front of Queens' Borough Hall.

While the storm raged around "Civic Virtue," Frederick MacMonnies was finishing his design for the 130-foot-high monument commemorating the Battle of the Marne, which was paid for by the contributions of four million Americans. MacMonnies made the model and submitted detailed drawings of the total design, but the actual carving was done by Edmundo Quattrocchi. A titanic nude female, representing a defiant France, turns eastward toward Germany and holds in her arms a mortally wounded nude male figure. By the time it was carved and in place in 1936, MacMonnies' career was virtually over, though a few portrait busts—such as that of James McNeill Whistler, in the Hall of Fame at New York University, and one of the architect Thomas Hastings, in the New York Public Library—date from the 1930's.

In the spring of 1937 the sculptor contracted pneumonia and died on May 22. His career had begun auspiciously enough, and in the busy years of the 1890's he had been acclaimed one of the outstanding young sculptors of America. But he, like his contemporary fellow artists, lived through a period that saw a fundamental change occur in Western art, a change that was more profound and far more rapid than the change that occurred between the ancient and medieval worlds, or between the Middle Ages and the Renaissance. Incapable of converting to its principles, MacMonnies and the others were soon left behind with a moribund style that was no longer suitable for the expression of 20th-century ideas.

Paul Wayland Bartlett (1865–1925) was the son of the sculptor, critic, and teacher Truman H. Bartlett, who was himself rather well known in his day. For more than twenty years the elder Bartlett taught modeling at the Massachusetts Institute of Technology, but he is perhaps best known for his book *The Art Life of William Rimmer, Sculptor, Painter, and Physician*, published in 1882. He produced several monumental statues, such as the Wells and Clark figures in Hartford; and as a little boy, Paul often sat in his father's studio, watching him model one of his portrait busts in that characteristic Civil War-era academic naturalism. Truman Bartlett was determined that his son would not be educated in the United States, and so in 1874 nine-year-old Paul was sent to Paris, where he lived with his mother for the remainder of his youth.

Paul was only fourteen when he exhibited his work—a bust of his grand-mother—for the first time at the Paris Salon of 1879. In the following year he enrolled in the drawing and modeling classes at the Ecole des Beaux-Arts, where he studied with Pierre Jules Cavelier. Becoming fascinated with the animal sculpture then popular among Frenchmen, he began studying with the famous Emmanuel Frémiet at the Jardin des Plantes. He soon became so adept at modeling animals that he was employed by Georges Gardet, another animal specialist, with whom he frequently went from studio to studio, to model the animals required for statues being created by other sculptors. As a result, Paul Bartlett became steeped in the French manner of modeling before he was twenty.

In 1887 Bartlett came to the attention of critics and connoisseurs with his group "The Bear Tamer" (Fig. 12.5), which was shown at the Salon. The theme may be traced back to Henry Kirke Brown and John Quincy Adams Ward, whose search for a truly American subject led them to represent the American Indian with an animal. Bartlett, too, found the subject intriguing and modeled a young, nearly naked Indian happily engaged in training a snarling little bear cub. The twenty-two-year-old sculptor demonstrated his mastery of anatomy in the human figure, and his special talent for modeling in lively masses is revealed in the Indian's hair and in the shaggy form of the bear. The liveliness of the surfaces and the suggestion of forms—rather than a literal depiction of them—were characteristics of the art then being taught in Paris. A comparison of this statue with Ward's "Indian Hunter" (Fig. 7.18) shows the latter is dependent upon realistic details, whereas in the former the details are subdued in favor of lively surfaces and with a much richer feeling for modeling. Bartlett sent his "Bear Tamer" to the Columbian Exposition in 1893, along with another Indian piece called "Ghost Dancer"—a young naked Indian, with a feather at the back of his head, dancing in the hypnotic frenzy of a primitive ritual.

The two Indian pieces show the sculptor's liking for poetic, historical, and ethnological subjects. Unlike many American sculptors who did mostly portraiture, Bartlett's career resembled that of Daniel Chester French, for both concentrated on symbolic images instead of likenesses of their contemporaries. Although he respected the portrait statues by Ward and Saint-Gaudens, Bartlett expressed his disdain of that type of art several years later, speaking of it as "commercial" sculpture:

The commercial influence is damning. It is this rock which threatens shipwreck to the rational development of sculpture in America. The trade in sculpture, wholesale and retail, commenced a little after the close of the war of 1861 and the death of Lincoln. Every city, every village wished to have its monument of the heroes of the war . . . Thus our country is encumbered more and more with indifferent sculptures and grotesque figures of no artistic value whatever.
[Quoted from "What American Sculptors Owe to French Art," *The New York Times*, February 9, 1913, Magazine Section, p. 13]

With few exceptions those portrait statues that Bartlett did undertake were not of contemporary subjects but imaginary portraits of men from other ages. In the late 1890's, for example, he modeled statues of Michelangelo and Columbus; around 1912 he worked on a dramatic statue of Benjamin Franklin, and very late in his career he did a great bronze image of the 18th-century English jurist Sir William Blackstone, which was followed by one of the colonial financier Robert Morris. Adeline Adams, in her brief biography of Paul Bartlett for the *Dictionary of American Biography*, pointed out that Bartlett was fortunate because "he was not called upon to celebrate contemporary frock coats and trousers. He appreciated this immunity. His romanticism abhorred the prosaic, and refused to come to grips with it."

Paul Bartlett's first great opportunity came a few years after the Columbian Exposition when he was commissioned to do two of these imaginary portraits —"Michelangelo" and "Columbus"—for the rotunda of the Library of Congress. These statues established the sculptor's reputation in America, and from the time of their completion he was ranked as one of the leaders of American art. "Michelangelo" (Fig. 12.6) was an image of great power that reflected the titanic will and the artistic soul of the man. Dynamic yet pensive, he is represented in the working attire of a Renaissance sculptor; the figure itself suggests the robust liveliness of Michelangelo's own image of Moses. All details were again subordinated to the whole in this heroic—almost Olympian—vision of the great Michelangelo. Lorado Taft, after declaring that all previous portraits had failed to do justice to the subject, described the image poetically:

This man might have carved the "Moses," might have toiled alone for years on the scaffolding of the Sistine Ceiling, might have lived "the tragedy of the Tomb," might have withstood the arrogant Julius, . . . might have wept over unhappy Florence . . . . Such a man one finds in the "Michael Angelo" of Paul Bartlett . . . .

[*History of American Sculpture*, p. 381]

Bartlett's "Columbus" was also endowed with a dynamic quality that more than overpowered any details of the costume; in this respect it is more successful than MacMonnies' "Shakespeare," which stands near by. Bartlett made both statues larger than the commission specified, and they are therefore larger than the others in the upper level of the rotunda. There was a great deal of interest in the statues when they were completed, and their merits were proclaimed in newspaper and magazine articles of the day.

Bartlett's reputation in France had increased throughout the 1890's. Frequently represented in the annual Salons in Paris, in 1895 a number of small bronzes of animals, fish, batrachians, and crustaceans drew wonderment and praise for their jadelike patinas, from critics, connoisseurs, and fellow artists. He had cast them himself in the cire-perdue method, further impressing his contemporaries with his all-round skills as a sculptor. In that same year Bartlett was awarded the Legion of Honor in recognition of his artistry. But it was his equestrian statue of the Marquis de Lafayette (Fig. 12.4), which was set up in the court of the Louvre, that really endeared him to the hearts of Frenchmen.

In 1898 school children all over America were asked for penny and nickel contributions to pay for a statue of Lafayette, more or less as a reciprocal gift to the French nation for the Statue of Liberty, which had been erected in New York harbor in 1886. About $50,000 was subscribed, and in 1899 the committee named Paul Bartlett as the sculptor. Bartlett had been working in a studio in busy, noisy Paris, but to do the "Lafayette" he chose the quiet little village of Saint-Leu, about twenty miles north of the capital. There, in late 1899 and early 1900, he worked away in pleasant solitude. Pressure was exerted to have the statue completed by the opening of the Paris Exposition in 1900, and though this was impossible, he did have a painted plaster model ready by opening day.

For a year Bartlett worked at Saint-Leu on his equestrian group. One small model followed another, each more detailed than its predecessor, until the sculptor arrived at the one he wanted. The half-size model was then sawed into parts, which were taken to various studios in Paris to be enlarged; they were reunited when the plaster group was set up on the pedestal, and all pieces fit perfectly. The unveiling ceremonies (for the plaster model) were held on the Fourth of July, 1900, in the garden setting, with the magnificent palace of the Louvre forming a background on three sides. The French and American dignitaries, the committee of approval and acceptance, Bartlett's fellow sculptors—all were ecstatic over this newest member of the equestrian fraternity. All, that is, except Bartlett himself; he was not to find a satisfactory solution to the "Lafayette" for another seven years.

His "Lafayette" of 1900 was dressed in fancy attire with too many frills, and the three-cornered hat detracted from the subject's face; moreover, the horse was wrong, and the sculptor decided to use a sturdier breed for his model. A seemingly endless number of sketches were carried to varying degrees of completeness as the plaster model continually deteriorated on its pedestal. There were other commissions that occupied Bartlett all the while, and the committee of Americans appointed to supervise the project grew increasingly anxious to have their statue finished and cast in bronze. Bartlett ignored them all as he worked out the problems before him. He covered the fussiness of the Louis XVI costume with a great overcoat, and he removed the hat from the head to afford a clearer view of the sensitive features. He wanted his image to represent the idealistic, aristocratic youth who had been so steadfastly dedicated to the cause of the American colonies. Finally he was satisfied, and in 1907 the American ambassador to France, the President of the French Republic, and other guests who had assembled in the sculptor's studio were shown the revised model for the statue. They were pleased, but the great moment for the statue had been back in 1900 at its first unveiling. Only Bartlett and a few others realized the great improvement of the second model over the original. There was even less attention paid a year later, in June 1908, when the bronze equestrian "Lafayette" was finally set in its place in the Louvre garden. As a humorous comment, for those who had chided him for being so slow in bringing the project to a conclusion,

Bartlett placed a turtle on the plinth in front of the left rear hoof of the horse; the turtle—symbol of slow but steady progress—can barely be seen from the ground level.

Bartlett had continued to work in or near Paris during the years 1900 to 1907, and in his studios he produced a statue of General George McClellan for the city of Philadelphia and one of Joseph Warren for Boston. There were also two full-length marble portraits for the State House, Hartford, Connecticut—John Mason, the military Puritan, and Governor John Winthrop, Jr. In 1908 he was summoned to America to execute the sculptures of the pediment of the New York Stock Exchange.

John Quincy Adams Ward's design, approved in 1903, represented "Integrity Protecting the Works of Man," and because of the classicism of the building, a quasi-classical style was adopted for the sculptures. Either because there were too many other pressing commissions in Ward's studio, or because Ward's seventy-seven years prevented him from executing such a big job, Bartlett was called in to execute the full-size models from Ward's design. There was a difference of opinion between the two men regarding the style, but Ward insisted on adherence to the classicism he had specified, with the admonishment that when Bartlett got his own pediment to design he could choose whatever style he wanted. So Paul Bartlett spent most of 1908 and 1909 making the models in a style essentially foreign to his own.

As his work on the Stock Exchange figures was ending, Bartlett did receive his very own pediment commission. In February 1909 his design for the long-empty pediment of the House of Representatives wing of the United States Capitol was approved. Persico's personifications of America, Hope, and Justice stood in the great central pediment; Crawford's program on the Senate wing re-enacted the progress of American civilization. It was decided that the House pediment should represent the present, and the central theme accordingly revolved around the flourishing of the American people under the benevolent and watchful aegis of a peaceful democracy. The central group consists of a robed woman (Peaceful Democracy) guarding a nude child (Genius), who sits at her feet and holds the torch of immortality. In her left hand, the woman has an olive branch (peace) and a shield (preparedness). Beside her is the altar of peace, and behind it is an olive tree. The group on the left represents Manufacturing and Navigation, the one on the right represents Agriculture. Waves tucked into the corners refer to the two oceans. In the design accepted by the congressional committee, an Indian hunter stood at the left of Peace, carrying a slain deer over his shoulder. This may have seemed too much like the Indian hunter in Crawford's Senate pediment, or perhaps Bartlett realized that his pediment was too crowded; in any event the Indian was removed, as was one of two oxen. This simplified and improved the composition considerably.

Bartlett went back to Paris to execute the central figure and the Agriculture side of the pediment, but by 1914 he had returned to America and opened an enormous studio in Washington, D.C. While a small army of stonecutters translated his plaster models into Georgian marble, he modeled the Manufacturing half of the pediment.

The style, of course, is unlike that of the pedimental decorations by Persico and Crawford. It is lighter and more picturesque, and enriched by the fine details of the wheat field, the garlands of fruits and flowers, the olive tree, the details of the foundry, and the lapping waves. Bartlett's style may be described as more colorful than the cool, reserved, precisely contoured neoclassical images of the other pediments. The French influence, especially in the richly modeled surfaces, is apparent. Bartlett refused to compromise his style—as Ward had insisted upon doing at the New York Stock Exchange. He endowed his pediment with that decorative, poetic touch typical of most of his work; he gave his Americans a quiet dignity, and he made them heroic yet unpretentious. He achieved a harmonious composition that was richly sculptural. His contemporaries were captivated with the strength and charm of the total effect.

The other major project of Bartlett's studio in the years before World War I was the group of six heroic personifications for the attic of the entrance on the main façade of the New York Public Library. At the left and right stand two bearded old men, representing Philosophy and History, and between them are two pairs of women: Romance and Religion on the spectator's left, Poetry and Drama on the right. Standing over 10 feet in height, these figures were truly monumental and heroic personifications of the world awaiting within the magnificent new library. Most of the work was carried on in a large rented studio in the Bronx, and the figures were finished and translated into marble by 1915.

In 1915–1916, Paul Bartlett was at the height of his career. In 1917 he was elected to the National Academy and the next year he became president of the National Sculpture Society, a position honored by all American sculptors—except those who embraced the "inanities" of the wild "modern art." Next to Daniel Chester French, Bartlett was the most respected of American sculptors, a conservative bulwark against the tide of the new aesthetic. In an address given in 1913 Bartlett had warned against what he called the "subversive tendencies of the newer art movements in France," and he lamented that young sculptors returned from study in Paris with no grounding in the fundamentals of their art:

. . . they have been lured into circles where . . . mental aberration is deliberately cultivated; where intellectual impotence passes for genius, and theories take the place of talent. It is learned that they have frequented studios in which drawing is done with closed eyes, in order to give better expression to the soul.

[*The New York Times*, February 9, 1913, Magazine Section, p. 13]

Among the works that occupied Bartlett in his last years was the "Quadriga," which was placed atop the triumphal arch erected in honor of General John Pershing's return in 1919. The entire structure and its decorations were made hastily of impermanent material and have long ago disappeared. But it was an honor for Bartlett to be assigned the crowning group of the monument. In 1921 his statue of Alexander Agassiz was unveiled in Boston, and in the same year the enormous marble block of his "Benjamin Franklin," for Waterbury, Connecticut, was finished. In the latter the sculptor attempted to show his subject at a dramatic moment of brilliant inspiration, but the dynamic pose somehow seems at odds with the commonly held image of the quiet, practical Quaker. Far more successful was the bronze statue of Franklin's contemporary Sir William Blackstone, the English barrister, judge, and commentator on the law. The dynamic quality in this statue is in the noble bearing of the subject rather than in his excited attitude. The "Blackstone," executed in Bartlett's London studio in 1923–1924, was a gift of the American Bar Association to its British counterpart, and was set up in London in the Royal Law Courts, near the subject's former chambers. The last of Bartlett's statues was the "Robert Morris" for Philadelphia, unveiled in the fall of 1925.

In late August of that year Paul Bartlett stumbled and fell on the lawn of a friend's house in the Ardennes. He cut his wrist on a rock, but it was only a scratch, and no one thought anything about it. In three weeks blood poisoning had set in, and on September 20, at the age of sixty, he died. The ranks of the conservative element in American sculpture thus lost one of its more gifted standard bearers.

Herbert Adams (1858–1945) spent his youth in New England, where he attended school at Fitchburg, Massachusetts, then went to the Institute of Technology at Worcester, and finally to the Massachusetts Normal Art School. His serious pursuit of art began about a decade after the end of the Civil War— when America was beginning to launch into a vigorous new era of materialistic growth and artistic activity. Very little is known about Adams' career in the late 1870's and early 1880's, but in 1885 he went to Paris, where he remained for five years. At the Ecole des Beaux-Arts he studied with the renowned Mercié, and within two years he had his own studio. From these years dates a bronze fountain (1888) of two boys playing with turtles, for the city of Fitchburg, Massachusetts. The work that brought him his first acclaim, however, was a lovely and exceedingly feminine bust of Adeline V. Pond (in the Hispanic Society of America), who was soon to become his bride, and who would later be famous as Adeline Adams, author and critic. The bust was shown at the Paris Salon of 1888. Although it is executed in marble, the precise contours and smooth surfaces, the lack of expression of the neoclassical marmorean effigies, and the dry objectivity of pre-Civil War naturalism, are no longer present. Instead there is a lively, alert countenance, a sparkle in the eye, the promise of a smile; and the marble has been rendered in a way that suggests the spontaneity of a wax or clay sketch. There is a remarkable softness to the flesh, the hair has a silky quality, and a gossamer fabric envelops the shoulders. In this bust, Herbert Adams created a new type of feminine portrait that would, in a few short years, make him famous among American sculptors.

Adams returned to America in 1890, and at the Columbian Exposition of 1893 he was represented by the bust of Adeline Pond and two others—"Primavera" (Fig. 12.7) and "Saint Agnes." These were Adams' conception of the ultimate in feminine beauty, and they were at once accepted as a new ideal image of womanly grace and loveliness. Adams departed from the pure white of his predecessors' marble images by tinting certain areas of the "Primavera" and "Saint Agnes." These touches of color made the portraits even more decorative and much livelier than the ashen blandness of those wrought a quarter of a century earlier by Hiram Powers or William Rinehart. The gown that barely covers the shoulders of the "Primavera" is polychromed blue, and the bandeau in her hair is gold. The pupils of the eyes have color; the palest of tints are on the lips and brows; and the hair is a soft brown. A later bust called "Marianna," a girl masquerading as an 18th-century marquise, seems to take its coloration from a French Rococo portrait, with its soft tints of rose, light blue, and gray. All this was considered a brilliant artistic achievement and praised for its vivaciousness. MacMonnies had created a new kind of female figure in his dancing "Bacchante," also largely French-inspired, and Adams achieved as much with the feminine portrait bust. Both were in contrast to the bold naturalism of Saint-Gaudens' neo-Renaissance style and the cool aloofness of Daniel Chester French. The softness and decorative qualities of this early work by Adams may be traced to the work of such Frenchmen as Camille Lefèvre, and François Larche; the idea of polychroming the image may stem from the work of Louis Auguste Rivière. About 1893, Adams created "La Jeunesse," now in the Metropolitan Museum of Art. The gown of this piece was wrought in fruitwood and ornamented with paste jewels and twisted wire. The tinted portrait of Julia Marlowe should also be added to the list of ideal busts.

Soon after he returned to America, Adams began teaching at the newly established Pratt Institute in Brooklyn, and he remained on the faculty of the art school until 1898. Quincy Ward, Saint-Gaudens, Olin Warner, Daniel Chester French, and MacMonnies were all in New York City then, and all enjoying success. If Adams' star did not shine as brightly as theirs, it nevertheless glowed with an ever-increasing luster. During this period he was influenced more by Saint-Gaudens than by any of the others, as may be seen in his 1894 marble relief "The Singing Boys" (Fig. 12.8). Adams' relief relies more on a soft delicate modeling than on the linear element favored by Saint-Gaudens. But Adams' debt to Saint-Gaudens is unmistakable, and includes even the decorative use of the inscription that identifies the three Campbell boys.

In the late 1890's Adams was forced to give up his teaching to attend to his many commissions. He was given the task of completing the Congressional Library's bronze doors, which were left unfinished at Olin Warner's death. In keeping with the mode of personifying abstract concepts, Adams decorated the valves with robed female figures who represent Truth and Research. Next, he did the winged "Victory" for the triumphal arch erected for Admiral Dewey. Adams was represented at the Pan-American Exposition at Buffalo (1901) by the group known as "The Age of Enlightenment," an allegory depicting "the blessing, in a modern sense, of religion, education, and the family." According to the *Art Handbook* of the Exposition:

This group symbolizes the intellectual character of an intellectual age. A female figure representing Learning sits with an open scroll on her knee and instructs a boy and a girl. On one side is a figure with a lyre, representing the Arts. A palette and the masks of Comedy and Tragedy are at her feet. In her left hand she holds a laurel wreath. On the other side is Science with one hand resting on a globe and the other on a book.

These were prestigious commissions, and as the new century opened, Herbert Adams stood among the leaders of his art. In addition to his portrait and ideal busts of women, he had proven himself in monumental sculpture. He was given the commission for the bronze statue of William Ellery Channing for Boston's Public Garden. It is a bold design, with a fine large mass created in the full-length ministerial robe and its ample sleeves; a spirited vigor informs the figure, and the head is a sensitive portrait.

That Adams could achieve a truly sculptural form is seen in his portrait statue of Professor Joseph Henry (Fig. 12.10) for the Library of Congress. The head of Professor Henry is strongly modeled and well constructed, with an exciting texture and a boldness in the rendering of the hair. The great academic robe also has an interesting texture, blended—about the shoulders, chest, and sleeves—with a delicate linearity and well-designed folds. The impact of Saint-Gaudens is very apparent here. By this time Adams had opened a studio in the quiet hills of Cornish, New Hampshire, just across the ridge from Saint-Gaudens' summer studio-residence.

In 1911 Adams' quiet and pensive bronze image of William Cullen Bryant (Fig. 12.9), seated in large masses of enveloping robes, was unveiled in its neo-Renaissance niche; the niche had been designed by Thomas Hastings, one of the architects of the New York Public Library. The monument is erected against the rear wall of the library building. The exedra-like setting unfortunately deprives the statue of the monumentality that it does possess, and the bigness of the figure is not sensed until one stands close enough to it to block from view the great urns at the sides and much of the architectural setting itself. But monumental it is, and moving too, in its inspired portrayal of the famed poet and friend of artists.

The "Channing" in Boston, the "Henry" in Washington, and the "Bryant" in New York represent the apogee of Adams' career, attained in the first decade of the 20th century. In these three monuments he approached the creative powers of Saint-Gaudens (d. 1907) and J. Q. A. Ward (d. 1910), and it appeared as if he were to be their successor in the art of the portrait statue. But it was not to be, and although he remained a much-respected sculptor in the following decades, his position was assailed by the advance of modern art. Adams created other works during the first decade of the century—such as the bronze doors for St. Bartholomew's Church, New York, a number of symbolic figures for the Brooklyn Institute of Arts and Sciences, and the bronze doors for the American Academy of Arts and Letters. But he never appproached the symbolic art of Daniel Chester French to the same degree that his portraits challenged those of Saint-Gaudens and Ward. He attempted to enter the age-old contest to create the most ideal nude female figure, submitting as his entry "The Nymph of Fynmere" (Cooperstown, New York) of 1916 to join the Dianas and the Bacchantes, the Clyties and the Captives; but he did not pursue this form of expression.

Like others of his generation, Herbert Adams was called upon to create personifying images, such as those robed maidens bearing wreaths and flags for the war memorials at Fitchburg (1917) and Winchester (1927), Massachusetts. By no means at his best in these monuments, still his contemporaries thought highly of them. His McMillan Fountain in Washington, D.C., of three graceful, diaphanous-robed maidens standing with their backs to each other was awarded the medal of honor by the Architectural League in 1916. After World War I had ended, Adams' greatest period was over; his art was being replaced by a new mode of sculptural expression.

During the years between the two World Wars, Adams was preoccupied with a contemporary American theme, but a rather curious one for a serious artist—the debutante. He was probably seeking to return, as it were, to the successes he had enjoyed earlier with his ideal images of lively, fashionable women. But the motif was not taken seriously by others and seemed inconsequential in comparison with the universal ideas and problems that then haunted men. The "Bride" of 1938 would fall into the same category as the numerous versions of the "Debutante" (1925, 1935, 1943). There were a few portrait busts from these years, such as the "Will Rogers" of 1937, and some decorative work like the "Sea Scape" of 1935 at Brookgreen Gardens. He also made several designs for medals. Meanwhile, he was twice made president of the National Sculpture Society, and was named honorary president for life in 1933. But the battle for leadership in American sculpture that raged between the National Sculpture Society and the proponents of abstract art was being won by the abstractionists. Seen from a historical vantage point, everything that took place in the career of Herbert Adams after 1920 was, if not an anticlimax then at least passé. He died in 1945, at the age of eighty-seven.

Charles Grafly (1862–1929) was the youngest of eight children born in Philadelphia to Dutch-German parents. He grew up in the environment of a Quaker home and was educated at a public school. His artistic talent had only begun to reveal itself when young Charles saw sculpture displayed at the Philadelphia Centennial of 1876. Three years later his father, a craftsman himself, arranged for Charles to begin an apprenticeship in the Struthers stone yard. He was then seventeen years old. It was in the stone yard that his career was determined as he became adept at carving architectural ornament; some of the stones that make up the profusion of decoration on the Philadelphia City Hall were carved by young Grafly.

Realizing the limitations of the craft he was learning, Charles took some formal instruction at the Spring Garden Institute. Then, after five years in the stone yard, he was ready to commit himself fully to his art, and he began studying at the Pennsylvania Academy of the Fine Arts. Thomas Eakins was then teaching drawing from the nude figure and anatomy from the dissected corpse; Grafly was a student at the Academy in 1886 when the controversial painter precipitated a scandal in his women's drawing class by removing the loincloth from a male model. Thereafter it was Thomas Anshutz who taught the drawing classes, continuing the Eakins tradition of mastery of the human figure without the gloss of antiquity's idealism.

These years prepared Grafly well for his study in Paris, which began in 1888. In his anatomy lessons at the Pennsylvania Academy he had learned the fundamental structure and form of the human figure; in the art schools of Paris his proclivity toward ideal subjects was first nourished. At the Académie Julian he studied with the then renowned sculptor Henri Michel Chapu, and he continued his study of the human figure in the drawing classes of Adolphe Bouguereau and Fleury at the Ecole des Beaux-Arts. Toward the end of this two-year period in Paris he modeled the heads of Saint John and Daedalus, which he exhibited at the Salon of 1890. They received little attention there, amid all the works by men with fine artistic reputations; but when Grafly returned to America later that spring, the Pennsylvania Academy took notice of them and bought the plaster "Daedalus," which was later cast in bronze.

However, Philadelphia was not Paris, and the artist life in the city did not offer the exhilaration of the Left Bank and the Parisian studios. By fall of that year he had returned to France, and after acquiring a studio of his own he began working on a life-size nude female figure. His statue was titled "Mauvais Présage" when it was shown at the Paris Salon of 1891, and when exhibited at the Columbian Exposition in Chicago two years later it was known by its English version, "A Bad Omen." Although Grafly was destined to achieve distinction in sculptured portraiture, by the early 1890's it was clear that he preferred to work with the ideal figure in images that expressed some basic element of human existence. In this he became a kindred spirit of George Grey Barnard.

After remaining in France for two years, he returned to the United States to teach. Before leaving, however, he toured Europe's famous art collections to prepare himself for his new work. During the next three years much of Grafly's creative energy was absorbed by his classes in drawing and modeling at both the Pennsylvania Academy and the Drexel Institute, but his work began to attract attention beyond Philadelphia. In 1892 he modeled an exquisite bust of his mother that possessed the bold truthfulness, the strength of form, and the sensitivity of the portraiture of Thomas Eakins. This was one of the pieces he exhibited at the Columbian Exposition in Chicago in 1893, and in recognition of Grafly's talent in both portraiture and ideal work, he was awarded a medal. In that same year he became a charter member of the National Sculpture Society, and he produced the bronze statuette of Aeneas and Anchises (Fig. 12.11), whose rippling surfaces recall the Romantic and dramatic emotionalism of the work of Auguste Rodin. But he still longed for Paris.

Grafly was married in the late spring of 1895, and shortly afterward he and his bride embarked for France. He took a studio that was reached by entering an old gateway at 115 rue Notre Dame des Champs, going past the lodge of the concierge, through another gateway, and into a picturesque courtyard. In this low rambling building the sculptor began work on his first monumental and symbolic piece—"Vulture of War." There was no commission for this heroic group; it was an idea the artist had had for some time. Grafly frequently created his symbolic pieces on his own, foreshadowing that principle of modern art that holds that the greatest art comes from within the artist himself, independent of the requirements and conditions that usually accompany a commissioned work. Lorado Taft recognized this in 1903 when he wrote in *History of American Sculpture:* "Mr. Grafly . . . persists in developing these strange fancies of his in spite of considerable cost. He seems to think that this is what sculpture is for—the expression of one's own ideas in form—and he protests that he does it because he 'must.'" The group consists of a central figure representing War, who swings a scythe in the form of a man; across the blade of the scythe is the limp figure of a dead woman, who symbolizes the death and destruction that always accompanies war. On the back of War is perched the hideous vulture, patiently waiting "to reap from the carnage his impious harvest." Thus, Grafly sought to express the vital, emotionally charged concept of man's inhumanity to man through the traditional means of personification; the day when symbolism and abstract concepts would be expressed through abstract or nonobjective forms was still a decade or two away.

The "Vulture" won him recognition wherever it was shown—at the Paris Exposition of 1900 (where it won a gold medal), at Buffalo's Pan-American Exposition of 1901, and at the St. Louis Fair in 1904. At these same world expositions Grafly exhibited his group "Symbol of Life," which was completed in 1897 in his studio in Philadelphia. It represented two nude figures—a young man and a young woman—striding side by side in energetic posture. This may well have been the sculptor's optimistic counterpart to the pessimistic "Vulture." The man holds a true scythe—symbol of the peaceful pursuit of farming and of toiling for food for his family; the woman holds an ivory orb from which springs a shaft of wheat—symbol of fecundity. Another work of these years was titled "From Generation to Generation"—a boy and his grandfather, both deep in thought as they gaze at the winged dial of a clock.

Grafly's reputation was by then virtually nationwide. At the Botolph Club in Boston in 1901, for example, a large number of his works were assembled, including a strange, enigmatic figure for the Fountain of Man, which he had made for the world's fair in Buffalo that year. At the Pan-American Exposition the complex iconographic program of the sculptural monuments dealt with such allegories as the savage, the despotic, and the enlightened ages of man, and Grafly was assigned the task of treating man himself (Fig. 13.5). In his crowning figure for the fountain, he chose to illustrate the dual nature of man, a theme that had also fascinated George Grey Barnard. He enlarged upon this idea with thirteen additional figures, all of it being described by Karl Bitter in the official *Art Handbook* of the Exposition:

The central feature, the Fountain of Man, is composed of a number of groups surmounted by the single figure of a "Man the Mysterious," portrayed with two faces and two bodies, emblematic of the two natures of man. It is partly veiled, creating the impression of mysterious dignity. The pedestal upon which the figure stands is borne by a striking group typifying the Five Senses. Below this is a large lower basin, and outlined against its cavernous shadows may be discerned through the dripping waters the writing forms of the virtues struggling with the vices. The whole rises to a height of fifty-three feet.

Grafly's image of Man is indeed a mysterious one, and few if any of the general public, artists, or critics who saw it could perceive its total meaning. Two figures of men are addorsed to form one being, swathed in drapery that conceals the union of the two bodies. Only Grafly himself fully understood the fine points of his symbolism—such as the handle-like cap that joins the two heads—but the primary meaning of the two natures of man, good and bad, active and passive, is clear enough. The writing pairs of virtues and vices at the bottom further suggest the coexistence of such opposites as love and hatred, courage and cowardice, within man. The sculptor's intention to affiliate his Man with an ancient image of the Egyptian priesthood—in the costume, the rigid stance, and the pegs in the hands—is quite clear, but his reason for the alliance is not. In this monument, as in many of his symbolic works, Grafly sought to "reveal the forces in life that have manifested themselves through the ages." But, the difference between Grafly's symbolism and, say, that of Daniel Chester French is that Grafly's symbolism was very personal and often intelligible only to him, whereas French created personifications that were just as universal, but whose meaning was far less obscure. Even Lorado Taft called Grafly's symbolism "exasperating" and chastised him, remarking that "a pure, wholesome, reasonable art does not take such liberties with nature, even in order to convey a psychological idea."

In the "Fountain of Man," Grafly reached what was perhaps the apogee of his symbolic sculpture. There were other forays, of course, such as "In Much Learning," which was shown at the St. Louis Fair of 1904, along with the pert nude female seated within the throne of an oyster, which the sculptor called quite simply, "Truth." For the New York Customs House he created uncomplicated personifications of France and Great Britain; these figures were done around 1905. But about this time a major change occurred in Grafly's work. His interest shifted from symbolic imagery to portraiture, and the later part of his career is concerned largely with portrait busts and a few full-length figures. At the Louisiana Purchase Exposition of 1904, he exhibited as many portraits as imaginative works. In addition to his wife's likeness, there were the bronze heads of Dr. Louis Starr,

Joseph R. DeCamp, and James McManes. His reputation in portraiture grew quickly, as if America found the change refreshing and welcomed it. One of his finest is the bronze bust of Edward Willis Redfield (Fig. 12.12), which was made in 1909. The modeling is both sensitive and strong, and there is an expression of alertness and liveliness in the eyes and at the mouth. The breadth of modeling in the masses and planes eliminates distracting details, which portraiture of the mid-19th century had dwelt upon, with the result that his sculptured heads were true works of art instead of merely good likenesses.

Adeline Adams, the critic, called Grafly "the foremost American sculptor of male portrait-busts"; as such, he would have held a position equal to the one that her husband, Herbert Adams, then enjoyed as a sculptor of portraits of women. But there was actually greater substance in Grafly's fine portrait heads. Adeline Adams also described Grafly's method of taking a bust: "He cared little to have his subjects 'pose' before him. With his mastery of construction he 'caught the likeness' as they walked at ease about his workshop." (Quoted from the *Dictionary of American Biography*.) In 1917, in his *Modern Tendencies in Sculpture*, Lorado Taft praised Grafly's portraits, saying, "In his hands the soul gives up its secrets," and declared that in comparison most of the other contemporary portraiture looked like "decaying vegetables" and "frostbitten pumpkins."

The simple truthfulness, unencumbered by details or frills, that Grafly first learned as a student in Thomas Eakins' drawing classes, developed into one of the finest portrait styles of the day. His bold but refined naturalism is seen in his portrait of Hugh Breckenridge (Fig. 12.13), in which the softer modeling of the French school is quite evident. The same may also be observed in a number of bronze likenesses of his artist friends in the Philadelphia Museum of Art: "Paul Wayland Bartlett" (1910), "Frank Duveneck" (1915), and "Childe Hassam." Between 1900 and 1910 Grafly produced three pieces for the Smith Memorial in Fairmount Park, Philadelphia—a standing figure of General John Fulton Reynolds and two large busts of John B. Gest and Admiral David D. Porter, all in bronze.

The Armory Show of 1913—with its "riot of deformities," as some viewed it—came and went, with virtually no impact on Grafly's work. In 1915 he prepared the model of a statue for a memorial to The Pioneer Mother, a sturdy standing woman, with a little boy and girl clinging to her skirts. In the following decade there were additional portrait busts, but his major project was the Meade Memorial in Washington, D.C. The marble monument, dedicated in 1925, has a heroic figure of General Meade as the focal point, with two groups of allegorical nude and seminude figures behind him. Loyalty, Fame, Chivalry, and Progress accompany him, and winged War is flanked by muscular youths who represent Energy and Military Courage. Crowning the group is an eagle within a wreath, reminiscent of the standards carried before the generals of ancient Rome. The allegorical groups at the sides are generally similar in concept to the figures George Grey Barnard made for the Pennsylvania State Capitol building in Harrisburg, and they also recall William Sievers' monument to "Maury, Pathfinder of the Seas" (1927–1929), which is in Monument Boulevard in Richmond, Virginia. But 1925 seems late for a sculptor to employ allegorical forms to express abstract ideas.

The last major piece that occupied Charles Grafly was a standing bronze figure of President Buchanan (1927), destined for Lancaster, Pennsylvania. The artist considered it one of his most successful works. By the time of its unveiling he was sixty-five years old. Two years later, while crossing a street in Philadelphia, he was hit by a car, and he died shortly afterward in the hospital. His reputation had first been established by his symbolic pieces; then later he won distinction with his portraits. But in time, the march of 20th-century art passed him by. At his death, however, he was still one of the most respected sculptors of the academic old guard.

In the late 19th century there were several forces working upon the course of American sculpture, as it experienced regeneration after the doldrums of the post-Civil War era, and certainly the French influence was of enormous importance. There was the decorative element in both style and subject matter, the invigorated naturalism in portraiture, and the use of personification, all of which have already been mentioned. A fourth element was a highly romantic and expressive one, that was unleashed through the supercharged spirits and titanic figures of George Grey Barnard. Like Rodin, he electrified his figures with the most powerful emotions that mankind may experience, filling them with love or hate, anguish or fear, joy or sorrow. Both Rodin and Barnard were primarily concerned with the spirit rather than the matter of man, but they employed the flesh in a bold dramatic fashion to express what dwelt within.

George Grey Barnard (1863–1938) grew up in the Midwest. Born in Bellefonte, Pennsylvania, he was moved about as a child when his father, a Presbyterian minister, took pastorates in Illinois, Iowa, and Wisconsin. While still a boy he amused himself with his hobby of taxidermy, creating a little museum of stuffed birds and animals in the barn of the parsonage. There are also reports of small creatures he modeled in clay or mud, and even a portrait bust he made of his younger sister that seems to have astonished everyone. But no one in the family gave much thought to his pursuing a career in sculpture, and eventually he was taken to a local jeweler to learn the skills of the engraver. He seems to have enjoyed his work and soon became quite proficient at it, but he had already begun to dream of becoming an artist some day. The family could not afford to send him to art school, but George's heart was set on it; he saved a little money, and when he was seventeen years old he set out for Chicago and art school. This was the beginning of lean years during which Barnard lived the life of a struggling art student, with only his skill as an engraver earning him enough for the barest necessities. But he reveled in this life and worked hard. When he was not engraving inscriptions on gold and silver vessels or jewelry, he was in the classrooms of the Chicago Art Institute, drawing and modeling. He was profoundly impressed by some large casts of sculptures by Michelangelo, an influence that was to bear fruit in some of his earliest marble pieces.

Chicago was not one of the art centers of the United States in 1880, and few sculptors were then working there. Many years later Barnard recalled that only a few statues existed in Chicago when he studied there: One was of Sir Walter Scott; and the others were of Indians and were carved by a man named Richards. It was this same Richards who taught Barnard how to use the mallet and chisel, and it was in Richards' studio that Barnard carved the portrait heads of two children. His recompense for these portraits was sufficient to pay his way to Paris in 1883.

There was quite a colony of American sculptors in Paris in the mid-1880's—Paul Bartlett, Edwin Elwell, Frederick MacMonnies, and Herbert Adams; Augustus Saint-Gaudens was there part of the time, as was Daniel Chester French. Of these, MacMonnies seems to have been his closest friend, but Barnard kept largely to himself, living in extremely impoverished circumstances and working with fierce intensity. For over two years he studied at the Ecole des Beaux-Arts and in the atelier of the elderly Pierre Jules Cavelier. About his only known work of this period is the crouching figure "Boy." Barnard made remarkable progress during these years, and it was only natural that someone would eventually recognize his special talents, even though he withheld his work from the annual exhibitions at the Salons. In the spring of 1886, Alfred Corning Clark, the man who was to be Barnard's benefactor for the next ten years, saw his clay statue "Boy."

Clark's first encouragement came with a commission to put the "Boy" into marble; Barnard was overjoyed as he purchased the large marble block, for he was confident this was the beginning of great things for him. And he was right. Before long he took a fine studio at 12 rue Boissonade, where in 1887 he executed his first major commission—the memorial to the Norwegian poet Severin Skovgaard, which was eventually set up in Langesund, Norway. Skovgaard had been a friend of Alfred Corning Clark's; Barnard, too, had known him and his family intimately and had made several visits to the Skovgaard home in Norway. The subject of the memorial was Brotherly Love, represented by two nude male figures standing at the sides of a vertical stone slab; they turn toward one another with faces concealed but with hands touching, in a manner both tortured and sensitive. The contortions of these muscular figures suggest the profound emotions within. The influence of Michelangelo and the dynamic spirit within his marmorean giants is evident; this is especially noticeable in a smaller copy that Barnard made for Clark in 1894, in which the figures only partially emerge from the rough-hewn rock, very much like Michelangelo's "Slave"; but the figure style itself is more reminiscent of Rodin.

Up to 1894 Barnard was content to work in his studio under the patronage of Alfred Corning Clark. He apparently did not need to seek approval and acclaim from the general public or his fellow artists, and therefore he remained largely an unknown figure within Parisian art circles. But in 1894 Barnard made his appearance with a great crescendo as critics, artists, and public all marveled at the awesome power and expressiveness of his "Two Natures" (Fig. 12.14).

The title of "Two Natures" was taken from Victor Hugo's "Je sens deux hommes en moi," and Barnard's group represents, quite typically, the different forces that dominate man's soul or inner being. Barnard found such subjects far more fascinating than the rendering of the objective appearance of things. The history of the group goes back to the early part of 1888; by spring of that year Barnard had finished his studies for what he then called his "group of Liberty." In these initial stages there was never any suggestion of the two-natures theme, and even the "Liberty" was soon transformed into a "Victory" group. The central motif is that in all conflicts victor and vanquished suffer alike. One man triumphs over the other, but on the face of the standing figure there is no expression of victory, nor is there one of defeat in the face of the reclining figure. By June of 1888 more than two tons of clay had been put into the full-size model, which was nearly 8½ feet high. Barnard later reminisced in an interview that his own blood went into the group, for as he would claw at the clay to shape various parts, his fingers would rake over the wires of the armature, leaving his blood to mix with the clay. Perhaps the anecdote is somewhat exaggerated, but it suggests the gusto with which Barnard worked. Indeed, he wrote home that he had built up the two tons of clay into the full-size model in only two days.

Work on the group lingered over the next three years; it remained under damp cloths much of the time and not reaching the finished state until the early spring of 1891, when it was cast in plaster. Once this was accomplished, the sculptor was anxious to have it translated into marble; for Barnard, the modeled clay represented life, whereas the plaster replica was the death of the piece, and the marble version was its resurrection. At this point Alfred Corning Clark commissioned it to be put into marble, and Barnard departed for Carrara in May 1891. It was to be another three years, however, before the group would be finished. The plaster group—still unnamed as far as can be discovered—was sent to Carrara, where Italian stonecutters blocked out the rough forms. By the middle of 1892 the two figures stood in the center of Barnard's studio in Paris, where he himself found a great delight in working down to the final form the enormous hulking shapes of his two protagonists. Word about the magnificent group was already spreading among students and artists, but work advanced at a slow pace. Meanwhile other figures in the studio continued to emerge from marble blocks. There was the small version of "Brotherly Love" for Clark, and two equally Michelangelesque figures entitled "The Elements"; these two figures were derived from an ingenious design for what was called the "Norwegian stove," studies for which date from 1891 and recalled Rodin's tormented figures of the "Gates of Hell." In the meantime Barnard had fallen in love with Edna Monroe of Boston (who was to become his wife in 1895), and the artist found himself quite distracted from his work by her beauty and charm. It was not until May 1894 that he could put down his mallet and chisel and write home to his parents that the work was done. A little over a month later it was sent to the Salon. As the huge figures left his studio and were taken into the street, people stared in awed silence; even before the work's presentation at the Salon, George Grey Barnard was confident of its success.

Barnard sent six pieces to the Salon: "the group," the two "Elements," "Boy," a bronze bust (one of Barnard's rare portraits of this period), and a plaster head of one of the figures of "the group." The struggling giants were placed in an excellent location and were at that time labeled "Je sens deux hommes en moi." "Two Natures," as the group has come to be called, was among the most spectacular successes of the Salon that year; Barnard received praise from all sides—even from Rodin himself—and the sudden appearance of a genius was proclaimed in numerous articles in the French press. Virtually overnight George Grey Barnard ceased to be an unknown: He was immediately elected an associate of the Société Nationale des Beaux-Arts and was suddenly a major figure in the world of European and American sculptors.

In 1896 Barnard's friend and patron, Alfred Corning Clark, died; his estate made a gift of the "Two Natures" to the then embryonic collection of American sculpture in the Metropolitan Museum of Art. In that same year an exhibition of Barnard's work was held in New York City, but in spite of his growing fame, his reception there was considerably less enthusiastic than at the Paris Salon of 1894. Barnard had been warned by Rodin and others to remain in Paris and not to return to America, but he had not taken their advice.

The major projects of the years 1896 to 1900 were "Hewer" and the nature god "Pan." The latter recalls the languishing gigantic figures of Michelangelo and represents the pagan god in a powerful, sensuous image in which both human and animal characteristics exist in equal portions. The "Pan" was commissioned by Clark, who died before it could be cast in bronze; it is now on the campus of Columbia University. In 1895 Barnard modeled a group titled "Primitive Man," comprising more than half a dozen figures in a viking-type ship, which is being attacked by a huge sea serpent. During the next few years several of the figures were enlarged slightly, but ultimately only one was to be finished and wrought on a heroic scale; this was the "Hewer," a primitive man who was shown carving an oar from a piece of wood. Barnard liked the theme of primitive man, perhaps because it allowed him to explore basic man, with his fears and struggles, his virtues and his vices—a man seen naked of soul as well as of body.

"Hewer" was completed in marble in 1902, and Barnard later created a kneeling "Primitive Woman" as his mate. Both these figures are now in a private collection in Pocantico Hills, New York. There is a supple, masculine beauty to the form of the Hewer, exquisitely modeled, with every fiber of the taut body concentrated on the labor at hand. Lorado Taft, who reproduced a large illustration of the clay model, may well have realized the position of this figure in the history of American sculpture when he wrote that "no other nude figure of the strength of 'The Hewer' had up to this time [1903] been done or even conceived in America."

Around the turn of the century Barnard's work was shown at the major expositions at home and abroad. As part of the American Fine Arts exhibition his "Two Natures," along with the "Pan," returned to the Paris Exposition of 1900. At Buffalo's Pan-American Exposition he was represented by two groups—"Primeval Niagara" and "Niagara Today"; these groups, placed at the base of the tower that was crowned by Herbert Adams' "Goddess of Light," were made of the impermanent staff material and have long since disappeared. The "Two Natures," and the "Pan" were also displayed at Buffalo, the former winning a gold medal. His "Hewer" was shown at the St. Louis Fair of 1904, and a bronze copy of it was made for Cairo, Illinois. During these years, 1901 to 1904, Barnard had succeeded Augustus Saint-Gaudens' as instructor of sculpture at the Art Students League in New York. Meanwhile, in his own studio he began to work on the small-scale models for the sculptures of the capitol at Harrisburg, probably the most important commission of his entire career.

The Harrisburg commission was the kind Barnard had dreamed of all his life—highly symbolic and expressive of lofty virtues and vile sins, vast in scope, comprising a large number of nude figures and (at first, anyway) an iconographic program of great complexity. It was a commission worthy of a challenge to Michelangelo in his finest days, when he was working on the Julius Tomb or the Medici Chapel figures. Barnard liked such comparisons; in fact, around 1910—when the sculptures were completed—he boasted (in an erroneous statement) that "Michelangelo did only nineteen figures in all his life. The big plan we agreed upon had in it sixty-seven figures." In the same interview he reminisced about his first meeting with the architect and the commissioners:

They had filled in the plans with a lot of stock figures that may be found everywhere . . . . Within ten minutes I had sketched out a plan of work that met with hearty approval. It wasn't so impromptu, tho, for in the plan I concentrated a lifetime of study and thought. I was glad to put together what I had been thinking and studying about for years.

[Quoted from "Barnard's Mighty Sculptures for the Pennsylvania Capitol," *Current Opinion*, vol. 49, 1910, pp. 207–209]

The original plan, however, was far more grandiose than the one that finally materialized. Originally there were to have been four groups of sculptures: An enormous bronze composition along the skyline of the main entrance façade was to represent the Apotheosis of Labor, for labor and industry had contributed significantly to the development of the state; below this were to be four pairs of caryatids symbolizing the types of labor. Flanking the main entrance were to be two large groups representing "some allegorical conception," primarily concerned with primitive peoples; these were the ones the sculptor ultimately produced. Finally the wing entrances were to be flanked by the four groups of peoples who had settled the state—English, Quakers, Scotch-Irish, and Germans or Dutch. In an effort to conserve both time and money, the plan was quickly reduced by the commissioners to the two allegorical groups for the main entrance, with the outrageous demand that Barnard have all his work completed in three years, or by 1905. Barnard was so anxious to have the commission that he agreed to virtually all terms; on December 12, 1902, he signed the contract, which was to pay him $100,000 (instead of the original $300,000) for the entire project.

During the course of the next few years the small models for the two groups took form in his New York studio. They were to represent "The Broken Law" and "The Unbroken Law" and were to be "symbolic of man's destiny on Earth," his drives, desires, and passions. Recalling the processions on the Last Judgment tympana of Gothic cathedrals, where the resurrected souls of the blessed and damned march off either to heaven or hell, Barnard's two groups possess either the joyous confidence of the virtuous or the anguish of those who led evil lives. The assemblage of "The Broken Law" begins at the back of the procession where Adam and Eve stand amid the lush-bowered garden setting, suggestive of Eden, from which they and their descendants were expelled. The other figures march off, bearing burdens, writhing in pain, or concealing their faces in shame for their sins. Among these figures of "the Paradise that fails because it is not the fruit of Man's Labor," there is a large peacock, symbol of human vanity, and a figure representing the annihilation, or the "lost soul." Opposite these tormented souls is the group "The Unbroken Law" (Fig. 12.16), in which youthful hope, expectation, and confidence, plus family felicity, are the dominant themes. This group could also be described as Labor at Rest, or Love and Labor, most clearly embodied in the man at the rear, who rests his arm on his scythe; but brotherhood and parenthood are also present, along with the youthful antithesis of the "lost soul."

By 1904 the iconographic program and the general design of the two groups had been worked out on a small scale, and Barnard and his family departed for France, where the full-size models would be made and the marble statues finally carved. He did not go to Paris, but chose the seclusion of the little town of Moret-sur-Loing, near Fontainebleau. There he worked over the next several years, frequently with as many as fifteen assistants and models in the barn which he had converted into a studio. Then in 1906 came news of the Harrisburg scandal of the misuse of funds for the capitol, and all payments were stopped immediately. The state's initial payment of $20,000 had been modest enough, considering the expense of the large blocks of marble, their transportation costs, and the operation of a sizable studio. Barnard's investment in both time and money was already enormous when the entire project suddenly appeared to be in jeopardy. His workmen agreed to remain with him, in hopes of being paid at a later date. At this time Barnard began selling the medieval antiquities, which he picked up as he toured the French countryside or else acquired from dealers. In a relatively short period he not only turned a profit of some $20,000—enough to pay his bills and his assistants—he also laid the foundation of his own extraordinary collection of medieval statues, sculptured capitals, reliquaries, crucifixes, and the like, which would ultimately become the basis of The Cloisters museum at the northern tip of Manhattan Island.

Thereafter work progressed well, and through the intervention of a number of prominent New Yorkers, who thought it would be a national disgrace to allow the project to collapse, the state of Pennsylvania agreed to honor its contract with Barnard. The marble cutting proceeded throughout 1909, and by the spring of 1910 the completed sculptures were shown at the Salon in Paris, where their enthusiastic reception equaled that accorded his "Two Natures" in 1894. The venerable Rodin described them as magnificent, and President Theodore Roosevelt expressed his pride in the artistic genius of his countryman. During the winter of 1910–1911 the huge groups were erected on the façade of the capitol in Harrisburg, under the direction of Giulio Piccirilli. A grand celebration was organized for their official unveiling on October 4, 1911, a day designated as Barnard Day. Throngs of spectators assembled as a band played "The Barnard March" and a chorus of school children sang "The Barnard Groups." While flags waved in the warm fall sunshine orators praised the sculptor. So pleased was the state that, on learning of the large expenses incurred by the artist, it awarded him an additional $80,000. All things considered, although not of the grandiose scope he had originally planned, George Grey Barnard was quite satisfied as he gazed at his groups in place.

Barnard had also worked on a few other sculptures during those years, and an exhibition of his work was held in Boston in 1908. The new art museum on Copley Square showed some of his most exciting pieces, among them "Brotherly Love" and "Maidenhood"; and across the way, beside Trinity Church, his marble "Hewer" was displayed. There was a gala opening attended by President Eliot of Harvard and Governor Guild. Barnard himself was there, for the difficulties of the Harrisburg project had brought him back to America for a brief visit. William Howe Downes reviewed the exhibition, and few critics have better understood the essence of Barnard's art than he:

... it is the sheer humanity of his creations which takes hold of us, and gives us a fresh realization of the divinity of human nature, its boundless possibilities, and its glorious destiny . . . . It reminds us of the gospel that man is made in the image of God; that his capacities are godlike; and that, no matter how far he may stray from the right way of life, there is always hope for him . . . . One of the vital words that Mr. Barnard's work has for us is that the only kind of beauty that is a joy forever is moral beauty . . . .   [*World's Work*, vol. 17, 1909, p. 11268]

Barnard participated in the Armory Show of 1913 in New York City, exhibiting a marble replica of his "Prodigal Son" group from the Harrisburg sculptures, plus several pieces from "The Urn of Life," which included figures of "Solitude," "Mystery" and "The Birth." He was one of the few Americans represented in the show whose work seemed to fit in among the strange new forms and color patterns.

For the New York Public Library, which during the years 1913 to 1917 offered one of the major sculptural programs of the country, Barnard created the figures representing the Arts. They were placed in the south pediment of the Fifth

Avenue façade, but the sculptor felt that the firm of Donnelly and Ricci had bungled the job of cutting them in marble.

The next project George Grey Barnard undertook stirred up one of the most heated controversies of early 20th-century American art. Charles P. Taft had given Cincinnati $100,000 to erect a memorial to Lincoln, and the commission went to Barnard. Barnard set out to create his own image of the subject. All photographs, he said, had been retouched and were therefore useless to him, so he finally decided to use the life mask Leonard Volk had made in 1860. For two years he searched for just the right model for the figure; finally, near Louisville, Kentucky, Barnard found a six-foot-four-inch forty-year-old farmer, who had been splitting rails all his life, and persuaded him to pose. The statue was completed in the early part of 1917, cast in bronze at the Roman Bronze Works in Brooklyn, and set up in Cincinnati's Lytle Park soon afterward (Fig. 12.15). It was then that the controversy broke. Barnard was attacked from all sides for creating a portrait of Lincoln that showed him as a coarse, imbecilic dolt, with oversized hands and feet, and clothes that were excessively baggy and rumpled. The expression on Lincoln's face was meant to be one of profound thought, but the critics interpreted it as vacant stupidity. The furor increased when it was proposed to send a replica to London to commemorate one hundred years of peace between the two nations; if it was not considered a fitting image to be shown among Americans themselves, many remonstrated, it certainly should not be presented to foreigners. Some defended the "Lincoln," but more attacked it, and in the eyes of most of his contemporaries Barnard's only serious attempt at portrait statuary was a miserable failure. Copies eventually did go to Manchester, England, and to Louisville. In 1919 the sculptor executed the marble head of Lincoln that is now owned by the Metropolitan Museum of Art, and many years later he worked on a colossal head (16 feet high) of Lincoln, which he always hoped would be set up along the Palisades overlooking the Hudson River. But this wish was never fulfilled.

By 1920 the major part of George Grey Barnard's career was behind him, although he remained active in his New York studio, and his imagination expanded with the passing years. In 1925 he sold most of his collection of medieval art for $600,000 to John D. Rockefeller, who in 1937 presented it to the Metropolitan Museum of Art; they, in turn, installed it at The Cloisters. Barnard had been instrumental in obtaining the Romanesque Hall for the Philadelphia Museum of Art, and during his lifetime many of his medieval sculptures were displayed there. After his death some of these pieces were purchased for the Philadelphia museum.

The earlier commissions and remuneration for his work, plus the sale of his medieval collection to Rockefeller, had left him well-fixed financially. But money in large amounts was a necessity for one who dreamed on the scale that Barnard did; and he had yet another vision of a sculptural project that would surpass all others: the supercolossal Rainbow Arch. For seventeen years he had worked on the design and the final models, and in his will he stated that the bulk of his $750,000 estate should go toward its execution and erection on a site near The Cloisters in Fort Tryon Park. But much more money was needed before work could begin on the final execution of the project. The Rainbow Arch, "dedicated to the Gold Star Mothers of America, as a shrine to our nation, our state and our city," was to be made of marble and would be 100 feet high and spread some 60 feet at the base. There were to be sculptural groups at each side of the arch. All of this was to be placed at the rear of a 350-foot plaza that would also contain a bronze Tree of Life, 40 feet high. Within the arch would be a tomb, and on top of the tomb would lie the marble figure of a dead soldier. Before his death in 1938, Barnard saw a number of the pieces cast in plaster, and in his will he suggested that the Piccirilli brothers of New York City do the carving. When additional funds were not forthcoming in the years after his death, it was made a condition of the sale of the rest of his medieval collection to the Philadelphia Museum of Art that that institution would store the many parts of the arch for at least ten years. But no further attempt was ever made to reactivate the grandiose scheme.

Barnard had once said that he saw all the work of his career as a continuum, and in theme and style—from the early "Two Natures" to the unrealized Arch at the end—there was a continuity. He had explored the depths and the heights of human emotions, and recorded them forever in white marble. He had virtually no affinity with his academic contemporaries. Others may have equaled or surpassed his skills of rendering material forms, but none, save Rodin himself, could rival the expressiveness of his moral tableaux.

All of the sculptors who have so far been discussed in this chapter fell very much under the spell of the Parisian schools of the late 19th century. One of their brotherhood, however, chose to go to Munich to study, with the result that there is the decided influence of German neoclassicism in much of his work. This was Charles Henry Niehaus (1855–1935) who, in a way, represents a continuation of the old tradition of academic realism in portraiture. He was essentially a portrait sculptor, and in the numerous pieces he executed for Statuary Hall and other locations in the Capitol he did indeed perpetuate the prosaic statues and busts typical of the Civil War period. But he belonged to the generation of American sculptors who came to prominence between the Centennial of 1876 and World War I, and at times he, too, was caught up in the Beaux-Arts spirit and style.

Niehaus' work might be described as something of a combination of the naturalistic portraiture of Ward and the symbolic imagery of Daniel Chester French. His touch was not as refined as that of Saint-Gaudens, and he did not have the latter's feeling for delicate linear design; but like Saint-Gaudens, he was so pursued with commissions for portrait statues from the very beginning of his professional career that he was not often allowed to explore the personification of abstract concepts, although his most interesting sculpture belongs to that category.

Born of German immigrant parents who had settled in southern Ohio, Charles Henry Niehaus was set to work at an early age as a carver—first of wood and then of marble. When his special artistic talent revealed itself, he began attending the McMicken School of Design in Cincinnati. Then in 1877 he set out for Europe for further training. He chose Munich with its Royal Academy, where emphasis was placed on the ideal figure and the study of the antique—a situation quite different from the Parisian school of living models. Little is known of Niehaus' work at the Royal Academy, but he did win a first prize for a figure called "Fleeting Time." After receiving his diploma he embarked on a tour of Europe that carried him from one major collection of sculpture to another. But by 1881 the twenty-six-year-old Niehaus was eager to return to America to see what opportunities might await him.

In the summer of 1881, President James Garfield was assassinated. His fellow Ohioans, anxious to demonstrate their affection for the man, at once commissioned two statues of him—one, in marble, was to be the gift of the state to Statuary Hall in Washington; the other, in bronze, to be paid for by public subscription, was to stand in a prominent place in Cincinnati. Niehaus, a native Ohioan, was selected to do the statues; in addition, the state commissioned a second marble statue, that of William Allen, also destined for Statuary Hall.

America was not the place for Niehaus to pit himself against his first great challenge. Once more he rejected Paris, this time choosing Rome. Perhaps it was because two of his commissions were to be executed in marble that he chose Italy, with its excellent white stone and its well-trained carvers; or it may have been the traditions of ancient art that drew him there, for among his major works completed in Rome between 1883 and 1885 are three images of classical inspiration. His training in Munich had taught him that the ideal subject taken from mythology or history offered a greater challenge than the portrait. Consequently, during these years he modeled a figure titled "Caestus," another called "Athlete Scraping Himself with a Strigil," and a third, "Silenus." The "Caestus" is a nude athletic figure of bold naturalism, resembling statues of ancient Roman athletes and thereby possessing the two essential elements advocated by the Royal Academy in Munich. The figure takes its name from the Latin *caestus*, which are leather straps, often studded or leaded, that Roman boxers placed around their fists to protect their hands and increase the damage to their opponents. The original was modeled in 1883 and, according to the sculptor, six replicas were cast in bronze; but at present the whereabouts of only one is known: the Metropolitan Museum of Art has a 38-inch-high copy. The swan song for such work of academic classicism had been sung at the Philadelphia Centennial of 1876, and by the time Niehaus created his "Caestus," American art had largely turned to a lighter variety of French classicism; but in the following decades the statue became a much-admired piece, being shown frequently at the several international expositions held in America, as well as at the National Academy of Design in 1903. The "Athlete with Strigil" was well received at the Columbian Exposition of 1893 (where it won one of its five medals) and at the Pan-American Exposition in 1901. Work of this type was still highly esteemed in Rome, where these pieces won the sculptor membership in the L'Associazione della Artistics di Roma.

Circumstances did not often allow Niehaus to experiment with images of ideal subjects, but one instance was "The Driller" (Fig. 12.18) for the Drake Monument, erected at Titusville, Pennsylvania, to commemorate the discovery of oil there. A 10-foot-high nude youth kneels to pound a drill into the ground. In the raw, rugged naturalism of the image one is reminded of the "Warrior," which sits at the base of Ward's Garfield Monument in Washington, while the figure seems rather academic when compared with the muscle-rippling Rodinesque "Hewer" of George Grey Barnard. Nevertheless, it is one of Niehaus' finest efforts. Niehaus also made one of the large groups for the West Esplanade of the Pan-American Exposition at Buffalo in 1901. In his "Mineral Wealth" (Fig. 12.17) a half-dozen nude male figures are busy with the activities involved in the discovery and refining of gold, and a robed maiden invites men to prosper through the gifts of nature. Photographs of this group show that Niehaus could design and model in the Beaux-Arts style, which dominated the sculpture and architecture at the Exposition.

Thirteen years later Niehaus turned again to classical mythology for inspiration. For the Francis Scott Key Monument in Baltimore, he created an "Orpheus" that was to stand 24 feet high atop a pedestal of about the same height. His model for this statue is now in the National Collection of Fine Arts in Washington. Several artists—among them Rhind, Lukeman, Fraser, and Packer—entered the competition for the Key Monument, which was to be commissioned by the city of Baltimore as part of its celebration, in 1914, of the centennial of the writing of "The Star-Spangled Banner." Niehaus' design was selected as the best of all those submitted. That the figure of Orpheus, famous musician of mythology, should crown the monument is quite fitting. Key's poem itself had been set to a musical score entitled "Anacreon in Heaven," and a critic writing in the July 1917 issue of *Art and Archaeology* explained:

In this memorial the sculptor has paid a tribute not only to the poet who wrote the song, but by representing a colossal figure of Orpheus, he has paid an equally splendid tribute to the genius of music . . . . Thus he has given us an Orpheus instead of presenting the world with one more unlovely portrait of a mere man.

Other heroic and ideal works by Niehaus included "The Triumphant Return" for the left front pier of the Dewey Arch in New York. But it was for his portraiture that he was to become best known, and we must now return to the years 1883 to 1885 to pick up this strain of his work.

It was the two portrait statues of Garfield and the one of Allen that sent Niehaus to Rome in 1883. There, in the three years that followed, he modeled them in his studio in the Villa Strohl-Fern near the Porta del Popolo and the Villa Borghese. The "Garfield" for Cincinnati was to stand out of doors in Piatt Park, and was therefore to be cast in bronze. This allowed greater freedom for the sculptor, and he portrayed the subject in the pose of an animated orator with the papers of his speech held in his right hand. The head is well modeled and possesses both a delicate sensitivity and a profound gravity, but unfortunately it has too much competition from the large mass of the rest of the figure. Moreover, the problem that had long plagued American sculptors—the representation of contemporary dress—also troubled Niehaus, following as he did the older line of Ward rather than the new solutions discovered by Saint-Gaudens. In the marble image that stands in Statuary Hall, it is the same—a rather unexciting image, dominated more by the clothing style of the day than by the spirit of a great man. Lacking the verve and the sculptural form that Saint-Gaudens and others were then instilling into American portrait sculpture, it perpetuates the dry naturalism that characterizes so many of the statues in the Capitol. As if he were consciously following the tradition of Statuary Hall, Niehaus' several other marble portraits in the Hall all possess the same dry naturalism. Those who were in charge of assigning the commissions for such portrait statues were satisfied with that type of imagery, however, for Niehaus executed no less than six marmorean images for Statuary Hall. Especially in the "Allen" from Ohio and the "Morton" from Indiana is the unexciting, lifeless portraiture of post-Civil War American sculpture to be found.

That Charles Niehaus could rise above the limitations of the "tradition of Statuary Hall," however, is evident in a few of his works. His portrait of the venerable master and leader of the American school of sculpture at the turn of the century, John Quincy Adams Ward (Fig. 12.19), contains a vitalized naturalism, which eventually developed in Ward's own work as he, too, conquered the spiritless objectivity of mid-century naturalism. There is a spirit in this portrait that was lacking in the marble Garfield; moreover, the sculptor achieved a lively design in the tucks and folds of the smock, endowing the drapery with a varied richness and a feeling for sculptural form.

Perhaps his greatest triumph in monumental portraiture is the image of Doctor Samuel Hahnemann, seated in a classical exedra, which was designed by Israels and Harder, in Washington, D.C. At a meeting of the American Institute of Homeopathy in 1892, a committee was appointed to receive funds for a bronze statue to honor the founder of the science of homeopathy, and a sum of $50,000 to $70,000 was estimated as necessary. Eight years later the money had been raised, and Charles Niehaus was chosen as the sculptor. A report on the matter, published in 1900, read in part:

... by the advice and assistance of the National Sculptors' [sic] Society, through its distinguished president, Mr. J. Q. A. Ward, a competition was had under the supervision of the following committee of artists and architects, viz., Messrs. Daniel C. French, George E. Bissel, Olin N. [sic] Warner, Thomas Hastings and Russell Sturgis, leading to the submission of twenty-five models, by as many artists, both home and foreign.

It was obviously a major commission and an enormous challenge to those who competed. All twenty-five entries were exhibited in New York City, and both houses of Congress passed resolutions to accept the statue for the Capital when it was finished. The competition caused a great deal of excitement among sculptors on both sides of the Atlantic, and it was a moment of great joy for Niehaus when he received word that his design had been chosen. He represented the brilliant scientist wearing a long academic gown, seated and deep in thought, with his head resting on his right hand. By enveloping the figure in the robe he eliminated the problem of contemporary dress and was able to concentrate attention on the head of his subject. Niehaus modeled the head from a portrait bust that had been made by the Frenchman David d'Angers; it has some of the verve found in the sculptor's portrait of Ward, and one critic commented in 1896 that "the face is marked by the majesty and pensive thoughtfulness that are the finest possession of a wise and benevolent old age." The statue was cast by the Gorham foundry, as were the flanking panels, which represented four periods in the life of Hahnemann, and the entire monument had its unveiling in Scott Circle in 1900. Niehaus was at the height of his career, and his fame spread as the statue was shown about the country—at the exposition in Buffalo in 1901 and at St. Louis in 1904. This portrait statue was to bring him many more commissions in the ensuing years, and perhaps it was the avalanche of new work that prevented him from ever equaling the peak he attained in his "Hahnemann."

A list of works from the prolific years of 1890–1910 is far too extensive to enumerate here, but among the more important ones are a set of bronze doors for the Library of Congress, a statue of Gibbon, in 18th-century attire, and a Michelangelesque "Moses" for the same edifice, all done in the 1890's. The Astor Memorial doors for Trinity Church, New York City, were begun around 1892 and in six panels represent scenes associated with Trinity Church and Saint Paul's Chapel. In Buffalo, New York, his seated "Lincoln" is a fine character study in the thoughtful countenance; the figure is reminiscent of Randolph Rogers' earlier statue of Lincoln in Philadelphia's Fairmount Park. Niehaus' eclectic nature is again found in his statue of "Farragut," done in the late 1890's, which is so like Saint-Gaudens' image of the admiral that the one could properly be termed a variation on the other. Niehaus' "Farragut" was erected in Muskegon, Michigan. Similar but far more original and dynamic is the bronze "Admiral Perry" in Buffalo. For the capitol at Hartford, Connecticut, the sculptor's studio created marble statues of Hooker and Davenport, in which he illustrated two different types of the Puritan spirit. The former, a layman in waistcoat, pantaloons, and a great mantle, carries a Bible in his left hand; the latter, a minister of the faith, is dressed in a full-length clerical robe and also holds a Bible.

The list of works continued with a bronze statue of John Paul Jones (Washington, 1912) and equestrian statues of Ulysses S. Grant (New York City) and Nathan B. Forrest (Memphis). The Grant group, consisting of a foot soldier walking on either side of the general, who is astride his mount, received the hearty endorsement of General Frederick Grant, the subject's son. Another of Niehaus' Civil War memorials, "Planting the Standard," stands in Newark, New Jersey. In 1907 his statue of President McKinley was unveiled in front of the subject's tomb in Canton, Ohio; it was modeled from a photograph taken of McKinley as he made his speech at the Buffalo exposition just before he was assassinated. For the city of St. Louis Niehaus executed an equestrian statue in staff material of the patron saint of the city for the fair of 1904, and also a group representing the Apotheosis of Saint Louis a couple of years later; a bronze replica of the equestrian statue was dedicated in 1906.

His style remained academic, and he never experimented with abstraction, which began to appear in America in the second and third decades of the century. One of the best examples of this prolongation of an outmoded style is the pedimental group that Niehaus made for the state capitol building at Frankfort, Kentucky. In the seventeen figures he resorted to the old academic method of symbolic personification to tell the story. "Agricultural Abundance," a classical female in robes, holds a horn of plenty, and another classical maiden represents Kentucky, with Progress kneeling at her side. The state's interest in animal husbandry is indicated by two enormous bulls and two splendid horses; its past is represented by a pair of Indians who crouch in fear as they watch the approach of civilization. The whole complex of figures and its boastful iconography somehow seem much more at home in the world of the mid-19th century, when Thomas Crawford designed his pediment for the United States Capitol, than it does in the 20th century. The later years of Niehaus' career remain in obscurity; he died in 1935 at the age of eighty.

Of the six men discussed in this chapter, five represent an expansion of the Beaux-Arts style in American sculpture, with each bringing to it a distinctive flavor of his own personal style. Charles Grafly was second only to Augustus Saint-Gaudens in his excellent portrait heads; MacMonnies, Bartlett, and Adams worked on a grander scale in their exposition sculpture, their large architectural commissions, their ideal images, and their imaginary and contemporary portrait statues. And George Grey Barnard added a unique and enriching element with his powerful, emotional compositions of dynamic figures that carried on the tradition of Michelangelo and Rodin. The one element that united these five men was their debt to contemporary French sculpture. The modeling techniques, the lively surfaces, and the new kind of personifying imagery, which Saint-Gaudens, French, and Warner had found so stimulating, likewise inspired these men and did much to form their individual styles. The sixth man considered here—Charles Henry Niehaus—was also touched by the French influence, but not as strongly and then only in some of his ideal pieces or in his decorative sculptures for the great expositions. But taken all together, their individual differences notwithstanding, these six men brought a great variety and breadth to American sculpture between the Philadelphia Centennial of 1876 and the next major dividing point in American art and history—the Armory Show of 1913 and the beginning of World War I in 1914. They were joined in all of this by a whole legion of other sculptors who are perhaps not as well known but who, when taken collectively, represent an important element in late 19th- and early 20th-century American sculpture. It is to these men that we now turn.

[FIG. 12.1] "Nathan Hale," by Frederick MacMonnies (1890). Bronze. Courtesy, Art Commission of the City of New York.

[FIG. 12.2] "The Triumph of Columbia," or "The Barge of State," by Frederick Mac-Monnies (1893). Columbian Exposition of 1893, Chicago. Courtesy, New-York Historical Society, New York City.

[FIG. 12.4] "Marquis de Lafayette," by Paul Bartlett (1899–1907). Bronze, reduced replica of the statue at the Louvre, Paris. Collection, Corcoran Gallery of Art, gift of Mrs. Armistead Peter, III.

[FIG. 12.3] "Bacchante with an Infant Faun," by Frederick MacMonnies, small replica of the original (1893). Bronze. Courtesy, Cincinnati Museum of Art.

[FIG. 12.5] "The Bear Tamer," by Paul Bartlett (1887). Bronze, 68½" high. Collection, Corcoran Gallery of Art, gift of Mrs. Paul Wayland Bartlett.

[FIG. 12.6] "Michelangelo," by Paul Bartlett (c. 1898). Bronze. Courtesy, Library of Congress.

[FIG. 12.7] "Primavera," by Herbert Adams (1893). Polychromed marble. Collection, Corcoran Gallery of Art.

[FIG. 12.8] "The Singing Boys," by Herbert Adams (1894). Marble, 36" high. Courtesy, Metropolitan Museum of Art, bequest of Charles W. Gould, 1932.

[FIG. 12.9] William Cullen Bryant Memorial, by Herbert Adams, sculptor, and Thomas Hastings, architect (1911). Courtesy, Art Commission of the City of New York.

[FIG. 12.11] "Aeneas and Anchises," by Charles Grafly (1893). Bronze. Courtesy, Pennsylvania Academy of the Fine Arts.

[FIG. 12.10] "Professor Joseph Henry," by Herbert Adams (1911). Plaster cast of bronze statue in the Library of Congress, 78″ high. Courtesy, National Collection of Fine Arts, Smithsonian Institution.

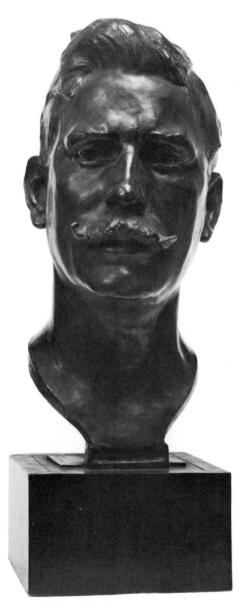

[FIG. 12.12] Edward W. Redfield, by Charles Grafly (1909). Bronze. Collection, Corcoran Gallery of Art, gift of Edward W. Redfield.

[FIG. 12.13] Hugh Breckenridge, by Charles Grafly. Bronze. Courtesy, Pennsylvania Academy of the Fine Arts.

[FIG. 12.15] "Abraham Lincoln," by George Grey Barnard (1917). Bronze. Lytle Park, Cincinnati. Courtesy, Cincinnati Park Board.

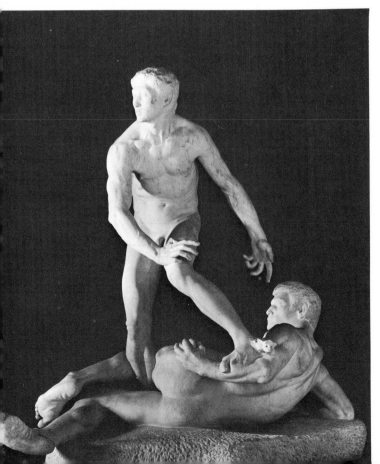

[FIG. 12.14] "Struggle of Two Natures in Man," by George Grey Barnard (1889–94). Marble, 101½″ high. Courtesy, Metropolitan Museum of Art, gift of Alfred Corning Clark, 1896.

[FIG. 12.16] "The Unbroken Law," by George Grey Barnard (1902–10). Marble. State Capitol, Harrisburg, Pa. Courtesy, State of Pennsylvania; photo, Index of American Sculpture, University of Delaware.

[FIG. 12.18] "The Driller," by Charles Niehaus. Plaster, 91″ high. Courtesy National Collection of Fine Arts, Smithsonian Institution.

[FIG. 12.17] "Mineral Wealth," by Charles Niehaus (1901). Pan-American Exposition, Buffalo, N.Y.; no longer extant.

[FIG. 12.19] "John Quincy Adams Ward," by Charles Niehaus. Plaster, 30″ high. Courtesy, National Collection of Fine Arts, Smithsonian Institution.

13

Mansions, Monuments, and the Beaux-Arts Style: Part II

THE COLORFUL ERA BETWEEN THE CENTENNIAL OF 1876 AND THE YEARS JUST PRIOR to the outbreak of World War I was exceptionally productive in American sculpture. The nation had at last become conscious of sculpture as an art form, and with marvelous gusto and exuberance incorporated it into architecture, public squares, plazas, and other aspects of the American scene. Sculpture was needed to adorn the several spectacular expositions that crowned the period like jewels, as well as the magnificent edifices built to house the commercial, financial, and industrial enterprises of this gilded age. Sculpture was also part of such projects as the triumphal arch erected to welcome Admiral Dewey to New York upon his return from the Philippines, the Library of Congress, and the Appellate Court Building in New York City.

This demand encouraged many young artists to go into sculpture, thus swelling the ranks of sculptors to an unprecedented number. Lack of scholarly studies on these men makes an accurate analysis of their work difficult. Of the many sculptors discussed in this chapter, several may later emerge—as the perspective of time sharpens the judgment of their contributions—as meriting a more prominent place than given here. In general, these sculptors followed one or the other of the two major trends of the era—that is, their work was dominated by the decorative elements of the Parisian schools and by indigenous naturalism in portraiture.

One of the most gifted and prolific of this new wave of sculptors was Karl Bitter (1867–1915). In addition to creating numerous individual pieces on his own, he was instrumental in the planning and organizing of some of the largest sculptural programs of the period. Bitter possessed a special decorative sense, a rare ability in administration, and a style that well expressed the excitement, the adventurous daring, and the self-confidence of America itself—qualities that made him exceptionally qualified to take charge of such projects as the sculptural decorations for the Pan-American Exposition at Buffalo, the Louisiana Purchase Exposition at St. Louis and the Panama-American Exposition at San Francisco. His activities in the National Sculpture Society also made him one of the most prominent artists of his day. Bitter's later work is especially significant, for it represents the first step toward abstraction of form in American sculpture.

Bitter was born in Vienna, the son of middle-class parents whose hopes that their son would some day enter the law or the clergy were defeated by his inability to master Latin. Even as a boy, Bitter was always creating with his hands. Eventually he enrolled at the School for Applied Arts, then later at the Academy of Fine Arts, where he acquired a skill in decorative architectural work. After serving a year in the Austrian army he came to America at the age of twenty-one. Hardly able to speak a word of English and knowing no one who could assist him, Bitter was at that point just another immigrant craftsman, virtually penniless, but equipped with a determined will and a few tools of his trade. With the aid of some drawings and several photographs of his work, he soon found employment with a firm that specialized in architectural decoration. His work was exceptional, and he quickly came to the attention of the most celebrated architect of the period, Richard Morris Hunt—mansion maker to America's millionaires. Hunt helped Bitter establish a studio where he could execute the ornament to adorn the finest residences of Fifth Avenue and other enclaves of fashion. The architect's style incorporated a wealth of decorative carving, and Bitter's talent was earnestly encouraged. Probably the most famous edifice for which the young Viennese did much work was Commodore Vanderbilt's luxurious mansion, "Biltmore," in North Carolina. Before long, other architects began to commission Bitter's work, but it was to Hunt that the sculptor owed the greatest debt for his prodigious success and his early acclaim.

John Jacob Astor had bequeathed the funds for three splendid bronze door-ways for Trinity Church, and Richard Morris Hunt was named to select the sculptor. The architect announced a competition open to all sculptors in America, and among the entries was one submitted by his protégé. Bitter's relief, "Expulsion from Paradise," was selected, and in March 1891 the committee commissioned him to do the Broadway entrance doors, the most important of the three sets. Bitter, in America only a few years, was thus catapulted into the forefront of the large body of talented young sculptors.

He had barely begun to work on the whole design for the Trinity Church doors when Hunt called him away from them to assist in a project that would add even greater distinction to his reputation. The American art world was at that time excited over the grandiose plans for the Columbian Exposition in Chicago, scheduled to open in 1893. Well over a year in advance, architects and artists began to design its buildings, fountains, and promenades, and to Richard Morris

Hunt fell one of the choicest assignments—the Administration Building at the head of the Court of Honor. Hunt selected Bitter to be in charge of the twenty-two colossal groups of sculpture, which were to provide "a most charming inter-ruption to the architectural masses" (Fig. 13.1). Early in 1892 Bitter and eight other sculptors began working in a closed-off section of the Forestry Building; there he and his crew produced the enormous Rude-like allegorical groups enti-tled "The Elements, Controlled and Uncontrolled," which flanked the entrances to the Administration Building (Fig. 13.3). He also supervised his assistants as they executed (after his models) twelve groups, representing the Arts, Industry, Re-flection, and other nude or seminude heroic female personifications, in staff—a mixture of plaster and straw—built over wooden and iron armatures. And at the base of the great dome sat eight "angelic groups that trumpeted the victory of peace." It was a major sculptural program, a baptism of fire for a sculptor whose previous efforts had been confined to ornamentation on a much smaller scale. But Bitter proved equal to the challenge, and ever after had more commissions than he could accept.

With the conclusion of his work in Chicago, he returned to New York and finished the Trinity doors in 1894. He had become a charter member of the National Sculpture Society in 1893, and in that same year produced the numerous terra-cotta figures that were to fill the long pediment of Pennsylvania Station in Philadelphia. His biographer, Schevill, wrote that the subject of the pediment "represented Fire and Water tamed and harnessed to the service of Man—certainly a theme eminently appropriate to a railway station." In those days railroad stations were frequently the pride of the cities they served, and enormous sums were devoted to their decoration.

While continuing to do decorative work for the architects, Bitter received his first portrait commission, a statue of Dr. William Pepper (Fig. 13.2), retiring provost of the University of Pennsylvania. A model was shown at the National Sculpture Society in 1895, but the statue was not completed until 1898. Pepper is shown seated, leaning to one side, and deep in thought, a forceful, animated figure. No brooding or remorseful man this, but one whose thoughts are charged with a potent energy. The head is rendered in the reinvigorated naturalism characteristic of the last quarter of the century, and the large masses of the academic robe have a fine sculptural quality. Bitter was anxious to create a work of art as well as a likeness; in the eyes of his contemporaries, he succeeded admirably. He was not destined to become famous as a sculptor of likenesses, however, but rather as one who made images that translated their loftiest ideas and ideals into tangible, visual form.

New York City had built itself an enormous, noble, neo-Renaissance palace of art called the Metropolitan Museum. To adorn the attic high above the main entrance, Karl Bitter created four robed figures that personified Architecture, Sculpture, Painting, and Music; for other parts of the Fifth Avenue façade he designed medallion portraits of Michelangelo, Raphael, Dürer, Velasquez, Rem-brandt, and Bramante. Richard Morris Hunt had died by then, but the leading architects of the day turned to Karl Bitter for the ornamentation of their buildings. While working on the figures for the Metropolitan Museum of Art, for example, Bitter also modeled the colossal caryatids that personified the White, Negro, and Malayan races for the St. Paul Building in New York City. His studio, which by 1896 was in Weehawken, New Jersey—where he also built a fine house and riding stables—bustled with men enlarging his clay models, making plaster casts of them, carving them in stone, constructing great armatures, mixing plaster and clay, and modeling details for various commissions. Bitter's talent as an organizer of men and projects was obvious in his own atelier, and before long he was called upon to manage the efforts of a whole corps of sculptors and their studios.

In New York City, the 19th century was brought to a festive close with Admiral Dewey's triumphant return from the victory at Manila Bay. The National Sculpture Society offered to provide the city with a sculpture-adorned triumphal arch at the point where Fifth Avenue joined Madison Square. With the exception of Saint-Gaudens, all the eminent sculptors of the day participated, and it fell to Bitter to create the "Combat" group, which stood against the front of the pier on the right (Fig. 13.4). At the command of a young officer, sailors manned a shielded cannon; above billowing clouds of smoke stood a classical goddess—helmeted, winged, bearing a spear in one hand and a Medusa-headed shield in the other. The scene represented American warriors assured of victory under the protective guidance of an ancient deity.

Ten years after his arrival in America Karl Bitter received a still more lustrous distinction by being named chargé d'affaires of the sculptural projects of the brilliant spectacle that inaugurated the new century—the Pan-American Exposition in Buffalo (1901). Whereas at Chicago in 1893 there had been only a large collection of essentially independent motifs, Bitter brought all the sculpture of the Buffalo Exposition within one magnificent iconographic program that encompassed such themes as man's dominance over nature and the genius of man himself. In the *Art Handbook* of the exposition, Bitter declared that the intention from the beginning was that the sculptures "must give inspiration to the mind and assist the reason which has been appealed to by the contents of the buildings. The sculpture should give us here . . . . a conception which step by step and link by link, should lead the receptive mind to grasp one big idea and ignite a fire of true and lasting enthusiasm." All the sculptures should be related thematically to a unified plan, or to "one big idea," and the many related themes were knit together by the organizational genius of Karl Bitter.

The main entrance and the Triumphal Causeway were "given over to an apotheosis of the United States, an allegorization of national pride." Nature was the subject in the West Esplanade, representing the abundant natural resources of the nation, man's dependence upon them, and his gratitude for them; an example of this may be seen in Niehaus' "Mineral Wealth" (Fig. 12.17). The East Esplanade (Fig. 13.5) told of the emergence of man from primitive chaos to the benevolent modern form of government, which was, of course, seen at its best (so the patriots firmly believed) in the United States; these sculptural themes were associated by their location with the Ethnology Building and the U.S. Government Building. Next came the Court of Fountains and the Mall, whose sculptures extolled America's ingenuity and inventiveness, as well as her industriousness; the crowning monument here was the great Electric Tower. And finally there was the Plaza, the doorway between the exposition proper and the midway, where the practical side of life gave way to "the more poetical, which shows us the temperament of the people, their games and their sports and their varied amusements." Throughout the plan sculptured groups and figures explained these "big ideas," whose central theme was that America, blessed with the riches of her natural resources and the home of an enlightened form of government, offered the opportunity for the genius of man to reach its fullest potential. Citizens of less fortunate nations, it was thought, might profitably contemplate this sculptural philosophy and carry the lessons back to their less fortunate homelands where progress was stifled and human misery perpetuated under dictatorships.

Nearly fifty sculptors—including almost everybody of any prominence whatever—provided the small models for some group or statue that would become a part of the over-all iconographic plan. In his Weehawken studio, Bitter and his chief asssistant, Gustave Gerlach, directed a large crew of artists and artisans. Bit by bit the statues grew to enormous size in the easily workable staff material (Fig. 13.7). They were then cut into sections and shipped by rail to Buffalo, where still another crew assembled and installed them. Bitter's own contribution to the sculptures of the exposition was a pair of equestrian "Standard Bearers"—helmeted, seminude youths holding aloft their flags while riding huge rearing mounts. As with many other exposition groups, when seen individually the "Standard Bearers" are not very impressive; but when seen as part of the total architectural and sculptural program they are much more effective. In addition, Bitter sent a "Gladiator" and a piece called "Gay Music" to the Fine Arts Exhibit at the exposition, and his bronze "Dr. William Pepper" was placed outside the Fine Arts Building.

After his work on the Pan-American Exposition was completed, Bitter married Marie A. Schevill of Cincinnati, and in the summer of 1901 they went abroad. Though he had not achieved the status of Ward, Saint-Gaudens, or Daniel Chester French, Bitter now was unquestionably one of the leading sculptors of America's younger generation. In 1903 he was elected to the National Academy of Design; three years later he was elected president of the National Sculpture Society, succeeding Daniel Chester French, who had in turn succeeded John Quincy Adams Ward.

Bitter's marble Hubbard Memorial for Montpelier, Vermont, was completed in 1903. Although its image of Thanatos—a personification of death, seated, swooning, and swathed in the ample folds of a diaphanous garment—has been compared to the quiet enigmatic woman of Saint-Gaudens' Adams Memorial, Bitter's figure is of an essentially different character, being more overtly dynamic and dramatic. On the block behind the figure a few lines from William Cullen Bryant's poem "Thanatopsis" were inscribed. A replica of this monument and a plaster version of the Villard Memorial (whose "Barnardesque" marble original was set up in Sleepy Hollow Cemetery near the Hudson River) were shown at the Louisiana Purchase Exposition.

Bitter had found an immense satisfaction in serving as the organizer of the Pan-American Exposition's plan, and he again acted in that capacity for the Louisiana Purchase Exposition in St. Louis in 1904. The over-all sculptural theme of the St. Louis fair was the Winning of the West—from the time of the indigenous Indians and the coming of the Spanish explorers and French missionaries, through the transfer of the Louisiana Purchase from Napoleon's France to Jefferson's United States, to the settlement of that vast territory by the pioneers. Numerous sculptors again provided models for various groups, which were enlarged by Bitter's assistants in an abandoned railroad roundhouse in Hoboken, then shipped by rail to St. Louis. The only piece Bitter himself created especially for the exposition was a relief, placed at the base of the great shaft dedicated to peace, representing the signing of the treaty that added the Louisiana Territory to the United States.

Although the supervision of the sculpture for the exposition kept him busy during 1902–1904, other works progressed in his Weehawken studio. The major undertaking was an equestrian statue of General Franz Sigel, commissioned by American citizens of German descent. The group seems small and does not possess the solemn dignity of Henry Kirke Brown's "Washington" or Saint-Gaudens "Sherman," which stand in other plazas in New York City. Bitter's "Sigel" was unveiled on Riverside Drive in October 1907.

In 1908 he was commissioned by the city of New York to do the statue and reliefs for the Carl Schurz Memorial overlooking Morningside Heights. The memorial provides an interesting contrast between the strong naturalism of the image of Schurz in contemporary attire and the reliefs at either end of the exedra, which are rendered in the style of archaic Greek compositions. The sculptor thereby distinguished between the real man and his ideals, which are done in an eclectic style. The panels are among the earliest examples of the use of the stylized forms of archaic Greek art, which offered yet another historic style to inspire and influence American sculptors. Bitter's adaptation of the archaic Greek style may again be seen in the pedimental groups for the Wisconsin state capitol at Madison, on which he worked between 1908 and 1910.

During this period—several years before the famed Armory Show of 1913—Bitter was beginning to experiment with abstraction of form, a step of immense significance for American sculpture. A strong stylization in low-relief had appeared in the two figures that Bitter created to adorn the doorway of the First National Bank of Cleveland (1908). In their angular axes, in the straight and rigid lines of many of the folds, and in the stark simplification of hands and features of the face and body, one finds stylizations that are in part concessions to the architectural setting they embellish. These figures are extremely important, for they represent one of the first attempts at a true abstraction of the forms of nature.

Bitter's experience as a sculptor of architectural decoration made him sensitive to the architectonic forces that surrounded his adornments. Anxious to have his sculptures work harmoniously with the new architectural theory, which was based on the beauty of the simplicity of geometric designs—excluding all of the revival styles of the 19th century—Bitter incorporated this geometric simplification into his figural designs. Since he did this only in work that embellished buildings, it seems safe to assume that the abstraction of form was largely a result of his effort to create a style of sculpture compatible with the new nonrevival architectural style. But in any case, it was a definite step toward abstract form by an American sculptor who had previously worked in the style of the Ecole des Beaux-Arts.

It was a very important step and in following years this sculptural stylization gained momentum, reaching its fullest realization in the work of Paul Manship. Its significance in 1908, however, is that it is the beginning of the tendency to compromise late 19th-century naturalism with the experiments in abstraction of form that were being carried on in Europe during the first decade of the 20th century. Although many American sculptors of the early years of the new century were totally unwilling to admit the validity of abstract—to say nothing of nonobjective—form, a few recognized some potential in it and even absorbed it on a modest scale into their own work. Bitter was a pioneer in this respect, for the figures that sit on the lintel of the doorway of the Cleveland bank are abstractions in form, as well as in the things they symbolize.

But Karl Bitter was not to explore fully the possibilities of the abstraction of form in the few years of his life that were left. In those sculptures not intended to decorate architecture Bitter remained faithful to the conservative tradition, which tended to ignore what were considered the anti-naturalistic inanities of the new art. For example, the memorial dedicated to Dr. Burrill Angell (1910) in Ann Arbor, Michigan, is extremely reminiscent of Saint-Gaudens' bronze high-relief plaques of McCosh and Bellows in the 1880's. The forceful, invigorated naturalism of Saint-Gaudens is also found in Bitter's full-length portraits of Senator Dryden in Newark, New Jersey (1912), of President Tappan at Ann Arbor (1913), and of President Andrew White of Cornell University (Ithaca, 1915). Nor is the abstract element found in the statues of Lord Somers and Lord Mansfield (1910), Alexander Hamilton (1913), or Thomas Jefferson (1914)—all for the interior of the County Court House in Cleveland—or in two other statues of Jefferson that Bitter did for St. Louis (1913) and the University of Virginia (1914). When the invitation to participate in the Armory Show of 1913 went out to American artists, the piece Bitter selected to represent him was the portrait bust of Dr. White; although it was catalogued to appear in the exhibition, it did not arrive and was not shown. But it is revealing that Bitter chose one of his naturalistic pieces, rather than one that tended toward the more modern abstraction of form. Clearly he did not see himself as one of the revolutionary modernists.

The last few years of Karl Bitter's life were extremely active. He was named to the Art Commission of New York City in 1912, and from 1912 to 1915 he was the director (mainly in an advisory capacity) of the sculptural projects of the Panama-Pacific Exposition at San Francisco. There were numerous commissions. Besides those mentioned above, some of the more impressive ones are the Barnard-like Thomas Lowry Memorial in Minneapolis (1915), the Prehn Monument (1911) for Passaic, New Jersey, and the Kasson Monument (1915) for Utica, New York. In the last winter of his life he worked on two important fountain commissions: The Depew Fountain for Indianapolis was filled with the joy and decorative spirit of late 19th-century French sculpture; the lovely nude for the Pulitzer Fountain, at the Plaza at Fifth Avenue and Central Park South, belongs to the academic school of the early 20th century. The Plaza figure—representing Pomona, the goddess of abundance—was modeled in the Weehawken studio, which had been deserted some time earlier when the Bitter family moved back to New York City. The sculptor had sequestered himself in the old studio, and in the early days of the spring of 1915 he finished the statue, the last he was to do. He rejoined his wife and their three small children for a joyful reunion. One evening soon afterward as Bitter and his wife left the opera to return home, they were run down by an automobile that had gone out of control. Marie Bitter was not injured seriously, but her husband was crushed beneath the wheels. Abruptly and prematurely his life ended at the age of forty-seven.

Philip Martiny (1858–1927), who worked with Karl Bitter on several large sculptural projects, exemplified the decorative sculptor of the late 19th and early 20th centuries. It was he who carried sculptural ornamentation on architecture to heights that surpassed even Bitter. At the Columbian Exposition in Chicago, America first became aware of his brand of lively, gay, colorful sculpture through the numerous pieces he created for McKim, Mead, and White's Agricultural Building (Fig. 13.6). Martiny came to America in the early 1880's, already a well-trained artist who had studied and worked in his native Strasbourg (Alsace) in ateliers that specialized in the Parisian Beaux-Arts style of ornamental sculpture. He was in his twenties when he became an assistant in the studio of Augustus Saint-Gaudens, who had been impressed with the excellence of Martiny's decorative wood carvings for the interior of the Vanderbilt house. Saint-Gaudens soon put him to work on the famous statue of the Puritan. Martiny, along with Frederick MacMonnies, was one of Saint-Gaudens' assistants when Saint-Gaudens moved his studio to Cornish, New Hampshire. After Saint-Gaudens had designed a piece, it would frequently be turned over to Martiny to be enlarged and carried to near completion with the master all the while making changes. Saint-Gaudens no doubt placed a sobering restraint on the young man during those few years, for Saint-Gaudens' sense of design was more delicate and refined than was Martiny's, and Saint-Gaudens' sculpture demanded far more in the way of structural form. This discipline was probably good for Martiny, but it did not significantly alter his decorative style.

A few of Martiny's own early works are known, and they do reveal the influence of Saint-Gaudens'—for example, the relief portrait of Charles James Osborn (1888) at Yale. The older sculptor was mainly engaged in the mid-1880's in bas-relief and medallion portraits, and Martiny would have had ample opportunity to observe these works in the studio, in fact, he may well have worked on some of them. In Saint-Gaudens' studio Martiny met the leading architects of the day—McKim, Mead, and White—and did the decorations for their Agricultural Building at the 1893 Chicago fair. The number of pieces he devised, their complexity and scale, and the relatively short time in which he did them constitute an astonishing accomplishment. Martiny by nature worked very fast, in contrast to the plodding, painstaking Saint-Gaudens. A critic, in one of the illustrated art handbooks of the exposition, wrote of the near-phenomenal feat:

In less than a year's time he was to cover the long-stretching cornices and façades . . . with the richest ornamentation ever seen in America . . . . Mr. Martiny proved that wealth and grandeur of sculpture can be attained by the duplication of ideas in similar architectural positions, for although his important groups appear several times on the fronts of Agricultural Hall, yet the very unity of appearance assures the observer that sculpture was here used in its true, subordinated relations—that is, it was the Agricultural temple as a whole which was to be admired. [*The Dream City*, 1893]

By using his primary groups several times Martiny reduced his task considerably. For instance, the motif of the "Four Races," each comprising four graceful, nearly nude maidens representing the peoples of the four continents, crowned each of the four corners of the building. His large "Ceres" groups—composed of two elegant, lightly draped female figures who sit beside an oval cartouche bearing the name of the goddess while two *putti* hold up lavish garlands of flowers and fruits—were also repeated along the cornices of the façades; in their floweriness and elegance these groups have a noticeable Rococo flavor, as do the groups of the "Four Races." There were also enormous groups of men with teams of horses or oxen along the skyline of the building, all appropriate to the theme of agriculture. In addition, sixty figures of robed women, spaced at intervals along the attic, represented abundance; and sixty more along the four façades represented the zodiac. Finally, there were colossal groups symbolic of the four seasons. Martiny's ability to produce so much sculpture in his studio in such a short time was impressive, but more important, nearly everyone was impressed with the quality of his sculpture. His reputation was clearly established, and for the next twenty-five years his talents were to be in great demand.

For the fair in Buffalo in 1901 Martiny made the decorative and popular "Fountain of Abundance" (Fig. 13.8). At the one in St. Louis in 1904 he was represented by the two heroic quadrigae symbolizing "The Progress of Art" and "The Progress of Commerce," as well as by a large group, "Apollo and the Muses," that was placed over the main entrance of Festival Hall. Other projects of these years included numerous pieces for the colorful interior of the new Library of Congress in Washington, chief among them being the two torch-bearing, robed maidens on the newel posts of the staircase, the twenty-six fanciful pastoral reliefs with their *putti* and festoons for the balustrade, and several figures around the base of the great dome. In 1899 he produced the figure of Confucius for New York's Appellate Court Building, and in the same year his more staid and monumental Soldiers' and Sailors' Monument was unveiled in Jersey City. Not long afterward his two groups, with John Jay and Alexander Hamilton as the central figure in each, were set in place atop the New York Chamber of Commerce Building, and in them he returned to his more decorative style. The same is true for the many sculptures he worked on between 1903 and 1908 for the Hall of Records Building in New York City. For this noble edifice he created eight cornice figures of famous New Yorkers, sixteen symbolic figures, the two seated figures of "Justice" and "Authority" for the entrance, and two groups representing "New York in its Infancy" and "New York in Revolutionary War Times." The upper-level figures were placed amid festoons and swags, cartouches and richly carved capitals. In all of it he achieved a Baroque grandeur, and in the finest sense he added sculptural color and enrichment to the edifice. Henry Kirke Bush-Brown carved some of the other figures for the building.

In 1919, New York City bedecked itself in glorious adornment to welcome home the troops returning from Europe. Martiny's contribution was a large spirited group entitled "Our Allies," which was made of staff and placed atop the Flatiron Building. In the last decade of his life he worked on two large war memorials, the main feature of each being a bronze doughboy; one was for Abingdon Square in Greenwich Village, and the other for Chelsea Park.

Scattered throughout his career of decorative architectural work and war memorials were several fine portraits, such as one of President William McKinley for Springfield, Massachusetts, and one of Vice-President Garrett Hobart for Paterson, New Jersey, both created soon after the turn of the century. In the former he followed a French tradition in the design, which consisted of a robed female figure of "Fame" reaching up toward a portrait bust of the subject with a palm branch, the emblem of peace. But Martiny never made a speciality of portraiture, and his critics have rightly observed that he frequently failed to achieve a poignant, penetrating study of his subject's personality.

Philip Martiny was unquestionably at his best when he could allow his innate decorative sense the full freedom of design, which was frequently possible in some of the large sculptural projects he produced in the years 1893 to 1915. He brought the full range of ornamental work of the French Beaux-Arts style to America and was unquestionably its finest exponent. It ran throughout almost the entire body of his production, which in its number and scale was almost unbelievable. Martiny died in 1927 at the age of sixty-nine.

Another who obtained fame and fortune through decorative architectural sculpture was Isidore Konti (1862–1938). After studying at the Imperial Academy in his native Vienna and then in Rome, Konti came to America in 1891 with several monumental sculptural commissions already behind him. He went at once to Chicago, where he worked on the elaborate architectural decorations of the

Columbian Exposition; as a result of his training in Europe, he was well prepared for the type of work required for the decorative projects of a great international exposition. He was to continue in that line even after he settled in New York City and for a few years became Karl Bitter's assistant. During this period Konti executed pieces on his own, mainly figures destined to decorate architecture, such as the reliefs of 1894 for Grace Church and for the Home Life Insurance Building. For the Dewey Arch he created three figures representing the West Indies, the East River, and the North River (Fig. 13.4), thus participating in one of the major sculptural projects of the end of the century. When Karl Bitter was named director of sculpture at the Pan-American Exposition of 1901, Isidore Konti was assured of representation there; in addition to four groups for the Temple of Music, he also made the group of the "Despotic Age," which was part of the Ages of Man theme of the East Esplanade (Figs. 13.5 and 13.12). A small bronze replica of the "Despotic Age" exists in the Corcoran Gallery of Art. Karl Bitter explained the iconography of the group in the official *Art Handbook*:

[The] chariot of State [is] drawn by four men representing the mass of the people, the peasant, the artisan, etc. On the chariot is seated the Despot, whose governing power is being represented by a Fury, scourge in hand, forcing the people in the yoke to draw the heavy burden; in the rear of the chariot are chained Justice and Truth.

This was typical of the spirit of personification that dominated American monumental decorative sculpture during this period. Work such as this occupied most of Konti's time in the next several decades.

The sculptor continued to produce ideal figures or personifications, such as "The Brook," which he sent to the National Sculpture Society exhibition of 1902 and to the St. Louis Exposition two years later. There were also pieces entitled "Orpheus," "Inspiration," "Pan and Cupid," and "Awakening of Spring," all dating from the early years of the 20th century. Of "The Brook," Lorado Taft wrote:

Mr. Konti is always refined, but this coy figure is a veritable embodiment of sinuous grace. Carefully studying nature, the artist . . . [eliminated] all offensive realism, all accidents of the individual body, and [permitted] the figure to stand for just what it is, a beautifully sculptured form.   [*History of American Sculptures*, p. 464]

In 1909 Konti was elected to the National Academy. From 1912 dates his figure of a seated male nude, "Genius of Immortality," a piece exhibited widely over the next several years and now in the Metropolitan Museum of Art. He is represented at Brookgreen Gardens by a bronze figure of a young faun, seated and playing a pipe. His architectural and decorative work continued with two groups for the ballroom of the Astor Hotel and the figures of Justinian and Alfred the Great for the Cleveland Court House. Funerary monuments dedicated to the Reverend Morgan Dix and Bishop Horatio Potter are in New York City's Trinity Church and Cathedral of St. John the Divine respectively. Konti's few portraits include a bust of George Fiske Comfort in the Metropolitan Museum of Art. A portrait statue of Governor F. T. Nicholls is in Baton Rouge, Louisiana; and for the city of Ljubljana, Yugoslavia, he made the memorial to Anastasius Grün. From his studio in Yonkers issued a steady production of decorative architectural and garden sculpture. His art was devoid of any harsh realism and clearly belonged to the Beaux-Arts school. Konti lived to be seventy-six and died in Yonkers in 1938.

Frederic Wellington Ruckstull (originally Ruckstuhl; 1853–1942) was two years old when his parents emigrated from Alsace, France, to the bustling river town of St. Louis on the Mississippi. As a child he was fascinated with carving and hoped to be apprenticed to a stonecutter, but his father was determined that Frederick should become a missionary. At the age of eighteen, after trying hard to imbue himself with religious zeal, young Ruckstull realized—with some relief—that the ministry was not for him. He began clerking in a store during the day, and at night he modeled in clay, relating in his autobiographical sketch—published in the back of his book, *Great Works of Art* (1925)—that one of the earliest of these was "Penelope Waiting for Ulysses," after Flaxman's Homeric drawings. As his interest in sculpture became more serious, he entered evening art classes at Washington University and joined the St. Louis "Sketch Club." Finally in 1882, when he was twenty-nine years old, he decided to go to Paris to study.

Arriving in the French capital, he was accepted at the Ecole des Beaux-Arts; before attending a single class, he went to see the annual Salon exhibition where he was at once disillusioned at the quality of the sculpture. With the self-confidence that he was to possess all his life, and fully convinced that he could do better sculpture than anything he saw there, he decided to return to St. Louis to earn money enough to stay and work in Paris for three years. About a month later he returned to Missouri, where for the next several years he sold toys by day and modeled nights and Sundays. A bust of Nick Vedder, from Washington Irving's "Sleepy Hollow," drew such admiration from a local group of amateur artists that many of them agreed to subscribe five dollars a month to send Ruckstull to Paris. There, in the spring of 1885, he entered the Académie Julian.

At the Académie he had drawing lessons with Boulanger and Lefebvre, and drew independently from the sculptures in the Louvre. After a year he took private instruction from Tholemaar, Dampt, and Mercié, and recalled in his autobiography: "I could have become the private pupil of Rodin; but, as his works, all but a few, repelled me by their ugliness and brutal mannerisms, I preferred to be under the influence of the refined, poetic Mercié." Here the sculptor reveals his early bitter hatred of the modern art, which he later referred to as "lunatic art," the work of madmen whose vulgarities resulted in a total "deformation" of the human figure. He chose then, in the late 1880's, to follow the traditional line of the academies, and attempted to defend that line throughout his life against the swelling tide of abstract and nonobjective art.

Ruckstull's first major piece, on which he began work in 1887, was a standing nude female figure. Entitled "Evening," it belongs very much to the academic tradition; it won an honorable mention at the Salon in the spring of 1888, thereby confirming the sculptor's belief that he had chosen the true path in art to follow. Returning that summer to St. Louis, with the plaster cast of "Evening," Ruckstull acquired the patronage of a woman whose portrait bust he was modeling; with her financial support he returned to Paris to put his statue into marble. He did most of the carving himself, a project that occupied him for well over a year. In 1890 he was also working on another classically inspired statue called "Mercury teasing the Eagle of Jupiter." This and "Evening" were sent to the Salon of 1891, where they received high praise but no medals, due to a decision—by part of the committee, led by Bartholdi—that foreign entries should not be awarded prizes. During this period Ruckstull became good friends with many of the leading French sculptors of the academic brotherhood—such as Aubé, Dalou, and Gardet—and frequently met with them at their studios or at a wine shop operated by Mme. Binet. Also, he came to know Rodin "before he had been foisted into the international notoriety he later enjoyed."

After the close of the Salon Ruckstull returned to the United States, setting up a studio briefly in St. Louis. By the fall of 1892, however, he had established himself in New York City, where he soon entered into the thick of artistic activities. His "Evening" won a medal at the Columbian Exposition of 1893, and he soon became one of the more prominent sculptors in America. Ruckstull maintained, for example, that he had "fathered" the foundation of the National Sculpture Society in 1893. Though there is some dispute about this point, he did play a significant role in helping to bring together rival factions that existed within the ranks of American sculptors. *The New York Times* reported on May 31, 1893, that on the preceding day numerous American sculptors had met at the Fencers Club with W. Russell Sturgis acting as chairman and Frederic Ruckstull as secretary. An executive committee of seventeen members was appointed, seven of whom were professional sculptors: J. Q. A. Ward, Augustus Saint-Gaudens, D. C. French, John Rogers, Herbert Adams, Olin Warner, and Frederic Ruckstull; the remaining ten were architects (Hunt, White, and Hastings), laymen, amateur artists, and men in some way connected with various areas in which sculpture was involved—such as bronze foundries. The objectives of the organization, as reported in *The Times*, were:

To spread the knowledge of good sculpture, foster the taste for, and encourage the production of, ideal sculpture for the household, promote the decoration of public bldgs., squares, and parks with sculpture of a high class, improve the quality of the sculptor's art as applied to industries, and provide from time to time for exhibitions of sculpture and objects of industrial art.

During the following two decades the National Sculpture Society was to develop into one of the most powerful artist organizations in the United States, in one way or another participating in the largest collaborative sculptural projects of the period—at Buffalo, at the Louisiana Purchase Exposition in St. Louis, at the Library of Congress, the Dewey Arch, the Appellate Court Building, the New York Customs House, and others. In 1895 the Society began holding its own exhibitions, which became one of the major artistic events of the year. Moreover, it became the official guardian of the older traditions in sculpture and entrenched itself against the relentless advance of the new "modern" art. In time it became an ultraconservative group that would allow virtually no compromise with the abstractionists and nonobjectivists. In the war to establish the primacy of one set of aesthetics over another, Frederic Ruckstull was a foremost spokesman for the academicians, with countless lectures and articles in which he ridiculed the works of such men as Rodin, Matisse, Brancusi, Picasso, Cézanne, and Archipenko.

Ruckstull loved to involve himself with large sculptural projects and was, in fact, often their prime mover. Such was the case with the Dewey Arch (Fig. 13.4), hastily erected in six weeks. Charles R. Lamb was the architect, and Ruckstull was the director of the sculptural work. Sponsored more or less by the National Sculpture Society, twenty-seven sculptors volunteered models for groups to adorn the arch; of these, seven groups were selected: Ruckstull and George Bissell provided the Army and Navy groups respectively, which stood some distance in advance of the arch; the four groups on the two piers were by Niehaus ("Triumphant Return," on the left), Bitter ("Combat," on the right), Martiny ("Departure for War," on reverse side), and French ("Peace," on reverse side); the crowning group atop the arch was the quadriga by Ward, "Naval Victory." All of this was made of impermanent staff and has long ago disappeared, although it was Ruckstull's hope that the city would commission the arch to be put into granite and marble. Another large scheme, of which Ruckstull declared he was the organizer and director, was the group of statues for the Appellate Court Building in New York City. To the complete satisfaction of the architect and the judges of the court, Ruckstull worked out "a coherent scheme," which was then parceled out to several members of the Sculpture Society. Ruckstull himself did the personifications of Wisdom and Force, which bear rather strong resemblances to Michelangelo's "Moses" and the Medici portraits in San Lorenzo, Florence.

It was also Ruckstull, according to his "Autobiographical Notice," who in 1899 urged the commissioners of the Pan-American Exposition to appropriate money for "a sculpturesque decoration of their buildings, grounds, etc." The directors responded by visiting New York, where the National Sculpture Society was their host; Ruckstull wrote that after dinner he showed lantern slides of "the progressive use of sculpture at every exposition of the world since 1851 . . . ; and they went home and quickly set aside $225,000 for sculpture. Nearly all of this went to the members of the Sculpture Society." Ruckstull's share in the vast sculptural array there—coordinated by Karl Bitter—was the quadriga atop the U.S. Government Building, "America Welcoming the Pan-American Nations" (Fig. 13.5), which he executed in Paris during "a delayed wedding trip to Europe." In 1902 he was named Director of Sculpture for the Louisiana Purchase Exposition in his home town of St. Louis, but after "conditions out there became so irksome" he resigned, and Bitter was named in his place.

Interspersed among these enormous projects were a good many lesser but still monumental works—portraits and fancy heroic pieces. In 1895 Ruckstull had won the competition for an equestrian statue of General John F. Hartranft for Harrisburg, Pennsylvania. The working model was made on the farm of a friend in New Rochelle, but Ruckstull went to Paris in 1897 to produce the full-size statue. The result was a dignified if unexciting equestrian portrait, whose design was also used in the equestrian statue of General Wade Hampton (1906) for the State House lawn in Columbia, South Carolina.

In the first two decades of the 20th century Ruckstull created several portrait statues and heroic monuments for the Southern states, which were beginning to erect memorials to their heroes and ideals. He made Confederate monuments for Baltimore and for Little Rock, Arkansas; and for the city of Columbia he produced a memorial to "the South Carolina Women of the Confederacy" (1911) and another that honored Revolutionary generals from that state—Sumter, Marion, and Pickens (1912). These were placed not far from his equestrian "Hampton." The memorial dedicated to Confederate women (Fig. 13.9) depicts a sorrowful but resigned woman seated in a chair of some elegance; a winged goddess holds a wreath above her head, and curly-headed *putti* at either side bring her bouquets of flowers. The woman has a deep and distant look upon her face; in her expression one may read the bitter experience of the South, of the loss of a way of life, and of sorrow for her men who went to war while she was left only to wait and hope. It is an academic figure of the type fostered by the French schools of the late 19th century, for Ruckstull throughout his life adhered to this tradition. The richness of modeling and decorative details are also derived from the Ecole des Beaux-Arts.

In portraiture, too, there were numerous commissions from the South where a conservatism in artistic taste and a remoteness from exposure to the strange new forms of modern art found in the work of Ruckstull an art to its liking. Ruckstull perpetuated the rather prosaic naturalism of an earlier generation of American sculptors when he made his marble statues of John C. Calhoun (1910) and Uriah M. Rose (1917), which were sent to Statuary Hall by the states of South Carolina and Arkansas respectively. Very late in the sculptor's career, the state of South Carolina commissioned its second marble statue—"Wade Hampton" (1929)—which was also destined for Statuary Hall. For the state of North Carolina, Ruckstull made a portrait statue of Charles D. McIver, which was cast in bronze in 1911; it, too, possesses that quiet unobtrusiveness characteristic of much of his portraiture. In his autobiographical sketch he went to great lengths to point out that he did not like clever technique, lively surfaces, or any kind of personal stylistic mannerisms:

I am, by instinct, opposed to all *mannerisms*, in . . . any statue, done to make it instantly *recognizable* as the manner of Monsieur So and So . . . . Originality in Conception and Composition, of course. But mannerism—in surface technique—never! Hence I strove to produce works, which should be impersonal.

[Quoted from *Great Works of Art*, p. 537]

Between 1909 and 1912 Ruckstull did four marble busts of prominent North Carolinians that were placed in the State House in Raleigh, thus adding to the large body of works that made him one of the South's main sculptors in the years preceding World War I. After the war, Ruckstull's activities as a sculptor decreased. In 1923 he produced still another quasi-classical personification, "America Remembers," which was erected in Stafford Springs, Connecticut. But by then he was seventy years old, and although he lived until 1942—to the age of eighty-nine—his career as a sculptor was essentially over by 1920.

In 1925 he published an accumulation of his fiery, sarcastic attacks on modern art in *Great Works of Art and What Makes Them Great*. Much of this material came from articles he had written for *The Art World*, a magazine he edited. *The Art World*, whose first issue appeared in October 1916, lasted only a few years and was dedicated to the defense of academic art, maintaining a constant attack upon modern, socialist, and communist art. In his Preface to *Great Works of Art*, he wrote, "The problem of how to stem this drift, in America, towards a complete topsy-turvying of the art world, appeared to me ever more pressing; and . . . it did not take much urging to determine me to make the effort to combat this intellectual pest called 'Modernism.' " Ruckstull, one of the arch-reactionaries in a war that brought two diametrically opposed artistic theories to a head-on confrontation in the first quarter of the 20th century, passionately fought off the insurgent art throughout the period of greatest conflict. He was the outstanding spokesman for a great many artists of his day; but in time the modernists won out, and Frederic Wellington Ruckstull began to slip quietly into oblivion, just about the time—1929—the Museum of Modern Art opened its doors in New York City.

John J. Boyle (1851–1917) was also represented in several of the large sculptural projects at the turn of the century, and belonged to the group that created colorful, imaginary sculptures in the Beaux-Arts style. Boyle was born of Irish parents in New York City, but grew up in Philadelphia. The paternal side of the family had a long tradition as stonecutters, and after his father died, young John turned to that craft to help support his mother and the other children at home. In time he rose from stonecutter to stone carver, all the while studying art in the classes of Thomas Eakins at the Pennsylvania Academy.

By 1877 he had saved enough money; he went to Paris to study at the Ecole des Beaux-Arts. He remained there for three years, improving his art and attaining some recognition through his portrait busts. Boyle then returned to Philadelphia, where he began work on a group that excited him because of the wild, untamed nature of its subject—the "Indian Family," or "The Alarm" as it is also called. It was commissioned by Martin Ryerson, a prominent citizen of Chicago, who had a special fondness for the Ottawa tribe. Boyle was a happy choice as the sculptor to immortalize this Indian and his family, endowing them with great vigor and verity in a massively formed group rich in authentic details. To obtain this truthfulness—unquestionably one of the real strengths of the group—he visited the Indian people to make studies of their habits, customs, and appearance. His group comprised a stalwart brave, standing alert to danger, while his squaw holds a papoose in her lap; the hunter's shaggy dog stands at his side, as alert as his master. In typical late-19th-century fashion, this image of raw and forceful naturalism was placed upon a classical pedestal, complete with cornice, triglyphs, and metopes, in a curious amalgamation of styles. More than one critic observed that it would have been better to set it upon a rugged boulder, viewed, as Lorado Taft imagined, "half concealed amid shrubbery, where one might come upon the dusky household as unexpectedly as in those already legendary days when similar statuesque figures made our forests even more darkly silent by their mysterious presence." (*History of American Sculpture*, p. 407.) Clearly, America was ready to romanticize these people whom they formerly feared and hated. "The Alarm" was one of the early manifestations of this change of heart.

So powerful an impact did this group make when it was shown in Philadelphia that the city ordered a similar group—"Stone Age in America" (Fig. 13.13). The piece was modeled in Paris, where it received an honorable mention at the Salon of 1886, and the finished bronze statue was set in place in Fairmount Park in 1888, this time upon a rough boulder instead of a classical pedestal. In Boyle's original model, the woman was defending her children against a huge eagle that flapped its great wings as it lay supine on the ground. But when a photograph of the design was seen in Philadelphia, it was decided that the national bird, symbol of American greatness, should not be shown as defeated by an aboriginal woman, and the sculptor was asked to substitute some other menace. Boyle was not very happy about the recommended alteration, but he complied. The group lost much of its forcefulness, however, for the little bear cub does not pose the same threat as the eagle would have. Sculpturally there is again a powerful arrangement of bold masses; the group is picturesque yet without excessive detail. This was typical of Boyle's work, for he understood the meaning of sculptural form. It is again found in his two heroic groups, "The Savage Age in the East" and "The Savage Age in the West," which he created for the Pan-American Exposition in 1901 (Fig. 13.5). Several critics lamented that these groups, enlarged in the plaster-based staff, were never put into a permanent material. Boyle's groups, along with those by Konti and MacNeil representing the "Despotic Age," were designed as foils to the exposition's celebration of the democratic form of government and the good life in a civilization where law, order, and social conscience prevailed—referring, of course, to the United States of America, whose building stood just beyond these statues. Boyle was at his best when rendering subjects of this kind, and his groups were described in the official guidebook in the following way:

A group of aboriginal warriors armed with rude weapons and surrounding a female captive are depicted in an attitude of attack. A savage woman with a headdress of feathers is beating a drum while a child lies dead behind her. A band of Goths are bearing away the captive woman whose protectors they have slain, symbolizing the lawless and brutal customs of the Savage Age.

Thus America proclaimed with boastful pride the superiority of her system of government by contrasting it to the lawless, savage ages of the past. Boyle was at the height of his glory in such imagery, but these two groups were to be his last excursions into such subjects, and he turned thereafter to more prosaic work.

Boyle's activities at the Columbian Exposition in Chicago in 1893 had been limited to some of the decorative work on the Transportation Building, but he was represented in the Fine Arts exhibition by a group, entitled "Tired Out," of a mother and two children; it was awarded a medal at Chicago, and a bronze replica of it is in the Pennsylvania Academy. "Tired Out," along with his "Stone Age," was also shown at the Pan-American Exposition in 1901. In the late 1890's, the main projects in his Philadelphia studio were the bronze statues of Plato and Bacon for the upper ring of the rotunda of the new Library of Congress. Upon completion of these, which seem to lack the boldness of his earlier aboriginal groups for Chicago and Philadelphia, he turned his efforts to a seated bronze image of Benjamin Franklin, which was presented to Philadelphia by one of its more prominent and successful merchants, J. C. Strawbridge. Lorado Taft praised this statue, saying it was the finest representation of the subject, except for the one by Houdon; he wrote that Boyle had given posterity the "amiable personality" of Franklin, the "quiet, thoughtful, humorous, and, above all, sane man of perfect balance." "Franklin" was probably the most successful of Boyle's portrait statues, and he proudly displayed it in 1904 at St. Louis, together with his "Indian Hunter" and "Stone Age." Several portrait busts also date from the end of this Philadelphia period in his career.

In 1902 John J. Boyle moved his residence and studio to New York, where he took an active part in the artistic life of the city. He had been a charter member of the National Sculpture Society, and for two years, 1906–1908, he served on the Art Commission of the city of New York. The last major project he undertook was the monument to Commodore John Barry, commissioned by Congress for Washington, D.C., in 1906 (which had a stipend of $50,000). The handsome, heroic bronze statue of the naval hero, wearing a long mantle and resting his right hand on his sword, is set on a pedestal, which is decorated with a robed woman standing on the prow of a ship; she wears a liberty cap and carries the laurel branch of victory in her right hand, with an eagle at her right side. The portrait statue accompanied by such a personification is definitely French in origin, recalling the work of Mercié, Louis Barrias, Eugène Piron, J. B. Champeil, or Charles René de Saint-Marceaux. The memorial was unveiled in May 1914, President Woodrow Wilson delivering an address. Within a year the sculptor became ill, and he died on February 10, 1917.

When Lorado Taft published his *History of American Sculpture* in 1903, his reference to Alexander Milne Calder was confined to half a sentence: He stated only that Calder had "furnished most of the sculptural decorations of the enor-mous [Philadelphia] City Hall, as well as a 'General Meade' in Fairmount Park." The immense scope of the City Hall sculptures alone would seem to have entitled Calder to more recognition than this; hundreds of sculptures—from capitals for pilasters to truly colossal figures and groups—were executed after his designs, either by him or under his supervision, and virtually covered one of the archi-tectural wonders of the century. But John McArthur's City Hall, acclaimed as one of the most exquisite designs of its day when first drawn up, came toward the end of the era dominated by the style of the Second Empire. As it rose in the last quarter of the century, story by sculptured story, its style became increasingly unpopular as America turned from its curious architectural Victorianisms to what it considered the purer and more elite designs of Richard Morris Hunt's châteaux and mansions for private houses and McKim, Mead, and White's cool, pristine Renaissance palaces for government and institutions of higher learning. (In truth, although one phase of eclecticism had merely replaced another, the artists, critics, and patrons of the time recognized, nevertheless, a great change.) In the twenty-three years between the acceptance of McArthur's design and the Columbian Exposition, Calder devoted himself almost entirely to the sculptures for the Phila-delphia City Hall. He cast his lot with that one grandiose project, which turned out to be a brilliant swan song to an artistic era, with the result that he was inseparably bound to a style that Lorado Taft and his contemporaries found grossly outdated. The result was that his son, Alexander Stirling Calder, and his grandson, Alexander Calder, reached the very pinnacle of success with their art, whereas Alexander Milne Calder became increasingly consigned to obscurity.

Alexander Milne Calder (1846–1923) was born in Aberdeen, Scotland, and received his first training in carving stone from his father, a tombstone cutter. Young Calder sought a higher form of the art, however, and in 1864 he went to Edinburgh, where he studied at the Royal Institute and worked with John Rhind—the father of the sculptor John Massey Rhind. After three years Calder went to London, and then to Paris to study; he arrived just after the new addi-tions to the Louvre had risen in all their glory, virtually creating the Second Empire style, which later formed the basis of McArthur's design for City Hall. He returned to London and is reported to have studied at the South Kensington School and to have worked on the carving of the Albert Memorial, an archetype of Victorian monument art. In 1868, at the age of twenty-two, he and his young bride journeyed to the United States.

The Calders settled in Philadelphia, where Alexander began taking classes with Thomas Eakins at the Pennsylvania Academy. The sculptor later recalled this period:

While modeling for a number of the leading architects of Philadelphia and New York during the next three years, I became a citizen, and with the exception of a season in New York, have resided in Philadelphia ever since. In 1872 I was engaged by the late John McArthur, architect, to design and model groups for the new City Hall

[Quoted from a brief "Autobiography" in the Registrar's Files, Pennsylvania Academy of the Fine Arts]

John McArthur must be credited with the concept of an architecture that was covered from top to bottom with decorative sculpture, and Calder merely followed the lead of the architect. But McArthur seems to have given Calder considerable leeway in designing the countless individual pieces and in working out much of the complicated iconographic program. Allegory, personification, and symbolic images make up a jumble of Baroque classicism in the style of the Second Empire. In the vicinity of the law courts one finds the visage of Moses, the great lawgiver, and an image of Justice, and near by is a wide-eyed owl with its legendary store of wisdom; also present are the motifs of sword and scales. In the area of the prison are heads of ferocious animals, warning evildoers of the punishment that follows crime, and figures representing Pain and Sorrow invite them to repent before they fall in the wake of their own wickedness. There are statues, reliefs, and panels that depict the history of the state of Pennsylvania and its rise to a mighty center of the arts, commerce, agriculture, industry, and mining—nearly all in allegory and personification. Here and there are portraits of men who made the state great: Benjamin Franklin and Benjamin Rush, Thomas Mifflin, Nicholas Biddle, and many others watch over the affairs of the city from their brackets, keystones, niches, and occuli. There are images of earth, air, fire, and water, and of the four seasons, as well as innumerable animals. Higher up on the central pavilions of the four façades are personifications of the continents and statues of the New World's explorers. Rising from the square lower portion is the high tower, which has at the base of the dome four groups of figures that pertain to the early settlement of the area; these multitonned, twenty-four-foot giants represent the Swedes and the Indians. And finally, standing highest and tallest of all, is the thirty-seven-foot statue of William Penn himself, surveying from his lofty perch Philadelphia and miles around.

After 1877 Calder occupied one of the building's rooms, destined to serve as a law court, for his studio and worked on the premises amid the construction. As to style, Calder went from the classical in his personifications (Fig. 13.10) to the naturalistic in his images of American workmen, whereas his architectural motifs—such as pilasters, capitals, and window frames—have all the luxuriant richness that the Second Empire style allows (Fig. 13.11). In brief, his work ranged through the whole scale of mid-19th-century academic classicism and naturalism, but it never acquired—with the passing of the years—the new academism of the Beaux-Arts style. One indication that Calder's style had fallen from favor is that McArthur's successor did not care for Calder's work; the new architect had the great statue of Penn turned away from the sun (much to Calder's displeasure), so that his face is in perpetual shadow. Moreover, in spite of his vast experience with architectural sculpture, Calder did not participate in any of the enormous sculptural projects for the expositions at Chicago, Buffalo, and

St. Louis, nor was he involved in the Dewey Arch or the Library of Congress, where the Beaux-Arts style ruled the day. As the new age of American sculpture dawned in the 1880's and 1890's, Calder was left behind.

Besides the sculptures for Philadelphia's City Hall, Calder did a few other pieces. To the Fine Arts exhibition of the Philadelphia Centennial of 1876 he sent "several figures and a carved panel in stone—birds attacked by a snake. . . ." In 1881 his model won the competition, out of eighteen entries, for an equestrian statue of General George G. Meade; the spirited bronze image of the general, which stands in Fairmount Park, is not one of the more successful equestrian monuments in America. The rest of Calder's production is confined to portrait busts, such as those of General Meade, Samuel C. Perkins, Ernest Goodman, and John McArthur, Jr. For the Academy of Natural Sciences he designed the Ferdinand D. Hayden Geological Fund Medal. The great pleasure of his last years was in watching his son, Stirling, rise to a prominence in America's sculptural activities that he himself never experienced.

Like Alexander Milne Calder, John Massey Rhind (1860–1936) came to America from Scotland with several years of experience as a professional sculptor. Rhind, a third-generation sculptor, was a native of Edinburgh, where his father and brothers worked as decorative sculptors. He had left Scotland to study in London, where he received instruction from Dalou, with whom he also worked in Paris in the mid-1880's. Returning to England and Scotland briefly, Rhind married the daughter of an architect, for whom he was working, and with his bride departed for America in 1889. Considering his proclivity for decorative architectural sculpture, he could not have arrived at a more propitious time. American architects, following the Beaux-Arts style, were beginning to incorporate decorative sculpture into their architectural designs, and John Massey Rhind was soon to become one of the leading carvers of such ornamentation.

The total production of Rhind's first decade in the United States testifies both to his popularity and to his prolificacy. His first commission was for the chapel decorations of the General Theological Seminary on West 21st Street, New York City; but it was the next project that really brought him to the attention of connoisseurs and his fellow artists. Rhind was one of three winners in the competition (sponsored by the Astor bequest) for the three sets of doors for Trinity Church; Karl Bitter and Charles Niehaus were the other two. This was quite a celebrated competition, seen by many as a re-enactment of the one held some five hundred years earlier for the doors of the Florentine Baptistry. Rhind's competition panel, which was a fine display of modeling, design, and skill in the rendering of nude and robed figures, showed him to be a sculptor of great promise. For the next two years he worked on the several panels that made up his set of doors.

This success was followed by a commission for a memorial fountain in Albany, dedicated to the memory of Rufus King. It was the venerable John Quincy Adams Ward that named Rhind as one of four sculptors who should compete for the commission, indicating that Rhind's abilities had already been recognized by the man then acknowledged to be the dean of American sculptors. Next came the six figures for the American Security Building—robed female personifications of Peace, Truth, Honesty, Fortitude, Self-denial, and Fidelity—which decorated the attic above the grand Ionic colonnade; in their architectonic quality they recall the maidens on the side porch of the Erechtheum. In the mid-1890's Rhind was also working on the decorations for the Alexander Commencement Hall at Princeton—a large mural complex executed in Italian Gothic style. The theme of the design was the arts and sciences taught in the university; the figure of Learning sits in the center, accompanied by other personifications, who represent Language, Theology, Law, History, Philosophy, Architecture, Painting, Poetry, Music, and Geometry. In style it is yet another revival from the past, this time from the late Middle Ages; Rhind, in good 19th-century fashion, felt free to draw from any historic style of the past.

Also in the 1890's Rhind did an enormous statue of John C. Calhoun, to go atop a towering shaft in Charleston, South Carolina. For the city of Syracuse he produced an elaborate design of a Soldiers' and Sailors' Monument, with Victory crowning a high circular shaft and four military groups standing at the base; and he created a fine portrait statue of merchant-philanthropist Stephen Girard for Philadelphia. He also entered an ambitious model in a competition for a monument to General William Tecumseh Sherman, to be erected in Washington, D.C.

The intense pace of production in Rhind's studios in New York City and in Alpine, New Jersey, near the Palisades, continued throughout the first quarter of the 20th century. By 1900 John Massey Rhind had already become famous for both public monuments and architectural sculpture. Around the turn of the century he spent two years on four bronze figures of Hudson, Wolfe, Stuyvesant, and DeWitt Clinton for the Exchange Court Building in New York, each figure about 10 feet high. His statue of Robert Burns is in Pittsburgh; Philadelphia has his bronze images of H. H. Houston (Fig. 13.14) and John Wanamaker, as well as two great eagles on the Smith Memorial in Fairmount Park. For Hartford, Connecticut, he created the Corning Fountain with its noble stag atop the central pedestal, and four kneeling Indians in the basin. Another fountain, very much in the "French flavor" of Versailles, was designed for George Gould's estate, "Georgian Court," in Lakewood, New Jersey; its main feature is a group of nymphs playing about a boat. The city of Newark, New Jersey, has his unusual equestrian group of General Washington standing and meditating beside his horse; the group—which has no base, but stands directly upon a mound of earth—was dedicated in November 1912, with President William Howard Taft as the guest of honor.

The almost unlimited range of Rhind's activity is demonstrated in the bronze copy of Verrocchio's celebrated "Colleoni," which he made for the city of Newark. The citizens of Newark had been looking for some way of celebrating the 250th anniversary of their city; Rhind, who had long been an admirer of the "Colleoni," calling it the finest statue of its kind in the world and reporting that he had once stood spellbound before it for hours, convinced a Mr. Christian Feigenspan that it would be an appropriate gift to commemorate the anniversary. When a critic wrote that American artists concurred that the $70,000 spent on the project could not have been put to a more worthy purpose in advancing American art, there was already a small group in sharp disagreement—a group that held there was nothing creative in such art and that worse than being an eclectic revival image, it was purely imitative. But the objections of this group were scarcely heard.

Late in his career Rhind was occupied with two projects of straight portraiture. He joined the legion of sculptors whose portrait statues stand in that rather uninspiring congregation in Statuary Hall when he modeled the full-length image of Dr. Crawford W. Long at the request of the state of Georgia; it was finished in marble and set up in the Capitol in 1926. The other project was the sculpture for the McKinley Memorial in Niles, Ohio. The main piece was the standing marble figure of the President, shown as if about to deliver his last address at the Buffalo Exposition. It stands in the center of an open Doric court, which was designed by the firm of McKim, Mead, and White. In addition, Rhind modeled portrait busts, which were cast in bronze, of over forty of McKinley's close friends and fellow statesmen—among them Sir Henry Bessemer, Warren G. Harding, John Hay, Theodore Roosevelt, Elihu Root, William Howard Taft, George Westinghouse, and Joseph Green Butler; Butler was the man primarily responsible for the creation of the McKinley Memorial in Niles.

That John Massey Rhind was both prolific and successful—judged by the number of commissions he received and the reputation he enjoyed among his fellow sculptors—cannot be denied. He was mainly a sculptor of architectural decorations and public monuments, and was widely acclaimed in each of these fields. But his work today seems rather unexciting, and it appears that he never achieved a real feeling for the beauty of sculptured form. Although he lived until 1936, he was firmly anchored to the academic naturalism and the Beaux-Arts style of the 19th century. The arrival of the new art, with its special emphasis on sculptural form, had not the slightest influence on his work.

Among the most imaginative sculptors of this period was John Gutzon Borglum (1867–1941), who was born in Idaho and grew up in the wild expanse of the great American West—a fact that was to have a decided impact on his early work in sculpture. After attending college in Kansas and studying for a few years at the newly established Mark Hopkins Art Institute in San Francisco, he went to Paris to study painting. He eventually turned to sculpture, however, and entered the Académie Julian, where Mercié was one of his teachers. His interest in the wild beauty of animals was encouraged there, for Barye was then immensely popular and Frémiet was teaching animal sculpture in the Jardin des Plantes. Though scorning the highly decorative element of French sculpture, Borglum absorbed much of the art of Rodin. After six years abroad, he returned to the United States in 1893, in time to exhibit his "Indian Scouts" at the Columbian Exposition in Chicago. A second trip to Europe soon followed, with part of his time being spent in England; and by 1902 he was established in New York City.

Gutzon Borglum was then thirty-five years old and had already been overshadowed by his younger brother, Solon. In 1903 Lorado Taft gave him no more recognition than to mention his name once in passing—and then mistakenly grouped him with "other names of foreign flavor." It was not until 1904 that Gutzon Borglum came to the attention of the American public, artists, and critics when he exhibited seven sculptures and a collection of eleven gargoyles at the Louisiana Purchase Exposition in St. Louis. Among his entries was a statuette of John Ruskin, moody and withdrawn, wrapped in a blanket and a large coat, bearded, and looking very much the stern old patriarch. The forms are massive and possess a surface that retains the roughness of the sculptor's first spontaneous creation. For such a small piece—it is only 15 inches high—it has a remarkable monumentality. Its boldly sculptured forms seek to express the spirit of the subject, just as Rodin had done in his statue of Balzac. This treatment of form was to appear frequently in Gutzon Borglum's work, as in the "Dancer" and "Figure," in the Corcoran Gallery of Art, and in his marble "Figure of a Woman," in the Cincinnati Art Museum. In all these pieces, but especially in the last named, his work possesses a certain affinity with that of George Grey Barnard. The "Figure of a Woman" only partially emerges from the rough-hewn marble block, and the full forms and pronounced *contrapposto* further suggest the influence of Barnard and Rodin.

The piece that attracted the most attention at St. Louis was the "Mares of Diomedes" (Fig. 13.15), which was executed in a highly naturalistic and detailed style, in marked contrast to the statuette of Ruskin. It is a large piece (over 5 feet high) and contains the six thundering, flesh-eating horses of Diomedes in wild flight, accompanied by a single rider. Borglum wanted to convey the idea of brute force being conquered and directed by the human mind. Though the subject is ostensibly the last of the labors of Hercules, A. T. Gardner astutely observed that "the classical title and the nude rider cannot disguise the fact that the real subject of this sculpture is a cowboy stampeding a herd of broncos. The allusion to Greek mythology was an afterthought . . ." (*American Sculpture*, 1965, p. 101.) The group was cast in bronze by Gorham, and there are several small replicas, one of which is in the Newark Museum. The sculptor made another large horse group, "Texas Cowboys," which commemorates the cattle drives along the Chisholm Trail to the railheads in Abilene, Wichita, and Dodge City, Kansas. This monument, erected in San Antonio, Texas, is 32 feet high and 40 feet long; it consists of two cowboys riding their ponies as they drive a segment of the herd, represented by several longhorn cattle bunched closely together. It dates from the late 1920's and is reported to have cost $100,000.

That Gutzon Borglum did not approve of the over-all sculptural work at the St. Louis fair is seen in a letter, dated November 15, 1911, to his friend Robert H. Davis; after writing that he had done all he could to secure for himself the directorship of sculpture for the San Francisco fair, which was scheduled to open four years hence, he concluded:

Quite seriously I think it will be a crime if some New York or other academic votary is given that task and is permitted to establish the borrowed and garbled art of this coast beyond the Rockies. That's not simply sentiment—but those mountains ought to screen out this cheap and stolen stuff that was made for a day for St. Louis and Buffalo and Chicago . . .   [Courtesy, New York Public Library]

The position was ultimately awarded to Karl Bitter, and Borglum's hope of creating a sculpture different from that of the academic decorators was squelched. Probably his marked individuality, his quick temper and outspoken manner, and his sharp criticism of most contemporary American sculpture alienated him from the leading sculptors who clustered around the National Sculpture Society.

Borglum carved the "Twelve Apostles" for the enormous Gothic church of St. John the Divine in New York City, along with other decorations for the same building. But toward the end of the first decade of the 20th century he began to turn increasingly to portrait sculpture and away from animal and ideal pieces. In 1908 a joint committee of the Library of Congress accepted his six-ton marble head of Abraham Lincoln. This giant head reportedly led a number of Southern women to commission a portrait of similar scale of General Robert E. Lee; this in turn evolved into the ill-fated project in which Borglum was to carve an enormous image of Lee out of the live rock of Stone Mountain near Atlanta, Georgia.

Although the original commission was solely for a colossal figure of General Lee, Borglum, in typical fashion, soon enlarged the design to include additional figures along the whole side of the dome-shaped mountain. Borglum was at the height of his glory with a project of these dimensions, and at one time he talked excitedly of more than two thousand figures in the composition. The cost was estimated at $2,000,000. Sensitive chemicals were poured down over the face of the area to be sculptured, and from a distance of 600 feet a projector cast an image of Borglum's design across the huge wall of stone. In May 1917 he wrote his friend Robert Davis that the scaffolding then extended over a length of 500 feet, and that he would soon be working on an expanse of mountain wall that was 800 feet high and 2,000 feet long. Work was interrupted by World War I, and it was not until 1923 that Borglum returned to his mountain. But by then dissension surrounded the project—partly because Borglum refused to include a Klansman among the many figures and partly because of the great expense involved. Although in the end Borglum would not be denied his dream of carving gigantic figures from the live rock of a mountainside, he was dismissed in 1925, whereupon he promptly smashed all his models. Taken to court on that account by the state of Georgia, he won the case when he explained that the models were his personal property with which he could do as he pleased, and that he could be found guilty only if he had destroyed the carvings on the mountain, which did indeed belong to the state. The state of Georgia was therefore left with a half-carved mountain-side, and Augustus Lukeman was called in to finish it. But after Lukeman had completed the figures of Lee and Stonewall Jackson, financial considerations terminated the project.

In 1908, the same year that Borglum completed his huge head of Lincoln, his spirited equestrian portrait of General Philip Sheridan was unveiled in Washington, D.C.; some fifteen years later he did another version of Sheridan for the city of Chicago. Borglum did not lack commissions, and his portraits commanded high prices; in a letter to a Mr. Bispham he reported he was charging $2,500 to $5,000 for a portrait bust in bronze, and for the equestrian "Sheridan" in Washington, Congress paid $50,000. Borglum is represented in Statuary Hall by three full-length portraits: one of Zebulon B. Vance of North Carolina (1916), a marble image of Alexander Stephens of Georgia (1927), and a bronze of John C. Greenway of Arizona (1930). Also destined for Washington was his bronze portrait statue of William Jennings Bryan, wrapped in a mantle, with the head set forward in a gesture of determination and the right hand held aloft in an oratorical gesture. The "Vance" and the "Bryan" are the best of the group, each possessing a boldness of sculptured masses and a strong animation. His seated figure of Lincoln is at the Court House in Newark, New Jersey, and in Newark's Military Park stands his "Wars of America" memorial (Fig. 13.16). Typically, in the "Wars of America," Borglum carried the war-memorial monument to a much greater size and complexity than had yet been done in the United States. Dozens of figures and horses make up this lively composition of fighting men, who wear the uniforms of all of America's wars from the Revolution to World War I.

Gutzon Borglum's dream of carving images out of a mountainside was realized with the colossal portrait heads of the four Presidents on Mount Rushmore in South Dakota: Washington, Jefferson, Lincoln, and Theodore Roosevelt (Fig. 13.17). Borglum originally planned to carve full-length figures of the four men, each 450 feet high; but this idea was soon abandoned. The carving was done with dynamite and with jackhammers, which operated from a power line that ran three miles to the town of Keystone. A camp was established at the base of the mountain, and a cable car ran up and down the 1,300-foot-high wall. President Coolidge had dedicated the site on August 10, 1927, and on the Fourth of July, 1930, the unveiling ceremony for the first of the great portraits—Washington's—was attended by more than two thousand people. Jefferson's was finished in 1936, Lincoln's in 1937, and Theodore Roosevelt's in 1939. Borglum, assisted by his son Lincoln, continued to work on the project until his death in 1941. In 1940 Congress voted another appropriation to complete the Mount Rushmore sculptures, which cost approximately $1,520,000. When someone asked Borglum about the great expense of these mountain portraits he replied sharply, "Call up Cheops and ask him how much his pyramid in Egypt cost and what he paid the creator. It was inferior work to Mount Rushmore."

John Gutzon de la Mothe Borglum remained active as a sculptor until almost the very end and survived his brother Solon by twenty years. He died of coronary sclerosis in a New York hospital, following an operation.

The early years of the life of James Earle Fraser (1876–1953) coincide with the history of the railroad camps of Minnesota and the ranch lands of South Dakota. He was born in Winona, Minnesota, where his father was in charge of pushing the railroad ever westward through desolate country. The family lived a rather nomadic existence for several years as the railroad continued its steady progress; but about 1880 the elder Fraser bought a ranch in South Dakota, and there young James spent the next ten years. The many impressions of the railroad gangs at work and in camp, of the ever-present Indians, of the great herds of plains' animals, of wild beasts, and of the natural magnificence of the land of nature were never to leave him. Years later, he recalled modeling little figures and animals in chalky clay, a substance native to South Dakota, which in time attained the hardness of stone; the more practical-minded homesteaders frequently formed bricks of this clay with which to build their homes.

After attending school for a few years in Minneapolis, Fraser went to Chicago, where he studied drawing and modeling at the Art Institute and worked in the studio of the sculptor Richard Bach. But his restless spirit let him stay only about six months, and when he was nineteen he set out for Paris.

Three of the next five years were spent in the modeling classes of Falguière and others at the Ecole des Beaux-Arts. Fraser was thrilled when his "Head of an Old Man" was accepted at the Salon of 1898 and prominently displayed along with other busts by the leading sculptors of the day; to his further delight it was awarded the prize of the American Art Association of Paris for the best piece at the Salon by an American. His next excitement came when his renowned countryman Augustus Saint-Gaudens, who was then occupying a studio in Paris, invited him to become his assistant. For two years Fraser worked with the famous sculptor on such projects as the equestrian "Sherman" for Central Park and the low-relief "Stevenson" portrait for Edinburgh; and when Saint-Gaudens returned to the United States in 1900, Fraser came with him to spend another two years in his studio in Cornish, New Hampshire. In 1901 when the commissioners of Buffalo's Pan-American Exposition wanted a special medal struck to honor the fine display of work there by Augustus Saint-Gaudens, they asked James Fraser to design it. The impact of the discipline and sensitivity of his master's style is clearly evident in Fraser's medal. It was also the first of many medals Fraser was to design, perhaps the best-known being the Victory Medal awarded to nearly five million people after World War I.

The Saint-Gaudens medal pleased the commissioners, and shortly after Fraser left Cornish to establish his own studio in New York, they asked him to produce a large bronze vase to commemorate the Pan-American Exposition. Commissions then came from the Louisiana Purchase Exposition for a statue of Thomas Jefferson and an equestrian statue of a Sioux Indian astride his pony, the latter group destined to stand in a prominent place in the Court of Honor.

By 1904 the Indian was no longer the feared heathen savage but the heroic, ill-fated warrior of the plains. Belatedly the white man began to sympathize with the Indian's plight and romanticize him as America's "noble savage." For the next great fair, the one in San Francisco in 1915, Fraser created "The End of the Trail" (Fig. 13.18), a statue that epitomized these feelings and brought him widespread fame. The subject was inspired by a passage from Marion Manville Pope: "The trail is lost, the path is hid and winds that blow from out the ages sweep me on to that chill borderland where Time's spent sands engulf lost peoples and lost trails." The sculptor sought to express the utter despair of this conquered people by showing the warrior and his mount at the end of their journey—"a weaker race . . . steadily pushed to the wall by a stronger [one]," as Fraser himself put it. It was the sculptor's dream to have it cast in bronze and placed on some prominent cliff near San Francisco, looking down on the Pacific Ocean—"driven at last to the edge of the continent. That would be, in very truth, 'The End of the Trail.'" Although no such commission was forthcoming, the great popularity of Fraser's sculpture led art-print publishers to pirate the image and sell it for an estimated gross of $150,000—more than enough, Fraser observed, to have his statue cast in bronze. Several small copies were cast in bronze, and one of these is in Brookgreen Gardens; a full-size cast stands in Waupun, Wisconsin. The sculptor's interest in the West he had known in his youth was indicated a couple of years earlier in his design for the five-cent piece, with the head of an Indian on one side and a buffalo on the other—typically American motifs.

James Fraser next turned to portraiture. From 1906 to 1911 he taught at the Art Students League, but was eventually drawn from the classroom to his own studio in MacDougal Alley to keep up with the deluge of commissions. He made a specialty of children's portraits, which had his own gentle lyrical touch blended with the low-relief design he had acquired from Saint-Gaudens. Examples of this are the portrait of the Harry Payne Whitney children on horseback or the one of Horatio Brewster, which was shown at the National Academy exhibition of 1902. There were numerous portraits of prominent men and women, such as the bust of E. H. Harriman, the relief of Morris K. Jessup, and—most famous of all—the bust of Theodore Roosevelt of 1909–1910. Fraser and Roosevelt found a common interest in the great outdoors and in athletics, and their close relationship is seen in the portrait bust, which captures the vigor and vitality of Roosevelt. For the final marble version, however, the sculptor lamented that he was instructed to "generalize" his image so it would harmonize with the other busts of the Vice-Presidents for the Senate wing of the U.S. Capitol. Thirty years later Fraser was again to portray Theodore Roosevelt, this time in an equestrian group that showed him as explorer and hunter; the bronze statue stands in front of New York City's American Museum of Natural History, with which Theodore Roosevelt was closely connected.

The Armory Show of 1913 made as little impression on Fraser as it did on most American sculptors of his generation. He was represented by a frame of medals, a bronze horse, and a marble image of "Grief." But he was soon back at work on portraits—the statue of John Hay (1914) for Cleveland; one of Thomas Jefferson for the capitol steps in Jefferson City, Missouri; and portraits of Lewis and Clark for the same state. His "Alexander Hamilton" was placed in front of the Treasury Building in Washington, and his "John Ericsson" (Washington, D.C.) is seated at the base of a tall shaft, at whose top are three figures—"Vision," "Adventure," and "Labor." In 1938 Fraser made a marble statue of Benjamin Franklin for the Franklin Institute in Philadelphia, and he did a statue of George Washington for the 1939 New York World's Fair. To adorn the great pylon of Chicago's Michigan Boulevard Bridge, he created "The Pioneers," a group of homesteaders, determined and unflinching, setting out from that great midwestern center to seek their fortunes on the prairie. His sculptures adorn the National Archives and Supreme Court Building in Washington. And for the Bank of Montreal, in the early 1920's, he created a stylized classical goddess of Victory to stand in the center of McKim's Doric atrium, an ensemble that the critic Royal Cortissoz described as having the "majesty of a temple." The marble goddess has nothing of the colorful, flowery Beaux-Arts style about her; the style is instead characterized by the union of naturalism and abstraction that attempted to achieve a compromise with the new art of the 20th century.

Fraser, however, never really made any significant contribution to the development of modern art. His style remained essentially bound to tradition, although he lived into the 1950's. One thing that gave him great personal satisfaction in his later years was being put in charge of organizing a memorial exhibition for the Century Association, celebrating the centennial of the birth of Augustus Saint-Gaudens. This was held in 1948, by which time James Earle Fraser had laid down his modeling tools forever. He died five years later in Westport, Connecticut, at the age of seventy-seven.

Lorado Taft (1860–1936) is remembered mainly as the author of *The History of American Sculpture*, first published in 1903. His was the first book to give a full treatment to American sculptors and sculptures of the 19th century, and with penetrating insight, well expressed, he provided a wealth of information to which future historians of sculpture in the United States will always turn. As a sculptor, however, he has fallen into virtual obscurity, except perhaps in the Chicago area, where his works are known best.

The son of a minister and educator (and later professor of geology), Taft was graduated in 1879 from what is now the University of Illinois. On receiving his master's degree in 1880, he went to Paris, where he studied at the Ecole des Beaux-Arts for the next three years. He returned home for a year, then went back to France for another two years of independent study. In 1886 he established his studio in Chicago and began teaching at the Art Institute. He enjoyed lecturing on the history of art, especially on the history of sculpture, and before long his lectures were extended to the University of Illinois in Urbana. Throughout his career, lecturing, teaching, writing, and participating in the activities of various art organizations occupied much of his time.

He first attracted national attention when for the Horticultural Building at the Columbian Exposition in Chicago he created two groups: "Sleep of Flowers" and "Awakening of Flowers." For the next four decades, Taft's studio was busy with poetic ideal pieces and large-scale symbolic works. His "Solitude of the Soul" group (1901), consisting of four nude figures emerging from the stone, is not unlike the style of George Grey Barnard, whose figures were sometimes only partly freed from the stone. In this is seen a certain feeling for sculptural form, even in an abstract sense, which is fully realized in the artist's enormous cast-concrete "Fountain of Time" in Chicago's Washington Park (1922). But more typical is the style of the Beaux-Arts, neo-Renaissance classicism of the 1912 "Fountain of Columbus" in front of the railroad station in Washington, D.C. In the gigantic Columbus and the two kneeling figures flanking him, there is simplification of form that approaches abstraction. The sculptor did the same thing in the enormous figure of Time (which stands in front of the "Fountain of Time") in which the enveloping robe minimizes the amount of naturalistic detail and increases the monumentality of the figure. But despite this simplification and stylization, Taft remained a staunch supporter of the conservative group and constantly rallied to the defense of the National Sculpture Society. He called Daniel Chester French the dean of American sculptors, and fiercely attacked the wild men of modern art. In his Scammon Lectures at the University of Chicago in 1917, he railed against the grotesqueries of Brancusi, Archipenko, and Matisse. He was a far more articulate spokesman than Ruckstull for the conservative group that clustered around the National Sculpture Society.

To Lorado Taft, abstraction meant a simplification of nature for purely formal purposes, usually to obtain an increase in monumentality or movement. He could not abide deformation of natural forms to a point where the integrity of the human figure was jeopardized. He was not a realist, and stressed that his own style depended upon "a feeling for mass and a preference for sculptural interpretation, rather than a literal or realistic one." Among the works by Taft that should be noted are the gigantic "Black Hawk" (1911) in Oregon, Illinois; the "Fountain of the Great Lakes" (1913) in Chicago; and the "Thatcher Memorial Fountain," unveiled in 1917 in Denver, Colorado. "Young Lincoln" (1927) stands in Urbana, as does "Alma Mater" (1929), which he created for the University of Illinois. For the town of Elmwood, Illinois, the place of his birth, he made a Pioneer Monument, and for Baton Rouge, Louisiana, he produced two groups, "Patriots" and "Pioneers," for the capitol. After a very active decade in the 1920's, Taft's career as a sculptor tapered off. He died in 1936.

One of the finest sculptors in the Boston area during these years was Bela L. Pratt (1867–1917), son of a Norwich, Connecticut, lawyer. His first serious training came when he enrolled in the Yale School of Fine Arts at the age of sixteen, and studied for four years under Professors John Henry Niemeyer and John Ferguson Weir. By his twentieth birthday he was studying at the Art Students League, where he remained for three years, attending the classes of William Merritt Chase, Kenyon Cox, Edwin Elwell, and Augustus Saint-Gaudens. During this period he was for a while an assistant in the studio of Saint-Gaudens, and thereby gained extremely valuable professional experience. In 1890 he went to Paris, studying at the Ecole des Beaux-Arts and working in the studios of Chapu and Falguière. After two years he returned to America to teach modeling at the art school of Boston's Museum of Fine Arts.

Bela Pratt returned just in time to get in on the sculptural decorations for the Columbian Exposition in Chicago, and he soon was at work on two large groups for the Peristyle, just behind Daniel Chester French's colossal "Republic." The groups, which represented the "Genius of Navigation," were done in the Beaux-Arts style. Pratt's success in the invention and modeling of these two groups established his reputation among American sculptors, and thereafter he had as many commissions as he cared to undertake. A decade of intense effort and productivity followed, with more than fifty pieces being done in his Boston studio.

There were bas-relief portraits, in the manner made popular by Saint-Gaudens, such as the "Daughters of F. C. Shattuck" (1893), "Mrs. Shattuck and her Daughter," and "Children of William Slater" (1894). His most famous portrait bust is of Bishop Phillips Brooks (1899), which is in the Brooks House at Harvard; it was this portrait that Pratt used later (1916) for his full-length bronze statue of Brooks that stands in the park opposite the Merrimack Valley Textile Museum in North Andover, Massachusetts. Pratt lacked the delicate sense of linear design that Saint-Gaudens possessed, and instead he endowed his works with a voluminous largeness, as may be seen in his bronze statue of Edward Everett Hale (1912) in Boston's Public Garden (Fig. 13.19). Pratt did several portraits for Harvard University, some of which were copies of busts by other sculptors; among the finest of his own design was that of Colonel Henry Lee (1902). The same institution owns his bas-relief portraits of John Codman Ropes (1902) and Louis Agassiz (1911).

Though Pratt was much respected for his work in portraiture, he was better known for his ideal subjects and for his decorative work for architecture. In 1894 he produced a life-size image of Our Lady of Sorrows for the shrine at Auriesville, New York, and two years later a bronze personification of Victory for the battleship *Massachusetts*. During a period of study and work in Paris in 1897, he modeled an academic nude figure of Orpheus playing his lyre as he mourns the loss of Eurydice. In 1911 he executed two heroic bronze women, representing Art and Science, which were placed at the main entrance of the Boston Public Library. He made numerous decorations for the Library of Congress in 1895–1896 and for the Pan-American Exposition of 1901. These, too, were fashioned in the spirit of decorative architectural work as it was taught in the last quarter of the century in the schools of Paris. For the Congressional Library he made six heroic spandrel figures—personifications of the arts and sciences—to go above the main entrance, and a 12-foot-high figure representing Philosophy, for the rotunda. For the pavilion he made bas-relief medallions of the "Four Seasons," which W. H. Downes praised as "full of spirit, refinement and true decorative character." On the exterior of the Liberal Arts Building at the Buffalo Exposition were several robed maidens and nude youths that Pratt had modeled, and atop the building his winged goddess danced lightly upon an orb; lower down was his group "Floral Wealth," showing Flora waving a festoon of blossoms while she rides in a flower-bedecked chariot, accompanied by *putti* and several personifications. Lorado Taft found this group quite objectionable, but admitted that "the misfortune lay largely in the subject. One is at a loss to know how an impressive sculptural mass can be built around so light and ephemeral a motif as a flower." (*History of American Sculpture*, p. 493.) But Taft praised the marble statue of a little girl, seated and deep in thought, which Pratt exhibited at the Fine Arts gallery.

Soon after the models for the Pan-American projects were finished, the sculptor was at work on an exceptionally fine figure of a soldier for a memorial to the boys of St. Paul's School in Concord, New Hampshire, who had served in the Spanish-American War. Far superior to most of the country's military figures on pedestals, it possesses a verve, a dignity, a youthfulness, and a genuine sensitivity, none of which are obscured by the careful details of the uniform. Pratt returned to the Beaux-Arts style in his Butler Memorial, with its two heroic classical maidens somewhat cramped in their small niche, one representing War, the other Peace. The strength of the piece is again in the massiveness of the sculptural form. Pratt's last major project was the statue of Alexander Hamilton for the memorial in Lincoln Park in Chicago. He continued to be active as a sculptor until his death in 1917.

William Ordway Partridge (1861–1930) was a sensitive poet, an actor, an articulate lecturer, a knowledgeable author and critic, and a gifted sculptor. He was well educated, with an outlook that was international rather than narrowly national and provincial. His parents, who were wealthy, were living in Paris at the time of William's birth; but he was educated at private military academies in the United States, and later at Columbia. When, at the age of twenty-one, he decided to make sculpture his profession, he took off for several years of study in Florence, Rome, and Paris.

By 1889 he had established a studio in Milton, Massachusetts. Not much is known of his first years as an artist, but among his earliest pieces was a softly modeled portrait bust, which was put into marble, of Chief Justice Melville Fuller (1891) for the U.S. Capitol. His impressionistic tendencies were already present. In 1892 he modeled the head of an old woman, a kind of genre piece, and called it "Nearing Home" (Corcoran Gallery of Art). That same year found him in London, where he was fascinated with a study of Shakespeare, a pre-occupation soon to bear fruit in a seated, casual, and thoughtful image of the great writer for the city of Chicago. Partridge made his debut as a sculptor at the 1893 Columbian Exposition, where he showed the model for his "Shakespeare," portrait busts of Edward Everett Hale and James Russell Lowell, and the model for his statue of Alexander Hamilton, which was soon to stand in bronze in Brooklyn. His "Shakespeare" and "Hamilton" transcend the weaknesses of earlier costume pieces by American sculptors to become living images of the men themselves, and they drew much attention to the sculptor, then thirty-two. These successes were soon followed by an equestrian statue of General Ulysses S. Grant for Brooklyn (1895) and the Kauffmann Memorial for Rock Creek Cemetery in Washington. In all of these Partridge remained true to the naturalism, infused with either vitality or pensiveness, characteristic of American portrait sculpture of his day.

By the turn of the century his work had taken a decidedly impressionistic turn, with a loose sketchiness and a spontaneous modeling, often leaving much of his subject only partially defined. This is noticeable in several portrait busts of British authors—Tennyson, Keats, Scott, Shelley, Milton, and others—where the face itself is strongly modeled but the hair and attire remain in a very rough "unfinished" stage. Lorado Taft criticized him severely in writing about a statue of Nathan Hale that Partridge made for St. Paul, Minnesota: "Portions are left barely outlined. With increasing distance from the head . . . the treatment becomes more and more summary, so much so, indeed, as to waive anatomical truth." (*History of American Sculpture*, 1903, p. 431.)

What Partridge searched for, and what Taft never came to understand, was the sheer joy of a sculptor who found in his first spontaneous sketches the fulfillment of creating meaningful form. Partridge sought the essence of his subject, plus a lively, fresh, impressionistic treatment of sculptural form—rather than the bold naturalism that Taft and many others worshipped. This looseness, this rejection of superficial detail, is clearly seen in Partridge's little statuette of Thomas Jefferson (Fig. 13.20) in the New-York Historical Society, a forerunner of the larger bronze statue he made for Columbia University. In this he went yet another step beyond the flickering, lively, decorative surfaces of MacMonnies' "Nathan Hale." The representation of material substance gave way to a sculptor's delight in the suggestiveness of only partially realized forms and a richness in the effect of modeled clay.

Partridge produced a second statue of Hamilton, this one for the Columbia University campus as a companion to the Jefferson, and also the Schermerhorn Memorial for the same institution. A variety of other sculptures issued from his New York studio, such as portrait busts (many imaginary, like those of Whittier, Goya, and Beethoven), decorative pieces (a "Satyr" for a Newport country club), and religious subjects (a "Pietà" for St. Patrick's Cathedral in New York City). In 1921 his "Pocahontas" was unveiled in Jamestown, Virginia, and five years later his bronze statue of Samuel Tilden stood just off Riverside Drive in New York. His last statue was that of Lord Gardiner for Saybrook, Connecticut.

One of the more prolific creators of memorial statues and portrait busts was Frank Edwin Elwell (1858–1922). Raised by his grandfather, a blacksmith, in the Concord of Emerson, Thoreau, and the Alcotts, young Elwell—like Daniel Chester French—received his first artistic instruction from Abigail May Alcott. The love he long harbored for these extraordinary people is seen in the busts he created many years later of Louisa May Alcott and Henry David Thoreau, now in the Public Library in Concord. As a young man he was sent to work in a Boston firm that manufactured surgical instruments, but his interest was always in sculpture. The general acclaim given a couple of his portrait busts provided the encouragement—and Louisa Alcott provided the funds—to send him to study abroad. Arriving in Paris in 1878, he attended the classes of Falguière and Jouffroy at the Ecole des Beaux-Arts. This Parisian period was climaxed by the statue "Aqua Viva"—a water carrier of the streets of Pompeii. Modeled in 1883, it was cast in bronze the following year and shown at the Salon in 1885. This was the first of Elwell's monumental works, which were soon to attract a large following in the United States.

By 1885 Elwell was in New York City, where for a while he shared a studio with Daniel Chester French and began teaching at the National Academy of Design and the Art Students League. His major work in the late 1880's was a monument for Edam, Holland—called "Death of Strength"—of an angel standing over a dead lion; this type of imagery followed the lofty, symbolic, and academic example of numerous French monuments then being erected. In the early 1890's Elwell worked on a literary group, "Dickens and Little Nell," which he sent to the Fine Arts exhibition of the Columbian Exposition of 1893; the piece, cast in bronze and thereafter placed in a park in Philadelphia, contains much anecdotal charm. Also shown at the Chicago fair was his marble "Intellect Dominating Force," or "Diana and the Lion." Other imaginary and symbolic subjects of his include "Egypt Awakening" (1896), "Orchid Dancer" (1898), "New Life" (1899), the personifications of Greece and Rome for the New York Customs House, and the "Kronos" and "Ceres" for the Pan-American Exposition in Buffalo.

Elwell's portrait busts are similar in style to those by Daniel Chester French, such as the marble busts of Simeon B. Chittenden (1890) at Yale and of Vice-Presidents Levi P. Morton (1890) and Garret A. Hobart (1900) in the United States Capitol. His portrait statues include the equestrian "General Winfield Scott," unveiled in 1896 at Gettysburg, and statues of Admiral Davis and General Steele at Vicksburg. In Orange, New Jersey, is his statue of Abraham Lincoln, and in Newark is the Dodd Memorial. For two years, beginning in 1903, Elwell was curator of Ancient and Modern Sculpture at the Metropolitan Museum of Art, but he was not temperamentally suited to the position. Except for his close friendship with French, Elwell was frequently at odds with his fellow artists and became involved in a personal controversy with the National Sculpture Society. By the second decade of the century he had withdrawn from active work as a sculptor. He died at the age of sixty-four in 1922.

In 1888 Giuseppe Piccirilli left Massa, Italy, to bring his large family to America. He was a stonecutter by trade, and his six sons learned the craft as they grew up. In New York City the family operated a stone-carving shop similar to a number of other Italian ateliers in the 19th century. Lorado Taft wrote that the scene of family life at the Piccirilli residence resembled "a Florentine household of the Quattrocento," and another critic described the Piccirilli atelier in an article on the carving of Daniel Chester French's "Lincoln":

Built around a substantial brownstone house formerly the dwelling of the Piccirilli family, and flanking on either side a picturesque courtyard, rise the great studios. Once within this busy hive, where the sculptors and their many assistants work . . . , you leave behind . . . the life of the city and feel transported into an entirely foreign atmosphere; and it is not a great stretch of the imagination to feel that this place resembles, with its granite, its antique busts and plaster reproductions . . . more the ancient "botega" where the old Italian masters of the Renaissance carved their masterpieces, than anything which our modern city can offer.
   [W. M. Berger, "Making a Great Statue," *Scribner's Magazine*, vol. 66, 1919, p. 430]

By the time of Taft's *History*, in the opening years of the new century, a couple of the sons—Furio and Attilio—were more than just skilled artisan marble cutters.

Before coming to America Attilio Piccirilli (1868–1945) had attended the Accademia di San Luca in Rome for several years, and in the last decade of the century he was the first of Giuseppe's sons to establish himself as a creative sculptor. He learned much by helping enlarge the models of other sculptors, and by the late 1890's he was producing work of his own design. His first commission was the statue of McDonough for New Orleans. At the Pan-American Exposition of 1901 he exhibited three pieces: "Dancing Faun" (1895), "Young Faun" (1898), and the model for the Maine Monument, which now stands at a corner of Central Park. The Maine Monument was a large-scale undertaking, with numerous personifying figures and naval motifs about the prow of a ship, climaxed at the top by Columbia riding triumphant in a shell-shaped chariot drawn by sea horses. One of the more popular motifs was a group of a "Mother with her Child," which the sculptor often exhibited separately. Work on the project extended over a decade, but all the while other commissions occupied Attilio. At the Louisiana Purchase Exposition, for instance, he exhibited three marble busts and a marble faun. As with several of the brothers, Attilio maintained his own studio where he executed his own pieces, but the Piccirillis continued to operate a common atelier in the old brownstone in the Bronx. It was this fraternal atelier that enlarged and carved in marble the designs by Paul Bartlett for the Senate pediment of the United States Capitol, as well as the pediment for the New York Stock Exchange, which Bartlett modeled from Quincy Ward's design. The brothers also communally produced several statues to adorn the new Parliament Building in Winnipeg.

Among Attilio's architectural works are the figures of Indian Literature and the Indian Law Giver for the Brooklyn Museum, a pedimental composition for the

Wisconsin State Capitol Building, and some lunettes for the Frick mansion on Fifth Avenue; in 1935 he experimented with a new material for sculpture in the glass reliefs he produced for the Palazzo d'Italia in Rockefeller Plaza. Of his few portrait statues, there is one of Governor Allen in Baton Rouge, Louisiana. In the 1930's, Attilio's work was very popular among wealthy patrons of conservative tastes and among the academically inclined sculptors. He took an interest in the affairs of several of the leading professional organizations, and was a member of the National Sculpture Society, the Architectural League of New York, and the National Academy of Design.

Henry Kirke Bush-Brown (1857–1935) was reared by his aunt Lydia and his uncle Henry Kirke Brown, the sculptor, at their home in Newburgh, New York. He received his first training there in his uncle's studio, and after moving to New York City he attended classes at the National Academy of Design. The years 1886 to 1890 he spent in Europe, mainly in Paris and Italy; in Italy he completed the marble statue of Richard Stockton, which had been designed by his then-deceased uncle.

Bush-Brown first achieved national recognition through his group "The Buffalo Hunt," which was exhibited at the Columbian Exposition of 1893 in Chicago. Thereafter he received several sizable commissions, the most important being the equestrian statues of General George C. Meade (1896) and General John F. Reynolds (1898) for Gettysburg Memorial Park. Years later he executed another equestrian statue for Gettysburg, the "General John Sedgwick," unveiled in 1913. In the late 1890's he participated in two of the major sculptural projects of New York City, producing the figure of Justinian for the Appellate Court Building and the one of Commander Hall for the Dewey Arch. He was represented at the Buffalo Exposition of 1901 by an ambitious group titled "Truth," and at the St. Louis fair by a more modest piece in marble, which he called "Infant Conversation." Another equestrian statue, "General Anthony Wayne," was erected at Valley Forge in 1908.

Two years later Bush-Brown moved his studio to Washington, D.C., where over the next couple of decades he executed memorials for Stony Point and Hudson, New York, one of a "Mountaineer Soldier" for Charlestown, West Virginia, and a "Lincoln Memorial" for Gettysburg. There were many portrait busts from these years, including one of his uncle, which is now in the Hall of Fame, New York University. The last years of his life were spent in organizing and commenting on the letters to and from his aunt and uncle.

Bessie Potter Vonnoh (1872–1955) represents an element in American sculpture quite removed from the pretentious memorials and elaborate architectural decorations of most of her contemporaries. Her fame was based on her intimate little groups of young mothers and infants, and on her groups of children at play. Although her lifelong work was essentially limited to these themes, she, like Mary Cassatt, was able to achieve in them an exceptionally fine expression of the warm joy of motherhood or the wholesome beauty of young children absorbed in some wonder of nature.

Bessie Potter was born in St. Louis in 1872. About 1890 she went to study with Lorado Taft at the Art Institute in Chicago, and she later assisted him in his work for the Columbian Exposition of 1893, where she exhibited a couple of her own portraits. To Bessie Potter, the most significant event at the fair was her exposure to the loosely modeled little figures by the Russian sculptor Paul Troubetzkoy. These inspired her to attempt small-scale genre pieces and the little groups of mothers and children (Fig. 13.21), which in time achieved enormous popularity, culminating in an exhibition of her work at the Brooklyn Museum in 1913. In 1896 she produced what was to become the most popular of all her statuettes— "The Young Mother" (Fig. 13.22). A great many replicas of it (14 inches) were made in plaster and bronze, and it was the source for several other statuettes that were variations on the same theme. The flickering surfaces and spontaneity of modeling reveal the influence of the contemporary French manner.

In 1899 Bessie Potter married the painter Robert Vonnoh and thereafter lived in New York City. Her "Young Mother" was exhibited regularly during these years—at the National Sculpture Society show of 1898; at the Paris Exposition in 1900, where it won a bronze medal; and the following year at the Buffalo Pan-American Exposition, where it received an honorable mention.

In the 1920's and 1930's, Bessie Potter Vonnoh modeled several groups of children, which were the central themes for fountains; one is at Ormond Beach Park in Florida; one, the Burnett Fountain (1937), is in Central Park. For the Roosevelt Bird Sanctuary at Oyster Bay, Long Island, she made another fountain (1925), in which a little girl holds up a bowl from which the birds may take a drink. The statue of a nude little girl, entitled "Water Lilies," done in 1913, was set up in Brookgreen Gardens in 1934. Bessie Potter Vonnoh occasionally did a portrait bust—such as the one of Major General S. W. Crawford for the Smith Memorial in Philadelphia, or the James S. Sherman for the United States Capitol. She was obviously more at home in such work as the pert little bust of Hester (in the Cincinnati Art Museum)—a bright-eyed beautiful child, full of wonder and love, wearing a big ribbon in her bobbed hair. In all her genre pieces the sculptor sought a quick spontaneous impression, rather than a labored naturalism. Although she lived until 1955, her career as a sculptor came to an end in the 1930's.

Bessie Potter Vonnoh was like nearly every one of the sculptors discussed in the last three chapters in that the major characteristics of her style were derived from the Parisian schools and ateliers of the last quarter of the 19th century. The sculptors considered in the next chapter will bring to a close this period in American sculpture, which was dominated by the Beaux-Arts style, with its rich modeling, flickering surfaces, lavish decorative element, lively naturalism, and affinity with the neo-Renaissance, neo-Baroque architectural revival. These sculptors were united by a common interest in indigenous themes and subject matter, and thus constitute something of a phenomenon in the history of 19th-century American sculpture.

[FIG. 13.1] Administration Building, Columbian Exposition, Chicago (1893). Richard Morris Hunt, architect; Karl Bitter, sculptor. Courtesy, New-York Historical Society, New York City.

[FIG. 13.2] "Dr. William Pepper," by Karl Bitter (1895–98). Bronze. Courtesy, University of Pennsylvania.

[FIG. 13.3] "Air," by Karl Bitter (1893). Northern entrance to the Administration Building, Columbian Exposition, Chicago. Courtesy, New-York Historical Society, New York City.

[FIG. 13.4] The Dewey Arch, New York City (no longer extant). Architect, Charles R. Lamb; sculptor in charge, Frederic Ruckstull; contributions by numerous other sculptors (1889). Courtesy, New-York Historical Society, New York City.

[FIG. 13.5] East Esplanade, Pan-American Exposition, Buffalo, N.Y. (1901). Center, "Fountain of Man," by Charles Grafly; four groups (left to right): "The Savage Age in the East," by John J. Boyle; "The Despotic Age," by Hermon MacNeil; "The Savage Age in the West," by John J. Boyle; "The Despotic Age," by Isidore Konti. "America Welcoming the Pan-American Nations" (quadriga atop dome), by Frederic Ruckstull. Courtesy, New-York Historical Society, New York City.

[FIG. 13.6] Columbian Exposition, Chicago (1893). Far end of lagoon, the colossal "Republic," by Daniel Chester French; near end of lagoon, "Triumph of Columbia," by Frederick MacMonnies; at right of lagoon, Agricultural Building, by McKim, Mead, and White, with sculptural decorations by Philip Martiny. Courtesy, New-York Historical Society, New York City.

[FIG. 13.7] Decorative sculptures being enlarged for the Pan-American Exposition, Buffalo (1901). Courtesy, New-York Historical Society, New York City.

[FIG. 13.8] "Fountain of Abundance," by Philip Martiny (1901). Pan-American Exposition, Buffalo. ("Love on A Snail," in spillway, by Janet Scudder.) Courtesy, New-York Historical Society, New York City.

[FIG. 13.9] Memorial to the South Carolina Women of the Confederacy, by Frederic Ruckstull (1911). Bronze. State House, Columbia, S.C. Courtesy, State of South Carolina; photo, Index of American Sculpture, University of Delaware.

[FIG. 13.10] Model for the "City of Philadelphia," by Alexander Milne Calder, for City Hall (1872–94). Plaster. Courtesy, Archives of the City of Philadelphia.

[FIG. 13.11] Model for "Asia," by Alexander Milne Calder, for City Hall (1872–94). Plaster. Courtesy, Archives of the City of Philadelphia.

[FIG. 13.12] "The Despotic Age," by Isidore Konti (1901). Pan-American Exposition, Buffalo. Courtesy, New-York Historical Society, New York City.

[FIG. 13.13] "Stone Age in America," by John J. Boyle (1886–88). Courtesy, City of Philadelphia.

[FIG. 13.14] H. H. Houston," by John Massey Rhind. Bronze. Courtesy, Archives of the City of Philadelphia.

[FIG. 13.15] "Mares of Diomedes," by Gutzon Borglum (1904). Bronze, 62″ high. Courtesy, Metropolitan Museum of Art, gift of James Stillman, 1906.

[FIG. 13.16] "Wars of America," by Gutzon Borglum (1925–26). Bronze. Newark, New Jersey. Courtesy, Essex County Park Commission.

[FIG. 13.17] Presidential portraits, Mount Rushmore, S. Dak., by Gutzon Borglum (1930–41). Courtesy, United States Department of the Interior; photo, National Park Service.

[FIG. 13.18] "End of the Trail," by James Earle Fraser (replica of the original of 1915). Bronze. Courtesy, Brookgreen Gardens, S.C.

[FIG. 13.19] Edward Everett Hale, by Bela Pratt (1912). Bronze. Courtesy, City of Boston; photo, Index of American Sculpture, University of Delaware.

[FIG. 13.20] Sketch for a statue of Thomas Jefferson by William Ordway Partridge. Plaster, 20½″ high. Courtesy, New-York Historical Society, New York City.

[FIG. 13.22] "The Young Mother," by Bessie Potter Vonnoh (1896). Bronze, 14½″ high. Courtesy, Metropolitan Museum of Art, Rogers Fund, 1906.

[FIG. 13.21] "Motherhood," by Bessie Potter Vonnoh. Bronze. Courtesy, Art Institute of Chicago.

Cowboys and Indians;
Lions and Tigers

IN REFERRING TO THE IMPETUS GIVEN TO THE THEMES OF COWBOYS, INDIANS, AND WILD animals through the sculptural decorations at the Columbian Exposition of 1893 in Chicago, Beatrice G. Proske wrote in her book *Brookgreen Gardens* that it was then and there that the sculptor-decorators were first "called upon to extol the pageant of their country." Chicago especially was acutely aware of the future of the expansive and rich American West, and the nation in general could already look back upon a chapter in its history that had but recently come to a close. From that time on, the West was thought of as a part of civilized America, and the country began to reminisce nostalgically about the exciting era just ended—and to suffer the first pangs of national conscience for its deplorable treatment of the Indian. By 1893 an acceptable solution had been found to the "Indian question," at least as far as the white man was concerned, who no longer living in fear of bloody reprisals for his misdeeds could well afford to take a more dispassionate view of the red man. By then the Indian could therefore be observed historically, with all the color and romance that had once surrounded him as a "noble savage" before he became the scourge of the intruder who continually annexed his lands. There was a renewed interest in him—not so much for humane reasons as for the part he played in the Western panorama—and artists and writers began to take him as their subject. In the late 19th and early 20th centuries there were several American sculptors who found the lore, the dress, the customs, the very being of the red man a new and fertile theme, and we shall consider them presently. But first a few words must be said about how the Indian regained the image of "noble savage" that Lord Byron and James Fenimore Cooper had given him.

Among the first of the American artists to represent the Western Indians was

George Catlin, who found them a fascinating and a noble people. For a long time he lived among them, doing hundreds of sketches, and later he wrote two volumes about his experiences. Even then, around 1840, he could foresee the dim future for the Indian as civilization moved relentlessly westward. Less than a decade later, of course, when the news from Sutter's Fort, California, reached the East, "the way to gold led through Indian territory." By 1856 the "iron horse" had nosed its way across the great Mississippi, over a bridge that unified the East with the Western territories. Catlin, in his *Letters and Notes on the Manners, Customs and Conditions of the North American Indians* (London, 1841), lamented the inevitable expiration of what he had come to love:

Many are the rudenesses and wilds in Nature's works, which are destined to fall before the deadly axe and desolating hands of cultivating man . . . . Of such "rudenesses and wilds," Nature has no where presented more beautiful and lovely scenes, than those of the vast prairies of the West; and of *man* and *beast*, no nobler specimens than those who inhabit them—the *Indian* and the *buffalo*—joint and original tenants of the soil, and fugitives together from the approach of civilized man; they have fled to the great plains of the West, and there, under an equal doom, they have taken up their *last abode*, where their race will expire, and their bones will bleach together.

Continuing with the theme of the good life of those "children of nature" who lived in a natural wonderland uncorrupted by civilized man, he wrote: "It is here that the buffalo dwell . . . and with them live and flourish the tribes of Indians, whom God made for the enjoyment of that fair land and its luxuries."

But that land of luxuries was to invite the destruction of the Indian. The white man's desire for wealth changed his view of the good and noble red man to "the only good Indian is a dead one," or at best that uncharitable and unromantic attitude expressed in the New York *Tribune* by Horace Greeley in June 1859 while on a tour of the West:

I have learned to appreciate better than hitherto . . . . the dislike, aversion, and contempt wherewith Indians are usually regarded by their white neighbors. It needs but little familiarity with the actual, palpable aborigines to convince any one that the poetic Indian, the Indian of Cooper and Longfellow, is only visible to the poet's eye. To the prosaic observer, the average Indian of the woods and prairies is a being who does little credit to human nature—a slave of appetite and sloth . . . . As I passed over those magnificent bottoms of the Kansas, . . . and saw their owners sitting around the doors of their lodges in the height of the planting season, . . . I could not help saying, "These people must die out—there is no help for them. God has given his earth to those who will subdue and cultivate it, and it is vain to struggle against His righteous decree."

Deprived of his lands, decimated by the white man's diseases, and his buffalo rapidly vanishing, the Indian struck out against his enemy. But the white man always retaliated, gradually reducing and wasting the Indian population through big and little Indian wars. By the time of the Columbian Exposition, the West had been secured for the white man and his civilization, and many had begun to feel that the Indian had been disgracefully treated. Hamilton Wright Mabie wrote to the editors of *Century Magazine* in 1889 that "the long and terrible story of injustice to the Indians has at last borne its fruits in an awakened public conscience." The time was ripe for a kind of artistic eulogy to the vanquished red man of the plains. Judge Lambert Tree, presenting Cyrus Dallin's "Signal of Peace" to the city of Chicago, declared to the commissioners of Lincoln Park what might well have been a kind of charge to the artists of America:

I fear the time is not far distant when our descendants will only know through the chisel and brush of the artist these simple untutored children of nature who were, little more than a century ago, the sole human occupants and proprietors of the vast northwestern empire of which Chicago is now the proud metropolis . . . . It is evident that there is no future for them except as they may exist as a memory in the sculptor's bronze or stone and the painter's canvas.

[Quoted from *Scribner's Magazine*, June 1915, p. 781]

Before the Columbian Exposition, the Indian had appeared only a few times in American sculpture: in Horatio Greenough's "Rescue," Hiram Powers' "Hiawatha," Crawford's despondent "Chief" for the U.S. Capitol pediment, Clevenger's "Indian Chief," Palmer's "Dawn of Christianity"; H. K. Brown had modeled his "Indian and Panther"; Quincy Ward did an "Indian Hunter"; in the 1880's there was John J. Boyle's "The Alarm" and "Stone Age in America," Bartlett's "Bear Tamer," and H. K. Bush-Brown's large group "Indian Hunting Buffalo."

The Indian's counterpart was the cowboy, a new type of hero-in-the-rough who was uniquely American. It was the hard-riding, happy-go-lucky, tough-fighting, freedom-loving cowboy that appealed to the imagination of such men as Frederic Remington and Charles Russell. But by 1893 the cowboy, as Remington had known him, was also disappearing from the West; he then became a subject for the sculptor, as did the pioneer, both men and women, to whom bronze memorials were erected from Massachusetts to Oregon.

Nor did the wild animals of the West escape the attention of the sculptor, who joined the sportsman, the zoologist, and the photographer in stalking the tawny cougar and the mountain goat, the elk and the moose, the grizzly bear and the prairie dog. Those sculptors who were less adventurous stalked their subjects in the zoological gardens of New York, Philadelphia, and Paris. American sculptors thus added new breadth to portraiture and the academic monument of the preceding generation with subjects as new as the West itself.

In his chapter devoted to Hermon Atkins MacNeil, J. Walker McSpadden used the subtitle "The Sculptor of Indians and Monuments." The epithet was well applied, for MacNeil was to become as known for his portrait statues and memorials as for his images of Indians. MacNeil (1866–1947) was born near Chelsea, Massachusetts. After attending the public schools he entered the State Normal Arts School, and on completing the four-year course, he was appointed instructor in modeling at Cornell University. He held the position for three years, at which time he decided that study abroad was essential to his development as a sculptor.

MacNeil arrived in Paris in 1888, and during the next three years, studied with Chapu at the Académie Julian and then at the Ecole des Beaux-Arts with Falguière, absorbing much of the impressionistic modeling of the French school. When he returned to the United States in 1891, he went to Chicago to assist Philip Martiny in his sculptural decorations for the Columbian Exposition; in time MacNeil was assigned to do some figures of his own design for the Electricity Building, an opportunity that thoroughly delighted him.

During the next three years MacNeil became absorbed in the subject of the American Indian. Carl Rohl-Smith, who had also done sculpture for the Electricity Building, had earlier made a bronze group known as the "Indian Massacre," which had been erected near the Pullman mansion in Chicago; and A. Phimister Proctor had made an equestrian group of an Indian scout, which stood along one of the main lagoons of the fair. Many Indians attended the Columbian Exposition, some to take part in ceremonial affairs, but most to perform in Buffalo Bill's Wild West Show. MacNeil was evidently fascinated with them. About a year after the close of the Columbian Exposition, he chanced to meet on the street one of the Wild West Show Indians who had remained in Chicago. His name was Black Pipe, and he was destitute; MacNeil persuaded him to pose for him in his studio. The result was a life-size high-relief portrait, the first of his Indian sculptures. Another piece for which Black Pipe posed was to bring the sculptor to the attention of the critics and his fellow artists; this was "Primitive Chant"—an Indian in breechcloth, hopping from foot to foot as he plays his flute. A marvelous rhythmic grace flows through the entire figure, which MacNeil caught in a moment of complete abandon and executed in a style best described as raw naturalism.

For the next ten to twelve years the Indian was to be MacNeil's primary theme, and he took an extensive trip through the Southwest to study the subject at first hand. He visited the Moquis and the Zuñis, observing their daily life, their customs, their dress, their various ceremonies. When he returned to Chicago (where he began teaching at the Art Institute), MacNeil was fired with an enthusiasm to create more images of the American Indian. Commissions were still scarce, and he was overjoyed when he was engaged to create four reliefs to adorn the new Marquette Building. The scenes represented the Jesuit priest's life among the Indians during the earliest days of the white man's settlement of the Chicago area. MacNeil's compositions were filled with the vitality that came from the artist's strong feeling for his subject; though somewhat coarser than Saint-Gaudens' elegant bas-reliefs, they possessed a fine quality of design in their contrast between linear and massive forms.

In 1895 Hermon MacNeil married one of his students—Carol Brooks, who was herself a sculptor—and at about the same time he learned he was the recipient of a one-year scholarship in Rome. As it turned out, he and his wife were to spend three years there, under the auspices of a Rinehart Scholarship. But study in

Rome did not mean the same thing to Hermon MacNeil that it had meant to the American sculptors of preceding generations. Throughout his career MacNeil remained essentially French in his naturalism and method of modeling, and he clung firmly to his love for the Indian as a subject all during his years in Rome. While there he did model a bust titled "Agnese Mattelia," which is reminiscent of the feminine portraiture of Herbert Adams; also, in fulfillment of one of the Rinehart Scholarship requirements, he made an ambitious relief based on a lofty theme, "From Chaos came Light." But his two major pieces from these years were inspired by the Indian of his native America, and not by pagan mythology or ancient history.

The "Sun Vow" (Fig. 14.1) is a group of an Indian sitting at the side of his adolescent boy who has just shot an arrow toward the sun. Here again, one finds the ethnological accuracy, the naturalism, and the French modeling of his earlier work, while there is no trace of any Roman influence; it is no youthful Apollo who makes his vow, but truly an American Indian, with feathered bonnet and moccasins, braided hair, and large-nosed, bony face. The same is true of the "Moqui Runner," a little bronze statuette of an unidealized red man dashing across the desert, carrying in his hands "a loathsome tangle of serpents"—an image, according to Lorado Taft, of "savagery personified." Taft also wrote that the "Sun Vow" was "good enough and important enough to assure its author of a permanent place in the history of American art."

In 1899, after three years in Rome, MacNeil closed his studio at the Villa dell' Aurora and went to Paris for a year, before returning to America. There his French tendencies in modeling were reinforced, and there his reputation received added luster when his "Sun Vow" and "Moqui Runner" were praised at the Exposition of 1900. The "Sun Vow" won a silver medal and afterward became one of MacNeil's most popular works. While on exhibition at the Art Institute in Chicago, the bronze original was purchased by architect Howard Shaw for the grounds of his home in Lake Forest, Illinois, and shortly thereafter a replica was ordered by W. T. Evans for his estate, Wentworth Manor, in Montclair, New Jersey. These statues eventually made their way into the art museums of Chicago and Montclair, and at least ten other replicas are to be found in various museums around the country. The "Sun Vow" and the "Moqui Runner" were both exhibited at the Pan-American Exposition in Buffalo in 1901, and the former was shown at the Louisiana Purchase Exposition in St. Louis in 1904.

Before MacNeil's return to America, New Yorkers had been given a preview of his work when "From Chaos came Light" and another of his Indian pieces done in Rome, the "Moqui Prayer for Rain," were shown at an exhibition held at the Metropolitan Museum of Art in 1899. When he came home in 1900 to establish his studio in New York, he was already a respected sculptor. Soon after his return he was asked to do the pedimental decorations for the Anthropological Building at the Buffalo Exposition, as well as the powerful group "Despotic Age" (Fig. 13.5), which stood opposite Boyle's "Savage Age" in front of the U.S. Government Building. Karl Bitter, director of sculpture at Buffalo, described the group in the *Art Handbook:*

The spirit of despotism with relentless cruelty spreads her wings over the people of the Despotic Age, crushing them with the burden of war and conquest and dragging along the victims of rapine. A half-savage figure sounds a spiral horn in a spirit of wild emotion.

MacNeil was also commissioned to design the official gold medal struck in celebration of the Pan-American Exposition. On one side a youthful woman stands beside a buffalo—representing the triumph of the intellect over physical power. On the reverse side a North American Indian offers a peace pipe to a South American Indian. Interestingly, MacNeil chose to depict the idea of Pan-American friendship through images of the red man, not the white man.

The year after the Buffalo fair, MacNeil created pieces for the exposition in Charleston, South Carolina; but more important was an exhibition of his works at Pratt Institute, in response to a great popular interest in his work. Of the twenty-two pieces shown, seventeen were of Indian subjects. Only two statuettes, "Dancing Greek Figure" and "Zephyr," betrayed any influence of his Roman period, but even these bore no trace of Italian neoclassicism.

MacNeil's decorative sculptures for the St. Louis fair of 1904 included a statue of an Indian boy running beside a buffalo, as well as several groups personifying Music, Art, and Sculpture. These, like all the plaster exposition sculptures, disintegrated after exposure to the elements. For Portland, Oregon, he created a monumental group titled "The Coming of the White Man" (Fig. 14.2). A proud defiant Indian warrior stands solidly with arms folded across his chest, peering at the horizon, while the medicine man at his side excitedly points toward the intruding white settlers in the distance.

By 1910 MacNeil's work with the theme of the American Indian had virtually come to a close. For the Panama-Pacific Exposition in San Francisco in 1915, he modeled the signs of the zodiac in stylized forms that reveal the influence of the new abstract art. By 1915 MacNeil was already doing the portraiture and monument decorations that would occupy the rest of his career. McSpadden reported a conversation with the sculptor in his studio in the early 1920's; after discussing the long frieze for the Missouri state capitol, the author asked the artist if he ever did Indian subjects any more: " 'No, only incidentally,' he said regretfully. 'This frieze will have some Indian figures, but my larger work has crowded out my figure studies. It has not been my choice, but as the gods have decreed.' " (*Famous American Sculptors*, p. 323.)

When MacNeil designed the new U.S. quarter in 1916, he put the eagle on one side and the Goddess of Liberty on the other; unlike James Fraser, who three years earlier had chosen an Indian portrait and the buffalo as proper themes for the American nickel, MacNeil reverted to a classical personification. And in 1922 when he created an ideal piece called "Into the Unknown," the subject was not the red man, but an academic classical nude.

Hermon MacNeil's reputation in portraiture rested mainly on two monuments: the McKinley Memorial in Columbus, Ohio, and the bronze statue of Ezra Cornell on the campus of Cornell University in Ithaca, New York. The former, executed soon after the turn of the century, consists of a full-length portrait of the President—his right thumb hooked in his pocket, his left hand holding his speech—in an image that is quietly animated. The figure stands on a pedestal in the center of a quasi-classical exedra; at the extremities are fine bold bronze groups representing Industry, Prosperity, and Peace. In the statue of Ezra Cornell, produced around 1915–1917, MacNeil approached the powerful, living naturalism of Saint-Gaudens, and one is reminded of the latter's standing "Lincoln"; the "Cornell" (Fig. 14.3) possesses an exquisite characterization of the subject, as well as a fine sense of structure. By the sculptor's own admission it was one of his happiest ventures into portraiture. Other commissions were the "Judge Burke Memorial" for Seattle, the portrait of Judge Ellsworth for Hartford, Connecticut, and the bronze figure of General George Rogers Clark, which stands within a circular Doric temple in Vincennes, Indiana. For Hartford he also produced a bronze high-relief portrait of Senator O. H. Platt amid symbolic figures. MacNeil and A. Stirling Calder each executed a portrait statue of Washington to adorn the piers of the Washington Arch in New York City; MacNeil provided the image of the subject as the military commander who led the colonies to victory, and Calder represented him as President. For Waterbury, Connecticut, MacNeil made the bronze figures for the memorial dedicated to the "Pilgrim Mother and Pilgrim Father," and for Chicago's West Park he produced a heroic statue of Père Marquette, which was unveiled in 1926. In the course of his career he created several war memorials, among them the Soldiers' and Sailors' Monument in Albany and another in Whitinsville, Massachusetts. In Charleston, South Carolina, his group commemorating the "Defenders of Fort Sumter" was unveiled in October 1932, but it was not as successful as his earlier work. Another of his war memorials stands in Flushing, New York (1925), while his Army and Navy groups decorate the two great pylons alongside the parkway in Philadelphia. MacNeil made the groups "Intellectual Development" and "Physical Development" that stand outside the entrance of Potter Gymnasium on the campus of Northwestern University. In the 1920's he produced a bas-relief frieze about 130 feet long for the Missouri state capitol, representing the first settlers who "received supplies and renewed strength from Missouri" as they crossed the Mississippi and headed West. The Supreme Court Building in Washington contains a marble pedimental group of his design.

MacNeil's career ended in the 1930's. The Fort Sumter Memorial was his last major project. Only a few portrait busts—such as "Dr. Elmer E. Brown" (1933) at New York University or "John Stewart Kennedy" (1933) at the New York Public Library—were done after the monument. The earlier strength of his naturalistic style and his fondness for Indian subjects gave way in his later years to a strange and generally unsuccessful attempt at "academic stylization." The Fort Sumter Memorial, big and heroic, is formally quite displeasing and totally uninspiring as a work of art. His greatest period of artistic creativity was over by the time of World War I; thereafter he seems to have lost touch with the subjects and the stylistic influences that provided him with real inspiration.

Alexander Phimister Proctor (1862–1950) was born in the province of Ontario and grew up in Denver. Colorado was as raw, rough, and untamed in those days as it was beautiful, possessing the natural loveliness of flowering spring valleys and wooded mountainsides, awesome winter blizzards, and the bleakness of snow-bound cabins. As a boy, Proctor observed the Indians stoically maintaining a centuries-old primitive coexistence with the forces of nature, yet constantly yielding to the encroachment of the white man's world. That world, in the territory of Colorado in the 1870's, consisted of roaring mining camps, of grizzled prospectors and hunters, of the drunken jubilation over a strike, and of the trapper's lonely solitude. Young Proctor knew intimately all the facets of life on the frontier that he would one day immortalize in bronze.

Far more than the lessons taught in Denver's Broadway Grammar School, the boy loved to trek through the forest in search of big game—elk or grizzly bear. While in his teens, he and a friend went on a camping trip into the Yosemite Valley where they hunted and sketched and climbed mountains, reveling in that virtually untouched, majestic paradise. And although a stronger calling eventually lured Proctor from his spacious West to crowded New York City, he never forgot the rich life of the red man and the white man in Colorado, California, and Oregon. He modeled a few pieces on his own, but he clearly needed professional training if he wanted to make a career of sculpture, and in 1888 he went East to study at the Art Students League and at the National Academy of Design in New York City. But there were, of course, at that time no teachers at either institution who offered instruction in the modeling of such subjects as cowboys, Indians, and wild animals.

Proctor's first real opportunity came in 1891 when he was invited to do some of the decorative sculpture for the Columbian Exposition in Chicago. There, during the next two years, he produced more than thirty-five models of animals of the American wilderness, including moose, elk, mountain lion, and even a pair of Alaskan polar bears. And overlooking the waters of the main basin of the fair stood his two equestrian statues—one a cowboy, one an Indian scout. In the Fine Arts exhibition his bronze "Charging Panther" (Fig. 14.5) attracted a good deal of attention. There can be no doubt that Proctor added a new ingredient to American sculpture, for while others in his profession were creating robed maidens and assorted neoclassical personifications, Proctor brought to the attention of the world the strength and beauty of the wild animals of America. Moreover, his cowboy on his pony and his Indian scout scanning the horizon were among the first monumental equestrian statues to give dignity to those subjects from the American West. In creating these images, he employed a simple naturalism that included all the rich detail peculiar to his subjects.

In 1893 Proctor won a designer's medal in recognition of his special contribution to the exposition. That year he also won the hand of a lovely Chicago girl. With his bride he departed for Paris, where he studied in the ateliers of Denys Pierre Puech and Jean Antoine Injalbert for over a year. At the request of Augustus Saint-Gaudens he returned to model the horses for the equestrian statues of General Logan and of General Sherman in Central Park. Awarded the Rinehart Scholarship for study abroad, Proctor again went to Paris, where he worked in the Académie Julian and the Académie Colarossi.

So imbued was he with the scenes and life of his youth in the West that he never succumbed to the abstract themes of the Parisian schools. He modeled a "Lioness," standing in an alert pose; this is dated 1897. He had his "Panther" with him, plus a charming little "Faun" only a few inches high; and the art world of Paris saw in these pieces a continuation of the work of their own beloved *animaliers*, Barye and Frémiet, whose models, however, had come from the zoos and academies of Paris. Another very popular work of Proctor's was his equestrian "Indian Warrior," about 42 inches high, replicas of which were cast in Paris by Pazin and in America by Gorham. The "Indian Warrior" was among the several bronzes that won him a gold medal at the Paris International Exposition (1900); for this exposition he supplied the quadriga that decorated the United States Building. In that same year he was made an associate member of the National Academy of Design, and he returned to New York City to open a studio.

By the turn of the century, cowboys, Indians, and wild animals were recognized as legitimate subject matter for sculpture. Carrère and Hasting's design for the McKinley Monument in Buffalo called for four large lions, and Proctor was asked to do them. Those who attended the Pan-American Exposition in Buffalo in 1901 could have seen his collection of nine small bronzes, most of which were of animals. Proctor's decorations for that exposition were two groups representing Agriculture and Industry; these were not pseudo-neoclassical, academic personifications but actual scenes from the field and the forge. For the Bronx Zoo he made numerous reliefs and animal heads, and an entrance to Brooklyn's Prospect Park was adorned with a pair of his dozing panthers. Probably his most famous feline sculptures of this period were the two tigers he produced for Princeton University to replace the weathered old wooden lions that guarded a doorway to one of the campus buildings. For the tigers he won the much-coveted gold metal annually awarded by the Architectural League of New York.

At Theodore Roosevelt's insistence Proctor modeled two bison heads for the White House, to replace the British lions that had long decorated one of the fireplaces. The sculptor and the President shared a love of outdoor life and hunting, and they became good friends. When Roosevelt's Cabinet held a farewell dinner for their chief, their gift to him was Proctor's bronze "Charging Panther," a drawing of which was later used as the frontispiece for one of Roosevelt's books. Many years later, Proctor was to make an equestrian statue of the old Rough Rider for the city of Portland, Oregon. Between 1912 and 1914, Proctor made the four heroic bison that decorate the Q Street Bridge in Washington, D.C.

These enormous beasts, about 8 feet high and 14 feet long, reveal the keen eye of the hunter-naturalist turned sculptor, who had often studied the animals in their native habitat. They were neither abstractions nor generalizations, but were the reincarnation of the shaggy bison themselves.

In 1914 Proctor closed his large prosperous studio and left New York for Idaho, California, and Oregon, where he spent many happy years. Though there were still vast areas where he could roam and hunt, there were also large cities and a citizenry who took pride in the land they had tamed and the civilization they had established. As a result, Proctor found no scarcity of commissions for his type of art in the Far West. For the plaza of Denver's Civic Center he made a bronze memorial, "Buckaroo," or "Bronco Buster"—a woolly-chapped cowboy with right hand flung high, riding a diving, spinning, bucking pony. It was erected on a site where the artist recalled having seen herds of wild antelope graze and (in earlier days) a band of Utes with newly won scalps at their belts ride into town, and near where he himself had gone to grammar school and played ball as a boy. The "Bronco-Buster" was a popular piece, and small replicas of it—about 28 inches high and signed and dated 1915—were cast by Gorham. The large version was later joined by Proctor's Indian on horseback, "On the Warpath." In the years 1919–1922 he modeled the "Circuit Rider," a memorial dedicated to the early itinerant preachers of the Northwest and erected on the State House grounds in Salem, Oregon; also the buckskin-clad "Pioneer," which stands on the campus of the University of Oregon. In 1922 his "Teddy Roosevelt as a Rough Rider" was presented to the city of Portland by Joseph N. Teal, a long-time friend of the President.

In 1925 Proctor went to Rome where he spent two years as artist in residence at the American Academy. In his studio he modeled the monument entitled "Pioneer Mother" (Fig. 14.4), which was given in 1928 by a local benefactor to Kansas City, Missouri. Another product of these two years was the equestrian statue of Sheriff Til Taylor for Pendleton, Oregon. Once again the sculptor's intimate knowledge of his subject allowed him to render it with great authenticity. Proctor's art was always based more on his own direct observation than on any academic lessons; if such works as the "Pioneer Mother" or the "Sheriff Til Taylor" seem so unaffected as to be artless, it is because Proctor knew the unpretentious character of his subjects; he wished to render them in as natural a manner as possible. Nevertheless, he infused into the "Pioneer Mother" a heroic determination and fortitude.

These pieces were followed in the early 1930's by an "Indian," cupping water from a stream while alertly looking about, which was placed in a natural setting in Saratoga State Park. The "McKnight Fountain," representing an Indian kneeling to examine the trail beside a bearded old trapper in buckskins, was destined for Wichita, Kansas. They were executed in Proctor's New York studio, with the Indian he had brought East with him, Big Beaver, serving as the model for his red men.

In 1936 President Franklin D. Roosevelt dedicated Proctor's Robert E. Lee Memorial in Dallas, an equestrian group composed of the general riding his horse, Traveler, followed by a young aide also mounted. By that time, the seventy-four-year-old sculptor had already decided to move his studio across the continent once more, this time to Seattle. This accomplished, there remained but one major project in his career.

When historian J. Frank Dobie and oilman Ralph Ogden wanted to commission a monument to the beautiful, spirited mustangs of the West, they turned to Alexander Phimister Proctor. The sculptor and part of his family moved to Texas, where the wiry ponies could be observed in large numbers. There he modeled the "Monument to the Mustangs," which is composed of seven wild horses thundering in frenzied flight across the plain. Because of World War II, the bronze was not available at once, but by 1948 the group had been cast and was unveiled on the campus of the University of Texas. At the ceremony, J. Frank Dobie told what he, Ogden, and the sculptor found symbolized in the "Mustangs":

As I behold these glorious plunging creatures that Phimister Proctor has arrested in enduring bronze, they inspire in me a kind of release and elation. I am free with them and with the wind, in spaces without confines . . . . Like the Longhorn, the mustang . . . has been bred out of existence. But here, beautiful and free, he lives for centuries to come.   [Quoted from *Montana the Magazine of Western History*, 1964, p. 23]

Two years after his "Mustangs" was unveiled, Proctor died, leaving behind more than a score of vivid images of the beautiful wild creatures, the Indians and cowboys, the hunters and pioneers who had made up the West of his youth.

Another who came out of the American West was Solon Hannibal Borglum (1868–1922), younger brother Gutzon Borglum. Solon grew up in Fremont, Nebraska, where his father was a physician. The boy frequently accompanied his father on the long circuit of calls through the prairie, and would play with Indian boys while the elder Borglum attended to the sick. He came to know ranching far better than his books, and while still in his teens, he was put in charge of a ranch that his father owned in western Nebraska. All the still beauty and remoteness of the land, the intense heat of the summer sun and the blinding fury of the winter storms, the camaraderie of the cowboys around campfires and the loneliness of night watch over the herds, the affectionate relationship that developed between horse and rider, the fascination of Indian and animal life—all this and more made up the world of young Borgum as he grew to manhood. It was very much to his liking, and though Solon had frequently made sketches of cowpokes, Indians, and animals, he had never considered any other way of life—until the brief return visit of his brother, Gutzon, who had been studying sculpture abroad. Gutzon was much impressed with Solon's sketches and eventually persuaded him to give up ranching and take up art. Shortly thereafter, in the mid-1890's, Solon Borglum left the ranch to study with his brother in California. But after opening his own painting rooms in Sant' Anna, he soon found he was maintaining his studio only on Saturdays, and the rest of the week he was roaming the open spaces and camping with cowboys and Indians.

His first taste of artistic success and recognition came one Saturday when a local citizen chanced to catch him in his studio and commissioned him to paint his portrait. The finished portrait drew praise and more commissions. Before long he had amassed a fortune of $60; and with the money, and some misgivings, he climbed aboard a train bound for Cincinnati, Ohio.

He studied day and night at the art school in Cincinnati, quickly attracting the attention of his instructor, Louis Rebisso, a sculptor noted for his equestrian statues of Generals William Henry Harrison, Ulysses S. Grant, and James B. McPherson. Rebisso, an Italian by birth and long a professor of sculpture at the Cincinnati Art School, invited Solon Borglum to work in his studio, and there the young artist gained much practical experience. Borglum had always had a great interest in horses, and in Cincinnati he was regularly found at a government stable, where he had obtained permission to sketch and take measurements. At the place where the city disposed of dead animals, Solon dissected the creatures in order to learn more about their anatomical structure. One of his first pieces of sculpture, "Horse Pawing a Dead Horse on the Prairie," won a prize in the school exhibition. Another prize, which carried with it a modest stipend, financed his trip to Paris.

For a few months Solon Borglum attended the Académie Julian, studying with Puech and with the animal sculptor Frémiet. But he was to reject the orthodox course of study, and later wrote of this period:

. . . when I got [to Paris] I was suddenly dismayed. I saw that the most any artist can do is to live and work with nature, and I said to myself, "*that* is what I must do at home. Why have I come?" And the whole time I stayed, I struggled not to let my work lose its stamp of American life.
[Quoted from "Solon H. Borglum: Sculptor of American Life," *Craftsman*, July, 1907, p. 382]

While in Paris Borglum continued to make statuettes of horses, such as the "Little Horse in the Wind," which was purchased for the Cincinnati Art Museum in 1898. A group of two cowboys and their mustangs, entitled "Lassoing Wild Horses," was sent as his first entry to the Salon in 1898; the next year he sent "Stampede of Wild Horses," which was acclaimed by the critics and awarded an honorable mention by the jury. Parisians were quite taken by this fresh new art and subject matter from western America; perhaps their interest had been whetted by the two appearances in recent years of Buffalo Bill's Wild West Show. It was in Paris, then, that Solon Borglum achieved his first recognition.

It was also in Paris that he found a bride, whom he took back to America for a summer's tour through the Sioux encampments on a reservation in North Dakota.

Indian life now joined cowboys and wild horses as the subject matter of his sculpture. One of the three statuettes he showed in the Fine Arts Department of the U.S. exhibit at the International Exposition in Paris in 1900 was awarded a silver medal. It was called "Horse and Indian," or "On the Border of White Man's Land," and a replica of it is owned by the Metropolitan Museum of Art. A lone Indian peers over a rise in the terrain at some unwelcome intrusion upon his hunting grounds. He is filled with curiosity, yet aware of the danger before him, every fiber of his body taut. Borglum successfully avoided the more hazardous pitfalls of late 19th-century academic French art, for without sensationalism, sentimentality, or melodrama he rendered this dramatic scene of the confrontation of civilization and primitive life on the Western frontier. The entire story is revealed without recourse to "literary sculpture" or an excessive picturesqueness. Borglum's naturalistic style achieves its strength through his familiarity with his subject.

In 1900 Solon Borglum established a permanent studio near New York City. The American public first saw his work when he exhibited eleven pieces at the 1901 Pan-American Exposition in Buffalo; not long afterward, he had another exhibition at the Keppel Gallery in New York City. Several of his earlier statuettes were shown at Buffalo, but two new pieces took the nation's fancy: the thundering, horn-locking, ground-pawing bronze "Fighting Bulls," and the cold, haunting, white marble "Burial on the Plains." His success at the exposition was followed by his election to the National Sculpture Society the same year. A similar collection of nine Western subjects was shown at the St. Louis Exposition in 1904; more important were his four large groups representing cowboy and Indian life that decorated one of the main concourses. In one, a grizzled old plainsman huddled close to his horse in a wintry group called "The Blizzard," or "A Peril of the Plains"; a second, "Cowboy at Rest," showed a young cowhand lying prone beside his standing horse. The other two were of Indians: one was a moving scene of a brave talking to his young son; and the other, the most impressive of all, was "Sioux Indian Buffalo Dance." A small bronze replica, 38 inches high, of the "Buffalo Dance" is reproduced through the courtesy of the Kennedy Galleries (Fig. 14.6). Borglum captured all the colorful detail of a dance in which those powers of the red man's universe were implored to send the life-sustaining buffalo to his people once more. Hooded and cloaked in a buffalo hide, a wiry medicine man, clad only in breechcloth and moccasins, crouches to make a mighty leap, his body tight as a coiled spring; an old man chanting beats a drum at the rear of the group, and a stalwart chief stands on the other side. C. H. Caffin, in *International Studio*, June issue, 1903, wrote of the sculptor:

His groups have little of the ordered arrangement of traditional composition, nor does the modeling show facile skill or refinement. His work, indeed, is much more an expression of nature than of art; the frank, untrammelled expression of a natural artist giving utterance to the fullness of his thoughts.

This summary is true enough, for Borglum remained dedicated to his promise to hold to his native way of rendering those subjects that were truly American, and he never adopted the Beaux-Arts style.

During the years after the St. Louis Exposition, Solon Borglum worked on two equestrian monuments. The first to be unveiled, on May 25, 1907, was of General John B. Gordon, on the State House grounds in Atlanta, Georgia. The second, of Rough Rider Bucky O'Neill riding high atop the arched back of a bucking bronco, was dedicated about a month later, in Prescott, Arizona. Gutzon Borglum, in his memorial letter in *The New York Times*, March 5, 1922, described it as "the finest heroic group of its kind in America." Only in the work of Frederic Remington, which was on a much smaller scale, can one find a challenge to that claim. Solon Borglum created another equestrian statue, "The Pioneer," for the Court of Honor at the Panama-Pacific Exposition of 1915 in San Francisco; it depicted a sturdy frontiersman, with rifle in readiness, riding across the Western plains.

Solon Borglum, nearly fifty years old when the United States entered World War I, served as a canteen volunteer. Frequently he went among the troops along the front lines, where he was twice gassed. Afterward, France awarded him one of her highest medals of honor. Returning to America, Borglum took charge of an art school for the rehabilitation of the men who had served in the American Expeditionary Forces. He seems to have enjoyed teaching and did a great deal of it in the last years of his life. He even designed a book, *Sound Construction* (published posthumously in 1923), in which he provided hundreds of illustrations of comparative anatomy. Regarding his own work from 1919 to 1922, there was a curious departure from his subjects of Western life in favor of ideal themes. Among the last pieces he worked on were "Aspiration," "Inspiration," and "Little Lady of the Dew." In January 1922 he had a sudden attack of acute appendicitis; he died a few days later, after an operation, at the age of fifty-four.

The sculptor who more than any other captured the grave dignity and the nobility of the American Indian was Cyrus E. Dallin (1861–1944); his great series of four equestrian statues carried the imagery of the red man to its finest expression in sculptural form. Dallin in these works achieved a true monumentality, bestowing upon his subjects those innate qualities that had been almost wholly obscured to the eyes of the white man during the decades of hatred and conflict.

Dallin's parents were pioneers who in the 1850's had moved into the vast prairies of the West and helped to establish the little settlement of Springville, about forty miles south of Salt Lake City. There, in 1861, in the crude frontier town encircled by a high adobe wall, Cyrus Edwin Dallin was born, and there he grew up. The adobe wall was never needed for defense against the Utes who were commonly found camping in the vicinity, and the sculptor recalled many years later that while the rough and boisterous cowboys frightened him on several occasions when he was a little boy, the Indians never did. On the contrary, young Cyrus played games with the Indian boys and frequently went to their encampments and into their wigwams; among other pastimes, they would model little animals from the soft clay along the riverbanks. As a youth, Cyrus came to respect the red man, finding a beauty in his primitive arts, as well as a dignity and integrity in his way of life that was often lacking in the life of his own people. Through the years of his teens, then, his world was circumscribed by the raw life of the miners and cowboys and by the solemn, proud Utes.

Young Dallin's father operated a mine in the beautiful Wasatch Mountains. Cyrus, who worked at odd jobs around the mine, was present one day when the men struck a vein of white clay, and he soon modeled two lumps of it into portrait heads. They attracted the curiosity and admiration of the entire region, and when they were shown at the local fair that summer, they brought their creator his first patrons: Two men put up the funds to cover the cost of Cyrus' train fare to the East, plus a little spending money. In the company of a group of Crow Indians, who were headed for Washington, D.C., to see the "Great White Father," Dallin journeyed across the continent to Boston.

Boston in 1880 overawed Dallin at first. But he was soon studying with the sculptor Truman Bartlett, and assisting him in his studio to help pay for his instruction. To earn extra money, Dallin eventually found a job in a nearby terra-cotta factory. After two years he opened his own studio, which showed enough profit over the next six years so that the sculptor could afford to go to Paris for further study. From this period date the earliest of his Indian subjects. One of these won a medal when it was shown at the American Art Association in New York City in 1888. In the fall of that year he went to France.

In Paris, the influences of Chapu and the Académie Julian were apparent in Dallin's "Apollo and Hyacinthus" and "Awakening of Spring"; these were academic subjects that meant little to the man from the Utah Territory, but he persevered in his studies in order to master technique and the elements of composition. Then Buffalo Bill's Wild West Show came to Paris in 1889, and Dallin rediscovered the American Indian; he became the subject of Dallin's first major statue—the "Signal of Peace," the first of his four great equestrian monuments. Dallin later recounted:

The origin of that statue goes back to my boyhood, to a day when I witnessed a peace pow-wow between the Indian chiefs and the United States Army Officers. I shall never forget those splendid-looking Indians arrayed in their gorgeous head-dresses, riding up to the army camp . . . . In making my model of "The Signal of Peace," I used, to a certain extent, one of the Buffalo Bill Indians; in putting into it that dignity typical of the Indian, I had in my memory the chiefs who rode up to the peace pow-wow many years before.
[Quoted from W. Long, "Dallin, Sculptor of Indians," p. 568]

In representing his Indian chief with spear pointing upward in a signal of peace, Dallin meant the group to show the trust and good will the Indian offered the white man at their first meeting. The head and figure are truly those of the

Indian, modeled with a simple and strong naturalism and without the clever, lively surface treatment of the French school. The sculptor re-created the proud, brave warrior chieftain as he had known him in his youth. Even the scrawny pony is a careful rendering of the kind ridden by the Plains Indians.

Although the "Signal of Peace" drew much favorable comment from Parisians in 1890—just before Dallin returned to Boston with it—it was at the Chicago Columbian Exposition in 1893 that America became aware of it. Judge Lambert Tree purchased the statue and made a gift of it to the city of Chicago, where it still stands in Lincoln Park. The group established Dallin's place among the nation's most promising young sculptors; and that same year he was elected to the newly formed National Sculpture Society.

Not long afterward Dallin and his wife, the former Vittoria Colonna Murray of Boston, returned to his beloved Utah Territory, where he produced part of the "Pioneer Monument" for Salt Lake City and also the "Angel" on the dome of the Mormon Temple. But he felt that he needed still more training, and so in 1897 the Dallins departed for Paris. This time Cyrus studied under Jean Dampt. Dallin was represented at the Salon that year by a curious and charming little equestrian statuette of Don Quixote, and the following year by a marble bust of a young lady. But his interest in Indian themes continued, and in 1898 he was working on the second of his major equestrian monuments—"Medicine Man." It won high praise at the Salon of 1899 and was given a place of honor and a gold medal at the great Paris Exposition of 1900. According to reports, several Austrians were empowered to purchase it for their country, only to be disappointed when it was obtained for Fairmount Park in Philadelphia, where it may be still seen today (Fig. 14.7).

In Dallin's series, the "Medicine Man," unlike the naïve chief of the "Signal of Peace," warns that there may be danger in the presence of the white man on Indian lands. The expression on his face and his upraised right hand suggest a solemnly murmured incantation as he watches from his pinnacle as still more white men with their women, children, wagons, and livestock make their way farther and farther into Indian territory. On seeing this statue, spectators were impressed with the strong naturalism combined with the moving sentiment of the group: The former is a forceful image of the red man, without any modeling tricks or display of virtuosity of style; the latter epitomizes the strange, foreboding, yet heroic medicine man. Critics and artists alike had long agreed that the equestrian group was the sculptor's greatest challenge, and in the "Medicine Man" Dallin carried the Indian theme to a truly monumental level of artistry. No one had accomplished that before; other attempts at large-scale Indian subjects had suffered from too great a reliance on picturesqueness. Also the equestrian statue had previously been limited to portraits of military leaders; Dallin expanded the motif to include an American ideal subject filled with all the romance, color, and grandeur befitting a monumental art.

Dallin returned to the United States in 1900, bringing with him his latest triumph and the silver medal it had won in Paris. He exhibited the "Medicine

Man" at the Pan-American Exposition in Buffalo the following year and at the St. Louis fair in 1904. It was for the St. Louis Exposition that Dallin made the third of his equestrian Indian statues, "The Protest," which unfortunately was never put into permanent material. This, the most spirited of the quartet, lacked the solemn grandeur of the others, depicting something more momentary than monumental; perhaps that is why it was never cast in bronze. William Howe Downes described the scene as the time when the Indian had become

. . . fully cognizant of his peril and plight. His peaceful advances have been of no avail. He must accept the prophecy of the seer of his tribe. He now arrays himself against the enemy, and, with clenched fist, his steed rearing on its haunches, he hurls defiance at his foe. This is the war stage; the conflict with the frontiersman has begun. [Quoted from "Mr. Dallin's Indian Sculptures," *Scribner's Magazine*, vol. 57, June 1915, p. 782]

The last of the four Indian equestrian groups, and probably the most moving, is "The Appeal to the Great Spirit," which stands in front of the Museum of Fine Arts in Boston. First shown at the National Sculpture Society exhibition in Baltimore in 1908, it was awarded a gold medal at the Paris Salon the following year. Like Fraser's "End of the Trail," it summarizes the utter despair of the Indian's situation. After meeting with treachery and broken promises, after suffering continual defeat in armed conflicts, and being totally unable to halt the oncoming enemy, he seeks help out of utter hopelessness from some more just and potent power than mere man, either red or white; he appeals to the Great Spirit who rules the universe. With head thrown back and arms outstretched, the Indian pleads his case. This was one of the most profoundly stirring pieces of sculpture in its day. Moreover, it was so popular that the house of Caproni, which turned out thousands of plaster casts of ancient and modern sculptures in the late 19th and early 20th centuries, produced replicas of it in three different sizes at modest prices. As it appeared within a year of the unveiling of Saint-Gaudens' "Sherman" in Central Park, it might be said that in 1907–1908 the equestrian statue in American sculpture reached its zenith.

When Cyrus Dallin returned from Paris in 1900, he settled in Boston and taught at the Massachusetts State Normal Art School. His statue of Sir Isaac Newton was cast in bronze about this time and placed in the rotunda of the Library of Congress. In addition to his equestrian Indian statues there was the "Cavalryman" of 1905, destined for Hanover, Pennsylvania; the next year he won the competition for the Soldiers' and Sailors' Monument for Syracuse, New York. In the second decade of the century he continued doing Indian subjects: An "Indian Hunter," stooping to cup some water in his hand for a drink, was placed in the public gardens in Arlington, Massachusetts; there was an Indian bowman, called "Marksman"; one entitled "On the Warpath" was cast in bronze in 1935 and placed in Brookgreen Gardens; another, "Scout," was exhibited at the San Francisco Exposition of 1915. His statue of Anne Hutchinson, in Pilgrim dress and holding a Bible, with a little girl at her side, was modeled in 1914; the funds were not available to have it cast in bronze, however, until 1920, when the governor of

Massachusetts accepted it for the Commonwealth and it was erected on the State House grounds. Toward the end of World War I Dallin was working on a statue of a defiant doughboy entitled "Captured but not Conquered." But none of these attained the sculptural or expressive heights of his "Medicine Man" or his "Appeal." Only his statue of Massasoit, commissioned by the Imperial Order of Red Men, approached the greatness of the two earlier pieces; stalwart, confident, and heroic, the bronze figure of the great war chief who made peace with the Pilgrims in 1622 was set up on a boulder on Coles Hill in Plymouth to commemorate the 300th anniversary of the event.

In 1921 Cyrus Dallin was sixty. During the next twenty years, however, three major pieces were to issue from his studio. From 1928–1929 dates the "Spirit of Life"—a robed woman holding heavenward a newborn child—which was placed beside a pool in a private residence in Brookline, Massachusetts; it represents one of Dallin's rare academic ideal pieces. His aged mother, herself a pioneer woman from the earliest days of the state's settlement, posed for the monument of the "Pioneer Women of Utah," completed in 1931; and in 1940 his equestrian statue of Paul Revere was unveiled in Boston. This statue brought the career of Cyrus Dallin to a close. With the possible exception of the "Paul Revere," he is remembered only for his images of Indians and Indian life, and it was in them that he made his finest sculptural statements.

The man who best depicted the life of the cowboy in the West of the 1880's and 1890's was a latecomer to the art of sculpture, having first made a name for himself as an illustrator and painter. This was Frederic Remington (1861–1909), who, in the words of Theodore Roosevelt, "portrayed a most characteristic and yet vanishing type of American life. The soldier, the cowboy, the rancher, the Indian, the horses and the cattle of the plains will live in his pictures and bronzes, I verily believe, for all time." His work as a painter extended over about a quarter of a century, but he did not take up sculpture until fourteen years before his death.

Born in Canton, New York, Remington grew up in Ogdensburg, where his father was Collector of the Port and editor of the local newspaper. As a boy he read with great excitement the accounts of the Western adventures of Catlin, Lewis and Clark, Irving, and Gregg, traveling with them page after page. Probably because his father had been a colonel in the army, young Remington wanted to go to West Point; his father wanted him to be a civil engineer, but Frederic's inability to master the multiplication tables dashed all hopes for either career. Yale was finally chosen, and he enrolled in the School of Fine Arts; a friend later recalled that "his eminence at that institution was on the football field rather than in the art classes." Remington was robust, athletic, and vigorous by nature; he was blond, handsome, and tall, though the large frame of his youth gave way to obesity in the last years of his life. His father's death brought an end to his college education, and at the age of nineteen he set out on his first trip through the West.

In 1880 Remington, who seems to have had no inclination at that time to become a professional artist, wandered about in what was still very much the wild West. In nearly every respect the West lived up to the exciting pictures he had formed of it as a boy. He first clerked in a general store and soon began sketching the scenes around him; this pastime became all the more enjoyable when he took a job as cowpoke on a cattle ranch. About this time he decided to become an artist and record the West in his art. He returned to New York to study at the Art Students League, but within a year he was back in the land of the cowboy and Indian. In the March 18, 1905, issue of *Collier's Weekly*, Remington reminisced about those early days:

I knew the railroad was coming—I saw men already swarming into the land. I knew the derby hat, the smoking chimneys, the cord-binder, and the thirty-day note were upon us in a resistless surge. I knew the wild riders and the vacant land were about to vanish forever . . . . Without knowing exactly how to do it, I began to try to record some facts around me, and the more I looked the more the panorama unfolded.

Within a short time Remington had fallen in with the cowboy way of life on the open range. This life included the Indian, both at peace and at war, and the blue-uniformed "pony soldiers," who were sent to enforce the peace in the West; it also included the hunters and trappers, as well as the missionaries out to convert the Indians. These were the years of the last of the great Indian wars in which the red men were led by the fierce Geronimo. Remington's first commission came from the editor of *Harper's Weekly* for a picture illustrating an incident of the Geronimo campaign; it was the first of many that appeared in *Harper's* throughout the 1880's and 1890's. Other magazines soon asked for his illustrations, most of which were done in black and white, though he did a few modest-size oil paintings. The magazine *Outing*, for example, paid him $10 apiece for his pen-and-ink drawings; and he was chosen to do the illustrations for Teddy Roosevelt's articles about life among the cowboys. This was at a time, the artist remarked later, ". . . when most people didn't know whether cowboys milked dairy cows or fought in the Revolution." And he added, "I knew more about cowboys then than I did about drawing." "Crow Indians Firing into the Agency" and "Cowboys Coming to Town for Christmas" are examples of the many engravings made from his paintings; they appeared in *Harper's Weekly*, November 5, 1887, and December 21, 1889, respectively. *Century Magazine* in 1889 published an article written and illustrated by Remington, in which he told about his experiences in the sun-baked desert territories of the Southwest. Through the wide circulation of these periodicals, the name of Frederic Remington soon became associated with all the excitement that the terms "cowboys and Indians" and "the wild West" evoked. His pictures possessed an authenticity, for he was always a stickler for employing accurate details. By 1891 he had become such a popular personality that an article about him appeared in the January 17 *Harper's Weekly:* it told of the many Western items in his studio that he used to achieve verity in his art:

The trophies of his many visits and errands to the West hang all about the walls and litter the floors delightfully. Axes, clubs, saddles, spears, bows and arrows, shields, queer water-tight baskets, quaint rude rugs, chaparrajos, moccasins, head-dresses, miniature canoes, gorgeous examples of beadwork, lariats and a hundred other sorts of curios from the desert and the wilderness . . . [were scattered about].

All this paraphernalia was essential to the factual reportorial art Remington practiced. Factuality was the cornerstone of his art, far more than cleverness of style or composition. His paintings and sketches were never sentimental or melodramatic, for the artist believed that the subject itself contained all the drama and excitement necessary. "When I began to depict the men of the plains, white and red," he later wrote, "this Western business was new to art and we had the dread background of the dime novel to live down." Remington's way of telling the story of the West was to show it as it really was. This straightforward method of making images was established while he was still a painter and illustrator, and it remained pivotal to his art when he became a sculptor.

Before he was thirty Remington had been a rancher and lived the life of the cowboy; he had crossed through the country of the Apaches when they were on the warpath; and he had been captured by Indians in Dakota territory. He had traveled among the peaceful Indian encampments and reservations, and he had ridden with the army in combat against the war parties, always with his sketch-book at hand. But by 1891 he showed signs of settling down in the house and studio he had purchased in New Rochelle, New York; he called it "Endion," an Indian word meaning "the place where I live." In 1893 the American Art Galleries exhibited and placed on sale one hundred of his famous paintings and sketches of life out West. Within a decade Remington would command an annual retainer of $25,000 from one periodical alone. But he had not yet tried his hand at sculpture, and his first effort came only a good while after he had established his reputation as an illustrator.

It started in the summer of 1895 when Frederic Wellington Ruckstull was modeling his equestrian statue of General Hartranft in a tent set up in the backyard of one of Remington's neighbors. Remington, fascinated with the day-to-day progress of the horse and rider, eventually yielded to an irresistible temptation to plunge his hands into the soft clay and shape something from it. In Remington's own words: "I was impelled to try my hand at sculpture by a natural desire to say something in the round as well as in the flat. Sculpture is the most perfect expression of action. You can say it all in clay." (Quoted from P. Maxwell, *An Appreciation of the Art of Frederic Remington*, p. 407.) Thus began the sculpture career of Frederic Remington. His subject matter, of course, was cowboy life on the prairie, the rough-and-ready trooper, the Indian, and the horses they rode.

His first attempt in clay was one of the most popular pieces he ever produced—"Bronco Buster" (Fig. 14.8). More than two hundred of these were cast in bronze at the Roman Bronze Works in New York. This example is 23 inches high; another, of which about six copies were cast, is 32 inches. Charles de Kay once wrote about this statuette that the artist had "approached sculpture from the pictorial rather than the monumental side." Remington certainly did endow his sculpture with all the rich and authentic detail that had made his paintings so popular, and referring to it as realistic genre, de Kay was moved to comment that "one cannot expect in such literal transcripts of fact the largeness of heroic sculpture." But though the pictorial qualities of "Bronco Buster" could never be denied, and though it never attained a true monumentality, Remington revealed in this first essay in clay a definite feeling for sculptural form. His daring spirit is seen in the ambitiousness of a first effort—an equestrian group with the horse rearing on its hind legs—and the artist admitted that it was "a long work attended with great difficulties on my part." He liked very much the vital, expressive reality he could capture through sculpture, and within a year after completing this first piece he wrote to William Coffin: "I propose to do some more, to put the wild life of our West into something that burglar won't have, moth eat or time blacken. It is a great art form and satisfying to me, for my whole feeling is for form." (Quoted from *Century Magazine*, June 1896.)

Although he found the new medium very much to his liking, Remington continued to paint and to do magazine illustrations. The January 24, 1897, issue of the *New York Journal* contained "Cuban War Sketches, Gathered in the Field by Frederic Remington"; and in the August 6, 1898, issue of *Harper's Weekly* there appeared a large engraving of the "'Storming of San Juan Hill.' Drawn by Frederic Remington, Special Artist for Harper's Weekly with General Shafter's Army." In 1899 he was sent to Havana as a special correspondent for *Collier's Weekly* to paint the scenes and write about the American occupation forces there—the soldiers, their horses, the scenes of camp life, and some of the local color of Cuba.

By that time several more of his bronze statuettes had appeared, such as "The Wounded Bunkie" (1896), which shows two troopers on horseback, one of them wounded, fleeing from Indians; another piece, "Wicked Pony" (1898), is a bucking bronco that has thrown its rider to the ground. There were a couple of Indian subjects, "The Scalp" (1898) and "The Cheyenne" (1901). Remington chose "Bucking Bronco" and "The Wounded Bunkie" to send to the 1901 Pan-American Exposition in Buffalo, where they attracted the interest of visitors from all over the nation; many people knew his illustrations in magazines, but few had seen his sculpture. They were drawn to his sculptures of the West the way an earlier generation had been attracted to the genre groups of John Rogers.

In 1902 Remington produced another of his popular pieces, "Comin' Through the Rye," sometimes called "Off the Range" (Fig. 14.9). The bronze group of four fun-loving, six-gun-shooting, hard-riding, yelping cowboys, about 27 inches high, dates from 1902, but the idea goes back to a painting the artist had done thirteen years earlier, "Cowboys Coming to Town for Christmas"; the engraving of the painting had appeared in the December 21, 1889, issue of *Harper's Weekly*.

Remington himself had known and loved this life in earlier days, and with the detail-conscious eye of the illustrator, he captured the spirit of the group in a naturalism that contains both truth and art. The dash of the cow ponies—by no means the thoroughbred stock of Eastern stables—adds to the frenzied excitement, as only five of the sixteen hooves touch ground. Remington's sculpture was indeed based on his own observation rather than on the principles of art taught in the schools. Charles de Kay, writing about another piece, in the January 8, 1910, issue of *Harper's Weekly*, explained that

Remington's daring violation of many of the rules of sculpture in an effort to produce a literal scene can go no farther than the large group of buffalo, pony and Indian . . . . An old buffalo bull has hoisted a pony on his shoulders so that all four hoofs of the horse are off the ground, while the buffalo is still rearing. At the impact . . . the nude rider has been hurled into the air above his steed. Thus buffalo supports horse, and the Indian soars above both. The rule that sculpture ought to represent momentarily suspended action, if action is needed, has been broken without remorse.

The same applies to "Comin' Through the Rye," in which the ponies seem to touch down on earth scarcely at all. This was a new subject for art, and Remington made up his own rules as he went along.

Large-scale staff replicas of "Comin' Through the Rye" were made for two of the great Western fairs, the one at St. Louis in 1904 and the Lewis and Clark Exposition in Portland, Oregon, in 1905. By then the wild West of the cowboys and Indians had become only a memory, and the nation looked back on that era with a certain nostalgia. But Remington could remember the old days of the West, and he continued to paint and model it in vivid imagery.

"The West is no longer the West of picturesque and stirring events," he once wrote around 1904, lamenting that "the romance and adventure have been beaten down in the rush of civilization . . . . The Cowboy—the real thing, mark you, not the tame hired hand—disappeared with the advent of the wire fence, and as for the Indian, there are so few of him that he doesn't count." He continued that he had no interest in the new, civilized West, concluding that his "West passed utterly out of existence so long ago as to make it merely a dream." He frequently spoke in terms of "my West," which had indeed ceased to exist by the turn of the century, and Remington knew he was one of the few men who could still re-create a vision of it.

His illustrations were in great demand, and between 1905 and his death five years later he painted several pictures for *Collier's*, which were often reproduced on the cover. His sculpture, too, continued to have popular appeal, and in 1905 Knoedler's Art Gallery held an exhibition of nine of his bronzes. By 1907 he had made about fifteen statuettes, including "The Rattlesnake," which shows a horse about to throw its rider as it is startled at the sight of a rattlesnake on the ground, and "The Outlaw," a cowboy riding a bucking bronco; it is estimated that some ninety replicas of "The Rattlesnake" and between twenty-five to one hundred replicas of "The Outlaw" were cast in bronze.

One of Remington's last groups was the "Trooper of the Plains, 1868," (Fig. 14.10), which he did in 1909. The earlier remarks about composition pertain here, for the statuette nearly defies gravity as the horse gallops across the prairie with all four hooves off the ground. Horse and rider have become so much one that they create a kind of western American version of the mythical centaur. The horse is rather scrawny, with an awkward neck, a head that seems too large, and bulging frightened eyes; but such was the nature of the Western pony. As for the wiry trooper himself, gun drawn as he rides into battle, every detail is accurately rendered in the paraphernalia about his person and saddle. He is a hardened, squint-eyed, moustached old trooper, one of the iron men who eventually secured the West. The artist once said, "I only knew the soldier as a part of my West, and the West and the soldier closed together." The "Trooper of the Plains" was a kind of eulogy in bronze to a kind of soldier that existed no more. About eleven replicas of it were cast by the Roman Bronze Works in New York City.

The husky athlete of earlier years had become quite stout by 1909, but he still loved the outdoor life, and he and friends would hike through the wooded hills of Westchester County. He was a popular club man in New York, often dining with other celebrities. In 1908 he sold his New Rochelle home and moved to Ridge-field, Connecticut, where he built a new house. He was to enjoy it for only six months. One day in January 1909 he suddenly became ill; he was operated on for acute appendicitis and died soon afterward. Much of the nation mourned the loss of the man who recreated so vividly the old wild West.

In the late 19th and early 20th centuries zoologists, sportsmen, photographers, and even artists were roaming the remote parts of the world in search of wild animals. Zoos were growing in number and size, and museums of natural history were displaying stuffed animals of the wilderness in their natural surroundings. Wealthy hunters and business tycoons, and even an American President, were traveling to the far-off jungles of Africa and to the still-wild areas of the American West for the thrill of stalking big game. The "stay-at-home" sportsmen contented themselves with Sunday afternoon family trips to the zoo.

Such large-scale fascination with the animal kingdom was bound to be reflected in art, and the sculptor who first took it up as his exclusive subject was the Frenchman Antoine Louis Barye (1796–1875). His initial success, after years of rejection, came in 1831 when his "Lion devouring a Gavial" was shown at the Salon and purchased for the Luxembourg Palace collection. From then on he was famous for his vivid portrayals of animal life in all its violence, grace, and natural beauty. Barye never left France and barely strayed beyond the limits of Paris, but in his spare time—when he was not employed making clock and furniture ornaments—he attended the lectures on zoology at the Paris zoo in the Jardin des Plantes. He never had the benefit, therefore, of studying animals in their natural habitat. Barye's success was often in spite of sharp criticism from the art academies, where his animals were viewed as insignificant subjects and his style as artless realism. He was very popular among American collectors, however; and in

1873 the Corcoran Gallery of Art in Washington ordered a bronze replica of everything Barye had ever modeled.

Barye was indisputably the founder of the group known in France as the *animaliers*. He was, in the words of the critic Ernest Peixotto the first "to replace mere convention by truth and reality, to observe animals closely and record in bronze a profound knowledge of their forms, [and to impart] to his groups . . . an incomparable dignity of line and mass." By the end of his career he had made the wild animal an acceptable subject for the sculptor. Cain was his successor, but it was Frémiet and his classes at the Jardin des Plantes that had the greatest influence on American *animaliers* in the late 19th century. Frémiet—animal sculptor, member of the Académie des Beaux-Arts, professor of animal drawing at the natural history museum—is represented in America by two equestrian monuments: the "General John E. Howard" in Baltimore and the "Joan of Arc" in Philadelphia. But in France he was better known for his sculptures of wild animals, which were sometimes carried to melodramatic extremes: He once sent to the Salon a group of a huge shaggy gorilla carrying off a helpless woman. American sculptors, however, avoided any hint of sensationalism in their animal pieces, feeling that the natural beauty of the animals and their way of life in their native habitat offered a sufficiently exciting imagery. Nevertheless, several American sculptors studied with Frémiet, from whom they gained much valuable instruction. And though animal sculpture had its origins in Paris, the United States developed its own school of *animaliers* around the turn of the century.

The first American sculptor to take animals as his principal—almost exclusive—subject was Edward Kemeys (1843–1907). Fascinated by the beauty of wild beasts, with their potential violence and the instincts that gave each species a personality of its own, Kemeys regarded America's wild fauna much as Remington had regarded the cowboy or Dallin had the Indian—as a magnificent part of the nation's heritage that was disappearing before civilization's relentless advance. There were others who specialized in animal sculpture—Edward Potter, Frederick Roth, Eli Harvey, Albert Laessle, and Anna Hyatt Huntington, for example; and Phimister Proctor, Solon Borglum, and Henry Kirke Bush-Brown frequently undertook animal subjects. But Kemeys occupies a special place historically, for his first efforts date from the early 1870's.

Edward Kemeys was born in Savannah, Georgia, and grew up in the area of New York City. His interest in animals seems to have manifested itself when, at age thirteen, he was spending the summer on a farm in Illinois, which in the mid-1850's still had some of the wildness of the frontier about it. Years later, after he had served as an artillery officer in the Civil War, he went back to Illinois to make an unsuccessful attempt at running his own farm. Returning to New York City, he found employment with the engineers who were then laying out Central Park, and in his spare time he would visit the small Central Park Zoo. One day in 1871 while visiting the zoo, Kemeys chanced upon a man modeling the head of a wolf, and he experienced a sudden desire to model the forms of animals.

Edward Kemeys' first major work met with instant success when the Fairmount Park Association purchased his "Hudson Bay Wolves" (Fig. 14.11), a group that captured all the snarling ferocity of two wolves fighting over the carcass of the latest kill. The style is one of simple, direct naturalism, altogether devoid of clever modeling and surface techniques; it remained a constant characteristic of Kemeys' work, even after his trip abroad a few years later. Instead of going off to France with the money he had received for the "Wolves," he headed for what he recognized as his true source of inspiration—the western American wilderness and its animals. With banjo, gun, and sketch pad, he traveled around; at one time he joined a big-game hunt, whose trophies provided him with specimens of elk, bear, buffalo, and antelope to dissect and study. Eventually his money ran out, and he returned to New York where he set up a small studio. By the time the Philadelphia Centennial of 1876 opened, Kemeys had three more pieces ready to exhibit: "Coyote and Raven," "Playing Possum," and "Panther and Deer." The last-named was his second major work, and he took it to England with him in 1877 and sold it to a Londoner. He journeyed next to Paris, where he had planned to study; but he stayed only briefly, because he cared neither for the kind of teaching in the schools nor for the caging of animals at the zoological gardens. He wanted to render the wild beasts as he found them in nature, not in some cage. His "Bison and Wolves" was acclaimed at the Salon of 1878. The following year he returned to America, firmly convinced that his method of working entirely from nature with a minimum of artifice was truly the best way. On the entire trip, only those works by the recently deceased Barye seemed worth studying.

Again opening a studio in New York, he began a period of great productivity, doing small pieces mostly, with an occasional large one. Prospective patrons could see his collection of small models in his studio and select the one they wanted to have enlarged and cast in bronze. In 1883 Kemeys produced one of his most popular studies, "Still Hunt," which portrays a large American mountain lion crouched, ready to spring upon its prey (Fig. 14.12). The city of New York purchased the statue and had it mounted on a large boulder in Central Park, in a setting quite appropriate for the great bronze beast. Americans were quite smitten by this kind of imagery from the untamed western reaches of their own land, just as they would be a decade later by the statues and statuettes of cowboys and Indians. The subject was taken from America itself and rendered in a naturalism Americans could appreciate. Its success was almost inevitable.

Kemeys had a very close affinity with the animals he modeled, be they bear or bison, wolf or wildcat, antelope or raccoon, panther or mountain goat; and part of his success was attributable to his ability to penetrate to the depths of animal behavior and psychology. This may be seen in the group titled "Jaguar Lovers" (1888) in the Corcoran Gallery of Art. The special feline power and grace of the jaguar seems to have captivated him, for he made many studies of it. About this same time he received and executed the commission for the great bison head that was to decorate the bridge of the Union Pacific Railroad at Omaha. In 1892 he moved his residence and studio to Chicago, probably at the inducement of commissions for the Columbian Exposition; there he remained working in his studio, "Wolfden," for eight years, with frequent trips into the wild areas of the West. In the grand scheme for the sculptural decorations of the exposition grounds, Kemeys joined Proctor in producing animal sculptures, such as the several wild-cats he designed for entrances to bridges. But the main exhibition of his work was in the Fine Arts Building, where no less than a dozen of his animals were shown. In addition to the "Still Hunt" and the "Panther and Deer," there was a "Jaguar and Boa-Constrictor," a "Panther and Her Cubs," a "Bison," and several bears. He was awarded one of the coveted medals of the Columbian Exposition, and he received another medal at the Louisiana Purchase Exposition in 1904, with fifteen examples of American fauna. One of his major commissions while in Chicago was for the two standing bronze lions (1895) that guard the main entrance to the Art Institute.

Kemeys' last major work was a fountain group for Champaign, Illinois: an Indian flanked by a deer and a panther prays for rain. This was one of the sculptor's rare attempts at the human form. In 1900 Kemeys moved East again, this time to Washington, D.C. Not long afterward, his health began to fail, and his activity in the studio was greatly curtailed. He died in 1907 and was buried at Arlington National Cemetery with full military honors. Lorado Taft, writing as Kemeys' career drew to its close, summed up the quality and character of his art in these words:

Self-trained as he is and indifferent to the methods of other men, Mr. Kemeys makes no pretense to clever technic. One scrutinizes his work in vain for those passages of beautiful modeling which form the secondary charm of Barye's little masterpieces . . . . [His] summary, impressionistic treatment has its own particular appeal. It conveys with an element of rugged forcefulness a sense of movement which none but a master can express by means of careful modeling.

[*History of American Sculpture*, p. 471]

Like Edward Kemeys, Eli Harvey (1860–1957) devoted himself almost entirely to animal sculpture. Instead of seeking his subjects in the wilds of the American West, however, Harvey found them mainly in the zoos of Paris and New York. He was born in Ogden, Ohio, and went to art school in Cincinnati, taking painting with Noble and sculpture with Rebisso. But at this time and for several years to follow, Harvey was more interested in painting than in sculpture. When in 1889 he went to Paris—where he was to remain for eleven years—he entered the painting classes of Lefebvre and Constant at the Académie Julian and also attended the Académie Delécluse. Later he studied with Frémiet at the Jardin des Plantes and began to make animal sculptures. His first piece to be sent to the Salon was "Young Lion and Rabbit" in 1897; the next year he was represented at the Salon by his "Jaguar Rampant," which became one of his most famous works when it was exhibited throughout the United States. Just before returning to America in 1900, he executed a charming little group called "Lion Cubs," and by the time he left Paris he was firmly committed to animal sculpture.

Eli Harvey set up his sculpture studio in New York City. In the year following his return he was represented by five animal studies at the Pan-American Exposition at Buffalo, all of which drew a good deal of attention. During that same year he attempted uniting the human figure with one of his wild creatures in a group called "Prometheus," but aside from another group, "Discord"—a lion, a python, and a man locked in a death struggle—he thereafter excluded man from his work. During 1902 and 1903 his major project was the sculptural decorations for the lion house at the New York Zoological Park, but he also found time to model a few more little animal groups, which were among the nine pieces that he sent to the Louisiana Purchase Exposition in 1904. All nine were modeled from members of the feline family and won for Harvey a medal. In 1912 a New York gallery held an exhibition of about three dozen of his animal pieces and he won another medal at the San Francisco Panama-Pacific Exposition in 1915. By this time Kemeys had been dead eight years, and Harvey now headed the list of America's *animaliers*.

For the Eaton mausoleum in Toronto, Eli Harvey modeled a pair of heroic lions, and for the New York Zoological Society he made a powerful gorilla. The Order of Elks commissioned him to create a statue of the elk, and so pleased were they with the result that they ordered numerous replicas made. Although Harvey lived to the age of ninety-seven, his career essentially ended when he moved to Alhambra, California, in 1929.

A prominent and capable *animalier* in his day was Frederick George Richard Roth (1872–1944) who frequently portrayed the clever or humorous aspects of animal life. He was born in Brooklyn and was educated in Germany, studying at the fine arts academies in Vienna, Austria, and in Berlin. By the time his studies ended in 1894 he had already been a professional sculptor for some years, but his work did not attract much attention until he created the tour de force of the Pan-American Exposition of 1901—the "Roman Chariot." In this group, four horses dash forward, with only a few hooves touching ground, and one wheel of the chariot is in the air in the furious race, which almost unseats the driver. Though people were impressed with the group, several critics questioned whether a subject of such vigorous movement was really proper for the art of sculpture. One critic asked whether this most impressive group had not "forced the medium beyond its characteristic limits." In any case, it brought Roth to the forefront of America's younger sculptors, and he was thereafter in constant demand. For the fair he created two other heroic groups—the "Resting Buffaloes" and "Stallion and Groom"—but no one paid as much attention to them as to the "Roman Chariot."

The Metropolitan Museum of Art has a group of small and charming bronze animals by Roth that date from the first few years of the 20th century; there is a pair of elephants performing on their platform of wooden tubs, and a performing bear, as well as a couple of amusing little pigs. Still another of these, a polar bear, was exhibited at the 1904 Louisiana Purchase Exposition, where it, like nearly all animal sculptures, enjoyed a great popular success. Roth continued working with the polar-bear motif and in 1905 modeled a group that was instrumental in his being elected to the National Academy; this same group won the National Arts Club prize in 1924, and ten years later a bronze replica of it was set up in Brookgreen Gardens. Like Eli Harvey, Roth modeled from animals in nearby zoos; he was strictly an artist and not a sportsman-artist like Edward Kemeys or Phimister Proctor.

In 1910 Roth modeled the horse for Augustus Lukeman's "Kit Carson" equestrian portrait in Trinidad, Colorado. For the Panama-Pacific Exposition at San Francisco in 1915, he collaborated with Stirling Calder and Leo Lentelli to produce the magnificent groups of the "Nations of the East and West." Soon afterward he became a modeling instructor at the National Academy of Design, a position he held for three years.

Roth was frequently a prize winner, twice being awarded the Ellen P. Speyer Award at the annual exhibitions of the National Academy, which carried a $300 stipend for "a painting or piece of sculpture portraying an act of humaneness toward animals, or a painting or piece of sculpture of animals." Interestingly, the *animaliers* had their own prize of recognition at the National Academy shows. In 1924 his image of Balto, the Eskimo dog, won the Speyer Award, and he received it again in 1942 for his statue of Saint Francis. In 1931 he won the National Arts Club prize again, this time for his "Elephant."

In the late 1920's Roth did an equestrian monument of George Washington for Morristown, New Jersey. During the depression he served as chief sculptor, under the auspices of the Works Progress Administration, for the New York City Department of Parks. The results of these years—1934 to 1936—were two groups of sculpture especially designed for children: One was from *Alice in Wonderland;* the other was from *Mother Goose.* By then Roth was in his mid-sixties, and although he continued working almost to the time of his death in 1944, his career was essentially over. In addition to being a member of the National Academy of Design for nearly forty years, he was a member of the National Sculpture Society (for a while serving as its president) and of several other national arts organizations.

Edward Clark Potter (1857–1923) is mainly known for his collaboration with Daniel Chester French on a number of equestrian commissions, for which French would make the rider and Potter the horse. French usually received far more recognition for these monuments, because they were executed from his original designs, and because the commissions were actually awarded to him. But Potter was much more versatile than his work with French indicated. He created several equestrian groups on his own, as well as a good many portrait statues and a few ideal pieces.

It was in French's studio, in 1883, that Potter got his first professional training as a sculptor, although he had previously studied art for a brief period at the Boston School of Fine Arts. He remained with French for two years, leaving to take employment at the Proctor marble quarry in Vermont, where he supervised the cutting of French's figures for the Boston Customs House. In 1887 he went to Paris, where he studied the human figure and animal sculpture with Mercié and Frémiet respectively; after two years he considered his work ready to be shown and sent a "Sleeping Faun" to the Salon of 1889. Remaining in Paris until 1891, he returned to America to establish a studio in Enfield, Massachusetts, and before long he resumed his association with French.

French and Potter collaborated on a number of groups for the Columbian Exposition at Chicago, the major piece being the Columbus quadriga (atop the grand colonnade) in which Potter made the horses and the outriders. They also worked together on the heroic animal groups along the Court of Honor, each of which comprised an enormous animal, either a horse or an ox, with an attendant figure. The figures—a farmer, a Negro teamster, an Indian woman, and a classical version of America—were the work of French, but the critics also applauded Potter for his fine accompanying beasts. This partnership was resumed later in the decade with the equestrian statues of General Grant for Philadelphia's Fairmount Park and of George Washington, which the D.A.R presented as a gift to France on July 4, 1900. The equestrian "General Hooker" of 1903, destined for the State House grounds in Boston, and the "General Devens," which was unveiled July 4, 1906, in Worcester, Massachusetts, were also collaborative efforts. Although the rider and the proper expression of his personality are the most important part of any equestrian portrait, it is also important to achieve the proper expression in the horse, as well as an image that is anatomically and structurally accurate. The spirit of the group as a whole depends on the successful union of the horse and rider. Potter always sought to endow his horses with the proper personality in an equestrian portrait, and the horse he modeled for the "General Grant" is quite unlike that of his "DeSoto" statue, made for the St. Louis Exposition of 1904. Similarly the quiet horse that carried Potter's "General Slocum" of 1902 is not the same as the sturdy "Work Horse" or the classic chariot horses of the quadriga of the Columbian Exposition. His special skill at rendering the horse was generally recognized, and in addition to the equestrian groups mentioned, he made three more on his own—"General McClellan" of the Smith Memorial in Fairmount Park; "General Custer" (1910) for Munroe, Michigan; and "General Kearny" for Washington, D.C. In a little more than twenty years he turned out five equestrian groups of his own and six in collaboration with Daniel Chester French—a remarkable production.

Just before the turn of the century Potter modeled the fine animated portrait statue of Robert Fulton for that circle of luminaries high above the rotunda of the Library of Congress. He was represented at both the Buffalo Exposition in 1901 and the one at St. Louis in 1904; at the latter he was awarded a medal for his "Bull and Lynx." In addition to the "Fulton," other portrait statues include "Governor Austin Blair" in Lansing, Michigan, and "Colonel Raynal Bolling" in Greenwich,

Connecticut. Though these are quite competent as portraits go, Potter's work lacks excitement and sculptural dynamics. The same is generally true in the sculptor's more colorful commissions, such as the "Zoroaster" for New York's Appellate Court Building or the "Indian Philosophy" and "Indian Religion" for the Brooklyn Institute. Although he was best known to his contemporaries for his horses and oxen, Potter produced other animals, too, such as the pairs of lions he made for the Pierpont Morgan Library, for the residence of Collis P. Huntington, and for the front of the New York Public Library; toward the third pair the critics were less than kind. Perhaps his highest achievement was the "General Slocum" at Gettysburg, of which Lorado Taft wrote that there was "no more impressive sculpture upon the famous battlefield."

Another sculptor especially noted for his horse studies was Amory C. Simons (1866–1959). Born in Charleston, South Carolina, he went north to study at the Pennsylvania Academy of the Fine Arts under John J. Boyle and Charles Grafly. Thereafter he went to Paris to study with Puech and Dampt and Frémiet. His first recognition came around the turn of the century when his work won honorable mention at the Paris Salon of 1900 and at the Buffalo Exposition in 1901. The two spirited little bronze horses in the Metropolitan Museum of Art reveal his mastery of the forms of the horse and also show that he absorbed something of the Parisian surface technique in his modeling. His "Haut Ecole" represents an elegantly groomed circus horse going through its paces with style and spirit. Unlike some of the other *animaliers*, Simons preferred the elite beauty of the thoroughbred to the Western horse of the cowboy or the Indian pony.

Herbert Haseltine (1877–1962) also made a specialty of modeling horses. He received his first encouragement in the arts from his father, the landscape painter William Stanley Haseltine. Born in Rome, Herbert grew up and went to school in Italy and graduated from Harvard in 1899. He then went abroad to study in Munich, in Rome, and finally in Paris at the Académie Julian. Before 1905 he had studied drawing and painting, but at the suggestion of his teacher Aimé Morot he tried modeling. He took to it avidly and was represented at the Salon by "Polo Players." Thus began his career in sculpture and also his preoccupation with the horse as his subject matter. The Whitney Museum of American Art owns one of his bronze pieces titled "Un Puyazo," which he did in 1912. His work was interrupted for several years during World War I, and from the war came such pieces as "Les Revenants" (1920), in the Philadelphia Museum of Art. It is a procession of ten paired horses led and followed by riders in military uniform; there is a modern quality in its sketchiness and the suggestiveness of its forms.

Haseltine began to experiment with the abstraction of form during the 1920's, and he is best known for his stylization of horses. This stylization is due largely to the sculptor's fascination with ancient Egyptian art rather than to a conversion to the true principles of 20th-century abstraction. Examples of this type of sculpture are to be found in both Phillips Academy (Andover, Massachusetts) and the Philadelphia Museum of Art, and three especially fine pieces are owned by the

Metropolitan Museum of Art. Haseltine is also noted for several large-scale statues, such as the equestrian "George Washington" in front of the National Cathedral in Washington and his portrait of the celebrated race horse Man o' War in Lexington, Kentucky.

Whereas most American *animaliers* were concerned with the larger specimens of the animal kingdom, Albert Laessle (1877–1954) chose his subjects among the small creatures of the riverbanks and the domestic animals of the barnyard. So naturalistic was his rendering of them that on at least two occasions he was accused of making casts from nature's originals. Laessle could find a kind of drama and humor amid life in the barnyard, and his small bronzes became quite popular for their charming expression of animal personalities; this came from an intimate knowledge of their ways.

It all started in Charles Grafly's sculpture class at the Pennsylvania Academy when Laessle became fascinated with a huge snapping turtle a fellow student had brought in for Grafly's dinner. The creature was given a reprieve when Laessle asked to borrow it as a model for what was to be his first composition—a turtle and a crab contending for the body of a dead crow. When it was placed on exhibition, probably in the year 1901, the critics insisted it was a cast. All was set right, however, when Laessle soon afterward produced a second group, known as "Turtle and Lizards" (Fig. 14.13), which was modeled in wax. In this he created a sort of microcosm of the world of the turtle surrounded by snails and salamanders and such things, and with all of the dramatic struggle for survival that maintains nature's balance.

Laessle sent the "Turtle and Lizards" to the Louisiana Purchase Exposition, where it attracted much interest in the Fine Arts exhibition. It was probably that excellent little piece that won for its creator the Pennsylvania Academy's major prize of the year, the Stewardson Scholarship, which allowed Laessle to study in Europe in 1904; the Academy bought the model and had it cast in bronze for its own collection. Following the precedent of Barye and the group that gathered at the Jardin des Plantes, Laessle continued to make small groups of animal life. An example of his work during this period is the "Turning Turtle," now in the collection of the Metropolitan Museum of Art. It shows a tortoise on its back and struggling to regain its proper position. The Parisian critics maintained the little sculpture was cast from life; Laessle later recalled being rather pleased at this, for both Barye and Rodin had been similarly accused by the critics. Laessle's concierge had loaned him a turtle to serve as his model; as was then a common practice among Parisians, she kept the creature in her cellar to eat the bugs and insects.

In 1907 Laessle returned to Philadelphia, and for several years he worked in the studio of Charles Grafly. Grafly's influence may be seen in the style of the portrait busts Laessle did over the years; but, despite the success of these, Laessle's first love was modeling commonplace animals. In the barnyard Laessle found many a subject, such as the "Chanticleer," a brash, strutting, crowing rooster, in the collection of the Pennsylvania Academy. There is also the statue "Billy" (1915), a goat, which now stands in Rittenhouse Square.

Laessle was awarded a gold medal in 1915 at the International Exposition at San Francisco for his little animal studies, and in the same year he received the Pennsylvania Academy's fellowship prize. Three years later he won the Academy's Widener Memorial gold medal; his work won gold medals in Chicago in 1920 and in Philadelphia in 1923, as well as other national and international honors. From 1921 to 1939 Laessle was an instructor at the Pennsylvania Academy, and he maintained his own studio not far from the Philadelphia Zoological Gardens. There he enjoyed the privilege of keeping some clay and modeling the animals whenever he so desired. During these years much of his energies were absorbed by his teaching, although there were such works as the "Dancing Goat" (1928), now in Brookgreen Gardens. Albert Laessle died in Miami, Florida, in 1954 at the age of seventy-seven.

Probably the most prolific of the animal sculptors is Anna Vaughn Hyatt Huntington (1876–   ), whose career extended through the first four decades of the 20th century. Born in Cambridge, Massachusetts, where her father was a professor of paleontology at Harvard, Anna Hyatt was surrounded by animal life from the lowest forms on up the zoologist's scale. After studying the violin for several years, she was drawn to modeling in clay, a pastime that soon became her chosen vocation. For a while Anna received instruction from the Boston sculptor Henry Kitson, known for his portrait statues around New England; then she went to New York to attend Hermon MacNeil's classes at the Art Students League. At this time she also had the benefit of criticism by Gutzon Borglum—a criticism that was especially valuable in rendering the horse. One of the first pieces to bring Anna Hyatt recognition, in fact, was the group of two horses entitled "Winter Noon"; created in 1902, it is now in the Metropolitan Museum of Art. This little bronze group was shown at the St. Louis Exposition of 1904, along with "Men and Bull," a collaborative effort executed with Abastenia St. Leger Eberle, with whom she was then sharing a studio in New York City.

Before this time her subjects seem to have been confined to images of dogs and of those domestic animals observed in the rural surroundings of the Hyatt summer home on Cape Ann. But around 1905 she became fascinated with the beauty found in the great cats of the New York zoo, particularly a prize jaguar called Señor Lopez. A group of two tigers, entitled "Tigers Watching," dates from this period, and several replicas, each 7 inches high, were cast in bronze. These studies continued when she went to France, where she took a studio at Auvers-sur-Oise. Her early version of the "Reaching Jaguar," which was not cast in bronze until 1926 (the year it was given to the Metropolitan Museum of Art), was exhibited at the Paris Salon in 1908; that same year, in Italy, she created a "Lion" that was commissioned for a high school in Dayton, Ohio, where it was placed on a boulder on the grounds.

Returning to America, she worked for a while with the graceful form of the greyhound. But her interest was on a small model for an equestrian statue of Joan of Arc, which received honorable mention from the Salon in Paris in 1910. A committee in New York City had for some time had the necessary funds to commission a heroic-scale monument to the Maid of Orleans, which was to be a gesture of friendship to the people of France; but neither sculptor nor design had been agreed upon until Miss Hyatt's model came to the committee's attention. Over the course of the next few years her original model was refined and revised until the finished product emerged: It now stands on Riverside Drive in New York. The sculptor sought to represent the slender, armor-clad figure of Joan of Arc—standing erect in the stirrups and holding aloft her sword of destiny—as a being fired with a spiritual zeal. She is neither muscularly powerful nor bellicose, but seems merely to have given herself over to the will of God; the sword she carries seems less the means of her victory than the emblem of her strength. Her mount is a sturdy, spirited European war horse, fastidiously rendered, as are the details of the armor worn by the rider. The work inclines perhaps too much toward a historical picturesqueness; a greater feeling for sculptural form is more often found in some of the artist's smaller animal pieces. Nevertheless, contemporary critics and connoisseurs found a great deal that was praiseworthy in this image of the "unconquerable spirit of France." The French ambassador was present at the unveiling on December 6, 1915, and the sculptor was decorated with the Purple Rosette of the French government. In 1922 a replica was set up in Blois, France, and Anna Hyatt was made a Chevalier of the Legion of Honor. Several other replicas exist throughout America, and there is one in Canada; a small version is in Brookgreen Gardens. There is a full-size bronze copy in Gloucester, Massachusetts, which is a memorial not only to the men of the area who had served in World War I, but also to the career of the sculptor, whom the residents of the area have long counted as one of their own. Anna Hyatt produced one more equestrian statue—that of El Cid—which was erected in Seville, Spain, in 1927, with a reduced copy again being placed in Brookgreen Gardens.

Many more honors and awards were bestowed upon Anna Hyatt, following the triumph of her "Joan of Arc." She received the Rodin Gold Medal from the Plastic Club of Philadelphia in 1916, and she twice won the Saltus Prize at the National Academy of Design, of which she was a member. In 1923 she married railroad heir Archer M. Huntington, and they went on an extended ocean cruise on their private yacht. Back in New York, she resumed her work. By then the careful naturalism of her earlier work had begun to give way to a slight simplification of animal forms. Her "Fighting Bulls" received the Shaw Prize at the National Academy show in 1928, and the following year she received the "Grand Cross of Alfonso XII" from the Spanish government; in 1930 she won the Gold Medal of the American Academy of Arts and Letters, and two years later Syracuse University gave her an honorary Doctor of Arts degree in recognition of her work.

During the late 1920's and up to 1937, Anna Hyatt Huntington was occupied in producing two sizable collections of her work, one destined for the Hispanic Society in New York and the other for Brookgreen Gardens in South Carolina. The latter, a nature preserve with floral gardens, was originally intended to contain only a collection of her sculptures, but eventually its scope was broadened to include (and become an outstanding collection of) most of the important American sculptors who were active between the late 19th century and about 1940. Most of her pieces at Brookgreen Gardens are of animal subjects. Of special interest is that they were cast in aluminum; she thus was one of the first American sculptors to cast their works in that metal.

In 1936 the American Academy of Arts and Letters sponsored a retrospective exhibition of her work in New York, and another was later held at the Virginia Museum of Fine Arts. Having reached sixty, she still continued to work in her studio. Her "Greyhounds Playing" was awarded the Widener prize at the Pennsylvania Academy in 1937; for a fountain in Brookgreen Gardens that year she made a group of four alligators. In 1940 she was given a special medal of honor by the National Sculpture Society. Only a small number of her works and of her honors and prizes have been mentioned here.

The period in American sculpture that we have been considering formed an entity in itself, yet it is also a period of transition between the old outworn order and the new. Its art was dominated by the style of the Ecole des Beaux-Arts and the other Parisian schools and ateliers, which constituted the last great flowering of eclecticism. It offered a new, rich kind of modeling and lively surface effects, but there was never any fundamental change in its attitude toward sculptural form; it was the same as had existed for centuries. These sculptors' attempts to render abstract concepts never carried them to a successful use of abstract form; they chose instead to present these concepts in the time-honored form of the quasi-classical figures called personifications.

American sculpture in the late 19th century introduced a new liveliness into an art that had exhausted itself in the Civil War era, and it advanced to the very brink of the modern movement. But the Ecole des Beaux-Arts, the National Academy of Design, and the National Sculpture Society never led their followers into the exciting new movements of abstract and nonobjective form. In that confrontation of the old and the new styles of art, the abstractionists and nonobjectivists emerged the victors because the 20th century needed a new kind of art to express the feelings and values of a new kind of society. A winged personification of Mercury could no more adequately express the age of the jet airplane than a neoclassical representation of Justice could convey the forceful sentiments against social and political injustice or the conflicts between peoples. America, like most of Europe, needed a totally new conception and vision in art to express the vital dynamic forces of the 20th century. The men discussed in the next two chapters provided this art.

[FIG. 14.2]"The Coming of the White Man," by Hermon MacNeil (1905). Bronze. Courtesy, City of Portland, Ore.

[FIG. 14.1] "Sun Vow," by Hermon MacNeil (1898). Bronze, 73″ high. Courtesy, Metropolitan Museum of Art, Rogers Fund, 1919.

[FIG. 14.3] "Ezra Cornell," by Hermon MacNeil (1915–1917). Bronze. Courtesy, Cornell University, Ithaca, N.Y.

[FIG. 14.4] "Memorial to the Pioneer Mother," by A. Phimister Proctor (1928). Bronze. Courtesy, Board of Park and Recreation Commissioners, Kansas City, Mo.

[FIG. 14.5] "Charging Panther," by A. Phimister Proctor (c. 1892). Bronze. Collection, Corcoran Gallery of Art; gift of James Parmelee.

[FIG. 14.6] "Sioux Indian Buffalo Dance," by Solon Borglum (small bronze replica of the group made for the Louisiana Purchase Exposition at Saint Louis in 1904). Courtesy, Kennedy Galleries, Inc., New York City.

[FIG. 14.7] "Medicine Man," by Cyrus Dallin (1899). Bronze. Courtesy, Fairmount Park Association, Philadelphia.

[FIG. 14.8] "Bronco Buster," by Frederic Remington (1895). Bronze, 23″ high. Courtesy, New-York Historical Society, New York City.

[FIG. 14.9] "Comin' Through the Rye," by Frederic Remington (1902). Bronze, 27¼" high. Courtesy, Metropolitan Museum of Art, bequest of Jacob Ruppert, 1939.

[FIG. 14.10] "Trooper of the Plains, 1868," by Frederic Remington (1905). Bronze, 25" high. Courtesy, Metropolitan Museum of Art, bequest of Jacob Ruppert, 1939.

[FIG. 14.11] "Hudson Bay Wolves," by Edward Kemeys (c. 1871). Bronze. Courtesy, Commissioners of Fairmount Park, Philadelphia.

[FIG. 14.12] "Still Hunt," by Edward Kemeys (1883). Plaster model, 21″ high, for the bronze replica in Central Park, New York City. Courtesy, National Collection of Fine Arts, Smithsonian Institution.

[FIG. 14.13] "Turtle and Lizards," by Albert Laessle (c. 1902). Bronze. Courtesy, Pennsylvania Academy of the Fine Arts.

Between the Wars:
At Odds with Tradition

AMERICAN SCULPTURE IN THE 1920'S AND 1930'S UNDERWENT A TRANSITION FROM the century-old academic eclecticism to the modern art of the post-World War II era. Two rival factions existed: the entrenched, more or less official art, which came out of the National Academy and the National Sculpture Society; and the rebellious new art, which in the early years found only a few champions, but which gained strength constantly as it explored uncharted realms of artistic expression.

Modern art began in Europe about 1905–1910, emerging out of the painting of the Post-Impressionists, and displacing the false start of Art Nouveau. In painting there had been such men as Cézanne, Van Gogh, and Gauguin to form the new art's foundation. But in sculpture the naturalism of the arch-Romantic Auguste Rodin dominated the scene, and if modern art was violently opposed to anything, it was opposed to naturalism and romanticism. The young sculptors, then, faced a negative situation in which they were compelled to rebel against the greatest living master of their day. They drew some inspiration from Cézanne's experiments with the analysis of form, and a few of them became Cubist sculptors, at least for a while. But though a number of American sculptors quickly embraced the broad philosophy of the new art, they resisted Cubism. The brilliant Boccioni had prepared his "Technical Manifesto of Futurist Sculpture" in 1912, but its influence was more on the general movement of modern art than on any particular American sculptor.

The key to the new sculpture in America, therefore, is the theory of simplification and abstraction of natural form, which represents a far more moderate course than that taken by much of European art during this period. In the United States,

[5 5 4]

there was no contemporary counterpart to Brancusi's Cubistic "Kiss" or "Madame Pogany," and it took even Archipenko—who settled permanently in America in 1923—a long time to win acceptance of his quasi-Cubist style. American sculptors seemed determined to advance toward a modern art at their own pace, without accepting directly any European movement, such as Cubism, Expressionism, or Futurism. Although this was an exciting period with many fine sculptors, the United States did not really reach the forefront with an international modern style until after World War II.

The country benefited from the many foreign sculptors who made their homes in the United States: Elie Nadelman, Archipenko, Robert Laurent, José de Creeft, and Gaston Lachaise all began their careers in Paris before crossing the Atlantic. And American-born sculptors spent a varying number of years in Europe, primarily in Paris, where they found a larger coterie of fellow participants in—and enthusiasts for—the modern movement than existed in the United States. It was through the European artists who came to the United States and the American artists who went abroad to study that America became aware of the new experiments toward a truly modern art.

The celebrated Armory Show of 1913 had surprisingly little influence on the evolution of modern sculpture in the United States. By the time it arrived, most of America's modern sculptors were already set on a course of simplification and abstraction of natural form, and most of them found nothing there that they had not seen years earlier in Europe. The Armory Show was more enlightening to the general public than to the artists themselves, who were already well aware of the *avant-garde* experiments in Paris. The Armory Show came and went; while it left the American public in something of a dizzying recoil, the sculptors themselves went about their business of working out their own forms of modern art. They certainly did not boycott the exhibition, and indeed they found it exciting and encouraging to the general cause of modern art in the United States. But the big noise over the show came not from the new artists of the 20th century, but from members of the entrenched old guard like Lorado Taft and Frederic Ruckstull, and the reactions of amazement came from the public. It is sometimes forgotten that there was a conservative side to the Armory Show; although Gaston Lachaise, Elie Nadelman, Alexander Archipenko, and William Zorach were represented, Karl Bitter, George Grey Barnard, Solon Borglum, James Earle Fraser, Bessie Potter Vonnoh, Jo Davidson, Mahonri Young, and Arthur Lee were also.

In the 1920's and 1930's the human figure remained the primary subject for artistic expression, followed by animal forms, whereas portraiture—long the mainstay of American artists—became less important. Memorial statues of politicians and war heroes did not become altogether extinct, but they absorbed increasingly less of the artistic energies of our most gifted artists, who sought to express themselves more and more in creations of their own imagination. The modern movement was given direction by the artist's personal search for expression and the basic elements of Art with a capital *A;* the new art was not created to please the general public or the millionaires who were slow to realize the potential of the modern experiments. Rather, it flowed from the artists themselves, who were bound to find a new form of expression relevant to 20th-century man in spite of himself. The naturalism and romanticism of earlier movements disgusted most of the *avant-garde* because those styles had become ends in themselves and had lost the vigor and vitality needed for the expression of modern ideas. A new aesthetic was required, and this was the generation that would carve it.

The expression "carve it" is appropriate, for the new aesthetic, which was based on the fundamentals of sculpture, was in large part derived from the new technique of *taille direct*, or direct carving. In Paris about 1907 Brancusi began carving directly in wood and stone, as did Henri Laurens and Modigliani in the following decade. Several Americans also found the new method highly suited to developing the form they sought. By 1913 Robert Laurent had taken up direct wood carving, applying the technique to stone about 1920; he was followed by William Zorach and John B. Flannagan. New effects were achieved; a new attitude toward the material was formed; and a new aesthetic of simplified, somewhat stylized, massive form evolved. The academicians continued to work in clay, and as often as not turned the finished model over to artisans who made the plaster cast of it and then put it into marble or bronze, neither of which possessed any of the intrinsic qualities of the original clay.

In the search for basic and fundamental principles of sculpture, a new respect for the unique qualities of diverse materials was born. Moreover, the artisan middleman was eliminated as the sculptor attacked the block directly, working, refining, and finishing the piece himself. The modern sculptors held that they gained a greater integrity and a more direct intimate relationship with their finished piece when they themselves carried the creative process through the various stages from the selection of the block to the finishing of the details. They achieved a certain bold, undiluted, almost primitive effect, which found acceptance at once among a generation of sculptors who suddenly discovered the naïve forcefulness and expressiveness of primitive art, and who rejected the previously sacred dictum that ultimate beauty rested in classical Greek art.

The term "modern art" need not necessarily exclude a naturalistic style if it possesses a freshness, a vitality, a good sculptural form. Just as the paintings of Andrew Wyeth have regained a respectable place for naturalism in American painting, so it is possible for the portraitist Jo Davidson to create good art in the 20th century without submitting to either abstraction or nonobjectivism. Naturalism had long been a part of the American tradition in art, and its deep-rooted strength was partially responsible for the more conservative brand of modern art that developed in the United States between the wars. But because at one time it had lost its poignancy does not mean that it could not—or cannot in the future—be revived by the touch of a truly creative, imaginative artist who has something to express in plastic form.

Between the two World Wars, the two American sculptors who continued to infuse life and spirit into naturalistic portraiture were Jo Davidson and Malvina Hoffman. Both were intimately aware of the new experiments in abstract art that were being carried on in Europe, but each maintained an integrity to a personal style, working diligently to make a living art of it. Neither could really be called academic, as neither was a product of any of the academies, nor did either create his art through mere adherence to academic principles. Naturalism remained alive in their hands because they put vitality into meaningful sculpturesque form—one of the essentials of great art whether realistic, abstract, or nonobjective.

Jo Davidson (1883–1952), born in New York, frustrated the wishes of his parents that he become a doctor by pursuing the art of sculpture. One day in New Haven, where he was preparing to enter Yale to study medicine, he wandered into the empty sculpture room of the School of Fine Arts: "I found the clay bin, put my hand in it, and touched the beginning of my life," he wrote in his autobiography. Soon afterward he found a job doing the most menial tasks in the studio of Herman MacNeil, but he learned there little more than the practical procedures of mixing plaster or building an armature. It seems MacNeil, who was then working on sculptures for the St. Louis fair, gave him virtually no instruction in either modeling or the principles of art.

Although Davidson did some modeling in clay at the Art Students League, he did not actually receive formal criticism there either. Then, in about 1906, one of his first serious efforts, a statuette of David, was commissioned to be put into bronze and was given a good place in the League's annual exhibition. This success gave Davidson his first real encouragement, and he took a modest studio of his own on East 23rd Street, living an impecunious existence and surviving on the free lunches that went with nickel beers in those days. At that time one of his friends was the colorful Sadakici Hartmann, later to become an eminent critic and historian of American art. Throughout his life, Davidson was to attract and be attracted by people of strong character and rare gifts, developing an insatiable desire to know those who made the world go round. This fascination with the personalities of his sitters was one of the prime ingredients in the success of his portraiture.

In 1907, the year in which Picasso created his "Demoiselles d'Avignon," Jo Davidson, then twenty-four, went to Paris. He eagerly entered a sculpture class at the Ecole des Beaux-Arts and, after only a few weeks withdrew, disappointed with the teaching there. He worked on his own without the benefit of criticism by anyone from the academies. Commissions came slowly, but he was in love with life, with Paris, and with his work; he was becoming a colorful figure amid the Bohemian world of the Café du Dôme, with his burly black beard and his Great Dane, Sultan, a stray who adopted him one night on the streets of Paris. He married a French girl, the sister of one of his artist friends. In his work, he was absorbed with universal themes of the struggle and toil of mankind, and he was represented at the Salon of 1909 by a statuette entitled "La Terre."

In time he began to acquire a reputation for his ability to model a portrait bust in a single sitting, and commissions came his way. Although he worked on large ideal works throughout his life, he was evidently a portraitist by nature; his likenesses of people were far more successful than his imaginary subjects. Exhibitions of his work in London and New York did little to secure him either reputation or money, but at least they were a beginning. In his autobiography, *Between Sittings*, he recalled that period:

Portrait making began to occupy the major part of my time. My approach to my subjects was very simple. I never had them pose but we just talked about everything in the world. Sculpture, I felt, was another language altogether that had nothing to do with words. As soon as I got to work, I felt this other language growing between myself and the person I was "busting." I felt it in my hands. Sometimes the people talked as if I was their confessor. As they talked, I got an immediate insight into the sitters.*

Jo Davidson's work was next seen in New York at an exhibition held at the Rinehardt Galleries in 1913, and also in the enormous international exhibition of modern art that some of his friends were organizing. He sent seven sculptures to the Armory Show that year, and unlike many of the artists of the National Academy and the National Sculpture Society, he thrilled at the arrival in America of this bold new art. His work seemed to him to be as alive and as contemporary as Marcel Duchamp's "Nude Descending a Staircase," or Brancusi's "Madame Pogany," or any of the other 1,600 entries. His own exhibition moved next to the Rinehardt Galleries in Chicago, and the International Exhibition of Modern Art soon followed to the same city. Amid the hullabaloo over the wild new art, Jo Davidson's more conservative sculpture made its impact.

Early in 1914 Davidson modeled the likeness of Lord Northcliffe, tycoon of the London newspaper world. He included this bust in an important exhibition of his work held at the Leicester Galleries that June along with a number of other portraits, among which were those of Ambassador Walter Hines Page, Rabindranath Tagore, Israel Zangwill, and Georg Brandes, as well as an enlarged version of "La Terre." "Portraiture became an obsession," he later wrote. "Meeting and knowing people meant becoming acquainted with their thinking. My life became richer by association with a great variety of people. I made life-long friends in the British capital and discovered there what friendships really meant." The exhibition was a success. Davidson was beginning to attain an international reputation just as hostilities broke out between Germany and the Allies.

During the war he served for a while as an illustrator-correspondent at the front, then returned to the United States, where he modeled the likeness of Woodrow Wilson as he worked in his office at the White House. In 1918 Davidson conceived the plan of modeling the portraits of the most eminent wartime leaders, and arrangements were made through friends at Washington for him to go to Europe to begin with General Pershing and Marshal Foch. The latter enjoyed the encounter immensely, and when Davidson had finished, Marshal Foch

---

* Unless otherwise noted, quotations by Davidson are taken from *Between Sittings*, and are quoted here through the courtesy of Dial Press.

added his own signature alongside the artist's, thereby establishing a precedent the sculptor was to follow with many subsequent busts.

I look back on this period and wonder where I got the energy. I had now done, within the year, Masaryk, Wilson, Foch, Tardieu, General Dawes, Harbord, Pershing, Bliss, Colonel House, Baruch, and a statuette of my friend Colonel Réquin . . . . The speed with which one sitter replaced another, each being a distinct personality, taught me to simplify more and extract the essentials needed to make a portrait . . . . My studio seemed at times to be a branch of the Quai d'Orsay and the Crillon.

At the Genoa Conference in 1922 the sculptor added several "Bolsheviks" to this group.

In 1920 Davidson modeled the excellent portrait of his friend Gertrude Stein (Fig. 15.1). "To do a head of Gertrude Stein was not enough—there was so much more to her than that. So I did a seated figure of her—a sort of modern Buddha." While he was doing her portrait, she would come to his studio and read from a manuscript, once writing a prose portrait of Davidson himself. He was quite flattered, for he found her a "very rich personality." In a different way, he found the ancient John D. Rockefeller—whose profile reminded him of Ramses II—to be equally fascinating. When he was a guest at the home of the old man in the summer of 1924, they talked quietly about all manner of things and joked a bit and listened to the organ. The result was a colossal marble bust, commissioned by John D. Rockefeller, Jr., and placed in the Standard Oil Building in New York.

Another important series of busts by this "plastic historian" came about when George H. Doran, of Doubleday, Doran and Company, got the idea of having Davidson do the likenesses of eminent British and American writers. Davidson was delighted with the proposal, for it meant getting to know more interesting people. First came James Joyce, "frail, detached and the essence of sensitivity"; then Hugh Walpole, Frank Swinnerton, Rudyard Kipling, Sir Arthur Conan Doyle, Aldous Huxley, Arnold Bennett, H. G. Wells, and Christopher Morley. Davidson's perceiving eye caught both the physical likeness and the spirit that dwelt within, through a naturalism that was as selective as it was sensitive. In a general reference to his work he wrote:

In making portraits, some intrigued me more than others. I would get some quickly and others would evade me. Some sitters give themselves with ease—others resist. I once said facetiously that some of my sitters were short stories, and others were novels. It takes two to make a bust. The important thing is the rapport between the artist and the sitter.

More of the world's great men sat for Davidson, and most of them found the sculptor as likable and interesting as he found them. Gandhi once said to him, after looking at photographs of his work, "I see you make heroes out of mud," to which the artist replied, "And sometimes vice-versa." In the White House in 1933, which impressed him as "a friendly place, alive, gay and human . . . [with] barking dogs and voices of children," Davidson modeled the likeness of Franklin

D. Roosevelt as he began his first term as President. He also did Albert Einstein at Princeton. The death of his wife left Davidson restless and quarrelsome for a while, but eventually he returned to his work. He modeled a statue of one of his literary favorites, Walt Whitman, which years later was set up in New York's Bear Mountain State Park. And he did a statue of his friend Will Rogers, one of the few fine portrait statues to be placed in Statuary Hall in this century (Fig. 15.2). Davidson had never done a bust of Rogers, and whenever he broached the subject, the humorist would reply good-naturedly, "You lay off of me, you old head-hunter." A replica of the statue went to the Rogers memorial in Claremore, Oklahoma.

In April 1941 Jo Davidson sailed for South America to do a series of portraits of presidents of ten Latin American countries. After returning to the United States he settled down for a few years on a farm in Bucks County, Pennsylvania, with his new wife, a former sweetheart from his art-school days. Following the end of World War II he and his wife went to San Francisco, where delegates from all over the world were meeting to draft the constitution of the United Nations; Jo Davidson had hoped to add some more likenesses to his "plastic history" there, but a heart attack put an end to such plans. After his recuperation the Davidsons returned to France, to the sculptor's beloved house and studio, "Bécheron," near Paris. He dreamed of continuing his "plastic history" with busts of members of the French Resistance, but only one portrait resulted. In 1947 he worked on the model for a memorial to Lidice, a monument to those the Nazis slaughtered there and in the Warsaw Ghetto, and to the tragedy of all the Jews during the war. This took a great deal of his energy and dedication, but in the end nothing came of it.

The American Academy of Arts and Letters held a retrospective show of his work in the late 1940's, a glorious finale to his forty years of "busting" the world's important men and women. About two hundred pieces were shown at Rockefeller Center, with the proceeds going to the United Nations Children's Appeal. He later did busts of Dwight D. Eisenhower, Helen Keller, Marshal Tito, and a few others. By the end of his career, Davidson's work was quite conservative in comparison with the nonobjective forms of contemporary American sculpture; but in its spirit, vitality, and sculptural form it possesses the stuff of which fine art is made.

Malvina Hoffman (1887–1966) would undoubtedly have wished to be remembered for her large, heroic works and especially for her heads and figures that make up the "Hall of Man" collection at Chicago's Field Museum; but the heroic works somehow lack that spark of imagination that might carry them beyond mere convention, and the heads and figures, although competent, seem to be more an ambitious anthropological exercise than great art. However, in her portrait busts of prominent figures of the 1920's and 1930's she achieved something truly fine and creative in her art. One day after beginning her studies as a painter, she modeled the likeness of her father, a gifted concert pianist, whom she adored. She sent the finished bust to the National Academy exhibition of 1910, and its success encouraged her to continue in sculpture. A bust of Samuel Grimson—musician friend of her father's, whom she was to marry fifteen years later—had been modeled in 1909. Both of these contain the fluid impressionistic surfaces of the French style.

After studying at the Art Students League, and after helpful criticisms from Gutzon Borglum and Herbert Adams, she went to Europe in 1910 with the single purpose of studying in the studio of Auguste Rodin, the great French master. When she finally gained admittance to Rodin's studio she showed him a couple of photographs of her work and told him that if she could not study with him she would return to America. According to the account in her autobiography, *Heads and Tales*, Rodin looking up from the photographs of her portraits then said, "Character seems to interest you. You have studied these men well." For the next year she worked under his criticism with free run of his studio. She drew a lot that year and modeled some, without coming under the spell of the strong personal style of Rodin. In 1911 her "Russian Dancers" won a prize in Paris. She returned to America that year and studied dissection at a medical school to improve her knowledge of human anatomy; a year later she was back in Paris, where she was to remain until 1914.

Malvina Hoffman sometimes observed Rodin as he modeled a portrait, often making as many as six or seven studies to catch the expression he felt portrayed the sitter's personality. This search for a spirit, or soul, as well as for a likeness, soon began to appear in her own portraiture, which in time she executed in her own studio. These were exciting years for her, being drawn into the circle of "Pavlowa, Nijinsky and Diaghileff's Ballet, Gertrude Stein and Matisse, Brancusi," and others. She became infatuated with the ballet, primarily through her friendship with the great Pavlowa.

In 1914, Malvina Hoffman supervised the arrangement of the Rodin exhibition in London at Dorchester House; the excitement about this rather overshadowed the exhibition of her own work, which was being held at the same time at the Leicester Galleries. With the outbreak of war, she returned to the United States—never again to see Rodin, who died in 1917. She had brought with her from Paris a spirited sculpture called "Bacchanale Russe," which represented Pavlowa and Mordkin dancing. Six replicas were cast in bronze, and it became immediately popular. A small replica is in the collection of the Metropolitan Museum of Art; a large version is at the Luxembourg Museum in Paris. When exhibited at the National Academy of Design in 1917, it won the Julia A. Shaw Memorial Prize "for the most meritorious work of art in the Exhibition by an American woman." It possessed nothing of the profound depth and emotion of Rodin, and was more reminiscent of MacMonnies' "Bacchante" than anything else. Malvina Hoffman next began a series of panels representing pairs of dancers, based on her close observation of Pavlowa and Mordkin, both of whom were quite interested in her work. She also made a war monument called "The Sacrifice," a curious medieval tomb sculpture of a dead knight lying on his back with a robed, hooded woman—presumably the mother of the fallen warrior—kneeling at his head. It was commissioned to be put into marble as a gift to Harvard from Robert Bacon (of whom Malvina Hoffman did a portrait bust) but was placed instead in the Cathedral of St. John the Divine in New York. Two heroic but academic and unexciting figures representing "The Friendship of English-Speaking People" were placed in the pediment of Bush House in London and unveiled in June 1924.

In 1930, the directors of the Field Museum in Chicago asked Malvina Hoffman if she would travel around the world doing sculptural studies for the "Races of Man." Excited by the proposal, she set to work on it at once. During the next five years she traveled to the far parts of the earth, modeling the heads and figures of Africans, Polynesians, Asians, Caucasians, and other racial types, executing 105 heads and some full-length figures or groups that were cast in bronze and set up in the Field Museum. This project attracted much interest, but as works of art, these pieces—like most of her ideal works—were not as successful as her many portrait busts.

Like Jo Davidson, Malvina Hoffman modeled the likenesses of many of the most notable men and women of her time, concentrating on those who were prominent in the arts, in the humanities, or in society. A collection of twenty-eight plaster replicas of her portraits is in the New-York Historical Society and includes the early portrait of her father, Richard Hoffman, and one of her mother (1918), which more than any other shows a trace of Rodin's influence. One of her most sensitive works is that of Pavlowa (Fig. 15.3). Both the face and the hands portray the delicacy and grace of the incomparable ballerina; it is much more successful than the fantasy-like "Mask of Pavlowa," with its elaborate tiara and necklace, which also dates from 1924. The bust of Pavlowa was modeled with deep insight into the beauty and genius of the subject, a true character study that goes well beyond its naturalistic style to capture the essence of the great dancer. Malvina Hoffman also did a portrait of Pavlowa's partner, Michael Mordkin, and three different studies of the famed pianist Paderewski—one as a friend, one as a musician, and one as a statesman. All again are poignant character studies.

The sculptor's naturalism extended over a wide range, from the vigorous and dynamic image of the Yugoslavian artist Mestrovic and the genteel, fashionable portrait of Mrs. Edward Harriman, to the bold strength of Pierre Lecompte Du Nouy. These possess a simple and direct naturalism, which is imbued with a spirit and personality, all contained in a fine sculptural form. The "Robert Bacon" possesses the same strength of character and form found in the Du Nouy portrait; the likeness of Henry Clay Frick was placed in the McKinley Memorial at Niles, Ohio, and that of Dr. Harvey Cushing is at Yale. The "Edward Harkness" for the Columbia-Presbyterian Medical Center in New York is an exceptionally good example of her work, as is the bust of the publisher Adolph S. Ochs and the one of Wendell Willkie, which was placed in the Willkie Memorial Building in New York City.

Malvina Hoffman, who was a member of the National Academy of Design and the National Sculpture Society, won numerous prizes and medals, and was awarded honorary degrees from five different American colleges and universities. Long active as an author, her last book about her life and work was published in 1965, the year before her death.

Another who remained dedicated to the traditional naturalism in American sculpture was Arthur Lee (1881–1961), who was born in Trondheim, Norway, one of a large family. His parents brought him in 1888 to the United States, where they settled in St. Paul, Minnesota. In 1901 he went to New York City to study at the Art Students League; four years later he went to Paris. After his return to America in 1910 his work began to attract attention.

Throughout his career, he was to concentrate on a search for beauty in the human figure, meaningfully expressed through sculptural form; as a result of this all-absorbing interest, he did few portraits and avoided commissions for public monuments. At the Armory Show of 1913, for example, he exhibited statuettes of Hercules, an Ethiopian, and an Aphrodite, all in bronze, and a "Virgin," in plaster. In 1914 he went back to Paris, where he continued his work in spite of the war, remaining there until 1917. From this period dates one of his finest works, "Volupté" (Fig. 15.5), a female torso in marble. As the name implies, "Volupté" represents the full bloom of womanhood, softly sensuous with graceful contours. Head, arms, and lower legs were omitted as unnecessary to the expression of the loveliness of the womanly form, for Lee was seeking to reproduce its natural beauty in three-dimensional form rather than any of the academic "isms," which too often had become ends in themselves.

In the 1920's and 1930's, Arthur Lee's work was much respected by the more traditional sculptors. In 1924 he was the winner of the Widener Gold Medal at the Pennsylvania Academy; he received the same award four years later for one of his most popular pieces, "Rhythm," a supple figure of a nude youth. In 1937 he won the Saltus Prize at the National Academy exhibition for his monumental nude woman titled "Great Fortune," which one critic described as a ". . . powerful, balanced and decidedly modern bronze figure." The "modern" element results from a certain affinity with the heroic female figures of Gaston Lachaise, for Lee obviously emphasized the womanly aspects of the figure while including a slight abstraction of the forms. But that was the extent of Lee's compromise with the abstractionists, for his love of the human figure would not permit anything that deviated from its own natural form. Arthur Lee lived until 1961, but his active career as a sculptor ended long before.

The main theme in the work of Mahonri Young (1877–1957) was man at his labors. Born in Salt Lake City in the same year that his famous grandfather Brigham Young died, Mahonri grew up in the Mormon settlement. Encouraged in his interest in art, he copied the illustrations he found in the popular periodicals of the day and took some drawing lessons. His awareness of sculpture was stimulated by the presence of Cyrus Dallin in Salt Lake City in connection with the Pioneer Monument, and in 1899 the twenty-two-year-old Young left Utah to study at the Art Students League in New York for two years. In Paris he studied drawing and painting at the Académies Julian and Delécluse, and it was not until he took a trip to Italy that his interest focused on sculpture. Although he continued to do drawings and watercolors, his main artistic efforts thereafter were sculptural.

He first attracted attention in the United States when his "Shoveler" and "Man Tired" were exhibited at the American Art Association. In this same period he did the bronze "Stevedore" (Fig. 15.4) of 1904. The work is rich in modeling, and the sculptor's disregard of minute details gives a kind of monumentality to even this small piece (16 inches high). Such richness of modeling and sculptural form are salient features of Young's style. It is also found in the "Man with Pick" in the Metropolitan Museum of Art, and in the "Driller" at Brookgreen Gardens. Although subjects such as these were drawn from the working class, Young, like Abastenia St. Leger Eberle, did not become involved in statements of social comment; instead, he simply found the human figure in action an inspiration, whether his subject be at labor or in a prize fight, as in his "Right to the Jaw" and "The Knockdown."

In 1911 Young's "Bovet Arthur—A Laborer" won the Barnett prize at the National Academy for the best sculpture by an artist under thirty-five. The following year he took a trip to Arizona, where he became interested in doing cowboy and Indian subjects. The painted plaster statuette titled "Man Shoeing a Horse," which he exhibited at the Armory Show of 1913, was inspired by his western trip. In his studio in New York he designed and modeled the memorial Salt Lake City erected to the seagulls that had once saved the Mormons' crops from locusts. He sent two of the reliefs for this monument to the Armory Show, along with "Man with Boys on His Shoulder," "Old Rembrandt," and a painted plaster piece titled "Mother and Son." Young, who received a silver medal at the Panama-Pacific Exposition in San Francisco in 1915, continued to take his subjects mainly from men at their labors: He did "Man with a Wheelbarrow," "The Forge," and "The Heavy Sledge." "The Rigger," in Brookgreen Gardens, was modeled in 1922 and was shown at the large Centennial Exhibition of the National Academy of Design in 1925. Young had been elected a member of the National Academy in 1923; he was also a member of the National Sculpture Society and of the National Institute of Arts and Letters.

One of Young's few portraits—his bust of Emil Carlsen—received the Maynard Portrait Prize at the National Academy in 1932. His ponderous marble statue of his grandfather was unveiled in the Capitol's Statuary Hall in 1950, with the features and clothing of the seated figure simplified nearly to the point of abstraction. Young, by his own admission, wanted to remain close to nature, and therefore he did not experiment very much with abstraction. Mahonri Young was eighty years old when he died in 1957.

Paul Manship (1885–1966), an extremely talented sculptor, pursued a path that led directly between the ultraconservative, old-guard realist-academicians and the wildly experimental and adventurous *avant-garde* of modern art. His strong personal style had elements of both camps, but in time he was hailed as the savior of the more traditional group. His subjects and even his style sprang from antiquity and were therefore acceptable to the men of the academies, yet his work incorporated something of the simplification and abstraction of the new art. In the end, however, the latter would allow no compromise, and Manship was branded, in the most derogatory sense, an "academician." But there is no denying he was a good sculptor—gifted and imaginative, a fine technician and craftsman.

Paul Manship grew up in St. Paul, Minnesota, and went to the local Institute of Art for his first art lessons. There he soon developed a preference for sculpture over painting, and by the time he went East in 1905, he had decided to become a sculptor. Likable and precocious, he had just turned twenty when he became an assistant in the studio of Solon Borglum. He also worked with Isidore Konti for a while, and at the Pennsylvania Academy of the Fine Arts he studied with Charles Grafly. His progress was rapid, and in 1909 he was awarded the most coveted of all prizes, the American Prix de Rome. The American Academy in Rome, established in 1894, consisted of two parts: a School of Fine Arts and a School of Classical Studies; the prize provided $1,000 a year for three years of study there, plus a travel allowance and lodging and a studio at the Academy. It was the first of many major prizes and awards that Manship was to win during his long career.

Once in Italy, Manship immediately began a love affair with Rome in particular and antiquity in general. He had completely bypassed Paris, the École des Beaux-Arts, and the powerful influence of Rodin. Instead, Manship found a source of inspiration in the graceful maidens in the frescoes of Pompeii, in the decorative figures in the vase paintings, and in the elegant classic beauty of Roman bronze statuettes. Especially stimulating to him were the simple, rather abstract figures of archaic Greek art, with their decorative stylizations of the hair and drapery. So infatuated with this art did he become that he traveled to the eastern Mediterranean to see the archaic Greek art, and became the first American sculptor to choose its aesthetic principles over the classical art of Phidias and Polykleitos. In Egypt he discovered another stylized art of antiquity; indeed, the oriental Indo-Greek, the Minoan, and the Assyrian styles also came to influence his style in time. Back in his studio in Rome he began to incorporate all he had absorbed into a very personal style. When he returned to the United States in 1912, he brought with him a number of carefully finished pieces that contained the elements of his new and original style.

Manship's success was immediate. At the exhibition held by the Architectural League in 1913 he became the newest prodigy on the American art scene; no less than ten of his works were shown in the Academy Room, and their subjects revealed the revived inspiration of antiquity. There was a "Centaur and Maid" and a "Mask of Silenus"; the latter clearly possessed an archaic Greek influence, as did the flat, linear folds of the garment with zigzag hems, in the popular group called "Playfulness." "Woodland Dance" represented a prancing centaur and a lithe wood nymph; and the "Duck Girl," a fountain figure, was clearly inspired by classical—not archaic—Graeco-Roman art. Kenyon Cox noted that "it reminds one of the best Pompeian bronzes"; he also admired the simplified contours. Cox closed his review with the prediction that if the work of this newly discovered genius did not suddenly crystallize into a clever mannerism of itself, then much could be expected from its creator in the years to come. The "Duck Girl" received the Widener gold medal in 1914 when exhibited at the Pennsylvania Academy, and the city of Philadelphia purchased it for Fairmount Park.

In 1913 Manship also showed his work at the National Academy exhibition, where his "Centaur and Dryad" was awarded the Barnett prize—the only prize given for sculpture. An even greater honor came that year when the piece was purchased by the Metropolitan Museum of Art. The sculptor was then only twenty-eight years old, and the art world was indeed impressed that the work of one so young should enter such a distinguished collection. In the midst of all these accolades and awards came the Armory Show of 1913—in which Manship did not participate; but that by no means diminished his general popularity. Americans liked his work for its craftsmanship and its lyrical aesthetic appeal. His style somehow fitted the time, and his brand of abstraction—unlike the brutal distortions of so much of the new art—reaffirmed the forms of nature. The marked stylization of forms into decorative patterns and rhythms is apparent in the "Centaur and Dryad."

Manship's next personal triumph came in 1916 with his one-man exhibition at the Berlin Photographic Gallery in New York City; nearly 100 of the 150 pieces were sold. The stellar attraction was his newly created "Dancer and Gazelles" (Fig. 15.6). There is a flavor of Asian—especially Indian—art in the central figure, seen in the rhythm of the torso and arms, in the denial of weight and mass as the toes barely touch ground, and in the long sweeping, curving contours of the drapery. Even in the gazelles' delicate forms one senses Near Eastern prototypes. The piece is altogether well conceived in the composition, in the harmonious union of its parts, and in the extremely refined and sensitive design, with fine contrasts between volume and linear motifs—a sort of symphony in curves. The surfaces are finished with the sculptor's impeccable craftsmanship. Critics praised it as a well-executed piece that was both naturalistic and abstract; the promise many had seen earlier in Manship was being fulfilled as he established a new standard by which much of American sculpture would be judged in the next two decades. In 1917 the "Dancer and Gazelles" won the Barnett prize at the National Academy, and no fewer than a dozen replicas (most in a smaller scale) were sold.

Honors continued to be heaped upon Paul Manship as his position as the leader of the younger men of the academic group became more evident. In 1918 the Metropolitan Museum of Art again honored Manship by selecting him to design the J. P. Morgan Memorial. The American Institute of Architects presented him with its gold medal in 1921, and in 1922 he was appointed the annual professor of sculpture at the American Academy in Rome. And when the American Numismatic Society met in 1924 Paul Manship was given the Saltus award for excellence of design in medallions and medals.

By 1924 Manship was maintaining a studio in Paris, but he frequently worked in Rome. Here he completed one of his most famous sculptures, "Diana," whereas its companion piece, "Actaeon," was finished soon afterward in Paris. He had been working with the Diana and Actaeon themes since 1911, and they finally took finished form in the two heroic groups that were the main attractions of an exhibition of his work, at New York's Scott and Fowles Gallery, in 1925. With these two pieces Manship's style attained both maturity and monumentality. The archaic Greek influence exists in the stylization of the dogs that attack the fleeing Actaeon, as well as in the inset eyes of both man and beasts. Characteristically the composition is decoratively rhythmic, and "its charm is that of a shrewdly organized silhouette." Royal Cortissoz, reviewing the exhibition for the New York *Herald Tribune*, wrote of the aesthetics of Manship's style:

An eclectic still, as he probably always will be, ineffably refined, sophisticated, a master of his craft through whom the influences of all the historic schools have seemed to flow, he yet preserves as his central merit a rich and altogether personal feeling for beauty . . . .

Henry McBride of the New York *Sun* saw another aspect of Manship's work and lauded the workmanship of the sculptures, saying that it was his superb technique that appealed to the general public.

Manship was trying to find a style of sculpture that would be compatible with contemporary American life and the settings being created for that life. In an article about the American Academy in Rome, published in *Art and Archaeology* in 1925, he said that one thing young American sculptors needed to learn was to become a part of the total flow of contemporary life—to learn how to create statues that worked with the designs of garden landscape, city plazas, and especially with the new architecture of the 20th century.

The Minoan-like "Flight of Europa" in 1925 was another Manship success, and in 1926 he did the "Indian Hunter with Dog" (Fig. 15.8), in the style of the "Actaeon" group. The original was executed as a fountain destined for St. Paul, Minnesota. An image of fleetness, gracefully sleek, a glittering tour de force of technique, bold yet delicately decorative, it remains a work of art while finding a certain affinity with the metallic brilliance of the machine age. The head of the dog is modeled with a simplification and stylization that approach the contemporary work of Zorach or Warneke. Manship's abstraction, however, sprang from a different source, and its limits were well defined; it could not be lured beyond what is seen in the "Indian Hunter with Dog."

At the end of the 1920's Manship was made a Chevalier of the Legion of Honor. His fame spread in 1935 with an exhibition of his sculpture at the Tate Gallery, London's museum of modern art.

Manship did not do many portrait statues for public memorials, but there were a few, for example, "Lincoln as a Youth" for the plaza of the Lincoln National Life Insurance Building in Fort Wayne, Indiana. His major commission of the mid-1930's was for a figure to adorn the new Rockefeller Plaza in New York. Paul Jennewein had been commissioned to execute decorations for the nearby British Empire Building, a part of the new architectural complex. The statue by Manship was to form the focal point of the plaza, and the result was a colossal gilded bronze image of Prometheus. Glittering and floating, truly godlike, framed within the sprays of the fountain, it became one of the spectacular sights of New York City in the 1930's. Manship's "Prometheus" somehow belongs to that era of Radio City Music Hall; only a few years earlier, however, William Zorach and Robert Laurent had experienced bitter disappointment when the manager of the Music Hall had refused to accept their heroic nude abstractions.

The exhibition of Manship's work at Averell House in New York in 1933 was characteristically successful, although the critics were divided. Royal Cortissoz, old-guard critic of the *Herald Tribune*, was rather disappointed in the sculptor's later work:

Latterly something seems to have modified the color of his dream. Was it the modernistic hypothesis that has troubled the waters everywhere? It would seem a plausible surmise, because the new things here show a decided trend toward that "simplification" that we have all heard so much about.

But Cortissoz was unnecessarily apprehensive; though there may have been some diminution of decorative qualities in Manship's work of the 1930's, it was in favor of a greater monumentality rather than an increase in abstractionism. His style was essentially unaltered in the groups he created for the New York World's Fair in 1939—"Moods of Time"—simplified and stylized form, inspired by nature but conditioned by a flavoring from one of the historic styles of the past.

A retrospective exhibition of Manship's work was held at the National Institute of Arts and Letters, New York City, in 1945—just as World War II was ending and a new era was beginning for modern art in America. Manship, in his sixtieth year, was awarded a gold medal by the society in recognition of over three decades of work. He was hailed as the elder statesman of the academic group and was recognized as having effected a stylistic revolution in American sculpture, bringing to it something fresh and full of vitality. But his revolutionary triumph was a temporary one, and in the hands of less talented men the style became dry and pedantic. Moreover, the truly modern movement had gained momentum, and its art was coming of age in the United States. By 1945 Manship's greatest contributions had been made, and it was time to make way for younger men with other ideas to express in another kind of plastic form.

As heir to the style of Manship, Paul Jennewein (1890–   ) remained very close to the traditional academic fold. Jennewein—former vice-president of the National Academy of Design and for many years the president of the National

Sculpture Society—possessed a conservative decorative style that was in great demand from about 1920 through the 1940's.

Jennewein came to the United States in 1907 from Stuttgart, Germany, and the next year began studying at the Art Students League. In 1912, after winning the Avery Prize awarded by the Architectural League, he went on a two-year tour of Germany, Italy, France, and Egypt; but Rome captivated him most of all. Back in the United States he won the Prix de Rome in 1916, and for the next five years he studied at the American Academy in the Eternal City, employing much of the classical style in many of his own works. The art of the ancient Graeco-Roman world underwent a kind of metamorphosis under his touch, becoming decorative, somewhat stylized, and curvilinear; antiquity was to experience yet one more revival at his hands, sometimes curiously merging with a kind of Art Nouveau decorative quality. All this is apparent in his bronze statuette in the Metropolitan Museum of Art titled "Cupid and Gazelle," modeled in Rome in 1919. Other works from his years at the American Academy are "The First Step," "Repose," "Comedy," and "Hercules and Bull," all more or less classically inspired.

Jennewein's success continued. Shortly after he returned to America in 1921 he opened a studio in New York City, and the next year his "Nymph and Faun" won the competition for the Darlington Fountain in the national capital. Commissions were plentiful: There was the seated, sword-bearing nude for the war memorial in Barre, Vermont; the figure "The Puritan" was erected in Plymouth, Massachusetts; and a statue of Governor Endicott was produced for the city of Boston. For buildings in Harrisburg, Pennsylvania, and Fort Wayne, Indiana, he designed and modeled several panels, and thereafter his talents were in great demand for decorative architectural bronze reliefs. In 1926 his "Baby with a Squirrel" won a medal at the Concord Art Association exhibition, and the following year he was again awarded the Architectural League medal. His continued interest in classical themes may be seen in his "Greek Dancer," modeled in Rome in 1926. In Brookgreen Gardens there is a bronze statue of an Indian and an eagle that was made in 1929 as a study for a war memorial in Tours, France; three years later when it was shown at the Pennsylvania Academy it was awarded the Widener gold medal.

In the early years of the 1930's Jennewein was occupied with the polychromed terra-cotta pedimental decorations for Philadelphia's new art museum. The classical design of the edifice itself called for a classical motif in the pediment, and Jennewein was the natural choice for such a project. Zeus stands in the center flanked by Demeter, Ariadne, Theseus, Aphrodite, Cupid, and Adonis. Looking back from our historical vantage point, the whole idea of creating classical images of Greek gods and goddesses to adorn a 20th-century building now seems strangely out of step with the times; it was this sort of art that, according to many contemporary artists and critics, retarded the development of a vital modern art in America. But Jennewein was not alone to blame, for a committee of Philadelphians approved the architects' designs for the building itself, and given the low triangular space to decorate—surrounded by neoclassical architecture—there was little else the sculptor could do. Everything considered, Jennewein fulfilled his responsibilities adequately enough, deriving his inspiration from the rather severe style of Greek sculpture of the first half of the 5th century B.C. Interestingly, these were the beginning years of the Museum of Modern Art (founded 1929) in New York City; the two institutions were obviously dedicated to antithetical principles. By no means is it implied that the regal Philadelphia Museum of Art is of poor design or that Jennewein's sculpture is bad, but they do represent something of an anomaly from the course of 20th-century American life.

Paul Jennewein played an increasingly important role among those artists sincerely dedicated to the conservative trend in American sculpture. In 1939 he received the medal of honor from the Pennsylvania Academy of the Fine Arts, and three years later he was awarded the Saltus medal at the National Academy of Design exhibition for his little bronze piece titled "The Secret," an infant whispering to a stork; he again won the Saltus award in 1949 and the Watrous gold medal in 1960.

Among Jennewein's many works are war memorials in Providence, Rhode Island; Worcester, Massachusetts; and Rochester, New York. In Washington, D.C., the Department of Justice Building is decorated with his reliefs and figures, and there are two panels by him in the White House. He designed a set of bronze doors for the British Building in Rockefeller Center, and the decorative grille at the door of the Brooklyn Public Library is also his work. His sculpture adorns a fountain at City Hall in Kansas City, Missouri, and examples of his work are in the Dauphin County Court House, Harrisburg, Pennsylvania. His work is characterized by a marked gracefulness, strong linear rhythms, and smooth, highly polished surfaces. He is currently (1968) recognized as the head of the academic school of American sculptors.

The work of Alexander Stirling Calder (1870–1945) belongs to two very different movements in the history of American sculpture. He began his career in the Beaux-Arts style of the end of the 19th century, then changed some thirty years later—about 1920—to the modern school, which advocated the simplification and abstraction of natural form. Although he grew up in and about his father's studio while Alexander Milne Calder was designing the sculptures for Philadelphia City Hall, Stirling's hope was to attend West Point in preparation for a military career. When this did not work out, he turned to art, but he was as interested in the theater as he was in painting or sculpture. In 1886 he entered the Pennsylvania Academy, where he had the benefit of some instruction from the gifted artist and teacher Thomas Eakins. After four years at the Academy he went to Paris, where he studied under Chapu at the Académie Julian for a year, and then with Falguière at the Ecole des Beaux-Arts. Returning to Philadelphia in 1892, about the time his father was concluding work on City Hall, he found American sculptors in a whirl of industry and excitement on the eve of the World's Columbian Exposition at Chicago. He sent a couple of minor pieces to the Chicago fair in 1893, but by then he was already at work on two large commissions—a fountain for the University of Pennsylvania and a rather uninspiring portrait statue of the eminent physician Dr. Samuel Gross, to go in front of the Army Medical Museum in Washington. He next created six heroic portrait images of prominent Presbyterians for the Witherspoon Building in Philadelphia. In 1898 his son Alexander, the future mobilist, was born, and three years later Stirling Calder exhibited a charming statue of the boy, called "Man Cub," among his other works at the Pan-American Exposition in Buffalo. It is an intimate portrait executed in a highly selective naturalism.

In 1903 Stirling Calder became an instructor at the School of Industrial Art in Philadelphia. During the first decade of his professional career he had established a local reputation, but it was the exposition at St. Louis in 1904 that brought him national recognition. He served on its advisory committee for sculpture and won a silver medal for his decorative sculptures, the most important of which were "Philippe François Renault," the French explorer, and "The Missouri, Queen of the Rivers." In Philadelphia, his marble zodiac sundial, supported by four maidens in diaphanous garments, was placed in Fairmount Park. Poor health necessitated his moving to California in 1907, and there he did several Indian subjects. He also was commissioned to do six spandrel figures representing Nature, Art, Energy, Science, Imagination, and Law for the arcade entrance to the Spanish Renaissance-style building of the Troop Polytechnic Institute in Pasadena.

About 1910 Stirling Calder settled in New York to teach at the National Academy of Design and later at the Art Students League. He took a studio in the famed old Studio Building on 10th Street, where painters and sculptors had worked since the 1850's. When the Armory Show was held in 1913, Calder was already working on his grandiose and exotic designs for the Panama-Pacific Exposition, which was to open two years later in San Francisco; instead of absorbing any of the new art that suddenly appeared before him, his wonderfully fantastic groups "The Nations of the East" and "The Nations of the West" were the epitome—and one could almost say the swan song—of the Beaux-Arts style in America. The two groups, each containing about a dozen figures, were colorfully resplendent. The "West" group had equestrian outriders of cowboys and Indians, flag-bearing explorers and scouts, and oxen pulling a covered wagon that was crowned by symbolic personifications; the "East" was represented by a bejeweled elephant amid elaborately costumed Arabian horsemen, desert tribesmen on camels, and Asian warriors. In addition, he did a "Fountain of Energy," on top of which a muscular nude personification of Energy rode a prancing horse while small figures of Fame and Glory trumpeted from his shoulders. Stirling Calder was assisted by Lentelli and Roth, and most of the work was done in the New York studios. Although Karl Bitter was in charge of all sculptured decoration for the exposition, Calder supervised the work as it progressed in the various studios in New York. But Bitter died before the San Francisco fair opened, and Calder was given the responsibility of bringing the entire sculptural program to a successful conclusion.

At Bitter's death Calder took over another of the late sculptor's projects—the

Depew Fountain in Indianapolis. He followed Bitter's general scheme, but re-worked the design according to his own ideas. Eight children dance in a ring around a gay nymph, who beats time to their merry step with a pair of cymbals while fish leap from the water of the basin. This gleeful pastoral poetry set in plastic form has an affinity of spirit with MacMonnies' celebrated "Bacchante," as well as in the Carpeaux's fountain in Paris, with its timbrel-playing Apollo ringed by mirthful dancing maidens. As the second decade of the new century drew to a close, Calder still clung to the 19th-century Beaux-Arts style. This may be seen in another important commission of the same period—the gaines and mermaids that decorate the curious coastside fantasy known as the "Island" on millionaire James Deering's estate at Miami:

> The "Island" is a limestone structure designed like a Venetian barge, and built in the waters of Viscaya Bay, at this point quite shallow, confronting the series of terraces which lead up to the house. The sculpture comprises the two prows of the barge, colossal in size, six figures on the balustrade and four gaines on the boat landings.
>
> [*International Studio*, April 1919, p. XLV]

The first trace of influence from the abstractions of modern art are found in the group Calder did in 1918 for one of the piers of the Washington Arch in New York. The main figure of the first President is rather conventional, but the low-relief personifications of Wisdom and Justice, seen over his shoulder, are decidedly stylized in an effort to make them harmonious with the architecture. Thereafter the new experiments in simplification and abstraction appeared with increasing regularity, as Stirling Calder, then about fifty years old, began to pick up the spirit of modern art. If he was never wholly converted to it, it is not surprising considering his age and the degree to which he was committed to the academic Beaux-Arts style. A kind of classic modernism, not unlike that of Maillol, is found in his "Woman Scratching her Heel," in the Metropolitan Museum of Art. No ideal of the Beaux-Arts style is subscribed to here, but rather the beauty lies in the sculptural form itself.

When the Swann Memorial Fountain (Fig. 15.7) was dedicated in Philadelphia's Logan Circle in 1924, it was evident that Stirling Calder had made a stylistic transition. The dominant characteristic was a stylized decorative rendering of the figure with "sharp edges to define planes and accentuate pattern." The three figures, which represent the three waterways of Philadelphia—the Delaware and Schuylkill rivers and Wissahickon Creek—are a compromise between the traditional and *avant-garde* styles, which were earnestly beginning to contend for supremacy in the United States. It is to Calder's credit that he could see the possibilities of the new art and welcomed its virtues into his own style, for many of his conservative colleagues shut it out altogether. In a very brief period he had synthesized his former manner with the theories of simplification and abstraction, and created what was for him a genuinely new style. Still, it was a compromise, and although Stirling Calder was to remain active for another fifteen years, his brand of modern art was to progress only slightly beyond what he had achieved in the Swann Memorial Fountain. It would be for his son, whose wire figures were then beginning to attract attention, to push ahead the frontiers of modern art.

Throughout the rest of the 1920's and during the 1930's, Stirling Calder's services continued to be in great demand. In 1928 he was working on statues of four famous performers in their most celebrated roles for the I. Miller Building in New York: Mary Pickford in the role of Little Lord Fauntleroy; Ethel Barrymore as Ophelia; Marilyn Miller as Sunny; and the opera star Rosa Ponselle as Norma. Also in 1928 he began work on a monument to Shakespeare, with adjunct figures of the jesting Touchstone and the pensive, moody Hamlet; it was unveiled in Philadelphia's Logan Circle in 1932 and awarded the McClees prize by the Pennsylvania Academy. Another award in 1932 came from the Architectural League of New York for his heroic statue of Lief Ericsson, which the people of the United States presented to Iceland in celebration of the 1,000th year of its parliament. Calder's decorative stylization is especially noticeable in this monument, a plaster copy of which may be seen in the National Collection of Fine Arts in Washington. Perhaps the most abstract of all his works is the "Native Dance" (1938) in Brookgreen Gardens. The last piece he worked on was a monumental head of Winston Churchill; by then the sculptor had passed his seventieth birthday. He died in St. Luke's Hospital in New York in 1945. In an age when no quarter was given in the life-and-death struggle of two opposing forms of art, when artists ferociously defended one group and attacked the other, Stirling Calder was one of the few who left the conservative camp to find a new invigorating strength in modern art.

With this discussion of Stirling Calder we conclude our study of the "academic abstractionists." We turn now to those men who from the beginning divorced their work from the academic tradition to forge a new style out of the formal principles of simplification and abstraction of the forms of nature. Because there were no guidebooks for them to follow, they had to work out the theory as they went along. They were truly loners among a great array of artistic theories. These men shunned academic principles, and they could not accept the theories of such modern movements as Cubism, Constructivism, or Futurism. Three men— Robert Laurent, William Zorach, and John B. Flannagan—must be seen as pioneers, for their art represents the first appearance of a true modern art in American sculpture. Robert Laurent (1890–   ) was the first to introduce direct carving into American sculpture; he was followed by William Zorach and John B. Flannagan. With these three men working independently, a new movement emerged that had no manifesto and, to this day, has no name to single it out; but it broke completely with the past and forged a new set of aesthetics.

Robert Laurent was born in Concarneau, a small town in Brittany. His prodigious talent was recognized at the age of twelve by an American painter and collector, Hamilton Easter Field, who persuaded Robert's parents to let him take the boy back to America, where Field could see to the development of Laurent's special gifts. Field became like a father to young Robert, and he carefully nourished the boy's genius. While still in his teens Laurent was sent to Paris during the exciting years of the first appearance of the Fauves, the Cubists, the stormy Futurists and the other explorers and experimenters. He knew Picasso and many of the other leading art revolutionaries. By 1908 he was in Rome studying at the British Academy and with Hamilton Field and his friend Maurice Sterne. Along with his two mentors, young Robert discovered primitive art, and Sterne told him of the South Seas and the things he had seen in the Orient—all of which exposed Laurent to expressive art forms far beyond the confines of Graeco-Roman art. When Robert showed a special talent for carving wood, he was apprenticed to a famous Roman frame carver, Giuseppe Doratori, from whom he learned the fundamentals of craftsmanship. He was then about twenty years old.

Laurent's first serious wood carving, a bas-relief entitled "Negress" (1913), possesses a pseudo-primitive style that has a bit of the spirit of some of Gauguin's wood carvings. Consciously primitive in style, its subject is derived from a source not only beyond the classical heritage but also beyond the periphery of civilization itself. Two years later it was among the works that made up his first one-man show at the Daniel Gallery in New York. Through the twenty press notices the exhibition received, and especially from the laudatory critique of Henry McBride, Americans learned of the new sculptor in their midst. Dr. Albert Barnes bought one of his pieces for his collection, and in 1917 Forbes Watson acclaimed the rise of a new talent at the Whitney Studio group show. During those years Laurent exhibited regularly in New York, often along with Hamilton Field. When the United States entered the war, Laurent joined the Naval Aviation Corps. This eventually brought him to his native Brittany, where he met and married his beloved Mimi.

Back in his Brooklyn studio he resumed his work. In 1921 he carved a head in stone, thus initiating direct carving in that medium, a technique taken up by Zorach two years later. The "Head" (reproduced in *Arts*, vol. 1, 1921, p. 12) and other stone carvings were included in his one-man show at the Bourgeois Gallery in 1922 which Zorach undoubtedly saw since he was then working in New York.

Hamilton Field died in 1923, leaving Robert Laurent two houses in Brooklyn and a farm in Maine. Thus began his attachment to Maine, where he had a summer art school at Ogunquit for many years. About the same time he began teaching at the Art Students League and introduced into the sculpture classes direct carving in wood and stone—an extremely important step for the dissemination of the new method among the younger artists. His quiet manner, perceiving eye, and gentle criticism made him a most popular and successful teacher.

In 1928 Robert Laurent had a one-man show at the Valentine Gallery, and his sculptures began to go into some of the most important private collections in America. It was, incidentally, about 1928 that John Flannagan began carving directly in stone, after carving in wood for several years. By 1930 Laurent and

Zorach were formulating an articulate sculptural form of expression through abstraction, simplification, and respect for media, devoid of the elegant decorative elements that characterized the work of Paul Manship. Flannagan, meanwhile, in the remote seclusion of Ireland, was turning fieldstones into creatures of dynamic sculptural beauty.

In the early 1930's Robert Laurent was working on a commission for Radio City Music Hall, as were William Zorach and Gwen Lux. Laurent's subject was a girl with a goose, which he executed in plaster rather than in clay; the final version was to be cast in aluminum. When completed, the "Goose Girl" and the other two works caused a near-riot in the art world when the manager of the theater refused to accept them because they were nudes. Critical opinion eventually forced him to place them in the Music Hall, but they were consigned to inconspicuous locations.

A good example of Laurent's work in the mid-1930's is the bronze statue titled "Kneeling Figure" (Fig. 15.11). Although only 23 inches high, it possesses a remarkable monumentality. This is achieved by simplifying all the parts and enlarging them into massive, voluminous forms, without deforming them. When he modeled this piece Laurent was obviously thinking as a sculptor, not as a decorator or illustrator, for the bold masses reveal a true love of plastic form. He further emphasized the forms' three-dimensional quality by the subtle use of planes. All this is characteristic of the sculptor's mature art.

In 1936 Laurent participated in a group show in Rochester, New York, in which works by Gaston Lachaise, Georg Kolbe, Wilhelm Lehmbruck, Charles Despiau, and William Zorach were also shown. Two years later his "Kneeling Figure" won the Logan Prize at the Chicago Art Institute. In Philadelphia, meanwhile, his "Spanning the Continent" was erected as part of the Samuel Memorial in Fairmount Park, to which John Flannagan contributed a statue called "Gold Miner." Laurent's group represents a pioneer man and woman striding onward, westward, with vigor and determination; the sculptor wished to express the relentless surge of the tide that settled the great western territories. The facial features are stylized in a manner that suggests the strength and perseverance of these sturdy people.

By this time—the late 1930's—Jacques Lipchitz had had his first one-man show in New York, David Smith had made his first revolutionary experiments with welded-metal sculpture, and Alexander Calder had begun to exhibit his mobiles. In the years just before World War II, a new phase of modern sculpture dawned in America. Laurent, then approaching his fiftieth birthday, had many years of fine work ahead of him, but he was no longer one of the leaders of the revolution.

In 1940 Laurent carved the exquisite alabaster figure "Seated Nude" (Fig. 15.12). In the poised dignity and the massive volumes of this nude female figure, Laurent attained a kind of 20th-century classicism that was in every sense modern and in no way eclectic; it represents the unification of the beauty of the human figure with the pure beauty of sculptural form. It is a highly original work of art that grew out of his experiments in simplification and abstraction.

He was still teaching at the Art Students League in 1941 when another one-man exhibition of his work was held at the Valentine Gallery. The next year Henry Hope, chairman of the Art Department, persuaded him to join the faculty of Indiana University in Bloomington. He was to remain there, teaching sculpture during the academic year, for over twenty years. His efforts were mainly devoted to teaching during these years, and one of his last pieces was a fountain group titled "Venus," which was placed on the campus of Indiana University. Laurent was always a quiet man, more reticent than many of his contemporaries who have drawn more attention to themselves. But the facts of history are that Robert Laurent was one of the real pioneers of modern sculpture in America.

William Zorach (1887–1966) was one of the first American artists to participate in the modern movement, to understand fully its aesthetics, and to break completely with the traditional art of the academies. His story begins in Eurburg, Lithuania, where he was born to impecunious parents. His father, who had worked a freight barge up and down the Niemen River, decided to seek his fortune in America, to which he journeyed alone, eventually sending for his wife and children in 1891. Life was better in Port Clinton, Ohio, although the family income remained meager. William was sent to public school, where a teacher recognized his talent for drawing and suggested he be apprenticed to a lithographer. This was arranged, and during 1903–1906 while he was working at the Morgan Lithograph Company, he also began attending night classes at the Cleveland Art School. Going to New York City in 1907, he studied painting at the National Academy of Design for two hard years; then in 1910 he went to Paris.

Those were exciting years in the French capital. Unlike many other American artists, William Zorach did not turn away from the experiments in color and form then being conducted by the Fauves and the Cubists. He was not interested in sculpture at first, and began developing a kind of personal, abstract style of painting, as close to Cubism as anything else, but not really following its analytical theories to the letter. Returning to Cleveland in 1911, he worked and saved for a year, and in the winter of 1912 went to New York City, where he married Marguerite Thompson, a girl he had met in Paris. She, too, was a painter, and they opened a studio where they could both work. By traditional standards they were both "wildly modern" in their art and were among the few abstractionists working in America in those days—even before the opening of the famed Armory Show of 1913. To that famed exhibition William sent two abstract paintings and Marguerite one.

During these years, though William Zorach was developing an acute sense of abstract design, he was reluctant to give up nature, which even then—as throughout his career—was to be the original point of departure in his art. Unlike many of his European counterparts who ran pell-mell down the path of abstraction to nonobjective form, Zorach was to emerge from these experiments with a renewed devotion to nature. His aesthetic soul had been purged of academic clichés by the cauterizing modern art, and it left him and his art clean to develop a fresh and independent and meaningful art of his own. It was at that point, in 1917, that fate turned him toward sculpture.

That summer, on a farm near Plainfield, New Hampshire, he picked up a piece of wood and for a diversion carved it with a pocket knife. The result was a low relief executed very much in the quasi-Cubist style of his painting. Archipenko was doing stylistically similar things at that time, but he and Zorach were destined to develop in quite different directions. There is a strong trace of the influence of primitive—especially African—art in Zorach's earliest pieces, which is not surprising considering the great interest it held for many of the modern artists. Zorach admitted admiring the beauty of African wood carving, and its influence reappears in his mahogany "Figure of a Child" done in 1921, especially in the way the finished work reflects the original shape of its material. Soon this respect for the material and its original form became an integral part of his own quite personal style, undoubtedly as a result of his carving directly into the wood—and later stone. This direct carving, initiated by Laurent, marked the beginning of a new technique for sculpture in America. A little over a decade later when David Smith made his first experiments with welded sculpture, the revolution in the techniques of modern sculpture was complete.

This early phase of Zorach's work in sculpture reached its zenith in 1922 in a mahogany group of "Two Children," 36 inches high, in the collection of Theodore Frost. That year, when he gave up oil painting altogether for his new-found medium, Zorach was thirty-five years old and had never had any formal training in sculpture. He was simply drawn to it, and plunging in, began to work toward his own means of expression. It was a bold and daring move that in itself deserves admiration. Two years later he made his first essay at working directly in stone with a portrait of Marguerite carved from a block of Tennessee marble.

Zorach's "Child with Cat" (Fig. 15.9), also carved from Tennessee marble, dates from 1926, and in it the essential elements of his style reached their maturity. "Real sculpture," Zorach had written in *Arts* the year before, "is something monumental, something hewn from a solid mass, something with repose, with inner and outer form, with strength and power." He liked the simple contours and compact mass of a block of stone, whether quarried or found in a field; and even in a piece such as this, which is only 18 inches high, there is a monumental massiveness. Direct carving is very demanding, but the sculptor thrilled as he saw his own creation emerging from the raw material. The very hardness of the stone, plus the effort involved in working it, helped him keep his forms simple and bold. Often the raw material itself might suggest certain forms or subjects or procedures of working it: The peculiar coloration of a stone, the grain of a piece of wood, or the original shape of the raw material could stimulate the artist by the inherent sculpturesque qualities. Zorach would then work the piece, freeing the image that he sensed within the stone or log. The original shape of a piece of dark Labrador marble, for example, suggested the little "Pigeon" of about 1930. Many of the stones came from the fields near Robinhood, Maine, where Zorach took his family each summer. A comparable attitude toward the union of subject matter and the original shape of the stone, its compactness and the simplicity of the finished piece, may be found in the untutored yet sophisticated abstractions of the Eskimo carver.

When Zorach saw one or another stone he inclined toward certain basic subjects, such as the loving embrace of a mother and child, or the affection between a child and her pet. He had an especially deep feeling for the beauty of the female nude. His work was, in fact, the result of a profound sensitivity to life—always avoiding the theatrical and sensational, but always expressive. He had never embraced the credo of "art for art's sake" in his painting, and in his sculpture, too, pure form alone was not sufficient. In addition to the beauty of his simplified, compact forms abstracted from nature, he infused his work with an expressive content, sometimes gentle, sometimes heroic. This is not to be confused with Expressionism which normally connotes violence or dynamic force in art history parlance.

In 1924 Zorach had his first one-man show at the Kraushaar Galleries in New York; another came four years later, and the more advanced critics and patrons became aware of a new art in their midst—an art that had its roots in America and was not merely a brilliant but temporary artistic sunburst like the Armory Show. Between 1927 and 1931 Zorach carved his group called "Mother and Child" from rose-colored Florida marble; 65 inches high, it was to test the principles of his art on a heroic and monumental scale. Compact and massive, out of respect for his material and from a feeling that sculpture should have volume, with the forms of nature undergoing simplification and abstraction, the piece epitomizes the work of William Zorach. It was shown in 1931 at the Downtown Gallery in New York and at the Art Institute in Chicago, where it received not only the Logan prize for sculpture, but also critical acclaim and recognition for an art that was then bold and new. Zorach and his sculpture were by no means established and famous in those days, and he was one of several artists who were individually engaged in an ideological battle against an entrenched conservatism for the acceptance and survival of their art. The awarding of the Logan prize to Zorach's "Mother and Child" was an encouraging sign of the times for the modern sculptors. The statue has been in the collection of the Metropolitan Museum of Art since 1952.

The year 1931 was also an important one for Zorach's career, for it was then that the first piece of his sculpture was purchased for the permanent collection of a major art museum, the Whitney Museum buying his walnut wood "Pegasus," done in 1925. The next year, however, his "Spirit of the Dance"—a large kneeling nude woman—was rejected by the manager of Radio City Music Hall, along with nudes by Robert Laurent and Gwen Lux. Newspaper critics and museum curators protested so vigorously that the manager was forced to accept them; but the incident serves as a reminder that the artist's struggle to obtain the American public's acceptance of the nude was by no means over in the 19th century.

In 1929 Zorach began teaching at the Art Students League. He was a fine teacher who taught for more than thirty years, and his influence may be seen in the work of numerous students. The major achievements in his own work during the early 1930's were the superbly formed and exquisitely simple "Torso" (1932) of Labrador granite; the charming group called "Affection" (1933) of a little girl hugging her dog; and the bronze group of a nude man and woman entitled "The Embrace" (1933). In 1936 his commissioned group for a memorial to the pioneer women of Texas was refused in general because of its nudity, and in particular for such inane reasons as the woman wore no wedding ring. His colossal image of Benjamin Franklin for the new Post Office in Washington had a better reception; but somehow the period style of Franklin's costume seems incompatible with Zorach's sculptural style, and the pink Tennessee marble leaves something to be desired. At the New York World's Fair of 1939 he was represented by an even less successful heroic group of several figures and two horses, called "Builders of the Future."

In the early 1940's Zorach began a series of heads and masks that extended over the next two decades. One of the most striking of these is the black granite "Head of Christ" which is 15 inches high (Fig. 15.10). It is a visage of calm imperturbability and benevolence, with eyes that are truly all-seeing; the hard granite and the pronounced structure of the face make it a strong characterization. It is a personal image that is eminently successful, just as the sculptor's granite head of "Moses" (1956) is the most original conception of that subject since the one by Michelangelo. In addition to the usual massiveness and simplification of nature that characterize Zorach's style, there is in the "Head of Christ" a sensitive refinement of the abstracted features.

Zorach returned regularly to the theme of mother and child, as in "The Future Generation" (1942–1947; Whitney Museum of American Art) and in one of his highest achievements, the granite "Devotion" (1946; Collection of Mr. and Mrs. Laurence S. Rockefeller). The subject of the love of man and woman recurs in the marble "Youth" (1936–1939) and the extremely sensitive "Lovers" (1958), a piece that is far more monumental than its less than 11-inch-length would seem to allow. Among his larger projects was one in 1949 for the memorial to the Jewish martyrs, which was to be placed on Riverside Drive in New York, but no decision was ever made on his design. His four floating figures and groups (1952–1953) for an exterior wall of the Mayo Clinic in Rochester, Minnesota, are probably his most successful venture into sculptural adornment for architecture.

In 1958 when William Zorach received the Avery Award from the Architectural League he had already passed his seventieth birthday and could look back on a career in which he had pioneered into the uncharted future of modern art. In 1961 he received the gold medal of the National Institute of Arts and Letters and the Widener medal from the Pennsylvania Academy; he was also the recipient of honorary academic degrees from Bowdoin and Colby colleges and of a citation from Bates College in Maine. All this recognition was indeed well earned, for his contribution to the maturity of modern art in America was an enormous one.

Like Zorach, John B. Flannagan also possessed an affinity with the raw stone, which he could transform into images of all kinds of creatures. He, too, developed a style based on the simplification and abstraction of the forms of nature. To Flannagan, there was a kind of pantheistic existence in the rocks of the field, and no subject, be it toad or grasshopper, was too lowly to stimulate his genius. He could find the same spirit of motherliness in a monkey holding her offspring to her bosom that he found in the scene of the human mother quietly observing her sleeping child. All life came within his purview as an artist, and as an artist he sought to reach the essential form and character of each creature he portrayed, employing a monolithic style that suggested the eternal continuum of life on earth.

John Bernard Flannagan (1895–1942) was the son of a Fargo, North Dakota, newspaperman who died when the boy was five years old. Unrelenting poverty, which forced his destitute mother to place him and his two brothers in an orphanage, was to plague him the rest of his life. Even as a boy in the children's home, his talent for carving images manifested itself, and in 1914 when he was old enough, he made his way to Minneapolis, where he studied painting briefly at the Institute of Arts. When the war came along he joined the Merchant Marine, in which he served until 1922. Resuming his study of painting in New York, he seldom had money for food and often had to seek shelter for the night. When Arthur B. Davies found him he was on the verge of starvation and was packed off to the Davies farm, where good food and nearly a year's employment as a handyman helped him to recuperate. His benefactor encouraged him in his painting, and one day suggested that Flannagan try his hand at wood carving. It was the beginning of his career.

Back in New York Flannagan's impoverished way of life continued, although he was generally able to ignore it because of the extreme pleasure and excitement he found in his work. He showed his carvings for the first time in a joint exhibition at the Montross Gallery, along with Davies, Glackens, Kuhn, Prendergast, and Sheeler, and became acquainted with the artists and dealers in New York. He could have had a steady income by holding a job during the day and working on his sculpture at night, but this he refused to do; he wanted to force himself to live by his art alone—and "turn stone into bread," as he frequently quipped.

Through Carl Zigrosser, Flannagan made an arrangement with E. Weyhe whereby Flannagan would receive a weekly check and in return would give the Weyhe Gallery all of his sculptures as he produced them. A balance sheet—often totaled in red ink—was kept as sales were made and credited to the sculptor's "account." Flannagan thus had the larger burden of his indebtedness removed through an agreement that lasted until 1937 and was completely to his satisfaction. His correspondence with Weyhe was usually through Carl Zigrosser, who became his lifelong friend and confidant, ever ready to assist the artist. Flannagan's letters to Zigrosser, some of which have been published in *Letters of John B. Flannagan* (1942), reveal the warmth of the sculptor's nature, his humor, his sadness and depression, and his euphoria and excitement over his work.

About 1928 John Flannagan discovered the immense satisfaction of carving directly in stone; thereafter stone was to remain his favorite medium. Flannagan seemed to possess a natural inclination to express beauty and character through simplification and abstraction, and he joined Laurent, Zorach, Nadelman, Archipenko, and others in adding yet another vital force in the reaction against the traditional academic art. This is evident in two of his earliest stone carvings, the sandstone "Pelican" and the granite "Chimpanzee," both of 1928. The summer of 1929 and the following winter were spent at Woodstock, New York, where his exploration of the craft of direct carving was facilitated by the abundance of different kinds and colors of stones found along the wooded slopes of the Catskills. His personal style was developing, and with characteristic articulation he wrote of his work to Carl Zigrosser that year:

My aim is to produce a sculpture . . . with such ease, freedom and simplicity that it hardly feels carved, but rather to have always been that way. That accounts for the preference for field stone. Its very rudeness seems to me more in harmony with simple direct statement. There are often necessary compromises, but the shape of the stone does not determine the design. More often the design dictates the choice of stone because I like to have them appear as rocks left quite untouched—and natural.

[Quoted from *Letters of John B. Flannagan*, p. 20]

In a more practical vein, he admitted years later that there was an economic factor involved in his use of fieldstone, since it could be had merely by carrying it away, whereas quarried stone would have been expensive. An example of his work at this time is the "Elephant," carved from a piece of bluestone 15 inches wide (Fig. 15.13). The original rounded contour of the stone may still be imagined, for the sculptor made maximum use of the natural configuration of the rock, and reshaped it as little as possible.

Through Zigrosser and the Weyhe Gallery, arrangements were made for Flannagan to go to Ireland, the land of his forefathers. He and his wife found a quaint little cottage and studio near Connemara, and they loved to roam about the beautiful countryside, searching for stones to be carried or hauled back to the studio. Some were green, some white, some black; marble and granite awaited them wherever they wandered. If they came home to find a cow or a goat in the kitchen, their shouts in evicting the beast were mingled with laughter. Flannagan found the ever-present animals of Ireland—the dogs and cats, the cows and goats, the donkeys and colts—an inspiration to him. He had already realized that inspiration could come from all forms of life and refused to limit himself to the human figure. He worked in intense contentment, writing to Zigrosser at one time that he hoped to have thirty-seven pieces finished by the end of his first six months in

Ireland. His cursed insomnia was greatly reduced, and his drinking had nearly ceased.

By the spring of 1931 he had tired of the inconveniences of beautiful, stony Ireland. He had to send his chisels more than fifty miles away each week to get them sharpened, and once his pieces were finished the procedure for getting them shipped out was hectic. However, after being back about a year in the United States he was awarded a Guggenheim Fellowship, and he used it to return to Ireland. This time he settled in Dublin. This, too, was a productive period—as always, intensely so—and the strain of it would eventually lead to disaster. The major work of this second visit to Ireland was a mountain goat entitled "Figure of Dignity"; many years later when it was acquired for the Metropolitan Museum of Art, the sculptor punned that the headlines should read "Metropolitan gets Flannagan's goat!" The regal image of the Irish mountain goat was carved from a block of granite—except for the horns, which were cast in aluminum and applied. Only a minimum was carved away from the original block, for direct carving inspired in Flannagan, as in Zorach, a respect for the stone itself. But Flannagan was not a cerebral abstractionist (as the Cubist sculptors were), and he felt that the warmth of his subject and the spontaneity of his execution took the edge off of cold, intellectual abstraction. One piece followed another, most of them being sent back to the Weyhe Gallery as soon as they were finished. In a letter to Julianna Force of the Whitney Museum, he spoke of twenty-five or thirty works he hoped to have completed by the end of that spring. He was driven to increased exertion by the realization that his work was maturing, that he was finally reaching a valid means of expression. The mental and physical strain notwithstanding, he had for the time being found a wonderful peace for himself. But his application for a continuation of the Guggenheim Fellowship was not successful, and he returned to the United States in June 1933.

A year of severe stress followed, caused by the intensity of his work and his impecunious situation, and aggravated by marital difficulties. It reached a climax in his total nervous breakdown and confinement in a mental institution in September 1934. This was the first of two major calamities that made his life wretched. He was in sheer misery in the sanitarium, primarily because he was not allowed to work at his sculpture. He complained to friends that the doctors had taken away his lifeblood when they refused to let him work, and he mocked the psychiatrists who believed that the source of his problem was his intensity over his sculpture. Toward the end of his seven months of "incarceration," however, he was allowed to model in clay, and apparently for the first time became excited about that medium and the casting of it in metal. But casting was to prove too expensive, and there were only a few bronzes during the next decade.

After his release from the sanitarium he spent the summer in remote and quiet Woodstock, where he slept well and enjoyed working on several different pieces. By August he was back in New York City, occupied in his studio with such fieldstone subjects as "Baby," "Pelican," "Flea," and "Head of a Colt"; November and December were spent in Boston and the nearby Quincy stone quarries. Among his most successful efforts of this year were "The Nun" and a mother and child, which he called "Full Hands." He was divorced from Grace, his first wife, who was given custody of their daughter; he soon married again, however, and Margherita was to be his constant companion for the few years that remained of his life.

Flannagan's attention was next absorbed by the commission that was to be a part of the Samuel Memorial in Philadelphia's Fairmount Park; the main group, "Spanning the Continent," was to be executed by Robert Laurent. Flannagan's subject was to be the "Gold Miner," the model for which was approved in November 1937. Progress on the statue was delayed when the sculptor suffered a broken leg in an automobile accident, but the "Gold Miner" was finally set up in the summer of the following year. Flannagan usually refused large memorial commissions, explaining that he had no experience with such things; in truth, he abhorred the "hero statue" of the 19th century and its 20th-century successor. He much preferred his small animal pieces, for which he felt a profound intimacy. It was as if he portrayed the mysteries of life itself in his little creatures, as in the "Triumph of the Egg" (Museum of Modern Art), or as if he had created a new kind of imagery for the concept of miraculous rebirth, as in "Jonah and the Whale" (Fig. 15.14); both of these pieces date from the summer of 1937 when he was working in rural Ridgefield, Connecticut. He had found the stone that eventually became the "Jonah" more than two years earlier, and carried it home with him; it lay around the studio for a long time, gathering dust, until the sculptor visualized the image that its shape, coloration, and texture contained. It needed only a little reshaping to obtain the form of the whale, and a few incised lines completed the image. Flannagan's stated credo is obvious in this piece, to represent as much character as possible while altering the original or primitive form of the rock as little as possible. His insistence upon the appropriateness of the stone may be observed in "Jonah and the Whale," for the bluestone has the general coloration of a whale; likewise the gray-white granite of "Triumph of the Egg" is equally fitting. The blackish bluestone of the "Snake" that he carved for R. Sturgis Ingersoll in 1937 was equally well chosen.

During the winter of 1938–1939 he was trying hard "to stay on the water wagon" because he had so much work he wanted to get done, such as the "Woman's Head" and the "Woman and Horse." Then in Boston in 1939 came the second major calamity: He was struck by an automobile and seriously injured. Four operations followed to relieve the pressure on his brain, but he was left with a speech impediment and a complete loss of balance when standing or walking. During the convalescent months that followed he despaired of not being able to return to work. His letters to friends, while never indulging in self-pity, were pathetic pleas for them to intercede to obtain some kind of curatorial or administrative position for him. But in time he was able to return to work, although his former energy was gone and he tired very quickly. He experienced a kind of childish delight in 1940 when it was possible for him to purchase an air compressor and automatic chisel that facilitated his carving in stone; arrangements had been made by Curt Valentin of the Buchholz Gallery, and in return Flannagan agreed to repay the gallery with six stone pieces and three bronzes. He was again preoccupied with bronze-cast pieces in an attempt to broaden his art beyond the limiting scope of his stone carving. The prime example of this effort was the bronze "Not Yet," a mother and infant group that somehow took on the contours of a stone piece in spite of the sculptor's insistence that the two media must be treated differently.

Flannagan seems to have been drawn closer to his Catholic faith during these difficult years, seeking and encouraging friendships with priests, and in 1941 working on a group of the "Pieta." He busily prepared for a one-man show that was coming up in March 1942 at the Buchholz Gallery, and was anxious to have a large number of works for it. The retrospective exhibition was terribly important to him, and he worked at a feverish pace. But he was not to see it. Two months before it opened, because of strain, pain, exhaustion, depression—or a combination of all of them—he could no longer cope with a life that had been beset by adversity. In January 1942 he took his life by asphyxiation.

John Flannagan's contribution to the development of modern art in America was not revolutionary. He created no school; he left no heir-apparent to perpetuate his personal style. But he gave American art one more creative genius who could see anew, and envisage fresh images that might express 20th-century sentiment far more poignantly than could the academic tradition. To the next generation of American sculptors he left a strengthened position for abstract art. Today Flannagan's work is greatly appreciated. It is a pity that there were so few in his own day whose eyes could see the lyrical, often humorous, and always eternal beauty in his sculpture.

By the early 1920's, José de Creeft (1884–   ) was also carving directly in stone, and when he came to the United States in 1929 he added considerable strength to the movement that had centered on Laurent, Zorach, and Flannagan. He was born to impoverished Castilian parents in Guadalajara, the Valley of Stones— "from which," his friend Alexander Calder quipped many years later, "he must have carved his way out." After a couple of unsuccessful apprenticeships he was determined to become a sculptor, and by the age of eighteen he was in Madrid studying at the Bellas Artes and wandering through the halls and galleries of the Prado. The impish, jovial manner of "Pépé" de Creeft did not mesh well with the sober Augustina Querol, in whose sculptural studio he was employed for a while, and Madrid was no longer the place for him.

So in 1905 José de Creeft went to Paris, where he found a room near the quarters of a couple of his countrymen, Pablo Picasso and Juan Gris, who soon became his good friends. He studied for a while at the Académie Julian, where his "Torso" won a prize in 1906. Under the influence of the dynamic new art then being born in the studios of his friends, he left the academy to begin his own first essays in abstracted form. But de Creeft had to seek employment or starve, and he took a job at the Maison Greber, where he repaired broken or badly restored statuary. The experience of working constantly in stone was extremely valuable. But the war years brought hard times, and not until the demand arose for monuments to the dead did the situation improve.

After the war he was commissioned to carve an 18-foot-high *poilu*, or French doughboy, out of granite. It was then, in the early 1920's, that he began to carve directly in stone. One of the earliest specimens of this work is the granite group titled "Maternity" (1922) in the Metropolitan Museum of Art. It is characterized by the massiveness and voluminosity of the stone itself, for de Creeft had already understood the respect the artist must have for the material he worked with. Just as with Robert Laurent and William Zorach—and at about the same time—de Creeft began to evolve a new aesthetic out of his new method of working, his respect for the material, and his search for the basic principles of the art of sculpture. De Creeft was fast approaching his mature style when one day he suddenly purged his studio by destroying almost every piece in it because it did not belong to his new way of working; he reportedly announced to friends that he felt he had been born anew, ready to commence a new era in his work.

He exhibited regularly at the salons of the avant-garde, such as the Salon des Tuileries, where he set up his work alongside that of Lipchitz, Despiau, Bourdelle, and others. In one of these the prankish Pépé placed a "Picador" (1925) that was made out of stove pipes and other metal scraps; he thereby invoked the displeasure of his friends, who felt that his joke might tarnish the seriousness of their art in the eyes of those who came to the Salon. The next year de Creeft left for Majorca at the request of a wealthy painter who wanted him to supervise the renovating of a castle the painter had purchased. The sculptor found plenty of time for his own work, and an abundance of challenging stones as well, executing altogether some two hundred pieces during his three-year stay. When he sailed for the United States he took with him about three tons of sculpture.

His first one-man exhibition in America was held in 1929 at the Art Museum in Seattle, Washington; it was followed soon afterward by another at the Ferargil Gallery in New York and by a third in Chicago, where it was sponsored by the Art Club. De Creeft was immediately known on both coasts and in the Midwest as well, but unfortunately all this coincided with the stock-market crash and the ensuing depression. There were very few sales, even though the genius of the sculptor was recognized and heralded. Moreover, in his work at Majorca he had inhaled too much stone dust, and a protracted illness was the result. When in time he re-emerged, both he and his work were filled with a dynamic vigor.

His first one-man exhibition since 1929 was held in 1936 at the Passedoit Galleries in New York, the gallery that was to represent de Creeft in the art market. Industrious, with a zest for work that equaled his zest for life, de Creeft produced sculptures at a rate that would almost permit a one-man show of new things each year. In 1936 he was experimenting with the technique of beaten lead—again working the material directly and achieving a boldness reminiscent of his stone pieces, yet capitalizing fully on the greater pliableness of the soft lead. Examples of this are found in the head of a "Slave" (1936) and his "Reclining Nude" and "Saturina," both of 1938.

In the floating, rhythmic forms of the 1939 group titled "Cloud" (Fig. 15.15), one sees the essential character of de Creeft's style. Carved of green stone and standing 13½ inches high, it reveals that the sculptor subscribed to the simplification and abstraction of natural form. De Creeft organized his rounded, full-bodied, curving masses into a splendidly conceived composition of repeating curves; the beauty of sculptural form itself has clearly replaced the beauty of academic naturalism and academic eclecticism. Sculpture like this, of the late 1930's, marked the triumph of the fresh, original, creative work of such men as Laurent, Zorach, Archipenko, Lachaise, Flannagan, and de Creeft over the conservatives of the academies.

De Creeft's work in stone continued with the black Belgian granite head titled "Maya" (1937; Wichita Art Association) and the "Acrobats at Rest." Two especially fine pieces are the green serpentine "Astonishment" of 1941 and the black Belgian marble figure of a Negress, "I Am Black but I Am Beautiful," of 1942. De Creeft frequently used a Negro woman as his model, but he was often attracted by the special features of other races, too—as in the "Peruvian Girl" and the "Maya." In his stone carvings de Creeft would obtain the highest polish on some parts and leave other areas virtually untouched—as if to leave a reminder of the natural character of the material from which the image emerged. He frequently achieved several textures with the patterns of his chisel marks, adding great variety to his work. These roughed-out sections were as much a part of de Creeft's design as the white areas Cézanne left on his canvas, and in each a feeling of completeness prevailed.

De Creeft had developed a great love for the beauty of rocks as he found them, and he would ride about the countryside looking for fieldstones to bring back to the studio. How he would lament it when he found an especially fine one that was already employed as part of a gateway or a porch. Those stray, rough, unwanted jewels of nature that were brought back to his studio often sat about the place gathering dust for a year or two before the sculptor had clearly visualized the images within them. In this respect, again, his approach was similar to Flannagan's.

In 1950 de Creeft executed a gray granite statue of a "Poet" for Fairmount Park in Philadelphia; his bronze "Alice in Wonderland," 16 feet high, for a New York City park dates from 1960. A retrospective exhibition of de Creeft's work was held in 1961, at which time he received a Ford Foundation Award. The show clearly demonstrated the role that José de Creeft had played in bringing a new means of expression to American art.

In 1935, in the middle of the depression, the Guild Art Gallery was launched with a daring exhibit of the work of two gifted and unknown sculptors—Chaim Gross and Ahron Ben-Shmuel, both advocates of direct carving. Ahron Ben-Shmuel

(1903–   ) learned stonecutting in a dusty quarry while still in his teens, and it was natural that as his artistic instinct grew he should employ the technique so familiar to him. He turned to sculpture in the mid-1920's. Among his earliest works are the "Pugilist," in black granite, and the "Torso of a Boy"; both pieces, now in the Museum of Modern Art, reveal that the young sculptor was embracing the theory of simplification and abstraction of natural form. The similarity of his approach to that of Zorach or Flannagan may be seen in his "Seated Woman," a blocky granite carving of 1932. The massiveness and the true character of the original stone have been disturbed as little as possible. Ben-Shmuel soon branched out into other media—wood, terra cotta, and bronze—but perhaps with less success than in stone. His bronze "Figure of Job," for instance, in the Philadelphia Museum of Art, seems ungainly and extremely mannered, with none of the subtle beauty of form of his work in stone.

Chaim Gross (1904–   ) made the natural qualities of wood and the chisel marks of the carving a part of his distinctive style. Gross came to America from Austria in 1921, at the age of seventeen. He studied at the Art Students League, at the Educational Alliance Art School, and at the Beaux-Arts Institute of Design for four years; in 1927 he began teaching at the Beaux-Arts Institute. From that year dates his acrobatic "Mother and Child at Play" in the Newark Museum; even then his work possessed the blocklike, monumental interlocking forms and the basic sculptural principles that were to characterize his style for the next several decades.

Gross revived the art of wood carving, which had either died out or become a folk art in the course of the 19th century. His subjects were frequently gymnasts or circus performers—sometimes riding unicycles, sometimes stacked vertically, two and three figures high. A one-man show at the Gallery 144 in 1932 was followed three years later by the more important exhibition, shared with Ben-Shmuel, at the Guild Art Gallery. Gross' "Circus Girls" of 1934, carved from lignum vitae, was one of the pieces shown. Gross also had a one-man exhibition in Philadelphia in 1935, and one of the outstanding works of that year was his "Handlebar Riders" (Fig. 15.16). Through these exhibitions Chaim Gross was attaining a reputation for his merry little sculptural masterpieces in which his sheer joy in carving wood was obvious.

In 1935 Gross was also working on his model of the "Alaskan Snowshoe Mail Carrier" for the new Post Office Building in Washington, D.C., for which Zorach was executing his statue of Benjamin Franklin. Although the figure was to be cast in aluminum, Gross could not free himself from the style he had established as a wood carver; one critic observed that his "Alaskan Mail Carrier" was ". . . a much less personal work than most of his wood-carvings and only reminiscent of them in its excellence. . . ." The "Mail Carrier" was awarded a national prize in 1936, and his "Offspring" won a silver medal the next year at the Paris Salon. In 1938 he produced a lovely ebony statue of Lillian Leitzel, which the Metropolitan Museum of Art subsequently purchased when it won second prize at the Artists for Victory exhibition in 1942. For the 1939 New York World's Fair, Gross created two groups to adorn the French and Swiss buildings. Again returning to the circus for his subject, he carved "Girl on a Wheel" (1940), which was also purchased by the Metropolitan Museum of Art two years later.

Gross joined the faculty of the Brooklyn Museum art school in 1942, where he was to teach for many years, but he also maintained his own studio on East 9th Street in New York City. By 1950, the year in which he created his wooden statue "Adolescent," the postwar avant-garde had passed by Gross and others of his generation. Nevertheless, during the 1950's he received numerous prizes and honors. A fine example of his later work is "Happy Mother" (1958) in the Philadelphia Museum of Art. The vigorous acrobatic subject is retained; but the use of bronze instead of wood allowed the sculptor greater freedom, and he expanded the range of his art enormously by capitalizing on the virtues of the cast metal. Gross had already published his autobiography, *A Sculptor's Progress*, in 1938 at the age of thirty-five; in the 1950's he wrote *The Technique of Wood Carving* and *Fantasy of Drawing*.

The direct carvers, who brought a new aesthetics to American art in the 1920's, made a daring break with the academic tradition. But they represented only one segment of the modern movement. Another group worked mainly in metal and explored many diverse forms of expression. We turn now to it and to such men as Elie Nadelman, Alexander Archipenko, Hugo Robus, John Storrs, and Gaston Lachaise.

Previous to the posthumous retrospective exhibition at the Museum of Modern Art in 1948, the work of Elie Nadelman was either largely forgotten or seldom taken seriously. There were a few, however, who recalled the sculptor and his creations when they represented the ultimate spearhead of the revolutionary avant-garde movements in art. By 1948 his doll-like creations had been absent from the showplaces of modern art for nearly two decades; in the meantime modern American sculpture had come of age, and the debt owed to Nadelman was seldom remembered. Between 1905 and 1920 the story of Elie Nadelman was one of brilliant professional and personal success. But then in the 1920's, while Picasso and Matisse were continually pushing their work into richer forms of expression Nadelman seemed to slip comfortably and complacently into a lower gear.

Elie Nadelman (1882–1946) was born into a cultured home life in Warsaw, Poland, and after attending the gymnasium was sent to the high school for liberal arts. After a couple of years at the Warsaw Academy of Art, he tried in vain to find inspiration at Cracow and then at Munich. In Munich, he discovered the Aegean antiquities at the Glyptothek and the folk-art doll collection at the Bayerisches Museum, both of which were to be important influences on his work. When in 1903 he went to Paris he finally found the artistic atmosphere he craved, and his development thereafter was prodigious and meteoric.

Nadelman got to know Picasso, Matisse, and most of the other young artists working there, but he remained generally aloof from their cafés and studios and other haunts. His closest friendship seems to have been with Leo Stein, who was among the first to recognize Nadelman's talent and collect his work. By 1905 he was engrossed with his own personal quest for an understanding of the fundamentals of sculpture, which led to an analysis of volumed form and, of singular importance, contours. Much of the time he worked with pen and ink, drawing the human head or figure in an arrangement of concavities and convexities and curved lines. This led to a kind of proto-Cubism, which by 1907 was already well advanced. It is reported that when Leo Stein took Picasso to Nadelman's studio in 1908, Picasso saw there a head whose planes had been carefully reshaped to the point of abstraction and simplified in a consciously analytical manner. (By that time Picasso had already painted his "Demoiselles d'Avignon.")

Nadelman was always aware of the place he should occupy in the history of modern art; in 1921 he published a portfolio of his work in which he wrote:

These drawings, made sixteen years ago (1905), have completely revolutionized the art of our time. They introduced into painting and sculpture *abstract form*, until then entirely lacking. Cubism was only an imitation of the abstract form of these drawings and did not attain their plastic significance. This influence will continue to be felt more profoundly in the art of the future.
[Quoted from L. Kirstein, *The Sculpture of Elie Nadelman*, 1948, p. 14]

In his first years in Paris he seems to have been thoroughly involved with an analysis of form, and by 1905 or 1906 he may have been in advance of Picasso in this respect; by 1907 each was well along in developing the major premises of their styles, and they were soon joined by Georges Braque, Juan Gris, and others. Nadelman, however, was the only sculptor who at this early time was consciously analyzing abstract form.

By the time of his important and first one-man show in 1909 at the Galerie Druet, many recognized the handsome and engaging Nadelman as one of the foremost artists of the *avant-garde* movement. Leo and Gertrude Stein were among them, as was André Gide; later, Archipenko and Brancusi were to realize the importance of his experiments. With the success of his exhibition, Nadelman was heralded as the most progressive of the modern sculptors. Such pieces as his "Standing Female Nude" (Fig. 15.17) or its male companion were clearly objects of purposeful abstraction and analysis of forms, and already Nadelman's fascination with curve and countercurve, mass and countermass can be observed. These were eventually to evolve into the full, delicately rounded forms that characterized his mature style after he gave up the intellectual analysis of form that so often resulted in anatomical distortions.

In 1910 Nadelman first used the term "significant form" to describe his work, saying, "The subject of any work of art is for me nothing but a pretext for creating significant form, relations of forms which create a new life that has nothing to do with life in nature. . . ." The term, in the writings of the English critic Clive Bell (*Art*, 1914), was given broader scope in connection with the overall modern movement. Nadelman's next important exhibition was held in London at Patterson's Gallery, where Helena Rubinstein bought the entire collection. She placed the several pieces in her famous salons in major cities throughout Europe and America, and in subsequent years Nadelman set a new fashionable style for commercial decoration with the many sculptures he designed for her cosmetics houses.

Helena Rubinstein was of great assistance to Nadelman when he came to the United States after the onset of World War I. His work was already known in America from the twelve drawings and "Head of a Man" he had exhibited at the Armory Show, as well as through the publication in 1914 of his portfolio, *Vers l'unité plastique*. In the garage of the Rubinstein estate in Rye, New York, he made preparations for his first one-man show on this side of the Atlantic; it was held in 1915 at Alfred Stieglitz' "291" gallery and included "Man in the Open Air," the major creation of his first year in the United States (Fig. 15.18). Nadelman found an inspiration in high society, and during the remainder of the decade most of his works are of hosts and hostesses, couples dancing, orchestra conductors, and women seated elegantly on wire chairs or at the piano. Form, rather than subject matter, continued to be the sculptor's main concern, however, as mass and contour became increasingly sophisticated under his touch. In all his figures of this period the full torso tapers to delicate ankles and tiny feet and hands in an exquisite contrast.

An even more successful exhibition was held in 1917 at the Scott and Fowles Galleries, at which time one critic praised Nadelman's art as carrying "culture to the breaking point." This in a way was the crest of the sculptor's career. His abstractions were among the few experiments in modern art then being conducted in America; and the quality of his work, as well as the implications that his theories held for other artists, assured him at that time of a place in the very fore of the modern movement. At the Ritz-Carlton in New York, his work was shown again that year in an exhibition called "Allies of Sculpture," sponsored by a group of society women. Many of his pieces represented that society itself, with his figures possessing the usual curving contours around svelte spheroids. Nadelman was quite successful in rendering contemporary dress, which he abstracted and merged with the abstracted form of the figure itself.

In 1919 Elie Nadelman married a prominent and wealthy widow and moved into a fine house near the Hudson River in Riverdale. During the next decade he began to withdraw from the society of the *avant-garde*. He continued to work, however, within the framework of his established style, often rendering the robust figures of circus women in voluptuous masses of graceful curves; all forms were simplified and all details were virtually eliminated, yet there was a poetry of form and movement about them. He executed a few portraits in polished marble, employing his elegant style there, too, and establishing a mode that was frequently imitated by less talented men on a commercial basis. He experimented with painting on bronze, as in the "Bust of a Woman" of 1927, in which the eyes, mouth, hair, and ribbon-necklace were painted on. "Man in Top Hat" (1927), at the Museum of Modern Art, was also painted bronze, with its sharp, exquisitely modeled features and neatly trimmed beard, looking very much like a character out of a novel of Henry James, an author the sculptor greatly admired.

In the crash of 1929 the Nadelmans lost most of their material wealth; the sculptor's work suffered as well. He had kept himself apart from the mainstream of art in the preceding ten years, and in the 1930's he was still less inclined to accept commissions, arrange for one-man exhibitions, or even show his works in group exhibitions—even though he needed money. A second disaster occurred in 1935 when workmen, sent to remodel the studio on his Riverdale property (which he had lost in the crash), destroyed most of his sculpture out of ignorance of their artistic value. Many of his pieces were made of fragile papier-mâché or terra cotta, and crumbled at the slightest mistreatment. He had already withdrawn from the art world; now he became a recluse.

Nadelman was finally able to regain his Riverdale house, where he maintained a small sequestered studio, a place forbidden to the art world outside. He occupied himself with small, doll-like terra-cotta figurines, which remained unknown until after his death in 1946, when they were found in his studio in great abundance. They seem to be a combination of elements from a primitive eastern Mediterranean folk art and a sophistication of the Tanagra figures, infused with a thoroughly modern spirit.

Elie Nadelman, by coming to the United States in 1914, just after the Armory Show, contributed to the emancipation of the American sculptor from the academic tradition. When he first arrived he was unquestionably one of the leading figures of the international art movement; his personal brand of modern art won many friends while other, "wilder" forms, such as Cubism or Fauvism, tended to alienate most of the general public. His several one-man shows established his reputation in America and nourished the modern movement that was then beginning to emerge. Had he not withdrawn from the heart of artistic activity, his influence on modern American sculpture might well have been greater than it was.

As the new art unfolded in Paris during the years preceding World War I, Alexander Archipenko (1887–1964) began to apply Cubist principles to sculpture in a highly original manner. He was the son of an imaginative mechanic employed by the University of Kiev. After attending the art school of Kiev, Archipenko in 1906 went to Moscow, where he felt his creative energies stifled by the insipid naturalism and academic classicism being taught there. He next went to Paris in 1908, but there, too, he found the schools and the established idols of the academic art world not to his taste. Rodin, then at the peak of his popularity, was of no interest to him, and he could not endure more than a few weeks of classes at the Ecole des Beaux-Arts. Clearly, what he searched for would have to be found on his own—a situation faced by nearly all of the young men in their early experiments who were then beginning to give significant direction to modern art. In true revolutionary spirit, Archipenko embarked on a lifetime journey of experiments with forms and materials. New sources of inspiration were then being discovered: The archaic phase of Greek art replaced the classical style, and the influence of primitive art had already appeared in the work of Picasso; in addition, Archipenko found the severity and sculptural quality of ancient Egyptian art stimulating. The year before Archipenko's arrival in Paris, Picasso had painted his famous "Demoiselles d'Avignon," and in 1908 Brancusi exhibited his monolithic group titled "The Kiss"; Nadelman had already begun his analysis of form and was of considerable influence on the impressionable young adventurer. Archipenko, then only twenty-one, immediately joined the search for the new art.

Archipenko's "Crouching Figure" of 1909 demonstrates that by that date he had already begun the plastic reorganization of the human figure for the sake of a more meaningful sculptural form. He had begun to think of sculpture in terms of form, mass, planes, and the surrounding space, instead of in terms of subject matter and decorative details. It is possible that Archipenko never fully comprehended the significance of the art of Cézanne, at least not to the extent that some of his painter colleagues did, and his sculptural variation of Cubism was accordingly free to take an original course from the very first.

Archipenko held his first one-man show in Hagen, Germany, in 1910, for the Germans were among the most appreciative of his early work. His abstractions caused quite a stir, and he quickly became an acknowledged part of the *avant-garde* of modern art. That same year he opened his own school in Paris, to teach the new theories and principles that were evolving as his work progressed. His natural bent for teaching thus appeared early in his career; after settling in America he would devote the greater part of four decades to the instruction of young artists. Still he found time for his own work and participated in the exhibitions of the Cubists and Fauves. His massive "Seated Mother," with its exciting organization of planes, and "Repose," which was one of the pieces he sent to the Armory Show, were done in 1911. In 1912 his work was represented at Jacques Villon's Salon de la Section d'Or. His most adventurous experiment of that year was combining several new materials in a single piece of sculpture; inspired by a juggler of the Medrano Circus, he created an abstracted figure out of wood, glass, and metal in the earliest example of "varied media" sculpture. The Cubists were then making their collages out of scraps of paper and other materials, and Archipenko applied this practice to sculpture. Although it is not too successful aesthetically, the "Medrano" is extremely important historically and reveals the inventiveness and imagination of the sculptor as he blazed the trail of modern sculpture.

Archipenko sent four sculptures to the Armory Show in 1913, but the most important work of that date was the nearly nonobjective piece "Boxing Match." It clearly has affinities with contemporary Futurist sculpture—such as Boccioni's "Unique Forms of Continuity in Space"—in its massive, angular, and dynamically organized forms. But Boccioni denounced the work of Archipenko that very year when he wrote that the latter's Cubism had lapsed into an "archaic and barbaric" approach to the analysis of form; this was due largely to Boccioni's misunderstanding of what Archipenko tried to do within the framework of Cubism. The latter redeemed himself the next year with a very imaginative piece, the "Gondo-lier," which the Cubists and others discussed and praised thereafter for many years.

With the outbreak of World War I, Archipenko moved to Nice and estab-lished his studio there. It was in Nice that he created one of his most famous pieces, "Woman Combing her Hair," which shows his use of concave and convex surfaces played against one another and his use of open areas within the mass of his sculpture (Fig. 15.19). He was probably influenced by Nadelman, for the blocky, prismatic forms of Archipenko's earlier work gave way to sweeping curves, and the "Woman Combing her Hair" seems but the next logical step in abstraction beyond Nadelman's "Standing Female Nude" of 1909 (Fig. 15.17). One breast is convex and the other is concave, revealing his independence of natural form when seeking a meaningful arrangement of planes and masses; the head is suggested by a hole in the mass, foreshadowing Henry Moore's later work. With this piece Archipenko's experiments in true Cubist theory were carried as far as he was ever to take them; from that point on they were either variations on the same theme or something other than Cubism. The reorganization of matter for the sake of pure art was thereby completed within the artistic theory he then practiced. In the next few years Archipenko tried working with a more naturalis-tic but streamlined torso, which was usually executed in marble or shiny metal. His "Torso" of 1916, for example, in the Museum of Modern Art, is the most classic of all his sculptures.

In 1921 Archipenko went to Berlin, where he had long had an enthusiastic following—more so than in Paris, where strangely enough his imaginative cre-ations had little impact on modern sculpture. His influence on Rudolf Belling is obvious in the latter's "Dreiklang" in the Bayerische Staatsgemaldesammlungen. He remained in Berlin for two years, conducting a sculpture school, before mov-ing to America in 1923.

Though Archipenko was not as well known in the United States as in Europe, his works soon attracted the attention of critics and connoisseurs, who welcomed him as another talented purveyor of the new art. He was then past forty, and his style was for the most part set; there have been those who have said that nothing new came from the studio of Alexander Archipenko after his arrival in America. He continued to produce sculptures at a prolific rate, but his greatest contribu-tions had already been made by the early 1920's. Perhaps this was because much of his time and energy were devoted to teaching. Shortly after his arrival in the United States he founded his own art school where his theories and principles were taught to his many students. In 1933 he moved to California, where he maintained a studio for four years. He taught at Washington State University during the academic year 1935–36; then in 1937 he joined Moholy-Nagy to teach at the New Bauhaus School of Industrial Arts in Chicago. Two years later he was once more in New York, where he again opened his own school; and for nearly a quarter of a century it operated under his direction. Summers were spent at Woodstock, New York, where he also taught, and on numerous occasions he was a sculptor in residence at several universities around the country.

All this devotion to teaching does not mean that his own work ceased, nor did his imagination and inventiveness decrease. For example, the year after his arrival in America he produced what he christened "Archipentura," a combination of painting and sculpture; and as late as 1948—when he had his *78th* one-man exhibition—he brought forth his "modeling in light," in which he made sculptures of transparent and translucent materials with light emanating from within. The extent to which his own style underwent a constant metamorphosis during his first two decades in America may be seen in the sleek, metallic "Torso in Space" of 1946 (Fig. 15.20). Not only has the sculptor achieved a magnificent sophistication of form; he also has utilized the intrinsic beauty of the metal as successfully as Constructivists like de Rivera or Gussow. Dating from the 1950's, the "Dual" and the "Architectural Figure" are still reminiscent of the human form, but abstraction was carried further than before. They were painted with linear patterns, which added another element of design to the planes and volumes of the compositions. (See M. Seuphor, *The Sculpture of This Century*, 1961, p. 230, for illustrations of these two pieces.)

Aside from the intrinsic aesthetic value of the art Alexander Archipenko provided, he deserves special praise for his work as a teacher. Though his art may not have effected an instant revolution, his thorough understanding of the fundamentals of the theory of modern art was constantly at the disposal of young American sculptors who sought some entrée into its mysteries. In the 1920's and 1930's there were few men in the United States who had grasped the concept of sculptural form to the degree that Archipenko had, and fewer still who were motivated to pass it along to the next generation. When the chairman of the summer session of art at Mills College arranged to have Archipenko teach there in 1933, he wrote that the sculptor's presence announced the end of the realist-romanticist viselike hold on the training of young artists:

Archipenko, the artist whose name has been almost synonymous with "repellent, horrible, modern sculpture," begins to be seen as a courageous leader, a creative genius in the field of twentieth-century art. So long misunderstood and slandered, he now appears as a great artist whom an American college is proud to have on its faculty. Thus though he would hate the implication, Archipenko becomes the leader of an academy in collegiate circles.   [Warren Cheney, *Art Digest*, June 1933, p. 9]

In sweeping, sensuous, curving contour and in the polished sleekness of the bronze image, the sculpture of Hugo Robus (1885–1964) had much in common with the art of Elie Nadelman. Both Robus and Nadelman had a sensitivity for simplification, and both could incorporate a certain wit into their work. Robus studied at the Art School in Cleveland, Ohio, and also at the National Academy of Design in New York. He was then interested only in painting, and even during his years in Paris (1912–1914) he was generally bored with any modeling he had to do at the École de la Grande Chaumière; he did study sculpture with the famed Bourdelle one winter, but he admitted that he did so only to improve his concept of form in painting. After he returned to America he continued to paint for six years before discovering that sculpture was in reality the art for him. In 1920 he gave up painting for what he found to be the more rewarding search for form and expression in three dimensions instead of two.

For twelve years he worked at achieving a meaningful style of expression. All that time he remained in virtual obscurity, and never displayed his art before the public. Robus was not a fast worker; he would contemplate a sketch, or work out a design in drawings for long periods before actually modeling the piece. And as he did not present his sculpture to the public, the public could not buy it. To maintain his family and pursue his art, he made such items as jewelry, tableware, and batiks, which were marketable. (In some of his sculpture—for instance, the "Song"—there is something of a jewelry-craft flavor in the delicacy of the forms.) This craft work paid the bills and still left him several hours a day in which to work on his sculpture.

Some of the pieces from these years are the "General" (1922), a militant rider and horse, with suggestions of the Futurist sculpture of Boccioni, and "Walking Figure" (1923), a life-size figure with "its stylized and slightly distorted proportions pinched at the exactest places"; there was "Summer Afternoon" (1925), then "Spirit of Youth" (1928), which one critic compared to the Puckish, brazen "Yellow Kid" by the painter George Luks, saying it epitomized a part of life in the Roaring Twenties. In 1929 he did a piece called "Invocation," and with it a period in Robus' life drew to a close. The subsequent phase brought him and his sculpture out of isolation and into the galleries, for by the early 1930's he sensed that his work was becoming mature. His sculpture was represented at the 1933 show at the Whitney Museum, and from then on was perennially a part of the exhibition scene.

Two pieces from the early 1930's are "Song" (1932, brass), in the Metropolitan Museum of Art, and "Dawn" (1933, bronze). The "Song," probably Robus' best known sculpture, portrays a charming, innocent adolescent, completely uninhibited by any consciousness of nudity, leaning forward with hands clasped to pour forth her sweet melodic refrain. One can, in fact, fairly hear the notes that seem to issue from the mouth. The trim figure has a metallic sleekness—wrought out of respect for the medium employed—and a simplification and abstraction that resulted from the sculptor's search for expressive form. Long, graceful contours are unbroken by any trace of naturalistic details. The "Dawn"—a young girl standing, stretching, and yawning after arising from sleep—suggests the dawn of puberty, a kind of sexual awakening in a healthy, joyous sense, not as in the fearful, embarrassed imagery of Edvard Munch's painting on the same subject. The girl of Robus' "Dawn" has the first youthful fullness of the hips and the slight swelling of the breasts. The long sweeping contours, especially around the hips, suggest the influence of Elie Nadelman. This is also true of the "Woman Combing her Hair," a bronze piece in the Corcoran Gallery of Art in Washington (Fig. 15.21). Here too are found the long flowing curves, the well-rounded forms, and the sharp, cleanly designed features of the face that characterized Nadelman's work. The theme of a woman washing or combing her hair was a favorite with Robus, and he used it several times; there is a marble sculpture titled

"Girl Washing her Hair" (1933) of extremely simplified form in the Museum of Modern Art, and his bronze "Woman Doing her Hair" dates from 1956.

Hugo Robus' work continued with the violent "Seven Foolish Virgins" and the epitome of calm, "Maternal," representing a mother and child; both pieces were created in 1937. His work was not generally enjoyed by Americans, and it was almost another twenty years before he could live from the sale of his sculptures alone. The Grand Central Galleries arranged exhibitions of his work in 1946 and 1949. His parental group, "First Born" (1950), is grotesquely distorted. In that same year Robus received the Widener Prize at the Pennsylvania Academy, marking the beginning of a long-overdue recognition. His works now began to sell at good prices. In 1957 he was awarded a citation and grant by the National Academy of Arts and Letters, and three years later the Whitney Museum of American Art installed an important concurrent retrospective exhibition for him and José de Creeft. And then in 1963, the year before his death, the Whitney arranged another, larger, one-man retrospective show of his work. Hugo Robus thus lived to see his work both appreciated and recognized historically as a contributing force to the maturing of modern American art in the 1930's.

John Storrs (1885–1956) was a very gifted sculptor who in the early part of his career participated in the experiments of the Cubists. Largely an expatriate, he found Europe more congenial to life and more conducive to his work than the United States. Storrs had slipped into temporary obscurity until an exhibition at the Downtown Gallery in 1965 revived interest in his work. The Chicago-born Storrs was the son of an architect who amassed a considerable fortune in real estate development. His mother, herself a watercolorist, took John regularly to the Fine Arts exhibit of the World's Columbian Exposition of 1893; his tutor, who had painted one of the murals in the Women's Building, gave him his first art lessons. After John's graduation from high school, his father wanted to send him to the University of Michigan, but John persuaded the elder Storrs to give him and his sister, who studied music, a year in Berlin instead.

It was in Berlin that John Storrs turned to sculpture. After his return from travel through Spain, Italy, Greece, and Egypt, his father attempted unsuccessfully to make a real estate man out of him. But Storrs much preferred drawing to writing figures in account books, and so began taking night classes at the Art Institute. His father then gave in and sent him to study in Boston and then to the Pennsylvania Academy, where he worked with Charles Grafly. Next came Paris and the Académie Julian, which he soon deserted to study with the great Rodin in 1913; in a short time he became the master's favorite pupil. The highlight of his young life came at the Salon of that year when his marble portrait head of his mother was placed next to a portrait by Rodin. Works done during this year naturally reveal great influence of the Rodin style. Even after leaving the Rodin atelier he remained in close touch with him, helping him arrange for the large Rodin exhibition at San Francisco in 1915 and accompanying it there, showing a few of his own things, too.

It was the exhibition at the Folsom Gallery in New York that first made Americans aware of John Storrs; they did not like his work very much, but at least they were aware of it. His fellow Chicagoans received the show no more hospitably. Once out of Rodin's atelier Storrs quickly became involved with the work of the modern sculptors and painters. Just before the outbreak of World War I he began making Cubist sculptures; and he resumed them once hostilities were over. In fact, in the 1920's he was even doing nonobjective sculpture. No other American sculptor had previously ventured into such daring artistic experiments.

Storrs' brief period of success in the United States ranged over about a decade, from the mid-1920's to the mid-1930's. A few of his abstractions were shown in the international exhibition of modern art of 1926 at the Brooklyn Museum. His two most successful sculptures in the Cubist style were the "Sargent de Ville" (1923) and the "Gendarme Seated" (Fig. 15.22) of 1925; each was an exciting and ingenious conception of the human figure in terms of planes and masses, and no other American sculptor at that date was pushing the Cubist style to such an advanced stage. But unfortunately, Storrs' work throughout his career was uneven, and these brilliant experiments were not immediately followed by equally successful adventures in the analysis of form. Several years passed before he created anything nearly as exciting as these two pieces.

About this time Storrs was working on the colossal figure of "Ceres," which was cast in aluminum and placed on top of the Board of Trade Building in Chicago. In 1929 and again in 1931 he won the Logan Prize at the Art Institute, first with his "Two Figures," then with his Egyptian-like "Seated Torso." Chicago again honored Storrs by awarding him the commission for the enormous statue for the Hall of Science at the Century of Progress celebration in 1933; this academic monstrosity was curiously in direct contrast to the original experiments of the mid-1920's.

In the "Composition Around Two Voids" (Fig. 15.23) of 1932, Storrs is again at his best. It is indeed a bold essay in nonobjective form, especially considering the rest of American art at that date. As the title implies, the artist was not concerned with subject matter here, but rather with the analysis and organization of planes, contours, and volumes. It represents a sculpture of pure form in which the viewer finds beauty and inspiration in the sculptural form itself instead of in any subject matter it might portray. In such works as this—few though they were—modern American art had advanced a long way in the brief span of a quarter of a century.

John Storrs and his French wife lived in France as much of the time as they could, coming to the United States only when necessary. This irritated his father, and in his will he stipulated that if his son were to receive his annual allowance he would have to spend at least eight months of each year in the United States. Storrs resisted this lure to return home for seven years, supporting his family and his art by collecting and selling medieval antiquities. He loved France and found it more in step with his own advanced tastes and ideas. But eventually he gave in and spent the required time in America every year.

When the Germans invaded France at the beginning of World War II, John Storrs was put in a concentration camp. After being freed in 1945 he needed the latter half of the decade to recuperate, both mentally and physically. By 1951 when he returned to work, he was already over sixty-five. He died in Mer, France, five years later. He had been a highly respected artist in France, but he never became a major figure in the art of America, both because of his expatriation and because his work was too advanced for Americans who were moving into modern art at a rather slow and cautious pace in the 1920's and 1930's.

In the seventeen years between 1918 and 1935 Gaston Lachaise brought a unique ingredient to American sculpture. While Zorach might represent motherhood through the mutual love of parent and child, and Flannagan would envision images of eternal universal animal life in his stones of the field, the imagery of Lachaise can only be described as blatantly sexual in the robust women who seem so proud of their voluminous magnitude, like some present-day counterpart of a prehistoric idol of fecundity. Unlike the work of his American contemporaries, who dealt vaguely or hedgingly with the subject, Lachaise introduced sex and the gloriously abundant, fecundate female form directly into American art. Just as Sigmund Freud had brought sex into the light of open analytical discussion and out of the dark recesses of the subconscious or of things unspoken, Lachaise recognized it as one of the elements most basic to life itself, one of the truly appropriate subjects for the 20th-century artists. This was not sex in the erotic sense, but more in the fecundity-life-renewal sense. He was primarily concerned with the idea of womanhood, and for him that idea could only be expressed through the accentuation of the forms of the body; woman—the great mother-image—dwelt within a physical body, and Lachaise was dedicated to finding a form that would give this concept of womanhood a suitable physical manifestation. He could not separate the spiritual woman from the physical; this is where his "Woman" or "Mother" would differ from that of, say, Jacques Lipchitz, who treated universal motherhood in a far more abstract manner in his "Mother and Child." Lachaise's figures could be most provocative; a certain stance, or the way the arms were held would all too often be interpreted as eroticism when the sculptor's works were first shown, but to him that provocation, or invitation, was utterly natural to woman since time immemorial. Lachaise frequently admitted the influence of prehistoric art on his work, and something like the bulbous Willendorf Venus comes to mind; he looked upon his own work as a representation of the basic primitive urge that is fundamental to the perpetuation of life itself. To achieve this he needed the human figure in his art, but he abstracted it and exaggerated it wherever it suited his purpose.

While Lachaise had no followers who imitated his style, he opened the door for the expression of certain fundamental human urges in American art—a door that had previously been kept locked and bolted with the extreme caution of a priggish propriety.

Gaston Lachaise (1882–1935) was born in Paris. His father, a fine cabinetmaker, sent the boy to an arts and crafts training school; this was followed by several years at the Ecole des Beaux-Arts, where, according to the sculptor himself, he learned how to make "sweet-nothing compositions and soulless reminiscences of the classics." Soon after the turn of the century he fell in with that dynamic group of young artists in Paris who were seeking a new kind of artistic expression, and he discovered, along with them, new sources of artistic regeneration in the art of the primitives, the Orientals, and preclassical antiquity. He led the life of a Bohemian art student until Isabel came along; some years later he recalled:

At twenty, in Paris, I met a young American person who immediately became the primary inspiration which awakened my vision and the leading influence that has directed my forces. Throughout my career, as an artist, I refer to this person by the word "Woman."
[G. Lachaise, in *Creative Art*, August 1918]

In order to follow her to the United States—where she was to become his wife—he earned money by carving glass in the studio of René Lalique, known for his exquisite Art Nouveau designs. "Then in 1906 I left for America," Lachaise continued, " 'Wake up,' the interjection of a streetcar conductor, inducing me to act, should illustrate what I mean when I say that the new world is the most favorable place to develop a creative artist." This statement represents a declaration of artistic independence, whereby art in America is no longer to stay half a step behind its European counterpart, but begins to assume an equal position in the development of an international modern art.

The quickened spirit of Lachaise was held in check for a time while he was employed by the war-memorial maker of Boston, Henry Kitson. He spent most of his time modeling Civil War belt buckles or Spanish-American War leggings and the like. One of his own early pieces is the little (11 inches long) "Reclining Couple" (c. 1908–1910), which is Rodinesque in its modeling. Rodin's shadow fell mightily upon much of Parisian sculpture in the early years of the century, just when Lachaise was turning seriously to art as a career. Rodin's vigorous modeling and his passionate images of love and life recur continually in the work of Lachaise, although the former's naturalism has been translated into the latter's abstraction.

In 1912 Lachaise opened his own studio in New York and began to model his "Standing Woman," which many years later would be cast in bronze and purchased by the Whitney Museum. He sent a small plaster statuette to the Armory Show in 1913, and soon afterward began a seven-year tenure as assistant in the studio of Paul Manship. He still maintained his own studio, where he worked at night. Not much notice was paid to his sculpture until his first one-man show at the Stephen Bourgeois Gallery in 1918; even after that, when his work began to attract controversy Americans did not rush to buy his sculptures. Most critics were skeptical of his motives, his method, and even his ideal of womanhood; only Henry McBride of the New York *Sun* could perceive the grandeur of his two large plaster Venuses. Though Lachaise's work was not branded as scandalous, neither was it considered "safe." An example of this attitude came in the early

1920's when the sculptor modeled an allegorical figure for the Telephone Building, only to have it rejected on the pretense that customers might object to having their rates increased to pay for such a thing. Clearly, the officers of the utility company were not men of sufficient vision to seize "the chance to do a really gracious act for their subscribers," as McBride put it in an article in *The Dial*, June, 1927.

Although neither the 1918 exhibition nor the one in 1920 was a financial success, Lachaise left Manship's studio in 1921 to strike out completely on his own. In 1922 he modeled "Woman Walking" (Fig. 15.25), now in the Museum of Modern Art. Although only 18½ inches high, this little bronze has an imposing monumentality in the full forms of the body. There is an elegance and a rhythmic grace that may owe a debt to Manship; a trace of the simplified rounded forms, curving contours, and small hands and feet of Nadelman's sculpture are also present. But the total conception toward which Lachaise worked was entirely his own.

By 1927 Lachaise was beginning to reach the mature stage of his work. That year he created his large bulbous, gravity-defying "Floating Figure" (Fig. 15.24). Emphasis on the rotund volumes of the torso, breasts, and hips far surpasses anything of earlier years, and makes the "Woman Walking" of 1922 seem mild by comparison. The "Floating Figure" was one of the main sculptures of his show that year at the Intimate Gallery. Henry McBride again championed Lachaise's art; after chastising New Yorkers for a lack of sophistication that obscured their vision of the true beauty in the sculptor's work, he brought more of them around to an acceptance of, if not a desire to own, the art of Gaston Lachaise. Another one-man exhibition was held in 1928 at the Brummer Gallery. Lachaise's head of John Marin (1928) reveals the richness of modeling and the sensitive rendering of character of which he was capable. In 1930 he produced the greatly exaggerated, voluptuous, bump-and-grind "Burlesque Figure"; only 24 inches high, it possesses a monumentality that belies its size. The dynamic action of this figure was equaled the next year by "Torso," which is now in the Philadelphia Museum of Art. Lachaise's style seems to have reached full stride in 1932, attaining the classical phase, which shortly evolved into a mannerism of his own mature style. In that year he created several statues called "Standing Woman," which epitomize all the things he had been seeking to express in physical form. Robust and dynamic, yet poised, unabashedly proud, and looking down upon lesser humanity, this symbol of womanhood represents the most exciting and important functions of her sex.

Lachaise carried his imagery to near grotesqueness, however, in the "Kneeling Woman" (1932–1934); the enormous breasts are greatly emphasized by the pinched waist. But even such a figure as this never becomes bawdy, and with her uplifted arms she seems to be an idol praying for her continued fertility. Lachaise's women have too much the demeanor of goddesses, albeit fertility goddesses, and are too handsome to degenerate to the level of erotic symbols. Even the "Dynamo Mother," which confronts the viewer with her enlarged sexual parts, after the first shock will convey to him a sense of the overwhelming drive to reproduce that is instinctive in all forms of life. The name itself reveals Lachaise's intention. Both the "Kneeling Woman" and the "Dynamo Mother" are small, only 18 and 10 inches high respectively, but they are grandly monumental in form.

In 1934 Gaston Lachaise was occupied with some decorations for the RCA Building in Rockefeller Center, but much of his time was spent preparing for his large retrospective exhibition that was to open early the next year at the Museum of Modern Art. Many of the pieces mentioned were included, but most of them were only plaster casts, as the sculptor could not afford to put them into bronze. Several of them were cast in bronze many years later when exhibitions of his work were held at the Knoedler Gallery in 1947 and at the Whitney Museum, the Los Angles County Art Museum, and the Museum of Modern Art in 1963. The critics were not in agreement concerning the 1935 exhibition, but several concluded that "the sculptor's fixed idea on certain principles has become somewhat monotonous." Old-guard spokesman Royal Cortissoz referred to Lachaise's figures as "repetitious 'hosannas of the flesh,' " and further wrote in the *Herald Tribune* that Lachaise "demonstrates his capacity as a craftsman, but he does nothing else. Beauty as well as dramatic emotion go by the board, and all that is left is a mass of flesh." He obviously could not grasp what the artist tried to say in his sculpture. More attuned to the goals of modern art, however, was Margaret Breuning of the *New York Post*. She wrote that Lachaise was ". . . an artist who abandoned what he felt to be an exhausted civilization to align himself with the vitality of a new world, yet whose own vitality of expression has astonished and even shocked the same new world."

There is no way of predicting what Gaston Lachaise might have achieved had he not died in 1935 of leukemia, at the age of fifty-three. In the three decades that followed, his importance to the maturing and expansion of modern art in America has become increasingly clear. The strength of conviction of the artist and the strange beauty of his work added substance to a youthful movement that was not always certain of where it was going. Lachaise, along with several others, was instrumental in giving it direction.

The sculptors discussed in this chapter represent a heterogeneous group with regard to either their commitment to the academic tradition, their total separation from it, or their compromise between the two. This was the generation that fought the battle in America to see whether outworn tradition would prevail or the new art would establish valid forms and theories that would better express 20th-century man. The insurgents won, of course, after several decades of bitter contention, and laid the foundation on which post-World War II sculpture would rise to eminence amid the international modern movement.

Probably the most significant single accomplishment of the avant-garde sculptors discussed in this chapter was the return of plastic imagery to truly sculptural form. Through the efforts of the avant-garde sculptors America became aware of the potential beauty and expressiveness of sculptural form, and this did much to prepare the next generation for an appreciation of nonobjective sculpture—of the beauty and expressiveness of pure form.

[FIG. 15.1] "Gertrude Stein," by Jo Davidson (1920). Bronze, 31″ high. Collection, Whitney Museum of American Art, New York.

[FIG. 15.2] "Will Rogers," by Jo Davidson (1939). Bronze. U.S. Capitol, Washington, D.C. Courtesy, Architect of the Capitol.

[FIG. 15.3] "Pavlowa," by Malvina Hoffman (1924). Plaster, 22¼″ high. Courtesy, New-York Historical Society, New York City.

[FIG. 15.4] "Stevedore," by Mahonri Young (1904). Bronze, 16½″ high. Courtesy, Metropolitan Museum of Art, Rogers Fund, 1914.

[FIG. 15.6] "Dancer and Gazelles," by Paul Manship (1916). Bronze, 32¼" high. Collection, Corcoran Gallery of Art, Washington, D.C.

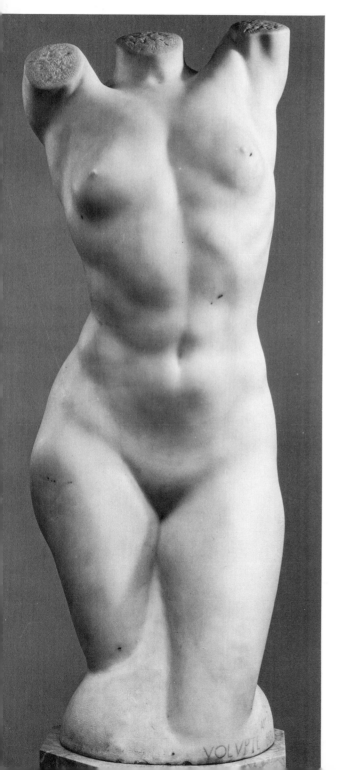

[FIG. 15.5] "Volupté," by Arthur Lee (1915). Marble, 38¾" high. Courtesy, Metropolitan Museum of Art, anonymous gift, 1924.

[FIG. 15.7] "Swann Memorial Fountain," by Stirling Calder (1924). Bronze. Courtesy, City of Philadelphia.

[FIG. 15.8] "Indian Hunter with Dog," by Paul Manship (1926). Bronze, 23¼″ high. Courtesy, Metropolitan Museum of Art, gift of Thomas Cochran, 1929.

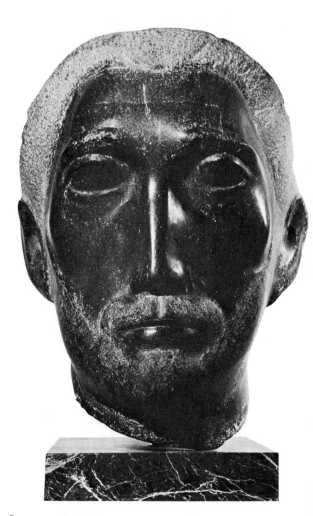

[FIG. 15.9] "Child with Cat," by William Zorach (1926). Tennessee marble, 18″ high. Collection, Museum of Modern Art, New York, gift of Mr. and Mrs. Sam A. Lewisohn.

[FIG. 15.10] "Head of Christ," by William Zorach (1940). Black porphyry, 14¾″ high. Collection, Museum of Modern Art, New York, Abby Aldrich Rockefeller Fund.

[FIG. 15.11] "Kneeling Figure," by Robert Laurent (1935). Bronze, 23½" high. Collection, Whitney Museum of American Art, New York.

[FIG. 15.12] "Seated Nude," by Robert Laurent (1940). Alabaster. Courtesy, Pennsylvania Academy of the Fine Arts.

[FIG. 15.13] "Elephant," by John B. Flannagan (1929–1930). Bluestone, 15″ wide. Collection, Whitney Museum of American Art, New York.

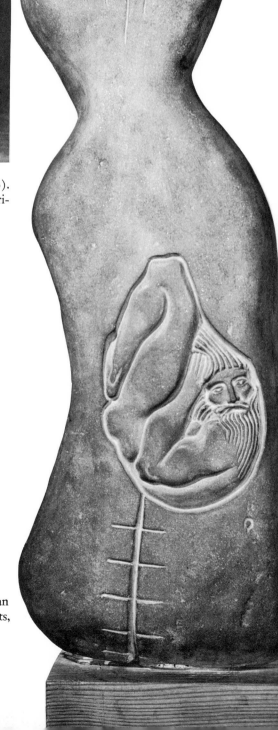

[FIG. 15.14] "Jonah and the Whale," by John B. Flannagan (1937). Stone. Courtesy, Virginia Museum of Fine Arts, Richmond.

[FIG. 15.16] "Handlebar Riders," by Chaim Gross (1935). Wood, 41″ high. Collection, Museum of Modern Art, New York, gift of A. Conger Goodyear.

[FIG. 15.15] "Cloud," by José de Creeft (1939). Greenstone, 13½″ high. Collection, Whitney Museum of American Art, New York.

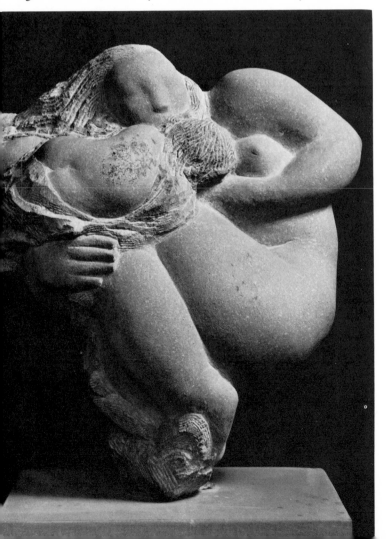

[FIG. 15.19] "Woman Combing Her Hair," by Alexander Archipenko (1915). Bronze, 13¾" high. Collection, Museum of Modern Art, New York, acquired through the Lillie P. Bliss bequest.

[FIG. 15.17] "Standing Female Nude," by Elie Nadelman (c. 1909). Bronze, 21¾" high. Collection, Museum of Modern Art, New York, Aristide Maillol Fund.

[FIG. 15.18] "Man in the Open Air," by Elie Nadelman (c. 1915). Bronze, 54½" high. Collection, Museum of Modern Art, New York, gift of William S. Paley.

[FIG. 15.20] "Torso in Space," by Alexander Archipenko (1946). Courtesy, Addison Gallery of American Art, Phillips Academy, Andover, Mass.

[FIG. 15.21] "Woman Combing Her Hair," by Hugo Robus (modeled 1927, cast c. 1958). Bronze. Collection, Corcoran Gallery of Art, gift of Mr. and Mrs. John Henry Berne.

[FIG. 15.22] "Gendarme Seated," by John Storrs (1925). Bronze. Courtesy, Downtown Gallery, New York.

[FIG. 15.23] "Composition Around Two Voids," by John Storrs (1932). Stainless steel, 20″ high. Collection, Whitney Museum of American Art, New York, gift of Monique Storrs Booz.

[FIG. 15.24] "Floating Figure," by Gaston Lachaise (1927). Bronze, 96″ long. Collection, Museum of Modern Art, New York, given in memory of the artist.

[FIG. 15.25] "Woman Walking," by Gaston Lachaise (1922). Bronze, 18½″ high. Collection, Museum of Modern Art, New York, gift of Abby Aldrich Rockefeller.

New Directions: American Sculpture Since 1946

MODERN SCULPTURE WAS BORN IN PARIS IN THE DECADE PRECEDING WORLD WAR I AND in Moscow in the first few years following the Revolution, although it soon found itself exiled from Russia. Paris was the great gathering place of the men who were to create the initial stage of modern sculpture. To them fell the task of finding new forms of expression to replace the eclectic tradition, the lifeless romantic realism, and the diluted art of the academies. Picasso and Brancusi were in Paris, as were Gonzales, Modigliani, and Zadkine; Nadelman and Csaky were there, Archipenko, Laurens, Pevsner, and occasionally Gabo; and Boccioni, Lipchitz, Matisse, and Duchamp-Villon as well. They had discovered new styles of art of the past which offered the inspiration that the Beaux-Arts style no longer held for them, and the domination of the classicism which had endured for five hundred years, since the beginning of the Renaissance, was thus brought to an end. Primitive Negro art of Africa, Egyptian sculpture, archaic Greek art, and so on, all possessed some form of abstraction which was compatible with their own concepts, and all were outside the realm of classicism and naturalism. But they did not allow the newly discovered historic styles to become new eclectic tyrants replacing old ones. All these men sought an art that was truly of the present and pointed toward the future. Thus a totally new means of artistic expression developed, displacing an earlier one, just as Renaissance classicism had once displaced the Medieval style. With the exception of a few enlightened souls, America was reluctant to participate in this revolution; what began in Europe before World War I did not really flower in the United States until after 1946. Only then did America in general really become aware of "modern art."

With the post-World War II period, the revolution in American sculpture that had been stirring for four decades was fully accomplished. This was done through the rugged determination of native American talent—like David Smith and José de Rivera—and the arrival of many gifted men who left Europe in the 1930's and 1940's to find sanctuary in the United States. These were men who had been at the very center of the modern experiments in the first part of the century—men like Jacques Lipchitz and Naum Gabo. Archipenko and Nadelman had already come over, and they were followed by Moholy-Nagy, and then Zadkine for a while. Several painters came and brought with them the seeds of the new aesthetic; there were Josef Albers, Marcel Duchamp, Mondrian, Chagall, Ozenfant, and others. They also brought encouragement to the small group of men who had stood alone, surrounded by an entrenched and hostile academy and a public that ridiculed abstract and nonobjective art.

The two most significant movements of the post-1946 period have been Abstract Expressionism and Constructivism. In the early decades of the century, Cubism was of fundamental importance in the rediscovery of form and the reinterpretation of nature, but it was a style mainly for the painter. It implied an organization of surface planes, and in the first few years after World War I it exhausted itself as far as sculpture was concerned. Even Lipchitz eventually gave it up to develop a style that could include expressive content; and Brancusi, an early participant in the Cubist movement, in time evolved a style other than Cubism. Constructivism in the 1920's, led by the Russian brothers Naum Gabo and Antoine Pevsner, spread from Moscow to Paris and through Europe; it was concerned with new concepts of space (as opposed to mass) as the major component of contemporary sculpture, and it opened up an infinite number of avenues of experimentation. Among the early movements of modern art, Futurism and the work and writings of the young Italian genius Boccioni were important because of their denial of the age-old principle that sculpture had to be composed of static volumes; that denial was underscored in 1920 when Gabo and Pevsner produced their *Realist Manifesto*, the foundation of Constructivism. The two movements mounted an attack on the concepts of time, space, and matter that had existed for centuries. But Boccioni, aged thirty-four, died in 1916, and Futurism in sculpture failed to coalesce into a movement thereafter.

There was also Fauvism, led by Matisse, but it was so largely based on color that it held little meaning for modern sculpture. German Expressionism had little impact on sculpture, aside from Lehmbruck and Barlach; the expressionism of the post-World War II period is an entirely different matter. Surrealism enjoyed a brief flourish in the 1930's, but its insistence upon overt symbolism was not the answer, as modern sculpture seemed to move irresistibly toward abstract and nonobjective form. In the years following World War II, painters and sculptors found themselves in control of nonobjective form; it was their new tool to use as they saw fit. Some chose to follow the lines of the Constructivists in pursuit of a largely formal analysis of space and time. Others gave forceful expressive content to nonrepresentational form, and this was called Abstract Expressionism. Hence the two major movements of contemporary sculpture in America emerged in the late 1940's and achieved maturity in the 1950's and 1960's.

In addition to the historical development of postwar sculpture, two other elements need to be considered. One concerns the use of new materials and new technology; the other concerns the *objet trouvé*, the "found object." Traditional means, like traditional styles, were no longer useful to the sculptors seeking an art that was truly of the 20th century. Modeling in clay, then casting in plaster or bronze, and even the more recent direct carving were not adequate for their new concepts of sculptural form. Men turned to the materials of the 20th century, such as metals and plastic, and their tools became the welding torch and metal shears. Sheet steel, tubing, wire, tanks of gas, torches, nuts and bolts, copper, tin, cluttered the sculptor's machine-shop studio. All of these seemed to possess an affinity with modern life. By virtue of their metallic substance or their daily use in 20th-century life, they seemed far more in touch with the reality of the times than cold white marble or cast bronze, which had both been tainted by academic realism. Marble and bronze also lacked the spontaneity desired in the new art—the sense of the original and direct creation of the artist without the intervention of artisans.

The second element—the found object—was incorporated to heighten the sense of reality. Real shoes on the image of a woman or a real doorway as the backdrop for a solemn figure created the ring of truth, the presence of reality, in compositions that were otherwise quite abstract. Junk heaps and trash dumps began to offer the sculptor ready-made forms that were expressive of certain aspects of 20th-century society, and he began to work them into a new kind of imagery.

In brief, after World War II the sculptor found himself in possession of new forms and new materials, and confronted with new social, cultural, political, and psychological conditions that were to find an outlet through his genius. A new sculpture was bound to come forth—and it did, in rich abundance.

Jacques Lipchitz (1891–   ) was already a noted sculptor by the time he left his adopted homeland, France, and came to the United States when the Nazis began to threaten. Born in Druskieniki, Lithuania, Chaim Jacob Lipchitz was the son of an engineer who belonged to a wealthy banking family. He was educated in Bialystok and Vilna, but because of anti-Semitic restrictions imposed by the Czar, Jewish boys were not permitted to enter the art school at St. Petersburg; moreover, his father was opposed to the boy's desire to become an artist. His mother, however, perceived his special talent and was convinced of it after a visiting professional sculptor praised his work; she quietly encouraged him in his early efforts. Young Lipchitz had not seen much sculpture, but he knew he wanted to make it himself. He thought that sculpture should be white because all the plaster casts he saw in the schools and elsewhere were white, so he painted his early works white in imitation of them.

Although barely aware of the art world beyond his homeland, he sensed that

Paris was the place to be, so in 1909, when he was eighteen, he secretly and illegally crossed the border and made his way to the French capital. Although the artistic revolution had already begun in Paris, Lipchitz knew little of it during his first years there. He turned instead to the Ecole des Beaux-Arts, the Académie Julian, and the Académia Colarossi, where he studied under the romantic-realists and turned out such sentimental academic pieces as the "Seated Nude" (1910) and the "Woman and Gazelles" (1912). About this time Picasso had modeled the first Cubist sculpture, in which the human head was diffracted into a series of planes and angles, with no care whatever for any sentimental attachment to the subject matter; Brancusi had carved his blocklike "Kiss" two years before; and Boccioni was then carrying the reorganization of form even further and more dynamically. Lipchitz seems at first to have been untouched by any of this, as well as unmoved by the work of Rodin.

He was recalled to Russia to perform his military service (from which he was soon released because of poor health) and returned to Paris in 1913, at which time he fell in with the group of rebels led by Picasso, Matisse, and Boccioni. He was then twenty-two and ready to begin his search for a means of artistic expression. Cubism offered the most exciting potential, and he joined the group practicing it. Among his friends were Picasso, Modigliani, and Juan Gris, and his studio in rue Montparnasse was next door to that of Constantin Brancusi. The extent to which Lipchitz absorbed Cubism may be seen in "Sailor with a Guitar" (1914), now in the Philadelphia Museum of Art; the figure is still recognizable, though definitely reorganized in terms of planes and masses. But two years later in his "Man with a Guitar" (Museum of Modern Art), the human element has been entirely sacrificed to a strict arrangement in vertical lines and planes, virtually identical to Cubist paintings of the period. In its emphasis on planes, the work reveals the great weakness of Cubism as a theoretical basis for sculpture, and the "Man with a Guitar" is anything but sculpturesque. Cubism was, however, the road to freedom from a sterile academic tyranny, and Lipchitz, along with the others, continued to follow it to see where it would lead. A significant feature of the "Man with a Guitar" was the hole the sculptor placed in it, for he thereby opened up the interior of such mass as there was; the possibilities of this were not immediately pursued, but years later the idea would become extremely important in his work. It may have come from Archipenko, who had done something similar in Paris several years earlier. In any event, it was yet another attack on the old academic principle that sculpture is surrounded by space but not integrated with it.

Cubism allowed exploration in many directions and the absorption of diverse elements. The influence of Boccioni, for example, is seen in Lipchitz' "Bather III" of 1916, which was acquired by Dr. Albert C. Barnes for his collection in Merion, Pennsylvania. Lipchitz' experiments with Cubism continued through the 1920's, although midway in the decade profound changes in his work took place. An example of his Cubist style in 1922 is the "Seated Man," in the Virginia Museum of Fine Arts, Richmond. Purely an abstract exercise and devoid of human qualities, it represents an art that soon became too theoretical for Lipchitz' intense sensitivity to life. Even in this solid chunk of granite there is little feeling for plastic form, since most emphasis was placed on the design and shape of the smooth, highly polished surfaces and the interrelationships of these two-dimensional planes. Though it is an excellent example of Cubism, it lacks the very qualities that were to dominate Lipchitz' mature work—the spirit of life itself and an absolutely monumental sculptural form.

In 1926 Lipchitz had his friend Le Corbusier, the architect, design a house and studio in the wooded Parisian suburb of Boulogne-sur-Seine; here Lipchitz lived with his young wife, Berthe. He worked in his studio—usually with the silent companionship of his dog, Maroud—and he and Berthe received friends and visitors from Paris and elsewhere. He was becoming known in Europe and in America, in the latter largely as a result of Dr. Barnes' acquisition of several of his works. But the harlequins and the guitar players were becoming increasingly sterile exercises for him, and he began to grope for more vitality in his art.

By nature he was a sensitive man, passionately sympathetic to all of life, and these very qualities began to appear in his sculpture, which at the same time began to grow in plastic dimension. This is first apparent in a piece entitled "Plou-manach" (Private Collection, Zurich), begun in 1925 after he, Berthe, and Le Corbusier returned from a summer in the small town of Ploumanach on the coast of Brittany. Finished the following year, its large rounded volumes herald a new robust sculptural quality, massive and dynamic and unlike the static planar character of his earlier work. Yet the reclining nude bather, modeled in relief in the upper part of the "Ploumanach," is clearly Cubist. It is in the other forms—those that represent the great boulders of the Brittany coast—that the new style begins to emerge. Although "Ploumanach" can hardly be called an Expressionistic piece, the new sculptural form achieved in it was soon employed for Expressionistic purposes.

In the second half of the 1920's, pure formal analysis became more and more insufficient to Lipchitz. His own life during these years was filled with the sickness and death of his father and sister, as well as of his close friend Juan Gris; he also saw his friend Pascin waste away the last years of his life and genius in frenzied debauchery. And the conditions prevailing throughout Europe seared his soul. All of this had an impact on the sterility of his Cubism, with the result that his work at last received the spirit that was to give it its powerful life. The mature phase of his work was near at hand.

Other important works from this period include the "Joie de Vivre" for the Vicomte Charles de Noailles' garden at Hyères, high above the Mediterranean coast. This piece, dancing and gaily lyrical, boldly sculptural but not completely freed of Cubism, would seem to be a reaction to all the misery that surrounded him during those painful years—as if to say that life must go on in his work, and the view of life on earth must remain positive and optimistic, even in the face of adversity. That Lipchitz began to realize such themes were indeed the proper goals for his art may be seen in the specter-like image called "Figure" (Fig. 16.2). It, like the "Ploumanach," was started in 1926 as a small sketch inspired by the rock formations on the coast of Brittany, with a reclining Cubist figure in the oval at the top. When Mme. Tachard visited his studio she spied the little sketch and asked the sculptor to make a large version of it for her entrance hall. This Lipchitz did, but the strictly Cubist motif of the sketch—the diffracted nude bather—was replaced by two haunting, mesmerizing eyes, and lower down, a suggestion of the female sex organ was added, thereby transforming what had been an inanimate study in mute form into a highly expressionistic image. With a beautiful interpenetration of space and massive form, Lipchitz created a superbly organized, bold, sculptural totem that is somehow human in part, yet not bound to the flesh as mortals are. It suggests a spirit, a conscience, a brooding, solemn being, in some manner connected with human existence but also apart from it. In this respect it is not unlike some of the African Negro sculpture that Lipchitz had long admired and collected. The structural organization of form, which the sculptor had long pursued through Cubism, was employed for expressionistic purposes, and his art grew immeasurably as a result.

The new element in Lipchitz' work became plain in 1930 when a retrospective exhibition of his work was held in Paris at the Galerie de la Renaissance. Relentlessly in the 1930's he pursued the new style he was pioneering, as may be seen in the "Mother and Child," in the Cleveland Museum of Art, and especially in the soul-moving, interpenetrating masses of the "Return of the Prodigal Son." The expression of human feeling became ever deeper in these pieces. Then came that gliding perforated mass, with its integration of space and form, known as "Song of the Vowels," a copy of which was purchased by the Nelson Rockefellers many years later. Formally as lyrical as a song itself, it is a symphony of rhythmic, curvilinear elements, organized into one of the most musical compositions that sculpture has ever known; here the expressive intent is that of the joy and gaiety music brings to the existence of man.

In 1934 Lipchitz' mother died of cancer. He reeled under the grievous blow, and for a long time was ill and could not work. Then slowly the optimism that dominated his view of all life returned, and he was able to resume his work. But by then the insane anti-Semitic cries of the Nazis in Germany were resounding throughout Europe; even in Paris there was much anti-Jewish feeling.

The work of Lipchitz was introduced to Americans on a large scale in an exhibition held in 1935 at the Brummer Gallery in New York. There were forty-two sculptures, chief among them being the "Song of the Vowels," "Jacob Struggling with the Angel," "Harpists," "Toward a New World," and the brilliant "Woman Resting on Her Elbows." Though some newspaper critics failed to recognize the genius that manifested itself in the collection, one art critic writing in the *Magazine of Art* (January, 1936) proclaimed Lipchitz "the most original and profound sculptor that the twentieth century has produced." It was an accurate assessment, for by 1935 no one had carried modern sculpture to such heights of formal and expressive power as Jacques Lipchitz. Far too few realized that Lipchitz had moved quietly to the forefront of modern sculpture.

The social and political situation in Europe worsened in the second half of the

1930's. Lipchitz was occupied much of the time with the colossal "Prometheus," which he was commissioned to design and execute for the Paris World's Fair of 1937; characteristically, he represented the fire giver triumphing over his vulture assailant. A smaller, revised version, "Prometheus and the Vulture," is owned by the Philadelphia Museum of Art; it dates from 1944 to 1953 and truly suggests the struggle of Olympians floating in some lofty celestial heights. Other mythological themes also interested Lipchitz, such as Europa and the bull. At the Paris exposition the sculptor had the honor of having one room in the Petit Palais devoted entirely to his work. But the situation outside the world of his art daily grew more ugly and critical. In 1939 came the outbreak of hostilities, and as the Nazi war machine advanced deeper into France, Lipchitz was forced to leave Paris and take refuge in Toulouse. Finally, in 1941, his art collection, his property, and much of his own work lost, he was persuaded by friends to come to the United States.

When Jacques and Berthe Lipchitz landed in New York, their reserve capital totaled $20. Lipchitz had only the clothes on his back and spoke no English. At first he was intimidated by the strangeness of New York; he missed Paris sorely, and felt very much alone. Then new friends and old came to help the Lipchitzes and make them feel welcome. He went to see Joseph Brummer at whose gallery his 1935 show had been held. Brummer was now dealing only in antique art, but he introduced the sculptor to Curt Valentin of the Buchholz Gallery. Valentin took several of the few drawings that represented Lipchitz' stock at the time, and sold them immediately for $600. With this Lipchitz had his start in the New World. He procured a studio in Washington Square and began to work feverishly to create a group of sculptures for a one-man show at the Buchholz Gallery early in 1942; this was to be his real debut in America, and how much more important it seemed to him than the show of 1935. Lipchitz, on the brink of greatness in his art, had been uprooted from all he loved, and his work had long been interrupted. Would he be able to take up from where he left off?

The exhibition was successful enough and clearly revealed that the sculptor's genius could obtain the necessary nourishment in his newly adopted land. But Americans at that moment were still stunned by the attack on Pearl Harbor and suddenly found themselves engaged in the war. The full impact of the art and presence of Jacques Lipchitz would not really be felt until the war was over. Commissions, however, came his way at once. He began working on a large "Prometheus and the Vulture" for the new building of the Ministry of Education and Health in Rio de Janeiro. It was to be his first great opportunity to make a monumental architectural piece, and he rejoiced in it as his 7-foot model took form. Then came a disagreement that caused the sculptor to disown the statue. The Brazilian government felt it would cost too much to have it thrice enlarged and put into bronze, so the model was ordered cast as it was. Lipchitz was furious and said that the small statue on the large building would look ridiculous. But there was nothing he could do, and with regret he turned to other work in his studio. Philadelphia acquired its version of the "Prometheus" when it was spared from the fire that destroyed the sculptor's studio many years later; R. Sturgis Ingersoll, a great admirer of Lipchitz, persuaded the trustees of the Philadelphia Museum of Art to buy the plaster model and have it cast in bronze.

The theme of life and growth, of nature, and the eternal image of mother earth was always with him, as in the spiny earth goddess titled "Blossoming" (1941–1942) or in the equally spiny orb called "Spring" (1942). The spiny attachments reveal a further penetration of, and integration with, the space that surrounds the form, and this form itself opened more and more to allow light and space to mingle with it in beautiful but forceful harmonies. This was pushed even further in "The Pilgrim" (1942) and the "Prayer" (1943), both dynamic in their jagged, open form. But for monumental work Lipchitz returned to the bold mass without the minor flourishes of the thorny forms. One of the most brilliant and monumental creations of the war years was his "Mother and Child II," a universal theme that over the years continually reappeared in the sculptor's work (Fig. 16.1). Examples are at Falling Water, Bear Run, Pennsylvania; at the Museum of Modern Art; and at the Philadelphia Museum of Art. Though it represents a human mother with a child on her back, raising her arms in prayer, the piece—being a double image—also forms a large bovine head and therefore represents a mother-earth figure that encompasses all existence. Since ancient Egyptian times the cow has been used to symbolize mother earth. Lipchitz used it here very adroitly and powerfully to expand his mother and child motif to cover all of life. The woman's arms become the horns of the cow-mother; her breasts, the eyes; her pelvic area suggests the nostrils; and the legs of the child become ears for the gentle cow. The abstracted forms are large and massive, and all distracting details are eliminated. Sculpturally it is an orchestration of bulging, compact, monumental volumes.

Unlike Zorach or Flannagan, Jacques Lipchitz did not see his images pre-existing in a block of wood or stone. Form came entirely from his own fertile imagination and creative power. From his first years in Paris he had always been a modeler, working with clay or one of its modern substitutes like plasticine. Although he had not cared for the work of Rodin back in 1911, by 1942 he revered Rodin as the greatest sculptor of the modern movement, equating him with Cézanne. Lipchitz could carve directly in stone and had often done it, but he felt more master of his material when working in clay. After the clay model had been put into plaster, he would rework the cast with kitchen knives and rasps, reshaping, simplifying, giving strong planar clarity to the shapes. Only then was the piece ready to be cast in bronze.

When the war ended, Jacques and Berthe Lipchitz returned to Paris to see what threads of their former life could be recovered. After the first glow of reunion with a few friends—most movingly with Picasso—the sculptor sensed an atmosphere of negation in Europe that was not compatible with his love of life and the poetic, positive strain that informed his work. For Berthe, who had never assimilated New World ways, it was a homecoming at last. Jacques had to leave Europe for the sake of all he lived for, and Berthe could not bear to leave France again for America. The two went their separate ways after twenty years together.

Before returning to Paris in 1946, Lipchitz completed the floating, lyrical, and sensuously embracing abstract shapes of "The Song of Songs," now in the Henry R. Hope collection in Bloomington, Indiana. It was followed on his return to America by the hosannah-singing forms of "Miracle II," with its seven-branched candelabrum radiating from the two Tablets of the Law, now in the Jewish Museum in New York City. Lipchitz was deeply moved when he was asked to create an image of the Virgin Mary for the French Church of Notre Dame de Liesse at Assy; it presented a challenge to him, for Christian iconography had never been a part of his repertoire. He made a haunting vision of the Virgin enclosed in an inverted heart form; on top, a dove descends, and cherubim and a lamb make up the base. All of it is in the sculptural style associated with Lipchitz' work. It is characteristic of the man that he obtained permission to inscribe on the back of the heart these words: "Jacob Lipchitz, Jew, faithful to the religion of his ancestors, has made this Virgin to foster understanding between men on earth that the life of the spirit may prevail."

Lipchitz' most monumental creation of the late 1940's and early 1950's was his "Sacrifice II" (Fig. 16.3). A brutish, monstrous being with thick, bull-like neck and tiny beady eyes holds a terrified, struggling chicken—the victim—and drives a huge knife into its breast. A second animal, a lamb—the traditional sacrificial animal of Christianity—whose time has not yet come and who seems oblivious to the fact that he may be the next victim, reclines complacently between the feet of the monster, totally unresponsive to the murder occurring before his eyes. It is a potent artistic language that this Jew, whose soul was tormented by the terror of Hitler's Europe, employed to express himself. He created an image that is equaled in our time only by Picasso's "Guernica."

By 1950 Lipchitz had established his home at Hastings-on-Hudson, had married again, and was the father of a little girl. In his studio on 23rd Street he completed the model for the Virgin of Notre Dame de Liesse and also a bas-relief, "Birth of the Muses," for Mrs. John D. Rockefeller III. He began work on the model of a large important commission for the city of Philadelphia, called "Spirit of Enterprise," which was to be a constant symbol to stimulate the citizens' initiative. He had found a great happiness in his work, his family, and his friends; then disaster struck once again. On January 5, 1952, his Manhattan studio burned down, destroying nearly all his work, including the models for the Virgin of Notre Dame de Liesse and the "Spirit of Enterprise." For a second time Fate seemed determined to efface all he had worked for and deprive him of his rightful place in the history of art. The sculptor felt as if a part of his own body had been destroyed in the conflagration. But the man who had so often made images of the Olympian fire giver was soon to see his work and his future rise like a geat Phoenix from the ashes of disaster.

American art museums collaborated to help Lipchitz start again, and his brother, Rubin, sent him some pieces that were in Paris. Philip Goodwin and Martin Lowenfish designed a new studio for him at Hastings-on-Hudson, and by 1953 Lipchitz had returned to work in it. He began to re-create the models for the Virgin and the "Man with the Eagle," in the "Spirit of Enterprise." The former was set in its place in the Church of Notre Dame de Liesse in the summer of 1955, and a second version was cast for Jane Owen's roofless church in New Harmony, Indiana. The "Spirit of Enterprise" grew to heroic proportions, reaching more than 12 feet in height, and had to be cast in twenty separate pieces, which were then welded together. It was to have been placed opposite another monumental group by Jacob Epstein, as part of the Samuel Memorial in Fairmount Park; but because the two were so dissimilar only Lipchitz' statue was set up there, and the Epstein group was erected at an entrance to the Art Museum. "Spirit of Enterprise" was placed on its pedestal in October 1960. After two years of intensive work following the fire, Lipchitz had a very successful one-man show at the Museum of Modern Art, and once again he was back on top.

In the mid-1950's he created a series called semiautomatics, small pieces of great vigor and enormous sculptural strength, often nearly nonobjective but throbbing with life, nevertheless. Wanting to create entirely with his hands, to develop a rich tactile power, Lipchitz had formed these by working the plasticine under water where his eyes were of no assistance, and he therefore could not turn the pieces into a visual sculpture; they were cast virtually as they emerged from the water, with only minor alterations of the forms. At the end of the decade, as he approached his seventieth year, a long illness made work impossible. As recovery progressed, he worked on a series of enchanting and highly imaginative little pieces called "A la limite du possible" in which he employed such motifs as flutes and artichokes in some of the most creative sculpture of his career. Even now, in his late seventies, he continues to create new images in his studio. The Donatello of the modern renaissance in sculpture, Lipchitz gave an undeniable validity to the expressive power of abstract sculpture. He arrived in America and began to work just as his creative energies were hitting full stride; in the years after World War II the quality and completeness into which his highly personal style had coalesced gave confidence to a new generation of younger sculptors.

The sculpture of David Smith is very different from that of Jacques Lipchitz—although both men were strongly influenced by Cubism in the early years of their careers, and both transformed it into a highly personal kind of imagery later on. But Smith belonged to the generation that followed Lipchitz', and Smith's sculpture took on more of the raw metallic substance of the 20th century than Lipchitz' modeled forms did. Smith emerged out of the milieu of a small avantgarde group in America in the 1920's, out of the early Cubist experiments with welded-metal sculpture, and out of his own practical experience in machine shops and automobile factories. From the time of the convergence of all these elements—about 1933—he forged his own course into unexplored regions of constructed metal sculpture in iron and stainless steel. His work does not have the small, refined, jewelry-like character of such Constructivists as Gabo, de Rivera, or Lippold, but is bold, heroic, hard-edged, sometimes rude and vulgar; in its metallic grandeur, however, it may also be poetic and lyrical. It is virtually impossible to categorize Smith's work, because he constantly changed direction, and he never stopped to formulate an ideology or write a manifesto. The shadow of Surrealism may appear from time to time in his work, but the spell of Cubism is usually much stronger.

Smith was brusque, yet warmly gracious to friends, vigorous, confident of himself and his art, and dedicated to the latter; he died prematurely just when his greatest promise was being fulfilled. In 1960 Hilton Kramer assessed Smith's position in the history of modern sculpture in an article in *Arts* (February, p. 22):

The sculpture of David Smith is . . . . a major contribution to the international modern movement, and at the same time the most important body of sculpture this country has produced . . . . He is one of the very few artists anywhere today whose work upholds the promise and vision of the modern movement at the same level at which it was conceived . . . . He is in the line of artists who are copious, energetic and unreservedly productive; artists who run the risk of vulgarity, repetition and garrulousness in the interest of sustaining an unchecked flow of new images and ideas.

David Smith (1906–1965) was born in Decatur, Indiana, where his father was a telephone company engineer by vocation and an inventor by avocation. As a boy he had a curiosity about mechanical things and enjoyed playing with the tools and gadgets in his father's workshop. He loved to sit at the edge of town overlooking the railroad tracks and marvel at the powerful great locomotives that puffed and chugged as they moved their enormous loads. He was only seven years old in 1913 when the Armory Show was held in New York and Chicago.

When he was eighteen, Smith went to Ohio University in Athens to major in art, but he left after a year because he felt they were not teaching art there. He next went to South Bend, where he was trained as a welder and riveter in the Studebaker automobile plant. Within a year, however, he was in the national capital, working by day for a finance company and in art classes at George Washington University at night. Later that year, 1927, he went to New York City and enrolled at the Art Students League, then the country's most progressive art school, where the theories of the European modernists were available to interested young painters and sculptors. He studied painting when he first arrived, and evidently gave no thought to sculpture. John Sloan and Richard Lahey helped him a lot that first year, but it was his teachers, the Czech painter Jan Matulka and the American John Graham, who were to influence him most. Matulka opened his eyes to the new art of Europe, especially Cubism; and Graham, always an inspiration, introduced young Smith to other influential forces in the persons of Stuart Davis, Maxim Gorky, William de Kooning, and Max Xceron.

David Smith wrote of those years many years later: ". . . we drank coffee and hung around together in New York City like expatriates. Graham lived summers at Bolton Landing. His annual trips to Paris kept us all appraised of abstract events, along with *Cahiers d'Art* and *Transition*." (Quoted from *Arts*, February, 1960, p. 44.) By the 1920's the modern movement had split into numerous elements, and the exciting talk at the cafés revolved around them all; at first, the big twenty-two-year-old Smith mostly listened, but as his confidence grew, he freely expressed himself. The discussions were about Cubism and Surrealism, Constructivism and the new direction of the Bauhaus, and the merits and failures of the men who led these movements. Smith had many paths laid open before him. For the remainder of the decade he chose one leading between the formal analysis of Cubism and the symbolic, nightmare imagery of Surrealism.

As his painting became more competent and more abstract, he began to apply odd scraps and found objects to his work, later recalling that his paintings refused to stay on the surface of his canvases. There were a few experiments with free-standing, painted wood constructions before he attempted his first welded-metal composition. He had been introduced to the area around Bolton Landing, New York, by John Graham in 1929. He loved its wooded mountainsides and Lake George, and he painted there almost every summer. He much preferred its landscape and people to those of New York City—his group of friends from the League excepted—and must have dreamed of some day having his own studio there. The summer of 1933, inspired by some welded-metal sculpture by Picasso, which he had seen in the magazine *Cahiers d'Art*, he borrowed some equipment from a local garage, and began to cut and assemble some of the rusty metal parts of a discarded wagon. The tools of the welder felt good and at home in his hands; he sensed at once that he had found his medium, and welded metal sculpture in America had its beginning.

About that time John Graham gave Smith a piece of sculpture by Gonzalez, one of several he had purchased in Paris. Gonzalez was all but unknown in America in the early 1930's, but Smith freely acknowledged the debt he and others owed the Spaniard. It was Gonzalez who taught Picasso and Gargallo how to weld metal into sculpture; Gargallo was famous in the 1920's for his metal constructions of abstract figures, and his work made a great impression on Smith when he saw it exhibited at the Brummer Gallery. Smith may have seen the show of Gonzalez' work at the Galerie des Cahiers d'Art in 1935, as he was then in Paris. In any case, encouraged by friends and teachers in America, and stimulated by the past and contemporary experiments of Cubist sculptors in Paris, David Smith began to fashion his own images in iron and steel. The old method of modeling in clay—never a part of Smith's training—was thus shunted aside to make way for a technique which in the evolution of 20th-century sculpture was to become even more important than direct carving.

The competency of Smith's first metal abstractions is remarkable; there was no fumbling or groping, no long period of searching. Though his sculpture was to undergo considerable evolution during the next decades, such early work as the "Head" (1933) shows a total and immediate comprehension of abstract art. Few in the United States in the early 1930's could say as much; among American sculptors, only John Storrs had previously penetrated the unexplored world of abstract sculpture to the same depths and with such daring originality. Instead of establishing a conventional sort of studio in lower Manhattan, Smith set up his machine shop at the Terminal Iron Works in the waterfront section of Brooklyn. His early creations—which drew reactions of wonder and incredulity from the metal workers and longshoremen in the vicinity—were definitely Cubist in style, more synthetic than analytical, but highly original. One of the finest pieces of this period is the "Untitled Composition" (1935).

In 1935 David Smith made his first trip to Europe, visiting London, Greece, Russia, and Paris. He saw much that stimulated him, but he later wrote in *Arts*, ". . . I matured enough to realize that no matter how inhospitable New York was to my work, my life and destiny and materials were there." He returned to America within a few months and began a period of enormous productivity. With cutting torch and welding iron, he ripped through great sheets of steel and put their strange, raw shapes together again, often incorporating found objects into the design—a rusty cogwheel, or a long wrench, or a hoop from a barrel, or the dented head of a steel drum. From those years came the linear "Reclining Figure" (1936) and the beautifully massive, sculpturesque "Unity of Three Forms" (1937), one of America's earliest masterpieces of nonobjective sculpture. Often the titles—always bestowed after the work was completed—were as non-representational as the sculptures themselves, as in the steel "Structure" of 1937, or the steel and sprayed-copper "Vertical Structure" of 1939. Just as often nature would also appear in a sophisticated abstract form, as in the steel and cast-iron "Head" (1938; Museum of Modern Art), which reveals a Cubist approach to abstraction.

David Smith held his first one-man show at the East River Gallery in New York in 1938. Critics and collectors were cautious and did not know quite how to take this new art form with its new technique and its raw materials from the steel mill and the iron foundry—so they took practically no notice of it for several years. It was a hard time for Smith; he never forgot those bitter years and the depression. He was driven further and further toward a political philosophy which was decidedly socialistic, as were many men in those difficult days. He saw the government's support of the arts (through the Works Progress Administration and the Fine Arts Section of the Treasury Department) as one of the brightest lights of a dismal period. For a while he was called a "Social Surrealist," but no restricting classification ever applied for very long to Smith's sculpture. The term Social Surrealist best applied to a series of fifteen bronze medallions, executed between 1937 and 1940, called "Medals of Dishonor." Inspired by collections of coins Smith had seen in the British Museum and by imprints from ancient cylinder seals, they represented such themes as war, hate, social injustice, and the like. Their titles are self-explanatory—for example, "Bombing Civilian Population," "Death by Gas," "War Exempt Sons of the Rich," or "Sinking Hospital and Refugee Ships." These were a reaction against the hypocrisy of the social order and man's inhumanity to man, which grew out of the Spanish Civil War and the emergence of the Nazis and the brutal aftermath of their rise to power in Europe.

The reliefs of the "Medals of Dishonor" were executed in a Surrealistic style but with an iconography that was painfully clear. One critic, after praising them, was moved to comment that at last America had an artist who could unite content with form, implying a certain dissatisfaction with pure nonobjective formalism. But such overt symbolism was not to endure long in Smith's work; after the completion of the series he employed more subtle imagery, and by the late 1940's he had begun to move away from social commentary altogether. His sculpture improved as a result, and his real strength was to reveal itself in his bright metallic abstract sculpture of form.

The "Medals of Dishonor" stimulated quite a bit of interest when they were exhibited in his one-man show at the Willard Gallery in 1940, but this was largely because they were executed in a traditional medium and in a style that had been around long enough to have acquired some understanding. But his welded-metal pieces still failed to arouse much of a following. In 1940 he decided to get away from "inhospitable New York" and bought some property at Bolton Landing. There he built a house and studio out of cement blocks, and he himself welded together the pieces that made the roof. He called his place "Terminal Iron Works." It was to be his residence and workshop for the next quarter century.

Money was not plentiful, but Smith had to have large stocks of material so he could work without restriction. The "Terminal Iron Works" looked more like a small-town machine shop than an artist's studio, with stacks of large sheets of stainless steel, piles of cast iron, strips of metal tubing, nuts and bolts, brass, copper, and aluminum; tools were strewn about on dusty workbenches, and hoses ran from cylinders of gas to several types of torches. There were grinders and polishers, bottles of acid, and cans of paint and waxes on steel shelving, as well as countless pieces of old metal, whose shapes were beyond description and whose original use defied explanation. These were gathered on trips throughout the area, where dumps and junkyards were ransacked for the treasures they might yield to the sculptor's perceiving eye. All of these things, or rather a selection from them, would experience a metamorphosis from machine-age products into dynamic works of art—or into an experiment toward that end.

During the war years, material for this kind of work was difficult if not impossible to obtain. Moreover, much of Smith's time was spent welding steel plates on huge armored tanks in a factory in Schenectady. The years after the war represented a period of exciting experimentation. Criticis have seen it as a very uneven period in his career when there were apt to be as many failures as successes. This was partly because Smith was restlessly searching for new avenues of aesthetic and technical expansion, and partly because of his compulsion to exhibit almost every piece he produced. "I never stop to decide what's good and what isn't," he once wrote; "I just do the work—I don't judge it. . . ." Cleve Gray explained this comment in his memorial of his last visit to the "Terminal Iron Works" one week before the sculptor died: "He meant that time would sort out the good from the bad, that wasn't the artist's job. The artist's job was to express himself unchecked by aesthetic judgments." (Quoted from *Art in America*, Jan.–Feb.

1966, p. 26.) If the quality was uneven during the late 1940's, the experiments were nevertheless necessary and important historically, for in time Smith emerged from this period of uncertainty with one of the most coherent and forceful personal styles of expression in postwar American sculpture, influential at home and in Europe and respected internationally. Successive Guggenheim fellowships in 1950 and 1951 freed the artist from having to earn a living by doing odd jobs or teaching, and he was able to sift through the work of the past several years and launch into fifteen years of consistently good work with a minimum of failures.

From about 1950 right up to his death in 1965, David Smith reached maturity in his work. It first appeared in the series known as "Agricola," which comprises about a dozen pieces. They, like much of his work of the 1950's, are decidedly linear and are best seen against the sky or an uncluttered wall. Three of his finest works, which have been called drawings in air because of their two-dimensional linear quality, are the "Hudson River Landscape" (Fig. 16.4), the "Banquet," and the lively "Australia," all from 1951. Their logic and order are masterfully worked out in linear patterns. Referring to the "Hudson River Landscape" (which is 75 inches wide), Smith explained the relationship of nature and his art in the following comments:

This sculpture came in part from dozens of drawings made on a trip between Albany and Poughkeepsie, a synthesis of ten trips over a 75-mile stretch. Later, while drawing, I shook a quart bottle of India ink and it flew over my hand. It looked like my river landscape. I placed my hand on paper. From the image that remained, I traveled with the landscape, drawing other landscapes and their objects, with additions, deductions, directives, which flashed unrecognized into the drawing, elements of which are in the sculpture. Is my sculpture the Hudson River? Or is it the travel and the vision? Or does it matter? The sculpture exists on its own; it is an entity.

["Thoughts on Sculpture," *College Art Journal*, 1954, no. 2, p. 99]

In 1952 and 1953 David Smith was working on a series entitled "Tanktotems," tall (ranging between 80 and 92 inches in height), gangly, linear forms set off by curved discs or parts thereof; "Tanktotem II" is in the collection of the Metropolitan Museum of Art. They derived their name from the fact that they reminded their creator of totem images and the discs resembled the convex ends of tanks. These, too, were basically linear, and the sculptor returned to the series continually throughout the decade, as in "Tanktotem VI," which was made in 1957–1959, and "Tanktotem IX" of 1960. But in a series entitled "Albany," dating from 1959, the linear element becomes thicker, and the flat discs and bars assume increased importance; one may perceive a movement toward simplification and an increased solidity that prefigure Smith's greatest masterpieces of the next decade.

It is in the "Cubi," "Zig" and "Menand" series that Smith achieved his greatest art. The "Cubi" group was begun in 1963 and is characterized by compositions of shining, burnished, stainless-steel rectangular boxes attached to one another, parallel to the axis of the main support, or perpendicular to it, or set at an angle to it (Fig. 16.5). A marvelous geometric order, simplicity, and harmony pervade the entire arrangement—as if one were visualizing in a single instant some great metallic symphony. Monumental in both scale and content, these glistening prismatic giants often were more than 8 feet high, and when finished, stood like 20th-century votive images about the meadow near Smith's Bolton Landing studio, silhouetted against the open sky or breaking the undulating line of the distant mountains. They are a testimony to man's ability to find beauty in geometric truths and in the harmony of pure geometric forms. The title of the series comes from the cubes stacked at angles in "Cubi I," and was the sculptor's invention of a term designating the multiples of the cube form. Nearly thirty pieces make up this group. The "Zig" (from *ziggurat*) series was more concerned with the angular interplay of metallic planes that were often coated in bright colors, which contrasted brilliantly with black or burnished metallic surfaces. These, too, frequently reached over 100 inches in height. The third series, the "Menand," which derives its name from a small town near Albany, is smaller than the other two by actual measurement, but equal to them in monumentality, for it too possesses a bold sculptural character. Made up of only a few volumed components, "Menand III" (Fig. 16.6) of 1963, recaptures the nonrepresentational beauty of the "Unity of Three Forms" (1937) and enlarges upon it. It is an indication of Smith's energy and industry that in a given year, such as 1963, he might produce a dozen or more heroic "Cubi," six or seven "Zigs" and about eight "Menands." In production Smith was indefatigable and outdistanced almost every other important sculptor, most of whom might create five or six major pieces a year. A large part of this enormous output was extremely successful. In 1964 Smith worked on yet another series of "bronze planes," which when silhouetted against the sky resemble abstract railroad signals, except for their handsome silver patinas. And along with these were individual pieces, often experiments, explorations of yet another fertile idea in metallic sculpture—such as the several lost wax bronzes of 1960 to 1962. It was a period almost incredibly rich in creation and exploration.

For years several critics and many artists, both American and European, had recognized Smith's work as one of the most exciting elements in modern postwar art. But fame came slowly, and buyers—both private collectors and museum curators—were extremely cautious. It was still necessary for the sculptor to teach, as he did at the universities of Arkansas, Indiana, and Mississippi in the academic years of 1953–1955, in order to make ends meet. He was constantly sending his work off to one-man shows, the largest of which was held in 1957 at the Museum of Modern Art. Two years later he won first prize at the international Bienniale of Modern Art in São Paulo, Brazil. In 1960 he had a one-man show at French and Company, and another in 1964 at the Marlborough-Gerson Gallery in New York. These exhibitions eventually began to bring Smith the belated recognition he deserved.

Smith's style, like that of so many 20th-century artists, was a very personal one made up of an imagery that sprang from his own imagination and aesthetic sense. In the 1930's he introduced new techniques and a new method of creative expression that others could employ in ways that best suited themselves. He did much to carry abstract art in America to a mature state, and he invented a style that was compatible with the 20th century, without making a fetish of steel and other metallic substances of our time. David Smith died on May 23, 1965, when the big yellow truck in which he hauled his supplies and works hit a utility pole. He was then fifty-nine, and to the very last excited about the things he wanted to do next.

Theodore Roszak crystallized the principles of the Abstract Expressionist movement into the leading and most dynamic sculptural style in America in the twenty-five years following World War II. Roszak (1907–   ) was born in Poznan, Poland, and brought to the United States at the age of two. The family settled in Chicago, where in time the boy was to receive his first lessons in art. While still in high school, he began attending classes at the Art Institute Professional School and eventually entered the regular curriculum as a full-time student specializing in painting. In 1926 he went to New York City, where for about a year he studied at the National Academy and on his own with George Luks. Of special significance at this point were the courses he took in philosophy at Columbia University, revealing an interest in the intangible forces that control men's lives. He was not especially impressed by the training he received in New York, and when he returned to Chicago in 1927, he was still largely unaware of the modern movement—by then more than two decades old. He resumed his studies at the Art Institute and during the summers maintained a studio in a corner of one of the old Columbian Exposition buildings. He was then occupied with lithography, and an exhibition of his prints was held at the Allerton Gallery in 1928. For a while he taught at the Art Institute.

The next phase of Roszak's career began in 1929 when he won the Anna Louise Raymond Fellowship for European study; it took him abroad for two years, and for the first time his eyes were opened to the glories of modern art. Still a painter, he found Cubist and Fauvist Paris interesting for six months, but Germany and Prague were more stimulating by far because of the Bauhaus experiments then being conducted there. The Expressionism of Kirchner or Kokoschka had little impact, but the potential of the new art of Klee and Kandinsky showed Roszak the way out of academic art. When he returned to the United States, his long student years were behind him; he had discovered the new aesthetics of the 20th century, and he was on the verge of beginning to work in sculpture. Roszak made a little sculptured "gimmick," which to his surprise won the Louis Comfort Tiffany award in 1931. With the money he won, he got married and settled in Staten Island.

In 1932 Theodore Roszak was invited to submit a piece to the first Biennial held by the new Whitney Museum of American Art, and has ever since been a regular contributor to the Whitney's exhibitions of modern art. An example of his stylized abstract painting of these years is owned by the Whitney Museum—"Fisherman's Bride" (1934). The first period of his sculpture dates from about 1937 to 1945, during which time he clearly belonged to the Constructivist camp. In 1938 he joined Moholy-Nagy's Design Laboratory in New York City as an instructor in two- and three-dimensional design, becoming fascinated with the problems of good design for the objects necessary to a 20th-century urban technological society. He became so steeped in the transplanted Bauhaus principles that his own art—his constructions—became experiments in streamlined forms and new materials, as in the "Bi-Polar Form" of 1940 or the "Vertical Construction" of 1943. But by the latter date he had become aware of the coolness of Bauhaus art, of its detachment from the emotional side of contemporary life and its complete exclusion of any Romantic element in art and design. All this in time left Roszak—by nature an arch-Romantic in his art—with a great feeling of vacuum in his constructions. They looked as cold to him, as devoid of man's spirit, as the machines of the new technological age that surrounded them. The search began to find a spirit and warmth for his art. These years had taught him one thing, however: it was sculpture rather than painting that he wished to pursue.

During World War II, Roszak worked on the assembly line of the Brewster Aircraft Corporation. He had learned to use the tools of the 20th century during the time he was devoted to the Bauhaus concepts and principles, and in the airplane factory he put this knowledge to practical use for a number of years. Therefore, when the time came for his important search for the spirit that was to give his art its greatness, the materials and instruments of the machine shop were far more natural and familiar to him than were clay or marble, mallet, and chisel. Moreover, he had the precedent of David Smith and a good many Europeans to encourage him.

With the end of the war, Roszak could once more devote his energies to his art. He was teaching at Sarah Lawrence College to support himself and his wife, and soon a daughter, but there was nevertheless time to work at his own sculpture. He began experimenting with the welding torch and various materials, and discovered the enormous potential of the technique. His forms increased in size over the earlier constructions, and he liked the effects of the fretted surface, the coloration, and all the special qualities that little by little began to build into a rich vocabulary of forms and textures. Unlike David Smith, Roszak worked very slowly, with many carefully detailed drawings preceding each piece of sculpture. But in spite of this it took only a few years for the artist to evolve one of the most original and dynamic styles of the present century. That he soon approached a mature plateau in his search for his new means of expression is readily seen in "Spectre of Kitty Hawk" (1946–1947) at the Museum of Modern Art (Fig. 16.7). No airplane or airplane part is recognizable in the piece, yet there is a soaring quality, a surging astronomic form that sweeps heavenward in a crescent from earth below; it suggests the realization of man's long urge to fly like a bird. Yet the spiky, jagged, tormented explosion of agonized form at its center reveals the corruption of Icarus' ancient dream and the Wright brothers' proud invention, for in two horrible World Wars the airplane had become an instrument of mass destruction. Thus are the name and the form self-explanatory, and anyone beholding the sculpture senses immediately the horror the sculptor sought to express. Roszak created a biting attack on a social order that among the many things it brought to the masses included mass destruction from the skies. The age of Abstract Expressionism had arrived in American sculpture.

Roszak continued to pursue his new-found form the next year with "Thorn Blossom" (1948; Whitney Museum of American Art), begun shortly before the birth of his daughter, Sara-Jane. It represents a lovely flower form in the center—his symbol of the joy and innocence of childhood—which can survive only if protected by the enormous, powerful thorn that rises over it. In much of his work, nature is the point of departure for the sculptor, but he soon frees himself from any specific representational form. There may be an organic quality, or a very real sense of animation, or both, but all objective details are eliminated, the form abstracted, and the expression of a universal truth or concept looms as the primary feature of the work. In a piece such as "Anguish," forms clash and react violently to one another. The surfaces are agitated and the entire work pulsates with a nervous centrifugal energy that disturbs whatever complacency the spectator may have enjoyed before confronting Roszak's image. In "Anguish," the artist does not represent one specific example of criminal violence or social injustice (although a particular event may have been the primary stimulus), but rather pricks the human conscience, and the thoughts of the serious observer turn to whatever injustice or violence may exist in his own experience. Expressionism was thus converted from the representation of material form (as in German Expressionism) to the representation of intangible ideas. As each piece slowly evolved, the sculptor's power to express his observations and judgments on contemporary life became keener, and his abstract vocabulary gained greater precision. His welded, burnished, acid-burned, filed surfaces continually gained effectiveness.

In the 1950's Roszak attained recognition as the leading Abstract Expressionist sculptor in America. The Pierre Matisse Gallery represented him, but one-man shows were rare because of the comparatively few pieces he produced. He was chosen to create the sculptural tiara to crown Saarinen's chapel at the Massachusetts Institute of Technology. The three spires rise 45 feet into the heavens above the nondenominational chapel, like a soul striving to gain reunification with the divine being whence it came. In reference to the Gothic tradition of religious architecture, Roszak visualized his spire as a great gargoyle pointed toward the sky, since in modern times that is where danger comes from. At the base are expressionistic reliefs cast in aluminum, which—the sculptor explained —although not visible from the campus, may be seen by God from his heavenly abode.

Roszak and his family spend the summers near Cape Ann, Massachusetts, where the sculptor reads and makes drawings, many of which eventually take form as sculpture. He is drawn to the area itself by a fascination with the sea—the life that inhabits it and the people that take their living from it. Old sea tales and such novels as *Moby Dick* or the ballad of "The Wreck of the Hesperus" also inspire the sculptor and fuse with the forms of seashore life into a nonnaturalistic, non-literary art. The "Nantucket Whaler," (Fig. 16.8) for example, suggests the foreboding, skeletal form of Moby Dick, the great white whale, which did in fact inspire the piece. Melville's stories had a profound impact on Roszak, and the drama woven around Captain Ahab and the phantom that ultimately destroyed him offered just the sort of psychological and physical violence that the sculptor in his abstract forms felt compelled to depict. The bold horizontal thrust, impel-lent and irresistible, is balanced by the frothy wave of a heavy sea. The sightless eye and the partly opened jaw make the monstrous mammal a menacing foe to any man who pits himself against such enormous natural strength. Yet nowhere does the sculptor actually give the literal details of either mammal or novel; instead he transformed all specifics into a broad universal statement that is so articulate in its form that its message is immediately clear to the spectator.

There was other sculpture inspired by the sea, such as the "Sea Quarry" or the "Sea Sentinel," the former from a passage in Melville's "The Encantadas, or Enchanted Isles." But the spiny, thorny plants of land continued to serve as points of departure for Roszak, as in the "Thistle in a Dream" (1955–1956). Like some great metal Rorschach blot, these sculptures are invested by the observer with his own interpretation; violence, anguish, pain, brute force, are frequently sensed, and sometimes there is in the midst of all the violence a gentle, poetic note, as in the "Thorn Blossom." Roszak's meaning is usually quite clear, and this has made his work a great favorite at the annual exhibitions; it is a kind of modern, abstract art to which people can relate emotionally. The show that brought Roszak to the attention of America in general was held in 1956, traveling from the Whitney Museum in New York, to Minneapolis, on to San Francisco, and finally to Seattle. It was a large retrospective exhibition with many of his earlier paintings and constructions, but the most fascinating and significant works were those done from 1945 on.

Another who belongs to the Abstract Expressionist group is Herbert Ferber (1906–   ). Born in New York City, he got his B.S. from Columbia in 1927 and his D.D.S. in 1930. His desire to become an artist crystallized as he began studying at the Beaux Arts Institute of Design. He picked up the new method of direct carving in wood and stone, and his favorite subject became the nude female figure. A trip to Europe in 1928 opened his eyes to the expressionism of Ernst Barlach, to Negro art in the ethnological museums, and to the contorted figures of Romanesque sculpture. All these elements were blended with his earlier training to form a continually evolving style in the 1930's. He carved compact, frontal figures and groups in awkward, straining positions, in a kind of figurative expressionism that suggested souls attempting to free themselves from some sort of social bondage. Like Roszak, in these early years Ferber was as much a painter as a sculptor, but in 1937, when his first one-man show was held at the Midtown Gallery, his commitment to sculpture was definite. By the early 1940's his style had become highly abstract, constantly moving toward a total elimination of recognizable objects. The sculpture of Henry Moore was at that time an important influence on him, as may be seen in Ferber's "Three-Legged Figure" (1945) or "Metamorphosis" (1946).

In the years after World War II, Ferber's sculpture experienced a kind of rebirth. He discovered the techniques of metal sculpture and began to develop a new style of expression; but he was careful never to allow the means to become an end in itself, frequently cautioning young sculptors not to confuse technique with the form and content of great art. His new work was shown to the art world in a one-man exhibition at the Betty Parsons Gallery in 1947, and again at the same gallery three years later. From these years date the "Apocalyptic Rider" (1947; New York University); the "Labors of Hercules" (1948), with its dominating clublike form, clearly suggestive of the ancient hero; the "Horned Sculpture" (1949); and "Portrait of Jackson Pollock" (1949; Museum of Modern Art). The "Flame" (1949) is a fine example of this period; it shows Ferber's complete independence of naturalistic objects and his achievement of an Abstract Expressionist style (Fig. 16.10). Made of lead, brass, and soft solder (with the blow torch and welding iron his chief tools) the statue is 65 inches high. The forms are forceful and dynamic, and space is incorporated into the very heart of the piece. Ferber's style, as seen here, is characteristically more linear than Roszak's.

The early part of the 1950's Ferber devoted mainly to the first of his large architectural sculptures. The congregation of B'nai Israel in Millburn, New Jersey, had a new synagogue designed by Philip Goodman, and Ferber was asked to make a large sculpture for one of the prominent exterior walls; the theme of the miracle of the burning bush was agreed upon, and the sculptor was given full freedom to interpret the subject in his own way. After Ferber had spent months making drawings and models, the large sculpture began to take final form in the artist's studio, which adjoined his apartment on Riverside Drive, overlooking the Hudson River. The forms that emerged were suggestive of both flickering flames and a leafy bush that would not be consumed; sparkling motifs here and there simulated the sparks that accompany the fire. The finished piece—more than 12 feet high by 8 feet wide—was placed against a wooden panel that nicely sets off the metallic tones of the lead and copper. The tension and dynamics that characterize Abstract Expressionism form the basis of a beautifully integrated composition of sharp, angular forms, and the sculpture suggests a kind of spiritual joy and wonderment.

In the mid-1950's, Herbert Ferber was interested in the problem of sculpture enclosed between a plane above and the base below—that is, between a rooflike plane that the sculptor created over the plane of the base, establishing a spatial relationship between them. Within this void he organized sculptural forms of exciting movement, which continually pierce the space in fascinating ways—as in "Roofed Structure with S Curve" (1954). This in time led to the Whitney "room" of 1961, in which the sculptor took as his spatial area the interior of a room, with the ceiling as the upper plane, the floor as a base, and the four walls limiting the space all around. Ferber's sculpture was woven about within the total space of this "room," so that when the spectator stepped into it, it was as if he were entering into the very depths, the spatial center, of the sculpture itself. But even then the four walls were too confining, and in 1962 the sculptor created a model for a kind of architectural sculpture, which he called "Environment." Intended to be three or more times the height of a man, this gigantic sculpture could be experienced not only from an exterior vantage point, but also from within the work itself; a person could walk under it, into it, and discover a multitude of spatial sensations heretofore unknown to him. Not only sculptural forms but also man himself could then penetrate the space imprisoned by the heroic sculpture—a great Abstract Expressionist giant. Whether this new conception of experiencing sculpture will become a reality in the parks and business plazas of the cities of this—or the next—century remains to be seen, but other sculptors, like Tony Smith, for example, have shown marked interest in its possibilities.

With his original and fertile imagination Ferber has become one of the leaders of the Abstract Expressionist movement in sculpture. One-man shows were held at the Betty Parsons Gallery in 1953 and at the Kootz Gallery in 1955 and 1957; in 1963 a large retrospective show of Ferber's work was held at the Whitney Museum of American Art and at the Emmerich Gallery in New York City. His work seems to be less inspired by the organic creatures of Roszak or the seed pods of Seymour Lipton than by a keen sensitivity to the endless potential of nonobjective form.

The work of Ibram Lassaw reflects a search for the cosmic order and harmony that dominate the philosophy of the artist himself. Lassaw's wiry mazes, golden-hued and delicately textured, set forth a doctrine that all things in the universe are interrelated, and he sees himself as a microscopic part of this continuum of life, matter, energy, and time. His airy constructions, like the universe and eternity, have no beginning, no end, and no great central climax—only a linear course through space, following geometric patterns that suggest order and harmony, with touches of color and textural variations that indicate life and activity. The eye may be arrested here and there momentarily, but then travels on endlessly, penetrating space, returning to the surface, moving up or down or horizontally, until it feels it has become a part of some great harmonic continuum. His art is therefore aimed at the expression of things more cosmic than Roszak, Lipton, or Ferber—a kind of celestial journey conducted by philosophy and physics and made tangible through the work of an alchemist-artist.

Ibram Lassaw (1913–   ) was born to European parents living in Alexandria, Egypt, who came to the United States in 1921 when their son was eight years old. He grew up in New York City and Brooklyn, and discovered the art of sculpture one Saturday when he wandered into a modeling class at the Brooklyn Museum. He was about fifteen when he became a member of the Clay Club, which met in a studio in a deserted building across from the Museum. This was his main source of instruction for the next four years, until he began attending the Beaux Arts Institute of Design, where he studied for a while with the conservative sculptor Edward McCartan. He was extremely encouraged one day in the early 1930's when someone bought a small wax nude figure for $15. But he did not sell another piece of his work for nearly two decades. Although he was surrounded by the conservatism of the academic tradition, he became aware of the developments of modern art in Europe through the periodical *Cahiers d'Art*, and he was especially fascinated with the work of Brancusi and the Constructivists. The modern movement stirred him as it did only a few American sculptors in those days. The radical abstract and nonobjective experiments were slow to be accepted even by artists in the United States, and Lassaw was one of the few who could foresee the potential.

In 1936 he was a co-founder of the American Abstract Artists group, organized mainly to provide some means of exhibition for the work of the avant-garde. The first show was held in 1937, and for the next fourteen years its annual exhibitions offered the best opportunity for Lassaw to present his work—which attracted very little attention all the while. Government-sponsored art projects helped keep him going during those years. His studio began to resemble more the shop of a metalsmith than the atelier of an artist. In 1935 he had purchased a forge, and following the example of Julio Gonzalez and David Smith, he began working directly in metal. He made shadow boxes, with brightly painted free-form shapes suspended in space by wires, and the concept of "colorformspace," as he called it, began to evolve. New plastic materials were used in Lassaw's experiments that sought to replace the traditional central mass with designs that pierced, enveloped, and altogether interwove space within the composition. As harbingers of things to come, there were even sculptures made of plaster-coated wire armatures, but this idea was not to coalesce into his mature style until after World War II. Typical of this period was his "Construction in Steel" of 1938, with suspended cut-out metal forms that are reminiscent of the art of Miró, Matisse, or Arp.

During and after the war, Lassaw worked a great deal in plastics, as in "Somewhere Window" of 1947, continuing to press further the interplay of space and form. Living and working in downtown Manhattan, in the very hub of avant-garde American art during those exciting postwar years, he was a founder of the Eighth Street Club, a gathering place for the rising young group soon to be known as the Abstract Expressionists. The moment of recognition for Lassaw finally came in 1951 when Sam Kootz saw his "Milky Way: a Polymorphic Space" (1950) in an exhibition at the Museum of Modern Art. Kootz was fascinated by the plastic-covered wire maze, with its intricacies of texture and its generally rectilinear movement in depth, and he arranged to give Lassaw his first one-man show at his gallery within a year. The sculptor's "golden webs" caught on, and ever since, Lassaw has been considered one of the leading sculptors of the postwar period.

"Galactic Cluster #1" (1958) is typical of the artist's work (Fig. 16.9) and represents his efforts to create a continuum of life, eternity, energy, and matter, plus a certain "acceptance of the universe." Geometric linear patterns rise to a height of nearly 3 feet. Although it may be called sculpture in line drawn in space, the texture and body of the line are of extreme importance; they constitute the mass of the sculpture and constantly delight the eye as it meanders through the space, which becomes inseparably interlocked with the piece. Sculpture such as this is built up from a wire armature, with pieces or sections added on with a welding torch or removed with cutting pliers. The sculptor bends and shapes the steel wire, and with bronze (which has a lower melting point than steel) and a fine-tipped torch he secures additional strength to the main frame. Lassaw soon found plastic unsuitable for the body and texture of his work and turned instead to metal. Drop by drop, molten bronze is added throughout the skeleton, and the piece hardens into a single inflexible unit. Next come the various metals that provide the desired texture and color; in his studio Lassaw has supplies of stainless steel, nickel, silver, chromium bronze, copper oxide, and so on. These, too, are added bit by bit as the "golden web" begins to reach its finished form. He also keeps a stock of chemicals that cause various reactions when poured upon the metal construction, providing different hues and intensities of surface coloration. Nitric acid, zinc chloride, lead acetate, potassium sulphide are among the many chemicals with which Lassaw creates the accents and color effects that add to the brilliance of his sculptures. Finally there may be some filing and burnishing for further refinement.

The "Milky Way: a Polymorphic Space" was the first piece Lassaw had sold since 1929, but from 1952 on, his work was in demand by private collectors and art museums, and for architectural decorations. In 1953 he created a piece to go on the wall of Philip Johnson's guest house at New Canaan, Connecticut; 9 feet long, 7 feet high, 3 feet deep, the "Clouds of Magellan" suggests some celestial system. The towering "Pillar of Fire" (1954) was designed for an exterior wall of Temple Beth El in Springfield, Massachusetts. Built in sections directly in metal, a copper and bronze coating was applied to the tongues of flame to achieve the desired color, which is as important to Lassaw as the right form. In his Manhattan studio (Sixth Avenue near 14th Street) he has continued to create such linear spatial mazes as "Procession" (1955–1956; Whitney Museum of American Art) and "Counterpoint Castle" (1957), and has shown his work annually at the major exhibitions. One-man shows were held at the Kootz Gallery in 1954 and in 1958. In the 1960's his sculpture took on more and more mass, moving away from the strictly linear design of the 1950's but still characterized by an interplay of space and volume.

In Lassaw's work Abstract Expressionism is not violent but dynamic. His sculptures are objects to contemplate at such times as the mind seeks to identify itself with cosmic purpose or one's place in the vastness of eternity and the universe—as in his "Kwannon" (1952) in the Museum of Modern Art. An interest in the teachings of Zen has influenced his work, and a profound personal interest in philosophy has given his work its direction.

The sculpture of Seymour Lipton is more earthbound and biomorphic than the work of Lassaw. Though Lipton's plastic ideas originate in his subconscious, the artist also admits to being inspired by organic life:

The bud, the core, the spring, the darkness of earth, the deep animal fountainhead of man's forces are what interest me most as the main genesis of artistic substance . . . . Thorns, bones . . . , sharp tensions, tusks, teeth and harsh forms develop and grow together in varying ways as new beings of sculptural existence evoking images and moods of the primordial insides of man—all towards a passionate intensity underlying the meaning of modern man.

[Quoted from *Magazine of Art*, vol. 40, Nov. 1947, p. 264]

His sculpture is a magnificent union of expressive form and equally expressive content, drawn from nature and his experiences and wrought in great metallic images. His art suggests the vitality, the fecundity, the violence, the irresistible drives; the lyrical and poetic, as well as the devastating, aspects of life. Bursting pods, blossoming flowers, shells, instruments of technology, the human psyche—all these elements and more may be fused together to express some aspect of life in general or 20th-century life in particular. This biomorphically dominated symbolism is revealed in bold, dynamic sculptural forms that command our contemplation by their very power, grandeur, and elegance.

Seymour Lipton (1903–   ) was born in New York City, and like Herbert Ferber, got his D.D.S. from Columbia University in 1927; and the young dentist gave no serious thought to becoming an artist. Then in 1932 he took up sculpture, learning on his own from the beginning. His first pieces, carved directly in wood and occasionally in stone, were characterized by an expressionistic distortion of the human figure. Although there were one-man shows of his sculpture in 1938 and 1943, it was not until after 1945—when he turned to working directly in metal—that he finally evolved his own personal means of expression.

Seymour Lipton's sculptures in the years just after the war were usually made of lead, as in "Dissonance" (1946). The human figure was still his main subject, but his themes were those of stirring emotions and anguish, and his forms were tortured and heavy. "Mortal Cage" (1947), a bronze figure floating as if in a trance, is another example from this period. Other titles are equally suggestive of the irresistible forces in nature and psychic experiences of man—for example, "Travail," "Moby Dick," or "Invocation"; in their forms are traces of the influence of Lipchitz and Moore. Lipton never went through a Constructivist period and seems always to have maintained a respect for mass and volume in his work, which was quite significant for the subsequent development of his style.

Lipton's new postwar work was exhibited at a one-man show held at the Betty Parsons Gallery in 1948. About 1950 he began to find more and more inspiration in the worlds of nature and of mental visions and experiences. In the process he freed himself from a reliance upon natural form, and consequently his images were not so much pictures of things as they were pictures of ideas. These ideas were concerned with the basic drives in man and nature—the urge to procreate, to defend, to kill, to complete the cycle of life from birth through growth to death and decay. Lipton's success with such subjects is found in his ability to put into powerful sculptural form a sensation of the pulsating quality of nature and life. A heroic sensuousness in Lipton's art strikes deep into man's subconscious with the realization of the glorious fertility of his own kind and the total organic world that surrounds him. Such a sculpture is "Sanctuary" (1953), an abstract organic form that suggests the lush fecundity of nature and her protective, nourishing ways during birth and infancy (Fig. 16.11); deep within the podlike shell is the sheltered creature. Whether it is some organism of the bountiful waters of the sea, or the newly formed blossom within some green plant, or the seed that patiently awaits fertilization, it is impossible to say and pointless to try to do so; it is the sculptor's concept of all such things.

To make his sculpture, Lipton starts with drawings that evolve into a small three-dimensional maquette, or model, made of metal; then he enlarges the maquette to whatever scale he thinks best. Pieces are cut to the proper shape from light-gauge sheet steel and welded together at the edges to make the basic form of the sculpture. The surfaces are then coated with either a golden bronze or nickel silver; the sculptor applies these finely textured, almost sensuous surfaces by holding a thin rod of the metal in one hand and his torch in the other, spreading the molten bronze or nickel over the entire surface until the coarser sheet steel is completely covered. If necessary, he hammers to reshape here and there. Large, relatively simple forms dominate, with virtually no linear or spiky motifs detracting from them.

The 1950's were prolific years for Seymour Lipton, as they were for most of the Abstract Expressionists, for the movement reached its full stride. The dynamic, impellent "Storm Bird" (Collection of Nelson Rockefeller) was done in 1953; the seven-branched "Menorah" for the Temple in Tulsa, Oklahoma, was created the following year. In 1956 he made the large statue for the Inland Steel Building in Chicago, plus the very powerful images of the "Avenger," the "Sea King" and the "Prophet." In contrast to the gentle, protective "Sanctuary," the "Avenger" is a harsh, sharp, almost brutal form, with great gaping jaws; it is violently animalistic, yet no specific animal is to be recognized. Likewise the "Sea King" represents no particular creature, yet its shell-like form and the manner in which it seems to propel itself through water suggest some awesome, powerful predator of the sea. Simplicity, boldness, and expressiveness in abstract design characterize these works. In 1958 Lipton was given a one-man show at the Biennale in Venice, a very high honor, and an indication of the international reputation of his work.

In 1960 Lipton was awarded a Guggenheim Fellowship and in 1961 a Ford Foundation Fellowship. During these years he explored more and more the world of the mind of man, although he continued to work with the organic forms of nature as well. His "Séance" (1961), for example, suggests the dreamy drifting of the mind amid the mysterious souls of the spirit world. The onrushing "Messenger" (1962), with its great rhinoceros horn, can only be a harbinger of evil, and the "Defender" (also 1962) is a great metallic being of titanic strength. Lipton's imagery is far from static; even dynamic seems too tame to describe the expectancy, the burst of energy, the explosion of tension, and the constant "becoming" of nature that are characteristic of his sculpture. His work achieved a great monumentality in such pieces as "Gateway" (1964), with its enormous seed in a 6-foot-high pod. "Archangel" (1963), commissioned for Philharmonic Hall in New York's Lincoln Center, is almost 9 feet high and suggests the sound of music in its large hornlike forms (Fig. 16.12). In such pieces as these Lipton has given the 20th century an art that is truly expressive of its own civilization. His work can be as contemporary as the skyward-bursting "Argonaut I" of 1962; it can depict fear and hate and violence, or love and poetry; or it can recall the cyclic events—of birth, growth, death, decay, and rebirth—of some enormous organism. A perfect unity of vital form and symbolic content, his works are always large and powerful, and the viewer is riveted in contemplation of the primary forces of life.

Reuben Nakian (1897–   ) is a latecomer to the Abstract Expressionist movement and represents a very personal branch of it. Not until the 1950's did Nakian enter the scene as a major American sculptor. Then past fifty, he had already gone through several rather conservative styles, and Abstract Expressionism had had a decade to develop into full bloom. Nakian, though not one of its creators, added to its breadth and richness.

The son of Armenian emigrants, Reuben Nakian grew up in or near New York City. While still in his teens he began doing odd jobs in an advertising agency and eventually graduated to commercial illustrating and lettering. After attending the Independent Art School he became in 1916 an apprentice in the busy studio of Paul Manship, where Gaston Lachaise was the first assistant. During the next four years he learned the fundamentals of the art and craft of sculpture, and from 1920 to 1923 he shared a studio with Lachaise. His work during the 1920's consisted mainly of animal sculptures, whose strongly stylized forms reveal Manship's influence. Nakian exhibited regularly at the major annual shows, and had his first one-man show at the Whitney Studio Club in 1926. At this time his work was modern in the sense that William Zorach's work was then modern—that is, a stylization of form often cut directly in stone, as in the "Calf" of 1929. By then he had met Edith Halpert, the redoubtable revolutionary art dealer who was assisting many of America's rising young artists through her now famous Downtown Gallery in

New York; during the early 1930's this remarkable woman helped Nakian along with several one-man shows of his work.

In 1931 Nakian was awarded a Guggenheim Fellowship. It allowed him to spend a year in Italy, where he was greatly impressed by ancient Roman portraiture and the romantic, erotic characters of classical mythology. Mythology was not to become a vital element in his art for many years, but on his return to the United States the impact of Roman portraiture was evident in his work. He had not gained much national recognition with his animal sculpture, but in the early 1930's a couple of series of portraits—one, a group of Nakian's artist friends; the other, Franklin D. Roosevelt and some of his Cabinet members and advisers— brought him a great deal of attention. The Museum of Modern Art owns Nakian's " 'Pop' Hart" from the earlier series and the "Harry L. Hopkins" from "The New Deal in Portraiture" series. The "Hopkins," though possessing the characteristic facial features, contains certain expressionistic elements, as the sculptor pushed his likeness beyond realism to serious caricature. A curious piece, which attracted widespread general interest, but which did nothing for his artistic career, was the heroic-scale plaster statue of baseball player Babe Ruth in the act of swinging his bat as he hit a home run. The statue, made in 1934 but later destroyed, was a stylized rendering of the figure, an attempt at the abstraction and simplification that was then the leading force in modern American sculpture.

About this time Nakian formed a close friendship with the painter Arshile Gorky, whose comments about Picasso and Surrealism caused Nakian to reappraise his own artistic theories. During the late 1930's and the early 1940's he did practically no sculpture; instead he concentrated on drawings, producing them in profusion. In this way he acquired the facility in draftsmanship that was to appear in his work in the 1950's.

In 1938 he began modeling a piece called "Europa and the Bull," which was completed in 1942 but subsequently destroyed; it marked the beginning of his preoccupation with this and other mythological themes. It was not until the postwar years, however, that he turned seriously to these subjects, and with a style that was fresh and original. The earlier conservative modernism was discarded, and an exciting flood of creativity began to pour forth. In 1948 he started a series of terra cottas based on the Europa theme. Beautifully sculpturesque and spontaneously modeled in the traditional material of ancient Greece, with more or less recognizable forms of Europa and the bull, they emerged from his kiln as fresh, lyrical interpretations of a mythical theme. Their imagery is intimately bound to numerous drawings that are calligraphic in their boldness and sureness. This theme and this type of work continued throughout the 1950's and into the 1960's. He also made a series of terra-cotta plaques, whose basic shapes were free form; into their smooth surfaces he incised—one might almost say slashed—images of languishing nude females, which, in their lustiness and voluptuousness, are true descendants of the classical tradition. But in the outburst of creative energy that created them and in their half-recognizable abstracted form they clearly belong to the Abstract Expressionist tradition of the 20th century.

A new monumentality of conception and size entered Nakian's work in 1954 with "La Chambre à Coucher de l'Empereur," a large (70 inches long), boldly modeled, nonobjective mass that trails majestically through space. It is quite typical that the romantic, poetic theme—so important to the artist—has evolved into nonrepresentational form. The same is true of other large pieces of this series, such as the "Olympia" in the Whitney Museum. In the "Voyage to Crete" (Fig. 16.13), the story of Europa and the bull again inspired Nakian, who modeled the large eight-foot-long sculpture in plaster during the years 1960–1962. Countless drawings on paper and in terra-cotta constituted a point of departure, but the result was a great, richly modeled mass, with only the vaguest suggestion—in the sensuous curve of Europa reclining on the back of the bull—of any recognizable form. The beauty of the work is in the powerful, bold sculptural form itself; the title merely adds an aura of exotic poetry.

This series continued in the mid-1960's with "The Birth of Venus," several versions of the "Judgment of Paris," a "Goddess of the Golden Thighs," and a piece called "Hiroshima." In these Nakian reached the height of his powers as a sculptor and made his finest, most poignant contribution to the Abstract Expressionist movement. Another large-scale series was constructed of steel plates that were welded at various angles to a maze of pipes. The "Rape of Lucrece," in the Museum of Modern Art, was the first of these (1955–1958); it was followed by the "Duchess of Alba" (1959), in the Los Angeles County Museum of Art, and "Mars and Venus," in the Egan Gallery. But this series was rather eclectic and lacks the originality of the modeled pieces.

Nakian's acceptance as a contemporary sculptor was accomplished in 1958 in a one-man show held at the Stewart-Marean Gallery in New York, his first large public display since the 1930's. "This exhibition establishes his full claim as a sculptor for the first time," wrote critic Hilton Kramer, who saw Nakian's work as adding luster but not depth to the Abstract Expressionist movement: "[Nakian] brings a kind of grandeur, an exalted level of discourse, to the current scene, but it comes as a brilliant adornment rather than a fundamental transformation of the period style" (*Arts*, Jan. 1959, p. 48). A large exhibition of Nakian's sculpture was held at the Museum of Modern Art in 1966, and the public received the full impact of his monumental bronze variations on a classical theme, his poetic drawings, and his terra cottas.

A second movement was to gain an important position in the history of modern American sculpture after World War II: Constructivism, whose origins found their crystallization in Russia in the years following the Revolution of 1917. Its first signs appeared as early as 1913 when Vladimir Tatlin made some compositions out of wood, glass, metal, and other materials. But under pressure from Communist authorities, he renounced his progressive new art in the early 1920's. It was actually Antoine Pevsner (1886–1962) and his brother Naum Gabo (1890–   ) who established Constructivism as a meaningful movement and gave it direction during the 1920's and 1930's. Pevsner had early decided upon a career in the arts, and in 1911, after attending the Moscow Academy of Fine Arts he went to Paris, where he observed and participated in the developments of the art world during those exciting years. Naum, the younger brother, was sent to Munich to study engineering, with courses that included mathematics, physics, and chemistry; he also learned to make three-dimensional models to prove theories and formulas. But Naum soon became more interested in the activities of the artists than in his courses in engineering. He met Kandinsky and saw the inception of the *Blaue Reiter* movement. And when he visited his older brother in Paris he met Archipenko and a host of other modern artists and heard their theories of art.

With the outbreak of war, both Antoine and Naum Pevsner went to neutral Oslo, Norway, where the latter changed his name to Gabo to distinguish himself from his brother. There the two worked together, Pevsner still a painter, Gabo a sculptor, in close fraternity, digesting and discussing the new artistic ideas they had recently discovered: there was the *Blaue Reiter* from Germany, Boccioni's Futurism, and Cubism from Paris, and from their native Russia came Malevich's Suprematism and the experiments of Tatlin. In Oslo in 1915, Naum Gabo made his first constructions: one was a "Bust" composed of intersecting planes of wood. Pevsner remained largely a Cubist painter for the time being. Then with the eruption of the Russian Revolution the brothers returned to Moscow to do their part for the cause of the fine arts.

For the first few years the modernists were in control of the arts, for the politicians were much too busy with other matters to pay much attention to such frills, and Lenin smiled condescendingly upon the strange art he could not understand. Pevsner was made a professor in the art school, along with Tatlin; Gabo opened his own studio not far away. The next three years were exciting and stimulating as the two brothers worked alongside each other and engaged in heated debates with Malevich, Tatlin, Rodchenko, and other gifted and creative artists in that chilly outpost of the *avant-garde*. As Gabo and Pevsner began to clarify their own theories they found Cubism unsystematic, even "anarchistic," and compromising with regard to naturalism; and they accused Tatlin of creating a kind of "machine romanticism" because of his monuments to the new machine age. They felt the greatest affinity with Futurism, but even its principles seemed to lead to too transitory an art. The result was the formation of their own movement, which some critic labeled Constructivism.

The doctrine of the art of Gabo and Pevsner was set forth in the *Realist Manifesto*, published in 1920 to accompany an exhibition of Gabo's sculptures and Pevsner's paintings, which was held in the band shell of a Moscow park. The fundamental tenets of the *Manifesto* were: the representation of the true reality of life must be based on time and space; volume and mass are not the only means of conceiving space; art must be dynamic as opposed to static; new forms and materials must be investigated for the expression of 20th-century concepts. In

Constructivist theory, the only reality is that of the basic elements of space and time, not a quasi-naturalistic world of appearances. Advocates of the theory would have agreed with Mondrian, who wrote that "to create pure reality plastically, it is necessary to reduce natural forms to the 'constant elements' of form and natural color to 'primary color.'" Science and technology had created the machine age, and contemporary physics was contributing to the formation of a new philosophy; Constructivism took all of this and attempted to reduce it to an artistic symbol or a means of expression. Nature was no longer to be the great inspiration of the artist; the greatest of all intangible elements known to man— space and time—were to form the basis of his knowledge of reality, and new materials and new forms were to be discovered for the expression of this reality. The concept of space was to be defined in plastics, metals, and cords, whereas time was to be suggested by the dynamic movement of form through space. Thus was the Constructivist theory established in 1920, and over the next twenty-five years it was to change very little.

The position the modernists in Russia had enjoyed in the post-Revolution years was soon challenged and overthrown. The old guard of academic realists had been lurking in the shadows during 1917 to 1920, but by the latter date had begun to find favor once more with a political party that wished to employ the services of the artist to present the doctrines of Communism to a people who were largely illiterate. The new art forms communicated nothing to the masses, and so they were rejected in favor of a "peoples' art" based on naturalism. This meant either a total compromise—which many such as Tatlin chose—or exile to a land where the artist was free to pursue his own aesthetic course without interference from the state.

In 1922 Gabo went to Berlin; he was joined by Pevsner, who left the following year for Paris, where he was to spend the rest of his life. This exodus from the birthplace of Constructivism occasioned the diffusion of its theory throughout Europe, to England, and eventually to the United States. In Paris, Antoine Pevsner turned to sculpture soon after his arrival in 1923. His art is characterized by abstract geometric compositions (in bronze, brass, copper, tin), which seem to trap space within their inner recesses or encircle it with finely wrought and polished rods and tubes of gleaming silver or nickel-plated metal. Gabo attended the Congress of Constructivism held in 1922 at Dusseldorf, where many of his concepts about aesthetics, materials, and the place of art in 20th-century life met with parallels in the teachings of Gropius' new Bauhaus school in Weimar and in the work and teachings of Moholy-Nagy. Likewise the Constructivist theory found an appreciation in Mondrian and van Doesburg. And in 1927 Americans became aware of the constructions of Gabo and Pevsner when they were well represented in the Machine Art Exhibition in New York City.

Naum Gabo remained in Berlin until 1932 when he moved to Paris for five years before settling in England in 1937. His style was established and well known by 1946 when he came to the United States, at the age of fifty-six. He can therefore hardly be counted as an American sculptor, but he was undoubtedly the greatest single influence on such artists as José de Rivera, Richard Lippold, and Roy Gussow, and on countless others as well. Gabo's transparent or translucent plastic and polished metal constructions, frequently geometrically laced with cord or wire in a tour de force of precision and changing patterns, created an impetus that was soon picked up by several American sculptors. The large "Gabo, Pevsner" exhibition held at the Museum of Modern Art in 1948 further stimulated an emerging abstract art in America into yet another direction of exploration.

The foremost extension of the Constructivist movement in the United States is the work of José de Rivera. But de Rivera's sculptures are dominated by theories he evolved on his own, as personal and individual creations—without capitulating to the "collective style" that Gabo saw as inevitable, and free of the negative conclusions of the Dutch neo-plasticists, Piet Mondrian and Theo van Doesburg. Moreover, unlike the mechanical constructions of his European counterparts, there is a warmth even in his metallic sculptures. Still, he would admit his debt to the Russian Constructivists and also to the Russian mathematician and physicist Hermann Minkowski, who was equally concerned with theories of time and space and their inseparableness. De Rivera's own theory is based on the belief that man has a natural inclination to create order and harmony; its most successful achievement is what he calls beauty. The artist seeks to achieve this elusive, almost indefinable quality. De Rivera's own search leads him into constructions of space, matter, time, and light, and into attempts to create perfect relationships among them. In the mature phase of his work they are gleaming, continuous linear trajectories that move through space in a perfect state of equilibrium, as if following some divinely ordained course. They are this, and are intended to be no more than this.

José de Rivera (1904–   ) was born in West Baton Rouge, Louisiana, the son of the chief engineer of a sugar mill. He grew up and attended public school in New Orleans, but whenever possible he would be at his father's side, working on some machine or learning the skills of the blacksmith. This training was to prove valuable to him later on when he turned to sculpture. In 1924, two years after graduating from high school, he left Louisiana to go to Chicago, where he worked for several years in foundries as a pipe fitter and in machine shops as a tool-and-die maker, always acquiring valuable experience with tools and metals.

De Rivera had not previously exhibited any special artistic talent, but in 1928 he began taking drawing lessons at night with John W. Norton, who soon recognized a gift that merited cultivation. (This was just the time in Europe when the Constructivists were challenging the age-old theories of static, solid form in sculpture.) De Rivera's drawings, of a quasi-Cubist style, had a strong sculptural quality to them, and Norton suggested he try something in three-dimensional design. José de Rivera made a cylindrical, rather mechanical, highly polished brass "Owl" (1930), which for a first effort possesses an exceptional feeling for the material and for sculptural form. His second attempt was a beautifully simplified figure (from waist to ankles) called "Form Synthesis in Monel Metal" (1930) that strongly suggests the influence of Brancusi in the sweeping curves of the abstracted form and in the glistening, reflecting surfaces. Clearly in these first works, de Rivera revealed a sensitivity for the beauty of polished metals and for abstract form. The third sculpture, also executed in 1930, was considered the most successful of all: the "Bust" was something of a cross between a Cubist sculpture and Brancusi's "Mlle Pogany." De Rivera was delighted when he was invited to exhibit the "Bust" in the American Painting and Sculpture show at the Art Institute in Chicago. Only his fellow Chicagoan John Storrs was executing anything so thoroughly modern in America at that time, though in a few years David Smith would begin his work in welded metal. By this time de Rivera had become interested in the fundamentalist theories of Mondrian and, of course, in the sleek metallic forms of Brancusi. In 1932 he took a trip through France, Italy, Spain, the eastern Mediterranean, and North Africa to see more of art both old and new, and by the time he returned he was determined to make sculpture his career.

His first major period came in the late 1930's. In 1938 he was commissioned, under the auspices of the Federal Arts Project of the WPA, to make a sculpture for Newark Airport. This piece, now in the Newark Museum, took the form of a highly stylized and simplified metallic bird, with straight wings spread high and wide in a V; it represents the embryonic form of many of the sculptor's nonobjective works of the 1950's and 1960's. Equally successful was a massive black granite free-form piece called "Life" (1938), an attempt at solid sculpture in stone. He evidently decided that this was not the type of sculpture he wanted to make, for he did not pursue it further, as if already accepting the Constructivist declaration that sculptural space need not be conceived in terms of static masses. It was also in 1938 that he made his first true construction, "Red and Black (Double Element)": two curving aluminum planes opposed to each other and attached at the center. This was much more to his liking, and after the war he would pursue this type of sculpture. That same year he was invited to send an example of his work to the annual Whitney exhibition of contemporary art, and he has since been represented in that show almost every year. His career was thus launched when he was about thirty-five years old, just as World War II came along. De Rivera served first with the Army in North Africa; then with the Navy, making scale models of ships.

De Rivera returned to art with a one-man show—his first in New York City—at the Mortimer Levitt Gallery in 1946. The remainder of the 1940's and the early 1950's were occupied with such compositions as "Yellow Black" (1946) and "Black and Red Construction" (1952), constructed of sheet metal cut in free forms and hammered into graceful curves. The surfaces were either polished to a high gloss, or painted in one of the primary colors or in black. Some of these pieces are similar to the work of Alexander Calder. There is a handsome lyrical quality to them that seems to invite the spectator to move around them, to observe the changing patterns of color, form, and space. His "Blue and Black" (1951) is in the Whitney Museum of American Art.

The work of José de Rivera in the 1950's and 1960's evolved into linear, tubular, polished metal compositions of the greatest elegance, such as "Construction 8" (1954) in the Museum of Modern Art, "Homage to the World of Minkowski" (1955) in the Metropolitan Museum of Art, and "Construction #93," of 1966 (Fig. 16.14), in the collection of Philip M. Stern. Such pieces, usually in stainless steel or aluminum, are demonstrations of the theory that sculpture may be wrought in terms of time and space as dynamic compositions, thereby rejecting the age old dictum that it must be composed of a static mass. Because of the high polish on these fluid metallic lines traveling through space and the way the surfaces catch and reflect light, their physical "matter" seems to be nearly eliminated. It presents a kind of mystical aesthetic experience of 20th-century physics and alchemy in which atoms and materialized energy, constantly re-creating itself, pursue a course through space and even time; it is this connotation that makes de Rivera's art so compatible with and expressive of the 20th century. His constructions are like a ray of light curving through and at the same time defining, space. Often his works are best appreciated when they are set in motion, rotating slowly before the observer. Movement through space becomes a tangible thing, as in time the tubular form moves fluidly, beautifully before the spectator's eyes. It does not occupy space so much as it describes it. The looping curve touches its base only slightly, almost denying the existence of gravity. The lyrical, sinuous, poetic line is determined not by any mathematical formula but by the sculptor's aesthetic sense. Only the materials and the techniques are products of the machine age; the form comes from the artist's feeling for order and harmony, presented in the simplest, most basic manner, without Romantic or Expressionist connotations.

De Rivera uses industrial materials and tools to create an art that is truly of the machine age, but he gives his form an elegance, a delicacy, and a grandeur that belong to the tradition of the ancient goldsmithery rather than to the crass work of the modern factory. His work has no iconography, and the sculptor himself has declared that his art represents nothing but itself—a beautiful linear form journeying continuously through time and space in a constant state of equilibrium.

De Rivera also created several works in collaboration with architects, such as the "Continuum" for William Lescaze's building at 711 Third Avenue, New York City, or the "Construction" for the Statler-Hilton Hotel in Dallas, both done in 1956. The latter is a large centrifugal, stainless-steel composition on a cadmium yellow base, with long arms that reach out in graceful curves toward infinity; its slow rotation (a complete cycle every six minutes) presents an ever-changing arrangement of line and space to the observer. For the Brussels World's Fair of

1958 he made one of his sophisticated, continuously curving tubular compositions, 48 inches in width. His exquisite stainless-steel continuum (1963) on its obelisk-like pedestal in front of the Smithsonian's Museum of History and Technology represents his art enlarged to a monumental scale. Recognition of de Rivera as one of the leading contemporary artists came with a series of exhibitions of his work. He was included in the "12 Americans" exhibition held at the Museum of Modern Art in 1956, had a one-man show at the Walker Art Center in Minneapolis in 1957, and was given a retrospective show at the Whitney Museum of American Art in 1961. José de Rivera's influence has been further spread by his several teaching appointments at leading art schools and universities.

Roy Gussow (1918–   ), native of New York City, went to the Institute of Design in Chicago for training in industrial design. After studying with Moholy-Nagy, he returned to New York where he worked under that great teacher of modern sculpture, Alexander Archipenko. Thereafter he became a teacher himself, and taught sculpture and elementary design at Bradley University and at the Colorado Springs Fine Arts Center; from 1951 to 1962 he was a member of the faculty of the School of Design at North Carolina State College in Raleigh.

In the years just after World War II, Gussow worked with free-form sculpture in terra cotta and red sandstone, such as the series called "Cycloid" and "Figure" of 1947. These were small nonrepresentational studies and concerned with the problem of arrangement of masses and hollows. More advanced and original, however, were his sculptures of the "Kinetic (capable of movement) Nutation" (nodding) series, which broke with the old concept of static form. Of one of these he noted: "Virtual volume created by movement of figure . . . . New forms based on speed—time and space. Volume implied, not actual." In 1947 he was also experimenting with open-form sculpture, as in the "Green Rhombus," a diamond-shaped metal sheet supported on three brass rods. By 1950 his sculpture was composed mainly of linear constructions as the "Kinetic Nutation" series continued; many of the pieces involved movement of some part through space. Although nonobjective solid designs were not altogether eliminated from his work in the 1950's, there was a concentration on constructions of rods, wires, and threads. These materials were merged with the space that flowed within their linear confinements, creating a dynamic unity in good Constructivist fashion. But he also thought of his wire forms in terms of "planar mass or massive plane, lines composed in space. Lines completely defining planes." This may be seen in the "Ambage" series (1951) of welded steel, and it was brought to a conclusion in the numerous pieces of the "Preperistalic" series (1951) in which virtual planes were created by increasing the number of wires or cords stretching between the structural frame. New experiences of form and space were constantly presented as the piece was rotated, or as the observer walked around the sculpture. The stainless steel "Metaphase" (1952) in the North Carolina Museum of Art, Raleigh, is a good example of this series.

By the start of the 1960's, Gussow's work was becoming known by being included in various exhibitions throughout the country. In 1962 he moved to the New York area and began teaching at the Pratt Institute in Brooklyn. He was represented by the Grace Borgenicht Gallery, which also handles the work of José de Rivera; Gussow and de Rivera became close friends. In 1964 the Borgenicht Gallery gave Gussow a one-man show; in 1967 the gallery held a two-man show of the sculpture of both Gussow and de Rivera. Gussow's interests in the 1960's returned to volume compositions, executed in highly polished chrome nickel steel, aluminum, or bronze. Exposure to the work of de Rivera may in part have been responsible for the brilliant delicacy, even poetry, that his work acquired in the jewel-like finish of the industrial metals. In 1961 he executed a 6-foot, free-form, stainless-steel sculpture for the garden outside the School of Design in Raleigh. Two years later he did a piece, commissioned by the architect, Max Abramovitz, for the rectangular pool beside the Phoenix Mutual Building in Hartford, Connecticut. The two exciting, space-piercing, interlocking shapes (one rising to a height of 8 feet) are deceptive because their actual volume is obscured by the light and reflections that play along their planes and angles. The dynamics of Constructivism are present in the elements of space, light, and glistening metallic surfaces, but a bold step has been taken to carry the Constructivist theory once more into sculptural mass.

Roy Gussow was headed in this direction years earlier when his linear sculptures became compositions in planes. It is in work such as this—or the series of "Three Columns" shown in the Borgenicht Gallery exhibition in 1967—that the sculptor reaches a mature form of expression.

The work of Richard Lippold (1915–   ) clearly belongs to the Constructivist style, but it occupies a place on the border between fine art and the highest level of design. Lippold, born in Milwaukee, was the son of an engineer. He studied at the Art Institute in Chicago and afterward worked as a designer of machinery for the dairy industry. In 1939 he established his own short-lived industrial design studio, but soon turned to teaching, first at the Layton School of Art in Milwaukee and then at the University of Michigan during the war years.

His first wire constructions came in 1942, a medium and form of expression he has pursued to the present time. Examples of this early work are "Gemini" (1947) at the Munson-Proctor-Williams Institute in Utica, New York, and "Variation No. 6" (1946), in brass, nichrome, and copper wire, in a private collection in New Haven, Connecticut. This type of construction continued into the 1960's with pieces such as the "Homage to Faberge" (1964) in the Virginia Museum of Fine Arts. A one-man show at the Willard Gallery in New York in 1947 brought Lippold to the attention of critics and collectors, but it was his "Variation No. 7: Full Moon" (1949–1950) that gave him international standing among contemporary sculptors (Fig. 16.15). This piece was shown at the Musée d'Art Moderne in Paris in 1950, as part of the exhibition of American art from 1900 to 1950. It was purchased by the Museum of Modern Art in New York and established the style for which the sculptor is best known. Its larger, more elaborate sequel, "Variation within a Sphere, No. 10: The Sun," was commissioned by the Metropolitan Museum of Art in 1953 and completed three years later. The former is 10 feet high and made of brass rods and nickel-chromium and stainless-steel wire; the latter, 22 feet wide and 5 feet deep, is composed of 22-karat-gold-filled wire, suspended by stainless-steel wires that are anchored to the walls, floor, and ceiling. Each is best seen in dark surroundings with specially arranged lights playing upon the metallic weblike constructions, as if reflecting the facets of some great wire jewel. There is, of course, no solid mass involved, and space is coexistent within the structure. The whole is suspended, with brilliant virtuosity, in a construction of dynamic tension.

Lippold's fine sense of design and his sensitivity to the potential in glistening metals, plus a structural geometry in his work that is in itself almost architectonic, have brought him commissions from (and through) several prominent architects to do decorations for their buildings. Walter Gropius was the first to recognize Lippold's special gifts when he asked him, along with Arp, Miró, Bayer, and Albers, to do a sculpture for the courtyard of the new Harvard Law Building; the spoked circles of "World Tree" was the result. In the 1953 London competition for the "Monument to the Unknown Political Prisoner," to which the world's finest sculptors submitted designs, Lippold's entry won third prize.

"Radiant I" for the Inland Steel Building in Chicago was completed in 1958, and two years later Lippold's decorative sculpture was installed in the Four Seasons restaurant in the Seagram Building, New York. Lippold worked on two very large commissions for New York in the early 1960's—the enormous explosion of glittering planes called "Orpheus and Apollo" in the spacious lobby of Philharmonic Hall in Lincoln Center, and the wire construction known as "Flight," which pierces the open space of one of the lobbies of the Pan-Am Building. Like the work of Harry Bertoia, that of Richard Lippold seems particularly compatible as decoration for 20th-century architecture. It is handsome, executed with exquisite craftsmanship, and possesses an appropriateness of scale and spatial qualities. But Lippold's work lacks any aesthetic philosophy of sufficient depth to challenge the viewer's intellect. It is attractive to the eye and indeed its creator seems content with a brilliant visual sensation.

Although the sculpture of Isamu Noguchi (1904–   ) belongs in a class by itself, his positive attitude toward space as sculpture, his belief that mass is not a necessary quality, and his tendency to "construct" in plastic design represent an affinity with Constructivism. But to assign his work to this or any other movement would be unjustifiable; his is an art forged from an Occidental-Oriental heritage into a 20th-century form of expression. His father was a Japanese poet who married an American girl of Scottish descent. Noguchi was born in Los Angeles, but at the age of two was taken to Japan, where he spent the next 11 years being educated in both Eastern and Western traditions. In 1917 he was sent to an experimental school, Interlaken, at Rolling Prairie, Indiana. He graduated from a nearby high school in 1922 and went to New York City, where the former director of Interlaken became a kind of foster father to him. Aware of Noguchi's inclination toward sculpture, his guardian arranged an apprenticeship for him in the studio of Gutzon Borglum. But within a year the boy was persuaded to begin premedical studies at Columbia. The call of sculpture was strong, however, and after a couple of years of college he returned to the serious pursuit of art.

The works Noguchi exhibited at annual exhibitions of the National Academy and the Pennsylvania Academy of the Fine Arts in 1926 and 1927 were competent if uninspired academic studies. The lack of vitality that he sensed in this academic art, plus a Guggenheim Fellowship in 1927 (renewed in 1928), led him to Paris, where he was introduced to the rich modeling of Rodin and, more important, to abstract art. He became the studio assistant to one of the most brilliant masters of modern sculpture, Constantin Brancusi, and from him learned the fundamentals of the beauty of pure form. As the potentials of new materials were revealed to him his work took a radical departure from the academic manner in such pieces as his nonrepresentational "Zinc Construction" of 1928.

In Paris, Antoine Pevsner had for some years been applying Constructivist principles to sculpture; moreover, in the eight years since his *Realist Manifesto*, the theories of Constructivism had spread throughout western Europe and by 1928 were challenging Cubism as the major doctrine of modern sculpture. Noguchi, of course, was aware of all this. He also got to know Giacometti and Alexander Calder, who was then creating his wire "Circus" figures and abstractions of animals. With Brancusi, Constructivism, and all the other influences, an exciting new world of form was opened to Noguchi; in time this would be fused with certain Oriental elements, which had always had a natural attraction for him.

When Noguchi returned to New York City, he did not plunge into experimentation with the new possibilities in sculptural form and space he had discovered in Paris; instead he turned to portraiture. A facile ability, a fine sense of modeling that found respectability as heir to the academic-Rodinesque tradition, and a "modern" form of characterization of his subjects led to almost instant acclaim and critical success. Portraits of George Gershwin and Anna Marie Merkel (both 1929) exhibited in New York and elsewhere brought Noguchi to the forefront of American portrait sculptors. Noguchi's comprehension of abstract form prevented his work from lapsing into the lifeless academic realism still being practiced in some quarters. Until about 1936 he supported himself very handsomely by his portraits. One of the finest examples of his work is the terra-cotta "Portrait of My Uncle" in the Museum of Modern Art, done in 1931 while Noguchi was on an extended visit to China and Japan.

This return journey of 1930–1931 to the Orient was his first since he had left Japan while still a boy. At Peking he studied Chinese calligraphy; after mastering its beautiful, expressive, nonobjective form he moved on to Japan. There he became fascinated with the forceful vitality of the prehistoric terra-cotta Haniwa figures. The influence of these may be seen in his "Erai Yacha Hoi!" (1931), also done in terra cotta. His master during this period was a notorious and expert forger of Japanese and Korean antiquities.

By the time he returned to America, Noguchi had acquired a mastery of the abstract and expressive elements of both East and West, and one might expect a fusion to appear in his sculpture. But again his work took an unexpected turn that seems unrelated to either influence. Though his portraiture continued with heads of the Mexican painter Orozco and of A. Conger Goodyear among others, he became increasingly preoccupied with a kind of social expressionism—an experience shared with many American artists during the years of the depression. His "Miss Expanding Universe" (1932) combines certain elements of Brancusi and ancient Japanese art, but it is also strong in social commentary. The twisted, anguished figure called "Death" is a powerful statement by the sculptor: In the shiny metallic surfaces of the 20th century he represented the naked, contorted, dangling body of a lynched Negro; its brutal realism and its sleek abstraction reveal the influence of both Rodin and Brancusi. This was strong imagery indeed, far from the placid beauty of his portraiture, and Noguchi began to lose favor among critics, patrons, and galleries. During the late 1930's he withdrew from the macrocosmic art world into his own little world to rethink and re-evaluate all that had happened in the brief decade since he decided to become a sculptor.

By the beginning of the 1940's Noguchi's commitment was made to nonrepresentational art. He began to construct sculptures out of driftwood, string, and other materials. It was an important step, for it entailed an investigation of spatial relationships, as well as a search for beauty and expressiveness in pure form. The last vestiges of naturalism and social realism were purged from his style, and the new style manifested itself in the hollow construction "Monument to Heroes" (1942), which resembles some totem or votary from an ancient Japanese shrine almost as much as it does a piece of modern, nonobjective sculpture. Significantly, its social comment is "stated symbolically instead of literally." Noguchi sharply resented the United States' treatment of the nisei, American-born Japanese, who after Pearl Harbor were placed in "relocation camps" for the duration of the war. In protest, he voluntarily entered for a brief time Camp No. 1 at Poston, Arizona. During the depressing period that followed his release he created the "Monument to Heroes" from fragments of bone, paper, and wood.

Beginning late in the war years, Noguchi made several stage designs for Martha Graham's modern dance presentations, such as "Herodiade," "Appalachian Spring," and "Dark Meadow." Inventive new forms began to appear on the stage as static but expressive counterparts to the movements of the dancers. It was in these that the form for the heroic "Kouros" (1945) in the Metropolitan Museum of Art had its inception. In it—a 20th-century hybrid inspired by the human dignity of an archaic Greek Apollo and the formal elegance of a Chinese calligraphic character—Noguchi finally attained that union of East and West, of nonobjective and prehistoric elements toward which he had been headed for so many years. A similar formal arrangement may be found in the "Humpty Dumpty" (Fig. 16.17) of 1946. Reaching a height of nearly 59 inches, with its parts carved from ribbon stone, it is a construction of free-form planes that pierce space at various angles while including space in the composition through perforations in the main piece. Noguchi's conception is fresh and original, a worthy descendant of the art of his former master Brancusi. Sophisticated simplicity, order, and harmony pervade the entire piece; those qualities that were beginning to form the basis of Noguchi's art. In a lecture delivered at the opening of an exhibition of modern sculpture at Yale University in 1949, he called "order" one of the main provinces of all great art: "I think of sculpture especially as the art of order—the harmonizer and humanizer of spaces. Order is the qualifier of space. It is the reality of matter, or a state of mind." (Quoted from *Art News*, March 1949, p. 55.) As a result of such sculptures as "Kouros" and "Humpty Dumpty," Noguchi returned to a position of prominence among modern sculptors.

During the 1950's, Noguchi's art experienced a continual enrichment, oscillating between nonobjective pieces stemming from Western traditions and Oriental-inspired abstractions. "Even the Centipede" (Fig. 16.16), for example, was the result of an extended visit to Japan in 1952. Composed of eleven separate pieces of *kasama*, a durable clay that has been used by Japanese sculptors and ceramists for centuries, the various components are attached to a vertical 14-foot wooden pole. Each section is a sculptured piece in itself, frequently enclosing space within its hollows; the total effect is of some ancient ritual totem while at the same time the head, legs, and tail of the centipede are also inventively suggested. Noguchi again struck a kinship here with the beautiful abstract form of prehistoric Japanese sculpture, but he nevertheless made it his own original creation in 20th-century forms.

During his 1952 visit to Japan, Noguchi created sculptures for the Peace Park Bridge in Hiroshima and a model for a memorial to those who perished in the atomic holocaust. His preoccupation with the idea of sculpture as an environment for civilized man is seen in the stone garden he designed for the UNESCO Building in Paris in 1958. Ideas that had their beginnings there were expanded in the early 1960's in the gardens incorporated into the design of two buildings by Skidmore, Owings and Merrill—the Beinecke Rare Book and Manuscript Library, at Yale University, and the Chase Manhattan Bank Plaza, in New York City. In discussing these projects he spoke of sculpturing space itself with whatever medium might be suitable, "be it trees, water, rocks, wire or broken-down automobiles." This philosophy represents a true extension of Constructivist principles into the reaches of everyday life.

In the 1960's, Noguchi's sculptures have taken on a form characterized by a severe simplification of nonrepresentational, quasi-geometric form; yet in all their austerity and abstraction they still possess a certain warmth—as in the stone "Square Bird-Bird E," or the handsome and elegant granite "Black Sun." Each springs from nature, or recalls some part of nature after its completion; but the form itself is contemplated purely for its sophisticated abstract beauty. They are sculptures of mass and volume, with highly polished surfaces and extremely simplified contours. In this, Noguchi carries on the work begun half a century earlier by Constantin Brancusi, and more than any other American sculptor he has a full comprehension of Brancusi's art. But with all the influences that have come to bear on Isamu Noguchi's sculpture, it remains his personal creation, capable of being diverted into some new and original form of expression.

Largely independent of the European Constructivists and their theories, Alexander Calder (1898–   ) developed his own highly original form of linear and planar compositions. His sculpture pierces or circumscribes space, and thereby creates space out of voids. Moreover, his work often includes movement through space, which by comparison makes even the sculpture of Boccioni seem static. And the materials he uses are those of the 20th century—wire and sheet metal, shaped to forms that possess a wit and expressiveness that equal the genius of Paul Klee or Joan Miró.

Alexander Calder was born in Philadelphia, the son and grandson of sculptors of renown. As a youth, however, he studied to be a mechanical engineer and graduated from Stevens Institute in 1919. He worked as an assistant engineer for the next several years, but during that period attended drawing classes, eventually turning to art as a career. His first professional efforts were line drawings, in the mid-1920's, for the *National Police Gazette*. His father's work, not yet freed from an academic style, had virtually no influence on him, and he went to New York where he studied at the Art Students League.

Although not really attracted to modern art Calder was attracted to Paris in 1926. Cubism and Constructivism were the two major movements then prevailing in modern sculpture, but he cared for neither. His work over the next several years took two forms: the serious wood carvings and the humorous little wire creations, which were done mainly as amusements for himself and his friends. It was the latter which in time evolved into one of the most original and significant sculptural styles of this century. His direct wood carvings, such as the "Horse," "Cow," and the acrobatic "Three Men High," are reminiscent of the simplification and abstraction of William Zorach, John Flannagan, Chaim Gross, and José de Creeft. He knew de Creeft in Paris and was undoubtedly influenced by him. But these carvings lack the *joie de vivre* that is found in his wire sculptures such as "Josephine Baker" (1926) or the "Hostess" (Fig. 16.18) of 1928. The former, the first of his line drawings in space, was meant to be hung by a thread so the figure would move in space; even Calder did not realize what this would lead to in a few short years. The sculptor's keen wit, so obvious in the 11½-inch "Hostess," was further revealed in his "Circus," a collection of wire figures and animals, many of which could perform when set in motion by their creator. Acrobats, activated by springs, leaped into action; an exotic dancer undulated about the set; a tightrope walker moved precariously through space, supported only by her taut wire; stretcher-bearers rushed in to fetch the lady target of the bungling knife thrower; and a man went around to clean up the droppings of the numerous circus animals. Calder would put on shows in his studio, sending his wonderful little performers through their paces to the utter delight of his audience. By 1930 his "Circus" had become one of the real successes of the art world of Montparnasse, as well as among the Paris intellectuals. Jean Cocteau, Fernand Léger,

Joan Miró, Piet Mondrian, Jean Arp, Jean Helion, Theo van Doesburg, and others were captivated by it, whereas none of them paid much attention to Calder's wood carvings. Such encouragement undoubtedly led him to try more serious experiments in wire sculptures. Although somewhat two-dimensional at first, the wire figures were soon to be extended in depth; in the meantime, he mastered the expressiveness of line traveling through space. Calder was barely aware of Gabo and Pevsner's Constructivism at this time and went about evolving the initial stages of his own line-space theory of sculpture. By Cubism he seems to have been totally unaffected.

Although Calder exhibited his work in America during these years, it was not especially well received, and consequently between 1926 and 1934 he chose to spend most of his time in Paris. In 1930 he went to Mondrian's white studio with its brilliant color-patch arrangements tacked up on the walls; it had a profound effect upon him, and for some time after that his work in sculpture gave way to the color experiments in painting that were his first adventures in nonrepresentational art. This was, of course, to have its impact upon the color of the mobiles that he began to create a couple of years later. Visiting Mondrian's studio was an experience in itself, like stepping inside a great piece of colorful sculpture with all objects carefully arranged within the space. Mondrian, however, did not think much of Calder's comment about how wonderful it would be if it could all be set in motion. Calder has always acknowledged his debt to Mondrian for the color theory that ever after was employed in Calder's sculpture. It was largely due to Mondrian that Calder made the step from representational to nonobjective art, but in time he found more in common with the more humanized abstractions of the Spaniard Joan Miró, who became his close friend.

At the exhibition of his work in 1931 at the Galerie Percier in Paris, little wooden balls and free-form metal shapes—Calder's first "stabiles"—revealed his new independence from representational art. The next year his first moving sculpture, the "mobiles," appeared. By then he had arrived at the fundamental principles of a Constructivist art that sliced through space with planes and circumscribed voids with wire. The basis for Calder's magnificent mobile and stabile art was thus laid in the early 1930's, and thereafter it would be a matter of variation, refinement, and essays toward monumentality within the idiom. He had successfully transformed his little wire caricatures and Mondrian's sophisticated color abstractions into his own highly personalized form of Constructivism, and the brilliant originality of his contribution to the expansion of modern sculpture was immediately recognized in Europe. In the United States recognition did not come until a decade and a half later—after World War II.

The years between the early 1930's and the end of the war were a period of experimentation, catharsis, and refinement of Calder's new style. In 1932 the idea of kinetic sculpture led him to explore motorization of his mobiles, so that they could be set in continual motion. Naum Gabo had attempted this as early as 1920 but had not pursued it; in time, Calder too decided that he did not like the precision and regularity—inherent in the motorization—with which the parts moved. This kind of abstraction was too mechanical, predictable, and dehumanized, and he rejected it in favor of constructions that were moved gently by currents of air. To achieve this natural movement through space, he continued to experiment with the delicate balance of weights and counterweights—composed of discs, balls, free-form shapes, and even found objects—hung at the extremities of flexible wire tendrils that stretched out in many directions at once. Usually the series of weights and balances were way off center, which facilitated their movement on the slightest impetus from air currents or the human hand. A pleasing state of equilibrium was always maintained, however, as an ever-changing composition of lines and shapes rotated through space. The found objects and pieces of free-form carved wood were eliminated as Calder worked closer and closer to the classic form of his sculpture. During the mid-1930's he gave most of his works the generic title "Mobile." This, however, was too impersonal and lacked the wit that was very much a part of the artist's personality. As the decade progressed, the Calder style moved toward its mature form, although still on a modest scale. Free-form shapes, reminiscent of the work of his friend Miró, danced their gentle ballet at the ends of long curving wires that swept them out into space. By 1939 the characteristic form of Calder's famous mobile had been established, as may be seen in the "Spider" (Fig. 16.20). The monumentality that would appear after the war was prefigured during these years in the standing stabiles such as "Whale" (1937; Museum of Modern Art) and "Black Beast" (1940; private collection); the main feature of these large sculptures was the broad extension of the free-form plane into space at various angles.

The Calders bought a farm in Roxbury, Connecticut, in 1934, though they frequently returned to France where they maintained a home. In addition to the evolution toward the archetype of his mobile, Alexander Calder was occupied in the late 1930's with designs for sculpture for the Spanish pavilion at the Paris International Exhibition of 1937, and with the models, which were never enlarged, for the New York World's Fair of 1939. A retrospective Calder show was held in 1938 at the Smith Art Gallery in Springfield, Massachusetts, as interest in his work began to grow in America. In 1942 a large exhibition of his sculpture was held at the Cincinnati Art Museum, then at the San Francisco Museum of Art; and there were shows at the Buchholz (1944) and the Kootz (1945) galleries in New York. But these were the war years; and although Calder continued to experiment, in a sense he and his fellow artists merely marked time. He made a temporary digression into modeling forms in plaster and casting them in bronze, but even here the basic concept of his sculpture remained the movement of linear form through space.

After the war a steady production of mobiles issued from Calder's studio, a prolific creation of exciting compositions of wire lines and exquisitely designed shapes, in black or the primary colors, floating as they moved into ever-changing spatial arrangements. Examples of this flowering of the Calder mobile are found in "Black Mobile with Hole" (1954), "Sumac" (1961), and "Roxbury Red" (1963).

These, like scores of others, are in private collections; Calder's works are extremely popular.

Since 1946 the artist has attempted to transpose his mobiles and stabiles into a monumental art. This must have been quite a challenge to him at first, for the successful result was by no means assured. But succeed he did, through a series of mobiles and stabiles commissioned for various architectural projects or urban plazas.

Before the 1950's there had not been many large commissions, mainly because there were so few architectural interiors that offered compatible settings for Calder's mobiles. Nor were there many plazas connected with large building programs that could have held his stabiles. But the new architecture that appeared after World War II was particularly accommodating, and Calder's sculpture has often proved especially suited to it. Opportunities presented themselves with increasing frequency for the projection of his style to monumental proportions. In 1952 he designed an acoustic ceiling composed of enormous brightly colored, free-form planes, for the auditorium at University City in Caracas, Venezuela. But of greater importance was his large mobile fountain for Eero Saarinen's General Motors Building in Detroit (1954) and, in 1957, the red and black "Mobile," 45 feet in diameter, for Kennedy Airport in New York.

A further indication of his international reputation was the purchase of "The Spiral" (1958), a standing mobile 30 feet high, to grace the city of Paris; and in 1962 his large and colorful motorized "Four Elements" was erected in the plaza outside the Moderna Museet in Stockholm. In 1963 he created a mobile for the interior of the Connecticut Bank and Trust in Hartford, followed the next year by one of his most joyous pieces, "Hello Girls!" for the Los Angeles County Art Museum; the latter is a standing mobile placed in a fountain, with jets of water set so that they strike the mobile and thus keep it in motion. The delightful "Ghost" that hangs in the great open central well of Frank Lloyd Wright's Guggenheim Museum was done in 1964, enlivening the void but destroying neither the spatial harmonies of the interior nor the view of the galleries on the opposite side.

The works mentioned above are for the most part enlargements, with careful attention to scale, of the sort of hanging or standing mobiles that Calder developed in the 1930's. Another form that emerged in the postwar period was the monumental black stabile. It culminates in such pieces as the "Black Widow" (1959) and in the gigantic "Teodelapio" (1962) for the city of Spoleto, Italy (Fig. 16.19); the model is in the Museum of Modern Art. The final, enlarged version, designed as a city gate, is more than 58 feet high, with plenty of space for traffic to move beneath what appears to be the belly of some great fantastic black monster that rears its head toward the heavens. Like so many of Calder's works, its adaptation to its setting is remarkable. There is no question about enlarging Calder's earlier mobile and stabile style to monumental scale, for the "Teodelapio," completed when the sculptor was sixty-four, is one of the largest and most successful examples of contemporary sculpture. It is the colossal example of Constructivist sculpture—not of the cold, impersonal European type, but having the warm animation and association with nature that Calder brought to most of his work.

There is also the Calder humor and wit, present since the early days of the "Circus," which is found in the splendid little "Rat" of 1952, and in many of the monumental black stabiles. It is a testimony to the sculptor's creative genius that within the framework of an idiom that might place limitations upon the variety of form and expression, Calder has achieved a breadth in his work in general and a marked individuality among many specific pieces. He is unquestionably one of the most original and gifted men in the entire history of American sculpture and belongs among the first rank of those international artists who have created an exciting new art for our time.

American sculpture in the 1960's has assumed diverse forms and materials as the spectrum of contemporary sculpture continues to broaden and take on increasingly subtle shades of expression. Cubism and Constructivism formed the basis of most modern sculpture up to the 1960's. But new movements are now stirring, and a great many artists are vigorously pioneering still newer forms for expressing themselves in particular and 20th-century society in general. At present their experimentation involves such variation of form and material that they frequently defy categorization.

One group, led by George Rickey (1907–   ), is extending the art of Alexander Calder into new conceptions of sculpture as form in motion. Rickey's "Dancing Waters," in the North Carolina Museum of Art at Raleigh, retains a clear affinity with nature, but another aspect of his work is virtually independent of nature; for example, in the "Three Lines" at the De Cordova Museum in Lincoln, Massachusetts, three pointed lances reach high toward the sky in a changing composition of rectilinear and geometric simplicity and grace. There is motion, but the forms are no longer those of Calder. Rickey rightfully considers himself an heir of the Constructivist movement, which had its beginnings when he was in his teens.

Harry Bertoia (b. San Lorenzo, Italy, 1915) often reflects an inspiration from nature in his work, as in the "Tree" or the "Landscape" (both in the North Carolina Museum of Art, Raleigh). In the latter piece there is a suggestion of toadstools and blooming things and trees, of things often experienced during a walk in the woods. Abe Satoru (b. 1926) also achieves a fine synthesis of nature and abstract form, as in his "Trees" in the Virginia Museum of Fine Arts in Richmond. But Bertoia is perhaps best known for the large gilded screens he creates for architectural interiors; one, for a New York bank, is 70 feet long. Such work clearly belongs to the Constructivist movement, but turned to the use of the interior decorator. Successful though they may be as decorative dividers of architectural space, they are sometimes guilty of a certain monotony, for they lack the expressive quality of Bertoia's "Tree" or "Landscape." His massive

Baroque fountain sculpture (1967) for the Philadelphia Civic Center is a handsome form, in every way sculpturesque.

Louise Nevelson (b. Kiev, Russia, 1900) has developed a very personal style of constructing nonobjective compositions in high relief out of scraps of wood and other materials, which are then painted a uniform color, often a medium to dark gray. Her compositions are built up from a "back wall," and in their variety of forms and inventive arrangements they offer an attractive spectacle to the eye. But she breaks with the Constructivist doctrine in that the forms do not pierce and enclose space so much as they form a wall along it. She is one of the few sculptors who has made a living art of relief sculpture in the 20th century.

Mary Callery (b. New York, 1903) has developed a kind of stick-figure style, with her figures often arranged along a single plane in the manner of David Smith's work of the early 1950's. Sometimes, however, as in "The Seven" (1956), her simple little figures enclose a void and penetrate space in good Constructivist fashion, but in such cases it seems to be stretching the usual definition of Constructivism to include her work under that label. Hence it is obvious that the major trends of the first half of the century begin in the second half to break down into variant forms that are seeking greater breadth and depth and are evolving new interpretations of old ideas.

David Hare (b. New York, 1917) turned to sculpture in 1944 after first going into color photography. Although he had an early flirtation with Surrealism, as Abstract Expressionism evolved in the postwar years he was drawn increasingly into its orbit. And as he worked continually toward greater abstraction, his sculpture became less dependent upon the Surrealistic symbol. He is often attracted to animal subjects, which he abstracts into images of subtle wit and good form.

Leonard Baskin (b. New Brunswick, New Jersey, 1922), who has gained a reputation as a fine graphic artist, also does sculptures—frequently of birds or of fantastic creatures that are both bird and man. Baskin's technique in modeling and carving follows conservative lines, whereas his style is both decorative and expressionistic. Baskin, long a teacher at Smith College, has a very personal style that ranges in imagery from humor to terror.

Dmitri Hadzi (b. 1921) reveals the influence of Jacques Lipchitz in the rich modeling and sculptural form of his "K.458, The Hunt." This piece decorates the lobby of Philharmonic Hall in New York's Lincoln Center.

Among the younger generation, George Segal (b. 1924) has continued to work with the figure, creating ghost-white imitations of mankind in highly expressive sculpture. There is often a feeling of intense loneliness surrounding his images, and he frequently incorporates actual architectural parts, such as windows or doorways, into the composition—as in "Girl in Doorway" at the Whitney Museum (Fig. 16.24). People sunbathing on a rooftop, truck drivers at work, an old woman watching the world go by from her rocking chair by the window—all these have been rendered in extremely somber images. The personality of the individual is eliminated as Segal's figures become symbols of 20th-century man caught in the social and psychological web of his own making.

There is also a movement in progress that seems determined to show United States civilization in its most mundane form; hence the paintings of soup cans and trading stamps and movie stars, and the sculptures by Claes Oldenburg of vinyl "French Fries and Catsup," the polychromed "Hamburger," the "Soft Type-writer," "Vacuum Sweeper," or "Tube of Toothpaste." While these may not be the highest achievements of technology, medical science, or social reform accomplished in America in the 1960's, they are all very much a part of contemporary life. Although they may cause us to consider whether a concentration on material wealth and mediocre taste should not be challenged, it remains to be seen if they are merely images of social commentary or an enduring art that will mean as much to future generations as it does today. Because it takes its subjects from the world of the masses, or from items popular among the broadest base of the population, such pieces have been labeled Pop Art.

One of the most gifted sculptors to come to the fore in the 1960's is Marisol Escobar. Except for about a half-dozen years in Caracas, her home has been in the United States, and her studio is now in New York City. She came to the attention of the art world in 1962 with an exhibition at the Stable Gallery, where her group called "The Kennedys" was especially popular. Her basic material is wood, usually left in large blocks, with only slight alterations to suggest a figure. From there, it is a matter of assemblage, or the application of objects—found or purchased—which creates a strange kind of reality in her images: Real shoes may be placed on the feet of her mannequins; an actual baby carriage may be set before a figure of a woman, as if it is being pushed by her; real or painted clothing is applied to the figure; and the likeness of the face may be drawn on the block, or it may be a photograph, or perhaps even a plaster mask of Marisol's own face. Her "Women and Dog" (1964) in the Whitney Museum of American Art (Fig. 16.21) is a fine example of her work in which she reflects so much of American society; in a subtle way she praises the material successes of middle-class America, but also depicts its tendency toward stereotyped living and personalities. She has an astute insight into contemporary life and incorporates actual everyday objects into her sculpture to achieve satirical images of wit, poignancy, and expressiveness. In her equestrian statue "John Wayne," for example, she captures everything that Western novels, Hollywood, and television have made of the legendary American cowboy, and she challenges Americans to consider whether this is the best they have to offer as their answer to Beowulf or El Cid. Marisol Escobar has created a rich, colorful, decorative, and expressive style that with penetrating accuracy achieves a sense of reality through the observer's identification with the many applied objects which he or she may own or wear or come into daily contact with.

The found object has been employed in works of art since the early Cubists worked sections of newspapers or other everyday artifacts into their paintings or assemblages; these were usually employed because of their contributions to the formal arrangement or composition. But of late, the found object has been used for its expressive and symbolic value, and often entire sculptures are made up of these discarded remnants of 20th-century civilization. Instead of searching for fine chunks of wood or blocks of marble, some sculptors today scour the rubbish heap and the city dump, the automobile junk yard and the sheds of wrecking companies for the materials of their art. Such is the case with Richard Stankiewicz (b. 1922), whose "Instruction" of 1957 is in the collection of the Museum of Modern Art (Fig. 16.22). Its form is sculptural, and it is deceivingly monumental for its 12-inch height. It is also quite expressive of several aspects of the 20th century, for the very parts from which it is wrought are actual products of our time.

Jason Seley (b. Newark, New Jersey, 1919) and John Chamberlain (b. Rochester, Indiana, 1927) are likewise currently working with the metallic discards of contemporary society, sometimes merely turning them into formal arrangements, but often endowing them with undercurrents expressive of planned obsolescence, the transitory nature of shiny chrome-plated goods, the ultimate wreck of a conscienceless materialistic civilization, and so on.

David Jacobs incorporated wit and satire into his "junk sculpture" piece entitled "If you wish to Dance you must pay the Fiddler, I'm just here to Blow my Horn" (Fig. 16.23). Out of a spring, an automobile horn, and odd bits of scrap iron and steel, Jacobs has created a funny little man—two legs, a torso, and a hand raised as if playing the horn, which seems to come out of the circular head. It is a jovial figure—brash, noisy, bouncy, and exuberant in the spring of the torso; without becoming encumbered with literal details of the human figure, the sculptor expresses the essential personality of a Damon Runyon character at whose tinny audacity we must smile good-naturedly.

There are other movements now evolving from the efforts of countless other contemporary American sculptors, who are gifted artists and who will carry sculpture into exciting new directions. They participate in a great renaissance of the art of sculpture that flowered in the years following World War II. For 2500 years the Western world has known only two distinct major styles—the Graeco-Roman and the Gothic; all the others have been eclectic derivatives of one or the other. Now we have a third, which at present is known only as the modern, or contemporary, style, with numerous subdivisions such as Cubism, Abstract Expressionism, Constructivism, and so on. But whatever it is finally called, it is a new art that points boldly to the future, an art that uses modern tools, technology, and materials to express in plastic form the emotions and sense of beauty of modern man.

[FIG. 16.2] "Figure," by Jacques Lipchitz (1926–30). Bronze, 85" high. Collection, Museum of Modern Art, New York, Van Gogh Purchase Fund.

[FIG. 16.1] "Mother and Child II," by Jacques Lipchitz (1941–45). Bronze, 50" high. Collection, Museum of Modern Art, New York, Mrs. Simon Guggenheim Fund.

[FIG. 16.3] "Sacrifice II," by Jacques Lipchitz (1948–52). Bronze, 49″ high. Collection, Whitney Museum of American Art, New York.

[FIG. 16.4] "Hudson River Landscape," by David Smith (1951). Steel, 75″ long. Collection, Whitney Museum of American Art, New York.

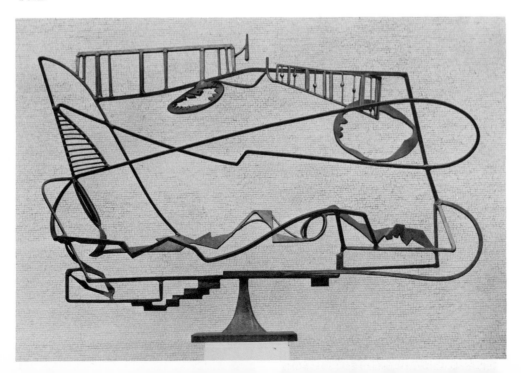

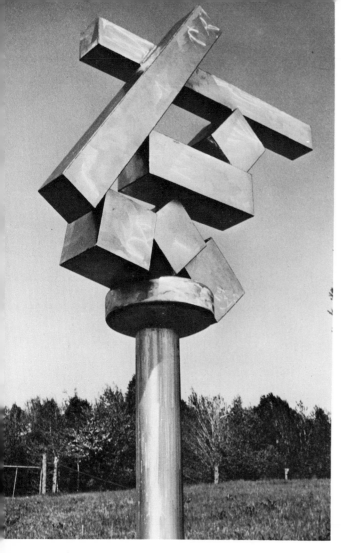

[FIG. 16.5] "Cubi XVIII," by David Smith (1964). Stainless steel, 108″ high. Courtesy, Dallas Museum of the Fine Arts; photo, Marlborough-Gerson Gallery, New York.

[FIG. 16.6] "Menand III," by David Smith (1963). Stainless steel, 25½″ high. Collection, Mrs. Raymond Goetz, Lawrence, Kans.; photo, courtesy, Marlborough-Gerson Gallery, New York.

[FIG. 16.7] "Spectre of Kitty Hawk," by Theodore Roszak (1946–47). Welded and hammered steel brazed with bronze and brass, 40¼" high. Collection, Museum of Modern Art, New York.

[FIG. 16.8] "Nantucket Whaler," by Theodore Roszak (1952–53). Steel. Courtesy, Art Institute of Chicago.

[FIG. 16.9] "Galactic Cluster #1," by Ibram Lassaw (1958). Bronze, nickel, and silver, 33" high. Courtesy, Newark Museum, Newark, N.J.

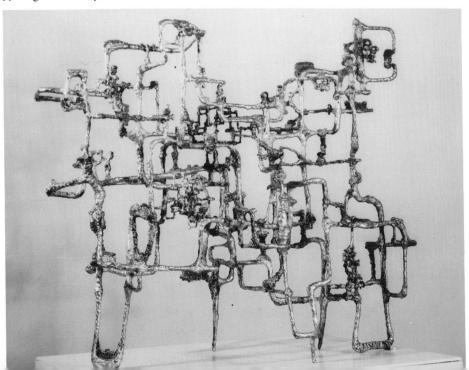

[FIG. 16.11] "Sanctuary," by Seymour Lipton (1953). Nickel silver over steel, 29¼″ high. Collection, Museum of Modern Art, New York, Blanchette Rockefeller Fund.

[FIG. 16.10] "Flame," by Herbert Ferber (1949). Brass and lead, 65½″ high. Collection, Whitney Museum of American Art, New York.

[FIG. 16.12] "Archangel," by Seymour Lipton (1963). Bronze on monel metal. Philharmonic Hall, Lincoln Center for the Performing Arts, Inc., New York.

[FIG. 16.13] "Voyage to Crete," by Reuben Nakian (1960–62; cast in bronze, 1963). 96″ long. New York State Theater, Lincoln Center, New York. Courtesy, Lincoln Center for the Performing Arts, Inc.; photo, Bob Serating.

[FIG. 16.14] "Construction #93," by José de Rivera (1966). Collection, Philip M. Stern; photo, Grace Borgenicht Gallery, New York.

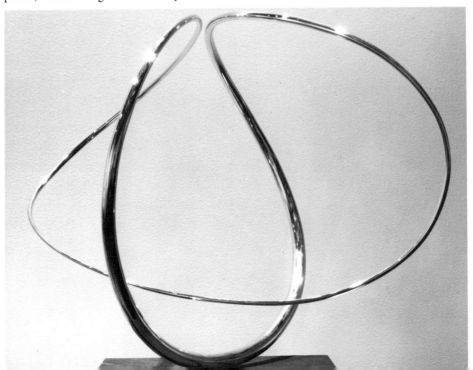

[FIG. 16.15] "Variation Number 7: Full Moon," by Richard Lippold (1949–50). Brass rods, nickel-chromium and stainless steel wire, 10' high. Collection, Museum of Modern Art, New York, Mrs. Simon Guggenheim Fund.

[FIG. 16.16] "Even the Centipede," by Isamu Noguchi (1952). Kasama Ware, each piece 18″ long. Collection, Museum of Modern Art, New York, A. Conger Goodyear Fund.

[FIG. 16.17] "Humpty Dumpty," by Isamu Noguchi (1946). Slate, 59″ high. Collection, Whitney Museum of American Art, New York.

[FIG. 16.18] "The Hostess," by Alexander Calder (1928). Wire, 11½″ high. Collection, Museum of Modern Art, New York, gift of Edward M. M. Warburg.

[FIG. 16.19] Model for the "Teodelapio," Spoleto, Italy, by Alexander Calder (1962). Painted sheet aluminum. Collection, Museum of Modern Art, New York, gift of the artist.

[FIG. 16.20] "Spider," by Alexander Calder (1939). Collection, Museum of Modern Art, New York, gift of the artist.

[FIG. 16.21] "Women and Dog," by Marisol Escobar (1964). Wood and various media, 72″ high. Collection, Whitney Museum of American Art, New York, gift of Friends of the W.M.A.A.

[FIG. 16.22] "Instruction," by Richard Stankiewicz (1957). Welded iron and steel, 12½″ high. Collection, Museum of Modern Art, New York, Phillip C. Johnson Fund.

[FIG. 16.23] "If you wish to Dance you must pay the Fiddler, I'm just here to blow my Horn," by David T. Jacobs (c. 1960). Steel and iron. Courtesy, Virginia Museum of Fine Arts, Richmond.

[FIG. 16.24] "Girl in Doorway," by George Segal (1965). Plaster, wood, glass, and aluminum paint, 113" high. Collection, Whitney Museum of American Art, New York.

Selected Bibliography

The Bibliography is divided into five general categories, plus a sixth category that is devoted to individual sculptors. There are numerous additional references within the text. An asterisk beside an entry indicates an extensive bibliography is contained therein on the subject or individual artist.

I. Surveys and General Sources

Compilation of Works of Art and Other Objects in the United States Capitol. Washington, D.C.: U.S. Government Printing Office, 1965.

FAIRMAN, CHARLES E., *Art and Artists of the Capitol of the United States of America*, Washington, D.C.: U.S. Government Printing Office, 1927.

*GARDNER, ALBERT T. E., *American Sculpture, A Catalogue of the Collection of the Metropolitan Museum of Art*, Greenwich, Conn.: New York Graphic Society, 1965.

GUNNIS, RUPERT, *Dictionary of British Sculptors*, Cambridge, Mass.: Harvard University Press, 1954.

*GROCE, GEORGE C., and WALLACE, DAVID, *Dictionary of Artists in America, 1564–1860*, New Haven, Conn.: Yale University Press, 1957.

*LARKIN, OLIVER, *Art and Life in America*, New York: Rinehart, 1949.

POST, CHANDLER, *A History of European and American Sculpture from the Early Christian Period to the Present Day*, 2 vols., Cambridge, Mass.: Harvard University Press, 1921.

QUINBY, FLORENCE COLE, *The Equestrian Monuments of the World*, New York, 1913.

SWAN, MABEL, *The Athenaeum Gallery, 1827–1873*, Boston: Merrymount Press, 1940.

*TAFT, LORADO, *The History of American Sculpture*, New York: The Macmillan Company, 1903.

II. Seventeenth Century to Early Nineteenth Century

BOLTON, ETHEL, *American Wax Portraits*, Boston and New York: Houghton Mifflin Company, 1929.

BREWINGTON, MARION, *Shipcarvers of North America*, South Saint Barre, Mass.: Barre Publishing Company, 1962.

CHRISTENSEN, EDWIN, *Early American Wood Carving*, Cleveland and New York: World Publishing Company, 1952.

———, *The Index of American Design*, New York: The Macmillan Company, 1950.

DUNLAP, WILLIAM, *History of the Rise and Progress of the Arts of Design in the United States*, New York: G. P. Scott and Company, 1834.

FORBES, HARRIETTE, *Gravestones of Early New England, and the Men Who Made Them*, Boston: Houghton Mifflin Company, 1927.

* LUDWIG, ALLAN I., *Graven Images*, Middletown, Conn.: Wesleyan University Press, 1966.

PENDERGAST, A. W., and PORTER, W. P., *Cigar Store Figures in American Folk Art*, Chicago: Lightner Publishing Company, 1953.

PINCKNEY, PAULINE, *American Figureheads and Their Carvers*, New York: W. W. Norton & Company, 1940.

REILLY, DAVID, *Portrait Waxes*, London: Batsford, 1953.

STACKPOLE, EDOUARD, *Figureheads and Ship Carvings at Mystic Seaport*, Mystic, Conn.: Marine Historical Association, 1964.

SWAN, MABEL, "Boston Carvers and Joiners," *Antiques Magazine*, LIII (1948), March, pp. 198–201; April, pp. 281–85.

III. MID-NINETEENTH CENTURY (1825–1875)

BELL, MILLICENT, *Hawthorne's View of the Artist*, Albany, N.Y.: State University of New York Press, 1962.

BENJAMIN, SAMUEL, "Sculpture in America," *Harper's Magazine*, LVIII (1879), 657–71.

CIST, CHARLES, *Cincinnati in 1841*, Cincinnati, Ohio: 1841.

CLARK, WILLIAM J., *Great American Sculptures*, Philadelphia: Gebbie & Barrie Company, 1878.

CLEMENT, CLARA, and HUTTON, LAURENCE, *Artists of the Nineteenth Century and Their Work*, Boston: Houghton Mifflin Company, 1889.

* GARDNER, ALBERT T. E., *Yankee Stonecutters: The First American School of Sculpture, 1800–1850*, New York: Columbia University Press, 1944.

GERDTS, WILLIAM, *A Survey of American Sculpture*, Exhibition Catalogue, Newark, N.J.: The [Newark] Museum, 1962.

———, "Sculpture by 19th Century American Artists in the Collection of the Newark Museum," *The Museum*, n.s. vol. 14, no. 4 (1962), 1–25.

HAWTHORNE, NATHANIEL, *Passages from the French and Italian Notebooks*, 2 vols., Boston: Houghton Mifflin Company, 1899.

HILLARD, GEORGE, *Six Months in Italy*, 2 vols., Boston: Ticknor, Reed and Fields, 1853.

LEE, HANNAH, *Familiar Sketches of Sculpture and Sculptors*, 2 vols., Boston: Crosby, Nichols and Company, 1854.

OSGOOD, SAMUEL, "American Artists in Italy," *Harper's Magazine*, XLI (1870), 420–25.

THORP, MARGARET, *The Literary Sculptors*, Durham, N.C.: Duke University Press, 1965.

TUCKERMAN, HENRY, *Book of the Artists*, New York: G. P. Putnam & Son, 1867.

IV. LATE NINETEENTH AND EARLY TWENTIETH CENTURIES

ADAMS, ADELINE, *The Spirit of American Sculpture*, New York: The Gilliss Press, 1923.

CAFFIN, CHARLES, *American Masters of Sculpture*, New York: Doubleday, Page & Company, 1903.

* MC SPADDEN, JOSEPH, *Famous Sculptors of America*, New York: Dodd, Mead & Company, 1924.

* PROSKE, BEATRICE, *Brookgreen Gardens, Sculpture*, Brookgreen Gardens, South Carolina, 1943.

SMALL, HERBERT, *Handbook of the New Library of Congress*, Boston: Curtis and Cameron, 1897.

TAFT, LORADO, *Modern Tendencies in Sculpture*, Chicago: The University of Chicago Press, 1921.

Expositions

ARNOLD, C. D., *The Pan-American Exposition Illustrated*, Buffalo, N.Y., 1901.

BARRY, JOHN, *The City of Domes*, San Francisco, 1915.

GRAY, DAVID, *Art Handbook: Official Handbook of Architecture and Sculpture and Art Catalogue of the Pan-American Exposition*, Buffalo, N.Y., 1901.

Columbian Exposition Album, Chicago, 1893,

Official Catalogue, Part II; Art Gallery, Annexes, and Outdoor Works of Art, Philadelphia, 1876.

Official Catalogue of Exhibitions . . . Department B, Art, Halsey C. Ives, Chief; St. Louis, Mo., 1904.

Official Guide to the World's Columbian Exposition, Chicago, 1893.

Official Illustrated Catalogue, Fine Arts Exhibit; United States of America, Paris Exposition of 1900, Boston, 1900.

Sculpture at the Exposition, San Francisco, 1914.

V. MODERN AMERICAN SCULPTURE

* *Index of Twentieth Century Artists*, published by the College Art Association, New York, 1933–1937.

BRUMMÉ, C. LUDWIG, ed., *Contemporary American Sculpture*, New York: Crown Publishers, Inc., 1948.

* GIEDION-WELCKER, CAROLA, *Contemporary Sculpture, An Evolution in Volume and Space*, New York: Wittenborn and Company, 1955.

GREENBERG, CLEMENT, "The New Sculpture," *Partisan Review*, 16 (June 1949), 637–42.

* HUNTER, SAM, *Modern American Painting and Sculpture*, New York: Dell Publishing Company, 1959.

MOHOLY-NAGY, LASZLO, *The New Vision*, New York: Brewer, Warren and Putnam, Inc., 1932.

———, *Vision in Motion*, Chicago: P. Theobald, 1947.

MUNRO, ELEANOR, "Explorations in Form: A View of Some Recent American Sculpture," *Perspectives, U.S.A.*, no. 16 (Summer 1956), pp. 162–70.

READ, HERBERT, *A Concise History of Modern Sculpture*, New York: Frederick A. Praeger, Inc., 1964.

———, *The Art of Sculpture*, New York: Pantheon Books, 1956.

* RITCHIE, ANDREW, *Abstract Painting and Sculpture in America*, New York: Museum of Modern Art, 1951.

———, *Sculpture of the Twentieth Century*, New York: Museum of Modern Art, 1952.

SCHNIER, JACQUES, *Sculpture in Modern America*, Berkeley, Calif.: University of California Press, 1948.

* SEUPHOR, MICHEL, *The Sculpture of This Century, Dictionary of Modern Sculpture*, New York: George Braziller, Inc., 1961.

SEYMOUR, CHARLES, *Tradition and Experiment in Modern Sculpture*, Washington, D.C.: American University Press, 1949.

VALENTINER, WILHELM, *Origins of Modern Sculpture*, New York: Wittenborn and Company, 1946.

Armory Show

* BROWN, MILTON, *American Painting from the Armory Show to the Depression*, Princeton, N.J.: Princeton University Press, 1955.

——, *The Story of the Armory Show*, Greenwich, Conn.: New York Graphic Society, 1963.

COX, KENYON, "The Modern Spirit in Art," *Harper's Weekly*, 57 (March 15, 1913), 10.

KUHN, WALT, *The Story of the Armory Show*, New York, 1938.

ROOSEVELT, THEODORE, "A Layman's View of an Art Exhibition," *Outlook*, 103 (March 29, 1913), 718–20.

STEIN, LEO, "The Panic in Art," *New Republic*, 1 (Nov. 7, 1914), 20–21.

VI. INDIVIDUAL SCULPTORS, ALPHABETICALLY LISTED

ADAMS, HERBERT

PEIXOTTO, ERNEST, "The Sculpture of Herbert Adams," *American Magazine of Art*, 12 (May 1921), 151–59.

"Herbert Adams," Pan-American Union *Bulletin*, 45 (July 1917), 93–104.

AKERS, PAUL

USHER, LEILA, "Paul Akers," *New England Magazine*, n.s. XI (1895), 460–68.

TUCKERMAN, HENRY, "Two of Our Sculptors, B. P. Akers and E. S. Bartholomew," *Hours at Home*, II (April 1866).

ARCHIPENKO, ALEXANDER

ARCHIPENKO, ALEXANDER, *Archipenko: Fifty Creative Years, 1908–1958*, New York: Tekhne, 1960.

HILDEBRANDT, HANS, *Alexander Archipenko*, Berlin: Ukrainske Slowo, Ltd., 1923.

AUGUR, HEZEKIAH

HAMILTON, GEORGE, "Hezekiah Augur," master's thesis, 1934, Yale University, New Haven, Conn.

BALL, THOMAS

BALL, THOMAS, *My Three Score Years and Ten, An Autobiography*, Boston, 1891.

PARTRIDGE, WILLIAM, "Thomas Ball," *New England Magazine*, n.s. XII (1895), 291–304.

BARNARD, GEORGE GREY

DICKSON, HAROLD, "Barnard's Sculptures for the Pennsylvania Capitol," *Art Quarterly*, 22 (1959), 127–47.
————, "Log of a Masterpiece, Barnard's 'Struggle of the Two Natures of Man,'" *College Art Journal*, 20 (1961), 139–43.
THAW, ALEXANDER, "George Grey Barnard," *World's Work*, 5 (1902), 2837–53.
TWOMBLY, MARY, "George Grey Barnard," *World's Work*, 17 (1909), 11256–67.

BARTHOLOMEW, EDWARD SHEFFIELD

WENDELL, WILLIAM, "Edward Sheffield Bartholomew, Sculptor," *Wadsworth Atheneum Bulletin*, Winter 1962, pp. 1–8.

BARTLETT, PAUL WAYLAND

BARTLETT, ELLEN, "Paul Bartlett: an American Sculptor," *New England Magazine*, 33 (Dec. 1905), 369–82.
WHEELER, CHARLES, "Bartlett," *American Magazine of Art*, 16 (Nov. 1925), 573–85.

BASKIN, LEONARD

O'DOHERTY, BRIAN, "Leonard Baskin," *Art in America*, vol. 50, no. 2 (Summer 1962), 66–72.
SPENCE, ROBERT, "Leonard Baskin," *Art Journal*, vol. 22, no. 2 (Winter 1962–63), 88–91.

BITTER, KARL

DENNIS, JAMES M., *Karl Bitter*, Madison, Wisc.: University of Wisconsin Press, 1967.
GREER, H. H., "The Work of Karl Bitter," *Brush and Pencil*, 13 (March 1904), 466–78.
SCHEVILL, FERDINAND, *Karl Bitter, a Biography*, Chicago: The University of Chicago Press, 1917.

BORGLUM, GUTZON

BORGLUM, GUTZON, "Art That Is Real and American," *World's Work*, June 1914; contains a biography of G. Borglum by G. Marvin.
————, "Moulding a Mountain," *Forum*, September 1923.

BORGLUM, SOLON

EBERLE, LOUISE, "In Recognition of an American Sculptor," *Scribner's Magazine*, 72 (Sept. 1922), 379–84.
SEWELL, FRANK, "A Sculptor of the Prairie," *Century Magazine*, 68 (June 1904), 247–51.

BROWERE, JOHN H. I.

HART, CHARLES, *Browere's Life Masks of Great Americans*, New York: Doubleday and McClure Company, 1899.
Life Masks of Noted Americans of 1825, by John H.I. Browere, New York: M. Knoedler and Company, 1940.

CALDER, ALEXANDER

* ARNASON, H. H., *Calder*, Princeton, N.J.: D. Van Nostrand Co., Inc., 1966.
SARTRE, JEAN-PAUL, "Existentialist on Mobilist," *Art News*, 46 (Dec. 1947), 22–23, 55–56.
SWEENEY, JAMES, *Alexander Calder*, New York: Museum of Modern Art, 1951.

CALDER, STIRLING

BOWES, JULIAN, "The Sculpture of Stirling Calder," *American Magazine of Art*, 16 (May 1925), 229–37.
HOEBER, ARTHUR, "Calder, A 'Various' Sculptor," *World's Work*, 20 (Sept. 1910), 13377–88.

CERACCHI, GIUSEPPE

DESPORTES, ULYSSES, "Giuseppe Ceracchi in America and His Busts of George Washington," *Art Quarterly*, vol. 26, no. 2 (1963), 140–79.

CLEVENGER, SHOBAL VAIL

BRUMBAUGH, THOMAS, "Shobal Clevenger: An Ohio Stonecutter in Search of Fame," *Art Quarterly*, vol. 29, no. 1 (1966), 29–45.
"Clevenger," *United States Magazine and Democratic Review*, VIII (Feb. 1844), 202 ff.
"Shobal Vail Clevenger, the Sculptor," *The Southern Literary Messenger*, V (April 1839).
TUCKERMAN, HENRY, "Clevenger," *The Columbian*, I (1844), 10–11.

COFFEE, WILLIAM JOHN

GROCE, GEORGE, "William John Coffee, Long-Lost Sculptor," *American Collector*, May 1946, pp. 14–15, 19–20.
RUTLEDGE, ANNA W., "William John Coffee as a Portrait Sculptor," *Gazette des Beaux Arts*, November 1945, pp. 297–312.

COGDELL, JOHN

RUTLEDGE, ANNA W., *Artists in the Life of Charleston, through Colony and State . . .*, Philadelphia: American Philosophical Society, 1949.

CRAWFORD, THOMAS

"Crawford and Sculpture," *Atlantic Monthly*, June 1858, pp. 64–78.
* GALE, ROBERT, *Thomas Crawford, American Sculptor*, Pittsburgh: University of Pittsburgh Press, 1964.
HILLARD, GEORGE, "Eulogy on Thomas Crawford," *Atlantic Monthly*, July 1869, pp. 40 ff.
LESTER, CHARLES E., *The Artists of America*, New York, 1846.

DALLIN, CYRUS

LONG, WALDO, "Dallin, Sculptor of Indians," *World's Work*, 54 (Sept. 1927), 563–68.
SEATON-SCHMIDT, ANNA, "An American Sculptor: Cyrus E. Dallin," *International Studio*, 58 (April 1916), 109–114.

DAVIDSON, JO

DAVIDSON, JO, *Between Sittings*, New York: Dial Press, 1951.
DU BOIS, RENÉ, "Jo Davidson," *International Studio*, 76 (Nov. 1922), 177–81.

DE CREEFT, JOSÉ

CAMPOS, JULES, *José de Creeft*, New York: E. S. Herrmann, 1945.
WELTY, EUDORA, "José de Creeft," *Magazine of Art*, 37 (Feb. 1944), pp. 42–47.

DE RIVERA, JOSÉ

ASHTON, DORE, "The Sculpture of José de Rivera," *Arts*, 30 (April 1956), 38–41.
∗ GORDON, JOHN, *José de Rivera*, New York: American Federation of Arts, 1961.

DEXTER, HENRY

ALBEE, JOHN, *Henry Dexter, Sculptor*, Cambridge, Mass., 1898.

EZEKIEL, MOSES

WRENSHALL, K. H., "An American Sculptor in Rome," *World's Work*, November 1909, pp. 12256–64.

FERBER, HERBERT

DENNISON, GEORGE, "Sculpture as Environment: the New Work of Herbert Ferber," *Arts*, 37 (May 1963), 86–91.
FERBER, HERBERT, "On Sculpture," *Art in America*, 42 (Dec. 1954), 262 ff.
GOODNOUGH, ROBERT, "Ferber Makes a Sculpture," *Art News*, 51 (Nov. 1952), 40 ff.

FLANNAGAN, JOHN B.

Letters of John B. Flannagan, Introduction by Wilhelm R. Valentiner, New York, 1942.
MILLER, DOROTHY C., ed., *The Sculpture of John B. Flannagan*, New York: Museum of Modern Art, 1942.

FOLEY, MARGARET

CHATTERTON, E. B., "A Vermont Sculptor," *News and Notes* (Vermont Historical Society), VII (Oct. 1955), 10–14.

FRASER, JAMES EARLE

"James Earle Fraser," Pan-American Union *Bulletin*, 46 (May 1918), 648–55.
SEMPLE, ELIZABETH, "James Earle Fraser, Sculptor," *Century Magazine*, 79 (April 1910), 929–32.

FRAZEE, JOHN

"The Autobiography of John Frazee," *American Collector*, 1946, September, pp. 15 ff.; October, pp. 10 ff.; November, pp. 12 ff.; excerpts from manuscripts in the New Jersey Historical Society and the New York Public Library.

FRENCH, DANIEL CHESTER

ADAMS, ADELINE, *Daniel Chester French: Sculptor*, Boston and New York: Houghton Mifflin Company, 1932.

CRESSON, MARGARET, *Journey into Fame; The Life of Daniel Chester French*, Cambridge, Mass.: Harvard University Press, 1947.

FRENCH, MARY A., *Memories of a Sculptor's Wife*, Boston and New York: Houghton Mifflin Company, 1928.

GABO, NAUM

GABO, NAUM, *Of Divers Arts*, New York: Pantheon Books, 1962.

Pevsner Gabo, Introduction by Herbert Read, text by Ruth Olson and Abraham Chanin, New York: Museum of Modern Art, 1948.

GRAFLY, CHARLES

DALLIN, VITTORIA, "Charles Grafly's Work," *New England Magazine*, 25 (Oct. 1901), 228–35.

TAFT, LORADO, "Charles Grafly, Sculptor," *Brush and Pencil*, 3 (March 1899), 343–53.

GREENOUGH, HORATIO

GREENOUGH, FRANCES, ed., *Letters of Horatio Greenough to His Brother, Henry Greenough*, Boston: Ticknor and Company, 1887.

GREENOUGH, HORATIO [Horace Bender], *Travels, Observations and Experiences of a Yankee Stonecutter*, Introduction by Natalia Wright, Gainesville, Fla.: Scholars' Facsimiles and Reprints, 1958.

TUCKERMAN, HENRY, *A Memorial to Horatio Greenough*, New York: G. P. Putnam & Son, 1853.

* WRIGHT, NATALIA, *Horatio Greenough, The First American Sculptor*, Philadelphia: University of Pennsylvania Press, 1963.

GREENOUGH, RICHARD

* BRUMBAUGH, THOMAS, "The Art of Richard Greenough," *Old-Time New England*, January–March 1963, pp. 61–78.

SHURTLEFF, NATHANIEL, *Memorial Inauguration of the Statue of Franklin*, Boston, 1857.

GROSS, CHAIM

GROSS, CHAIM, *The Technique of Wood Carving*, New York: Vista House, 1957.

* LOMBARDO, JOSEF, *Chaim Gross, Sculptor*, New York: Dalton House, 1949.

GUSSOW, ROY

GUSSOW, ROY, "Sculpture," *Student Publications of the School of Design*, North Carolina State College, vol. 3, no. 2 (1953), 9–18.

HARE, DAVID

GOODNOUGH, ROBERT, "David Hare Makes a Sculpture," *Art News*, 55 (March 1956), 46–49.

HARE, DAVID, "The Spaces of the Mind," *Magazine of Art*, 43 (Feb. 1950), 48–53.

HART, JOEL TANNER

PRICE, SAMUEL, *Old Masters of the Blue Grass*, Louisville, Ky.: J. P. Morton and Company, 1902.

HARVEY, ELI

MC INTYRE, R. G., "Eli Harvey—Sculptor," *Arts and Decoration*, 3 (Dec. 1912), 58 ff.

HOFFMAN, MALVINA

HOFFMAN, MALVINA, *Heads and Tales*, New York: Charles Scribner's Sons, 1936.
———, *Sculpture Inside and Out*, New York: W. W. Norton & Company, 1939.
———, *Yesterday Is Tomorrow*, New York: Crown Publishers, Inc., 1965.

HOSMER, HARRIET

BRADFORD, R. A., "Life and Works of Harriet Hosmer," *New England Magazine*, n.s. XLV (1911), 265 ff.
CARR, CORNELIA, *Harriet Hosmer, Letters and Memories*, New York: Moffat, Yard and Company, 1912.
THORP, MARGARET, "The White Marmorean Flock," *New England Quarterly*, June 1959, pp. 147–69.

HOUDON, JEAN ANTOINE

CHINARD, GILBERT, *Houdon in America*, Baltimore, Md.: Johns Hopkins Press, 1930.
HART, CHARLES, and BIDDLE, EDWARD, *Memoirs of the Life and Works of Jean Antoine Houdon . . .* , Philadelphia, 1911.

HUGHES, ROBERT BALL

CHAMBERLAIN, GEORGIA, "Portrait Busts of Robert Ball Hughes," *Art Quarterly*, 1957, pp. 383–86.
———, *Studies on American Painters and Sculptors of the Nineteenth Century*, Annandale, Va.: Turnpike Press, 1965.

HUNTINGTON, ANNA HYATT VAUGHN

LADD, ANNA C., "Anna V. Hyatt—Animal Sculptor," *Art and Progress*, November 1912, pp. 773–76.
PRICE, FREDERICK, "Anna Hyatt Huntington," *International Studio*, 79 (Aug. 1924), 319–23.

IVES, CHAUNCEY BRADLEY

Catalogue of the Important Sculptures by the Late C. B. Ives, New York, 1899.

JENNEWEIN, PAUL

CUNNINGHAM, JOHN J., ed., *C. Paul Jennewein*, Athens, Ga.: University of Georgia Press, 1950.

PARKES, KINETON, "Plastic Form and Color: the Work of Paul Jennewein," *Apollo*, 17 (Apr. 1933), 130–34.

JONES, THOMAS DOW

Memories of Lincoln, by Thomas D. Jones, and Reproductions of the Author's Two Busts of Lincoln, New York, 1934; reprinted from the *Sacramento Weekly Union*, November 4, 1871.

KEMEYS, EDWARD

HAWTHORNE, JULIA, "American Wild Animals in Art," *Century Magazine*, 6 (1884), 213–19.
MECHLIN, LEILA, "Edward Kemeys: An Appreciate," *International Studio*, 26 (Oct. 1905).

KONTI, ISIDORE

BRUSH, EDWARD, "The Art of Isidore Konti, Sculptor," *Fine Arts Journal*, 26 (May 1912), 330–35.
LEVETUS, A. S., "Isidore Konti: A Hungarian Sculptor in America," *International Studio*, 45 (Jan. 1912), 197–203.

LACHAISE, GASTON

GALLATIN, ALBERT, *Gaston Lachaise*, New York: E. P. Dutton & Company, 1924.
KIRSTEIN, LINCOLN, *Gaston Lachaise: Retrospective Exhibition*, New York: Museum of Modern Art, 1935.
LACHAISE, GASTON, "A Comment on My Sculpture," *Creative Art*, 3 (1928), xxiii–xxviii.

LAESSLE, ALBERT

MILLER, ROY, "A Sculptor of Animal Life," *International Studio*, 80 (Oct. 1924), 23–27.

LANDER, LOUISA

"Miss Louisa Lander's Work," *Cosmopolitan Art Journal*, vol. IV, no. 1, 1860.

LASSAW, IBRAM

CAMPBELL, LAWRENCE, "Lassaw Makes a Sculpture," *Art News*, 53 (March 1954), 24 ff.
SAWIN, MARTICA, "Ibram Lassaw," *Arts*, 30 (Dec. 1955), 22–26.

LAURENT, ROBERT

FROST, ROSAMUND, "Laurent: Frames to Figures, Brittany to Brooklyn," *Art News*, 40 (April 1941), 10 ff.
READ, HELEN, "Robert Laurent," *The Arts*, 9 (May 1926), 251–59.

LEE, ARTHUR

SLUSSER, J. P., "A Note on Arthur Lee," *International Studio*, 79 (June 1924), 171–76.

LIPCHITZ, JACQUES

*HAMMACHER, A. M., *Jacques Lipchitz, His Sculpture*, New York: Harry N. Abrams, Inc., 1960.
HOPE, HENRY, *The Sculpture of Jacques Lipchitz*, New York: Museum of Modern Art, 1954.
*PATAI, IRENE, *Encounters, The Life of Jacques Lipchitz*, New York: Funk & Wagnalls, 1961.

LIPPOLD, RICHARD

CAMPBELL, LAWRENCE, "Lippold Makes a Construction," *Art News*, 55 (Oct. 1956), 31 ff.
LIPPOLD, RICHARD, "Sculpture?" *Magazine of Art*, 44 (Dec. 1951), 315–19.

LIPTON, SEYMOUR

HUNTER, SAM, *Seymour Lipton*, catalogue, Marlborough-Gerson Gallery, New York, 1965, 36 pgs.
LIPTON, SEYMOUR, "Experience and Sculptural Form," *College Art Journal*, 9 (1949), 52–54.
RITCHIE, ANDREW, "Seymour Lipton," *Art in America*, 44 (Winter 1956), 14–17.

MC INTIRE, SAMUEL

COUSINS, FRANK, and RILEY, P. M., *The Woodcarver of Salem, Samuel McIntire*, Boston, 1916.
CUMMINGS, ABBOTT L., *et al.*, *Samuel McIntire, A Bicentennial Symposium*, Salem, Mass.: Essex Institute, 1957.
KIMBALL, FISKE, *Mr. Samuel McIntire, Carver, the Architect of Salem*, Portland, Me.: Southworth-Athoensen Press, 1940.

MAC MONNIES, FREDERICK

GREER, H. H., "Frederick MacMonnies, Sculptor," *Brush and Pencil*, 10 (Apr. 1902), 1–15.
LOW, WILL, "Frederick MacMonnies," *Scribner's Magazine*, 18 (1895), 617–28.
STROTHER, FRENCH, "Frederick MacMonnies, Sculptor," *World's Work*, 11 (Dec. 1905), 6965–81.

MAC NEIL, HERMON

HOLDEN, JEAN, "The Sculptor MacNeil," *World's Work*, 14 (Oct. 1907), 9403–19.
"The Art of MacNeil," *Craftsman*, September 1909.

MANSHIP, PAUL

MANSHIP, PAULINE, *Paul Manship*, New York: W. W. Norton & Company, 1947.
MURTHA, EDWIN, *Paul Manship*, New York: The Macmillan Company, 1957.

MARISOL

CAMPBELL, LAWRENCE, "Marisol's Magic Mixtures," *Art News*, 63 (March 1964), 38 ff.

MILLS, CLARK

BABCOCK, T. S., *Inauguration of the Mills Statue of George Washington*, 1860, "An Address by the Artist Clark Mills."

RUTLEDGE, ANNA W., "Cogdell and Mills, Charleston Sculptors," *Antiques Magazine*, March 1942, pp. 192–93, 205–7.

NADELMAN, ELIE

* KIRSTEIN, LINCOLN, *The Sculpture of Elie Nadelman*, New York: Museum of Modern Art, 1948.

MURRELL, WILLIAM, *Elie Nadelman*, Woodstock, N.Y., 1924.

NAKIAN, REUBEN

* O'HARA, FRANK, *Nakian*, New York: Museum of Modern Art, 1966.

KRAMER, HILTON, "Month in Review," *Arts*, 33 (Jan. 1959), 48 ff.

NEVELSON, LOUISE

SECKLER, DOROTHY, "The Artist Speaks: Louise Nevelson," *Art in America*, January–February 1967, pp. 33–42.

NIEHAUS, CHARLES

ARMSTRONG, REGINA, *The Sculpture of Charles Henry Niehaus*, New York, 1901.

WILSON, RUFUS, "Charles Henry Niehaus," *Monthly Illustrator*, 12 (June 1896), 391–400.

NOGUCHI, ISAMU

HESS, THOMAS, "Isamu Noguchi '46," *Art News*, 45 (Sept. 1946), 34 ff.

NOGUCHI, ISAMU, "Meanings in Modern Sculpture," *Art in America*, 48 (March 1949), 13 ff.

OLDENBURG, CLAES

FAHLSTRÖM, O., "Claes Oldenburg," *Studio*, 172 (Dec. 1966), 326–29.

ROSENSTEIN, HARRIS, "Climbing Mt. Oldenburg," *Art News*, 64 (Feb. 1966), 21–25.

PALMER, ERASTUS DOW

PALMER, ERASTUS DOW, "Philosophy of the Ideal," *The Crayon*, III (1856), 18–20.

RICHARDSON, H. E., "Erastus Dow Palmer, American Craftsman and Sculptor," *New York History*, XXVIII (1868), 324–40.

PARTRIDGE, WILLIAM ORDWAY

LANGDON, WILLIAM, "William Ordway Partridge, Sculptor," *New England Magazine*, n.s. 22 (1900), 382–98.

PARTRIDGE, WILLIAM, "Development of Sculpture in America," *Forum*, January 1896, pp. 554–69.

The Works in Sculpture of William Ordway Partridge, New York: John Lane Company, 1914.

PICCIRILLI FAMILY

LOMBARDO, J. V., *Attilo Piccirilli, Life of an American Sculptor*, New York and Chicago: Pitman Publishing Corporation, 1944.

POTTER, EDWARD

LANIER, HENRY, "The Sculpture of E. C. Potter," *World's Work*, vol. 12, September 1906.

POWERS, HIRAM

BELLOWS, H. W., "Seven Sittings with Powers the Sculptor," *Appleton's Journal*, I (1869), 342–43, 359–61, 402–4, 470–71, 595–97; II (1870), 54–55 and 106–8.
BOYNTON, HENRY, "Hiram Powers," *New England Magazine*, n.s. XX (July 1899), 519–33.
JARVES, JAMES JACKSON, "Hiram Powers," *Art Journal*, n.s. vol. XIII, 1874.

PRATT, BELA

DOWNES, WILLIAM H., "The Work of Bela L. Pratt, Sculptor," *New England Magazine*, 27 (1903), 760–71.

PROCTOR, A. PHIMISTER

PALADIN, VIVIAN, "A. Phimister Proctor: Master Sculptor of Horses," *Montana Magazine of Western History*, Winter 1964, pp. 10–24.
PEIXOTTO, ERNEST, "A Sculptor of the West," *Scribner's Magazine*, 68 (Sept. 1920), 266–77.

REMINGTON, FREDERIC

DE KAY, CHARLES, "A Painter of the West; Frederic Remington and his Work," *Harper's Weekly*, 54 (Jan. 8, 1910), 14 ff.
*MC CRACKEN, HAROLD, *Frederic Remington, Artist of the Old West*, Philadelphia: J. B. Lippincott Co., 1947.
MAXWELL, PERRITON, "An Appreciation of the Art of Frederic Remington," *Pearson's Magazine*, 18 (Oct. 1907), 395–407.

RHIND, JOHN MASSEY

BECKETT, J. A., "A Scotch-American Sculptor," *Art Interchange*, April 1902.
MAC DONALD, N., "A Genius of the Chisel," *Munsey's*, March 1896, pp. 671–79.

RICKEY, GEORGE

KEPES, GYORGY, *The Nature and Art of Movement*, New York: George Braziller, Inc., 1965.
RICKEY, GEORGE, "Morphology of Movement," *Art Journal*, vol. 22, no. 4 (Summer 1963), 220–31.
———, "The New Tendency," *Art Journal*, vol. 23, no. 4 (Summer 1964), 272–79.

RIMMER, WILLIAM

BARTLETT, TRUMAN, *The Art Life of William Rimmer, Sculptor*, Boston: J. R. Osgood and Company, 1882.

*KIRSTEIN, LINCOLN, *William Rimmer*, New York: Whitney Museum of American Art, 1946.

RIMMER, WILLIAM, *Art Anatomy*, Boston: Houghton Mifflin Company, 1877.

————, *Elements of Design*, Boston, 1864.

RINEHART, WILLIAM HENRY

ROSS, MARVIN C., and RUTLEDGE, ANNA W., *William Henry Rinehart, Maryland Sculptor*, Baltimore, Md.: Walters Art Gallery, 1948.

RUSK, WILLIAM S., *William Henry Rinehart, Sculptor*, Baltimore, 1939.

ROGERS, JOHN

BARCK, D. C., "Rogers Groups in the Museum of the New-York Historical Society," New-York Historical Society *Quarterly*, XVI (1932), 67–86.

SMITH, MR. and MRS. CHETWOOD, *Rogers Groups, Thought and Wrought by John Rogers*, Boston, 1934.

WALLACE, DAVID, *John Rogers, the People's Sculptor*, Middletown, Conn.: Wesleyan University Press, 1967.

ROGERS, RANDOLPH

D'OOGE, MARTIN, *Catalogue of the Gallery of Art and Archaeology of the University of Michigan*, Ann Arbor, Mich., 1892.

ROSZAK, THEODORE

ARNASON, H. H., "Growth of a Sculptor . . . Theodore Roszak," *Art in America*, 44 (Winter 1956), 21 ff.

GRIFFIN, HOWARD, "Totems in Steel, Interview with Theodore Roszak," *Art News*, 55 (Oct. 1956), 34 ff.

RUCKSTULL, FREDERIC WELLINGTON

RUCKSTULL, FREDERIC WELLINGTON, *Great Works of Art and What Makes Them Great*, New York: G. P. Putnam's Sons, 1925.

RUSH, WILLIAM

MARCEAU, HENRI, *William Rush, 1756–1833, The First Native American Sculptor*, Philadelphia: Philadelphia Museum of Art, 1937.

SAINT-GAUDENS, AUGUSTUS

CORTISSOZ, ROYAL, *Augustus Saint-Gaudens*, Boston and New York: Houghton Mifflin Company, 1907.

COX, KENYON, "Augustus Saint-Gaudens," *Century Magazine*, 35 (Nov. 1887), 28–37.

SAINT-GAUDENS, HOMER, ed., *The Reminiscences of Augustus Saint-Gaudens*, 2 vols., New York: The Century Company, 1913.

SIMMONS, FRANKLIN

BURRAGE, HENRY, "Franklin Simmons, Sculptor," *Maine Historical Memorials*, 1922, pp. 109–47.

CAMMETT, STEPHEN, "Franklin Simmons, A Maine-Born Sculptor," *Pine Tree Magazine*, 8 (Aug. 1907), 92–96.

THE SKILLINS

SWAN, MABEL, "Simeon Skillin, Senior, The First American Sculptor," *Antiques Magazine*, XLVI (July 1944), 21.

THWING, LEROY, "The Four Carving Skillins," *Antiques Magazine*, XXXIII (June 1938), 326–28.

SMITH, DAVID

GREENBERG, CLEMENT, "David Smith," *Art in America*, January–February 1966, pp. 27–32.

*HUNTER, SAM, *David Smith*, New York: Museum of Modern Art, 1957.

KRAMER, HILTON, "The Sculpture of David Smith," *Arts*, 34 (Feb. 1960), 22–41.

SMITH, DAVID, "Thoughts on Sculpture," *College Art Journal*, vol. 13, no. 2 (1954), 96–100.

STANKIEWICZ, RICHARD

KRAMER, HILTON, "Month in Review," *Arts*, 33 (Jan. 1959), 50–51.

"Richard Stankiewicz," *Art in America*, February 1956, pp. 46–47.

STORRS, JOHN

BULLIET, C. J., "Artists of Chicago, Past and Present," *Chicago Daily News*, March 16, 1935.

"John Storrs," *Art News*, 64 (April 1965), 15.

STORY, WILLIAM WETMORE

JAMES, HENRY, *William Wetmore Story and His Friends*, Boston: Houghton Mifflin Company, 1903.

PHILLIPS, M. E., *Reminiscences of William Wetmore Story*, Chicago: Rand, McNally and Company, 1897.

STORY, WILLIAM W., *Conversations in a Studio*, Boston: Houghton Mifflin Company, 1890.

——, *Excursions in Art and Letters*, Boston and New York, 1891.

TAFT, LORADO

GARLAND, HAMLIN, "The Art of Lorado Taft," *Mentor*, III (Oct. 1923), 19–34.

MOULTON, ROBERT, "Lorado Taft and His Work as a Sculptor," *American Review of Reviews*, 45 (June 1912), 721–25.

VALAPERTA, JOSEPH

WALL, ALEXANDER J., "Joseph Valaperta, Sculptor," *New-York Historical Society Quarterly*, July 1927, pp. 53–56.

VOLK, LEONARD

Biographical Sketches of the Leading Men of Chicago, Chicago, 1868.
VOLK, LEONARD W., "The Lincoln Life Mask and How It Was Made," *Century Magazine*, XXIII (Dec. 1881), 223–27.

VONNOH, BESSIE POTTER

HOEBER, ARTHUR, "A New Note in American Sculpture, Statuettes by Bessie Potter," *Century Magazine*, vol. 54, pp. 732–35.
"A Sculptor of Statuettes," *Current Literature*, 34 (June 1903), pp. 699–702.

WARD, JOHN QUINCY ADAMS

ADAMS, ADELINE, *John Quincy Adams Ward*, National Sculpture Society, New York, 1912.
SHELDON, G. W., "An American Sculptor," *Harper's Magazine*, 57 (June 1878), 62–68.
STURGIS, RUSSELL, "The Work of J. Q. A. Ward," *Scribner's Magazine*, 32 (Oct. 1902), 385–99.

WARNER, OLIN

BROWNELL, W. C., "The Sculpture of Olin Warner," *Scribner's Magazine*, vol. 20, pp. 429 ff.
ECKFORD, HENRY, "Olin Warner, Sculptor," *Century Magazine*, 37 (1889), 392 ff.
HITCHCOCK, RIPLEY, "Notes on an American Sculptor," *Art Review*, 1 (March 1887), 2 ff.

WHITNEY, ANNE

PAYNE, ELIZABETH PAYNE, "Anne Whitney, Sculptor," *Art Quarterly*, Autumn 1962, pp. 244–61.

WRIGHT, PATIENCE

LESLEY, E. P., "Patience Lovell Wright, America's First Sculptor," *Art in America*, October 1936, pp. 148–54.

YOUNG, MAHONRI

LEWINE, J. LESTER, "The Bronzes of Mahonri Young," *International Studio*, 47 (Oct. 1912), lv–lviii.
"Life as Mahonri Young Sees It," *Touchstone*, 4 (Oct. 1918), 8–16.

ZORACH, WILLIAM

*BAUR, JOHN I. H., *William Zorach*, New York: Frederick A. Praeger, Inc., 1959.
WINGERT, PAUL, *The Sculpture of William Zorach*, New York: Pitman Publishing Corporation, 1938.
* ZORACH, WILLIAM, *Zorach Explains Sculpture*, New York: American Artists Group, 1947.

Index

Page numbers in italics indicate illustrations.

[Index]

[Index]